A DICTIONARY OF PASTORAL CARE

THE NON-VANISHING IDEAL CASE

A DICTIONARY
OF PASTORAL CARE

EDITED BY ALASTAIR V. CAMPBELL

CROSSROAD · NEW YORK

1987

The Crossroad Publishing Company
370 Lexington Avenue, New York, N.Y. 10017

Printed in the United States of America

Library of Congress Cataloging-in-Publication Data

A Dictionary of pastoral care.

Includes bibliographies.
1. Pastoral counseling—Dictionaries. 2. Pastoral
psychology—Dictionaries. 3. Pastoral theology—
Dictionaries. 4. Counseling—Dictionaries.
I. Campbell, Alastair V. [DNLM: 1. Counseling—
dictionaries. 2. Pastoral Care—dictionaries. Wm 13
D55365]
BV4012.2.D57 1987   253.5'03'21   87-20186
ISBN 0-8245-0834-3

PREFACE

This publication is one of the major reference works in its field since the development over the past two decades of new approaches to pastoral care and counselling and the rapid expansion of pastoral education and training. As such it should fill an important gap on the library shelves of practitioners and universities and colleges as well as providing a companion volume to the growing body of literature on pastoral care. The aim has been to produce a volume of relatively modest size, but broad enough in scope to meet a variety of needs both academic and practical.

In a work with 300 separate entries written by 185 authors, drawn from a wide range of disciplines, it is inevitable (and probably also desirable) that there is a variety of approach and style in different entries. No attempt has been made to impose upon authors a normative view of the nature of pastoral care or to specify precisely how a subject is to be dealt with. Nevertheless, certain common features will be found in the *Dictionary*, determined by the following editorial policies:

First, the approach to pastoral care is *inter-denominational* and *inter-disciplinary*. Authors with Christian religious affiliations come from all the major denominations, and there are several authors from within the Jewish tradition. In addition, authors have been selected for their specialized knowledge irrespective of religious belief. The professions of law, medicine, nursing, social work and teaching are represented and the academic fields of philosophy, psychology, sociology and theology.

Secondly, an attempt has been made to provide a *broad and comprehensive theoretical background*. This has entailed a range of entries on the nature and history of pastoral care and its related disciplines (see PASTORAL CARE, NATURE OF and cross references). In addition topics have been selected from theology (e.g. CROSS AND RESURRECTION; GOD, DOCTRINE OF; INCARNATION), from philosophy, psychology and sociology (e.g. FREEDOM AND DETERMINISM; EMOTION; SOCIOLOGY OF RELIGION) and from the theoretical background of psychotherapy and counselling (e.g. ANALYTICAL PSYCHOLOGY; DEFENCE MECHANISMS; TRANSFERENCE), so that the reader can gain the benefit of specialist knowledge in these fields. We have deliberately not asked authors to draw practical implications for pastoral care in entries of this kind, leaving the reader to make the most appropriate and useful connections. The main purpose of such entries is to ensure that as rich a grounding in theory as possible is available in this *Dictionary*, without regarding any one discipline as the normative source of answers to the questions raised in the practice of pastoral care.

Thirdly, it is intended that the majority of the entries will be *relevant to practice*. This is not to be confused with the 'hints and tips' approach adopted by some pastoral manuals. What the reader should find is basic information on the kinds of problems commonly encountered in pastoral practice, whether the practitioner is a lay person or an ordained minister. Ministerial functions, such as preaching, sacraments and administration, are referred to, but the main focus is on the essentials of counselling and on aspects of helping and caring outside the 'safe

v

emergency' of the counselling session. A specific emphasis on social and political topics (e.g. HEALTH EDUCATION; PORNOGRAPHY; POVERTY; UNEMPLOYMENT) has been introduced to counteract the impression that the whole practice of pastoral care can be described in terms of individual therapy or counselling. Thus the practical relevance of the *Dictionary* depends upon the reader using it as both a source of information and a stimulus to creative experiment in pastoral care.

In order to use the *Dictionary* effectively it is suggested that, in addition to looking up the specific topic of concern, some 'browsing' to find unexpected topics will be helpful. Topics are listed alphabetically and cross references are provided both within entries and at the end of entries to guide readers to related topics which may amplify or modify the subject matter in question. Most entries have short bibliographies, which make no attempt at comprehensiveness (an impossible task in such a small reference work), but rather identify useful sources of further reading (and occasionally organizations to contact).

Editing a dictionary of this kind is a major undertaking, of which the magnitude is fully realized – fortunately perhaps – only in the midst of the project. I could not possibly have persevered with the task as editor without the constant and effective support of others. In particular, I am deeply grateful to Edward Glover, my assistant editor, who has worked with me from the commissioning stage on, and has spent countless hours on the details of editing copy of over 200,000 words in all. In addition to this major editorial work, he has been responsible for compiling, in collaboration with me and Derek Blows, the unsigned short entries which offer definitions of terms. Thus he has made a significant contribution to the content as well as the form of the *Dictionary*. I have also received constant stimulus and support from Derek Blows, and from the editorial staff at SPCK. They have helped me to clarify the overall policy of the *Dictionary*, and to select topics and appropriate authors. At the planning stage, I received relevant advice from a wide range of colleagues in the field, many of whom vetted and improved the topic list and were willing to become authors themselves. Finally, I wish to thank Elma Webster, whose secretarial skills ensured that the administration of the *Dictionary* was always in safe hands, and my wife Sally for her constant encouragement when I felt that I had undertaken a task too complex and time-consuming for my already busy academic life.

ALASTAIR V. CAMPBELL

CONTRIBUTORS

Rev. E.W.F. Agar is general secretary of the Church of England National Council for Social Aid.

Rev. Ian Ainsworth-Smith is chaplain at St George's Hospital, London.

Dr Cairns Aitken is professor of Rehabilitation Studies, University of Edinburgh.

Rev. Andrew F. Anderson is minister at Greenside Parish Church, Edinburgh.

Rev. Dr George F. Anderson is professor emeritus of Hebrew and Old Testament Studies, University of Edinburgh.

Dr Michael Argyle is reader in Social Psychology, University of Oxford.

David Armstrong is a consultant at the Grubb Institute, London.

Canon John R. Atherton is director of the William Temple Foundation, Manchester.

Rev. Dr D.J. Atkinson is college chaplain, Corpus Christi College, Oxford.

Rev. Michael Atkinson is research officer of the Board of Social Responsibility, Church of England.

Canon Norman Autton is chaplain to the University Hospital of Wales, Cardiff.

Very Rev. Peter Baelz is dean of Durham.

Rev. Paul H. Ballard is lecturer in Religious Studies and tutor in Pastoral Studies, University College, Cardiff.

Rev. Dr Peter Bellamy is chaplain/lecturer at the Queen Elizabeth Medical Centre, Birmingham.

Dr John Beloff was formerly senior lecturer in Psychology, University of Edinburgh.

David Black is a member of the Association of Jungian Analysts and a supervisor at the Westminster Pastoral Foundation, London.

Irene Bloomfield is a clinical psychologist and psychotherapist at University College Hospital and is clinical director of the Raphael Centre, London.

Rev. Canon Derek Blows is director of the Westminster Pastoral Foundation, a psychotherapist at University College Hospital, London, and a professional member of the Society of Analytical Psychology.

Rev. Peter Bowes is minister of Morningside Baptist Church, Edinburgh.

Rt Rev. Ronald O. Bowlby is bishop of Southwark.

Rev. Dr Kenneth M. Boyd is Scottish director and research fellow of the Institute of Medical Ethics.

The late Rev. Christopher Bryant was a member of the Anglican Society of St John the Evangelist and editor of *New Fire*.

Kay Carmichael is a social worker and writer.

Dr Michael A. Church is medical adviser, Scottish Health Education Group.

Rev. Dr Howard J. Clinebell is professor of Pastoral Psychology and Counselling, School of Theology at Claremont, California, USA.

Rev. Christopher Hamel Cooke is rector of St Marylebone Parish Church.

Roger Coward is senior lecturer in the School of Communication, Polytechnic of Central London.

Dr John L. Cox is professor of Psychiatry, University of Keele.

Dr Murray Cox is consultant psychotherapist, Broadmoor Hospital.

Yvonne Craig is adviser in Adult Education to the General Synod Board of Education.

Rt Rev. Mgr J.D. Crichton is a retired Roman Catholic priest.

Dr Sidney Crown is a consultant psychiatrist at the London Hospital.

The late Rev. John Dalrymple was a Roman Catholic parish priest and author.

Very Rev. A.H. Dammers is dean of Bristol.

Rev. Canon J.G. Davies is Edward Cadbury Professor emeritus of Theology, University of Birmingham.

Rev. William C. Denning is a Methodist minister responsible for the Maypole Farm Creative Art Centre, Bristol.

Jessie van Dongen-Garrad is senior lecturer in Applied Social Studies, University of Bristol.

Dr R.S. Downie is professor of Moral Philosophy, University of Glasgow.

Rev. John H. Drury is dean of King's College, Cambridge.

Rev. Alan R. Duce is Anglican chaplain at Lincoln Prison.

Dr Steve Duck is senior lecturer in

Psychology, University of Lancaster.

Moira Duckworth is a lecturer and supervisor at the Westminster Pastoral Foundation and a member of the Association of Jungian Analysts.

Rev. Canon Anthony Duncan is vicar of Warworth, Northumberland.

Rev. Denis Duncan is director of the Churches' Council for Health and Healing.

Rev. Canon G.R. Dunstan is emeritus professor of Moral and Social Theology, University of London.

Rev. Dr A.O. Dyson is professor of Social and Pastoral Theology, University of Manchester.

Rev. Dr Hugh A. Eadie is national executive officer, YMCA of Australia.

Rev. Dr Brian J. Easter is chaplain at Monyhull Hospital, Birmingham, and Middlefield Hospital, Knowle.

Rev. Dr John R. Elford is lecturer in Social and Pastoral Theology, University of Manchester.

Dr Ivan H. Ellingham is a psychologist at St Anne's Opportunity Centre, Reading.

Rev. Dr Heije Faber is *ordinarius emeritus*, Theological Faculty, Tilburg, Netherlands.

Christopher Fenton is a consultant to the Association for Pastoral Care and Counselling, and a member of the Group Analytic Society.

Dr David F. Ford is a lecturer in Systematic Theology at the University of Birmingham.

Rev. Dr Duncan B. Forrester is professor of Christian Ethics and Practical Theology, University of Edinburgh.

Rev. John Foskett is chaplain to the Bethlem Royal and Maudsley Hospitals, London.

Barbara K. Fowles is a psychotherapist and formerly principal psychiatric social worker, St George's Hospital, London.

Rev. W.H.C. Frend is professor emeritus of Church History, University of Glasgow.

Rev. Dr Albert H. Friedlander is dean of Leo Baeck College, London.

Monica Furlong is a poet, novelist and biographer.

Rev. Dr R.F.R. Gardner is a consultant obstetrician and gynaecologist, Sunderland District General Hospital.

Rev. Dr Robin Gill is senior lecturer in Christian Ethics and Practical Theology, University of Edinburgh.

Rev. David Goodacre is vicar of Ovingham, Northumberland.

Rev. Dr Roger Grainger is chaplain to Stanley Royd Hospital, Wakefield.

Rev. John Gravelle is deputy director of the Chelmsford Cathedral Centre for Research and Training.

Rev. Dr Graeme M. Griffin is professor of Church and Community, Ormond College, Melbourne, Australia.

Rev. George D.W. Grubb is minister of Craigsbank Parish Church, Corstorphine, Edinburgh.

Rev. Dr Colin E. Gunton is professor of Christian Doctrine, University of London.

Tony Hall is director of British Äencies for Adoption and Fostering.

Rev. David G. Hamilton is curriculum officer, Department of Education, the Church of Scotland.

Rt Rev. R.P.C. Hanson is emeritus professor of Historical and Contemporary Theology at the University of Manchester.

Rev. Geoffrey Harding was formerly director of the Churches' Council for Health and Healing.

Rt Rev. Michael Hare Duke is bishop of St Andrews.

Sister Barbara Harrop is a field worker with the Wellclose Square Fund, London.

Margaret Hebblethwaite is a freelance writer.

Dr S. Henley is a lecturer in Psychology, University College, London.

Rev. Dr John Heywood Thomas is professor of Christian Theology, University of Nottingham.

Dr Robert F. Hobson is a consultant psychotherapist at the Manchester Royal Infirmary.

Fr Simon Holden CR is the novice guardian, Community of the Resurrection, Mirfield.

Dr Walter J. Hollenweger is professor of Mission, University of Birmingham.

Rev. Michael Hollings is priest of St Mary of the Angels, London.

Rev. Bill Hopkinson is director of Pastoral Studies, Northern Ordination Course.

Rev. Dr J. Houston is lecturer in Systematic Theology, University of Glasgow.

Dr D.D. Howell was a consultant psychiatrist, St George's Hospital, London and is a training analyst of the Society of Analytical Psychology.

Dr Gerard J. Hughes, SJ is a head of the Department of Philosophy, Heythrop College, London.

Dr John M. Hull is senior lecturer in Religious Education, University of Birmingham.

Dr Michael Humphrey is reader in

Psychology, St George's Hospital Medical School, University of London.

Rev. Charles H. Hutchins is principal, Wilson Carlile College of Evangelism, London.

Rev. Dr Martin Israel is honorary senior lecturer in Pathology at the Royal College of Surgeons of England and priest-in-charge, Holy Trinity Church, London.

Michael D. Jacobs is lecturer in adult education at the University of Leicester.

Rt Rev. David E. Jenkins is bishop of Durham.

Ian McColl Kennedy is professor of Medical Law and Ethics, King's College, London.

Dr Robert L. Kratz is Helen and Joseph Regenstein professor of Human Relations, Hebrew Union College, Cincinnati, USA.

Dr Una Kroll is a deaconess of the Church of England and a medical practitioner.

Rev. Christopher Lamb directs the Other Faiths Theological Project, Selly Oak Colleges, Birmingham.

Dr David Lamb is a lecturer in Philosophy, University of Manchester.

Rev. Keith Lamdin is adult education officer, diocese of Oxford.

Rev. Peter Lang is rector of the parish of Christ Church, St Marylebone, London.

Rev. Kenneth Leech is field officer of the Board for Social Responsibility, Church of England.

Dr Marcus Lefebure OP is a Roman Catholic chaplain in the University of Edinburgh and a co-founder of the Wellspring counselling agency.

Rev. R. Murray Leishman is chaplain to the Royal Edinburgh Hospital (Psychiatric).

Rev. Dr Alan E. Lewis is a lecturer in Systematic Theology, University of Edinburgh.

Dr Emanuel Lewis is a consultant psychotherapist at the Tavistock Clinic, London.

Rev. Dr David Lyall is chaplain to the Edinburgh Northern Hospitals.

Rev. Dr J.I.H. McDonald is a lecturer in Christian Ethics and Practical Theology, University of Edinburgh.

Rev. T.S. McGregor is chaplain to the Royal Infirmary, Edinburgh.

Very Rev. John McIntyre is professor emeritus of Systematic Theology, University of Edinburgh.

Rev. Dr J.P. Mackey is dean of the Faculty of Divinity, University of Edinburgh.

Dr C.M. Una Maclean is reader in Community Medicine, University of Edinburgh.

Rev. Fraser Maclennan is assistant principal chaplain, Royal Air Force.

Dr Barbara J. McNeel is executive director, Opportunity Associates, Philadelphia, USA.

Rt Rev. Morris Maddocks is adviser to the archbishops of Canterbury and York for the ministry of health and healing.

Libby Malone is a solicitor and notary public in practice in Edinburgh and East Lothian.

Rev. Roger Marsh is chaplain to Marlborough College.

Rev. Louis Marteau is director of the Dympna Centre, London.

Dr James Mathers was formerly honorary lecturer in Pastoral Studies, University of Birmingham.

John T. Mead is senior lecturer in Social Psychology, Polytechnic of the South Bank, London.

Canon M.A.H. Melinsky is principal of the Northern Ordination Course.

Rt Rev. C.J. Meyer is suffragan bishop of Dorchester in the Oxford Diocese.

Rev. John P. Millar is lecturer and supervisor, Westminster Pastoral Foundation.

Rev. Dr Archie Mills is a clinical member and provisional teaching member (organizational development) of the International Transactional Analysis Association.

Rev. Bernard Mobbs is vicar of St Bartholomew's Church, Sydenham.

Dr Elizabeth R. Moberly works as a psychologist in Cambridge, in addition to being a poet and author.

Rachel Moss is a lay theologian and magistrate.

Rev. Dr George M. Newlands is professor of Divinity, University of Glasgow.

Rev. Dr Noel D. O'Donoghue is a lecturer in Systematic Theology, University of Edinburgh.

Canon Paul Oestreicher is secretary, Division of International Affairs, British Council of Churches.

Dr Joan O'Leary is an adult education consultant and a gestalt therapist.

Dr Ian Oswald is professor of Psychiatry, University of Edinburgh.

Rev. Dr Ruth Page is a lecturer in Systematic Theology, University of Edinburgh.

Dr Brian Parkinson is a post-doctoral research fellow in the Department of Psychology, University of Manchester.

Michael Parsons is a psychoanalyst in private practice, a member of the Royal College of

Psychiatrists, and associate member of the British Psychoanalytical Society.

Rev. Dr Stephen Pattison is lecturer in Pastoral Studies, University of Birmingham.

Rev. Michael Perham is secretary of the Church of England Doctrine Commission and rector of the Oakdale Team Ministry, Poole.

Ven. Michael Perry is archdeacon of Durham and editor of *The Christian Parapsychologist*.

Rev. Bryan Pettifer is principal of the St Albans Diocese Ministerial Training Scheme.

Rev. Hugo Petzsch is curate of St James the Great, Dollar.

Dr Brice Pitt is a consultant psychogeriatrician, Department of Psychological Medicine, St Bartholomew's Hospital, London.

Professor Sir Desmond Pond is chief scientist, Department of Health and Social Security, London.

Canon Ronald H. Preston is professor emeritus of Social and Pastoral Theology, University of Manchester.

Dr J.A. Raeburn is senior lecturer in the Human Genetics Unit, University of Edinburgh.

Fiona Raffaelli is a social worker with the Scottish Council for Single Parents.

Rev. Laurence Reading was formerly a staff member of the Church of England Board of Education.

Canon Martin Reardon is co-chairman of the English Association of Interchurch Families.

Peter Ribbins is a lecturer in Social and Administrative Studies in Education, University of Birmingham.

Joyce Rimmer is a lecturer in Social Work, University of Birmingham.

Dr Alex Robertson is senior lecturer in Social Administration, University of Edinburgh.

Rev. Warwick Ross is a postgraduate research student in the department of Christian Ethics and Practical Theology, University of Edinburgh.

Rev. Dr Nicholas Sagovsky is dean of Clare College, Cambridge.

Andrew Samuels is an author and professional member of the Society of Analytical Psychology.

Craig San Roque, a child psychologist and Jungian analyst, is a lecturer and supervisor, Westminster Pastoral Foundation.

Dame Cicely Saunders is medical director of St Christopher's Hospice, London.

Dr Ruth Schröck is head of the Department of Nursing Studies, Queen Margaret College, Edinburgh.

Rev. Tom Scott is administrator, Strathcarron Hospice, Denny, and executive officer (Scotland), National Society for Cancer Relief.

Rt Rev. Dr Peter Selby is suffragan bishop of Kingston-upon-Thames, London.

Rev. D.W.D. Shaw is professor of Divinity, University of St Andrews.

Dr Andrew Skarbek is a consultant psychotherapist, Runwell Hospital, Essex.

Ronald I.M.Smythe is a lecturer and supervisor, Westminster Pastoral Foundation.

Dr R.P. Snaith is senior lecturer in Psychiatry, St James's University Hospital, Leeds.

Rev. A. Brendan Soane is a lecturer in Moral Theology at Allen Hall, London.

Rev. Peter W. Speck is chaplain to the Royal Free Hospital, London.

Dr Faith Spicer is director of the London Youth Advisory Centre.

Rev. Dr Edward V. Stein is Tulley Professor of Pastoral Psychology, San Francisco Theological Seminary, USA.

Rev. Stephen W. Sykes is regius professor of Divinity, University of Cambridge.

Rev. Dr Gianfranco Tellini is rector of St Mary's, Dunblane.

Rt Rev. Hewlett Thompson is bishop of Exeter.

Dr Ian E. Thompson is senior educationalist, Scottish Health Education Group.

Joy Thompson is a member of the Institute of Group Analysis.

The late Rev. Dr Martin Thornton was canon chancellor of Truro Cathedral.

Canon Dr N.H. Todd is vicar of Rolleston and adviser on training to the bishop of Southwell.

Nicholas Tyndall is chief officer, National Marriage Guidance Council.

Rev. Dr Chad Varah, the founder of The Samaritans, is rector of St Stephen Walbrook, London and president of Befrienders International.

Robyn Vines is assistant director and head of clinical services, Cairnmillar Institute, Melbourne, Australia.

Canon Leslie G. Virgo is rector of Chelsfield and adviser on pastoral care and counselling for the diocese of Rochester.

Dr Eileen Vizard is senior registrar in Child Psychiatry, Great Ormond Street Hospital, London.

Rev. David Wainwright is diocesan officer for

Social Responsibility, diocese of Oxford.

Dr Gillian Waldron is consultant in Community Psychiatry, Tower Hamlets Health Authority, London.

Rev. Roland Walls is a member of the Community of the Transfiguration, Roslin, and a Roman Catholic priest.

Rev. Keith Ward is professor of History and Philosophy of Religion, King's College, London.

Dr J.P. Watson is professor of Psychiatry, Guy's Hospital Medical School, University of London.

Mary Welch is a professional member of the Society of Analytical Psychology, in practice in Lincoln.

Rev. John Wesson is rector of St Martin's in the Bullring, Birmingham.

Rev. Dr James A. Whyte is professor of Practical Theology and Christian Ethics, University of St Andrews.

Rev. Dr Chris Wigglesworth is a lecturer in Practical Theology, University of Aberdeen.

Jane Williams is an author and lecturer on theology and sexism.

Dr James Williamson is emeritus professor of Geriatric Medicine, University of Edinburgh.

Rev. Dr Brian Wren is a hymnwriter and author on worship, world development and peace.

Canon Frank Wright was formerly staff tutor in Religious Studies, Extra-mural Department, University of Manchester.

Rev. Dr Frances M. Young is a senior lecturer in the department of theology, University of Birmingham.

A

ABORTION AND ABORTION COUNSELLING

Abortion is the interruption of a pregnancy before the foetus is viable. Spontaneous abortion is frequent, criminal abortion has been commonly practised in almost all societies in all ages. However this article considers only legal abortion.

1. *Law.* Most governments have recently introduced legislation permitting the termination of pregnancy. The US Supreme Court has ruled this to be, in early pregnancy, a private matter between woman and physician. Most other legislatures allow abortion if there is a risk to maternal life, or of severe foetal abnormality, and on a variety of other grounds which in Britain are risk to the mother's physical or mental health, or to the welfare of her existing children. The details however are irrelevant, as once abortion is legal on any ground it becomes widely practised with scant regard for forensic considerations.

2. *Practice.* The existence of the option of termination has placed a new burden on pregnant women even when carrying a desired pregnancy. Often they have to resist pressure by family to seek abortion because of social or economic problems. It is an important function of pastor and doctor to identify and support such women against these pressures. Abortion during the first trimester of pregnancy, when the foetus is not yet fully formed, is technically easy, is usually performed under anaesthesia, and requires only brief hospitalization. In the second trimester it usually requires intra-uterine injections to initiate abortion, is technically more hazardous, emotionally traumatic, and repugnant to the nursing staff. It should require even more serious indication, such as marked foetal abnormality. Some severe congenital abnormalities can be identified early in pregnancy, and, if found, abortion is offered. Such investigations should be accepted only by the woman whose circumstances are such that she would be quite unable to cope with the life-long care of such a child. There is abundant evidence that some families break under that strain.

3. *Theological considerations.* On the grounds that the embryo from fertilization is alive and a person (or possessing 'personhood') many Christians forbid abortion under all circumstances, although usually making an exception where the mother's survival is in real danger. However, as medicine defines 'death' by the absence of cerebral electrical activity, it is difficult to define as alive an embryo before it develops electrical connections in its cortex at seven or eight weeks. Additionally, the realization that some 60% of fertilized eggs are discarded by nature makes it difficult to accord them the status in the divine economy demanded by some theologians. The sole biblical reference to abortion (Exod. 21.22–5 – the subject of varying interpretation since the first century) is held by rabbinic scholars to distinguish between the value of foetal and adult life. However there is no doubt that God takes an interest in prenatal life (Ps. 139.13–16; Jer. 1.5). The sanctity of life should therefore be preserved unless at the cost of other greater values.

4. *Counselling.* The woman unwillingly pregnant feels caught in a trap. She needs understanding compassionate unjudgmental rational advice. Remorse, which may be severe and lifelong, may follow abortion. It must therefore be discouraged in most instances. If her circumstances are indeed dire, a troubled conscience may be allayed by discussion of her God-given responsibilities to her existing children and to her husband, which may only be fulfillable by abortion. On the other hand it is vital to explore fully with her alternative help available with finance, housing, and babysitting from outside agencies, especially from a loving uncritical Christian congregation. As an abortion request is often an initial panic reaction it is important that without jeopardizing a possible urgent gynaecological appointment, there should be a couple of days for quiet reflection and exploration of the suggested alternatives. But timing is also important, since the later the abortion the more distressing it is likely to be.

The illegitimately pregnant woman will require especial help. Need far outstrips supply, but where realistic continuing support can be supplied throughout pregnancy this should be offered. Adoption must be explored. In addition to the pressing problems of shelter, money and emotional support, the possible long-term antagonism of mother to her child, and the potential deprivation for the child of a one-parent family, cannot be evaded. Abortion is usually unwise where the relationship to the putative father continues and is likely to lead to marriage. The story that it has broken up must be treated with scepticism. Future infertility makes earlier abortion a deep regret.

Compassion, which is mandatory, does not necessarily support abortion as the easy option. Our Lord's example when confronted with the adulteress (John 8.3–11) was linked to moral challenge. In all cases future behaviour must be considered; for the Christian this surely requires efficient family planning within marriage, and chastity outside.

Abortion, being directed towards the health of the woman and not motivated by hatred of the foetus, cannot rightly be defined as murder. Nevertheless some women feel guilty afterwards, and many will feel continuing ambivalence. It may be possible to let them see that their action was the best in the circumstances, but on the other hand there is often a continuing awareness of failure and sinfulness, for which the offer of forgiveness is the most appropriate help.

Cook, D., *The Moral Maze* (SPCK, 1982), pp. 86–132. Feldman, D.M., *Marital Relations, Birth Control and Abortion in Jewish Law* (Schocken Books, New York, 1974), pp. 251–96. Gardner, R.F.R., *Abortion: the Personal Dilemma* (Paternoster, 1972). Johnstone, B., Kuhse, H. and Singer, P., 'The Moral Status of the Embryo: Two Viewpoints', in W. Walters and P. Singer, *Test-Tube Babies, a Guide to Moral Questions, Present Techniques, and Future Possibilities* (Oxford, 1982), pp. 49-64. Noonan, J.T. (ed.), *The Morality of Abortion* (Harvard, 1970).

For the patient: Gardner, Rex, *What about Abortion?* (Paternoster, 1972).

REX GARDNER

See also: BIRTH; GENETIC COUNSELLING.

ACCEPTANCE

In psychotherapy acceptance is a concept of considerable complexity upon which the whole therapeutic relationship is built. It concerns the way in which the client's overall self-regard as one of adequate value comes about through the counselling process. The client may present with problems which basically convey a sense of little self-worth, even when complaining of ill-treatment by others. This lack of personal worth will be present in particular in a state of depression (q.v.).

The person needs to be able to feel that, whatever the difficulties, the counsellor accepts the client, in his or her own right. This involves the client not being required to meet any expectation from the counsellor. The client may have come to view himself or herself as a failure; socially, intellectually, academically, emotionally or professionally. Past experience may have taught that in the view of others – usually parents, teachers or those in authority – anything less than total success is inadequate and to be rejected, and therefore, since complete success is impossible, he or she is rejectable. In pastoral counselling this may include the imperative felt need to satisfy God.

Failure to be an adequate person will, in this self-view, include undesirable traits which are open to disapproval, such as resentment, envy and jealousy (often of siblings), anger and rebellion, and hatred. These emotions are part of a real personality which has been protectively hidden for fear of reprisal, but which need now to be revealed, tested in confrontation, and found to be congruent within the total person. What is acceptable is not the 'good', which may be experienced as false, but the 'real'.

Acceptance must be distinguished from condoning, which is not a genuine form of attributing value to the person. Behaviour aimed at deliberately provoking a judgemental response, so as to test out the integrity of the counsellor, should be pointed out to the client free of either condemnation or condoning. He or she can then admit to such errors and falsity of self, as and when able. Condoning acts which the client may come to regret would be likely to establish a negative false self, since the action would then appear approvable by the counsellor.

A further distinction to be made is that of collusion (q.v.) in which the counsellor may, consciously or unconsciously, support an attitude or an action of the client which does not really accord with his or her integrity. The counsellor may be seduced into colluding, for instance with an anti-parental or anti-spouse connivance which again no longer leaves the person free finally to make an objective judgement of these relationships.

The counsellor must be able to see, and to remember, that the client's view of significant persons in the past, or present, is as he or she sees and experiences them, for whatever subjective reason, not necessarily as they really are. It is his or her vision that the counsellor accepts; this must not be confused with facts.

Acceptance of the person involves a total and equal respect. It recognizes that the client contributes to the relationship not only possibly by payment, but also by giving the counsellor new experience, enabling a sharpening or modification of skills, and by affirming his or her role as a professional carer.

In the countertransference (see TRANS-FERENCE) of an accepting relationship, it is not required of the counsellor to always have a liking for the client although it is often not easy to work with one who is not likeable. There may be causes in the counsellor for strong reactions against the client; these must be recognized and prevented from blocking concern. The counsellor must be free of prejudice against racial characteristics, creeds and practices of other religions and cultures, and sexual deviations or eccentricities, if total acceptance is to be effectively conveyed. Further, it can be painful for the counsellor to find that the client may not easily accept the acceptance offered. The therapeutic experience, often unfamiliar to the client, may accentuate a sense of mistrust or guilt and unworthiness for a while, and this may take time and patience to overcome.

Cox, Murray, *Structuring the Therapeutic Process* (Pergamon, 1978). Rogers, Carl, *On Becoming a Person: a Therapist's View of Psychotherapy* (Constable, 1967).

BARBARA K. FOWLES

See also: CLIENT-CENTRED THERAPY; EMPATHY; JUDGEMENT.

ACCREDITATION
This is the process of certifying individuals or organizations as being competent to offer pastoral care and/or counselling, or to offer training in the field.

The Christian Church has generally regarded ordination (q.v.) as the principal authorization for ministry. Nevertheless the contemporary dialogue with the human sciences has resulted in more specialized approaches to pastoral care and counselling for which a different kind of certification or accreditation is sometimes deemed to be necessary. A sophisticated form of this may be found in the clinical pastoral education (q.v.) movement as it has developed in North America. The Association for Clinical Pastoral Education in the USA publishes Procedures and Guidelines for the accreditation of centres offering CPE and for the certification of CPE supervisors. Precise standards are set out for the different levels of CPE which may be offered (Basic, Advanced and Supervisory) defining entrance requirements, objectives, curricula and the quality of supervision (q.v.). Similarly, standards are laid down for the certification of CPE supervisors which normally comes via the preliminary and temporary status of acting supervisor.

This understanding of accreditation, while an integral part of a movement which has made a highly significant contribution to education for pastoral care, has not been without its critics. An influential figure in developments in Britain was the late Robert Lambourne, lecturer in Pastoral Studies in the University of Birmingham. At the time when moves were being made to bring together various British organizations for pastoral care (q.v.), Lambourne published an article in *Contact* objecting to the proposals as he understood them, for a national pastoral organization. He saw great dangers in copying American approaches to pastoral care, which he believed were based upon outdated clinical, medical and psychoanalytic concepts and practice. 'An accredited, hierarchical pastoral movement will be professional, problem-solving or problem-preventing, standardized and defined. What is required is pastoral care which is lay, corporate, adventurous, variegated and diffuse (Lambourne 1971, p. 24).

Lambourne's direct influence upon the development of pastoral care in Britain cannot yet be fully assessed. What is certain is that within the organization which was eventually formed (the Association for Pastoral Care and Counselling); there have been ambivalent attitudes towards accreditation. While the Association has had an Accreditation

Committee from its early days, few members have been prepared to subject their professional work to the scrutiny of their peers. Nevertheless, procedures have been developed for the accreditation of supervisors and trainess and more recently for pastoral counsellors. It should be noted however that, in the APCC, accreditation is not understood as a qualification or a symbol of status but as a tool for assessment, education and growth. The Westminster Pastoral Foundation has its own long-standing programme of accreditation leading to membership of its Institute of Pastoral Education and Counselling.

Foskett, John, 'APCC's Scheme for Accrediting Supervisors', (*Contact*, 77, 1982:4), pp. 30–4. **Lambourne, R.A.**, 'Objections to a National Pastoral Organisation', (*Contact*, 35, June 1971), pp. 24–31.

DAVID LYALL

See also: CLINICAL PASTORAL EDUCATION; ORGANIZATIONS FOR PASTORAL CARE.

ADDICTION

From *addictus*, pp. of *addicere*: assign, devote to. *Ad* – to + *dicere* – say. (1) To be an addict is to apply or devote oneself persistently or habitually; or to cause, to pursue or continue to practise continually (*Britannica World Language Dict.*, vol. 1) (2) An overdependence on the intake of certain substances such as alcohol or drugs, or performing certain acts, such as smoking. (3) The inability to overcome a habit or behavioural pattern (*Dict. Behavioural Science*).

In its broadest sense addiction is applied to all acts which are repetitive, compulsive and which create an overdependence which is difficult to break. An addicted person is one who is accustomed; inclined to the pursuit, practice or taking of anything: addicted to drugs.

One is addicted to that which has been allowed to gain a strong, habitual, and enduring hold upon action, inclination, or involuntary tendency. The term may then be applied to any human activity. It is possible to become addicted to work, religion, persons, food, sex and so on.

The term 'addictive behaviour' is now used to describe a range of activities whose similarities include a form of indulgence either as a defence against other aspects of personality or life which are seen as threatening or for short-term pleasure and satisfaction at the expense of long-term adverse effects. Of particular importance here for pastoral care must be the recognition that religion, or specific aspects of religion, can become an addiction which shields people from themselves and leads to a sense of euphoria and well-being. As with drug-withdrawal a person addicted to religion can suffer severe symptoms of breakdown when, for any reason, the addiction is exposed or broken.

A World Health Organization Bulletin of 1965 draws attention to the state of mind that is termed 'psychic dependence'. It is pointed out that, even with drugs, this mental state may be the only factor involved. With the use of drugs psychic dependence can and does develop without any evidence of physical dependence. (WHO *Bulletin* 32(5), 1965, pp. 721-33.)

The common and specific use of the term applies to the abuse of drugs. Definitions in this field both narrow and expand the concept: In 1950 the WHO described drug addiction as a state of periodic intoxication, detrimental to the individual and society, produced by the repeated consumption of a drug (natural or synthetic). Its characteristics include: (1) An overpowering desire or need (compulsion) to continue to take the drug and to obtain it by any means. (2) A tendency to increase the dose. (3) A psychic (psychological and sometimes physical) dependence on the effects of the drug.

Today's theories of addictive behaviour are multi-variate, taking into account such factors as: hereditary pre-dispositions, the physiology of addiction, cognitive expectancies, social learning patterns – all influence substance use and abuse, as well as other addictions. In established addiction there seems to be a life-dependency on the practice or drug, whether this is food, alcohol, religion or a person. Effective and lasting interventions are, therefore, difficult to find.

Addiction is caused by human weakness, not by drugs and is a symptom of a personality maladjusted rather than a disease in its own right. Usually people who become addicted are either hedonistic, psychopaths or psychoneurotics.

In addition to a personality so constructed as to make the individual susceptible to addiction, contact with an addicting drug is necessary, and the method of contact is extremely important. If a person learns about drugs and begins their use as a result of association with addicts, addiction is more likely to occur than if the drug is administered for medical reasons. This is another way of saying that addiction, like a contagious disease, spreads from person to person.

(H. Ishbell, quoted in Gross and Slater, *Clinical Psychiatry*).

Such an understanding underlines the addiction as serving an adaptive purpose in a person's life. Increasingly stress factors in society are leading to the medical use of drugs increasing addictive behaviour far more broadly than the 'addictive society'. Understanding of and attitudes to addiction tend to be subjective and highly emotional, influenced by society with bias and preconception.

There are four stages to pastoral care for persons who are addicted: (1) *Attending.* Attending to the problem by discovering as much as possible about addiction. Learning the language of addiction. Learning from those who are addicted by attending open meetings of the various groups established to help addicts. Getting to know the local resources. (2) *Relating.* Attempting to understand how the addict is feeling. Getting to know the person without condemning or condoning. (3) *Pattern making.* Helping the person to be more aware of the pattern of their addiction and what it does for them and to them. For most addicts it is only when the pain of addiction outweighs the apparent benefits that the person will be motivated to change. Only a person ready to change can be helped. Any action by the helper to relieve the pain can hinder the moment of recovery. (4) *Action.* Supporting action when desire for change is expressed. Encouraging reference to the general practitioner, local addiction centres, hospital or social service department. Those who can be helped to go to the appropriate voluntary group will find people who understand their problem, talk their language and will not be influenced by their manipulations. For some people a private clinic will be the place of choice for help.

It should always be recognized that addiction is a family and social dis-ease, and that the family can also be helped with these four aproaches.

Leech, K., *What Everyone Should Know about Drugs* (Sheldon, 1983). Miller, W.R.M. (ed.), *The Addictive Behaviour* (Oxford/Pergamon), 1980.

Addresses for further information and help with referral:

MIND, 22 Harley Street, London W1N 2ED. 01 637 0741.

The British Association for Counselling, 37a Sheep Street, Rugby, Warwickshire, CV21 3BX. (0788) 78328/9.

The Society for the Study of Addiction. Alcohol Concern. Both at 3 Grosvenor Crescent, London SW1X 7EE. 01 235 4182.

The United Council on Alcohol and other Drugs, 112 Albany Road, Cardiff. (0222) 49385.

From the local reference library: *Someone to talk to.* A directory of self-help, edited by Penny Webb. Mental Health Foundation, 8 Hallam Street, London W1N 6DH.

Directory Enquiries of British Telecom will supply telephone numbers of London and local centres for Alcoholics Anonymous, Gamblers Anonymous, Slimmers Anonymous, Narcotics Anonymous and so on.

LESLIE VIRGO

ADOLESCENCE
The period between childhood and adulthood.

It is characterized by rapid development of body and mind producing difficulties in the understanding of the self, of relationships with family and, sometimes, with society. The adolescent, in his or her move toward adulthood and autonomy, experiences new and often strange and worrying feelings. From being relatively peaceful in the setting of his family and school, he or she may become shy, awkward, argumentative, depressed, withdrawn or noisy, with bursts of energy and subsequent lethargy which may puzzle parents and other adult contacts.

The agenda of adolescence is discussed as follows:
(1) Separation from parents (or parent substitutes) and gaining of autonomy. (2) Deciding upon a life and work style. (3) Development of moral and ideological value systems. (4) Recognition of sexuality and the gaining of ability to deal with sexual feelings. (5) Ability to relate to other people at work and in friendship and ability to enjoy a long-lasting and committed relationship with one individual.

1. In early adolescence the child is still deeply involved in the family. Often changes of behaviour of young people are not purely a factor of their own change, but can be a reflection of problems of parents and other

members of the family. It is important, therefore, to assess the family dynamics in order to understand a young person's changed behaviour.

As adolescence proceeds, young people searching for an identity may make things very hard for their parents. They often apparently despise parental attitudes and value systems. They can be rebellious and, because of their need to test out their own values and yet to have sufficient boundaries at home, stir up dreadful battles. Just as in infancy, they need parents to give the space to experiment yet offer limits. There are times when adolescents need privacy, both physical and emotional, so that withdrawing from the family circle and seeking solitude is understandable. A preoccupation with body image, acne, greasy hair, clothes and being like the others suggests a need to accept the self and a difficulty in doing so. Parents often resent young people's choice of friends and their group activities, but the peer group can be of great positive value in so far as it enables the sharing of anxieties and sorrows, aspirations and ideas, with others going through a similar experience. Negatively, the peer group may be involved in dangerous or delinquent activities, perhaps by offering quick gains, excitement and peer-group acclaim. Drug experimentation is at present yet another factor in adolescence.

Adolescence is probably more difficult to negotiate in today's complex and urban society; very many parents are separated or divorced and children are often faced with added problems of dealing with step-parents and step-siblings. Divorce may be the best solution to some bad marriages and offer greater hope for young people, but it also causes great anxiety and anger and, frequently, demands an acceptance of the loss of a parent-figure.

2. As children grow away from the family they need to decide upon a job or career and where and how to live. The decisions concerning this are often extremely hard and frequently are a cause of battles in the family, particularly in those families with high aspirations for their children. Now that unemployment is a very likely event, at least at times, young people are frequently apathetic and depressed – the effect of not being needed in society being very destructive to the fragile ego. It is very important that young people

should be helped to develop sufficient inner strengths to deal with this lest they become less and less motivated.

3. In early adolescence concepts are difficult to grasp, and the development of the capacity to balance differing opinions can be lacking. Those children who lack sufficient 'good-enough' parenting may express their anger by adopting negative attitudes. In rather rigid, albeit loving families, children may attempt to throw over the systems taught them by parents and associate with people who hold different religious or political beliefs. The grief some parents suffer can be understood, but children from ordinary families do not become worse people for these changes of views and parents can be helped to accept that their children are still moral people.

4. The fairly sudden shift of hormone balance in adolescence has profound effects upon body size and shape and upon feelings. Girls begin their periods roughly between the ages of 10 and 14. The breasts develop and body-fat is laid down producing a more rounded appearance. There is often an increase in sweating, acne and other distressing problems. Boys delay growth compared with girls, but the final growth spurt can be very rapid. Muscles increase in power, limbs lengthen. The penis increases in size, hair develops and the boy experiences wet dreams as a result of the production of spermatozoa, etc. Both sexes can be very preoccupied with sexual matters; boys perhaps more directly. There is often an early phase of sexual play which does not suggest homosexuality, but soon boys seek a sexual partner. Girls may suffer difficulties in knowing how to handle the sexual demands of boys, and great pressure can be put upon them by young men and by the peer group and the media.

It is now very common for young people to have sex before marriage and has become quite normal for couples in love to live together before marriage. However, the young can be vulnerable to pressure from the peer group. If a family is undergoing stress, is extremely repressive or has no effective controls, teenagers may express their need for rebellion or their personal anxiety in early sexual activity.

It is well known that average normal young people do seek love and partnerships; a problem arises with the young because of their incapacity to take full responsibility for their actions, so that they are greatly at risk of pregnancy. Even if they have a good relationship with their boyfriends or girlfriends, they seldom use sheaths, and the steps to be taken to obtain the contraceptive pill are too great, especially as it may involve parental knowledge. They are in any case bad at taking the pill regularly. Doctors prescribing the pill for young people should take time to counsel adequately, and so enable the girl or couple to learn to be responsible for their own actions. A private study by the author showed that of all girls attending a youth counselling centre for contraception aged under 16, well over half came from broken homes.

It is not easy to help adolescents, but there is almost always a steady growth toward maturity and it is the task of the counsellor to enable this growth even if, at times, it means not interfering while the adolescent makes mistakes. In the long run, the adolescent from a 'good enough' family and very many from deplorable family backgrounds, muddle through to a useful maturity.

Farrell, C., 'My Mother Said . . .': the Way Young People Learned About Sex and Birth Control (Routledge, 1978). Laufer, M., Adolescent Disturbance and Breakdown (Penguin, 1975). Skynner, R. and Cleese, J., Families and How to Survive Them (Methuen, 1983).

FAITH SPICER

See also: CHILDREN: PASTORAL CARE; HUMAN DEVELOPMENT; MATURITY; PARENTING; REBELLION.

ADOPTION: AGENCIES AND LEGISLATION

Adoption is a way of enabling children to grow up in a permanent family if, for any reason, they cannot be brought up by the family into which they were born. It is a formal legal procedure by which all the rights and duties of the natural parents are permanently transferred to the adoptive parents by a court. The adopted child takes the adoptive parents' surname, inherits from them and loses all legal ties to his or her family of birth.

Adoption became legally possible in England and Wales in 1926 and in Scotland in 1930. Since then the laws have been amended, most significantly by the Adoption Act 1958 and the Children Act 1975, to reflect changes in social attitudes and needs.

There are at present 45 approved voluntary adoption societies operating in Britain. Each is entitled to make its own conditions for accepting would-be adopters, and practices vary. Many had a religious origin and operate along denominational lines. These vary in size and structure from the 'large nationals' – Barnardo's, National Children's Home and the Church of England Children's Society – to the small diocesan or independent societies.

In addition, all but a handful of local authorities currently act as adoption agencies and, when the Children Act 1975 comes into effect fully, all local authorities will have a duty to provide a comprehensive adoption service. This they will do by working in partnership with any existing voluntary societies in their area. Since February 1982 it has been illegal for adoptions to be arranged privately, i.e. without involving an adoption agency, except where the proposed adopter is a relative of the child.

Changes in adoption trends have been particularly significant over the past 15 years. After reaching a peak of almost 25,000 in 1968, the number of adoption orders in England and Wales declined to only 9,284 in 1981. More widespread use of contraception, and changes in abortion law, served to reduce the number of babies born unwanted by their parents. At the same time changes in social attitudes made it possible for more single mothers to keep and look after their children themselves (see SINGLE PARENTS). The result was a rapid decline in the number of illegitimate children adopted by 'strangers' – the group which has dominated the public image of adoption since 1926 – from 14,500 in 1968 to 3,300 in 1982. Of this last group only 2,000 were children aged less than one year old.

An equally significant trend was an increase followed by a rapid decrease in the use of adoption to formalize arrangements in reconstituted families following divorce, and to a lesser extent for illegitimate children when their single mothers married for the first time. In 1974, 15,000 of the 22,500 adoption orders (60%) were for step-parent adoptions of this kind; by 1982, following a change in the law which discouraged the practice, the number had dwindled to 5,800.

These demographic and social trends helped to revolutionize adoption law and practice during the 1970s. What in the late sixties had been a service for childless couples seeking to build a family of their own, became a service for children needing families. As the supply of healthy white babies for adoption dried up, adoption agencies began to recognize that there were nevertheless thousands of children in local authority care who needed and would benefit from life in a permanent family. Today, a majority of 'stranger' adoptions are of children with 'special needs' – children in public care or in hospital who, unless adopted, would be likely to remain in care for the whole of their childhood and beyond. Ten or even five years ago, many of the children adopted today would have been deemed unadoptable, e.g. mentally and physically handicapped children of all ages, older children and adolescents, and sibling groups.

Changes have also occurred in the characteristics of adoptive parents. Adoption agencies take great care to match each child with the capacities and interests of particular parents, whether a married couple or a single adopter of either sex. There is no longer a general ideal type of adoptive couple. The characteristics of adopters vary enormously in terms of social class, age (although they must by law be at least 21), income, marital status, family type and size, and home environment.

Since there is always a shortage of families willing to adopt children with special needs, adoption agencies have increasingly turned to local newspapers, radio, television and other methods to advertise the needs of children in care in the hope that suitable families can be found. Pastoral care may concern itself with this social need as well as paying attention to the day-to-day problems arising in adopting families and to the issues facing adopted children, especially in adolescence (q.v.).

Books and other information from British Agencies for Adoption and Fostering, 11 Southwark Street, London SE1 1RQ.
Bean, P., *Adoption: Essays in Social Policy, Law and Sociology* (Tavistock, 1984). **Smith, C.R.,** *Adoption and Fostering: Why and How* (Macmillan, 1984). **Tizard, B.,** *Adoption: a Second Chance* (Open Books, 1977).

TONY HALL

See also: PARENTING.

ADOPTION: EMOTIONAL ASPECTS

The adopted child has acquired a reputation for growing up emotionally disturbed, if not also a mischief-maker. However, there is no real reason why the experience of being reared by substitute parents *from early infancy* should lead to developmental problems or disordered conduct. It is not hard to understand how such an idea might have arisen, in

that adoptive status is often perceived as a source of stress by doctors, teachers, magistrates and other influential persons. In some cases 'adoption stress' is linked with delayed family placement such that the child's social and emotional development has already been hampered (Humphrey and Ounsted 1963). Yet the only national study (Seglow *et al.* 1972; Lambert and Streather 1980) has yielded an optimistic portrait of adoptive families in Britain, granted that none of these adoptees had reached adolescence (q.v.) at the time of the later report. Even when at least the first two years of life have been spent in an institution, without continuity of care from a dependable adult, adopted children seem to fare better than those restored to their original parent(s) after a similar period of group living (Tizard 1977).

Nevertheless, awareness of one's adoption may be a common cause of concern. Novelists and dramatists have long been attracted to this theme, which lies at the heart of man's search for a stable self-image. The provisions of Section 26 of the 1975 Children Act, whereby from the age of 18 onwards the adopted person has right of access to a copy of the original birth certificate, have not only stimulated curiosity among the genealogically deprived but also fed the anxieties of both adoptive parents and those parents who have given up a child for adoption. For a partially satisfied curiosity can lead to a search for absent relatives, with all the hazards of unforeseen confrontation. Those adopted prior to the Act are required to undergo counselling from an accredited social worker, which is intended to provide some kind of a safeguard. In the current decade there are signs of a more open attitude towards illegitimacy and adoption, so that the exaggerated secrecy of the transaction may come to be seen as undesirable. A recent study (Haimes and Timms 1985) commissioned by the DHSS has queried whether some of the anxieties of all interested parties might indeed be allayed by lifting the iron curtain which descends after the court order has been granted.

Child guidance workers, who see more than their fair share of young adoptees, have sometimes regarded children cut off from their roots as being consequently at risk of psychological disturbance. An up-to-date review of the literature (Humphrey and Humphrey 1986) has tried to correct such an impression on the grounds that, from the available evidence, supportive family relationships would appear to be an effective antidote. If it is only the more uneasy adoptions that lead to a compulsion to search for the unknown genetic parents, then mystification may be a less important factor than has hitherto been supposed. It could well be argued that *social learning* (i.e. feedback from significant others) contributes more than ancestral knowledge to one's sense of self.

Here prime emphasis has been laid on the adopted person's need of background information, since this is in tune with the spirit of our times. Another contemporary feature is the shortage of adoptable infants, with a growing trend towards placement of older children with a more or less firm grasp of their pre-adoptive history. This must lessen the temptation towards dishonesty and evasion on the part of adopters, only a small minority of whom in any case would want their children to start school in total ignorance of their family status. Concealment of adoption is no longer a serious problem, and competent agencies now make a practice of passing on a more comprehensive dossier about the children in their care than was usual in the past.

Given free communication within the adoptive family, are there other hidden sources of stress? Some couples may continue to grieve over their infertility, although by no means all adopters are biologically childless. Where doctors persist in heroic measures, such as *in vitro* fertilization, the unsuccessfully treated couple may find themselves adopting in a state of frustrated anguish. The careful vetting undergone by all prospective adopters prior to legal confirmation of their suitability is another possible stress factor, since it may encourage aspirations towards perfect parenthood or even doubts as to their entitlement to a child who is not their own. Moreover, adopted children were at one time more likely than others to be reared without siblings by elderly middle-class parents, and thus put under more pressure to succeed.

Happily, most children, given adequate parental care, can accommodate to a wide range of family circumstances. It is not wholly improbable that part of the anxiety about adoption is created by the conscientious professionals who are responsible for arranging it.

Haimes, E. and Timms, N., *Adoption, Identity and Social Policy: the Search for Distant Relatives* (Gower, Aldershot, 1985). Humphrey, M. and Humphrey, H., 'A Fresh Look at Genealogical Bewilderment' (to appear in: *British Journal of Medical Psychology*, 1986). Humphrey, M. and Ounsted, C., 'Adoptive families referred for psychiatric advice: (i) the children' (*British J. of Psychiatry*, 109, 1963), pp. 599–608. Lambert, L. and Streather, J., *Children in Changing Families: a Study of Adoption and Illegitimacy* (Macmillan, 1980). Seglow, J., *et al.*, *Growing up Adopted* (NFER, Windsor, 1972). Tizard, B., *Adoption: a Second Chance* (Open Books, 1977).

MICHAEL HUMPHREY

See also: ADOPTION: AGENCIES AND LEGISLATION; HUMAN DEVELOPMENT; IDENTITY; PARENTING.

AGAPE
See: LOVE.

AGEING
The gradual decay of the human organic system, becoming more marked towards the end of life, ending in the breakdown of the system and so death (q.v.).

The benefit of longevity as a result of medical advance brings with it the new medical and pastoral problem of the 'geriatric explosion'. In the UK about 15% of the population are aged 65 or over, and this proportion is increasing. Within this group the over-85s are increasing more rapidly than the 75+ group, which in turn is increasing more rapidly than the 65+ group.

In the past *gerontology* (the study of the phenomenon of ageing) and *geriatrics* (the medical care of the elderly) have been given scant attention in medical schools and nursing colleges. Many practitioners are ignorant of modern ideas on care of the elderly. Negative stereotypes have tended to cloud the distinction between acute and chronic illness, and the assumption that old age is inevitably a time of disability, dependency and loss of faculties has meant that often too little attention is paid to treatable conditions. Chronic instability of gait, incomplete bladder control, and a marked increased sensitivity to the unwanted effects of drugs become general in the over-80s group.

Common conditions include arthritis and heart disease. An important and yet still inadequately researched condition is dementia (q.v.). Physical disease may lead to emotional and psychological stress (q.v.). This is particularly true of cancer and strokes because of their dramatic consequences. Stress may result in manifestations of anxiety (q.v.) with agitation, restlessness and tremor, and may even lead to depression (q.v.) which is not uncommon in the elderly. Mental illness may exacerbate, or even take the form of a physical disease. A vicious circle is soon entered upon, made worse if the physical symptoms are misinterpreted. Inappropriate drug treatment results in an unwanted reaction to that drug, and the new symptom is treated with yet another drug.

Disease in old age may occur in atypical fashion, e.g. pneumonia without fever, chest pain or cough, or a heart attack without the characteristic central chest pain. Four cardinal features dominate the appearance of disease in the elderly, and these 'giants of geriatrics' are mental confusion, falls, decreased mobility and incontinence. Their occurrence, singly or collectively, may indicate the onset of an infection, of cancer, or other serious and potentially treatable condition.

The elderly are more likely to suffer from more than one disease at a time, and disease is more likely to result in disability (see DISABLEMENT). Old age is characterized by loss: of livelihood, spouse, fitness and faculties, of life in its broadest sense, and finally in the particular sense as a person faces his or her own death.

In responding to the needs of the elderly it is impossible to overestimate the role of the family. Contrary to popular opinion, family care today compares favourably with previous generations. All studies which have been carried out show that families generally do their best to support their elders. Daughters and daughters-in-law are the main source of support, and about two-thirds of elderly persons are in contact with their offspring daily and nearly 90% in the previous seven days. It is essential that families receive maximum support so that they may continue their caring role. Planned respite admissions and efficient community nursing services ensure families are kept within their limits of tolerance.

Important health services for the elderly include the general practitioner, hopefully co-operating with the district nurse and the health visitor. Others include the home help service provided by the social work department, meals on wheels, lunch clubs, and day centres, which not only help to ensure a proper diet (q.v.) but also offer opportunities

for social and recreational activitiy. Geriatric hospitals with both in-patient and out-patient facilities, and parallel developments in geriatric psychiatry, provide treatment and rehabilitation for the more seriously ill. More purpose-built accommodation for the elderly is being provided, e.g. sheltered housing, and opportunities exist for volunteer visiting (q.v.) of old people at home and in institutions.

The general aim is to enhance the autonomy of the elderly, to ensure they are given every chance to decide for themselves how and where they live and ultimately where they may die.

Bromley, D.B., *The Psychology of Human Ageing* (Penguin, 1966). **Mace, N.L.**, and **Rabins, P.V.** (eds.), *The Thirty-Six Hour Day* (Johns Hopkins UP, 1982).

JAMES WILLIAMSON

See also: DYING; HUMAN DEVELOPMENT; REHABILITATION.

AGGRESSION

A term applied to a variety of behaviours ranging from verbal insults, through prejudice, damage to property and physical abuse, to murder. In popular usage it also tends to be seen as a cause of such behaviours.

A distinction may be drawn between 'hostile aggression', the sole aim of which is to inflict injury, and 'instrumental aggression', in which the suffering of the victim is incidental to the attainment of some other goal. In either case the consequences are obviously a matter of public concern, and attempts to identify the causes of aggression as well as methods of controlling aggression are therefore of considerable social as well as scientific importance.

Determinants of aggression. Theoretical accounts differ primarily in terms of the relative emphasis placed on biological as opposed to social/environmental determinants of aggression. At one extreme are those who argue for the existence of an innate, biologically rooted, aggressive drive; at the other are those who attribute all aggression to antecedent events and/or concurrent environmental factors. It is increasingly clear that a full account of human aggression will have to take into consideration both biological and social factors and the likely complex interactions between them.

1. *Biological factors* include genetic, neuro-

physiological and biochemical influences. (1) Though difficult to demonstrate conclusively, it seems likely, particularly in view of evidence from animal studies, that genetic influences contribute to individual differences in human aggression. Evidence of the stability of aggressive tendencies over time and across situations is consistent with this view. (2) Certain aggressive responses, such as stamping the feet, clenching the teeth, and making fists, may be innately 'wired into' the neuromuscular system, since children born deaf and blind display these behaviours even though they have never had the chance to observe them. (3) Damage to or malfunction of certain parts of the brain may influence levels of aggression, as may ingestion of alcohol and other chemical substances. (4) In lower animals the administration of male hormones (testosterone and androgens) have generally been found to lead to an increase, and female hormones (oestrogens) to a decrease in aggressive behaviour. However, the relationship between hormones and levels of aggression in humans is not entirely clear and remains a matter for debate.

2. *Social/environmental determinants* of aggression include: (a) cultural attitudes towards aggression (reflected in national differences in homicide and suicide rates; (b) social expectations and pressures, which may lead even non-aggressive individuals to participate in aggressive actions; (c) child-rearing practices (a history of rejection and frustration, overly harsh or inconsistent discipline, *or* permissiveness and reinforcement for aggressive behaviour predisposed to high levels of aggression); (d) exposure to aggressive models, particularly when these are seen to be rewarded for aggression; (e) various stressful circumstances, for example exposure to insults and threats, frustration of important goals (particularly when this is perceived as arbitrary, intentional and caused by a responsible agent); (f) the presence of 'aggressive cues' such as individuals or objects (e.g. weapons) associated with aggression, particularly under conditions which are stressful or arousing in other ways.

Media violence and aggression. Opposing views hold that: (a) viewing violence enables viewers to discharge some of their own aggression and thus reduces aggression ('catharsis'); (b) viewing violence increases aggression by teaching new aggressive behaviours, disinhibiting aggressive responses, providing aggressive cues, altering value systems (encouraging acceptance of violence), distorting views about appropriate methods of conflict resolution.

Evidence from laboratory studies overwhelmingly supports the latter view. However, experiments in the 'natural environment' have indicated that the relationship between aggression and media violence is complex, and further research is needed to clarify various issues including the conditions under which media violence is most and least likely to facilitate aggression, and the differential effects of viewing violence on different individuals.

Controlling aggression. Methods of controlling aggression which appear to have met with some success include: training of responses that are incompatible with anger; 'empathy training'; training in the ability to think before acting; and exposure to prosocial models.

Bandura, A., *Aggression: a Social Learning Analysis* (Prentice Hall, New Jersey,1973). **Berkowitz, L.,** 'Some Aspects of Observed Aggression', in W.W. Hartup and J. de Wit (eds.), Origins of Aggression (Mouton, The Hague, 1978). **Eysenck, H.J.** and **Nias, D.K.,** *Sex, Violence and the Media* (Temple Smith, 1978). **Feshbach, S.** and **Weiner, B.,** *Personality* (D.C. Heath, Lexington, Mass., 1982), ch. 18. **Lorenz, K.,** *On Aggression* (Methuen, 1966). **Pervin, L.,** *Current Issues and Controversies in Personality* (Wiley, 1978), ch. 3. **Tinbergen, N.,** On War and Peace in Animals and Man (*Science*, vol. 160, 1968), pp. 1411–18.

S. HENLEY

See also: CONFLICT; REBELLION; VIOLENCE.

ALCOHOLISM
See: ADDICTION.

ALIENATION
The state, action or process of being estranged from oneself, others or God, often associated with anxiety (q.v.) or despair.

Tillich, P., *The Courage to Be* (Fontana, 1962).

AMBIVALENCE
A technical psychiatric term coined by Eugen Bleuler, which has now entered ordinary language to mean little more than uncertainty. Strictly, it implies having contra-

dictory feelings simultaneously towards the same object, e.g. both love and hatred. Ambivalence is still used as a technical term in psychotherapy, and appropriately enough it is evaluated both positively and negatively.

The positive evaluation depends on a picture of child development in which initially the child lives in a simplified world in which people and things are either good or bad (gratifying/frustrating, loved/hated, pleasurable/painful) and never both. Ambivalence is then an achievement, when the child can recognize that it is the same 'object' (mother, for example) who arouses in him *both* feelings of love (for her milk, her caring, etc.) and feelings of hatred (for her absences, limitations, etc.). A mature recognition of reality requires the realization that nothing is perfect, and perhaps also that nothing is unrelievedly evil. Such a realization makes relationship more difficult, in that feelings now have to be contained and not always acted on, but the difficulty results from a true perception of the world's complexity.

There are some adults who have failed to 'achieve' ambivalence in this way, whose feelings towards others are a succession of passionate idealization and raging denigrations, or (more stably) of loving feelings towards one person subtly balanced by hatred towards some other. This leads typically to a sort of cowboys-and-Indians, us-and-them view of the universe. The Christian picture of God and the Devil has often been misused to collude with an infantile picture of this sort (*see* COLLUSION).

Ambivalence ceases to be a positive achievement when it becomes excessive, that is, becomes so great that the person is unable to make decisions and commit himself or herself, either to a point of view or another person. When a history of failed commitments, or of endless doubts and scruples, begins clearly to repeat itself, then it may be that the challenge is *not* (as the person usually thinks) to 'make a decision and stick to it', but to examine the hidden reasons for a deep underlying fear of life.

Klein, Melanie, 'Love, Guilt and Reparation', in Klein and Riviere, *Love, Hate and Reparation* (Hogarth, 1937). **Winnicott, D.W.,** 'The Development of the Capacity for Concern' in D.W. Winnicott, *The Maturational Processes and the Facilitating Environment* (Hogarth, 1965).

DAVID BLACK

See also: DOUBLE BIND; DOUBT.

ANALYTICAL (JUNGIAN) PSYCHOLOGY

The term used by C.G. Jung (1875–1961) to describe his ideas about the psyche and his approach to analytic treatment.

Jung was one of Freud's earliest collaborators at a time when psychoanalysis (q.v.) was scarcely established as either a method of treatment or an accurate description of psychological process. Jung and Freud eventually broke off their relationship and a number of key disputes should be noted. (1) Jung could not agree with Freud's exclusively sexual interpretation of human motivation, preferring to see in what looked like sexual material something of a symbolic meaning. Eventually Freud granted this point. (2) Jung could not go along with an approach to psyche that was, in his view, excessively mechanistic and causal. Human beings do not live according to laws analogous to physical or mechanical principles. Jung was more interested in where a patient's life might be leading him or her (the final prospective viewpoint) than in the causes of the situation (the reductive viewpoint). (3) Freud had made too deep a division between 'hallucination' and 'reality'. Throughout his writings, Jung's concern is for psychological reality as experienced by the individual. In this context, the unconscious is not seen as an enemy but rather as somehow potentially creative and helpful. Dreams, for instance, cease to be regarded as deceitful, and instead are claimed to reveal the unconscious situation in the psyche.

Jung noticed similarities of his own unconscious material with that of his patients, and with the cultural motifs represented everywhere and throughout history. Such 'primordial imagery' forms one strand in Jung's concept of a *collective unconscious*. The word *archetype* refers to unconscious and irrepresentable patterns in the psyche. Jung was anxious to stress that archetypes are structures and need to be clearly distinguished from archetypal images such as motifs, representations, themes and metaphors. The archetype is psychosomatic. That is, it links body and psyche, instinct and image. This was important for Jung, since he did not regard psychology and imagery as 'correlates' or 'reflections' of biological drives. His assertion that images evoke the aim of the instincts implies that they deserve equal place. Archetypes form a core around which an individual's experiences may cluster. This

Jung designated a *complex*. The concept refers to the feelings and emotions generated by experiences in any one area of life. Thus everything that an individual experiences in relation to his mother, conditioned by the archetypal structure pertaining to child and mother, and continuing to have influence in adult life, is his mother complex.

As far as *ego* formation is concerned, this stems from the clash between external reality and instinctual impulses. Frustration is therefore of the essence to consciousness. One is not aware of anything until it is, in a sense, prohibited or out of reach. Although ego is vital in the integration of experience, it is not the whole of personality. The ego itself is enlarged by the passage of symbolic material from the unconscious into consciousness.

The capacity for such a move to take place lies in the *self*. The ego is subordinate to the self, and is said to arise out of it. The self means more than a sense of identity or continuity over time, which are matters dealt with by the ego. The self is the totality of the personality, psyche and soma, past and present, conscious and unconscious. It is also the means by which an individual achieves a sense of harmony and purpose. The postulation of a self answers the question: what holds an individual together? The self may be conceived of as a psychological form of homeostasis, a system that wants to keep in balance. In a way the self is a 'higher' personality than the ego. This is symbolized by such figures as Christ or Buddha who are as far above the ordinary person as the self is above the ego. The self is something we are moving towards as well as that from which we spring.

The notion of psychological movement leads conveniently to the image of life's journey. Jung used the term *individuation* to refer to the process by which a person becomes himself; the person he or she was 'intended' to be. Individuation also carries the meaning of having realized as many of one's potentials as possible. This suggests a relative concept and not a counsel of perfection; as many potentials *as possible*. This process was usually described by Jung as attainable only in the second half of life, but present-day analytical psychologists see individuation as a life-long process and as something natural and available to all. The concept has obvious clinical relevance, remembering the number of clients who feel oppressed by the mass nature of modern society.

The terms *anima* and *animus* suggest personifications of the man within the woman and the woman within the man. This imagery stems from Jung's own description of his encounter with such figures in dreams and fantasies. He came to recognize the figures which for him were female as useful guides to inner development. Later he observed the same phenomenon in women, only the figures were masculine. Traditional interpreters of Jung have suggested that anima and animus are psychologically analogous to the biological recessives in the genes whereby a person carries that which does not correspond to his or her anatomical sex. Anima and animus may also be understood as representing alternative modes of perception, behaviour and evaluation. For example, anima (Latin for 'soul') speaks of imagination, fantasy and play, while animus (Latin for 'mind' or 'intellect') speaks of focused consciousness, authority and respect for facts. The extent to which these qualities are truly linked to gender is much discussed by analytical psychologists. Anima and animus help a person on his or her journey. They connect the person as he or she is (ego) with that which he or she may become (self). As far as outward relationships are concerned, anima and animus spark attraction between the sexes. Men and women recognize and are attracted to their partners instinctively.

In *analytical treatment* Jung stressed the active involvement and psychological state of the analyst. He was the first to insist that the prospective analyst be analysed. The analyst's involvement should not be taken as implying over-enthusiastic sharing with the patient, or with ignoring transferences (q.v.), perhaps of an infantile kind. Rather Jung was arguing against a quasi-medical detachment. In his conception of analysis both participants are changed.

It is remarkable how prescient Jung was. Many of his theories and attitudes have been taken up by psychoanalysis and other disciplines. Analytical psychology is not a static body of ideas, and Jung's work has been furthered by succeeding generations of analysts. This is not to say that temptations to render him as a guru have been completely overcome. Nevertheless, perhaps because of a rapprochement with Freudian psychoanalysis, the professional clinical side has been accentuated in recent years. Jung's emphases on purpose and meaning, and on the moral necessity of facing the *shadow* (negative, evil and destructive) in oneself make him of special interest to pastoral counsellors.

Fordham, M., *Jungian Psychotherapy: a Study in Analytical Psychology* (Wiley, 1978). **Jacobi, J.**, *Complex, Archetype, Symbol in the Works of C.G. Jung* (Princeton UP, 1959); *Selected Writings* (Fontana, 1983). **Samuels, A.**, *Jung and the Post-Jungians* (Routledge, 1984).

ANDREW SAMUELS

See also: PSYCHOANALYSIS; PSYCHOTHERAPY.

ANDROGYNY
Having both male and female sexual characteristics. Represented in mythology by Hermaphrodite (*Ency. Brit.* vol. 3). True physical sexual ambivalence is very rare (Dennison), but in contemporary psychology human wholeness requires the liberation of personality characteristics normally associated with the opposite sex.

Dennison, W.M. (ed.), *Surgery in Infancy and Childhood* (Churchill Livingstone, 3rd edn 1974), p. 358. **Nelson, J.B.**, *Embodiment: an Approach to Sexuality and Christian Theology* (SPCK, 1979).

See also: BODY, THEOLOGY OF; FEMININITY/MASCULINITY; SEXUALITY AND SEXUAL DEVELOPMENT.

ANGER AND HOSTILITY
(1) *Anger* is an emotional reaction associated with the state of physiological arousal (increased pulse rate, heightened blood pressure, contraction of muscles, changes in digestion) provoked by frustration or threat. It may, but need not necessarily, lead to acts of aggression. (2) *Hostility* is an enduring attitude characterized by a readiness to attack (verbally or physically), which may be generalized or may be directed toward specific targets.

1. *Anger*. It has long been recognized that anger has powerful physiological concomitants. The Hebrew words '*aph* and '*anaph* refer to the nostril and thus to the snorting of anger, while *chemah* depicts the burning sensation anger creates; in Greek, *orge* refers to a thrusting and *thumos* to a boiling up; the English word derives from the Latin root *ang*, a narrowing, thus portraying the source of 'choking with rage'. The vividness of its bodily effects and its tendency to prime aggressive behaviour have made anger a

much feared and frequently deplored emotion. In Christian teaching human anger has been seen as tantamount to murder (Matt. 5.22) and as leading to intemperance and unrighteousness (Col. 3.8; Eph. 4.26; Jas. 1.19). Yet the God of love is depicted both in the OT and the NT as an angry God (in over four hundred references), and Jesus is described as angry with the Pharisees and with his own disciples (Mark 3.5; 10.13–16). A proper evaluation of anger depends upon a full understanding of its antecedents and its possible uses.

The physiology of anger is so similar to that of fear, that these emotions can be distinguished only when we recognize the cognitive element in this as in all human emotion (q.v.). People react angrily when they perceive a major threat or an intolerable frustration in a situation from which they cannot easily escape. Thus anger is often at its most powerful in domestic situations, since here people feel at their most vulnerable, fearing a loss of love and self-esteem. Anger and love are often interrelated and are by no means incompatible, in the way that love and hatred or love and indifference are. The moral and theological evaluation of anger depends not upon its origins but on the uses to which it is put. When anger leads to violence (q.v.), it cannot serve love. But equally the refusal to acknowledge the natural responses of anger leads to the concealment of resentment under a veneer of niceness. Moreover, there is evidence to suggest that the denial of anger may cause depression (q.v.) or psychosomatic problems (q.v.).

Anger can be used positively and creatively if it is seen as a warning signal that things are amiss in personal or social relationships, and if its arousing effect is used to promote honest and direct communication with those causing the hurt and frustration. In political situations, too, the anger of the oppressed can lead to a non-violent but uncompromising confrontation with injustice. The guideline for Christians is that, as members of one body, we must use our anger to 'speak the truth in love' (Eph. 4.25). This is especially true when we are aroused from our apathy toward the injustice which others suffer.

2. *Hostility*, unlike anger, has no positive part to play in human relationships. Often the origins of an attitude of hostility are obscure, but it seems likely that a failure to give direct

expression to anger (or even to acknowledge its presence) is a contributing factor. It is notable that in church groups, where anger is often denied, resentment toward fellow-members is common and hostility toward outsiders, in the form of prejudice (q.v.), is frequently found. Hostility is seen in an extreme form in paranoia (see PSYCHIATRY AND MENTAL ILLNESS), but it is more commonly part of the personality adjustment of people who feel permanently rejected and unloved, and is a frequent defence of the lonely and the elderly (see AGEING; DEFENCE MECHANISMS; LONELINESS). In times of war an attitude of hostility toward the enemy is encouraged by means of depersonalizing nicknames ('Japs', 'Jerries', 'Argies') and by emphasizing the threat they represent. Such an enduring attitude is necessary to sustain a war effort, outbursts of anger at attacks or atrocities being too episodic and unpredictable.

As a general rule, pastoral care must seek a greater acceptance and a more positive use of anger and a diminution of hostility in individuals and groups. In counselling (q.v.), the hostility of the client (or, on occasion, of the counsellor) can provide a useful starting point for a deeper understanding of the pain which a person experiences, or causes, in relationships. Usually, however, the aim will be to remove the need for hostility through empathy (q.v.) and acceptance (q.v.), so that the other person's positive personality resources can be expressed. Anger, on the other hand, is less destructive if it can be openly expressed and experienced. Although mere 'ventilation' is not an answer in itself, the person who does not deny anger is more likely to be able to create open and sensitive relationships and to seek them in return. The problem of 'chronic niceness' (Augsburger 1979, p. 8) in pastors and Christian helpers must be confronted by the reality of a God whose anger is not a denial of his love.

Augsburger, D.W., *Anger and Assertiveness in Pastoral Care* (Fortress Press, Philadelphia, 1979). **Bagby, D.G.**, *Understanding Anger in the Church* (Broadman, Nashville, 1979). **Campbell, A.V.**, *The Gospel of Anger* (SPCK, 1986). **Hanson, A.T.**, *The Wrath of the Lamb* (SPCK, 1957). **Storr, A.**, *Human Aggression* (Penguin, 1970). **Tavris, C.**, *Anger, The Misunderstood Emotion* (Simon & Schuster, New York, 1982).

A.V. CAMPBELL

See also: AGGRESSION;
EMOTION;   REBELLION;   VIOLENCE.

ANOINTING

A metaphor and a rite symbolizing the outpouring of God's gifts.

For the ancient Israelites, oil was a gift of God, one of the three essential sources of nourishment given by him to his faithful people (Deut. 11.14). It was considered to be a blessing (Deut. 7.13–14; Jer. 31.12), a sign of salvation (Joel 2.19) and the symbol of eschatological happiness (Hos. 22.21–3). It was used as a cosmetic (Amos 6.6; Esth. 2.12), a restorative (Ezek. 16.9) and as a medicine for open wounds and sores (Isa. 1.6). As fuel for lamps, it was a source of light (Exod. 27.20). It was seen as a symbol of love and beauty (Song of Sol. 1.3), of friendship (Prov. 27.9), of brotherly love (Ps. 133.2) and above all as a symbol of joy and happiness (Ps. 104.15).

In the Old Testament, anointing was used both as a rite of healing and purification and as a rite of consecration to God's purpose. According to Leviticus 14.1–32, it was part of the rites of healing and purification of a leper. The anointing of certain objects was seen as a mark of consecration and a sign of God's living presence (Exod. 29.36–7; Lev. 8.10. Cf. also Gen. 28.18–22). The anointing of a king by a prophet or priest was seen as a sign of God's election and of the consequent outpouring of God's spirit on the elect (1 Sam. 10.1–16; 16.3; 1 Kings 1.39). After the Exile, priests and in particular high priests were also anointed (a custom legitimized by the P source by backdating it to the anointing of Aaron and his children: Lev. 8.12. Cf. also Exod. 28.41 and Num. 3.3). The anointing of prophets was never a rite, but a metaphor for God's election and mission (compare 1 Kings 9.16 with 19.19. Cf. also Isa. 61.1). The very title of Messiah, the Anointed One, reserved by Judaism for the promised Deliverer of Israel, is to be understood in this metaphorical sense.

With regard to Jesus, the New Testament mentions only the metaphorical anointing received by him at his baptism in the river Jordan (Acts 10.38) and the royal anointing he received when, after his passion, he was made to sit at the right hand of the Majesty on high (Heb. 1.9). In Luke 4.1–21, Jesus claims for himself only the prophetic anointing related to the announcement of the good news. All Christians share in the anointing of Jesus. It is a *spiritual* anointing (through faith) which precedes any ritual anointing in

15

baptism. It consists in the penetration in the believer of the Word of Truth by means of the action of the Holy Spirit (compare John 14.6 and 16.13 with 1 John 2.20–27. Cf. also 2 Cor. 1.21). So sealed with the Holy Spirit, the believer is consecrated to God's purpose in fellowship with all other Christians (Eph. 1.11–14).

The link between anointing and the outpouring of the Spirit is at the basis of the symbolism of all Christian anointing rites. Throughout the history of the Church, anointing has been used in ordination and in the coronation of monarchs. As part of the rites of initiation, it has been used as a rite of purification and exorcism as well as a rite of consecration to God's service in the royal, priestly and prophetic community of the risen Lord. In some Churches (such as the Coptic Church) it has been used as part of the rites of marriage, to symbolize (a) the joy of human love, (b) the fruitfulness of the union of man and woman as participation in the royal condition of God as King of Life,, and (c) the priestly and prophetic role of human love 'in the Lord' as a sacrament of God's love for his people.

More commonly, anointing has been used throughout the history of the Church as a rite of healing for the sick (Jas. 5.14–16) after the example of the Apostles (Mark 6.13). Of these two classical biblical texts, the former clearly sets the charism of healing in a spiritual perspective by stating that the rite will effect the gift of salvation, the gift of healing, and the forgiveness of sins: 'the prayer of faith will save the sick man, and the Lord will raise him up; and if he has committed sins, he will be forgiven' (Jas. 5.15). The healing that comes from the Lord involves the healing of the total man: his mind, his soul and his body (Jas. 5.16).

Evidence of the continuation of the New Testament practice of anointing the sick was recently discovered in a 17-line Aramaic silver tablet from the first century. We also know that, during the first five centuries of the Common Era, the same practice continued in two different forms: the anointing of the sick person by either the sick person himself or by a member of his family in a domestic context, and the liturgical anointing by a bishop of presbyter (presumably in cases of more severe illness or in cases in which more specific spiritual help was being sought).

At the time of the Carolingian Reform, the rite became known as 'Extreme Unction'. It was administered by a recognized minister, together with Holy Communion ('viaticum', or 'food for the journey'), only to those in immediate danger of death. As the rite was administered only when the hopes of physical survival were slim, the spiritual aspect of the rite became consequently more important than that of physical healing. This new trend was strongly reinforced throughout the Scholastic period, during which the anointing of the sick became known as the *sacramentum exeuntium* ('the sacrament for those about to depart').

When, through the influence of the Tractarian movement, the liturgical anointing of the sick became more prominent in the Anglican Church, the medieval trend began to be reversed. Today, especially after the reform of Vatican II in the Roman Catholic Church, the anointing of the sick is seen, as in early times, as a healing rite for the total person. The recipients need not be any longer in danger of death. The rite itself is simplified to include as a rule only the anointing of the forehead and hands and may now be repeated, if in the course of the same illness the danger becomes more serious.

Gusmer, C., 'Liturgical Traditions of Christian Illness, Rites of the Sick' (*Worship* 46, 1972), pp. 528–43. **Mitchell, L.L.,** *Baptismal Anointing* (Univ. of Notre Dame, 1978).

G. TELLINI

See also: RITES AND RITUALS; TOUCH.

ANXIETY

An unpleasant emotion (q.v.) which is aroused by internal or external events which are felt to offer a real or potential threat to physical or mental well-being.

In psychotherapy (q.v.) the word has a technical emphasis best indicated by the German word *angst*, which also connotes anguish and dread. Because of its survival value as a danger signal, anxiety is one of the earliest differentiations of the infant's motivational structure, and is deeply rooted in the unconscious. Like other emotions, it is not only subjective but is also expressed in behaviour; and because it is so uncomfortable, such behaviour is often directed at escaping from it, or at least from an awareness of it, by largely unconscious techniques known as mental defence mechanisms (q.v.).

Whereas *fear* is aroused by a localizable

threat from which the victim feels an impulse to flee, anxiety is typically aroused by unknown or unconscious stimuli. Specific irrational fears, or phobias, express a defence mechanism which tries to 'bind' such free-floating anxiety to make it manageable.

Existentialists describe anxiety as a *fear of non-being*, and this can imply not only death but also a sense of meaninglessness and a sense of guilt (q.v.). Such a feeling of being in some way 'excommunicated' from the human community occurs at times to everyone, if only because of our finitude. The fear of non-being is not therefore to be seen as necessarily pathological.

A main source of anxiety is the *fear of being separated* from other persons who are felt to provide security. This element is probably present in some degree whenever anxiety is felt, stemming of course from early infancy when a child would be physically unable to withdraw from a threat even if he were able to locate it. Separation anxiety is therefore normal and healthy in small children (*see* HUMAN DEVELOPMENT), but its manifestation in later life is usually symptomatic of some other anxiety-producing factor.

Neurotic anxiety results from internal conflict (q.v.) between different elements or structures of the mental apparatus, of which at least one is unconscious. Such conflict typically occurs between innate impulses to behaviour judged unacceptable by the surrounding community (possibly aggressive or sexual) and the tendency to behave in patterns acceptable to it. Although the tendency is also innate, the patterns themselves have to be learned. These three aetiological perspectives are probably applicable in all cases. Erikson speaks of neurotic anxiety as a 'numbing loneliness, [sense of] isolation and disorganization of experience' – a description which might equally well apply to existential and separation anxiety.

Anxiety is aroused not only by threats to survival but also by real or imagined threats to the sense of personal identity accorded to an individual by his family or community. The various defence mechanisms evoked by it play a pervasive part in patterning inter-personal encounters and relationships, and also in structuring social systems and institutions such as family and workplace. Defence mechanisms try to bind anxiety or keep it from awareness; they do not abolish it. Since it is an emotion which (particularly if it is

unrecognized) spreads as if by contagion or infection, then to the extent that a social system is patterned by defences, it is likely to raise anxiety rather than lower it and thus establish a vicious circle.

Anxiety is an essential part of the human condition and cannot be eliminated. It can be turned to creative use and may promote maturation of the personality. The key notes of pastoral care for those whose burden of anxiety seems to be for the moment intolerable are two: a deliberate and compassionate sharing of the burden so as to lessen its weight on the sufferer; and an insistence on attending to, and if possible dealing with, the realities of the situation. Only in this context should measures to escape from or relieve the anxiety be considered.

Bowlby, J., *Separation: Anxiety and Anger* (Hogarth, 1973). Erikson, E.H., *Childhood and Society* (Hogarth, 1965). Menzies, I.E.P., 'A Case-study in the Functioning of Social Systems as a Defence Against Anxiety' (*Human Relations*, vol. 13, no. 2); reprinted as Tavistock Pamphlet, no. 3, (Tavistock, 1961). Rycroft, C., *A Critical Dictionary of Psycho-analysis* (Nelson, 1968). Tillich, P., *The Courage to Be* (Nisbet, 1952).

J. MATHERS

See also: DEFENCE MECHANISMS; DOUBT; GUILT.

APATHY

Apathy is a state, sometimes found in a distressed person, where all emotion and feeling appears to be absent. It presents as coldness, and can be mistaken for indifference, but should be understood as psychological protection against feeling rather than as lack of feeling. As such it is a powerful psychological defence mechanism (q.v.). Rather than there being no feeling within the state conveyed, there is likely to be a fear of too much feeling.

Apathy is often seen as a state of despair; an apparent indifference to possible future events or to the consequences of intended action; a sense that nothing matters, that nothing has meaning. It can lead to attempted suicide, whether intended or appearing as accidental, such as taking an overdose of drugs without caring about the result – 'It doesn't matter whether I wake up or not.'

Apathy shows itself in a lack of motivation; absence of energy; inability to carry out necessary tasks; and, generally, incapacity to function in an effective way. There is an absence of emotion of any kind towards others, a sense of lassitude, and often of helplessness. It is one aspect of depression (q.v.).

Apathy should not be confused with the condition of *belle indifference* which can be seen in psychosis (*see* PSYCHIATRY AND MENTAL ILLNESS), and which may be recognized by the person showing a bizarre casualness towards factual or supposed events of considerable seriousness; an attitude absurdly out of keeping with facts, or imagined facts. Mostly apathy is a condition conveyed by the neurotic rather than by the psychotic.

Apathy in the distressed person may induce helplessness and consequent anger in the counsellor, which is dealt with by recognizing the probable extreme pain and suffering against which the person is protecting himself or herself. There is a consequent need for the counsellor to establish, in time, a degree of trust in the person which would give enough assurance to allow him or her to experience some measure of true feeling. It is important to see that, rather than not suffering, the person is in fact suffering acutely.

Rycroft, Charles, *A Critical Dictionary of Psychoanalysis* (Nelson, 1968).

BARBARA K. FOWLES

See also: DEPRESSION.

ARMED FORCES CHAPLAINCY

The provision for religious ministry in the armed services.

Baptists, the Church of England (C of E), the Church of Scotland (C of S), Methodist, Presbyterian, Roman Catholic (RC) and United Reformed Churches provide chaplains from the ranks of their ordained persons to exercise a ministry to British Service personnel and their families wherever they are serving. The style of that ministry is recognizably that of their own denomination, although C of S and Free Church ministers are appointed to function ecumenically within that grouping in the Royal Navy and Royal Air Force, and in a unified department with the C of E in the army. Frequently they are commissioned in one of the Services or its reserve, but many are civilians appointed to a part-time ministry on a particular unit. Religious ministrations for Jewish personnel are co-ordinated by the Senior Jewish Chaplain to HM Forces. There are also people

appointed as full-time chaplains' assistants who may be members of religious orders. In this way the needs of the vast majority of those in the Judaeo-Christian tradition are met. Other faiths are not officially catered for, but chaplains act as referral agents in cases of expressed need.

Chaplains are non-combatant but have an important part to play in time of war 'in assuring that morality, compassion and humanity do not give way to retaliatory brutality . . . [and] that the human aspect of the logistic problems is not forgotten . . . When casualties, human suffering and stress are inevitable, it is vital that the chaplain continues . . . [a] pastoral and sacramental ministry . . . [and] . . . must be readily available to give spiritual comfort, counsel and advice' (A Service Order, August 1984). They are trained and exercised for such conditions.

In peace time they offer a wide spectrum of ministry including:

(1) *Worship.* They are responsible for conducting regular services, usually along denominational lines but there is a growing number of ecumenical situations and serious consideration is being given to the establishment of local ecumenical projects in some areas.

(2) *Rites and ordinances.* Candidates are prepared by their chaplain for baptism, dedication, marriage and confirmation according to the traditions of their faith and denomination. The C of E and RC churches each have a designated bishop to the Forces.

(3) *Visitation.* New entrants to the Services and those posted to new appointments are visited in their homes and work-places by the chaplain with a view to maintaining personal contact, which is essential in this type of ministry.

(4) *Hospitals.* The Forces have hospitals in the UK and overseas, and each has chaplains who minister to patients, their families and fellow staff members.

(5) *Religious education.* Chaplains have the task of providing an educational programme to the Services, and this is tackled in two ways: (a) *Padre's hours.* The overall training of personnel in the Forces emphasizes that of the whole person, and aims at producing an effective, rather than simply economically efficient, tradesperson. It is recognized that chaplains have a distinctive contribution to make here by conducting sessions for all,

commissioned and non-commissioned, undergoing initial and basic trade training. The aim is that the students should appreciate the importance of relating appropriately to God, their fellows and their own situation within the Services through an understanding of their faith. The chaplain works from an approved syllabus with full classroom facilities for back-up. (b) *Residential schools*. The Service chaplains have their own establishments, two of which are in the UK and one in Germany, in which they offer residential courses on such subjects as moral and welfare leadership, Christian foundation, and welfare counselling, as well as courses for ordinands and lay preachers, members of the Jewish faith, organists, youth leaders, Sunday school teachers, Service doctors, and in-service training for chaplains.

(6) *Pastoral counselling*. Service personnel need to have access to someone with whom they can discuss areas of their life in confidence, and who will offer them the time, attention and respect available to civilians through local clergy and counselling agencies. A young person struggling to a personal conclusion in areas which are experienced as genuine crises, the outcome of which could have serious career consequences, can turn to the chaplain for the necessary confidential counselling, who in turn increasingly has access to accredited supervision (q.v.).

Life for Service personnel and their families is disciplined, disruptive and sometimes dangerous. Commissioned chaplains, and their families where relevant, are fully integrated into that life both professionally and socially, and that identification is considered as being important in establishing credibility amongst those to whom they minister.

Smythe, J., *In This Sign Conquer* (Mowbray, 1968). Taylor, G., *The Sea Chaplains* (Oxford Illustrated Press, 1978). Zahn, G., *Chaplains in the RAF* (Manchester UP, 1969).

FRASER MACLENNAN

ART
The use of intellect, feeling and imagination to create visual, tangible or audible imagery that both communicates and evokes response. Painting, sculpture, music, drama, poetry and architecture typify this.

1. *Art as culture*. This tends to have a specialist and esoteric image. Many people are prevented from appropriating and exper-
iencing the received art of their community and are thereby denied access to worlds of truth, beauty and wholeness. It is a pastoral concern that these doors should be opened in order that the ordinary viewer may be enriched by seeing and hearing what artists are saying in their search for meaning, as they reflect, portray and comment.

Two important levels of response are to be encouraged: (1) A general or subconscious level where art is around in many forms as part of the environment, through pictures, music and architecture. (2) An aware and conscious level where, in this process of art appreciation, it is important to foster in individuals a trust in the validity of their own perception of the art form. They do not need instruction or permission in order to express opinion, develop values or respond in depth.

2. *Creative art*. The process whereby there is active engagement in, for example, painting or modelling, with or without training and skill, and where emphasis is upon imagination and intuition rather than upon rational and academic modes. It is a way of getting in touch with God, the self and one another which bypasses the normal communication stereotypes. Creativity is part of our human potential and is not itself a gift or skill possessed only by a talented minority.

Modes of expression: (1) Exploration, as a private and inward process for the individual. (2) Communication, as a sharing of perceptions with others in a way that is understood.

Therapeutic role of creative art. Non-verbal art forms have great value for the inarticulate and the disturbed, enabling exploration of feelings and an expression of what is beyond words. A deepening involvement in creative expression facilitates the discovery of inner resources; new possibilities of growth emerge and the life-style changes as awareness and sensitivity are cultivated. Since many assume that they are neither artistic nor creative, the discovery that they are can be quite dramatic. Art, drama and music therapy are now firmly established professions with practitioners working in psychiatric units and centres of healing.

The context for creative art. (1) An encouraging, accepting and affirming atmosphere is essential without judgement or competition. Performance, skill, achievement and excellence are unhelpful concepts for participants who may well believe they have no competence whatsoever. (2) Media. Powder paint, pastel, charcoal, modelling with clay, making simple music, sharing in drama, dance and movement, and writing poetry and stories are all valuable basic art forms. (3) The leader facilitates in a non-authoritarian manner but often needs to be quite directive to ensure an understood and safe framework for creating, reflecting and sharing. Deep and sometimes painful feelings may be exposed calling for great sensitivity and care.

Barker, Clive, *Theatre Games: A New Approach to Drama Training* (Eyre Methuen, 1977). **Franck, Frederick**, *The Awakened Eye* (Wildwood House, 1980). **Liebmann, M.**, *Art Games and Structures for Groups* (Bristol Art Therapy Group); also contains detailed bibliography for Art, Drama and Music Therapy; Copies (£3.70, including post and packing) from Marian Liebmann, 52 St Albans Road, Bristol BS6 7SH.

WILLIAM C. DENNING

See also: COMMUNICATION; FANTASY; IMAGINATION; INTUITION.

ASCETICAL THEOLOGY

The theology of training, or educating, the soul.

This terse definition by Kirk is filled out by others: 'the science of Christian progress towards perfection'; 'the development of the Christian life, and in particular with training in self-discipline and prayer' (q.v.); 'the systematic analysis of the life of grace under the Spirit'. Since the 18th century ascetical theology is variously treated as a branch of, or subsuming, or complementary to, moral theology (q.v.). Also the dividing line between ascetical and mystical theology is disputed. These distinctions are too arbitrary.

Ascetical theology is traditionally concerned with that growth in holiness (q.v.) which is possible for all Christians, sometimes presented in successive stages of repentance, spiritual culture and union with God. If moral theology becomes excessively legalist, cerebral, negative or minimalist, ascetical theology can (in principle) respond with a practical, developmental and positive attitude towards

spiritual growth. In the Catholic tradition ascetical theology draws upon biblical, patristic and scholastic resources. Later notable texts include Ignatius' *Spiritual Exercises* and Francis de Sales' *Introduction to the Devout Life*.

Protestantism has shown reserve towards ascetical theology, partly on the popular view that the whole ideal of asceticism is repulsive and false, and partly on the theological argument that ideas of 'progress in virtue and spiritual congeniality towards God' overvalue human effort and undermine the primacy of grace. In the modern period ascetical theology, often in the control of a male priesthood with a pliant laity, has to many seemed too individualistic, arcane, falsely world-denying, predominantly the affair of the professional ecclesiastic, pastor, confessor, and guide of souls. This is unfortunate.

For ascetical theology can and should: influence thinking about the psychology and subject-matter of Christian education (*see* NURTURE); assist bridge-building between rational thinking and moral power in Christian ethics; strengthen resistance to the tempting neglect of the experiential relationship with God in the work of pastoral counselling; and, overcoming clericalism, provide a valued resource for the practice of shared responsibility for each other's Christian growth in the mutuality of the church. Ascetical theology belongs within a broader pastoral theology (q.v.) which should enrich the church's own life and its social responsibility.

Sacramentum Mundi, vol. 1, pp. 110–16. *The Catholic Encyclopedia*, vol. 14, pp. 613–21. **Häring, B.**, *Toward a Christian Moral Theology* (Univ. of Notre Dame Press, 1966). **Harton, F.P.**, *The Elements of the Spiritual Life* (SPCK, 1932). **Hauerwas, S.**, *Character and the Christian Life* (San Antonio Trinity UP, 1975). **Rahner, K.**, *Theological Investigations*, vol. 3 (Darton Longman & Todd, 1967), pp. 3ff, 58ff.

A.O. DYSON

See also: SPIRITUAL DIRECTION.

B

BAPTISM
The rite of initiation into the Christian Church.

1. *The meaning of baptism.* Baptism is one of the two sacraments of the Church that originate in the words of Jesus (Matt. 28.19). It is the rite of entry into the Church, leading to participation in the other dominical sacrament, Eucharist (*see* COMMUNION), in which membership receives regular expression. As a sacrament, it expresses in symbolic ritual what the Christian believes happens in baptism, and focuses in a moment a timeless truth. The 'outward sign' in Baptism is dipping in water, a symbol of *drowning*. The baptismal candidate 'dies' to the old life and rises to the new. In so doing he or she enters into the experience of Christ in death and resurrection (Rom. 6.2–11).

In the early centuries this association of baptism with the Easter experience, and through it with the parallel deliverance of the Israelites from Egypt through the waters of the Red Sea, was more fully understood than in subsequent centuries, when the emphasis has come to be placed more on the secondary image of *cleansing*, an idea also present in the New Testament writings, though chiefly in relation to the ministry of John the Baptist (Mark 1.2–5). The new baptism rites of several churches restore to prominence the primary image of drowning. There is some disagreement in the Church about whether baptism is itself *complete* initiation or whether a further ceremony is needed. It is the gift of the Holy Spirit – another aspect of the Easter–Pentecost experience that links baptism to Christ's resurrection – that some see expressed in the Baptism itself, some in an anointing with 'oil of chrism', either at the time of baptism or later, and some in the laying on of the bishop's hand in confirmation. The disagreement is as much within churches (both the Roman Catholic Church and the Church of England) as between churches.

2. *The ritual of baptism.* Most Christian churches agree that valid baptism normally entails a threefold dipping in water (for which pouring may be substituted), though a single dipping (or pouring) is sufficient, accompanied by the formula 'I baptize you in the name of the Father, and of the Son and of the Holy Spirit'. Though all churches recognize the greater dramatic symbolism of 'total immersion', only the Baptist churches practise baptism exclusively in that form. Other subsidiary ritual has become attached to baptism, though water is the primary symbol. The Christian name is given. A sign of the cross is made. Sometimes oil is used. A candle lit from the Easter candle is given. Though for many centuries, baptism has normally been administered with only family and friends present, today baptism in the presence of the church congregation is again becoming the norm.

3. *Infant baptism.* Because baptism involves a conscious and explicit act of faith and commitment, some churches, notably the Baptist churches, administer it only to those old enough to speak for themselves ('believers' baptism'). But there is evidence of the baptism of children from early times, with adults ('godparents' or 'sponsors') making the vows for them, and this remains common practice. In popular thinking there is a need for infant baptism because of fear for the eternal fate of children dying unbaptized, though the Church has increasingly abandoned the sort of theology that lies behind such fear. There is a division today about the advisability of baptizing the infant children of parents who are not regular churchgoers. Some clergy are unwilling to do so where the parents appear unable to make the promises with integrity; others believe the approach for baptism provides a pastoral and evangelistic opportunity not to be missed. Some require evidence that baptism will lead to church commitment; others are content to minister to people at this key moment in their lives, when the birth of a child finds natural expression in a religious ceremony, without expecting a return in terms of church membership. In most churches a more rigorous preparation and follow up to baptism by the priest or minister, and by lay members of the Church, is being developed.

Emergency baptism. Where a child (usually a newly born baby) is in danger of death, baptism may be administered privately, if necessary by a lay person, using water and the 'Trinitarian formula'. A name is normally given. Where the child survives, the subsidiary ceremonies, together with the vows, should take place in the church on a subsequent date. Baptism is not repeatable, but where it is uncertain whether a person has been baptized, a conditional form is used ('N., if you have not been baptized, I baptize . . .').

Davies, J.G. (ed.), *A Dictionary of Liturgy and Worship* (SCM, 1972), pp. 44–64. Jones, C. *et al.* (ed.), *The Study of Liturgy* (SPCK, 1978), pp. 79–146. Fisher, J.D.C., *Christian Initiation: Baptism in the Medieval West* (Alcuin Club, 1965); *Christian Initiation: The Reformation Period* (Alcuin Club, 1970). Forrester, D.B. *et al.*, *Encounter With God* (T. & T. Clark, 1984). Hanson, A., *Church, Sacraments and Ministry* (Mowbray, 1975), pp. 36–55. Martos, J., *Doors to the Sacred* (SCM, 1981), pp. 161–202. Perham, M.F., *Liturgy Pastoral and Parochial* (SPCK, 1984), pp. 67–77. Whitaker, E.C. (ed.), *Documents of the Baptismal Liturgy* (SPCK, 1960); *Sacramental Initiation Complete in Baptism* (Grove Books, 1972).

MICHAEL PERHAM

See also: BIRTH; CHILDREN: PASTORAL CARE.

BEFRIENDING

In the general sense this means acting as a friend towards someone in need, but since 1953 befriending has had a technical meaning as a form of therapy based on listening, acceptance, understanding and empathizing, with no giving of advice or attempt at counselling techniques.

Before 1953, there were three recognized forms of therapy for depressed, anxious, lonely and possibly suicidal people: psychiatry (q.v.), which is a medical speciality and therefore allows the patient to be treated with drugs, electroplexy, or other medical resources; psychotherapy (q.v.), which may be provided by qualified medical and non-medical professionals, able when necessary to explore unconscious as well as conscious motivation in the patient; and counselling (q.v.), by non-medical professionals working with psychological insight but concerned only with problems of which the client is or can be made aware.

In 1953 a fourth form was discovered. Widespread publicity had been given in the Press to the availability of counselling for the suicidal and despairing at St Stephen Walbrook in the City of London. It soon became clear both that the need was greater than could be met by one man, and that counselling was not what 90% of those seeking help desired or required. They sought instead a listening therapy from one who had no professional status or authority but was simply a fellow human being who cared.

Compassionate amateurs had volunteered to wait with and upon those who came for counselling; they were unaware that listening in such a tolerant and warmhearted way was a new therapy, still less the one which would prove to be the most effective in suicide prevention. They were simply doing what came naturally to them. As soon as it was discovered that these carefully chosen people – if given a little instruction, properly supervised and with expert back-up – were the right people to make the first encounter with a caller in distress, whether on the telephone (q.v.) or face to face, they were put into the front line of suicide prevention, where they have remained ever since.

Where for the other disciplines training and qualifications are essential, for befriending selection is the important thing. The ordinariness and informality of this new (or rather newly schematized) therapy might have made it difficult for professionals to take seriously and accept; but they soon found that the patients who required professional help were whenever possible led gently to them, and their time is not wasted.

After 20 years of the efficacy of befriending being demonstrated by The Samaritans, other organizations concerned with social welfare began to take up the word and professionals began to recommend befriending for certain clients. After 30 years it is widely recognized that befriending is a preferred alternative to more specialized counselling in many cases.

An experienced befriender is a valuable therapist who respects the work of those using authority and skill in other forms of therapy but knows that his or her own, serving the distressed person on terms of equality, is valid and effective.

CHAD VARAH

See also: COUNSELLING; LISTENING.

BEHAVIOUR THERAPY

An approach to therapy in which therapists assume that behaviour is determined by contemporary events: both internal (thoughts, images and feelings) and external (environmental and interpersonal). Behaviour is a function of these two classes of variables, and once the antecedents (triggers) and consequences (results) of problem behaviour have been identified, it is possible to help a person change by modifying these in collaboration with client.

The approach takes at face value the problem a person presents and asks help with. The problem is viewed as a function of the person's present life situation, including both objective and subjective factors. These may be derived from the past, but consideration of the past is seen to be not always essential in helping people change.

Therapy is aimed at modifying present circumstances in a way that leads to the desired change of the problem. It entails: (a) a detailed focus on overt and specific problem behaviours; (b) a specific description of the circumstances surrounding the problem; (c) a precision in spelling out treatment goals; (d) a formulation of a specific treatment procedure appropriate to a particular problem; and (e) an objective assessment of the outcome of the therapeutic procedure.

Specificity is important in determining what the client wishes to change, what conditions determine the problem, what new behaviour needs to be learnt to replace previous maladaptive behaviour, and how far towards defined goals the patient has moved.

Specific *therapeutic procedures and techniques* have been developed on the basis of learning and cognitive theories to help a person confront and change his or her patterns of maladaptive behaviour. This requires a period of relearning, and readaptation to the environment, using new behaviours and cognitions which are not so counterproductive. The following techniques are some of those most frequently used: (a) systematic desensitization; (b) operant conditioning and extinction; (c) response prevention; (d) aversion therapy; (e) biofeedback techniques; and (f) cognitive strategies.

The *relationship between the therapist and client* is an equal, collaborative one in which the therapist helps the client to identify the goals which it is possible to work towards. Whilst the therapist assumes an active and directive role in treatment by teaching techniques, and reinforcing and modelling attempts at new behaviour, the client also participates fully

and actively in the behavioural analysis and planning of the approach to treatment of problems. Both are involved in assessing whether desired behavioural changes are achieved during therapy. The process of therapy does not exclude consideration of transference (q.v.) issues. For example, it may be necessary at times to interpret a client's dependence on the therapist's direction. However, transferential issues are not seen as the crucial focus of therapy, as in the case in some analytical approaches.

Behaviour therapy arose in the 1950s when, for some, there was a growing disillusionment with medical and psychoanalytic approaches to the treatment of mental illness. Since that time, flexibility in the use of different behavioural techniques, in conjunction with more recent problem-oriented approaches, has made such therapy more attractive, useful and successful in the treatment of the multitudinous problems-in-living that clients present with.

Goldfried, M.R. and **Davison, G.C.,** *Clinical Behaviour Therapy* (Holt, Rinehart & Winston, 1976). **Hersen, M.** and **Bellack, A.S.,** *Behavioural Assessment: a Practical Handbook* (Pergamon, 1976). **Wilson, G.T.** and **O'Leary, K.D.,** *Principles of Behaviour Therapy* (Prentice Hall, 1980).

ROBYN VINES

BEREAVEMENT
The state of loss following the death of a relative or friend.

Caring for the bereaved, and understanding the nature of grief, forms an important part of effective pastoral care. Pastors may have contact with the bereaved in a number of ways. He or she may be involved with the relatives and friends of a terminally ill person at or around the time of death. The pre-funeral visit and the conducting or facilitating of a funeral may, sensitively approached, be a very important service to the bereaved and a valuable basis for further pastoral care. Moreover, pastoral responsibility does not finish with the funeral. A number of studies suggest that many bereaved people find the worst and most vulnerable period is between six weeks and six months after the death. In addition, Colin Murray Parkes and others have suggested, on the basis of research, that many bereaved people would have valued more pastoral support than they felt they were offered.

There is great value in the pastor recognizing some of the key feelings associated with grief, provided that they are not just understood as chronological stages and always recognizing that no two people or groups of people will have identical reactions. Similar feelings may be experienced by those facing other significant losses, e.g. divorce or redundancy, events which have usefully been described as 'little deaths'. How the person who is bereaved as a result of death copes with the experience of bereavement will also be affected by their experience of previous losses and changes in their own life, whether or not these have involved the death of someone close to them.

Early reactions to bereavement are likely to include shock and disbelief, often expressed as 'I can't believe it' or 'It's not true'. The reality of the death or impending death may be denied. Frequently the pastor may have an important role in helping the bereaved person beyond the denial, possibly by mentioning the dead person by name, encouraging those involved to talk about the circumstances of the death, and by the avoidance of religiously loaded euphemisms, 'passed away' or 'with Jesus'. Professional helpers, relatives and friends, may prolong the denial of death by the use of sedation and diverting conversation. The rationale given is that the bereaved person should not be further distressed, but the effect is likely to be a delay in mourning, often to a time when it is less easily dealt with. Denial of death or its likelihood is very common with the newly bereaved and is influenced by a number of considerations, e.g. cultural factors, experience of previous separations and loss, and whether death took place suddenly or after some opportunity for preparatory mourning.

Anger (q.v.) directed typically at the medical profession, the hospital, other family members or occasionally the dead person, is a common reaction. Because of the perceived representative function of the pastor, he or she may provide a focus for the anger which may be directed at God or simply experienced as outrage that the death should have occurred at all. The fact that there is no perceived logic in such feelings may heighten the distress of the bereaved. Frequently the anger is best understood as a statement of pain to be heard and supported rather than an invitation to give a direct answer to the question, 'Why me?', or to justify God. Guilt (q.v.) is frequently associated with the anger, often expressed as, 'If only . . .'. Three areas of guilt and blame are frequently described: (a) 'real' guilt, where cause and effect are recognizable, e.g. in the family of a child who has been killed in a road traffic accident as a result of the parents' inattention; (b) 'exaggerated' guilt, less obviously connected with the death in a logical way, e.g. the widower who links his wife's death from cancer with his inability to love her more; (c) 'existential' guilt, often expressed in terms such as 'What have I (or the dead person) done to deserve this?' The three areas of course overlap considerably. Sensitive listening by the pastor can allow the intensity of the feelings to subside, in the absence of any easily given answers.

Sadness and emptiness are often present, and since they have less obvious external manifestations it is important that the bereaved can express these feelings in a pastoral context. Occasionally pastors may need to reassure people from a firm religious background that the expression of grief is not contrary to faith in the resurrection! (See CROSS AND RESURRECTION.)

The special contribution of the pastor also includes the need for the bereaved to undertake three important changes, and, if necessary, to provide scriptural, liturgical and counselling support to undergird and assist these changes:

(1) *Separation* from the dead person and also from the position and status that the bereaved person may have had by association, e.g. seeing the body of a dead person typically allows the bereaved to realize the reality of death and to be able to 'say goodbye' to the dead person. Many cultures have an agreed ritual way of doing this.

(2) *Transition* for the bereaved can involve much uncertainty and confusion in the attempt to discover and accept, with support, a new status, e.g. widow or orphan. Typically the funeral is the time when some of these transitions can be very tentatively attempted. The value of ritual is that it can provide a way of putting the unsayable into actions; its liability is that it is a generalized form of communication which does not speak to everybody equally usefully.

(3) *Reincorporation* into the community after a death will vary according to a number of factors, including the closeness of the bereaved to the dead person, any other

commitments, e.g. to looking after children, and the way in which the bereaved may experience their return as either being supported, delayed or hurried. Many mourners have felt a pressure to return to society and to be 'normal' before they really feel ready to do so. It is more helpful usually to think in terms of up to two years rather than the two or three months usually allowed. A difficulty which faces many people in northern European and North American culture is the lack of a structure within which to mourn and which might mark out the end of formal mourning. For this reason pastoral contact round the anniversary of the death and especially during the first year of bereavement around significant family occasions like birthdays and Christmas can be extremely valuable. The keeping of an anniversary of a death, maybe with a formal or informal religious ceremony, is an important pastoral function. The reincorporation can also involve the bereaved discovering a continuing relationship with the dead person which can be sustained and is different in quality and content from a denial of the reality of death. Pastoral care aims to help the bereaved find a future for their relationship with the dead person as well as affirming the past.

Mourning can sometimes fail to take place or be cut short, in which case it may be re-experienced later at the time of another death or loss. Pastors may also be involved with people under these circumstances, where the links with bereavement are more difficult to place but equally important. Mourning may be delayed if other responsibilities intervene. Pregnancy is now widely understood to be a factor which can inhibit mourning. For this reason pastoral care may involve helping to bury the dead metaphorically as well as literally. Prolongation of grief may mean that, for example, denial, anger, guilt or idealization may persist for many years. It can frequently help for a pastor or other helper to spend time retelling the events leading up to the death, the death itself, the funeral and feelings experienced at that time. For some people this may be sufficient to facilitate mourning. Pastors should, however, be aware of the need to seek psychiatric or other help or support if necessary.

The care of the bereaved inevitably means that the pastor's craft is to bring together theology and spirituality with a proper under-standing of sociological and psychological principles of growth, development and mental health. In care for the bereaved the pastor is required to develop skills in all these areas, whilst being faithful to his or her own humanity, limitations and personal experience of loss and grief.

Ainsworth-Smith, I. and Speck, P., *Letting Go* (SPCK, 1982). Lewis, C.S., *A Grief Observed* (Faber, 1973). Spiegel, Y., *The Grief Process* (SCM, 1978). Stephens, S., *Death Comes Home* (Mowbray, 1972).

IAN AINSWORTH-SMITH

See also DEATH: MEANING; DYING; HOPE.

BIBLE: PASTORAL USE

The Bible can be invaluable in pastoral care, yet it is often either misused or neglected. Many aspects of the understanding and application of the Bible are live issues in contemporary Christian theology and, far from dissuading, this should encourage a discerning pastoral use that avoids both the simplistic 'text for every problem' approach and equally a self-conscious avoidance of the special place the Bible has in religious experience. Counselling which has any Christian associations needs to be responsible in the place it gives to the Bible.

1. *Abuse of the Bible.* The hotel bedroom, 'Gideon' Bible contains a list of verses deemed suitable for various problems in life. Whatever emergency value this may have, it is a poor model for pastoral use. Some methods of counselling, which make almost exclusive use of confrontation, rely on alphabetical lists, e.g. anxiety, bereavement, comfort, with texts to match. The pastoral problems created by this approach should also be listed: absence of relationship, blocked expression of feelings, coerced responses, failure to listen, hasty diagnosis, premature advice, selective emphasis, superficial solutions, etc. More serious still is the attraction this approach has for the insecure pastor whose authority is shored up by the symbolic significance the Bible has for many people. Linked to this is the dependence (q.v.) encouraged by the pastor who is expected to know the 'correct' verse for each succeeding need. It is hardly surprising that such abuse has led many counsellors into leaving out use of the Bible from their work.

2. *Diagnostic use of the Bible.* 'Tell me what you find in the Bible and I will tell you what you are,' said Oskar Pfister. As part of a

counsellor's listening role, there needs to be a sensitivity to any ways in which the Bible is already influencing the one who seeks help. It may be providing answers, justifying attitudes or raising fears. Ministers in particular are likely to come across people who refer to phrases or incidents from the Bible, either in passing or to pose questions, some of which seem directly to raise religious issues. Rather than being waylaid in a discussion, or even worse a monologue, for which a theological education might seem the ideal training, the pastor can discover what is behind the use being made of the Bible and go on to help the counsellee recognize this. Oates (1953) and Switzer (1979) provide good case-studies. To find out why a story, a phrase or an image loom large provides a window into the conflicts that are part of the person's pain.

3. *Pastoral use of the Bible* really begins by taking its themes and images into the counsellor's own experience and reflecting on them. This can illuminate each facet of pastoral care, i.e. guiding, healing, nurturing, reconciling, and sustaining, and it will indirectly affect much of what is said and done. More explicit use will depend both on the counsellor's own appreciation of the value of different parts of the Bible and on the response of the counsellee. Where someone values the Bible as a source of help it could be argued that it is better to guide them to those aspects of the Bible which will support future choices, than to discount the potential it might have in facilitating their healing. The reassurance provided by many of the psalms, by Christ's words and actions, and by much else in the Bible can give great help in the sustaining work of a pastor, particularly in situations of bereavement. The affirmations of forgiveness and of God's love can be really valuable in situations where healing and reconciling is needed.

For this, and more especially in the task of nurturing, increasing recognition is now being given to the use of the Bible in group work. Methods range from simple discussion based on a Bible passage to role-play, simulation games and psychodrama. Useful examples of material are provided by Grigor (1980), Miller (1973), Weber (1981), and Wink (1981).

Grigor, Jean C., *Grow to Love* (St Andrew Press, 1980). **Miller, Donald E.** *et al.*, *Using Biblical*
Simulations, vols. 1 and 2 (Judson 1973, 1975). **Oates, Wayne E.**, *The Bible in Pastoral Care* (Westminster, 1953). **Oglesby, William B., Jr**, *Biblical Themes for Pastoral Care* (Abingdon, 1980). **Switzer, David K.**, *Pastor, Preacher, Person* (Abingdon, 1979). **Weber, Hans-Ruedi**, *Experiments with Bible Study* (WCC, 1981). **Wink, Walter**, *Transforming Bible Study* (SCM, 1981).

CHRIS WIGGLESWORTH

See also: NEW TESTAMENT AND PASTORAL CARE; PASTORAL CARE: HISTORY – THE REFORMED TRADITION; PREACHING AND PASTORAL CARE.

BIRTH

The moment when a child leaves the womb and is said to enter the world, whether by normal delivery or caesarian section.

1. *Care of the child.* In the last few decades increased attention has been paid to the child's psychological and emotional needs around the time of birth, so that its entry into the world is gentle and the physical closeness of its mother's body is continued, through close holding and breast-feeding.

No matter what views are held on abortion (q.v.), all Christians seem agreed that every child has full human rights at least from birth onwards, even if it is severely disabled (q.v.); some hospitals however have sometimes sedated and withheld food from the most severely disabled newborn babies. If urgent surgery is needed to save the life of a handicapped child, the parents' consent has to be asked.

Most Christian Churches administer baptism (q.v.) to babies. There is a move to make baptism more of a public, liturgical event and less of a private affair than it is in some traditions, in order to emphasize the importance of the entry into the Christian community. Some act of welcome by the local parish (a card or present, for example) can give additional expression to this. In case of danger of death, anybody (a parent or nurse, for example) can baptize, pouring water on the head of the child and saying, 'I baptize you in the name of the Father and of the Son and of the Holy Spirit'.

2. *Care of the mother.* Before the birth the mother needs good preparation. She needs to know what to expect from the medical staff (perhaps visiting the hospital, or discussing with the midwife who will attend her). She needs information about the physical events of labour, the emotional experiences of other

mothers and the means of pain control that are available (whether through relaxation (q.v.) or medical intervention). The National Childbirth Trust organizes classes throughout Britain. During the birth the wishes of the mother should be attended to as fully as possible, so that she is in a comforting environment. It is now normal practice to allow the father of the child to be present throughout the labour and delivery.

For the mother birth is often a peak experience (q.v.), and can be followed by a period of great excitement, renewed understanding of the meaning of life, physical exhaustion and emotional fragility. A time of upset and weeping is perfectly normal two or three days after the birth. (Post-natal depression is a later phenomenon, showing more long-term difficulties in adjustment.) The mother needs gentle, respecting care during the early period, because she is in a special time of suffering, grace and the beginnings of new love. She can expect to experience at least some ambivalent feelings about the new demands upon her.

Many mothers are now seeking early discharge from hospital, lagely because they feel more emotionally secure at home; others however find that their stay in hospital gives them a chance of rest that they would not find amid the pressures of home life.

Early bonding between the mother and child is of great importance, and can be hindered if the mother is not able to hold her baby much. Sometimes this is unavoidable, as when a baby needs to be in an incubator, but everything possible should be done to recognize, support and confirm the new mother–child relationship. The now obsolete rite of 'churching' was one way in which the woman's new maternal state was recognized after her confinement; it has largely dropped out of use, since it implied an impurity after birth which would not now be accepted.

3. *Theological dimensions.* Since baptism is spoken of as essentially a new birth (John 3.5), the experience of birth is an opportunity for a deeper understanding of what Christian initiation means. It also provides a uniquely privileged way in which a man and a woman can experience their co-operation with God in creation (q.v.). The specialness of the mother–child relationship, particularly at the peak moment of birth, has led some writers of spiritual classics to speak

of God as a mother: e.g. St Anselm – 'So you, Lord God, are the great mother . . . for you have brought it about that those born to death should be reborn to life'; Julian of Norwich – 'Our true Mother Jesus, he alone bears us for joy and for endless life, blessed may he be.'

Hebblethwaite, M., *Motherhood and God* (Chapman, 1984); 'Giving Birth' (*The Way*, vol. 24, no. 1, Jan. 1984), pp. 17–24. **Kitzinger, S.,** *The Experience of Childbirth* (Gollancz, 1962); *Giving Birth: the Parents' Emotions in Childbirth* (Gollancz, 1971). **Leboyer, F.,** *Birth without Violence* (Wildwood House, 1975).

MARGARET HEBBLETHWAITE

See also: ADOPTION; BIRTH TRAUMA; GOD, DOCTRINE OF; SINGLE PARENTS; STILLBIRTH AND MISCARRIAGE.

BIRTH TRAUMA

The experience of birth as a prototype of later anxiety conditions.

Freud proposed in 1926 that birth is a prototype of traumatic neuroses as opposed to those effected by inner conflicts. Otto Rank, an early follower of Freud, went further in saying that birth trauma was the precursor of all later anxiety problems. This view was rejected by Freud, and the subject has since occupied little space in the thinking of psychoanalytical orthodoxy.

In 1949 the analyst Nandor Fodor asserted that 'the change from pre-natal to post-natal life involved an ordeal as severe as dying', and he encouraged some of his patients to undergo an abreactive reliving of birth through their dream asssociations (*see* DREAMS). Donald Winnicott, English pediatrician and analyst pointed out the unconscious need of some of his patients to relive the experience of birth. The British School of 'Object-Relations', a development within psychoanalysis profoundly influenced by Winnicott, seems to allow a new look at birth trauma with its focusing upon much earlier transactions of the infant with his environment than was undertaken by Freud.

In 1966 Frank Lake (*see* CLINICAL THEOLOGY) claimed that his work with patients abreacting under the influence of LSD offered evidence that some neurotic conditions originated in birth trauma. In 1976 Stanislaus Grof, an American psychiatrist also using LSD with his patients, stated that specific correlations can be made between the infant's experience of the different phases of birth, and later psychological problems. In the 1970s a growth industry developed in the United States and

Britain called 're-birthing' or 'primal integration'. The object of this therapeutic approach is to relive the birth-process, to abreact 'held-in' emotional pain, and to establish new ways of relating to one's personal environment. The re-living experience has been undertaken by dream association, hypnosis, drugs and deep-breathing techniques.

Problems that can arise out of birth trauma hypotheses and therapeutic practices include a reductionist approach which virtually ignores other phases in human development, and the encouragement of a dramatic 'once for all', 'breakthrough' attitude in counselling and psychotherapy.

Fodor, Nandor, *The Search for the Beloved* (University Books, New York, 1949). Grof, Stanislaus, *Realms of the Human Unconscious* (E.P. Dutton, New York, 1976). Lake, Frank, *Clinical Theology* (Darton Longman & Todd, 1966). Rank, Otto, *The Trauma of Birth* (Warner Torch Books, New York, 1934). Wyss, Dieter, *Depth Psychology* (Allen & Unwin, 1966).

JOHN GRAVELLE

See also: CLINICAL THEOLOGY; HUMAN DEVELOPMENT; PSYCHOANALYSIS.

BLESSING

An authoritative declaration of divine favour.

A blessing is a bestowal of good upon either people or objects. The concept of blessing features prominently in the Old Testament and in places throughout the New Testament. It is a formula which occurs frequently in the stories of the patriarchs (Gen. 12—36), where various occasions for blessing are recorded. For example, it was used as a form of greeting at meeting or departing (Gen. 47.7ff.), and imparted especially at the climactic stages in life: at a birth (Ruth 4.13ff.; cf. Luke 2.34); a marriage (Gen. 24.60); and a death (Gen. 48.1ff.; 49.28ff.). Blessings were mediated through prophets, priests and kings. It was an important function of the early prophets to intercede for the blessing of Yahweh on the nation (1 Kings 18.41ff.; 2 Kings 6.24ff.; Amos 7.1ff.; Jer. 14). Blessings also played a prominent part in Israelite worship – at the consecration of Solomon's temple (1 Kings 8.14, 54), and at the close of worship as members returned to their homes (cf. Pss. 65; 115.12–15; 128; 129.8; 132). The words of the priestly Aaronic blessing were used at the end of every act of worship: 'The

Lord bless you, and keep you: the Lord make his face shine upon you, and be gracious unto you. The Lord lift up the light of his countenance upon you and give you peace' (Num. 6.24–6).

In the New Testament writings we find the Jewish custom of offering praise and blessing on various everyday occasions and in worship (Luke 2.28f., the 'Nunc Dimittis'; 2.34; 24.53; 1 Cor. 14.16). A prayer of blessing is recited at table before and after meals (Mark 6.41, feeding of 5,000; 8.7, feeding of 4,000; 14.22ff., the Lord's Supper). The concept of blessing in the synoptic gospels has three rather special features: (1) The blessing of children. Jesus lays hands on the children and blesses them (Mark 10.13–16). Blessing is therefore not restricted to adults, but embraces all stages of life. (2) The commissioning of the Twelve (Matt. 10.1–16). They are instructed to offer greetings of peace and well-being to the households they visit, and are given a two-fold commission to preach and to heal. They are to be evangelists and bearers of blessing. (3) The departure of the risen Jesus from his followers (Luke 24.50, 'he lifted up his hands and blessed them'). In the Pauline epistles (Gal. 3.8, 14; Eph. 1.3f.) the act of blessing is given a decisive christological form, while the author of the Epistle to the Hebrews recalls the Old Testament usage of blessing as found in the stories of the patriarchs (Heb. 6.7ff.), and frequently paraphrases Old Testament benedictions (6.14; 7.1–7; 11.20—12.27).

In current usage an act of blessing is frequently recited liturgically and at the end of the liturgy itself. The final blessing does not so much send the congregation away but rather sends them out to work and to witness for the faith. It is also customary to use the verbal formula of blessing for the sanctification of the outward and visible signs of the Church's sacraments – e.g. the water at holy baptism, the ring at holy matrimony, and the oil at anointing – as well as of religious objects and symbols (medallions, crucifixes, etc.). A house may be blessed before being inhabited or a dwelling in which psychic phenomena are thought to have occurred (*see* EXORCISM).

A form of blessing used in periods of emotional or psychic disturbance, physical sickness, pain, suffering, bestows a sense of peace and of grace which endows the person with the assurance of God's presence to strengthen, renew and heal in its fullest sense. When accompanied by the form of the laying on of hands (cf. Mark 10.16) the act of physical touch inspires confidence, tranquillity and hope. Expectant faith is strengthened, a faith which is the outcome of God having spoken good ('blessing', 'benediction'), enabling the patient to accept whatever may come. But for this very reason blessing should not be used as a way of obscuring fears or denying real conflict. In the various spheres of pastoral care outward signs and symbolic acts can be of real help and significance. A form of blessing can conclude a pastoral call or a pastoral counselling interview. A benediction can accompany prayers recited at the bedside of the sick. Used either with or without the imposition of hands, it can convey peace and confidence before an operation or in post-operative pain, distress and discomfort. In such a sacramental act of blessing, sick or troubled persons are able to offer themselves and all their needs to God in complete trust and absolute confidence. Since blessing can evoke a father/child relationship, it should not be used merely out of the pastor's need to establish a clear role. Rather, it should convey a relationship of empathy (q.v.) and identification, wherein the other is looked upon as an equal, a person of worth, as one to be valued and loved.

Hastings Dictionary of the Bible, article: 'Blessing and Curse' (T. & T. Clark, rev. edn 1963). **Richardson, A.**, 'Bless', in *A Theological Word Book of the Bible* (SCM, 1957).

NORMAN AUTTON

See also: COMMUNION; LITURGY AND RITUAL; TOUCH.

BODY, THEOLOGY OF

The theme of the body is pervasive throughout Christian theology. The incarnation (q.v.) marks the true human embodiment of Christ, the 'Word become flesh'. The traditional doctrines of the bodily resurrection of Jesus Christ, and the promised resurrection of the departed – with transformed bodies (1 Cor. 15) – contrast with belief in purely psychic survival and the ultimate dispensability of the body. Two somewhat different and extended meanings of the term 'body' are also of central importance. By baptism (q.v.) believers are brought into the Church, the 'body of Christ' (Eph. 1.23). Here the concept of the body emphasizes the corporate aspect of Christian membership, and the fact that it is more than merely a human association.

Additionally, communion (q.v.) marks participation in the sacramental body and blood of Christ (John 6.53).

The Christian faith offers a very positive evaluation of the human body. In this it may be contrasted with other faiths where the material creation in general and the body in particular are less valued or even regarded as evil. According to the Old Testament, the material creation is both real (not illusory) and good. Moreover, St Paul affirms that the entire universe is to 'enter upon the liberty and splendour of the children of God' (Rom. 8.21). In contrast to dualistic faiths, the Christian may affirm that the material world is to be redeemed. It is not to be redeemed *from*.

Salvation marks release from sin (q.v.), not from the material world. This affirmation is central to Christian doctrine, and yet at times its implications have been obscured, with a resulting ambivalence towards the body in general, and sexuality (q.v.) in particular. However, Christianity has 'an immensely positive bias toward embodiment' (Nelson 1979), and the responsible enjoyment of sexuality is an important part of this. The call to sexual morality is grounded in the understanding that the human body is 'a shrine of the indwellling Holy Spirit' (1 Cor. 6.19). Within sexual union, emotional maturity and respect for the sexual partner are important, and marriage (q.v.) is not justified merely on the grounds of procreation. Celibacy (q.v.) is a legitimate vocation, but is devalued when it is based on an aversion to sexuality.

Christian ambivalence towards the body has also been evident in the understanding of ascetic discipline. Self-control is a gift of the Holy Spirit (Gal. 5.22), yet at times it has been equated with mere bodily constraint. This marks a superficial and materialistic view of *ascesis*, which ought not to be an end in itself but a means to growth in self-giving and Christian love (*see* ASCETICAL THEOLOGY).

The bodily discipline of fasting has sometimes been ignored by certain sectors of Christendom, but curiously it has been rediscovered as a secular value, in dieting and in hunger-striking. For the Christian, fasting may not only undergird special times of prayer, but also has some noteworthy implications for the theological understanding of the body and the material world as a whole. In particular, it may be linked with the call for simple life-style and for responsible stewardship of material resources in a world where gross inequalities exist.

The Hebraic insistence on the person as a psychosomatic unity opposes any dualism in Christian theology, and acquires new significance in the light of contemporary explorations in psychosomatics. In the healing ministry of Christ, some sickness – though certainly not all – was linked with prior sin (John 5.14). There is now increasing evidence to suggest that much physical illness is stress-linked, or has some psychosomatic component. The quest for bodily health should take psychological and spiritual dimensions into account.

The theology of the body touches on numerous other concerns: the ethics of organ transplants; the propriety of cremation rather than burial; the rationale of sex-change surgery; genetic engineering; artificial insemination; the problems of sexism (q.v.); and many others. Christians will differ in their detailed response to these questions, while attempting to apply the general principles – in particular, the positive value of embodiment – that inform the mainstream of the Christian faith.

Nelson, James, *Embodiment* (SPCK, 1979). Robinson, J.A.T., *The Body* (SCM, 1952).

ELIZABETH R. MOBERLY

See also: FEMININITY/MASCULINITY; SEXISM; SEXUALITY AND SEXUAL DEVELOPMENT; SEXUALITY, THEOLOGY OF.

BOREDOM
See: APATHY.

C

CASEWORK
See: SOCIAL WORK.

CATHARSIS
Emotional release (Greek: *catharsis* = cleansing), for example crying, first used in psychoanalysis (q.v.) and analytical psychology (q.v.) but now accepted as an important prelude in nearly all types of formal counselling.

Clinebell, H.J., *Basic Types of Pastoral Counselling* (Abingdon, 1966), pp. 69–70. Jung, C.G., *Collected Works*, vol. 16 (Routledge, 1978).

CELIBACY
The voluntary renunciation of marriage 'for the sake of the Kingdom of Heaven'.

We do not speak of celibacy if a person is merely unmarried, but only when this state is embraced for religious reasons. The New Testament foundation is in Matthew 19.10–12, where Jesus speaks of the gift of remaining unmarried, which is not for all but is given to those who have made themselves eunuchs for the sake of the Kingdom of Heaven.

Celibacy grew in the Christian Church, connected with monasticism, offering an attractive absolute commitment after the possibility of martyrdom had ceased to be. In those centuries, when theology was much influenced by Platonism, some justifications for celibacy were offered which would not nowadays be accepted as either valid or healthy. They were connected with hatred/ fear of sex and with the denigration of women. Celibates today base their reasons for being so neither on fear of sex nor denigration of women but on at least five positive values.
(1) *Pastoral availability*. The celibate, having no family obligations of his or her own, is free with regard to both time and responsibilities to be 'got at' by people in need and may regard such people as his or her 'family'. Thus celibate pastors can share their homes with 'down-and-outs' or alcoholics, where it would be wrong for married people with a young family to do so. Also celibates are freer to be sent to live and work in undesirable places like remote mission spots or deprived inner city areas. Celibates are freer to join the marginals of society.
(2) *Single-mindedness*. Paul said, 'The unmarried man is anxious about the affairs of the Lord, how to please the Lord; but the married man is anxious about worldly affairs, how to please his wife, and his interests are divided' (1 Cor. 7.32–3).
(3) *Liberation for prayer*. There seems to be a connection between the practice of celibacy and the call to contemplation. A helpful background to that growth in non-possessive love which is the kernel of contemplative prayer is the practice of celibacy. The figure of Joseph, husband of Mary, caring for Christ who was not his son is symbolic here. Celibacy helps the one who prays to pass from 'having' to 'being' as the master idea of his or her life.
(4) *Liberation for prophecy*. It is easier for the celibate to live out a prophetic role in the world than for a married person with family responsibilities. The celibate can risk losing his or her life without counter-obligations to stay within bounds of prudent safety.
(5) *Gospel witness*. Just as the married state witnesses to some Gospel values, so the celibate state witnesses to others. There are two of these. First, celibacy reminds Christians of their future state in heaven where there will be no marriage. Secondly, celibacy reminds the world that human beings can love without sexual engagement, that not all love is sexual.

Celibacy is not without risk. Like all ideals its practice falls short. Celibates can become comfortable bachelors and old maids, increasingly out of touch with humanity, using their unmarried state as a barrier against their fellow men and women. It can be used to make themselves less available instead of more available. In practice, therefore, celibacy becomes a counter-witness to the gospel unless it is linked with gospel poverty – not only poverty of goods, but also poverty of ambition, career, fame, honour, power. In particular celibates have to be on their guard against the lust for power.

In the Roman Catholic Church celibacy has been an obligation for all priests since the 11th century. This obligation is much debated today, in view of the New Testament insistence that celibacy is a gift for some, not all. The most notable New Testament examples of celibacy are Jesus and Paul.

Goergen, D., *The Sexual Celibate* (SPCK, 1976). **Schillebeeckx, E.,** *Clerical Celibacy Under Fire* (Sheed and Ward, 1968).

JOHN DALRYMPLE

See also: SEXUALITY, THEOLOGY OF.

CHAPLAINCY
See: ARMED FORCES CHAPLAINCY; COLLEGE/UNIVERSITY CHAPLAINCY; HOSPITAL CHAPLAINCY; INDUSTRIAL CHAPLAINCY; POLICE CHAPLAINCY; PRISON CHAPLAINCY; SCHOOL CHAPLAINCY.

CHARISMATIC MOVEMENT
A spiritual renewal movement for the churches, stressing the doctrine of the Holy Spirit; a Christian variation of a world-wide religious upsurge in all religions and cultures.

1. *History and expansion.* Very soon after the emergence of the pentecostal movement at the beginning of our century (which itself tried unsuccessfully to be a renewal movement for all churches), small charismatic groups appeared in most European mainline churches. Some of the leaders of the early pentecostal movement remained in the ordained ministry of their respective churches until the end of their lives (the Lutheran Jonathan Paul in Germany, the Anglican Alexander A. Boddy in England, the Reformed Louis Dallière in France and others). Those beginnings however, never developed substantially and are neglected in most historical treatments of the Charismatic Movement.

Generally one dates the beginning of the charismatic movement in the early 1960s in the USA, although there were many isolated beginnings in England in the 1950s. The powerful public relations drive by the California-based Full Gospel Business Men's Fellowship International (a pentecostal lay organization), the ecumenical contacts of the pentecostal 'go-between' David J. Du Plessis with the World Council of Churches and the Vatican, the emergence of charismatic service organizations in many countries and a number of study conferences organized by the World Council of Churches (Bittlinger), made the specific expressions of charismatic spiritualities – with speaking in tongues (q.v.), baptism in the Spirit (q.v.) and prayer (q.v.) for the sick – socially more acceptable in mainline churches.

2. *Ecumenical character.* The ecumenical potential of the charismatic movement is significant. It is so far the only world-wide grass-roots organization of some size where ecumenical, catholic, evangelical and African-independent Christians meet. They discover that not only can they discuss but they can also pray and celebrate together. These ecumenical contacts are also responsible for the unsolved theological problems of the charismatic movement. It is obvious that the creation of ecumenical charismatic fellowships, sometimes even communities, especially between Evangelicals and Roman Catholics, as has happened in particular in the USA, in Ireland, France and Italy, is both an embarrassment and a source for rejoicing by church leaders and ecumenists. The embarrassment is caused by the fact that ecumenists and church leaders are alarmed when the people of God put the ecumenical appeals of their leaders into practice and begin to pray, act, celebrate and think together. When, as now happens, the charismatic movement hires its own staff, raises substantial amounts of money, and communicates its ideas and experiences to society at large through the media, many observers begin to detect clashes between some charismatic leaders and church authorities. The reaction to this is twofold. On the one hand some charismatic prayer groups develop into independent congregations, called 'house churches' in the UK and 'independent churches' in the USA. Others try to meet the concern of their ecclesiastical authorities by affirming that, as adherents of the charismatic movement, they are yet even more faithful to their Catholic, Anglican, Methodist, etc. traditions. They say that the Holy Spirit has not changed their loyalty and their theology. It has enlightened and strengthened it (McDonnell 1980).

3. *Significance for pastoral care.* It all depends on what the goal of pastoral care is. If it is to keep the existing churches together and to hinder as far as possible any fragmentation of the existing denominations, then pastoral care will try to interpret the respective ecclesiastical traditions and the existing power

structures in such a way as to make room for a reasonable middle-of-the-road charismatic spirituality. If, however, the priority of pastoral care is seen in the growth and development of the individual client, then there might be circumstances where the development of independent churches and groups appears inevitable, although in light of the high emotionality of some groups the positive effects can be outweighed by excessive dependency and denial of negative feelings.

Bittlinger, A. (ed.), *The Church is Charismatic* (World Council of Churches, 1982). **Hollenweger, W.J.**, *The Pentecostals* (SCM, 1972). **McDonnell, K.**, *Presence, Power, Praise: Documents on the Charismatic Renewal*, 3 vols. (Liturgical Press, Collegeville, Minn., 1980). **Thurman, J.V.**, *New Wineskins: a Study of the House Church Movement* (Verlag Peter Lang, Frankfurt, 1982). **Tugwell, S.** *et al.*, *New Heaven? New Earth? An Encounter with Pentecostalism* (Darton Longman & Todd, 1976).

WALTER J. HOLLENWEGER

See also: SPIRIT.

CHILDREN: PASTORAL CARE

Pastoral care is essential to the nurture of children. In the earliest phases, a caring, accepting relationship – especially between mother and child – provides the stable conditions in which 'basic trust' (Erikson 1950) can develop: trust in the mother, trust in others and trust in oneself. It promotes the confidence to make free choices and develop autonomy; and it provides a basis for the child's sense of identity. If mistrust is engendered, the consequences are shame, doubt, guilt and inferiority. Hence, all who are involved in the pastoral care of the child – parents, other members of the family, professional people such as teacher, nurse or minister – must reinforce the 'faith syndrome' (love, acceptance, trust, stability, confidence) as opposed to the 'fear syndrome' (unpredictability, rejection, guilt, hostility). Indeed, of all the qualities required for personal growth the greatest is *agape*: love as in 1 Corinthians 13. The growing child's moral and spiritual development continues to reflect relationships with significant adults, who define the bounds of acceptable behaviour and provide the authoritative reference points. Exaggerated moralism simply engenders guilt; nor should parental love ever appear conditional: e.g. 'Mummy won't love you if you do that'. Rather, '. . . children need security and freedom in the home if the impulses of self-giving are to grow in strength. They need the security that comes from an understanding affection at all times, the guidance that comes from rules wisely ordered and enforced with reasonable firmness, and freedom which enables them to grow in personal initiative and achievement' (Smith 1953).

Undoubtedly the pastor will meet many early casualties of the process. Strong disapproval or punitive measures may simply increase resentment and hostility, born of rejection. Patience and a readiness to listen and understand are likely to be more productive in the long term. A gesture of acceptance may be the beginning of a more positive relationship. The task is to build up the feeling of being wanted, of having worth. Industry is encouraged by having one's modest achievements recognized. Thus, the destructive sense of inferiority is checked and the sense of identity – of being someone – is reinforced; and the child is accordingly better fitted to face the next developmental tasks.

Erikson, E., *Childhood and Society* (Norton, New York, 1950). **Smith, J.W.D.**, *Psychology and Religion in Early Childhood* (SCM, 1953).

J.I.H. McDONALD

See also: HUMAN DEVELOPMENT; PLAY; TRUST.

CHRISM
See: ANOINTING.

CHRISTIAN SCIENCE
A system of religious teaching and practice evolved by Mary Baker Eddy (1821–1910), which is directed towards healing through spiritual understanding.

The founder of Christian Science and the Church of Christ (Scientist), Mary Baker Eddy, was an American brought up in New England. Injured in a fall on ice in 1866, she discovered, through a significant healing experience, the principles of health that she first described in her publication in 1875, *Science and Health with Key to the Scriptures*. She based her system on the words and works of Jesus, describing it in such phrases as 'divine metaphysics', 'the scientific system of divine healing', 'the law of God, the law of good, interpreting and demonstrating the divine Principle and rule of universal harmony'

(Eddy, 1910, pp. 111, 123; *Rudimental Divine Science*, p. 1). *Science and Health with Key to the Scriptures* has gone through many editions and, with the Bible, remains the chief authority of Christian Scientists. In 1875 the first Christian Science society was created and in 1879 'The Church of Christ (Scientist)' was given a charter. The Boston church remains the world headquarters of the movement. Branches are world-wide. 'Readers' conduct worship – there are no ordained clergy. 'Practitioners' offer healing ministry.

The basic standpoint of Christian Science is its proclamation of a clear distinction between what is real and what is apparent, but unreal. 'All reality is in God and His creation, harmonious and eternal. That which He creates is good and He makes all that is made. Therefore the only reality of sin, sickness or death is the awful fact that unrealities seem real to human erring belief, until God strips off their disguise. They are not true because they are not of God' (Eddy 1910, p. 472).

God, for Christian Scientists is all in all, divine Mind. Mind (which is synonymous with Spirit in Christian Science terminology), Soul, Life, Truth, Love, Principle are all that exist. Man is the expression of the Divine Mind. Matter is illusion. As evil is connected with matter it, like sin and death, is unreal. For Christian Scientists, sickness is false belief and suffering exists in the mortal mind. Disease and illness, because they are illusions and only in the human mind, will be cured by spiritual understanding and by prayer. Christian Scientists do not confine their faith to physical healing, but are concerned to recreate the whole being through spiritual insight and understanding.

Baker Eddy, Mary, *Science and Health with Key to the Scriptures* (1910). Braden, Charles Samuel, *Christian Science Today* (Southern Methodist UP, Dallas, 1958). Peel, Robert, *Mary Baker Eddy: the Years of Authority* (Holt Rinehart & Winston, New York, 1977). Wilbur, Sybil, *The Life of Mary Baker Eddy* (Concord Publishing, New York, 1908).

DENIS DUNCAN

See also: SPIRITUAL HEALING.

CHURCH, DOCTRINES OF

A group of theological interpretations of the significance of the worshipping assemblies of 'Christians' in the divine plan for humanity.

The raw material for doctrines of the Church is provided by a narrative or narratives telling in a single story the history of both the Old and the New Israel. The Church is a remnant 'selected by the grace of God' (Rom. 11.5), the inheritor of the promise (Acts 2.39), or the place where God has spoken his final word (Heb. 1.2). In each case a story must be told linking the saving events of Israel's history with the life of the new communities. This story provides the basis of the Church's identity, as called into being by God to bear witness to his new deeds in Jesus Christ, and to enjoy the fruits of communion with God.

The New Testament contains a remarkable richness of imagery relating to the Church, of which at least ten idea-complexes are of major importance, those of the sanctified, the faithful, slaves and servants, the people of God, the kingdom and temple, the household or family, the new Exodus, the vineyard and the flock, the one body in Christ, and the new humanity. More importantly the NT documents derive from, and reflect, different circles in the early Church, Pauline and post-Pauline, with varying attitudes to the Law and to formal structures of authority. Internal disputes were frequent, and the threat of error and schism was taken with great seriousness.

Already in the NT period account has to be taken of 'the routinization of charisma' (Max Weber), the social process whereby a prophetic movement achieves permanent institutional form by means of regular structures and internal discipline. Crucial for the sense of its own identity was the Church's long struggle with Gnosticism, a religious movement of the first and second centuries emphasizing in various forms the intellectual enlightenment by which the soul is released from its enslavement in an evil cosmos. In opposition to Gnosticism the Church developed an interlocking set of criteria for the preservation of its own distinctive identity, a canon of authorized writings, a summary of the apostolic gospel, and an apostolic ministry, the episcopate. It thus combined both a fixed written norm from the past, and a speaking contemporary authority.

Three inherent tensions in the doctrine of the Church have given rise to a series of variations in its historic form. The first is the tension between local and universal, that is, whether the Church is seen primarily in its embodiment in a specific community or whether its existence is thought of as, at least potentially, embracing the whole of humanity. At its extremes this tension has broken apart into, on the one hand, a purely congregational interpretation of the Church, and, on the other, one which so emphasizes the authority of the centre that no independent initiative is permitted to the local church. The history of the discussion of the papal claims up to the declaration of papal infallibility (1870) illustrates this tension.

A second inherent tension concerns the relation of the Church's mundane reality to its heavenly reality. Here again at its extremes a separation has taken place between those who simply identify the mundane Church and its organization, hierarchy and law with the true Church, and those who deny that the perfect Church of the heavens has any earthly correlate, so fallible and corrupt are all its members.

A third tension derives from the claim of the Church to holiness, which is in irresolvable conflict with its immersion in the complexities and compromises of human history. Here again the history of the Church shows, on the one hand, holiness movements which have retreated from normal society in order to set up a supposedly uncontaminated communal life and, on the other hand, compromised forms of Christian society, employing the ordinary methods of the political and social order to achieve dominance.

Although there is no intrinsic reason why the above tensions should lead to rival and contradictory doctrines, in fact the history of theology contains plenty of examples, notably at and since the Reformation. Roman Catholic understanding of the Church insisted that the Church is the specific foundation of Jesus Christ, having its own divinely given hierarchical order and constitution, centred upon the Pope, the successor of St Peter. It is the divine provision for human salvation, and its legitimate authority cannot be defied without endangering that salvation. Against this, Luther distinguished between 'physical external Christendom' and 'spiritual internal Christendom', salvation belonging only to the latter which may be entered alone by obedience to the word of promise addressed to the heart. The true Church exists wherever the word of God is preached and the sacraments duly administered. Against both Roman Catholic and Protestant regimes, on the other hand, Anabaptist groups sought to abandon the world of political power and realize a wholly new order.

In modern times strenuous efforts have been made to mitigate the confessional opposition set up at the Reformation. Of particular importance has been the recovery of the doctrine of the Kingdom of God, and the realization that the Church is a sign pointing to, but not identical with, the Kingdom. The Church is seen therefore, not as an end in itself, nor complete or perfect at the present, but on a journey; it is 'the pilgrim people of God' (Second Vatican Council). Also signficant in qualifying any tendency towards triumphalism has been the recovery of a sense of Christian ministry as service, specifically service to the liberation of humanity. Liberation theologies in Latin America, and black theologies in Africa and North America, have specifically focused on economic and racial injustice, as central dimensions of human bondage and seen the Church as an agent in struggles on behalf of the poor.

Contemporary theology continues to exhibit a variety of doctrines of the Church, expressive both of the original richness of imagery and the tensions inherent in its further development. On the whole, theology has been slow to incorporate insights derived from sociology of religion, which is in a position to help interpret its internal and external conflicts.

Dulles, A., *Models of the Church* (Gill & Macmillan, 1976). Jay, E.G., *The Church: Its Changing Image through the Centuries*, 2 vols. (SPCK, 1977). Küng, H., *The Church* (Burns & Oates, 1968). Moltmann, J., *The Church in the Power of the Spirit* (SCM, 1977).

STEPHEN SYKES

See also: BAPTISM; COMMUNION; COMMUNITY; CONGREGATION.

CLIENT-CENTRED THERAPY

An approach to counselling and psychotherapy developed in the United States by Carl Rogers (1902-) and his associates, sometimes referred to as 'Rogerian' counselling and psychotherapy.

Originally termed 'non-directive' therapy, the name 'client-centred' became preferred by Rogers in order to emphasize the exclusive focus in this form of therapy on the immediate inner experience (the 'phenomenal field') of the client. Since 1974, Rogers has attempted a further name change – from 'client-centred' to 'person-centred' – on the grounds that the psychological principles that he and his co-workers have elaborated in connection with the client in the counselling relationship have general application to all interpersonal situations.

Origin and development. In Rogers' opinion, client-centred therapy came into full-flower during the period 1938–1950, his work, *Client-Centered Therapy*, providing an important summation of development to this point. Influences on Rogers' thinking up to 1938 include: ten years professional experience as a psychotherapist (this first-hand experience constituted the most important influence on Rogers' thought throughout his career); in-depth exposure to the contemporary trends in psychology at that time, particularly to statistical methods on the one hand and Freudian psychotherapy on the other; attraction to the educational philosophy of John Dewey, Gestalt psychology, and the theory of therapy of Otto Rank.

In the 1940s Rogers originated the analysis of audio-recordings of interviews, and the continuing efforts of client-centred researches since the 1950s to study the 'raw data' of interpersonal interactions have yielded these results: (a) detailed elaboration of the process of psychotherapy; (b) evidence of the efficacy of client-centred therapy for schizophrenics; (c) the broader application of client-centred principles to personal growth or encounter groups, to education, and to politics and intercultural communication.

The therapy relationship. Primary importance in the practice of client-centred therapy is placed upon the character and quality of the therapy relationship. The relationship of client to counsellor is seen as that of person to person, not of superior to inferior as in the transference relationship of psychoanalysis. The client-centred therapist does not diagnose or interpret but seeks to create the ideal relational conditions for the release of the basic forces for growth which exist within the client. The human being at root is assumed to be rational and good. It is environmental conditions which warp a person.

Rogers identifies high levels of three therapist attitudinal conditions as essential ingredients in the optimally therapeutic counselling relationship: *accurate empathic understanding* – understanding the personal world of the client from within, 'as if' one were that person; *respect or unconditional positive regard* –

esteeming another in terms of that person's inherent worth; *genuineness or congruence* – possessing harmony between outward expression and deep-felt inner meaning.

Rogers has claimed that with respect to the therapist's contribution to the counselling relationship these core conditions are both necessary *and* sufficient for positive personality change. More recently, other client-centred theorists have suggested that the therapist variables of concreteness and immediacy of expression, confrontation and self-disclosure also have critical significance for the personal growth of the client.

Theory of therapy and personality change. Client-centred personality theory, as Rogers puts it, 'has always been a theory of the process by which change comes about in persons and their behaviour . . . not a theory of the structure of personality'. Rogers' own formal theory of personality thus stresses the notion of an innate actualizing tendency within the human organism which, under therapeutic conditions and in tandem with a valuing process related to the whole organism, acts as the motive force in the accurate symbolization of previously denied or distorted aspects of a person's self-concept. The changes which take place in the client's concept of self and, *ipso facto*, perception of the surrounding world, have been charted by Rogers as a seven-stage process. A person who reaches the final stage is said to possess the attributes of the 'fully-functioning person' (Rogers' equivalent to Maslow's self-actualizing person (*see* SELF-ACTUALIZATION)), attributes which not only represent the goals of psychotherapy, but which subsume the attitudinal qualities of the effective therapist, i.e. genuineness, empathy and respect.

Patterson, C.H., *Relationship Counseling and Psychotherapy* (Harper & Row, New York, 1974). **Rogers, C.R.**, *Client-Centered Therapy* (Constable, 1965); *On Becoming a Person* (Constable, 1974); *Encounter Groups* (Penguin, 1971).

IVAN H. ELLINGHAM

CLINICAL PASTORAL EDUCATION
A method of developing personal and professional growth in ministry, a distinctive feature of which is practical experience of ministry under supervision (q.v.), normally but not always in a hospital setting.

Clinical Pastoral Education (CPE) has its roots in the United States, early important figures being Richard Cabot, a physician, and Anton Boisen, a Congregationalist minister. In 1925 Cabot, who had earlier developed a 'case-method' approach for teaching medical students, wrote a paper, 'A Plea for a Clinical Year in the Course of Theological Study', advocating a similar approach to the training of divinity students. In the same year Boisen, then chaplain at Worcester State Hospital, Mass., and himself recovering from a psychotic breakdown, invited some theological students to work with him in the hospital during the summer vacation. This initiative sprang from a conviction that there were other ways of doing theology apart from reading books and that a study of the 'living human documents' of people in crisis would provide insights of pastoral importance. After an initial period of collaboration, Cabot and Boisen developed different approaches, the years 1930–46 being marked by bitter controversy between proponents of each school of thought. One group, consisting mainly of chaplains in general hospitals, emphasized the acquisition of pastoral skills and formed themselves into the Institute of Pastoral Care; others, mainly chaplains in psychiatric hospitals, focused upon the need for students to gain insight and self-understanding. This group became the Council for the Clinical Training of Theological Students. Obviously, these emphases were not mutually exclusive and after prolonged negotiation they came together in 1967 and, with two other denominational organizations, formed the Association for Clinical Pastoral Education.

There now exist between two and three hundred centres (normally general or psychiatric hospitals or prisons) in North America offering CPE courses. In these, students, pastors or lay people work under the guidance of a qualified supervisor, exercising a pastoral ministry, reporting back on these experiences of ministry to their peers and supervisors and finding themselves in a process of personal and professional growth. Many theological students benefit from a basic three months of CPE (and indeed many American seminaries require this for graduation); full-time hospital chaplains in the USA are normally required to have a year of this kind of training and an accredited chaplain-supervisor at least three years (see ACCREDITATION). Central to the process of CPE is competent supervision (q.v.). A typical CPE programme will consist of some didactic instruction in the field of

pastoral care and theology, the undertaking of a limited amount of pastoral work in the institution, an inter-personal group experience and supervision either individually or in the group setting. Written verbatim accounts of pastoral conversations may be used in the supervision process.

In recent years the influence of CPE has been extended in various directions. Internationally its methods and philosophy have affected the development of education for pastoral ministry, teachers of the discipline in many lands having had some direct experience of American CPE, or at least having been influenced by its literature. Indeed papers presented at international conferences have indicated an influence in some developing countries which has swamped approaches indigenous to local traditions and culture. In Britain the growth of CPE has not been widespread, though two London hospitals (St George's and the Maudsley) offer annual courses, and in Edinburgh University supervised hospital placements (q.v.) form an integral part of courses in pastoral care and counselling.

'Classical' CPE has also begun to exercise an influence upon education for ministry outside the hospital setting. Developments in field education owe much to the growing awareness of the importance of supervision and there have also been experiments in parish-based CPE. Some approaches to education for lay pastoral care (q.v.) also depend upon understandings of supervision developed in CPE.

While clinical pastoral education has undoubtedly made a major contribution to professional education for ministry, it has been criticized on the grounds that it embodies an individualistic approach to pastoral care, failing to take seriously the social and political context of the Church's mission. Recent publications however indicate an awareness of the need to apply CPE principles within a wider understanding of ministry which includes ministry within the structures of society (Coine 1983).

Coine, Simonne, 'Clinical Pastoral Education with the Poor' (*Journal of Pastoral Care*, vol. 37, June 1983), pp. 90-7. Nace, R.K., 'Parish Clinical Pastoral Education' (*Journal of Pastoral Care*, vol. 35, March 1981), pp. 58–68. Thornton, E.E., *Professional Education for Ministry: a History of Clinical Pastoral Education* (Abingdon, 1970).

DAVID LYALL

See also: ACCREDITATION; SUPERVISION; TRAINING METHODS.

CLINICAL THEOLOGY

A movement within pastoral counselling (q.v.) developed by the late Dr Frank Lake – psychiatrist and ex-missionary – and his psychiatric and pastoral colleagues from the Clinical Theology Association founded in 1966.

The movement is emphatic in its belief that the healing of a disturbed personality stems from a re-encountering of personal loss and pain produced originally by unsatisfactory relationships between the infant and his early personal environment. With the support of wise counselling, and the presence of the Holy Spirit, recognized or unrecognized by the client, it believes an effective process of grieving and 'letting-go' of unrealizable expectations can take place. Following this the construction of a new assumptive world minus the unrealizable expectations should be achieved.

Clinical Theology uses much of the language and understanding of neurotic development offered by the British School of Object Relations but departs from it in giving some prominence to the possibility of birth trauma (q.v.), or latterly intra-uterine trauma, as being prototypal experiences of loss and personal pain.

The Clinical Theology Association has taught and practised a number of different facilitating techniques ranging from a Rogerian style empathetic 'reflecting-back' method (see CLIENT-CENTRED THERAPY) to the 'deep-breathing' practices of Primal therapy. Critics have argued that its use of a multiplicity of therapeutic methods can be confusing to client and counsellor, both in the sense of offering too many options in a relationship which require secure consistency and in possible confusion about the therapeutic task arising from the different models of change underlying different techniques. The theological basis of the movement assumes, first, that parents, especially the mother, express on an emotional level the infant's experience of God, and secondly, that Christ's creative encountering of the personal pain of humanity is both a resource we need to claim, and an example of both spiritual and personal growth. It also believes that correlations can be made between, for instance, biblical understandings of man and psychodynamic analyses of personality.

The experience of anxiety–depression on the one hand and the Pauline description of justification by law and works on the other hand are seen to have common factors and an underlying similar dynamic. In an attempt to understand the different types of neurotic suffering that can be undergone, the Association has focused upon the schizoid personality as depicting the basic problem beneath other neuroses. Drawing upon the work of Melanie Klein, Fairbairn, Winnicott and Guntrip and assisted by the use of LSD abreaction in the early days of the movement, and later by Primal therapy methods of regression, it sees the detachment and introversion which the schizoid personality reveals as the result of deprivation of 'good enough' mothering.

In his voluminous writings Dr Lake developed an understanding of schizoid suffering and styles of personal functioning through a close examination of the work of Kierkegaard and other existentialists, and spiritual authors such as St John of the Cross. Amongst a number of criticisms of the movement's teaching, some people believe that it has used psychiatric, theological, existentialist, and psychoanalytical language as confusing alternatives, losing the rigour and consistency of each language in the process. Others believe that the emphasis placed by some members of the Association upon birth and intra-uterine trauma dangerously neglects a wider perspective of human growth and development. Yet others believe it has neglected the importance of group-dynamics in favour of individual histories. Nevertheless the Clinical Theology Association is regarded by many as having provided a most important catalyst in the development of pastoral care with counselling within Britain.

Frank Lake, *Clinical Theology* (Darton Longman & Todd, 1966); *Tight Corners in Pastoral Counselling* (Darton Longman & Todd, 1981); *With Respect* (Darton Longman & Todd, 1982).

JOHN GRAVELLE

COLLECTIVE UNCONSCIOUS
See: ANALYTICAL PSYCHOLOGY.

COLLEGE/UNIVERSITY CHAPLAINCY

A form of extra-parochial ministry exercised within institutions of higher or tertiary education.

Chaplaincies were rapidly developed during the 1960s in institutions created following the Robbins Report on Higher Education. While the structure and forms of chaplaincy were varied, certain common functions were undertaken and some significant theological themes were dominant.

1. *Forms of Chaplaincy.* A few colleges and universities appoint their own chaplains and provide appropriate resources and facilities. Some institutions are explicitly secular in their foundation and do not encourage chaplaincy work. The majority of institutions allow and encourage denominations to appoint chaplains. (1) Denominational chaplains may be appointed primarily to provide pastoral care for students belonging to their specific denominations, but frequently also join in ecumenical activities with chaplains and students of other denominations. (2) Chaplains appointed by institutions are expected to be chaplains to the whole institution regardless of religious, racial or any other difference. This form of chaplaincy can allow the chaplain more immediate and direct involvement in and identification with the institution.

2. *Functions of chaplaincy.* Common functions undertaken in most college/university chaplaincies include: conduct of worship; counselling (q.v.); organizing programmes of theological/cultural/social study; involvement with staff and student organizations.
(1) Conduct of Worship. Chaplaincies provide normal forms and orders of worship for students accustomed to worshipping regularly in a particular denominational setting. Experimental forms of worship using silence, drama, music, are usually organized on an ecumenical basis. Where institutions have their own chaplains, formal academic services are conducted with the symbols and regalia of the institution being used.
(2) Counselling. Chaplains may be perceived by students as neutral persons within the institution, thus becoming the recipients of personal problems in a setting of confidentiality (q.v.). Issues of adolescence (q.v.), sexuality and sexual development (q.v.), anxiety (q.v.) or apathy (q.v.) may be brought to chaplains, and liaison with other counselling services (where these exist) is often vital.
(3) Chaplaincy programmes often offer the main set of alternative perspectives in an otherwise monochromatic culture. Some programmes may offer areas of thought completely outside the academic disciplines of the institution, whereas others may relate disciplines to one another – e.g. science to theology or medicine to ethics.
(4) Involvement with staff and student organizations. Chaplains often seek direct involvement in the organizations of the institution. Such involvement may be 'professional', e.g. serving on a welfare committee, or 'personal' in the sense of showing an interest in other people's activities. Chaplains tend to seek a balance between being absorbed in their own programmes and isolated in their own buildings, and on the other hand being available to the whole institution.

3. *Dominant and Emergent Themes.* Because many chaplaincies were developed in the contexts of change – ecumenical, sociocultural, and political – they became 'experimental laboratories' for the testing of doctrines of Church (q.v.), means of evangelism and theological reflection in general. Certain themes may be identified:
(1) Christian Presence. '. . . to be present in the name of Christ spells death to the status quo, both in society and in the Christian community: we will not tire of pleading and working for the restoration of normal manhood as we see it in Jesus.' This statement (WSCF 1965, p. 234) conveys the approach of the World Student Christian Federation's approach to the developing academic communities. Within these communities Christian presence was to develop five distinctive characteristics: (i) 'openness' of mind to the plurality of the secular world; (ii) 'diversity' of approach to facilitate encounter with a range of de-humanizing issues; (iii) 'unity' – the rejection of the superimposition of denominational barriers in the Christian community 'present' in the world; (iv) 'experimentation' by which to discover the nature of Christ's presence in the world; (v) 'understanding with the Churches' – a plea that chaplaincies and student groups should be acknowledged as part of the Churches' total life and mission.
(2) Secular and religious – a false polarization. The adoption of the theme of 'Christian Presence' in many chaplaincies led to a deeper understanding of the secular world as the place of God's presence and activity. 'The world writes the agenda' became a slogan which both pointed up the urgent issues of race and poverty, but which also implied a deep faith that God's will could be heard and understood in the areas of life adjudged to be irreligious or secular. So by 1976 A.O. Dyson,

speaking at the Bradwell Consultation on 'The Language of the Church in Higher and Further Education', said, 'The distinctive aspect of the religious/secular view is above all the fixed and static boundaries between the two areas with a built-in impossibility of any serious reciprocal relation . . .' (Dyson 1976, p. 7). To overcome this polarization and to develop reciprocity of thought and action, chaplaincies have sought to become fully present in the academic communities.

The general approach of college/university chaplaincies is summed up by Jenkins (1975) when he describes them as helping the institutions of society 'to fulfill their function more effectively, without in any way impinging on their autonomy.'

Higher Education, report of a Committee under the Chairmanship of Lord Robbins 1961–63 (HMSO, 1963). *Student World*, no. 3 (WSCF 1965). **Dyson, A.O.**, 'The Language of the Church in Higher and Further Education' (The Bradwell Consultation, 1976). **Jenkins, D.**, *The British: Their Identity and Religion* (SCM, 1975).

TOM SCOTT

COLLUSION
A relationship in which both parties conspire consciously, or more probably unconsciously, to avoid confronting a pathological or immature aspect of their relationship.

The Latin derivation (*colludere* = to play or sport together) makes it clear that this is a kind of game (Laing). In a professional relationship, analyst and patient might avoid confronting the deepest and most disturbed aspects of the patient's condition and concern themselves with neurotic rather than psychotic material (Winnicott). The term is currently used to describe an unrecognized way of avoiding growth to greater maturity. The collusive relationship therefore meets the neurotic needs of both parties.

Just as the relationship between husband and wife or therapist and client can be collusive, so an individual and a group or two separate groups can operate on the same model of faulty perceptions. The parish priest or minister may need to be appreciated by his congregation as a caring parent, and there will be those in the congregation who find this a satisfying dependency. As long as both sides are convinced that this is desirable, they will contrive a theological rationalization for it and resist any questioning of it. Insight and

40

consequent growth are actively repelled.

A similar situation can arise in industry with a collusive conflict between management and workforce. The battle lines may become set and they are then the only way in which the two sides know how to relate to each other. It will be the task of effective consultancy to help those concerned to re-examine the collusive, and destructive, relationship which has been established. The same pattern can be observed operating in the international field.

Collusion can therefore be a function of any set of human relationships. Occasionally, by allowing a needful regression, it can prove helpful. For the most part, it is a blind engagement in an inadequate way which needs to be resolved by insight.

Berne, E., *Games People Play* (Penguin, 1970). **Laing, R.D.**, *Knots* (Tavistock, 1970). **Winnicott, D.W.**, *Playing and Reality* (Tavistock, 1971).

MICHAEL HARE DUKE

COMMUNE
A group of people having a common life.

The definition has the merit of being etymologically correct. But it does not distinguish between communes and communities, and in fact one of the principal definitions (*Shorter Oxf. Engl. Dict.*) of 'commune' is 'a community'. But its meaning in recent decades has tended to be limited to communities created in the last twenty-five years in Western countries, with the conscious intention of providing experimental alternatives to the defective ways of life felt to characterize both Western industrial society on the one hand, and the traditional and well established religious communities, such as monasteries and convents, on the other. Communes are in this sense essentially innovative and of comparatively recent origin. Even so, this distinction cannot always be maintained, there being communities originating in the 1930s, yet having today many of the features of the modern commune.

Common to all of these is a 'community of interest' having as its principle feature some aspect of that dissatisfaction with established ways of living referred to above. Within this general characteristic at least three particular strands of protest and of innovation can be discerned: (1) A wish to practise and to witness to a technological and agricultural way of life inspired by the ecological movement – the 'alternative society' as commended and portrayed by writers such as the late E.F. Schumacher – a way of life that can be sustained indefinitely because it does not damage the ecosphere or depend for its continuation on the increasing exploitation of limited and non-renewable resources such as coal and oil. (2) A wish to create and participate in a communal way of life wider and more genuinely sharing than the modern nuclear family. With this there tends to go a protest against the assignment of women to domestic and child-rearing tasks. (3) A wish to make real certain insights into the spiritual and psychological aspects of human nature felt to be ignored or inadequately recognized or practised by traditional religious communities.

Within these three strands a great variety of communes can be found. Some are primarily concerned with ecology and seek to become self-sufficient in food, energy and other resources. Others lay special stress on the quality of relationships and on feminist perspectives; though it is perhaps worth noting that studies indicate that attempts to increase the part played by men in child-rearing within the commune movement have not been particularly successful. Yet others, particularly those with an explicitly Christian commitment, seek primarily to be 'thera-peutic' in the sense of trying to provide for those in emotional and spiritual difficulties a supportive and healing milieu not generally available in established society. It is these which have the most obvious implications for pastoral care, seeking to demonstrate that no one can be fully healthy in a sick society. Yet this prophetic role can be discerned in all three types of commune, and is perhaps, for the established churches, the most important feature of the commune movement.

Abrams, P., and **McCulloch, A.,** *Communes, Sociology and Society* (CUP, 1976). **Clark, D.,** *Basic Communities* (SPCK, 1977). **Lockley, A.,** *Christian Communes* (SCM, 1976). **Mercer, J.,** *Communes: a Social History and Guide* (Prism, 1984). **Schumacher, E.F.,** *Small is Beautiful* (Blond & Briggs, 1973).

J.T. MEAD
See also: COMMUNITY; LIFE STYLE MOVEMENT; POLITICAL THEOLOGY AND PASTORAL CARE.

COMMUNICATION, VERBAL AND NON-VERBAL

1. *Verbal Communication* consists of the use of language, usually in conversation, but also in speeches, over the telephone and via writing. The basic types of utterance are (a) asking questions, (b) giving orders or instructions, and (c) providing information. There are several other uses, including the expression of emotions, and attitudes to the other, non-informative chat, social routines like apologies and greetings, 'performative utterances' (e.g. naming ships, declaring guilty), and 'latent utterances' ('as I was saying to the Prime Minister').

Speech varies from 'high' to 'low' usages. The high version, or 'elaborated code' in Britain, is used in more formal situations, and more readily by middle-class and educated people; it consists of more correct syntax, more elaborate utterances with subordinate clauses, more nouns and adjectives, com-pared with the low or 'restricted code'. Verbal skill consists, in part, of the careful construc-tion of utterances. For example, persuasion is done by arousing a state of need in the other, followed by showing how the desired behaviour would meet the need. Teaching is often done by stating a principle and follow-ing it with an example. Verbal skill also requires the correct management of conversa-tional sequences; for example a question may lead to an unsatisfactory answer, which then requires a follow-up question. The form of conversational sequences varies with the situation – e.g. informal talk between friends, psychotherapy, committee meetings – and the categories and rules of sequence are different for each. There are rules which specify the acceptable sequences of utterances, e.g. ques-tions lead to answers. While these rules are not yet fully understood, various maxims have been put forward by Grice (1975) and others, e.g. 'Make your contribution relevant to what has gone before;' 'Provide as much information and no more than is required.'

Another feature of conversational skill is politeness – not damaging another's self-esteem, or reducing his autonomy. The use of humour is also important – it can be used to avert conflicts, e.g. softening criticism, by discharging tension and offering a less threat-ening way of looking at the situation. Finally, speech is supported in several ways by non-verbal communication. Socially inadequate people are often poor conversationalists – they speak little, fail to initiate, e.g. don't ask questions, are unresponsive, produce uninteresting information about themselves, are unrewarding, disclose too much or too little.

2. *Non-verbal communication (NVC)* is the use of face, tone of voice, and other bodily signals, to send information either in combination with language, or alone. The other signals include gaze, posture, gesture, bodily movement, appearance, spatial behaviour, and smell. While a sender *encodes*, for example, his emotional state into a facial expression, the receiver *decodes* it. The process is partly outside conscious attention, especially for minor cues like pupil-dilation and head-nods; often the receiver is more aware than the sender. Some channels, like the face, are quite well controlled, while others, like tone of voice and posture, are not; the latter are regarded as 'leaky' channels, since they may reveal what has been concealed in better controlled parts of the body.

NVC is the main way in which emotions, and attitudes to others (e.g. like–dislike), are expressed. NV signals are more powerful than equivalent verbal ones here; the latter are virtually ignored if the two conflict. Facial expression for the 6–8 basic emotions are similar in all cultures; the main differences are in the 'display rules' governing when they shall be used. On the one hand gestures are very different in different cultures, as is proximity – Arabs stand nearer and face more directly, blacks stand further away. There are individual differences in accuracy of sending and receiving these NV signals: mental patients are bad at it, women are somewhat better than men.

NVC operates in a second way – to support and elaborate speech, and here the signals are more subtle and fast-moving. (a) A speaker accompanies his words with vocal emphasis, gestures, and other signals which elaborate on the meaning of the words, or make clear which of several alternate meanings is intended, e.g. 'Are you cold too?' to mean 'please come and warm me with your bodily warmth'. (b) Listeners send 'attention signals', such as head-nods and glances, to indicate that they are still attending, and facial expressions and grunts to indicate their reaction to what was said. (c) The synchronizing of utterances is achieved partly by NVC; for example the end of an utterance is signalled partly by a 'terminal gaze', by ending a gesture, and pitch change, though also by the grammatical form of the utterance. (d) Gaze

operates in two ways; it is both a signal (for the person looked at), and a channel (for the person looking). A terminal gaze is both a full-stop signal, and a means for the speaker to obtain feedback on the listener's reaction to the last utterance. (Kendon 1977)

Socially inadequate people, including many mental patients, often fail in the use of NVC – they look, smile and gesture little. They can be helped by social skills training, which includes coaching, especially in the use of face and voice.

Argyle, M., (1983) *The Psychology of Interpersonal Behaviour* (Penguin, 4th edn 1983). **Grice, H.P.,** 'Logic and Conversation', in P. Cole and J.L. Morgan (eds.), *Syntax and Semantics*, vol. 3: *Speech Acts* (Academic Press, New York & London, 1975). **Kendon, A.,** *Studies in the Behaviour of Social Interaction* (Indiana UP, Bloomington, 1977).

MICHAEL ARGYLE

See also: EMPATHY.

COMMUNION

1. Strictly, communion is the reception by worshippers of the elements of bread and wine in the central and distinctive Christian service of worship known variously as the Lord's Supper, the Eucharist, Mass, etc.

2. By extension, the service itself. This service goes back to the earliest strand of the Christian tradition (1 Cor. 23) and stems from the Last Supper which Jesus ate with his disciples (Matt. 26.26–38; Mark 14.22–24; Luke 22.17–19; cf. John 13). From the beginning, this ritual meal tied closely to the death and resurrection of Jesus. Whether the Last Supper was a Passover or not, both the Supper and the death and resurrection of Jesus were understood in the light of Passover themes, particularly Exodus, liberation, and the covenant establishing a new relationship between God and his people. Communion should also be understood in the light of the New Testament accounts of Jesus' table-fellowship; the feeding miracles, demonstrating God's gracious meeting of his people's needs and the narratives possibly reflecting something of the early Church's experience of the Eucharist; Jesus' conviviality and welcoming to his table of all sorts of people which caused so much offence among the religious folk of his day; the resurrection meals with the disciples which point to continuing real fellowship with the risen

Lord; and the 'banqueting parables' which suggest that the communion of the Lord's Table finds its fulfilment in the messianic banquet in the Kingdom to which many will come from north and south and east and west.

From the earliest days the Church continued with 'breaking of the bread' as a central part of its life (Act 2.42, 46). Obedience to the Lord's command to 'do this' as a memorial of him took a rich diversity of shapes and forms around the world, but always having at the heart the taking, the blessing, the breaking of bread, and the sharing of bread and wine, the repetition as closely as possible of the Lord's words and actions at the Last Supper. The theological understanding of the Eucharist has a complex and fascinating history which need not concern us here. In modern times the liturgical and ecumenical movements have led to a dramatic convergence in the practice and understanding of the Eucharist, which is well expressed in the World Council of Churches' Lima Document, *Baptism, Eucharist, and Ministry* (1982).

In this process, emphases of pastoral significance which were sometimes obscured in the past have been recovered. Patristic talk of the Eucharist as 'the medicine of immortality' sounds strange in modern ears, but in and through the sacrament many people experience forgiveness, reconciliation and renewal. The Eucharist creates and sustains the fellowship of the Church and integrates the individual into a community which has a past and a future, thus affirming a sense of identity and purpose. The Eucharist is also seen as a paradigm of the Christian life: the sharing of bread and wine involves a commitment to share food with the hungry; the care and acceptance of one another at the Lord's Table should be expressed in everyday life; the thanksgiving and reverent use of God's gifts should be reflected in behaviour at the family table. And the Eucharist is more than an exemplar or model for Christian living; it nourishes and upbuilds and heals the faithful for the fulfilment of their calling.

3. Communion is also used as a term for fellowship, translating the Greek word *koinonia*. Thus we speak of the communion of the saints (or communion in holy things), or communion in the Holy Spirit.

4. Communion is used to describe a fellowship of churches of the same tradition, usually in communion with one See, e.g. Canterbury or Rome.

Balasuriya, Tissa, *The Eucharist and Human Liberation* (SCM, 1979). Jungman, Josef A., *The Early Liturgy* (Darton Longman & Todd, 1960). Lash, Nicholas, *His Presence in the World* (Sheed & Ward, 1968). Willimon, William H., *Worship as Pastoral Care* (Abingdon/SPCK, 1979), ch. 8.

D.B. FORRESTER

See also: RITES AND RITUALS.

COMMUNITY

A widely used term in numerous contexts, often lacking precise definition. The immediate ancestry of modern usage is F. Tönnies, *Gemeinschaft und Gesellschaft* (1887, but only published in the United Kingdom in 1955). *Gemeinschaft* indicates a society of face-to-face relationships, with a marked involuntary element and a sense of rootedness, with clear role definitions, where benefits and misfortunes are shared, and the emphasis is on order and security rather than freedom. *Gesellschaft* indicates a society where relationships are specific, partial and utilitarian, more fragmentary and optional; an association rather than a community. The distinction marks a sense of regret for the loss of an alleged intimacy destroyed by industrial society with its urbanization and mobility.

A more objective categorization of types of community is possible: (1) Territorial – town or village. (2) Partial and limited – neighbourhoods. (3) Personal associations and networks of shared aims and values. (4) Minority groups – ethnic or communes. The values embodied in these four can be (a) conservative–hierarchical, emphasizing order and sanctions; (b) liberal – emphasizing freedom and autonomy, meritocracy and mobility as the weapon of the underdog; (c) radical – emphasizing equality, solidarity and communitarianism. Each type can express values (a), (b) or (c).

Each has problems: (1) can be stifling in its social control, or the more affluent setting themselves against the rest; (2) can be constricting as against intimacy and spontaneity; (3) can lead to *anomie* (Durkheim) or rootlessness, through lack of social norms; (4) can be closed and inflexible.

The Church as a *koinonia* (the nearest New Testament term to community) of those responding to the challenge of the Kingdom of God in the ministry of Jesus can express itself in all four forms of community, but in the United Kingdom today is mainly found in variants of (2) or (3). Its roots lie in the New Testament phrase, 'the fellowship of the Holy Spirit' (2 Cor. 13.14). It includes a sense of sharing in Christ's sufferings and blessings, and in love and service to one another. These latter were expressed in New Testament times by, for example, the so-called 'communism' of Acts 2 and 4 (living on pooled capital in the expectation of the *parousia* or return of Christ), and by the collection from St Paul's churches for the Jerusalem Christians who had impoverished themselves by doing so. The Church, which thinks of itself as a first fruits of how humanity is to overcome differences and live together, has to find ways of healing tensions within itself and without, and offering disinterested service at every level from the local congregation upwards. A *koinonia* ethic should: (a) offer love, security and significance; (b) test shallow and inauthentic forms of togetherness, belonging and co-operation; (c) judge hypocritical conceptions of community, e.g. racist or anti-feminist ones; (d) approach realistically the structural and institutional barriers in society, where genuine community requires a power balance rooted in justice, e.g. problems of inner-city areas cannot be isolated from wider structural facts and conflicts.

Cox, H.G., *The Secular City* (SCM, 1967). Dulles, A., *Models of the Church* (Doubleday, New York, 1974). Plant, R., *Community and Ideology* (Routledge, 1974). Thung, M., *The Precarious Organisation: Sociological Explorations of the Church's Mission and Structure* (Mouton, The Hague, 1976). Tönnies, F., *Community and Association* (Routledge, 1955).

RONALD PRESTON

See also: COMMUNE; CONGREGATION; CONFLICT.

CONFESSION

The act of acknowledging, in public or in personal communication, one's sins, in penitence, and with a view to obtaining forgiveness.

The confession of sins is an integral part of the Christian liturgy in East and West. The more specific personal confession, in the presence of a priest or minister, has been practised from early times in the Christian community. The association of the forgiveness of sins with the pastoral office is very ancient, and is mentioned in the Canons of Hippolytus and the Apostolic Constitutions. In the early Church penitential discipline was severe; the sinner was admitted into an order of penitents, but there was no sacramental means of coping with recurring sin. Repeated personal confession was, however, practised in the 5th-century Celtic Church. Although there are references in Origen (185–253) and in Leo the Great (c.459), there is no clear evidence of personal confession as a regular practice before the 6th century. In the West, the rule of an annual confession for mortal sin (the 'paschal precept') dates from the 2nd Lateran Council of 1215.

After the Council of Trent, confession was increasingly seen within the framework of canon law, as a judicial process. It was the 'tribunal of penance', and the priest was a judge. The practice did not disappear in post-Reformation Protestantism. Luther held it to be necessary. Wesley recommended it. Its revival in 19th-century Anglicanism led to fierce controversy. Bishop Samuel Wilberforce called it 'the crowning curse of popery'. However, the practice has become more widespread in the post-Second-World-War period, and is less confined to particular Christian traditions.

Since the Second Vatican Council, the emphasis has shifted from a legal to a pastoral approach. The Church is seen as the sacrament of reconciliation, and personal confession is one means by which the ministry of reconciliation is offered. The key document is the *Ordo Poenitentiae* of 1974. The changes it initiated are still in progress. There has been: a questioning of clerical and authoritarian models; a replacement of confessional 'boxes' by reconciliation rooms; a greater stress on corporate self-examination within the liturgy; greater use of the Bible; and the restoring of the laying on of hands, thus linking absolution with the other sacraments of strengthening and healing.

Confession of sin is increasingly linked to spiritual direction (q.v.). While they are not the same, they are rightly seen as parts of a process toward Christian maturity. While some view confession as an emergency measure, to be used only in cases of grave sin, it is now more common to see it as part of the ordinary developing Christian life. St Jerome called absolution 'the return of the Holy Spirit', while Origen called the confessor a *pneumatikos*, a person possessed of the

Spirit. This emphasis on confession as an integral element in spiritual progress is central to the current approach.

Those who hear confessions need to take great care over their lives of prayer and their inner spiritual disciplines. Preparation of body and spirit is of great importance. Gentleness and ability to listen are essential qualities. Confession is not the same as counselling: it is a sacramental act, the purpose of which is forgiveness and reconciliation to the Body of Christ. A penance is usually given as an act of commitment and gratitude. It should be simple and quickly fulfilled: it is not a punishment, nor is it a community service order. The confessional is not the place for lengthy advice or for preaching. Confessors should pray daily for their penitents, for the relationship is intimate and demanding.

The 'seal of the confessional' is absolute: no confessor must reveal anything revealed in confession. However, it is important to recognize the danger of a harmful 'privatization' of sin which prevents the person coming to terms with corners of his or her life. This is most common in the area of sexuality. Michel Foucault has argued that the privatizing of sex began in the confessional. It is important to see the relationship between personal confession and corporate wholeness.

Although children have been prepared for confession, especially in the Roman Communion, there is no evidence that children were absolved for the first 1200 years of the church's life. The new rites are clearly not designed for children, and most modern thinking sees confession as an adult sacrament.

Abeyasingha, N., 'Penance and the Holy Spirit' (*Review for Religious*, 33, 3, 1974), pp. 565–72. Gunstone, J., *The Liturgy of Penance* (Faith Press, 1966). Hepworth, M. and Turner, B.S., *Confession: Studies in Defiance and Religion* (Routledge, 1982). Leech, K., *Soul Friend* (Sheldon, 1977), Appendix. Ross, K.N., *Hearing Confessions* (SPCK, 1974). Thurian, M., *Confession* (SCM, 1958).

KENNETH LEECH

See also: GUILT; RITES AND RITUALS; SIN; TEMPTATION.

CONFIDENTIALITY

The principle which requires that personal information, revealed within a professional relationship or in pastoral care, should not be disclosed to others.

Any exceptions to this rule should be with the consent of the person concerned. Personal information here refers to aspects of a person's private life which are either normally hidden from others, or shared only with trusted friends or relatives.

Confidentiality is based upon the right of everyone to his or her own secrets. Pastoral care often creates relationships of trust which encourage those being cared for to be open about intimate aspects of their lives. The only proper response to this on the part of the helper is strict confidentiality. Sometimes an assurance about this may be required before trust can be established.

What at first seems a simple obligation becomes somewhat more complex on closer examination. The principle of confidentiality is observed differently in different situations, for instance in the medical and social work professions and in the sacrament of penance. It is usually taken for granted that personal information given to a doctor or social worker may be shared with colleagues. Adequate care requires this extension of confidentiality. Information given to a priest in confession (q.v.), however, must never be divulged.

Some situations of pastoral care require an extension of confidentiality similar to that observed in medicine or social work, as when a group or team are involved in care. At other times confidentiality will be absolute to one person only, particularly in counselling. Any person being helped should know what kind of confidentiality is being observed and that personal information is shared only with his or her consent. Those sharing personal information as members of a team must know that they are all bound by the obligation of confidentiality.

An extension of confidentiality may be required when the helper needs the advice of a third person about a difficult problem, or in routine supervision (q.v.) of pastoral care. The real identity of the person being discussed can often be disguised without impairing the usefulness of this exercise.

Difficult decisions about confidentiality may arise with children or adolescents when it seems imperative to involve parents for the well-being of the young person. Very rarely the obligation to keep confidence may have to be superseded when someone's safety is endangered by secrecy.

Biestek, Felix, *The Casework Relationship* (Allen &

Unwin, 1961), p. 81. **Dean, Harry** and **Margaret,** *Counselling in a Troubled Society* (Quartermaine House, 1981), pp. 48–50. **Duncan, A.S.** *et al.* (eds.), *Dictionary of Medical Ethics* (Darton Longman & Todd, 1981).

BERNARD MOBBS

CONFIRMATION
See: MEMBERSHIP OF CHURCH.

CONFLICT
A dynamic opposition of forces – social, interpersonal or intrapersonal. This article deals only with social conflict.

Functional sociology underplays conflict both at the micro-level (social roles and relations) and the macro-level (social and cultural systems) because of its stress on mutually sustaining systems. Dynamic sociology, in which Marx was a pioneer, deals more adequately with it. There can be the peaceful conflict of competition or of economic bargaining; or conflicts within and between institutions which can be resolved not mainly by reason but by a balance of power. There can be more regulated conflicts (as strikes) or less regulated and more disruptive ones involving political revolution or rebellion. In Marxist thought the social relations of production create class conflicts which spill over into every aspect of society. But, Marxism apart, conflicts arise because different groups in society have differing interests, and occasions arise when they conflict deeply and each party stands to lose what is vital to its cause if the other gains its objective. The art of politics is to make power serve justice, approximating to a common good. Serious conflicts arise to the extent it fails.

The Bible pictures human life as a conflict between good and evil. Indeed in both the Old Testament and the New Testament it is set in the context of a heavenly warfare. Jesus is engaged in God's battle against disease, 'demons', death – and hypocrisy – and the cross is the paradoxical herald of victory. His followers need to be armed for the continuing struggle (Eph. 6.10–20) which is to be carried on without hate, and by a church which is not a gathering of the like-minded but of those who may genuinely find themselves on opposite sides of social conflicts. The Church may also find itself in a situation so polarized that no neutrality is possible (e.g. South Africa); and occasionally an issue is so clear

that it would not be desirable. The Eucharist, at the heart of the Church's life, sets present conflicts in the world against the transcendent dimension of heavenly warfare but will not allow any escape from them. On occasion Christians may responsibly judge that they should object on grounds of conscience from direct participation in a conflict in which the authorities want to embroil them; where feasible the church should advocate a space which allows for this, under due safeguards and stipulations.

Bonino, J.M., *Towards a Christian Political Ethics* (SCM, 1983). **Dahrendorf, R.,** *Class and Class Conflict in Industrial Society* (Routledge, 1954). **Davies, J.G.,** *Christians, Politics and Violent Revolution* (SCM, 1976). **Niebuhr, Reinhold,** *Moral Man and Immoral Society* (SCM, 1963). **Preston, R.H.** (ed.), *Perspectives on Strikes* (SCM, 1975).

RONALD PRESTON

See also: AGGRESSION; POLITICAL THEOLOGY AND PASTORAL CARE; VIOLENCE.

CONFRONTATION
A counselling technique in which the counsellor challenges the counsellee's assumptions or self-perception by forcing a consideration of reality.

Clinebell, H.J., *Basic Types of Pastoral Counseling* (Abingdon, 1966), ch. 13 (includes further reading). **Egan, G.,** *The Skilled Helper* (Brooks-Cole, 1975).

CONGREGATION
(1) Any gathering of people or animals. (2) Technical secular usages, e.g. university congregation. (3) In Roman Catholicism formally for: (a) any of the departments of the Papal Curia; (b) certain orders within the church; (c) some groupings of monastic houses within a wider order. (4) In Protestantism, frequently to emphasize the corporate nature of the Christian community in contrast with clericalized and hierarchical usages of 'church': (a) historically (16th century) for the universal Church; (b) the local church or parish; (c) the wider worshipping community in contrast to the church members. (5) In modern popular usage: (a) any gathering for worship; (b) those who habitually attend a particular place of worship; (c) the membership of a local church.

The normal experience of Christian belonging is through a congregation or fellowship group of some kind. Thus the congregation is basic to any understanding of Church.

The NT term *ecclesia* is applied to both the whole Church and to particular fellowships in different places. Thus the local congregation is regarded as part of the universal and, of itself, a microcosm of the complete ecclesial reality. So the marks of the whole – love, peace, unity, reconciliation, etc. – are also the marks of the part. *Ecclesia* refers to a 'summoned gathering', underlining the biblical insistance that Israel and the Church are not voluntary societies but created by God's call into a covenant people.

Historically there have been many forms of ecclesiastical structure that have had different perceptions, styles and ethos of the local worshipping community. Broadly there are two main patterns. Episcopal and presbyterian polities tend to see the local unit as part of the wider organization. Congregational polities understand the congregation as the primary unit which is related to larger associations in ways that vary from the informal through to formal federation. The tension between these two approaches is a constant problem within traditions and ecumenically.

Contemporary Christianity has been marked by a rediscovery of the corporate nature of Christianity as the People of God. This has emphasized the importance of the congregation, for here the Church is normally constituted in worship and discovers itself in the fellowship of acceptance, sharing, service and common action. Faith (q.v.) is expressed and built up in the faithful community (q.v.). Hence the interest in 'base communities', prayer groups, parish communion, family worship, etc. At the same time Christians are having to adapt to a rapidly changing and increasingly secularized society. This has produced widespread, if uneven, changes in congregational patterns and groupings, including deliberate experimentation and ecumenical ventures. Also, within, alongside and sometimes deliberately separate, there has grown up the so-called 'alternative church'. There is thus now a very complex, theologically diverse and often disturbing variety of Christian groups, specialized agencies, worshipping communities and more formal congregations.

Not surprisingly, the congregation has also become a subject of interest in relation to the social sciences. By looking at such issues as the experience and function of worship, religious group dynamics, the place of religion in society and the setting and working out of goals, more and more is being understood of the dynamics of the congregation. The present weakness is in relating adequately the social sciences and theological perspectives.

In relation to pastoral care the congregation is clearly of considerable significance. Internally the structures and quality of its life of fellowship can provide the setting for meeting the needs of the group and individuals, making for maturity and spiritual growth. It is a community resource that can work to meet local needs, support initiatives and enable people to serve. It is also a witness to an understanding of healing and goodness based on the gospel. Many congregations have become centres of pastoral care. All can be places of caring.

Dudley, Carl S., *Making the Small Church Effective* (Abingdon, 1978). **Dulles, Avery,** *Models of the Church* (Gill & Macmillan, 1977). **Lambourne, R.A.,** *Church, Community and Healing* (Darton Longman & Todd, 1963). **Newbigin, Lesslie,** *The Household of God* (SCM, 1953). **Reed, Bruce,** *The Dynamics of Religion* (Darton Longman & Todd, 1978).

PAUL H. BALLARD

See also: CHURCH, DOCTRINES OF; COMMUNITY.

CONGRUENCE
In client-centred therapy (q.v.), the counsellor's integrity in self-presentation.

Rogers, C.R., *On Becoming a Person* (Constable, 1967).

CONSCIENCE: PHILOSOPHICAL ASPECTS
The ability to arrive at a view of what is morally right and wrong.

In the history of Christian tradition, discussions and disagreements about conscience have arisen on two related issues: in what this ability might consist; and what authority conscience enjoys.

Accounts of what conscience is fall broadly into two families. According to one version, conscience is nothing other than our normal powers of reasoning as applied to practical matters, and in particular to moral decisions. It is therefore not a special faculty with unique powers, but rather enjoys the ordinary powers and limitations of human reasoning generally. This position is defended by Aristotle, and by Thomas Aquinas in his account of the function of right reason (*recta ratio*) in the discovery of natural law. Writers in this tradition would generally stress that our reasoning powers in practical matters cannot arrive at the clarity which is at least theoretically possible in matters of logic or even in the physical sciences. Aristotle counsels against seeking greater precision in moral questions than the subject-matter allows, and Aquinas remarks that there is progressively greater difficulty in arriving at correct moral judgements the more detailed and specific these judgements try to be. It would commonly be held, however, that any normal adult would be clearly aware of at least general moral truths.

The alternative account of conscience regards it as a kind of moral sense or sensibility, on the analogy of our physical senses. Conscience according to this account grasps the moral quality of actions, or the truth of moral principles, directly and non-discursively. Joseph Butler gives one of the most authoritative defences of this position. It would be characteristic of this view to stress the clarity and certainty of judgements of conscience, and to align it with an intuitionist rather than a rationalist approach to morality. In principle, both views can be integrated into the Christian tradition, and each is compatible with the view that conscience is in some sense authoritative. There are, however, notable differences in the ways in which this is typically done by each account.

On the first, rationalist, account, reason is seen as one of God's gifts to human kind. The moral truths discovered by our human reasoning can to that extent be regarded as discoveries about the will of God for us. However, it would be acknowledged that our reasoning powers in general are fallible, and that this is true also of our moral reasoning. Our claims to discover moral truths may turn out to be in fact mistaken claims. Nevertheless, in the last analysis a human being can do no more than commit himself or herself to the truth as it is perceived to be. For this reason, Aquinas among others defended the view that we are bound to follow our conscientious judgement, even in cases where (as it turns out) that judgement is mistaken. Conscience is authoritative not because it always judges correctly, but because as rational beings we have no alternative but to do what, in our best judgement, we believe we ought to do.

On the alternative account, it is easier to claim that conscience is somehow infallible

(although it is not essential to this view to make such a claim), and that in a more direct sense it is the 'voice of God' within us. The authority of conscience is thus directly linked with the authority of God, and the duty to follow the dictates of conscience is immediately obvious. Especially those writers who, for theological reasons, believe that human reasoning is unreliable as a result of the Fall will stress that conscience is not a matter of human *reasoning* at all, but derives from the inspiration of the grace of God which makes our moral duty clear to us.

Aquinas, T., *Summa Theologica* I, 79, 12–13. **Baelz, P.**, *Ethics and Belief* (Sheldon, 1977). **Butler, J.**, *Fifteen Sermons*, sermon 1. **Donagan, A.**, *The Theory of Morality* (Univ. of Chicago, 1979).

GERARD J. HUGHES

See also: FREEDOM AND DETERMINISM; GUILT; MORAL ISSUES IN PASTORAL CARE.

CONSCIENCE: PSYCHOLOGICAL ASPECTS

From a psychological point of view, the traditional notion of conscience may be seen as having three aspects:

1. In psychoanalytic theory, one part of the mind, the superego, is formed in early childhood by a process of internalizing the attitudes and responses of the parents. Because the child's emotional world is primitive, and his understanding limited, these attitudes are often internalized in a form so primitive, violent, or distorted that they are not necessarily easy to recognize. Many of the irrational fears that children suffer have their origin in fantasies of guilt and punishment associated with this early superego. If things go well, its severity will be tempered as the child develops by his experience of parents and others who are able to be aware of the world's moral complexity. This awareness then is also internalized, and the primitive judgement can be moderated.

However, things do not always go well, and pastoral workers will be familiar with the phenomena of excessive 'conscience' – the person who must be always working, always earnest, always engaged in meticulous rituals, in ways which are inappropriate and alienating. In such cases, the activity is being used as a defence against the anxiety created by a powerful primitive superego, which is often of course projected outward onto God, authority figures, or the imperious needs of others.

In order to live satisfactorily, the child, and later the adult, has to acquire some separateness from the internal voice of the superego, and to refuse at times to be governed by it. The cost of such refusal is inevitably guilt (q.v.).

2. Psychoanalysis (q.v.) also uses another term, the ego-ideal, to point to a second aspect of what is traditionally called conscience. This rather vague term describes the person's own ideal for himself, derived from loved or admired (rather than judging and threatening) figures and images. It differs from the superego in that to fall short of the ego-ideal is experienced as a failure by the person himself, and not only by internalized others.

The distinction here, between superego and ego-ideal, has some plausibility, but is not easy to sustain in practice, and in psychoanalytic writings it often gets lost in theory as well. Non-technically, its value is that it allows us to see that one aspect of conscience has to do with guilt, another with aspiration.

3. These two aspects account for a great deal of what has traditionally been brought together under the notion of conscience. However, there is also (in Roger Brooke's words) 'a deeper guilt: to fail to respond to the self one has it in one to become'. This calls for a recognition of the most fundamental aspect of conscience, which goes beyond superego morality, and which may be got at by some such phrase as 'ultimate responsibility to oneself'. It is well described by Michael Polanyi in his discussion of commitment, when he says: 'The freedom of the subjective person to do as he pleases is overruled by the freedom of the responsible person to act as he must'. Such an authentic commitment is possible only by someone who is first able to feel internally free from both the constraints of the superego and the blandishments of the ego-ideal. Psychodynamically, it may be understood as deriving from identification with a loving, responsible parent-figure who is attentive to the true development of the child.

In the best religious thinking, it is perhaps one of the functions of God to be internalized as a responsibility-creating figure of this sort, rather than as the kind of rule-enforcing, punishing or rewarding parent who is internalized to form an excessive superego.

In practice, of course, all three of these aspects will be very entangled. It is only in the living struggle of decision-making that

they are likely to be, fleetingly, distinguished. Nevertheless, if they are not distinguished, 'conscience' all too often either becomes a deadening and guilt-producing tyrant, or is set aside as head-in-clouds 'idealism'.

Brooke, R., 'Jung and the Phenomenology of Guilt' (*Journal of Analytical Psychology*, April 1985). **Freud, S.,** *The Ego and the Id*, Standard edn, vol. 19. (Hogarth, 1923). **Klein, M.** and **Riviere, J.,** *Love, Hate and Reparation* (Hogarth, 1937). **Polanyi, M.,** *Personal Knowledge* (Routledge, 1958).

DAVID BLACK

See also: GUILT; HUMAN DEVELOPMENT; NURTURE, CHRISTIAN; PSYCHOANALYSIS; RESPONSIBILITY; SIN; TEMPTATION.

CONSCIOUSNESS

(1) Awareness. The totality of experience and mental processes of a person at a given moment (Sperling, 1957). (2) The perception of what passes in a man's own mind (John Locke). (3) Subjective life (Ornstein 1972).

The nature of human consciousness is far from being fully understood. What is clear, however, is that it cannot be conceived as a passive mirror of external reality, not least because conscious representation of objects and events can occur in the absence of external stimulation (as in dreams and hallucinations, for example) and because consciousness is extremely limited: 'It appears that at any given moment what is selected, filtered and admitted to full consciousness is only a small fraction of all that . . . which acts upon us' (Popper 1977, p. 130). Furthermore, 'All experience is already interpreted by the nervous system a hundredfold – or a thousandfold – before it becomes conscious experience' (Popper, p. 431). This (preconscious) selection and interpretation will be influenced by the individual's past history, his personality, needs, motives and expectations, as well as by aspects of the current environment. Consciousness is thus highly personal.

Evidence from split-brain experiments supports the notion of two major modes of consciousness which seem normally to coexist within each person, the one analytical, linear and rational in functioning, the other holistic, non-rational and intuitive. The analytical mode seems to have evolved primarily for the purpose of ensuring the biological survival of the individual. Creative achievements, however, seem to depend upon the complementary functioning of the two modes.

It has also been found useful to distinguish between different *levels* of consciousness. 'Preconscious' phenomena are capable of becoming conscious; 'unconscious' phenomena remain totally outside awareness. External stimuli which remain outside consciousness can nevertheless be registered by the brain and exert an influence upon behaviour (see Dixon 1981).

Some activities which are initially under conscious, voluntary control become habitual and less conscious (preconscious) with repeated practice. Under these circumstances 'divisions of consciousness' between two or more tasks become possible.

Alterations to the normal state of consciousness occur under a variety of conditions ranging from sleep (q.v.), through meditation (q.v.) and hypnosis (q.v.), to psychoactive drugs, trauma, brain injury and certain forms of psychopathological disturbance.

Dixon, N.F., *Preconscious Processing* (Wiley, 1981). Hilgard, E.R., Atkinson, R.L. and Atkinson, R.C., *Introduction to Psychology* (Harcourt Brace Jovanovich, New York, 7th edn 1979), ch. 6. Ornstein, R.E., *The Psychology of Consciousness* (Penguin, 1975); *The Nature of Human Consciousness* (W.H. Freeman, San Francisco, 1972). Popper, K.R. and Eccles, J.C., *The Self and Its Brain* (Springer International, 1977). Sperling, A., *Psychology Made Simple* (W.H. Allen, 1957).

S. HENLEY

See also: UNCONSCIOUS PATIENTS.

CONSENT TO TREATMENT

1. *Ethics:* It is a generally accepted principle that a doctor must respect the autonomy, the right to self-determination, of a patient. From this may be derived the more specific principle of the need for consent. Much that applies to medical practice can be extended to other forms of professional care, but the legal aspects are less well defined.

A patient's self-determination is safeguarded if a doctor (1) may not treat without consent, and (2) must respect a refusal of consent.

It is the obligation of the doctor to obtain consent. For consent (or refusal) to be real, and thereby valid, the doctor must ensure that it is (1) voluntarily given, (2) informed, and (3) the patient must be competent to give consent.

(1) *Voluntary* connotes the absence not merely of obvious force or duress but also of more subtle factors. These can be, for example, peer or family pressure, or can arise from the context the patient is in, as when a nurse asks a patient to take some medication because otherwise the nurse will be reprimanded.

(2) *Informed* connotes acceptance that an agreement (or refusal) made in ignorance of material facts cannot be relied upon. Disagreement exists as to the extent of the doctor's duty to inform. Some appear to accept the principle but claim that the problem of the proper quantum of information is insuperable, as the patient cannot be told all that the doctor knows. But a distinction exists between total and adequate information. Sound medical ethics would hold that the doctor must impart that information which will allow the patient's destiny to be charted by the patient. This contemplates a sensitive and thoughtful dialogue. Some suggest that the doctor must ensure that the patient understands what is said. This, perhaps, overstates the duty. The doctor need only do that which is reasonable in the circumstances. The duty to inform is also an aspect of the principle of truth-telling, which is another principle derived from respect for autonomy. The doctor must inform the patient of the circumstances of any condition before consent is valid. Some resist this proposition, arguing that truth-telling may sometimes harm the patient. Sound medical ethics would allow an exception to the doctor's duty to inform, only if the patient waives the duty, or there is clear evidence that the patient's physical or mental health will be harmed by the information in question.

(3) The patient must be *competent* to act autonomously. Disagreement surrounds the proper test for competence. Some suggest that, if below a certain age (e.g. 16) or mentally ill, then the patient is *ipso facto* incompetent. This 'status' approach to competence is flawed because it fails to examine and thereby respect the particular circumstances of the patient who may, for example, be 15 but may still be able to make reasoned decisions. Sound medical ethics defines competence as the ability to comprehend the nature and consequences of the proposed procedure. On such a test, a patient who is, for example, mentally ill may still be competent, if lucid and able to understand the treatment proposed. If the patient is

incompetent, the doctor must obtain consent from another. The person consenting, the proxy, must be someone who can be presumed to safeguard the patient's interests. Proxy consent, therefore, is justified as enhancing the patient's autonomy by forbidding the doctor from relying on any ill-considered decision made by an incompetent patient. Differences exist as to what a proxy may properly consent to. The competing criteria are: (a) what is in the best interests of the patient; (b) what is in the interests of the patient; and (c) what is not against the interests of the patient. The first criterion could well make some forms of non-therapeutic research (e.g. on children) impermissible. Some, therefore, prefer the third criterion, although this is not free from difficulties, e.g. in the case of compulsory treatment of a mentally ill patient.

2. *Law.* To a great extent the law reflects what has been suggested as sound medical ethics. The doctor is, in general, obliged to obtain the consent and respect the refusal of a patient. Failure to do so may expose the doctor to both civil and criminal liability. Some differences do, however, exist between the law and ethics.

(1) The law governing the quantum of information necessary for valid consent is in transition. It is still the law that the doctor need only inform the patient to the extent thought reasonable by responsible members of the medical profession. It is thought that this is insufficiently responsive to the claims of the patient and will, in time, be replaced by a legal requirement that the doctor must pass on that information which a reasonable patient in the particular patient's circumstances would wish to know.

(2) The law recognizes what is called the 'therapeutic privilege', whereby the doctor is absolved of the duty to inform if, in all the circumstances, it would not be in the interests of the patient's health to do so. Clearly, unless this legal exception is carefully circumscribed, it is capable of swallowing the principle.

(3) In law, someone may act as a proxy only if invested with this authority by law, i.e. a parent, guardian, Local Authority, or other, but not a relative unless so authorized. There is still some doubt as to what the proxy may in law consent to. One of the most troubling examples is where a proxy purports to refuse

further care on behalf of an incompetent patient, for instance, a severely handicapped new-born baby. The law, along with ethics, is still wrestling with the proper limits to the proxy's power. One further example of current legal uncertainty concerns the extent to which a proxy may legally expose a patient (e.g. an incompetent child) to research by purporting to consent on its behalf. It is thought that the test of whether a proposed intervention is not against the interests of the incompetent patient is the test gradually being adopted by the law.

Consent to Medical Care, Law Reform Commission of Canada (1980). *Making Health Care Decisions*, President's Commission for the Study of Ethical Problems in Medicine (US Govt Printing Office, 1982). *Sidaway* v. *Governors of the Bethlem Royal Hospital and the Maudsley Hospital and Others* [1984] 1 All E.R. 1018. **Kennedy, I.,** 'The Patient on the Clapham Omnibus' (*Modern Law Review*, 47, 517, 1984). **Veatch, R.,** *A Theory of Medical Ethics* (Basic Books, 1981).

IAN KENNEDY

See also: ETHICS, PROFESSIONAL.

CONSOLATION
(1) The process of being comforted. (2) The state of being comforted. (3) The pleasure and relief felt when distress is alleviated and comfort given.

The presence of God is the essential element in religious consolation and comfort. In both Old Testament and New Testament, 'comfort', of which 'consolation' is the more tender aspect, has its source in the compassionate love of God for his people, for the individual. In the New Testament, 'comfort' usually represents a Greek verb and noun, frequent in Paul's writing, which includes the element of strengthening or invigorating (Acts 9.31, 16.40; Rom. 1.12, 15.4; 2 Cor. 13.11, etc.). The element of tenderness is expressed in Matthew 5.4, 2 Corinthians 1.3ff., etc. For the Greek noun, the Authorized Version has 'consolation' fourteen times, interchanging 'comfort' and 'consolation' in 2 Corinthians 1.3–7. The New International Version of the Bible (in Acts 9.31; 16.40; Rom. 1.12; 15.4) uses the word 'encourage' or 'encouragement' underlining the 'invigorating' aspect. 'Comfort' is used in that version where the 'tender' element is present (Matt. 5.4; 2 Cor. 1.3ff.).

Consolation is expressed in the presence of

Christ as Messiah (Luke 2.24 – 'the consola- tion of Israel'). The Holy Spirit is his consoling presence (the Comforter). Christians are called to console each other (Rom. 1.12). There is consolation for the persecuted who are faithful despite tribulation (see John 16.33; Rom. 5.2–5). Suffering in Christ's name is sharing in his sufferings and brings consolation (2 Cor 1.3–5).

The Book of Common Prayer maintains the theme of consolation in the prayer after absolution ('Hear what comfortable words our Saviour Jesus Christ saith . . .').

In the Church's literature on spirituality, consolation is set against desolation, which represents the absence of God and the dis- quiet that follows from that. Israel's consola- tion (Luke 2.25) is the coming of the Messiah. Her rejection of him led to desolation (Luke 21.20). As well as being mediated by the presence of God himself, consolation comes through things associated with him – the Word and its promises, his servants and prayer.

Egar, H., *The Spiritual Exercises and the Ignatian Mystical Horizon* (Institute of Jesuit Sources, St Louis, Mo., 1976). **von Hügel, F.**, *The Mystical Element of Religion* (Dent, 1908). **Poulain, A.**, *The Graces of Interior Prayer*, tr. L.L. Yorke Smith, ed. J.V. Bainvel (Routledge, 1950). **Tanquerey, A.**, *The Spiritual Life*, W.H. Branderis (Society of St John the Evangelist, Desclee & Co, Tournai, 1930).

DENIS DUNCAN

See also: SPIRITUAL DIRECTION;
REASSURANCE; SUSTAINING.

CONSULTATION

The use of a person from outside an organiza- tion or a relationship to act as a consultant to enable the organization, group or individual to explore their situation from different perspectives and to support them in dealing with it. It may bear many of the characteristics of counselling (q.v.) particularly in so far as it may emphasize exploration and support and the enhancement of autonomy rather than the giving of advice and the offering of solutions.

See also: SUPERVISION, PASTORAL.

CONTRACEPTION

See: FAMILY PLANNING.

CONTRACT AND COVENANT

Two closely-related forms of voluntary, bind- ing relationship, which differ in the nature of

the promises made and the consequences entailed.

1. *Contractual bargain and covenantal commit- ment*. Individuals or collective bodies, such as companies, institutions or nations, will- ingly enter relationships of mutual obligation by two alternative modes of agreement. Moral seriousness, and often solemnity of manner, surround both forms of undertaking, since in either case the uncoerced act of speaking or signing the promise itself effects the accord and binds the parties to its requirements. But what becomes of promissory relationships when one party breaks its promises? A 'contract' is an equal, bi-lateral association, such as a treaty, pact or commercial bargain, where each side's responsibilities are con- ditional upon the other's faithfulness. When one party dishonours the agreement, the relationship, being essentially two-sided, is in effect already ended; and the innocent party, freed from further obligations, may become an adversary rather than a partner, invoking legal sanctions against the guilty.

In contrast (although the terms themselves are interchangeable in some usages), a 'covenant' is an unconditional commitment, which establishes personal relations capable of surviving their own imperfect fulfilment by one or both sides, through forgiveness, acceptance and renewal. The theological basis for such commitment, not terminable through lack of reciprocity, is the covenantal grace of God, who binds himself in the Old Testament to humanity, and especially to an undeserv- ing 'chosen people', promising and proving to be faithful unilaterally, despite the alienating infidelities of his partners. The New Test- ament affirms that God has overcome this alienation, reconciling sinful humanity to himself through Christ, and thus restoring and fulfilling the covenant which on his side was never abrogated.

This provides a divine norm for relation- ships of loving commitment between human beings at many levels. Especially, the concept of indissoluble marriage (*see* MARRIAGE, THEOLOGY OF), is grounded in analogies with God's covenant. Hosea's patience with an adulterous wife acts out God's faithfulness to faithless Israel. Conversely, the New Testament models the inseparable unity of husband and wife on that between Christ and his Church (Eph. 5.21–33); and the con- temporary churches, though ready, in different degrees, to recognize the reality of marriage breakdown, and the offer of divine forgiveness for human failure, also see forgiveness and reconciliation within marriage as essential to a relationship which is more than a legal contract and reflects God's covenant, as loving partners accept each other without conditions – that is, 'for better or for worse'.

2. *Conditional and unconditional acceptance.* Unfortunately, the Church has not always affirmed such unconditional acceptance in its own theology and practice. Assurance of God's love has often been withheld from those failing to satisfy conventional criteria of moral rectitude or to exhibit prescribed proofs of penitence for failure. The Reformation saw itself as recovering the good news of free acceptance 'by grace alone', from the legalism and scrupulosity of the medieval penitential system. However, subsequent Reformed theology itself sometimes qualified the grace of God. Calvinist 'federal theology' in the 17th and 18th centuries took 'covenant' (Latin: *foedus*) as its central motif but, ironically, tended to affirm a legalistic love which made repentance and faith the contractual preconditions of forgiveness, rather than its natural consequences. Critics of this interpretation, then and now, have focused upon its psychological effects: obsession with guilt-feelings, as the prerequisite for pardon; correspondingly defensive self-righteousness; insecurity about the reality of forgiveness; and fear of its forfeiture through new failure. Reverting to a more biblical understanding, contemporary pastoral theology has often interpreted the psychotherapist's non-judgemental acceptance of the patient as analogous to, even an instance of, God's unconditional love.

3. *Cheap and costly grace.* Love is as intolerant of licence as of legalism; and free grace is not cheap, but makes heavy demands for appropriate response. God's election of Israel was confirmed in the giving of the Law; and Jesus insisted that the forgiven sinner 'go and sin no more'. Likewise, Christian ethics describes love's inescapable call to 'costly discipleship'; and the counsellor who accepts a client unreservedly is not encouraging personal inadequacy, but aiming at greater maturity and more responsible living.

Bonhoeffer, D., *The Cost of Discipleship* (SCM, 1959). **Oden,** T.C., *Kerygma and Counseling* (Westminster Press, Philadelphia, 1966). **Torrance, J.B.,** 'Covenant or Contract?' (*Scottish Journal of Theology*, vol. 23 1970), pp. 51–76.

ALAN E. LEWIS

See also: STRUCTURE.

CONVERSION
Change of religious allegiance, usually from none whatsoever to active discipleship.

Whereas the theological emphasis is on the objective change in a person, much of the pastoral interest centres on the attendant subjective psychological experience and its implications.

The term is used in a variety of ways, and the significance of conversion is not the same for all religious groups; e.g. some will speak of 'life-long conversion' while a more evangelical tradition will lay more stress on a moment of decisive change. Scobie (1975) has identified three ways by which people become religious:

(1) *Sudden conversion.* Studies suggest that 30% of religious people undergo this experience. While some Protestant groups look for such an experience as an essential qualification for membership, others distrust its alleged association with strong social pressure, powerful persuasion and emotional arousal.

(2) *Gradual conversion,* in which a change of belief extends over a period of time and during which objections can be resolved and commitment accepted. Such a process may result in a personal crisis similar to sudden conversion, but such an experience is secondary to the part played by the gradual process.

(3) The third type, sometimes labelled *unconscious conversion,* is the well-established route of the individual exposed in his upbringing to religious faith and who accepts this faith with no personal crisis. For example, children attending Sunday School have been found less likely to experience sudden conversion. This type is comparable to William James's 'once-born' type of consciousness which develops 'with no element of morbid compunction or crisis'.

However it is categorized, conversion remains a profound and extremely complex process. Particular attention has been paid to identifying the mechanisms of the sudden conversion experience. Sargant's famous study alleged that the most effective techniques first created states of emotional exhaustion in the hearers and that, when in this condition, people are extremely susceptible. Against this, reports of wild emotional scenes are rarely encountered today outside fringe religious groups. Argyle (1958) has suggested that the skill and prestige of the speaker, the size of the meeting together with the use of emotional music all contribute to the success of mass evangelism. It is evident that psychological stresses skilfully applied can indeed produce dramatic changes in behaviour, and pastoral integrity demands that religious persuasion should avoid 'conditioning' techniques. The authentic communication of religious faith is not an attempt to abuse another's personality but to share profound conviction, reaching the will through the conscious mind.

Criticism has been levelled at the alleged spurious nature of much crisis conversion experience. In general it appears that religious conversion is more likely to be permanent if it is gradual. Studies however have shown that about 50% of those professing sudden conversion in recent large evangelistic meetings have been active church members twelve months later. This compares favourably with revivalist events of an earlier generation. Recently, mainstream Christian groups that encourage a conversion experience have laid even greater emphasis upon the support a convert receives and preparatory training for local churches on integrating new believers.

A conversion experience is frequently associated with adolescence (in evangelist Billy Graham's 1954-55 crusades in Britain, it is estimated that 60% of inquirers were under nineteen years of age). The alleged link between conversion and puberty has convinced some of the sexual nature of religion; conversion is thus explained in terms of the sublimation of recently awakened but suppressed sexual instinct. The evidence is by no means conclusive, since many have reported conversion experiences before the onset of puberty, and a substantial number of religious believers claim a conversion crisis in adult life. It is pastorally unsurprising that profound religious feeling should be associated with the adolescent concern about identity and experimenting with relationships (see ADOLESCENCE).

Personality variables in religious experience present a further area of interest. Argyle (1958) has suggested that people suddenly converted at public meetings are more easily

hypnotized and can be classified to some extent as hysterics. Sargant (1957) concluded that the healthy extrovert was most likely to undergo sudden conversion. Such a focus on the psychological aspects does not ignore or deny that in a genuine religious conversion there is objective change associated with new perceptions rather than a mere stirring of the emotions. But, from a pastoral point of view, the task of responding appropriately to an individual's stated experience may be greatly assisted by the recognition of age and personality factors.

Argyle, M., *Religious Behaviour* (Routledge, 1958). **Brown, J.A.C.,** *Techniques of Persuasion* (Penguin, 1963), pp. 223-43. **James, W.,** *Varieties of Religious Experience* (Longmans, 1902). **Lloyd-Jones, D.M.,** *Conversions: Psychological and Spiritual* (Inter-Varsity Press, 1959). **Sargant, W.,** *Battle for the Mind* (Heinemann, 1957). **Scobie, G.E.W.,** *Psychology of Religion* (Batsford, 1975), pp. 47-57.

JOHN WESSON

See also: EVANGELISM AND PASTORAL CARE; FAITH; PSYCHOLOGY OF RELIGION.

CORPORATENESS
See: COMMUNITY.

COUNSELLING
1. Traditionally and generally used of giving counsel or advice, as in spiritual direction (q.v.) and/or confession (q.v.), and in secular contexts such as career/vocational counselling, or other domestic and personal services (e.g. financial counselling). Although weighted on the side of advice and information-giving, such counselling sometimes uses the skills of counselling as defined below, not always having to be directive, and allowing the client to express emotional components even if the problem is a practical one.

2. More specifically, and increasingly widely used in the pastoral context, the term refers to a style of helping which emphasizes the client discovering his or her own solution to personal difficulties, without active direction or advice from the counsellor. The counsellor aims to listen carefully; and respond sensitively, so that the client is enabled to express emotional and other dimensions to the presenting problem and is encouraged to accept a potentiality for understanding self and for autonomy in making decisions ('the client knows best'). The expertise of counselling lies in facilitating such a process,

rather than in providing direct answers or information. Counselling is of greatest value with clients who are willing to accept such responsibility (when presented with the opportunity), who can express themselves verbally, who have some capacity for self-understanding, and where the difficulties presented are concerned mainly with relationships with others, or inner conflicts. Counselling as such, as opposed to longer-term psychotherapy, is especially appropriate for acute crisis situations, but not normally for chronic personality problems. It should also be distinguished from befriending (q.v.).

There are few full-time counsellors outside educational establishments (school and student counsellors). Most counselling takes place in voluntary agencies, such as the Marriage Guidance Council, Catholic Marriage Advisory Council, youth counselling services and pastoral counselling centres (often affiliated to the Westminster Pastoral Foundation). It is also an aspect of some professional activity – general practice, social work, the Church (see PASTORAL COUNSELLING), etc. Specialist counselling may also be available in particular situations (see ABORTION, RAPE COUNSELLING and SEXUAL COUNSELLING). Most clients are seen individually, although counselling can also be used with couples, families and groups – and some counselling schools indeed use groups by preference (see TRANSACTIONAL ANALYSIS, GESTALT THERAPY, ENCOUNTER GROUPS).

Although there are many schools of counselling (often having their origin in the United States), nearly all share similar basic techniques for listening to the client. The client who comes for counselling is normally offered a series of weekly sessions, in privacy and confidence, of about 45 minutes each. The client is encouraged to talk, not only about the 'problem', but about any aspect of the problem and of self. The counsellor's activity is minimal compared with ordinary conversations or interviews. He or she is concerned about the person, and not the problem alone, and encourages all thoughts and feelings to be expressed, especially those which are often withheld in social conversations. The counsellor adopts a warm and accepting stance, whatever is said, holding back any personal feelings of surprise, shock or criticism, preferring to comprehend the client rather than pass judgement. Many responses will be reflective, paraphrasing, summarizing and reformulating what the client has expressed, verbally and non-verbally, checking understanding of what the client meant to convey. The counsellor's capacity for empathy (q.v.) is crucial, as he or she tries to identify with the client's experience and to demonstrate this understanding by putting it into words. Where the client asks questions or seeks advice, the counsellor usually puts the initiative back to the client, encouraging the seeking of his or her own solutions, aware that any solution is rarely clear-cut, and that the different dimensions of any difficulty often need to be expressed (and understood) before painful feelings alleviate, or before decisions can be made. The skills involved in this type of listening and responding are also applicable to less formal counselling situations, and can be of considerable value in pastoral care (q.v.).

Where the major counselling schools differ is in the emphasis they give to what the client presents: some stress catharsis of emotion (q.v.), others the cognitive process, and even rationality and will-power. Some methods require a more active and confronting counsellor than others, even a person who directs the client in exercises which elicit more feelings, or alternative ways of looking at difficulties. Some are concerned only with what the client is experiencing in the here-and-now, while others seek the re-experience of past traumatic events, even as far as a type of rebirth (see GESTALT THERAPY; BIRTH TRAUMA).

In Britain the majority of counsellors are most influenced either by the work of European analytic schools (see ANALYTICAL PSYCHOLOGY, PSYCHOANALYSIS), or by the work of Carl Rogers (see CLIENT-CENTRED THERAPY), although insights from other theories are sometimes incorporated. The term 'eclectic' describes a counsellor who draws upon two or more models of counselling. Although too neat a distinction would be misleading, Rogers provides much useful insight into ways of listening and responding to the client (the process), while the analytic schools provide clearer models for understanding the content and some of the complications which may arise in the counsellor–client relationship.

Counsellors who are trained in Rogerian technique stress the actual relationship between themselves and their clients, and believe that their own positive regard (non-possessive love) for the client will help the client recover or gain regard and positive attitudes towards self. Expression of feelings is encouraged. The past is not relevant unless the client chooses to make it so, and there is little regard for the power of the unconscious (q.v.). The idea of making a psychological hypothesis, or attempting to formulate what has gone wrong within a frame of reference is generally frowned upon, at least in theory. Such counselling can be particularly effective where the disturbance of the personality is not profound.

Counsellors who are trained in analytic techniques, by contrast, are as interested in negative distortions of the counsellor-client relationship as indications of transference (q.v.) as in the positive relationship between them. They recognise the value of dependency (q.v.) as a stage towards autonomy, and give more credence to the influence of the unconscious and to fantasy (q.v.) as well as feelings. More prominence is given to the termination of counselling (q.v.) and its parallels with previous losses in the client's life. Such counsellors normally follow a model of human development (q.v.) which is more detailed than the Rogerian, and which assigns more significance to past damaging negative experiences. Such counselling is more applicable to clients who make connections between past and present experience.

The latter model of counselling comes close to psychotherapy (q.v.), and in the United States these two terms are often used synonymously. In Britain a greater distinction is made between them, albeit an unclear one, especially when counselling is engaged upon for longer periods, when it gravitates towards brief psychotherapy. Despite its avowed concern for the person rather than the problem, counselling is normally used in crisis situations, allowing the client to reflect upon immediate feelings and conflicts and to 'resolve' the problem, over a short number of sessions. In some instances counsellors need to refer clients for more specialized help, since their own training is limited, especially for dealing with very disturbed clients, and/or when personal problems are not amenable to talking alone.

Egan, G., *The Skilled Helper* (Brooks Cole, Monterey, 1975). Jacobs, M., *Still Small Voice* (SPCK, 1982); *Swift to Hear* (SPCK, 1985). Kennedy, E., *On Becoming a Counsellor* (Gill and Macmillan, Dublin, 1977). Mucchielli, R., *Face to Face in the Counselling Interview* (Macmillan, 1983). Rogers, C.R., *On Becoming a Person*

(Constable, 1981). Truax, C.B. and Carkhuff, R.R., *Toward Effective Counselling and Psychotherapy: Training and Practice* (Aldine, Chicago, 1967).

MICHAEL JACOBS

See also: BEFRIENDING; CRISIS THEORY AND INTERVENTION; PASTORAL CARE; PASTORAL COUNSELLING; PSYCHOANALYSIS; PSYCHOTHERAPY; TERMINATION OF COUNSELLING.

COUNSELLING: SPECIFIC FORMS
See: ABORTION COUNSELLING; GENETIC COUNSELLING; GROUP PSYCHOTHERAPY AND COUNSELLING; MARRIAGE AND FAMILY: CARE AND COUNSELLING; PREMARITAL COUNSELLING; RAPE COUNSELLING; SEXUAL COUNSELLING.

COUNTERTRANSFERENCE
See: TRANSFERENCE.

COVENANT
See: CONTRACT AND COVENANT.

CREATION
A doctrine which, in the Judaeo-Christian tradition, asserts that everything that is owes its existence to God.

The doctrine is based on the biblical data (e.g. in Genesis, Job, Psalms, Isaiah, John, 1 Corinthians, Galatians, Colossians, Revelation), and in the Christian tradition is to be linked with the doctrine of redemption, such that God's purpose in creation is none other than that disclosed in Jesus Christ. Except by the 'Creationists' who insist on a literal interpretation of Genesis, creation is now generally understood not as a biblical rival to scientific cosmogenies but as a statement of God's relation to humanity and the non-human world of nature; not, that is, as an account of 'how-it-all-began' but rather as an account of 'how-things-are'.

Distinctive features of the Christian doctrine include:

(1) *Creatio ex nihilo* (creation out of nothing). This distinguishes it from any idea that God is part of the world or identical with it (pantheism), and from any idea that there is or was some pre-existing matter out of which God was or is forced to create (dualism). It stresses the dependence of all creatures on God, and distinguishes God's creativity from that of humans, who, in order to create anything, need pre-existing materials.

(2) *Creatio continua* (continuous creation). What God originates, he sustains and directs

towards fulfilment. Not only is each new life, each new existence an act of God's continuing creativity, but life itself is dependent on God's creating activity at every moment. It is from this perspective that the doctrine of providence (q.v.) is generally treated (e.g. Calvin, Barth, Tillich).

(3) *The goodness of creation* (Gen. 1.31). Because the world is God's world, it has a fundamental order and reliability.

(4) *New creation*. This essentially NT emphasis draws attention to the new horizons and opportunities opened up for all creatures by the coming of Christ and the reconciliation God has accomplished in him.

In the second half of the twentieth century, theological attention has focused on 'creation', in two respects in particular. First, the concept of evolution which, in its earlier days, seemed to be a major threat to the intellectual acceptability of the traditional doctrine of creation is now seen as underpinning the understanding of creation, not as a 'once-for-all' event but as a continuing activity of God. 'Process' thinkers especially have drawn on insights from the metaphysics of A.N. Whitehead and his category of 'creativity'. God and the cosmos (and everything in it) are participants in the 'process of creation' wherein God, without denying their essential freedom, 'lures' all entities to fulfilment. They find it impossible to think of God other than as Creator, or of any living or change apart from the exercise of creativity. Second, while traditional teaching on creation has not been over concerned with the non-human world of nature, simply acknowledging that it owed its existence to God and seeing it as the setting or stage of the human drama ('the theatre of the glory of God' – Calvin), evolutionary ideas and ecological problems are alike forcing a change in theological interest. Because humankind is now appreciated as being part of the natural world, and because so much of the natural world seems to be threatened by human activity, if God is believed to be present in history, he must be acknowledged to be present in and related to nature as well. This raises the question of the destiny of the natural world (is it really of no consequence to God?) and, in turn, compels urgent concentration on human responsibility before God for its nurture and development (cf. Gen. 1.26; Job; Rev. 21.1).

In addition to its relevance to ecological problems, the doctrine of creation can be of key pastoral importance. Belief in God as creator can provide: stability; confidence in the reliability of the structures God has given and in the intelligibility of the universe; assurance of God's present activity in the tiniest atom as in the remotest galaxy; and, for human beings, the discovery that in every moment, however desperate, there is a creative possibility, a 'divine factor' (Tillich) which keeps the way to fulfilment open.

Barbour, I.G., *Issues in Science and Religion* (SCM, 1966), pp. 365–464. **Barth, K.**, *Church Dogmatics*, *III.i* (Oliver & Boyd, 1958). **Birch, L.C.**, *Nature and God* (SCM, 1965). **Gilkey, L.**, *Maker of Heaven and Earth* (Doubleday, 1959). **Hendry, G.**, *Theology of Nature* (Westminster, 1980) **Peacocke, A.R.**, *Creation and the World of Science* (Oxford, 1979). **Tillich, P.**, *Systematic Theology I* (combined vol., J. Nisbet, 1969), pp. 280–321.

D.W.D. SHAW

See also: GOD, DOCTRINE OF; PROVIDENCE.

CRIME

Crime (Greek: *krinein* = to judge or sift) describes society's assessment of culpable failure of relationship between citizen and State.

The judgement that crime has been committed is based on incidents – usually actions, but possibly words, omission, possessions or status. It is a complex and often confused response, consisting of three stages: description, explanation, proposed solutions.

(1) *Descriptions* usually include an agent causing, with guilty intent, specific harm within a jurisdiction enforcing sanctions. Descriptions can be affected by facts, witnesses' sympathies, moral climate, legal frameworks, feasible sanctions, mitigating factors, and types of offender.

(2) *Explanations* are only theoretical inferences. They are usually biassed towards determinism rather than free-will (q.v.). Biological theories emphasize instinctual drives; political theories emphasize state exploitation; psychological theories emphasize early learning; sociological theories emphasize group relationships rather than personal actions; economic theories emphasize rational intent. Choice, or integration, of such theories affects what is highlighted or overlooked, and collectively the theories contain complementary images.

(3) *Solutions* are often influenced by uncon-

scious or barely acknowledged emotional factors. Fear is most acute in responses to crimes of personal violence, but it underlies the variability in responses to crimes between, for instance, the dubious dealings of multinational corporations and more trivial but often more harshly judged social nuisances. This variability is perhaps capable of psychoanalytic explanation, but it is also affected by culture, contemporary values, media influence, political stability, and police attitudes.

In containing fear and preventing revenge, the State is the established arbitrator. The severest solution to crime in Western democracies is imprisonment. Its value may lie in the deterrent effect of degradation rituals associated with courts or custody, or in wider retributory needs within society, or in the distant hope that segregation may lead the convicted to reassessment through fair treatment and new opportunities. Noncustodial solutions comprise the largest proportion of court disposals and include suspended sentences, probation, community service and fines.

Crime prevention is an attempt at a broader solution. It involves increasing the level of the general perception of crime and can also be approached through individual help with problems which lead to crime (e.g. alcoholism) and through social welfare agencies. Combining Western liberties with urban independence limits more drastic prevention measures.

Victim studies are changing contemporary responses to crime. Sometimes victims invite crime (shoplifting) and sometimes they are well known to the offender (murder). Many victims do not report crimes. Legislation now offers compensation to victims of violent crime, so slightly redressing traditional focus on prosecution. Befriending (q.v.) agencies offer victim support. Prospects for victim/ offender reconciliation are also being discussed and experimented with in some countries.

Criminology, the theoretical study of crime, has evolved through many stages from the Lombrosian theory of 'the born criminal' to the modern concept of multi-factor causation. In the 1960s research narrowly emphasized social cures for crimes. Emphasis is now placed on incentives, making crime less profitable and legitimate endeavour more lucrative. Annual Comprehensive Criminal

Statistics for England and Wales indicate trends. Crime often relates to deteriorating urban areas, proximity of industry, unemployment, non-ownership of homes and poor community facilities. It is overwhelmingly committed by men. Women are criminals in isolation; men are orientated to groups. Serious offenders are usually under 25. Many criminals are related to each other and their family instability is common.

The definition of crime depends in the last analysis on relationships between moral and legal codes. *Morally*, crime is an action intuitively designated as evil. *Legally*, it is an action prescribed by law with the clarity and precision vital for justice. The rough congruence between the natural or moral concept of crime and the contents of criminal law is important. First, law must adjust to moral opinion in order to invest criminal acts with obloquy. The tendency to use the criminal law for regulatory offences, like traffic laws, deprives it of its moral quality, because the offences do not excite deep condemnation. Secondly, despite the precision of law, difficult cases still have to be decided in close association with their moral basis. Fair punishment must be both legal and moral.

Harding, J., *Victims and Offenders* (Bedford Square Press, 1981). Kadish, S.H. (ed.), *Encyclopedia of Crime and Justice*, 4 vols. (Free Press, 1983). Prinz, H., *Offenders, Deviants, Patients* (Tavistock, 1980). Radzinowicz, L. and King, J., *The Growth of Crime* (Hamish Hamilton, 1977). Wright, M., *Making Good* (Burnet, 1981).

ALAN R. DUCE

See also: POLICE CHAPLAINCY; PRISON CHAPLAINCY.

CRISIS THEORY AND INTERVENTION

1. *Crisis theory*. Crisis in a psychosocial sense, was a term first used by Caplan (1961) and stems from earlier work by Caplan and Lindemann on the psychological consequences of bereavement (q.v.) and grief. Caplan defines crisis as 'an upset in the emotional steady state of an individual or social unit caused by events which overwhelm pre-existing mechanisms for maintaining psychological equilibrium'. Such events tend to be sudden and unexpected and present new problems which cannot be solved without the development of new coping skills. Crisis exists when an acute

problem or set of problems confronting an individual or family unit contain, at the same time, both the opportunity for growth, healthy resolution and the development of new skills for coping with difficulties, and the danger of ill health, chronically impaired capacity for dealing with stress and relationships with others.

The period of crisis is divided into three phases; an initial rise in tension as the individual realizes that he or she is failing to solve the difficulty; a second stage of increasing anxiety and failure to cope, for example inability to work, breakdown of family relationships, and a search for solutions both within the self and from others, and a third stage where a solution is found which eases the anxiety. The third stage may solve the problem, for example a family working together to support an adolescent daughter in difficulties; or be a maladaptive solution, for example the adolescent daughter taking an overdose of tablets as a way of making her family take her seriously.

One of the important features of crisis theory is its emphasis on phase 2; the period of time when people acknowledge the severity of their difficulties and look to others for help. At this point, individuals are most suggestible and open to change and so may have the motivation to try new ways of behaving and to take difficult decisions which they normally cannot face. Crisis theory, therefore, indicates a point of maximum potential for change and the point at which intervention is most likely to be successful. Any crisis intervention must be geared for a quick response at the time that help is requested; delay in appointments and so on may mean that the crisis becomes resolved before help is offered. The entire period of crisis is short-lived, and continues for a matter of weeks only.

Crises are classified as situational, emotional, or developmental. Situational crises are those life events which involve readjustment, for example moving house, loss of job, illness or injury. Emotional crises involve psychological mechanisms such as confidence, competence and dependency. Examples of emotional crisis follow break down of marriage, bereavement, and other forms of loss, and involve the inter-play of external events and personality traits to a greater extent than situational crisis. Development crises are those transitions from one stage of the life cycle to another, such as adolescence (q.v.), marriage (q.v.), parenthood (q.v.), and retirement (q.v.). Such transitions require adjustment both in social and psychological spheres, and some individuals may be ill prepared for the change, for example, a marriage may develop serious difficulties on the arrival of the first child.

2. *Crisis intervention.* There is no specific treatment or specific type of person involved in crisis intervention. Everyone in a social network is called upon from time to time as friends or families to help others through crisis, and those in the helping professions – for example, clergy, doctors, social workers – frequently act in this capacity. Specific crisis intervention services, however, are increasingly becoming established in the UK, although they have been common in the USA for many years. Services range from those staffed by volunteers through to those established as part of psychiatric services and manned by professional specialists. They may offer help in many ways; from relatively remote and anonymous telephone counselling through individual therapy in drop-in centres, to team work with families in their homes. All are characterized by the ability to respond quickly to request for help.

Crisis therapy tends to be more active and confrontative than traditional dynamic psychotherapy (q.v.), and the emphasis is placed on current problems and available options for their solution. Past developmental difficulties are explored only where their understanding is essential to the current problem.

Crisis intervention is a useful development in mental health work, but its use requires careful evaluation. Studies on the effects of volunteer services have shown equivocal results; those on professional services tend to show that it is a more efficient way of delivering health services than traditional institutionally based psychiatric care, but have yet to show that outcome in terms of individual functioning is improved.

Aguilera, D.C. and Messick, J.M., *Crisis Intervention: Theory and Methodology* (Mosby, St Louis, 1974). Caplan, G., *An Approach to Community Mental Health* (Tavistock, London, 1961); *Principles of Preventive Psychiatry* (Basic Books, New York, 1964). Langsley, D.G. et al., 'Avoiding Mental Hospital Admission – a follow up study' (*American Journal of Psychiatry*, no. 127, 1971), pp. 1391–4. Raphael, B., 'Preventive Intervention with the Recently Bereaved'

(*Archives of General Psychiatry*, no. 34, 1977), pp. 1450–4.

GILLIAN WALDRON

See also: BEFRIENDING; COUNSELLING

CROSS AND RESURRECTION

The conjunction cross–resurrection, or negative–positive, is the source of Christian energy in doctrine, morals and spirituality. Religious power generally depends on conjunctions of opposites which surface in deliberately ambiguous images, reflecting the ambiguities of life and giving a frame to the betwixt-and-between states in which we often find ourselves. So St John's Gospel runs cross and resurrection together. The death of Jesus is simultaneously the breaking open of the water of life, his crucifixion is simultaneously his exaltation. The two major Christian sacraments work similarly. Baptism, though the beginning of Christian life, is a ritual dying with Christ from the world and a signing with the cross. Eucharist, which sustains Christian life, does so by participation in Christ's betrayed and broken body as the integrating factor of individual and communal life.

Christian pastoral work is bound to be deeply determined by the pattern of these rituals and their double symbolism. Anyone in trouble needs first to grasp the truth of their suffering with all possible clarity and objectivity. Because this is very difficult to do alone, the company of someone detached but sympathetic is helpful and normally necessary. It is only when the particular root of suffering has been located that any sort of cure is possible. But 'cure' is a very disputed concept and is the point at which the Christian pastor needs to refer again to the cross–resurrection symbol. In enthusiastic and simplistic versions of Christianity cure is often held to be miraculous, total and irrevocable. The 'cross' element disappears and the individual leads a 'resurrection' life of complete well-being. The transformation is over and done with. Crusading missions have offered this as a possibility, but it is unrealistic and inept. St Paul, the first practical theologian of cross–resurrection, was clear and insistent that we have yet to lay hold of resurrection, whereas the cross is still with us as our ongoing duty and discipline. His own life was still under the sign of the cross, real as his conversion was to him, and resurrection was a matter of hope. In his terms, then, cure is not so much a final resolution of ambiguities here and now as the patient capacity to live within them.

Reflection on these two concepts of cure, the complete and the yet-to-be-completed, discloses a conjunction within the cross–resurrection conjunction itself of which pastors need to be aware. It is the coming together of the realistic every day of brutal fact (cross) with the visionary and imaginative power of hope (q.v.) (resurrection). Religion works by keeping both in harness. But the work is tricky and demanding. If the two get confused or tangled, damage will result. It was a major part of Paul's achievement that he knew the difference between the two. Himself a visionary and a mystic, he was the sworn enemy of religious pretension and glamour. Modern criticism of religion, with its identification of myths and legends as such, also cuts down to size by making it easier for us to distinguish enough between the real and the imagined – not to separate them completely, but to investigate their inter-relation wisely. Indeed, the sting of suffering is usually in the disjunction between what a person believes or hopes and what is actually happening to him or her. To be able to distinguish one from the other, so that a patient can see what is happening to him or her and begin to cope with it in terms of belief is a major part of the pastor's skill. It is parallel to the work of the historian of Christianity, who investigates the interaction of events and interpretation in the New Testament: for example, in this instancce of cross and resurrection.

Finally, it is important to notice, on the cue of mentioning interpretation, that cross–resurrection is seen retrospectively. It makes sense after it has happened. It is the past interpreted later. So it is quite inappropriate to use it as a recipe or prescription, as if good always came out of trouble or, worse, as if it were worth inventing or increasing trouble to maximize good. It is as symbol (q.v.) and ritual (q.v.) that it has its most explicit expression. In pastoral situations it is trickier and more implicit, granted that its validity there is the real test of its value, and the quality of attention given by counsellor and patient is the key factor. Cross–resurrection is, after all, not so much a solution as a double sign.

Moltmann, J., *The Crucified God* (SCM, 1974).

JOHN DRURY

See also: DOUBT; HOPE; SALVATION AND PASTORAL CARE.

CURA ANIMARUM
See: PASTORAL CARE.

D

DEATH: DEFINITIONS

The absence of life, the irreversible absence of all vital signs.

1. *Biological* or *cellular death* is the cessation of simple life processes in organs, tissues and cells. Death in the biological sense may be a gradual *process*, with different organs dying over a period of time.

2. *Clinical death* is the formulation employed by physicians when determining the death of a human being, and refers to the permanent cessation of the integrated functioning of the organism as a whole. This must be distinguished from the cessation of function of the whole organism, that is, the sum of its tissues and component parts. Clinical death is an *event* involving the irreversible cessation of the complex integration and interaction of an organism's sub-systems.

Implicit in any definition of death are operational criteria for life and the irreversible cessation of life processes. Thus definitions of death must logically entail both necessary and sufficient criteria which specify the permanent cessation of particular vital functions. A definition must be such that a person can neither fulfil these criteria and still be alive nor be dead without having met the criteria. According to the terms of the definition these vital functions should include circulation, respiration, consciousness, and responsivity to external and internal stimuli. The following concepts of death are consequently defined in terms of the cessation of specific vital functions.

(1) *Systemic death* entails criteria and tests indicating cessation of heart-beat and respiration. Traditionally accepted as a yardstick of human death it is currently regarded as a prognostic indicator that total stoppage of the brain is imminent.

(2) *Whole brain death* entails criteria and tests which indicate the total and irreversible cessation of integrated brain function. This includes cessation of all neuronal components in the intracranial cavity, both cerebral hemispheres, brainstem and cerebellum. It involves a state where there is no capacity for consciousness combined with irreversible loss of respiration and heart-beat.

(3) *Brainstem death* is the physiological kernel of brain death and entails the death of all structures above the *foramen magnum*. The brainstem definition of death assumes that human death involves the loss of a critical and irreplaceable system essential to the integrated life of the organism as a whole. Since both the capacity for consciousness (q.v.) and the capacity for spontaneous breathing are brainstem functions it is impossible for the brain as a whole to survive the death of the brainstem. Despite the most vigorous form of therapy an individual cannot survive with dead brainstem. Conversely, evidence of brainstem function is an indicator of integrated life. It follows that definitions of death which do not specify irreversible cessation of brainstem function are inadequate and should not be interpreted as death but rather as states approaching death.

(4) *Cerebral death* or *persistent vegetative states* involve only the destruction of cerebral hemispheres, excluding brainstem and cerebellum. This state is often described as a 'lingering death', and in some sources it has been described as a form of brain death. This, however, is incorrect since a person in this state may still retain the capacity for spontaneous respiration and other related vital functions. Since *cerebral death* does not entail the death of the organism as a whole it is a necessary, but not sufficient, indicator of death.

(5) *Cognitive death* or *death of the person* refers to the alleged loss of personal identity in various states involving irreversible cessation of cognitive function. This is an unsatisfactory definition of death for the following reasons: (a) criteria relating to loss of personal identity are inherently vague and the subject of moral, philosophical, psychological, and theological controversy; (b) tests for loss of personal identity lack the diagnostic certainty found in tests for *systemic death*, *whole brain death* and *brainstem death*; (c) whereas 'death' is primarily a biological concept which is determined with reference to observations indicating total absence of vital functions, 'personal identity'

is a concept defined in terms of certain abilities and states of awareness in an organism which is still capable of functioning as a whole.

Ultimately there is only one kind of death: the irreversible cessation of integrated functioning of the organism as a whole. This entails the irreversible loss of the capacity for consciousness combined with loss of the capacity to breathe. Both of these are brainstem functions. Of the formulations considered above only a definition which specifies loss of brainstem function can meet these conditions.

Beecher, Henry K., 'A Definition of Irreversible Coma: Report of the Ad Hoc Committee of the Harvard Medical School to Examine the Definition of Brain Death' (*Journal of the American Medical Association*, no. 205, 1968), pp. 337–40. **Pallis, C.**, *The ABC of Brainstem Death* (British Medical Journal, 1983). **Veatch, Robert M.,** *Death, Dying and the Biological Revolution* (Yale University Press, 1976).

DAVID LAMB

See also: CONSCIOUSNESS; DEATH: MEANING; DYING; PERSON.

DEATH: MEANING

There is no one meaning of death in either the biblical witness or the Christian tradition. Neither is there one significance of death in pastoral practice. Death is used in the Bible to refer both to the end of physical existence for humans and for other living creatures and also to the condition of life lived in estrangement from God's purposes. It is not always clear which of these references is intended by a particular Biblical writer. Scholars are divided, for example, as to whether Paul's argument in Romans 5 and 6 is primarily about physical mortality or about our spiritual estrangement. One ancient tradition, based on this and other passages, sees death as an intruder into God's world, an alien presence which does not belong to the essence of human existence. This tradition, in which physical death is understood as punishment for sin, has dominated the Western Church since Augustine and tends to be associated with negative and fearful responses to death. Another tradition, more common in the Eastern Church but being rediscovered in the West in our time, acknowledges death as the natural and appropriate consequence of human creatureliness. This understanding permits a wider range of emotional and social

responses to death. The Bible contains many different responses to death including indifference, calm acceptance, fear, horror and even desire.

In human experience there is an essential ambiguity about death. It completes our span of life and makes fulfilment possible. But it can only do this by destroying life and our investment in it. Without death we could not be human but death takes from us all that is recognizably human. The reality of death gives point and urgency to our strivings but it also separates us from all the people and things which make life meaningful to us. Our responses, then, are likely to be ambiguous, ambivalent or confused. Pastorally it is important to recognize that in face of death we commonly have strong, complex and often contradictory feelings and attitudes. In bereavement the feelings we have about the other person's dying may well be different in quality from the feelings we have about our loss of the other.

The meanings we assign to death help shape our pastoral response to loss, to dying (q.v.) and to bereavement (q.v.). When, for example, death has been seen primarily in terms of its being the necessary prelude to judgement and to life beyond death, the care of the dying has tended to focus on issues of repentance and forgiveness. When death is seen more in terms of termination of earthly life, care tends to relate more to issues of quality of life before death. In either event it is the Christian conviction that the death of Christ has given new meaning to the human experience of death. Central to this new meaning is a sense of the trustworthiness of God even through the mystery of death and through our distorted experiences of dying.

In the contemporary Western world there is a renewed interest in the meaning of death following many decades of significant avoidance of death-related questions. The specific conditions of our living and dying are constantly changing and with the erosion and diffusion of older forms of religious belief it can no longer be taken for granted that the pastor shares a common frame of reference in regard to death with those to whom he or she seeks to minister. In the Middle Ages shared assumptions about death governed many aspects of life, but today, even among Christians, there is no one integrated set of beliefs to which all, or most, are likely to hold. Among secularists and adherents of non-Christian religions there is also a wide variety of meanings assigned to death.

Bailey, L.R., *Biblical Perspectives on Death* (Fortress Press, Philadelphia, 1979). Boase, T.S.R., *Death in the Middle Ages* (Thames and Hudson, 1972). **Griffin, G.M.**, *Death and the Church: Problems and Possibilities* (Dove Communications, Melbourne, 1978). Jüngel, E., *Death: the Riddle and the Mystery*, tr. Iain and Ute Nicol (The Saint Andrew Press, Edinburgh, 1975). Kaiser, O. and Lohse, E., *Death and Life*, tr. J.E. Steeley (Abingdon, Nashville, 1981). Pittenger, N., *After Death: Life in God* (SCM, 1980).

GRAEME M. GRIFFIN

See also: AGEING; BEREAVEMENT; DEATH: DEFINITIONS; DYING; FUNERALS; SUICIDE.

DEFENCE MECHANISMS
Operations of the ego which protect the personality from the excessive demands of either impulse or conscience.

The term was coined by Freud to describe certain neurotic symptoms in his patients, but healthy and adaptive use of these mechanisms is now regarded as part of normal mental functioning. They become pathological only when used in a destructive or maladaptive way to resolve inner tensions. They are part of the psychoanalytic system and assume such a view of the psyche. The ego (q.v.) is consciousness, while the id (q.v.) is a much larger area of amoral unconsciousness, the source of libidinal impulses. The superego (*see* CONSCIENCE: PSYCHOLOGICAL ASPECTS) is the seat of conscience, the source of moral constraint.

Repression consists simply in removing something from the domain of consciousness. It is a continuing activity which buries tension-causing psychic material in the unconscious and systematically keeps it there against all efforts of recollection. For example, a boy growing up in a family where interest in anything sexual was disapproved of might deal with sexually exciting events such as seeing the *au pair* undressing or early sexual play with girls by repressing the memory of them. Thus he avoids the anxiety aroused by the conflict between his libido (sexual impulse) and his superego (conscience, or internalized parental attitudes).

Regression is to return to a way of functioning which belongs to a stage of life before one was expected to deal with such anxiety-arousing situations. Normal adult life involves difficult judgements. Some characters retreat

from the maturity which these judgements demand into a kind of childishness. The implication is that when they make a mess of their lives people are not to be surprised or angry; such mature functioning cannot be expected of them.

Reaction formation is the constant attempt to be the absolute opposite of what one is avoiding, for example, to form one's character exclusively around the 'virtues' of sweetness and compliance.

Projection is the attributing of disapproved-of feelings within the psyche to another person. For example, to say, 'It is he being hostile towards me'.

Denial is considered as a defence mechanism but the word is used in various ways. Broadly it means refusing to appreciate something which is obviously significant, either an external factor or something in ourselves. It may be used of things which are denied by repressing them or by splitting them off. It is also treated as a defence mechanism in its own right when someone refuses to see any significance in what clearly remains important in their psyche.

Splitting means dividing an object, or indeed oneself, so that everything good resides in one area, and everything bad in another. The NT Pharisee who is 'not as other men are' (Luke 18.10) is a man who splits his ego. Anything about himself which might be bad is split off, so that he can see himself as entirely righteous. This technique combines with *denial* of the split-off elements and *projection* of these onto 'other men'. Splitting is sometimes observed in bereavement, as the bereaved finds it difficult to acknowledge negative as well as positive feelings towards the one lost. The negative feelings may be directed elsewhere, for example at doctors and nurses.

These descriptions are a simplification but one can see that all defence mechanisms have basically the same function, to avoid the anxiety (q.v.) aroused by psychological conflict. Other defence mechanisms have been described, but these are the chief ones. Certain of them are thought of as typical of particular disorders. For example, repression is associated with hysteria, and reaction formation with obsessionality. They are also related to stages of psychological development. Thus splitting and projection are features of primitive mental functioning, typical of the oral phase. Reaction formation is a more developed form of defence linked to the anal phase.

The recognition of defence mechanisms had an important effect on therapeutic technique. Resistance became something not merely to be overcome, but to be understood in terms of *how* it is carried out, so that light is shed on the client's character and his or her habitual modes of resolving conflict.

Freud, Anna, *The Ego and the Mechanisms of Defence* (Hogarth, rev. edn 1968).

MICHAEL PARSONS

See also: PSYCHOANALYSIS; PSYCHOTHERAPY.

DEMENTIA

A chronic disease, principally affecting the nerve cells in the brain, usually gradual in onset and of fairly long duration, ending only with the patient's death.

Dementia has been well described as 'an acquired global impairment of intellect, memory and personality, but without impairment of consciousness' (Lishman, 1978, p. 9). The symptoms vary in intensity and time of onset but can be described broadly under three headings: (1) The loss of short-term memory along with declining ability to acquire new memories. The long-term memory is often not so badly affected. (2) Impaired powers of reasoning. There is difficulty for patients' in assessing their sensory input (i.e. they are liable to be disorientated in space and time and to have little or no insight into their predicament). (3) Changes in feeling and conduct, with the result that patients' emotions appear blunted and their social behaviour changes its character, often becoming coarse.

The nebulous nature of these symptoms can make accurate diagnosis of dementia difficult and it is important that the disease is not mistaken for a remediable confusional state which presents in similar fashion in the elderly (as a result of psychological stress, malnutrition or metabolic disorders such as diabetes). Medical knowledge about the origin and causes of the disease is limited, consequently health services for the demented patient must be devoted to providing appropriate care. As the number of elderly in society increases so too does that proportion which is dementing. In spite of several informed reports about the urgent need for increased resources, no adequate provision has yet been made.

Pastoral attention must be directed primarily towards the patient suffering from dementia. This should go without saying, but there is a tendency to avoid confronting the problems of dementia by directing pastoral care towards the agents of primary care, relatives or nursing staff. Ministry with the dementing begins in acceptance of them as human beings, albeit ones who are often confused and 'messy'. Such ministry is concerned to overcome the distance created by our anxiety and the confusion resulting from our narrow image of humanity. Dementing people challenge our tendency to relate conditionally by their inability to conform to our expectations of a rational, coherent adult. The lack of a consistent grasp of reality by dementia sufferers means that ministry with them depends heavily, although not exclusively, on non-verbal communication (q.v.). The importance of simply being with the patient and of gentle reassuring human touch (q.v.) cannot be over stressed. Where conversation is possible it can be helpful to encourage the patient to reminisce about their life and former interests. This can serve to remind everybody concerned of the patient's individual character. The use of prayers familiar to the patient is also helpful, enabling participation in worship.

The second area of pastoral concern are the primary care agents, that is the relatives or nurses who bear the main burden of care. The predominantly long-term nature of the illness and the absence of any hope of recovery or remission can make such care very demanding emotionally. This is particularly the case for close relatives caring for a dementing spouse or parent at home. These carers experience a tension between their memory of the person they knew and the person they now live with. This strain can reach a peak when the relative realizes that the person they care for does not resemble, except physically, the person they thought they knew. This realization can mean that the grieving begins, yet the object of the grief is still alive and requiring care. The strain on a person caring for a dementing relative can be partially relieved by facilities available in varying degrees in most areas, such as the incontinent laundry service, home help, day care centres and planned respite hospital admissions. In some cases people feel guilt at accepting a hospital place for a dementing relative, even when this is the most sensible course of action. As a result of the heavy demands of domestic care relatives can become isolated from their friends and interests, and have difficulty picking up their life after the hospitalization or death of their dementing relative. Support groups (such as those run by the Alzheimer's Disease Society) can be a very useful resource for both relatives and nursing staff, providing an opportunity to discuss their experiences of caring for dementing people.

Carver, V., and Liddiard, P. (eds.), *An Ageing Population* (Hodder and Stoughton, 1978). Lishman, W.A., *Organic Psychiatry* (Blackwell, 1978).

HUGO PETZSCH

See also: ACCEPTANCE; AGEING; BEREAVEMENT.

DEMONIC, THE
See: EXORCISM.

DEPENDENCY
In counselling literature, a reliance of one party on the other in the counselling relationship, which may be beneficial or harmful depending upon the intensity, duration and context of the relationship.

See also: COLLUSION; COUNSELLING; TRANSFERENCE.

DEPRESSION
A psychological state of extreme low spirits characterized by a sense of hopelessness and despair; meaninglessness; constant, often unaccountable, weeping; poor or total lack of self-esteem which may mount to self-hatred; self-criticism and self-accusation; and loss of energy.

A depressed person may speak and move slowly and heavily, as if to do so were a great effort, as indeed it is. He or she may recount blackness of mood, evil and frightening thoughts and wishes; experience difficulty in having to speak, or be almost totally unable to do so. It will sometimes be difficult to meet the counsellor's gaze. The depressed person may not be able to eat or to sleep, and will find his or her mood is particularly bad on waking, lightening somewhat as the day goes on. He or she may have murderous feelings towards others, and/or express suicidal wishes or make suicidal attempts.

A severely depressed person showing

many or all of these symptoms, especially if there is a risk of self-damage, is in need of medical assistance since benefit can be had from the administration of therapeutic drugs, even if the apparent immediate cause of the depression is evident. The condition may contain a bio-chemical element, e.g. as sometimes found in the state which can follow childbirth, when the child as well as the mother may be at risk, and urgent and immediate medical action is imperative. Manic-depressive states, where depressive episodes alternate with euphoric ones, also need urgent medical attention.

Psychologically, a state of depression appears to arise in a vulnerable personality at times of stress, especially bereavement of some other form of loss. It has been compared to a state of mourning, and can be understood as a condition of repressed anger (q.v.) which would be dangerous if directed to the one who caused hurt or deprivation in the first instance, for fear of losing essential love and care. The anger is therefore turned in on the self, so that it is the self rather than the other who then becomes the object of destructive rage. Behind a person subject to states of depression there is often a considerable degree of maternal (or parental) deprivation (q.v.) which has resulted in low self-esteem, the apparent logic being that if one was worthy of close and continuing loving attention one would have received it, therefore lack of it, or loss of it, constitutes unworthiness. This may go with a belief that it must have been some antagonistic action on one's own part, albeit unknown or unrecognized, that drove the other way, or killed her off. Depressed persons often believe themselves responsible for all ills that happen to themselves or to those close to them, and that they bring about changes and separations by their bad thoughts and wishes. This is equivalent to the omnipotent, magical thinking which children do.

Reactive depression may arise at times of stress, such as illness, redundancy, change of employment, promotion, retirement, house purchase, or any other important life event. Change of any sort may result in depression since it often involves a loss of the familiar even if it appears not specifically to constitute a misfortune. The familiar has become a holding environment in which some of the self has been invested, and change comes to mean some loss of self. There may therefore also be fear that the diminished self may not be strong enough to withstand new demand, and wishes to withdraw from the risk of failure. Depression is often accompanied by anxiety.

The person in a state of depression is urgently in need of self-esteem. The counsellor must be able to accept the client's very real feeling of self-disgust, whilst making it clear that, although understanding it, he does not share it, nor would the person basically wish him to. The counsellor's task is to help the person to accept the experiences that have led to such a state of mind, to come to terms with the emotions which have been so fearfully repressed, and thus to discover that they can be consciously contained without causing severe destruction.

It requires long-term patience in the counsellor, to help the person to establish a trusting relationship that can withstand anger and fear of loss. The counsellor may be subjected to considerable attack as well as constant mistrust and betrayal. He or she may experience equivalent anger, disappointment and helplessness, but the main therapeutic tool is continuously to be there.

Bowlby, John, *Attachment and Loss*, vols. 1, 2 and 3 (Penguin, 1971, 1975). **Dominian, J.**, *Depression* (Fontana, 1976). **Freud, Sigmund,** *Mourning and Melancholia*, Collected Works, vol. 14 (Hogarth Press/ Institute of Psycho-analysis, 1957), pp. 239–58. **Rycroft, Charles,** *A Critical Dictionary of Psychoanalysis* (Nelson, 1968).

BARBARA K. FOWLES

See also: APATHY; BEREAVEMENT; GUILT; PSYCHIATRY AND MENTAL ILLNESS.

DEPTH PSYCHOLOGY

A generic term loosely referring to Freud's psychoanalysis (q.v.), Jung's analytical psychology (q.v.), and other related schools which employ the concept of the unconscious.

DETERMINISM

See: FREEDOM AND DETERMINISM.

DIET

(1) Habitual pattern of eating. (2) Type and quantity of food.

The word originates from the Greek *diaita*, meaning course of life. This is of interest as recent trends in health education (q.v.) stress the fact that healthy eating must be con-

sidered as an integral part of life-style. This includes, for example, the amount of regular exercise and rest taken, and habits such as smoking and drinking alcohol.

However, as applied to eating, 'diet' is used in three relatively distinct ways: (1) regular eating habits (e.g. 'He eats a healthy diet'). (2) A specific eating pattern prescribed for an illness (e.g. 'She is on a diabetic diet'). (3) A way of reducing food intake in order to slim (e.g. 'She is dieting again to get into her summer dress').

1. *Healthy diet.* This is a pattern of regular eating which satisfies all the basic needs of the body and is associated with optimum health. The authoritative guidelines to ensure adequate intakes, allowing for differences due to age, sex and biological variation, are given in documents such as the Department of Health and Social Security (DHSS) Report 15 on recommended daily intakes of food. Nutritional advice based on such guidelines has traditionally assumed that the main problems are likely to be of under consumption of specific nutrients leading to risks of malnutrition. Commonly expressed as Recommended Daily Intakes (RDIs) the main preoccupation has tended to be with achieving adequate intakes of nutrients such as vitamins, minerals and protein. Historically this approach has helped to achieve the considerable improvements in nutrition in the UK during this century. Good examples of its application are the existing welfare state legislation and food rationing during the Second World War.

Little attention, however, was given in such recommendations to the main current health problems, such as obesity, coronary heart disease and dental caries, which are related to over-eating. The important dietary component, dietary fibre, which is most likely to be lacking in the UK diet, was also ignored.

Within the last ten years most of these issues have been addressed separately in a series of authoritative reports but only recently has there been an attempt to combine these into one set of recommendations in a report prepared for the National Advisory Committee on Nutrition Education (NACNE). This report reviews the evidence of how different aspects of the UK diet affect health, concluding that on average people eat too much fat, sugar and salt than is good for them and not enough fibre. Quantitative nutritional guidelines for optimum intakes are given with suggested targets and realistic timetables for reaching these. The report also highlights the fact that nutrition is affected by so many factors and sectors of government, but there is no shared policy consistent with the best interests of health. For example, most existing agricultural policies, including subsidies, designed to protect farming interests favour high fat milk, meat and dairy products. Similarly, there are many bodies and industries whose only purpose is the promotion of single foodstuffs such as milk, sugar and meat. This largely accounts for the controversy that surrounded the publication of the NACNE Report and the fact that although it was circulated for professional discussion it was not endorsed by the DHSS, the Ministry of Agriculture, Food and Fisheries (MAFF), or the British Nutrition Foundation (BNF).

The issue of 'Diet and Cardiovascular Disease' is addressed in a more recent report prepared for the DHSS by the Committee on Medical Aspects of Food Policy (COMA). The recommendations of this report, which are substantially the same as the NACNE Report, have been accepted both by the DHSS and Parliament. The translation of these sets of recommendations into realistic, attractive and promotable patterns of healthy eating is the current challenge which faces everyone, but especially professionals such as dietitians, doctors and teachers, whose advice is likely to be sought.

2. *Therapeutic diets.* Many of the foods prescribed for specific illnesses are the same as those for a 'healthy diet'. For example, dietary fibre is prescribed for patients with severe constipation or more severe bowel conditions such as diverticular disease. This is also an example of a complete reversal in medical practice that has occurred within the last fifteen years due to new evidence on the effects of dietary fibre. Other examples are the dietary management of diabetes and peptic ulcers, which have also been radically changed. Some very specific diet treatments are required for people who, for instance, are allergic to certain foods or have an inherited genetic abnormality.

3. *Slimming diets.* The most common use of 'diet' relates to slimming because it is a major popular preoccupation. This has a partially sound health base since a high proportion of adults, especially as they get older, are over

the best weight for their health. However, it is the fashionable model image of slimness and beauty that causes the greatest concern, especially for women, as it is projected very widely on the media and through women's magazines. As a result, women tend to think they are unattractive if they feel that they don't match the model image and try to achieve it through dieting. An extreme and tragic example of this phenomenon is the dieting disease, *anorexia nervosa.*

A very wide range of slimming diets are promoted in books and magazines, and dieting foods are widely sold with many exaggerated claims. But weight-gain can occur only if one consistently eats more than one needs. Weight loss occurs only by eating less than that. The 'healthy diet' with more fibre and less fat and sugar is the best basis for those wishing to slim, and many people find that by making those adjustments they tend to lose weight anyway. In the NACNE report there are tables of acceptable weight ranges for men and women of different heights, to help people to set themselves reasonable and healthy targets. Those who are overweight by these standards and wish to lose weight are encouraged to do this steadily and gradually at not more than 2 lb. per week over a period of months. Crash diets are deceptive, rarely successful, and can be dangerous.

Diet and Cardiovascular Disease, DHSS Report 28 on Health and Social Subjects, of the Committee on Medical Aspects of Food Policy (COMA) (HMSO, 1984). *Proposals for Nutritional Guidelines for Health Education in Britain,* Report for the National Advisory Committee on Nutrition Education (NACNE) of the ad hoc working party under the chairmanship of Prof. W.P.T. James. (Health Education Council, 1983). *Recommended Daily Amounts of Food Energy and Nutrients for Groups of People in the United Kingdom,* DHSS Report 15 on Health and Social Subjects, of COMA (HMSO, 1979). **Burkitt, D.,** *Don't Forget Fibre in Your Diet* (Martin Dunitz, 1979)

M.A. CHURCH

See also: HEALTH EDUCATION.

DISABLEMENT: PASTORAL CARE OF MENTALLY DISABLED PEOPLE

There is no single definition of mental disability since criteria differ according to societal values. It is generally understood as a condition of varied intellectual impairment (70 I.Q. and below) accompanied by different levels of difficulty regarding learning and social adaptability. It need not involve physical or mental illness. Recent positive attitudes arise from this understanding of mentally disabled people. They are persons (q.v.) having the right to normal and fulfilled lives, including resources to make this possible. Research indicates that their full learning capacity has been underestimated, and they are able to improve in formal learning and personal character. They should be treated as members of the community, sharing its life opportunities as they are able. (See Mittler, 1979, chs. 1–3)

Christian care extends this by affirming that they share God's image, are embraced by Christ's redemptive work and accepted as they are in their humanity. An adequate pastoral care, expressed in the ministry of clergy, church members and professionals, must take account of the following:

(1) The mentally disabled are real people – widely varied in character and abilities, possessing full humanity, genuine emotions and sensitivities, able to give and receive love. Each is capable of growth in learning and relationships, needing widening horizons and enriching experiences. They are direct, vulnerable and trusting. Most know life's negative aspects, accept their limitations, and are often unaware of their mental disability. As people they experience life and others 'whole', understanding and learning in an action-orientated, participative way. In learning by doing concretely out of their immediate surroundings, they 'understand' more than they can express or explain. Many severely disabled people communicate expressively without words, though multiple disability increases difficulty here. They have, like us, the right to be accorded worth and appreciation – needing to belong and to share some responsibility and care for others.

(2) Pastoral care should support and share in active programmes for them – play, occupation, recreation, etc. – with explicit concern for the individual at every stage; especially regarding loss and bereavement, adolescent difficulties, guidance in relationships, and facing changes in accommodation and activities. Many mentally disabled people can deeply grasp spiritual realities, trusting and loving God in lifelong friendship, expressed concretely in worship and group activity. They know him as he upholds them, giving himself to them in accepting love. Pastoral care should share and articulate this

knowledge, showing God's concern for their whole life in a comprehensive, personal approach.

(3) Sensitive, appropriate communication (q.v.) is important – welcoming face and eyes, calm and interested tone, gentle touch and body-contact, accompanied by a consistent attitude. Through these, Christ's presence is encountered together. Humour and patience are assets, and sensitiveness about the pace of spiritual growth according to ability and circumstances. The elderly, overlooked and 'difficult' need particular attention. Care becomes mutual as 'carers' receive love and renewal from the disabled people. They are drawn to those with a relaxed, natural, well-rounded spirituality. This care-style is not exclusively ministerial, but 'incarnational' – the vocation of every Christian in contact with mentally disabled people.

(4) As all families are unique, so a mentally handicapped member affects each one differently. Earlier on, parents appreciate immediate practical help and professional guidance, sustained ungrudging friendship – room to adjust and give vent to their feelings. There is no readily discernable process of the child's acceptance within the family. Neighbourliness and pastoral listening help parents face the situation positively – sharing their traumatic experience, somehow knowing God's involvement in their pain. Appropriate pastoral care is continuous over years, giving parents, the handicapped and other children, a full place in the church. By offering undemanding friendship it provides a family 'extension', a network of natural relationships; enabling each family to reckon with and face future changes within a supportive group. A caring fellowship can help parents confront prejudice, offer 'sitting in', transport and other help in a natural way. Many families unknown to churches or institutions can be contacted through street wardens or community support schemes. (See Mittler 1979, Bayley 1973)

(5) Local church ministry to mentally disabled people begins by a warm welcome into fellowship and worship. They sense atmosphere and if they are wanted for themselves. They bring a naturalness, uninhibitedness and joy, participating in worship expressively by action-songs, colour and visual attraction. Many appreciate opportunities for quiet, too. They delight in and anticipate liturgical repetition requiring

response; offering their whole selves to God. Their presence reflects positively the Church's catholicity and inclusiveness in Christ. Many churches encourage mentally disabled people to receive holy communion as a supremely welcoming, incorporating event for the vulnerable. They appreciate this, like others, through the Spirit's presence. Leaders can demonstrate welcome in their own attitude to the disabled person. Difficulties regarding acceptance or disturbance, etc. are seen differently when anxieties are overcome by personal knowledge. Often, congregational education is necessary, enabling members to be agents for understanding and action in the local community. (Stubblefield 1965, Turner 1976, Easter 1983.) Mentally disabled Christians have the right to local church education, enjoying group sharing and smaller house fellowships. Presentation must be involving, story-like, Christ-centred and practically orientated, i.e. simple drama and dance, drawing, painting and crafts. (Marais 1976, Wilson 1975.) In residential accommodation worship can be devised for residents of varied abilities, in close adjustment to their life in co-operation with the staff. Small-group eucharistic worship for the severely or profoundly disabled that is short, dignified and part of a total visit, is much appreciated.

(6) Residential/training facilities. Chaplains are appointed to the hospitals for the mentally disabled. Adult training centres, hostels, etc. often 'adopt' local ministers or priests as chaplains. In all cases, chaplains require involvement in the organization's structure and life in order to care adequately. Identification with clients and staff is essential. From this stems a stance that counters the incipient dehumanization endemic to all institutions (see INSTITUTIONALIZATION), shows concern for the client's basic humanity, and stresses the essential ingredients of care.

Links can be forged with local church and community groups, their members befriending individuals, providing clubs, home hospitality and recreational contact. Councils of churches can speak for mentally handicapped people regarding resources and quality of care, take joint pastoral responsibility for different units or, when appropriate, organizing their own housing association; thus assisting the integration of specialised units into local communities.

Integration is essential if mentally disabled people are to contribute *their* pastoral care to

our society. Although on the edge, by their existence – in vulnerability, receptivity, transparency and unquestioning trust – they challenge the contemporary achievement-orientated, intellect-dominated 'normal' assumptions, judging others by relationship not status. They invite churches to look afresh at their understanding of 'common humanity', worship essentials, non-verbal communication, and at vulnerability as a living sign of Christ's presence. (*see* Müller-Fahrenholz 1979).

Bayley, M.J., *Mental Handicap and Community Care* (Routledge, 1973). **Easter, B.J.**, 'Communication and Community: a Study of Communication with Special Application to a Community for the Mentally Handicapped' (unpub. PhD diss., Univ. Birmingham, 1983). **Marais, E. and Marais, M.**, *Lives Worth Living* (Souvenir Press, 1976). **Mittler, P.**, *People Not Patients* (Methuen, 1979). **Müller-Fahrenholz, G.** (ed.), *Partners in Life* (WCC, 1979). **Stubblefield, H.W.**, *The Church's Ministry in Mental Retardation* (Broadman, 1965). **Turner, L.**, 'The Christian Ministry to the Mentally Handicapped', in **Millard, D.** (ed.), *Religion and Medicine*, 3 (SCM, 1976), pp. 2–20. **Wilson, D.G.** (ed.), *I am With You* (St Paul Publications, 1975).

BRIAN J. EASTER

See also: REHABILITATION.

DISABLEMENT: PASTORAL CARE OF PHYSICALLY DISABLED PEOPLE

The motto, 'disabled people are people', rightly places the emphasis on the person (q.v.) rather than on the disability. Disabled people are not a homogenous group any more than their able-bodied contemporaries, with whom they share the same range of difficulties and of material and emotional needs, including the need for friends and satisfying sexual relationships.

Some people experience, in addition, needs or difficulties which are directly related to the nature or severity of their disability. Those who become disabled later in life, through illness or accident, know what it is like to be able-bodied. This is in contrast to those who are disabled from birth, an experience which may limit their horizons literally and metaphorically, and which sometimes leads to relative emotional immaturity and unrealistic aspirations. Able-bodied people often have little understanding of disability. Consider the question, 'Do disabled people make you feel uncomfortable?' If so, their greatest handicap could be you and your attitudes.

This aspect of relationships is central to pastoral care with disabled people and their families. Attitudes in the community are often those of unacknowledged prejudice (q.v.) towards a minority group (about one in ten of the population in Great Britain) and the perception of disability as a stigma lingers on. These attitudes raise invisible barriers which exacerbate, or may create, difficulties affecting all aspects of disabled people's lives. The resulting vulnerability may be one reason why they, and sometimes the caring relative, are at greater risk than their able-bodied contemporaries of becoming depressed, anxious, hostile, verbally aggressive or ambivalent.

The onset of acquired disability, or the realization of the significance of congenital disability, may be likened to a bereavement (q.v.), and many disabled people benefit from early crisis intervention (q.v.) and from counselling (q.v.) as to a bereaved person. Newly disabled people usually need help in developing a new self-image in which they recognize that although they are physically changed with a different body-image, they remain people of worth. However, some resent such approaches and prefer practical help only.

Disabililty causes ethical, philosophical or religious problems. These include questions about abortion (q.v.) and euthanasia; about responsibilities of marriage (q.v.) or child-bearing (see FAMILY PLANNING), especially if the disability is hereditary (see GENETIC COUNSELLING); about the fact that the death rate among physically disabled people is five times that in their community. The most frequent question is, 'Why me?' This raises the problem of suffering in relation to a loving God, and those who ask want an honest discussion. (see THEODICY).

The concepts of a dominating future, over which we have no control, and of a manageable future, which we are able to influence, can be useful when co-operating with other professional helpers in a team (of which the disabled person should be the most important member). This approach shows in which direction change is possible and offers hope; while the range of professional skills and good interprofessional relationships (q.v.) extend the area of the manageable future.

Continued dependence (q.v.) on others is usually hard to accept; so, whenever possible, help should be reciprocal. Disabled people have their contributions to make to others, and helpers can assist them to identify their abilities (which may lie in personal relationships rather than in physical activities) and to find outlets for them. The social services tend towards segregation rather than integration in the community, and church congregations may react in the same way. 'It is the illusion of the strong, the whole, the healthy to see themselves in the centre and to see the handicapped as those on the margin . . . It is only when the witness of the handicapped is an integral part of the witness of the whole Church, that this witness is true to the Gospel of the Crucified who is risen, the risen Lord who is the Crucified' (Müller-Fahrenholz, pp. 24, 25).

Terminology in publications about disability is not uniform. The World Health Organization recommends the following usage: *impairment* – a medical condition affecting any part of the body, e.g. paralysis due to poliomyelitis, detached retinas; *disability* – a limitation of function, e.g. the inability to walk, or to see, as a result of suffering an impairment as above; *handicap* – the social disadvantages which result from having an impairment or disability, e.g. difficulty of travel or of getting a job, not being accepted as an equal.

Relationships and the Physically Disabled: an Introduction for Counsellors (published by the Association for the Sexual and Personal Relationships of the Disabled, 14 Peto Place, London, NW1 4DT, who are a useful source of information). **Berwick, L.,** *Undefeated* (Epworth Press, 1980); autobiography, congenital disability. **van Dongen-Garrad, J.,** *Invisible Barriers: Pastoral Care with Physically Disabled People* (SPCK, 1983). **Gibbs, K.,** *Only One Way Up* (Darton Longman & Todd, 1981); autobiography, acquired disability. **Müller-Fahrenholz, G.** (ed.), *Partners in Policy* (Heinemann Educational, 1971); especially ch. 4, 'Exchange and Stigma'. **Stewart, W.F.R.,** *The Sexual Side of Handicap: a Guide for the Caring Professions* (Woodhead-Faulkner, 1979). **Titmuss, R.M.,** *The Gift Relationship* (Allen & Unwin, 1970); especially ch. 13, 'Who is my stranger?' **Watson, W.C.,** *Disease and Social Disability* (Collins, 1972); medical information for members of the caring professions.

JESSIE VAN DONGEN-GARRAD

See also: DISABLEMENT: PASTORAL CARE OF MENTALLY DISABLED PEOPLE; REHABILITATION.

DISCIPLINE AS PASTORAL CARE

The concept of discipline in the Christian tradition is a complex one, holding together a variety of matters which are commonly treated separately today. The most familiar meaning of the term is the enforcement of a code of behaviour within the Christian community by church courts or by private penitential system. This form of social control was often extended into the broader society, so that the Church claimed the right to enforce morals through legislation and a call on the 'secular arm' for assistance in the exercise of discipline. A system of discipline co-ordinated the concerns of moral theology (q.v.), the confessional and ascetical theology (q.v.) – all of them dealing with aspects of the individual's moral and spiritual growth. Discipline also concerned itself with a range of matters which were traditionally labelled 'polity': issues of church order and boundary maintenance, and the shaping of a Christian society in which justice was done and the social order reflected and sustained Christian insights.

Discipline, in short, was concerned with disciplining individuals, with the repression of vice and the nourishment of virtue, with sustaining the fellowship of a true church and restoring repentant sinners, and with the structuring and maintenance of society at large as a 'godly community'. Thus most of what we know to-day as pastoral care was incorporated into discipline. This meant that the cure of souls tended towards legalism and was often highly judgemental. But, in theory at least, there was a strong affirmation of forgiveness, of the availability of absolution for the repentant sinner. Because pastoral care was to be conducted on a theological basis and in the closest relationship to the fellowship of believers, the worst excesses of individualism were usually avoided. The pastoral and the political were held together as two aspects of the same process.

The disciplinary procedures of the early Church, for which abundant evidence is to be found in the New Testament and the Fathers, were radically modified when Christianity became the official religion of the Roman Empire. The Church then shared responsibility for discipline with the state, or at least delegated to the state a range of offences and called upon the state to enforce certain penalties for enfringement of discipline. The elaborate structure of canon law grew up alongside a more flexible penitential system originating in Ireland and deeply influencing the developing of the confessional. The Inquisition was a particularly harsh instance of discipline as social control. The Reformers criticized the late medieval system of discipline as legalistic and encouraging false ideas of merit and justification by works. It was also seen as sacerdotalist and mechanical. The Reformed understanding of discipline is most clearly epitomized among the Calvinists who saw 'ecclesiastical discipline uprightly ministered' as one of the three marks of the true Church. The Scottish Books of Discipline, 1560–1578, dealt with the establishment of schools and the reform of the universities, the polity of the Church and the various responsibilities of ministers as well as discipline in the narrower sense, i.e. the enforcement of morals. Cases range from fornication through heterodox religious belief, gossip, cheating, to witchcraft and blasphemy. Ministers were expected to denounce from the pulpit not just the sins of the lowly but the oppressions and injustices of the powerful and the rich.

The system of ecclesiastical discipline survived in attenuated form almost into modern times, but was increasingly called into question. No one believes that a canon should be restored, but there are lessons of continuing relevance to be learned from the tradition of discipline, in particular that the pastoral and the political belong together, that pastoral care requires a theological basis and that it takes place in close relation to the life and worship of the Church.

Clark, I.M., *A History of Church Discipline in Scotland* (Lindsay, Aberdeen, 1929). **Forrester, Duncan, McDonald, James I.H.** and **Tellini, Gian,** *Encounter with God* (T. & T. Clark, 1983), pp. 148–50. **McNeill, John T.,** *A History of the Cure of Souls* (SCM, 1952).

D.B. FORRESTER

See also: PASTORAL CARE: HISTORY OF – REFORMED TRADITION; SIN.

DIVORCE: DOCTRINAL AND LEGAL ASPECTS

1. *Church law.* The attitude of a particular Christian tradition to the question of divorce is governed by its view of the nature of marriage (q.v.). The *Catholic* tradition describes marriage as 'an intimate partnership of life and love' which is 'rooted in the contract of its partners, that is, in their irrevocable

personal consent' (*Gaudium et Spes*, sec. 48). Roman canon law states that the 'essential properties of marriage are unity and indissolubility' (Canon 1056), and therefore, for a valid, consummated and sacramental marriage there can be no divorce. As Canon 1141 puts it: 'A marriage which is ratified and consummated cannot be dissolved by any human power or by any cause other than death.'

By contrast, the *Reformed* tradition, which underlies the practice of most Nonconformist churches, affirms the indissolubility of marriage not as an ontological fact ('a marriage cannot be dissolved'), but as a moral obligation ('a marriage should not be dissolved'). The Reformers, while affirming the divine intention for the permanence of marriage, allowed that the bond could be broken, and that divorce with right of remarriage might therefore be permitted for certain specified causes – usually sexual misconduct (cf. Matt. 19.9) and desertion (cf. 1 Cor. 7.15).

The *Eastern Orthodox* churches, in line with what they believe to be long-standing tradition, allow that some marriages can 'die', and grant divorce with right of remarriage in such circumstances as adultery, attempt on life, abortion without the husband's consent, continuing impotence, desertion for two years, apostasy or incurable insanity.

The *Church of England* has seen a continual tension since the Reformation between the indissolubilist (Catholic) and non-indissolubilist (Reformed) traditions. Had Archbishop Cranmer's proposal for a revised canon law (*Reformatio Legum Ecclesiasticarum* 1553) ever reached the Statute Book – it was allowed to lapse on the accession of Mary – this would have permitted divorce with right of remarriage for adultery, malicious desertion, prolonged absence without news, attempts against the partner's life and cruelty. In fact the Canons of 1603 only recognize divorce *a thoro et mensa* (separation from bed and board). No remarriage after such divorce was permitted. Despite this Church law, however, many influential churchmen believed that adultery dissolved the marriage bond, and that an innocent husband was free to remarry. Over 300 did so between 1670 and 1857 by obtaining a private Act of Parliament. The revised Canons of the Church of England (1964, 1969) affirm (Canon B.30) that 'marriage is in its nature a union permanent and lifelong . . .' They do not mention divorce,

remarriage or separation. Anglican pastoral practice has, however, been governed in recent years by an Act of Convocation (1957) formally reaffirming the Resolutions of 1938, which stated that marriage is indissoluble save by death, and that as a consequence remarriage after divorce during the lifetime of a former partner 'always involves a departure from the true principle of marriage as declared by our Lord'. The Convocations ruled that the Church should not allow the use of the marriage service in church in the case of a divorced person who has a former partner still living. This pastoral practice has been questioned by both the Root Report (*Marriage, Divorce and the Church* 1971) and the Lichfield Report (*Marriage and the Church's Task* 1978). In July 1981, the General Synod agreed that there are circumstances in which a divorced person may be married in church during the lifetime of a former partner, but asked for pastoral procedures to be prepared before the existing rules were changed. Several possible pastoral procedures have been discussed, but at the time of writing (July 1984) none has yet been generally agreed.

2. *Civil law (England and Wales)*. In 1857, Parliament abolished ecclesiastical jurisdiction in matrimonial cases, and established civil courts. The Matrimonial Causes Act (1857) made statutory provision for divorce with right of remarriage. It allowed that a woman could be divorced on the sole ground of adultery; if a husband was to be divorced, cruelty had to be shown in addition. The definition of 'matrimonial offence' was extended in 1937 to include desertion, cruelty and incurable insanity. In 1969 the Divorce Reform Act (consolidated into the Matrimonial Causes Act 1973) gave effect to some of the recommendations of the Anglican report *Putting Asunder* (1966). The new law substituted the principle of 'irretrievable breakdown' for that of 'matrimonial offence', but required the courts to be satisfied, as evidence of such breakdown, of at least one of the following facts: adultery which the petitioner finds intolerable; unreasonable behaviour by the respondent; two years' desertion; two years' separation with the consent to divorce of the respondent; five years' separation whether or not the respondent consents to divorce.

In 1977, amendment of Rules of Court

73

introduced a 'special procedure' by which almost all divorces may be dealt with by submission of a written affidavit to the registrar, without the need for the parties to go to court.

Under the Matrimonial and Family Proceedings Act 1984 no divorce may be obtained until one year after the marriage, but the previous restriction against granting a divorce within the first three years of marriage is reduced to one year. The grounds of the 1973 Act remain the same.

Reports: *Putting Asunder: a Divorce Law for Contemporary Society* (SPCK, 1966). *Marriage, Divorce and the Church* (SPCK, 1971). *Marriage and the Church's Task* (Church Information Office, 1978). *Gaudium et Spes* (Dec. 1965), Documents of the Second Vatican Council. *The Code of Canon Law* in English translation (The Canon Law Society Trust, 1983). **Atkinson, David,** *To Have and To Hold* (Collins, 1979). **Dominian, J.,** *Marital Breakdown* (Penguin, 1968). **Eekelaar, John,** *Family Law and Social Policy* (Weidenfeld & Nicolson, 1978, 1984). **Jones, Cheslyn** (ed.), *For Better, For Worse* (The Church Literature Association, 1977). **Kelly, Kevin T.,** *Divorce and Second Marriage* (Collins, 1982). **Puxon, M.,** *Family Law* (Penguin, 1963, 1971). **Schillebeeckx, E.,** *Marriage: Human Reality and Saving Mystery* (Sheed and Ward, 1965). **Thornes, B.** and **Collard, J.,** *Who Divorces?* (Routledge, 1979). **Winnett, A.R.,** *Divorce and Remarriage in Anglicanism* (Macmillan, 1958); *Divorce and the Church* (Mowbray, 1968).

DAVID ATKINSON

Addendum: HISTORY AND PRESENT LEGISLATION, SCOTLAND.

History. From the commencement of the Kingdom of Scotland until the Reformation, the law applied was Roman canon law. Marriage was based upon consent. The law did not recognize divorce but did recognize legal separation on the ground of adultery. Canon law, however, allowed that there could be reason why consent was never formed, e.g. error, insanity (*see* MARRIAGE: NULLITY). The courts dealing with the canon law were directly the responsibility of the bishop. After the Reformation the jurisdiction of marriage fell to the Commissary Court with a right to appeal to the Court of Sessions. Divorce was recognized for adultery and desertion. The law applied was based on canon law but this was developed greatly by case law. Until 1830 divorce was recognized only for adultery and desertion. Scotland was unusual in that, based on the idea of marriage

founded on consent, several irregular forms of marriage were accepted, including declaration in front of a witness by a promise of marriage with subsequent intercourse or living together and holding yourself as man and wife. This last practice is still a form of marriage in Scotland.

Present legislation. From 1830 matrimonial law changed slowly to allow marriage by ministers of all Churches and eventually by registrars in 1939. In 1938 grounds of divorce were widened to include cruelty, sodomy, bestiality. The final change in the law took place in the Divorce (Scotland) Act 1976 which declared there to be one ground of divorce, namely that the marriage had irretrievably broken down. However, the ways of establishing this breakdown – i.e. adultery, desertion, conduct, two years separation with consent and five years without consent – more or less followed the old grounds of cruelty, desertion and adultery. Subsequent changes in the law have been merely procedural, namely the use of only affidavits in undefended decrees, and the inclusion of divorce cases in the jurisdiction of sheriff courts.

LIBBY MALONE

See also: DIVORCE: PASTORAL ASPECTS; MARRIAGE AND FAMILY; MARRIAGE: NULLITY; MARRIAGE, THEOLOGY OF.

DIVORCE: PASTORAL ASPECTS

The rise in the divorce rate during the 20th century has fluctuated but shown a remarkable growth. In the period 1978–84 a high plateau has been reached, with divorces in the UK numbering some 150,000 annually. (Marriages in the same period numbered annually about 400,000.) Much of the previous stigma has therefore been removed from divorce, and as more and more families have personal experience of it, there is now less fear of the unknown.

However, the sense of failure, loss and sadness felt by most couples faced with marriage breakdown must not be underestimated. Each divorce marks the death of a relationship. It is generally accompanied by feelings of guilt, bitterness and let-down by at least one partner, and it may be followed by a period akin to mourning and bereavement (q.v.). Though the law does not now seek to ascribe fault to one partner (except in extreme cases) a sense of injustice may well be felt by at least one of the partners, and often one spouse requires support through experiencing shock or disorientation while the other sets up home with a new partner. Though divorce is primarily a matter for the couple, it affects other members of the family, who may be reduced to helpless onlookers during the marriage breakdown. Relationships between one spouse and the other's relations can be severed in every sense. Pastoral care may be required for these family members, particularly grandparents, and help should be available for the couple to talk about the implications of their divorce for the family.

In marriages where there are dependent children, the emotional and legal aspects of divorce are more complex. Practical arrangements for children are agreed by the court before a decree is granted. It awards 'custody', the right to make long-term decisions about the child, either to one parent or jointly; 'care and control' to the person with whom the child lives; and 'access' to the other parent specifying the detailed arrangements in cases of dispute.

Though most parents may initially agree about the custody of the children, disputes about them frequently occur after divorce. Counselling (q.v.) can enable divorcing parents to discuss the most suitable arrangements for their children and can help them to continue to be loving parents acceptable to their children even though living apart. A pastor or counsellor can also usefully act as child's confidant when no trusted friend, teacher or relative is available, for children often feel bewildered and unconsulted at this time and may try so hard to keep the peace at home that they bottle up their feelings at cost to their own emotional health.

Couples facing divorce have several formal sources of help. Most of them consult their doctor with medical symptoms at least once during the divorcing process. General advice is obtainable from Citizens' Advice Bureaux. Marriage counselling at a Marriage Guidance Council provides individuals, or couples together, time to talk about their difficulties, consider options open to them, improve their relationship if possible and decide about practical future arrangements, whether staying together or separating. Conciliation services exist in some towns to provide a neutral setting for couples to negotiate and agree plans for their children. Legal advice

and assistance is available from solicitors through the 'Green Form' scheme for people in financial hardship. Specialist solicitors, who act on behalf of one spouse, may be members of the Solicitors Family Law Association. When violence takes place or is feared, a court has power to issue an injunction to protect the threatened spouse.

These sources of help can provide practical assistance and emotional support. Decisions may have to be made on selling the matrimonial home and finding other separate accommodation. New financial arrangements have to be faced. Difficult issues of child management confront the parents at precisely the time when communication between them is likely to be most traumatic.

These practical questions may be the outward and visible sign of the confusion and uncertainty which the partners both feel. In counselling they can individually reflect on the reasons for the marriage breakdown, express their mixed feelings and, where they are ambivalent (see AMBIVALENCE) about divorce, explore the possibility of reconciliation. Whether or not formal help is sought, pastoral care and support can be provided through the informal network of friends and relatives. Divorcing individuals often need reassurance that the end of their marriage is not going to mean the end of their friendships. Depression and suicidal attempts are not uncommon. Uncertainty in the couple can be reflected in tentativeness by their friends. So positive support through a pastoral network is recommended. In the post-divorce phase individuals may need encouragement to persevere with previous social contacts or meet in self-help groups or join clubs for the divorced and separated. A church community can aim to give sensitive support to one partner, while not colluding (see COLLUSION) that all responsibililty for the divorce lies with the other spouse.

Though divorce signals the end of the marriage, it can bring relief from a dead or disabling relationship. New beginnings become possible for all members of the family, and some children report a welcome lifting of tension and improved relations with each parent after the separation.

Consumers Association, 'Divorce: Legal Procedures and Financial Facts' (*Which?* 1984). **Haynes, J.H.,** *Divorce Mediation* (Springer, 1981). **Oberg, B.** and **G.,** *I'm Leaving* (Norman & Hobhouse, 1982). **Shreeve, C.,** *Divorce: How to Cope Emotionally and*

Practically (Turnstone, 1984). **Switzer, D.V.**, *The Minister as Crisis Counsellor* (Abingdon, 1980).

NICHOLAS TYNDALL

See also: BEREAVEMENT; MARRIAGE AND FAMILY; DIVORCE: LEGAL ASPECTS.

DOUBLE BIND

A demand comprising two contradictory aspects forcing failure on the part of the one who receives the demand; often a feature of disturbed family relationships.

Laing, R., *Knots* (Penguin, 1972). **Satir, V.**, *Conjoint Family Therapy* (Science and Behaviour Books, Palo Alto, Calif., 1967).

See also: MANIPULATION.

DOUBT

Doubt is the state of withholding assent from both a proposition and its contradictory. As such it differs from disbelief which is a positive conviction of the falsity of a proposition. Methodical doubt has been used as a way of discovering the starting-point of philosophy and is thus to be distinguished from either an extreme philosophy of doubt (Pyrrhonism) or a moderate one (Scepticism). Similarly it is customary to distinguish between the various objects of doubt as theoretical and practical; and perhaps one ought also to distinguish between facts and values. However, religious doubt will then be a special kind of phenomenon inasmuch as it transcends both distinctions.

Practically it is often difficult to distinguish doubt from dogmatic negation, and scepticism in matters of morals can often be ally of moral failure. Writing to an inquirer Newman once remarked that doubt was a temptation. However, Newman was far from saying that a proposition assented to is not capable of being doubted, and in his famous work on assent he seems to think that it can be almost a virtue – as when he speaks of investigation as a duty for educated people. What he did see was that there is a doubting which 'excludes believing' and is already 'lost faith'. This doubt that is incompatible with assent is the doubt that puts us outside the circle of believers. It is most illuminating to see how Newman thus speaks of both the dubitability and the indubitability of assent. It is possible, he says, 'without disloyalty to our convictions to examine their grounds, even though in the event they are to fail under the

76

examination, for we have no suspicion of this failure'. It is thus important to see doubt as an issue of personal rather than merely intellectual importance. Even as an intellectual matter it has a personal dimension as an act of will. It is all too easy for us to imagine that the philosopher has done all that is necessary whereas proficiency in doubt is a task which I have to achieve and it is a task that lasts a lifetime.

In the New Testament doubt is often (e.g. Rom. 4.20f., 14.23; Jas. 1.6–8) seen as lack of faith, a lack of trust in the work that God will achieve. Similarly there can be a form of doubt that spells danger to theology, being all the more insidious in that it can be thought to be part and parcel of theology itself. So it is crucial to distinguish between the doubt that is an integral part of theology and the other that is an unnatural threat to theology. It is not clear whether doubt is a necessary part of theology because of the nature of the subject as a concern with an eternal mystery or whether it is because our theology is *theologia ektypa viatorum*. What is clear is that there is nothing to be gained from trying to escape this doubt and we must make it a life's work. By contrast, the second type of doubt is not merely to be avoided; it is to be combatted. The theologian must confess that he is a doubter of the second unnatural species but he should be sincerely *ashamed* of his doubt. The vision of the Kingdom is a vision of doubt overcome and the certainties of God's own life established.

Finally, we must return to the area of personal religion. Just as Newman saw the doubt that is incompatible with assent to be that which places us outside the circle of believers, so it must be said that it is in a man's *individual* existence that doubt especially assails him. It is not for nothing that we are enjoined by Scripture not to neglect the assembly of the saints (Heb. 10.25). Within the gathered group there is less room for doubt, and certainties are reinforced; but, though 'no man is an ilande, intire of itself', neither does he escape the solitude that makes up a significant part of his day any more than he can escape the inevitable solitude of his own subjectivity. Personal religion is a constant encounter and engagement with doubt, and as one's awareness of limitation increases with knowledge so too does doubt. The more we know of God the stronger and more subtle the attack from doubt. In the Genesis story there is a clear illustration of the way doubt can indeed be the temptation that Newman described; for the fall springs from that doubt of God's purpose which the serpent succeeds in creating. Just as in social existence any doubt which is not the product of neurosis is overcome by the social exchange of friendship, so can religious doubt be overcome in personal religion. The 'meaning of prayer' is precisely that we can be so schooled by this communication with God that God's communication with us reveals us those things which had been doubted.

To have spelt out something about the spiritual life and the theologian's task is to have shown something of what pastoral care will seek to enable. A final word about the role doubt plays in the pastor's and counsellor's own attitude is now necessary. The pastor's authority is the objectively personal nature of faith and what he aims to elicit in his pastoral care is a free relation that cannot live in the context of dogmatism. Confronted by uncertainty there is at times a need for us to emphasize the wisdom of a reduction of belief since it is not in a multiplicity of beliefs but in their unity within the Godhead that salvation lies. Finally, in any counselling, honesty and empathy (q.v.) are essentials, and it is only by sitting where his congregations sit that the pastor can care for them.

Barth, K., *Evangelical Theology: an Introduction* (Fontana, 1965). Guntrip, H., *Psychology for Ministers and Social Workers* (Allen & Unwin, 3rd edn, 1971). Lake, F., *Clinical Theology* (Darton Longman & Todd, 1966). Newman, J.H., *The Grammar of Assent* (Longman Green, 1891). Rogers, C., *Client-centred Therapy* (Mifflin, Boston, 1951). Rogers, C., *On Becoming a Person* (Constable, 1974). Wright, F., *The Pastoral Nature of Ministry* (SCM, 1980)

J. HEYWOOD THOMAS

See also: ANXIETY; FAITH.

DREAMS

Psychic phenomena normally, though not exclusively, experienced during sleep (q.v.).

Almost all cultures have found dreams fascinating, significant and mysterious. The Bible contains some early examples of dream interpretation (e.g. Gen. 40; Dan. 2). Most current use of dreams in pastoral care derives from the psychoanalytic or Jungian traditions. Sigmund Freud, the founder of psychoanalysis (q.v.), spoke of the dream as the 'royal road to the unconscious'. In the tradition he originated, the dream is regarded as a disguised statement in which many 'mechanisms' including *displacement* (in which, for example, one person may stand in for another) or *condensation* (in which two or more figures may be fused in one) twist and complicate a primary message from the unconscious part of the mind (the 'latent content' of the dream). The common picture of Freudians as regarding every long or hollow object as a symbol of the male or female genitals respectively is a caricature, but there is an expectation that the unconscious will be preoccupied with body-parts and sexuality, and with the dreamer's early relationships to parents and siblings.

Jungian psychology holds that dreams are *not* disguised statements, but are accurate statements in a symbolic language. The Freudian concern with the body, sex and early relationships is not rejected, but in addition Jungians would claim that the dream is overridingly concerned for the total life-journey of the dreamer (the 'individuation process') and may also bring up issues to do with culture, spirituality and religion. Understanding of the dream in both traditions derives from the associations of the dreamer, but Jungians would also emphasize that some dream images can only be understood by connecting them with the general heritage of symbolism, in mythology, folklore, fairy tales, etc, and that some 'big dreams' have reference not only to the dreamer himself but to his people or to some group of which he is a member (*see also* VISIONS). It is likely that in practice the difference between these two approaches is less great than it sounds in theory.

It is sometimes said that pastoral workers who are not psychotherapists should be wary of taking an interest in dreams that are told to them: dreams 'go too deep'. This view fails to take into account that it is often a dream which disturbs or challenges people into starting on the next development in their lives, and they may have a strong need to tell it, and to talk about their thoughts in connection with it. Two things should be borne in mind: (1) that there is no 'correct solution' to a dream, and to think one knows it is an unwarranted arrogance; and (2) that to tell a dream is a peculiarly intimate form of communication, and the way in which it is done is often as revealing as the dream itself. In particular, in a counselling relationship, the dream a person chooses to tell will often reflect something about his or her feelings towards the counsellor.

Freud, S., *The Interpretation of Dreams* (1900); in the standard edn of the *Complete Psychological Works of Sigmund Freud*, vols. 4–5 (Hogarth, 1953). **Hall, James A.,** *Jungian Dream Interpretation* (Inner City Books, Toronto, 1983). **Jung, C.G.,** *Dreams* (Routledge, 1982). **Sharpe, Ella,** *Dream Analysis* (Hogarth, 1937).

DAVID BLACK

See also: IMAGINATION; VISIONS.

DRUG ABUSE
See: ADDICTION.

DYING
The process by which the transition from being alive to the state of being dead is effected.

This transition may be virtually instantaneous (as with sudden death) or it may happen gradually (as with natural ageing or chronic illness). Establishing the point of death has recently necessitated a redefinition of clinical death (*see* DEATH: DEFINITIONS). This article is concerned with the time prior to that point, the response of the dying and of those offering pastoral care.

The dying person is faced with the necessity of letting go of family, friends, job, lifestyle and ultimately of life itself. In many ways the dying grieve for the impending loss of their own life and may, therefore, exhibit such reactions as denial, shock, numbness, bargaining, tears, anger, remorse, sadness and withdrawal, all of which one may identify in the reactions of the relatives before and after the death has occurred (*see* BEREAVEMENT). The response of the dying person commences when he or she knows, or suspects, that they are dying. This may be in response to direct information, intuition, the development of symptoms or the reactions of other people. Diagnosis of terminal illness may raise the question 'to tell or not to tell', with issues of confidentiality (q.v.) and trust (q.v.). Pastoral care centres on our preparedness to get close to those who are dying, discovering what they know and wish to know, and then having the courage to share reality with them or letting them tell us. In this way the dying may feel it is safe to express and share some of the fears and anxieties that they may have. Ideally this

relationship will be formed before the final stages of the person's life.

1. *Some of the commoner fears and anxieties*:
(1) Fear of loneliness, pain and suffering. Pain isolates and demoralizes and many fear they will not cope well. A variety of approaches may be needed including medication, information about causes and the involvement of the patient in his or her own management. Requests to end life prematurely are often challenging the quality of care given. Whilst we all have to die our own death, many of the attendant fears can be lessened if we feel that someone else is able to be there and prevent the isolation becoming acute.
(2) Loss of dignity and self control. Many people may fear loss of control over various bodily functions with accompanying loss of dignity. Regression to a child-like state and loss of independence may quickly sap morale. Although it may be beguiling to regress and be cared for, it can become irritating and smothering. Relatives may find it both satisfying and annoying and this can heighten any previous ambivalence in the relationship. The side-effects of treatment may also change the appearance and leave the dying person asking, 'Who am I?'
(3) Loss of family, friends, identity and one's body. 'I am a burden to you all,' may reflect the feeling that you are not who you were and that you are already 'dying in little bits'. The dying person may ask for no visitors, so as not to be seen in an altered state. There may be anger that one's body has let one down, or that others are so fit and well. Withdrawal and quietness are part of letting go of the family, and the dying may sleep or not be very communicative. Relatives need to 'give permission' to the dying to die and allow the letting go. People may have financial affairs to sort out, a will to write, things to say to each other, and old scores may need to be settled. An important part in restoring dignity is encouraging the dying person to have a say concerning the care arrangements and the place where he or she is to die. Cultural and religious factors will affect the way in which some people let go, e.g. a Buddhist may refuse drugs which might cloud the mind, in order to prepare for death by meditation, since the quality of the next reincarnation will depend in the way the present life ends. Many Christians will wish to see a minister in order to prepare properly

for death and to avail themselves of the ministry of word and sacrament.

(4) Fear of the unknown, or letting go into what? Here one has to consider the importance of hope (q.v.) and any understanding, or misunderstandings, about life after death. Many people are more afraid of the act of dying than of being dead and may seek reassurance about what they may have to face. Some may fear a punitive God and the prospect of judgement, whilst others may look forward to meeting God, whom they love, and others who have gone before them.

2. *Suggested pastoral aims*: (1) To reconcile. People frequently need help to re-establish broken relationships with themselves, others and God, through the assurance of forgiveness. (2) To sustain. The ministry of word and sacrament in the Christian Church (and the equivalent spiritual ministry in other faiths) is important if we are to be able to endure and transcend what is happening to mind and body and make sense of the experience. In this way the individual may be enabled to grow and attain true health/salvation. Such growth may only be achieved through dying and death. (3) To guide. Many people will rightly look to the religious leader, and others who practise their faith, for guidance both in what they do and in their understanding of God, and the after-life.

3. *Pastoral responses*. (1) The dying may wish to hear Bible reading and prayer, using familiar passages in a particular version. It is important to pray *with* not *over* the patient, whether conscious or not. (2) Baptism of adults as well as babies may be appropriate, in which case confirmation may be part of the rite. (3) The desire to 'put things right' may require a formal act of confession (q.v.) and absolution as an important part of letting go of the past. (4) Last receiving of holy com-

munion (q.v.) (known as *viaticum*, i.e. provision for the journey) may be appropriate. It may be accompanied by anointing (q.v.) and laying on of hands. It is important to liaise with hospital staff, GP, chaplain and family. (5) Marriage, by Archbishop's licence or Registrar General's licence is permitted *in extremis* only if the dying person cannot be moved to a place licensed for weddings. (6) Commendatory prayers at the time of the death should express confidence in Christ and his saving work, and commend the dying to God's mercy and love. Non-Christians may have similar affirmations of faith at this time. (7) Last offices – preparing for the disposing of the dead vary between cultures. The next-of-kin should be asked if they have any requests. In the case of the Jewish and Muslim communities, nursing staff should have no direct contact with the deceased, nor should they wash the body since this is done ritually.

Sensitivity and flexibility in our pastoral care, together with attention to our feelings and anxieties about relating to the dying, should enable us to give to the dying the space to face death in their own way and to facilitate letting go of this final part of their life.

Ainsworth-Smith, I. and Speck, P., *Letting Go: Caring for the Dying and the Bereaved* (SPCK, 1983). Burton, L., *Care of the Child Facing Death* (Routledge, 1974). Gordon, R., *Dying and Creating: a Search for Meaning* (Society of Analytical Psychology, 1978). Hospital Chaplaincies Council, *Our Ministry and Other Faiths* (CIO, 1983). Kübler-Ross, E., *On Death and Dying* (Tavistock, 1970).

PETER W. SPECK

See also: AGEING; BEREAVEMENT; DEATH: DEFINITIONS; DEATH: MEANING.

EDUCATION
See: CLINICAL PASTORAL EDUCATION;
HEALTH EDUCATION; LEARNING;
NURTURE; PASTORAL CARE IN SCHOOLS;
SCHOOL CHAPLAINCY; TRAINING METHODS.

EGO
In psychoanalysis (q.v.) that area of the psyche which is rational and self-conscious, but beset by anxiety (q.v.).

Freud, S., *New Introductory Lectures in Psychoanalysis* (Penguin, 1973), Lecture 31.

EMOTION
Involuntary experiential state usually involving disruption of normal planned functioning and typically accompanied by one or more of: autonomic response, facial expression, intense behaviour (approach or withdrawal), and magnified perception of the object of the emotion caused by heightened attention.

Although 'emotion' is easily recognized by people in their day-to-day activities, psychologists have found it difficult to agree on a definition for the term. A recent survey, for example (Kleinginna and Kleinginna 1981) lists 92 distinct definitions. Perhaps this problem relates to the fact that emotional experience is essentially under the control of systems to which conscious awareness has no direct access.

In ordinary language, there are roughly one hundred and fifty emotional terms, many of them synonymous, but several others representing subtle differences in the characteristics of the response described (Davitz 1969). Psychological theory, in contrast, usually reduces the variety of emotional experience to a basic set of six or so categories (Tomkins 1962), namely anger, happiness, sadness, fear, disgust, and surprise. According to this view, any other distinct emotional experiences are combinations or blends of these primary emotions (Izard 1977).

Emotion is often treated as a primitive, disruptive response which interferes with normal rational function. It is important to realize, however, that emotion can also serve as an organizing principle for behaviour.

Indeed, many would argue that each and every activity is accompanied by some degree of affective response and that it is impossible in practice to disentangle cognitive and emotional aspects of behaviour. A case should also be made for the positive influence of many emotional reactions (e.g. hope, love, dedication). Emotion is, however, traditionally contrasted with reason: mental activity can be thought of as having three distinct aspects, namely; cognition (reason), affection (feeling or emotion), and conation (motivation). This trinity of mind dates back to the early eighteenth century (Hilgard 1980).

In many ways, emotion can be seen as a private experience, which can never be fully shared with anyone else. Nevertheless, knowledge of the person's interpretation of his/her present situation, along with access to facial expression, overt behaviour, and non-verbal communication channels (tone of voice, posture, gestures, etc.) in a face-to-face encounter often allows fairly accurate empathic judgement (Zuckerman *et al.* 1979). In fact, there is evidence that these sources of information aid appraisal of one's own emotional state under certain circumstances (Laird 1974), so that to some extent the person making the judgement and the person having the emotional experience rely on similar kinds of information in decisions about characterizing emotions.

It is also worth mentioning that groups of people may 'collectively' experience an emotion by virtue of their common interpretation of the prevailing situation. Under these circumstances, the reaction may be intensified by perceptions of the emotional state of the others sharing the experience, and empathic reactions to these perceived responses (e.g. grief may become more intense as a function of the simultaneous distress of others). Secondly, there is evidence that crowding results in increased physiological arousal, which in turn heightens emotional responsivity, so that emotions may be more intense and volatile in situations where physical proximity to other people is high (consider, for example, the passions aroused at football matches). Thus, 'emotion' may be considered as a collectively as well as individually experienced phenomenon.

Davitz, J.R., *The Language of Emotion* (Academic Press, New York, 1969). **Hilgard, E.R.**, 'The Trilogy of Mind: Cognition, Affection, Conation' (*Journal for the History of the Behavioural Sciences*, 1, 1980), pp. 107–17. **Izard, C.E.**, *Human Emotions* (Plenum Press, New York, 1977). **Kleinginna Jr, P.R.** and **Kleinginna, A.M.**, 'A Categorized List of Emotion Definitions, with Suggestions for a Consensual Definition' (*Motivation and Emotion*, 5, 1981), pp. 345–79. **Laird, J.D.**, 'Self-attribution of Emotion: the Effects of Expressive Behavior on the Quality of Emotional Experience' (*Journal of Personality and Social Psychology*, 29, 1974), pp. 475–86. **Tomkins, S.S.**, *Affect, Imagery, Consciousness*; vol. 1: *The positive affects* (Springer, New York, 1962). **Zuckerman, M.** *et al.*, 'Posed and Spontaneous Communication of Emotion via Facial and Vocal Cues' (*Journal of Personality*, 47, 1979) pp. 712–33.

BRIAN PARKINSON

See also: ANGER; ANXIETY; EMPATHY; PAIN.

EMPATHY

The projection of one's feelings intellectually and emotionally into an object of contemplation in order fully to comprehend the object or person (cf. Greek: *empatheia*; German: *einfühlung – ein* (= in) + *fühlung* (= feeling).

The earliest use of this term in person-to-person counselling/pastoral care is probably C.R. Shaw's *The Jack Roller* (Chicago 1930) in describing work with problem boys. Contrasted with sympathy which is 'the attempt through imagination to put oneself in another person's place with all the fallacies which this necessarily involves' (p. 194), empathy enables the worker to see his client's life 'as the boy conceives it, rather than as an adult might imagine it . . . by entering into [the boy's] experience'. Sympathy projects categories from experience so that others feel that their situations are being made to fit our ready references, that the words are being received but the hearer is not grasping what it feels like to be them. Empathy is seldom instant and may involve a painful groping. 'To get inside them and live in them' (Lee 1968, p. 67). 'To understand the other from within rather than from without, yet to carry into the identification [the counsellor's] own strength and maturity' (ibid. p. 46).

Rogers (1959, p. 210) offered a technical definition of empathy as the ability to 'per-ceive the internal frame of reference of another with accuracy and with the emotional components and meanings which pertain thereto, *as if* one were the other person but without ever losing the *as if* condition'. Rogers linked empathy with genuineness and unconditional regard as essential qualities in counselling if a client is going to 'move away from a static fixed unfeeling impersonal type of functioning . . . towards a fluid changing acceptant experiencing of . . . feelings . . . and more realistic relationships to self, others and the environment' (1961, p. 66). Truax and Carkhuff (1967) called empathy, genuineness and acceptance (q.v.) the therapeutic triad, defining empathy as 'sensitivity to current feelings and the verbal facility to communicate this understanding'. Carkhuff produced an 'empathic understanding scale' and Truax an 'accurate empathy scale' with which to test specific counselling. Although raters using audio or video tape can produce different assessments, and to attempt to quantify empathy may be 'like using counting techniques to measure the level of love between two people' (Hackney 1978), the scales provide useful guidelines in learning empathic communication.

According to D.W. Winnicott (Davis & Wallbridge 1981), empathy originates in the parent's necessary sensitivity to the unspoken need of the speechless child; for mothers a way of life, and a component in all human relationships where there is a desire to be understood and responded to at depth. A sensible parent tries to grasp how a child feels and to see how the child can be enabled to solve his own problem. Sympathy can swamp a relationship or undermine confidence and be more emotionally satisfying to the sympathizer than supportive to the object of sympathy. In short, sympathy is feeling *for* someone in a shallow way that is inappropriate for pastoral care, while empathy is feeling *with* the object of care and requires accurate movement into his or her inner world. The extent, complexity and often contradictoriness of the other's situation is sensed while the carer remains separate and unintrusive, testing and retesting what it feels like to be in his or her shoes but avoiding walking off in them.

Winnicott argues that reliable empathy also arises from experiencing the mending of failure in full relatedness. A mother's mind will drop the baby, but such 'relative (not gross) human failures are necessary for the mother's reliability to be communicated to her infant' (Davis and Wallbridge 1981, p. 120). Winnicott postulates a necessary readaptation after the absolute dependency of the first six months of a child's life. If the mother continues to anticipate the infant's need by near total empathy she may force her child to regress or to stage a rejection. 'One minute [children] are merged with their mothers and require empathy, while the next they are separated from her and if she knows their needs in advance she is dangerous' (1960). Similarly the final service that the genuinely empathic counsellor performs is to fail the total expectation of the client so that conscious acceptance of a realistically imperfect relationship is internalized as a reliable interdependent separateness and counselling can be brought to an end.

Carkhuff, R.R., *Helping and Human Relations*, vols. 1 and 2 (Holt, Rinehart & Winston, New York, 1969). Davis, M. and Wallbridge, D., *Boundary and Space: An Introduction to the Work of D.W. Winnicott* (Penguin, 1981). Hackney, H.L., 'The Evolution of Empathy' (*Personnel and Guidance Journal*, 57, 1978), pp. 35–9. Lee, R.S., *Principles of Pastoral Counselling* (SPCK, 1968). Rogers, C.R., *On Becoming a Person* (Houghton Mifflin, Boston, 1961); in S. Koch (ed.), *Psychology: a Study of a Science* (McGraw-Hill, New York, 1959), pp. 184–256; 'Empathic: an Unappreciated Way of Being' (*Counselling Psychologist*, 21, 1975), pp. 91–103. Truax, C.B., 'A Scale for the Measurement of Accurate Empathy' (*Psychiatric Institute Bulletin*, 1, 12, University of Wisconsin, 1961). Truax, C.B. and Carkhuff, R.R., *Towards Effective Counselling and Psychotherapy Training and Practice* (Aldine Press, Chicago, 1967).

R.M. SMYTHE

See also: CLIENT-CENTRED THERAPY; COMMUNICATION; LISTENING.

ENCOUNTER GROUPS

Encounter groups have as their aim the fulfilment of human potential in the terms of humanistic psychology.

Such groups, unlike those operating on principles derived from conventional psychotherapy (q.v.), presuppose a membership which is 'healthy' and have as their goal, not the treatment of a 'sick' person, but the growth of members through a climate of trust (q.v.), and the use of a variety of techniques designed to enhance openness with oneself and others. The Encounter-group movement originated in the United States in the 1950s,

from a confluence of three streams of research into human behaviour.

The first stream was a posthumous contribution from the work of Kurt Lewin, a founder of the 'T'-group movement, whose groups were initially concerned with helping executives in industry to become aware of the inter-personal dynamics present in all groups and organizations. Later, the 'T'-group leaders became convinced that the 'feed-back' experience in their groups led to personal and inter-personal change in their members.

The second stream flowed from the investigations of Abraham Maslow (*see* SELF ACTUALIZATION, PEAK EXPERIENCES) into the possibility of what he called 'full self-actualization' and the realization of human potential. He believed that many more human beings are capable of going behind the satisfaction of basic physiological and inter-personal needs than is commonly supposed, and are able to achieve high degrees of creative attainment.

The third stream was provided by Carl Rogers (*see* CLIENT-CENTRED THERAPY) who, from his understanding of psychotherapy, believed that neurotic persons were basically healthy and have within themselves resources which can bring about change. For this to come about they must be provided with an environment of 'empathy' (q.v.), respect, and non-persecutory confrontation.

During the 1960s other influences entered into what was now being called the human potential movement, and the development of different therapies, such as the Gestalt (q.v.), Bio-energetic and Primal approaches. During this period Encounter groups often saw themselves as the heralds of a new age, and the answer to personal and spiritual alienation.

These groups present themselves in many different forms, some employing highly structured experiences, others such as those led by Carl Rogers, being largely non-directive. Styles of leadership can be markedly varied: one leader being confrontational and charismatic; another functioning in a 'low-visibility' manner and getting the group to make initiatives. But despite differences in the approach to leadership, structure and technique, certain common attitudes exist. They all focus upon the awareness of 'feeling' rather than intellectual understanding. This does not imply a denial of the crucial importance of thinking but is a deliberate concentration on the under-developed awareness of feeling in Western society. All groups stress the importance of 'here and now' rather than a 'there and then' preoccupation. All groups focus upon 'real' communications, rather than drawing attention to 'projections' (see TRANSFERENCE, DEFENCE MECHANISMS). The belief is that real communication will evaporate projections.

The Encounter-group movement has exercised some influence upon conventional psychotherapy, especially in group psychotherapy (q.v.) and family counselling (q.v.) where a number of its techniques are increasingly used. It has also influenced some human relations training organizations connected with the churches, such as the Richmond Fellowship and the Clinical Theology Association (see CLINICAL THEOLOGY). In the United States, the Growth Group, bearing many affinities to Encounter, has become a significant part of the life of some churches.

Reliable methods of assessing the effects of psychotherapeutic activity are notoriously difficult to discover, since the criteria of improvement to which therapists and clients appeal are often variable and subjective. But the investigation into the effects of Encounter-group experience related by Lieberman, Yalom and Miles (1973) is generally considered to be reliable. In one study upon which they report, it is considered that actual positive change occurred in about one-third of participants, one-third remaining unchanged, and about one third appearing to change for the worse in varying degrees. They also believe that there is a connection between adverse effects and a highly confrontational style of leadership.

The emphatically optimistic approach to personal development, often presented by Encounter-group leaders, could be seen as both naive and yet welcome: naive in the sense that sin and alienation from the source of our being and its creation is always present in human experience; welcome in the sense that religious faith calls for abundant life in body, mind and spirit.

Clinebell, H., *Contemporary Growth Therapies* (Abingdon, Nashville, 1981). Lieberman, M.A. *et al.*, Encounter Groups: First Facts (Basic Books, New York, 1973). Shaffer, J.B.P. and Galinsky, M.D., *Models of Group Therapy and Sensitivity Training* (Prentice-Hall, New Jersey, 1974).

JOHN GRAVELLE

See also: GROUP COUNSELLING AND PSYCHOTHERAPY; SUPPORT GROUPS.

ETHICS, PROFESSIONAL

Obligations of a moral nature which govern the practice of vocational groups and their members in making the specialized knowledge or skill professed available to the public; including, but extending beyond, professional etiquette, *viz.* conventions governing mutual relations within the profession.

The marks of a recognized profession are these: common possession of a body of knowledge and skill which practitioners are expected to develop, enhance and transmit to new aspirants; extensive autonomy under the law, conditional upon the exercise of oversight and discipline over identified members; recognition of a corporate ethics of conduct both between members and between each and the client or public; and entitlement in return to social satisfactions in status and material reward. Despite individual lapses and the swellings of corporate self-interest which have provoked cynics from Aristotle (*Nichomachean Ethics* V. vii. 13) to George Bernard Shaw ('All professions are conspiracies against the laity'), professional ethics are among the sinews of a free society; they sustain and extend (when they do not abuse) reliance on trust (q.v.); they limit coercive regulation and state control where human interests are best served by free and privileged communication.

Contemporary thinking on the subject stems from Dorothy Emmet's *Rules, Roles and Relations*, where she elucidated moralities attached to roles. The professional is a person of a special kind, made distinctive by the knowledge or skill which he or she possesses, and which he or she is both expected and authorized to exercise undeflected by self-interest or personal idiosyncrasy. The ethics are a complex of obligations: primarily to the client; generally to the whole society whose conventions and reliance upon trust sustain the professional relationship with the client; internally to colleagues in the profession, to maintain their corporate integrity and repute; and, over all, to the canons of truth proper to each scientific discipline or skill (Welbourn 1981). The ethics are first a corporate possession of the professional body; whether coded or conventional; and thence in the keeping of each practitioner, informing his or her conscience when occasion requires. They presuppose a relationship of covenant (*see* CONTRACT AND COVENANT) with the client: a commitment on the one side to serve the client's interest to the utmost of ability, and, on the other, to observe the discipline of the accepted regimen. Within this relationship there may exist a contractual relationship when a consideration, normally a fee (*see* PAYMENTS), is interposed. But in its ethical aspects the professional relationship is not contractual; some obligations stand, whether they are reciprocated or not (Dunstan 1979; Dunstan and Seller 1983; Reeck 1982).

Among the common features are these: (1) The client's interest is paramount up to the point where its promotion would gravely threaten an interest vital to society. (2) Confidences are to be kept inviolate, in that there must be no improper disclosure (*see* CONFIDENTIALITY). (3) There must be no betrayal, or improper personal advantage taken, of a position of trust. (4) No private or sectional advantage may be taken of the power which the professional worker has over clients in their vulnerability or dependency (q.v.). (5) A professional adviser is answerable for the advice he or she gives. (6) The induction of new members requires them to gain experience with actual clients – those responsible for their induction have a duty of care for those who may be at risk of harm from such inexperienced attention; and only those capable of discharging that duty should be entrusted with the responsibility of induction.

It has been pointed out that clergymen and ministers, though traditionally a profession, imperil their pastoral relationships if they succumb to the formal distancing of themselves, the detachment, which is a mark of some other professional relationships (Martin 1967). This is true, but they imperil also their pastoral standing and their order if they neglect the ground of their professional standing or calling, namely their theology. Despite the elements of professional ethics held in common, professions are discrete disciplines. Practice and the ethics of practice attach to role and context. Hybridization, or the uncritical lifting of norms out of one context into another, can only weaken and confuse. It would be as improper for the priest to ape the role of the doctor or social worker as it would be for them to assume the functions specific to a priest. The co-operation essential to good pastoral care assumes not

interchangeability but difference, in a mutual trust based on respect for the competence of each in his own profession (*see* Dunstan 1970).

Ainsworth-Smith, I. and **Perryman, J.,** 'Hospital Chaplains', in A.S. Duncan *et al.* (eds.), *Dictionary of Medical Ethics* (Darton Longman and Todd, 2nd edn rev. 1981). **Dunstan, G.R.,** 'The Doctor–Patient Relationship', in C. Wood (ed.), *Health and the Family* (Academic Press, 1979); (ed.), *The Sacred Ministry* (SPCK, 1970). **Dunstan, G.R.** and **Seller, M.J.** (eds.), *Consent in Medicine* (King Edward's Hospital Fund, 1983), see Index. **Emmet, D.,** *Rules, Roles and Relations* (Macmillan, 1966). **Franklin, A.W.,** *The Challenge of Child Abuse* (Academic Press, 1977). **Martin, D.,** *A Sociology of English Religion* (SCM, 1967). **Reader,. W.J.,** *The Rise of the Professional Classes in the Nineteenth Century* (Weidenfeld & Nicolson, 1966). **Reeck, D.,** *Ethics for the Professional: a Christian Perspective* (Augsburg, Minneapolis, 1982. **Welbourn, R.B.,** 'Medical Science', in A.S. Duncan *et al.* (eds.), *Dictionary of Medical Ethics* (Darton Longman & Todd, 2nd edn rev. 1981). **Wilson, B.,** *Religion in Secular Society* (Watts, 1966); 'The Paul Report' (*Crucible*, Feb. 1965), pp. 96f.

G.R. DUNSTAN

See also: CONFIDENTIALITY; CONSENT TO TREATMENT; PROFESSIONALISM.

EUCHARIST
See: COMMUNION.

EVANGELISM AND PASTORAL CARE
(1) To bring people to a personal faith in Jesus Christ and support them in discipleship. (2) To proclaim the gospel and look after the needs of people. (3) Proclaim the good news by supporting people in crisis. (4) Support people in adversity in order to make them Christians.

The above definitions demonstrate the basic tensions: (1) Does valid evangelism depend on response or is it mere proclamation? (2) Is pastoral care a means of making new Christians or supporting existing ones?

The 1918 Archbishops' *Committee of Enquiry into the Evangelistic Work of the Church* defined evangelism as 'to so present Christ Jesus in the power of the Holy Spirit that men shall come to put their trust in God through Him, to accept Him as their Saviour and to serve Him as their King in the fellowship of His Church.' This was taken over into the 1945 Report *Towards the Conversion of England* and makes the validity of evangelism dependent on its effects. John Stott has rejected this view: 'Evangelism itself is the proclamation of the historical, biblical Christ as Saviour and

Lord, with a view to persuading people to come to him personally and so be reconciled to God' (Anderson and Stransky 1975). Evangelism is proclamation whether there are visible results or not.

Mission and evangelism must not be confused. Mission is a wider concept than evangelism. It is the communication of Jesus Christ to the world. The Church must continually interpret him, avoid misrepresentation, limitation and distortion. Loving care, service to the world and witness to Christ's work (obligations on all Christians) make up mission. Evangelism with them is a part of mission dependent on personal initiative. Within mission, moral issues (q.v.) are encountered, discipline (q.v.) administered and pastoral care (q.v.) exercised. Traditionally polarization has existed between evangelism as personal response and as concern for the world. Since the late 1970s this polarization has been less evident as Evangelicals have demonstrated a greater social conscience and Roman Catholics have given more attention to personal faith in Jesus. The World Council of Churches has stressed contextualization, to see what gospel issues arise in a given situation, treating the gospel in a holistic way. Proclamation by word and life being global, local, personal, social and pastoral. The context provides the means and tool for evangelism and a front-line challenge for pastoral care.

The tension of whether pastoral care is offered in order to convert or whether we convert and then care is seen historically in models of pastoral care (q.v.). Initiatives for evangelism are possible through groups in the Church, confession (q.v.) and counselling (q.v.), as the Church pursues its ministry and worship. Pastoral care has in the main been seen as the role of the ordained ministry, but the more recent emphasis on lay ministry has changed that. Evangelism through local churches has often focused on the visit of a travelling evangelist, when it ought to be an on-going activity. If evangelism is defined in terms of results, it is necessary to resist the danger of unfair emotional pressure which denies people real choice; if it is defined only as proclamation, then care must be taken not to lose the element of challenge that forgiveness and reconciliation (q.v.) are to be found only in Christ.

Dayton and Fraser (1980) distinguish three elements which can usefully be employed in demonstrating the interdependence of evangelism with pastoral care: the *nature* of evangelism as the communication of the Good News; the *purpose* of evangelism – to give groups and individuals a valid opportunity to accept Jesus Christ; the *goal* of evangelism – to persuade men and women to become disciples of Jesus Christ and to serve him in the fellowship of the Church. By its *nature* evangelism is linked to pastoral care through baptism (q.v.), the cross and resurrection (q.v.), the Eucharist, forgiveness, healing (q.v.), and salvation (q.v.); in *purpose* through questions of free choice and determinism (q.v.), repentance (q.v.) and conversion (q.v.); in *goal* in terms of membership of the Church (q.v.). Styles of evangelism, like friendship, celebration, personal, crusade, home-group, all supply opportunities for initiative to bring people to faith in Christ. The motives for pastoral care, however, need to be kept under scrutiny so that support is not withdrawn when a person makes no commitment.

Anderson, G.H. and **Stransky T.F.**, *Mission Trends, no. 2: Evangelisation* (Paulist, New York and Eerdmans, Grand Rapids, 1975); for Stott's Lausanne address, see pp. 4–23. **Dayton, E.R.** and **Fraser, D.A.**, *Planning Strategies for World Evangelisation* (Eerdmans, Grand Rapids, 1980). **Douglas, J.D.**, (ed), *Let the Earth Hear His Voice* (Minneapolis World Wide Publications, 1975). **Newbigin, L.**. *The Open Secret* (SPCK, 1978). **Watson, David**, *I Believe in Evangelism* (Hodder, 1976).

CHARLES H. HUTCHINS

See also: BIBLE: PASTORAL USE; CONVERSION; MEMBERSHIP OF CHURCH: PREPARATION.

EVIL

In Christian theology, two main types of evil are usually distinguished. *Natural evil* is the suffering or frustration caused to sentient creatures by the processes of the natural world. *Moral evil* is suffering or harm caused by the free and responsible acts of rational creatures.

There are four main theories used by theists to account for the existence of evil. One is that evil does not really exist: that, if seen properly, it is really good, or that it is an illusion. However, it is hard to see severe pain as illusory or really good. Somehow, it must be opposed and eradicated if possible. So this view usually shades into the second, that evil is a necessary part of a very good whole, like seeming imperfections in a painting which contribute to the perfection of the whole. This view is mentioned by Augustine; is espoused by Plotinus in the 'Principle of Plenitude', according to which all degrees of being must exist in a perfect whole, even those with a small amount of goodness and much evil; and is revived by Leibniz, in his doctrine that this is the best of all possible worlds. This view hardly helps those who happen to be caught in the evil bits; and few are convinced that there could not possibly have been a better world. A third view, developed classically by Aquinas, is that evil is a privation of good; the lack of a good proper to something – like blindness in an eye. Again, however, pain does not seem to be just a negative reality; it is rather positive to be regarded as the lack of something. The fourth view is that evil is caused by forces opposed to God: an independent cosmic power; a fallen spiritual being; or the free choices of other people. The problem then is whether such forces are compatible with the existence of an omnipotent creator. Some, like Plato, think that God is not omnipotent but does the best he can with an independent material world. Or, like Whitehead, they may think that the world is made up of many diverse and often conflicting forces, which God simply tries to direct and organize, but can never causally determine. All four views assume that God is good. If God is not good, or is beyond human moral categories, there is no problem of evil; instead, there is the problem of why a morally neutral God should be revered or worshipped.

For most Christians, some view developed from the last three considerations seems most acceptable. We may say that God is omnipotent and does not ever will evil for its own sake. But he wills to create an intelligible universe, and therefore one which operates in accordance with general, mathematically expressible laws. He wills to create rational, free agents, and therefore allows random elements to exist in nature, which will later allow for the growth of freedom. And he wills the universe to be a multiplicity of creative individuals, and therefore permits the conflicts and failures which the emergent character of creativity engenders. In all these aspects of creation, the existence of some natural evil is a necessary condition or consequence of the great goods which God wills. Even an omnipotent being cannot

eliminate them without also eliminating those goods. Moreover, if moral freedom is a great good, God must create the possibility of the choice of moral evil. If it is actualized, his power cannot just obliterate it; but he may turn it to some greater future good.

We may say, then, that evil is parasitic upon good; it can only exist as a condition or consequence of greater goods. Those goods do not have to be the best possible; they need only be great enough to be worth choosing, even at the cost of redeemable evil. But Christians must never fall into the trap of thinking that they can passively accept evil. What is truly necessary must be endured; but, wherever evil can be opposed by human action, it must be opposed; for it is God's will that no evil which *could* be eliminated by creatures should exist. It is doubtless right sometimes to choose the lesser of two evils. But it is never right to choose evil, just because God will somehow bring good out of it (Rom. 3.8); or to permit evil, when it can be eliminated.

Ahern, M.B., *The Problem of Evil* (Routledge, 1971). **Farrer, Austin,** *Love Almighty and Ills Unlimited* (Collins, 1962). **Hick, John,** *Evil and the God of Love* (Fontana, 1968). **Tennant, F.R.,** *Philosophical Theology* (CUP, 1930). **Ward, Keith,** *Rational Theology and the Creativity of God* (Blackwell, 1983).

KEITH WARD

See also: CROSS AND RESURRECTION; EXORCISM; HEAVEN AND HELL; PAIN; SIN; THEODICY.

EXORCISM

'Christian exorcism is the binding of evil powers by the triumph of Christ Jesus, through the application of the power demonstrated by that triumph in and by his Church.'

1. This definition is taken from *Exorcism: the Findings of a Commission Convened by the Bishop of Exeter*. This report has compressed into it much of the historic wisdom of the Church and provides forms of prayer for those authorized to undertake this ministry.

The Bishop (Dr Robert Mortimer) stated in the Foreword to the Report: 'In 1963, I was much disturbed by the unhealthy and near hysterical publicity given by the national press to the question of exorcisms in the Church of England.' This was, in fact, not an isolated tendency, and the trend has continued over the years. Some improvement in the atmosphere has been gained through stress being placed on the healing aspect of this work and the use of the phrase 'the ministry of deliverance from evil'.

Cardinal Suenens provides a further definition, which is of particular relevance in the Roman Catholic setting, when he quotes from *The Dictionnaire de Théologie Catholique*: 'In the strict sense, exorcism is an adjuration addressed to the devil in order to force him to vacate a place, to abandon a situation, or to release a person whom he holds more or less in his power. The adjuration is made either in the form of a command given directly to the devil, but in the name of God or Jesus Christ, or in the form of a supplicatory invocation, addressed to God and to Our Lord, entreating them to order the devil to depart or to ensure that the order is executed.'

2. The experience of the early Church is recorded in the NT, e.g. Acts 13.10. Those who acted to help men or women who were oppressed by the devil were conscious that they were doing so in obedience to Christ, who had himself made this a recognized part of his ministry. The activities of exorcists were familiar to the Jewish people.

Christian exorcism assumes the power of evil as personified in the devil, or in his servants, demons. The power is active in the world and may at times have significant effects on both persons and places. It is, however, always subject to the power of God, who brings light and peace to replace the darkness and confusion of demonic influences. The intention of evil forces is always to distort the human personality, to accentuate its animal potentiality and to prevent recourse to the Holy Spirit.

The consciousness of the early Church, set in a pagan world, of the demonic influences which were part of the contemporary scene was never over-stressed, but was translated into normal liturgical practice, and particularly in Christian initiation. With the growth of infant baptism (q.v.) over the centuries, the practice has been retained in some cases, as, for example, in the Roman Catholic service, but has lapsed in some other forms.

3. Traditionally, within the framework of the historic Church it is the bishop who authorizes those who are to be responsible for exorcism, and no action without this authority should take place unless there is an extreme emergency. In the majority of cases, the exorcist will be a priest, but it can be a lay

person. The ultimate authority to cast out an evil force is from God and whoever exercises it does so as his servant. It is natural and appropriate for the Christian exorcist to do so in the name of Christ.

Both persons and places are affected. It should always be remembered that exorcism involves a direct and binding command to an evil presence to leave, without harming anyone, to go to its own place and to remain there for ever. Care should always be taken, therefore, to ensure that it is an evil force which must be disposed of rather than, in the case of buildings or places, the effects of unrest or grief which may have been caused in the past. In all cases when people are affected, pastoral after-care is essential.

While, as some may claim, religion decays, superstition flourishes and, in recent years, this has had a direct effect resulting in requests for help from those who have experimented with spiritualism, ouija boards, black magic, witchcraft and satanism. All of these can leave a mark which causes disturbance of the personality, depression, fear and anxiety, and often requires the exercise of an appropriate form of the ministry of deliverance. It cannot be stressed too strongly that involvement in any of these superstitious practices should be avoided. Unfortunately, it is the young who are not infrequently drawn in, and the effects are sometimes made worse by addiction (q.v.) to drugs.

4. It has long been recognized that a ministry in this field requires special training and preparation. Even so, those who exercise it may often need the assistance, through prayer and intercession, of others upon whom reliance can be placed. It would be unwise for any exorcism of a person to take place (other than in a grave emergency) without assistants.

Medical co-operation should always be sought and invited. It is essential that discrimination is made between situations where exorcism may be helpful and those where the most appropriate care is psychiatric treatment. Those who exercise a deliverance ministry should always avoid acting contrary to medical advice, and they should take all steps to establish whether those who say they are afflicted are, or have been, under medical care. Under modern conditions the factor of publicity also needs to be considered. Inevitably, if it is known that a person or place may be affected, the news media are attracted and anything following may be subject to sometimes dramatic and exaggerated statements. It should always be stressed that those who ask for help are entitled to privacy. All that they say must be regarded as confidential and any statements, other than those correcting inaccurate reporting, should be avoided.

Finally, all who undertake this ministry should be aware of the scientific basis of modern knowledge, which should be fully accepted. Nevertheless, it is recurring experience that situations can arise affecting people and places which for their solution require the application of Christ's healing power.

Exorcism: the Findings of a Commission Convened by the Bishop of Exeter (SPCK, 1972). **Jones, C.**, *et al.* (eds.), *The Study of Liturgy* (SPCK, 1978). **Richards, J.**, *But Deliver Us From Evil* (Darton Longman & Todd, 1974); this book provides a very exhaustive bibliography. **Suenens, L-J.**, *Renewal and the Powers of Darkness* (Darton Longman & Todd, 1983).

C.J. Meyer

See also: MAGIC; SPIRITUAL HEALING; SPIRITUALISM/SPIRITISM.

F

FAITH
Trust, belief, commitment, confidence, reliance, especially in relation to God.

1. *Bible.* In the OT, faith is the human response required by God's primary speech and action. It is first of all communal, Israel's faithfulness to the covenant (*see* CONTRACT AND COVENANT) with her God, Yahweh, who is himself faithful. It involves fear as well as trust (q.v.), hope and confidence in God's promises, exclusive worship of and loyalty to him and obedience to his law. In the NT, the OT meanings are continued, with a new reference to the gospel of Jesus Christ. Faith now includes acknowledging Jesus as Lord and Saviour, believing him, accepting the gospel, joining the community of his followers by baptism (q.v.), persevering in loyalty to him and expecting his return.

2. *Tradition.* The biblical elements were taken up in various ways. One common distinction was between the act of faith (*fides qua creditur* = the faith by which one believes) and the content of faith (*fides quae creditur* = the faith which is believed). The latter was made explicit through a complex process including: writing the books of the NT and their acceptance as the canon with the OT; summarizing essentials in 'the rule of faith', later developed into various creeds; decisions of church councils; writings of church fathers; and developments in worship and ethical teaching. Augustine's *Confessions* was a classic on the act of faith.

Medieval theologians explored both aspects of faith with rational, theoretical precision and much pastoral wisdom, partly due to experience of the confessional and self-reflective forms of spirituality. The Reformation centred faith anew in Jesus Christ, and insisted on its gift character. Salvation was through the free grace of God by faith in Jesus Christ, contrasted with reliance on works or any other preconditions (e.g. 'justification by faith alone', 'the cross tests everything'). A series of 'confessions' set out the content of faith.

3. *Modernity.* The post-Enlightenment era has seen many challenges to faith and attempts to respond to these. There were reductive accounts of faith (in biological, psychological, sociological, economic and philosophical terms). Some divided knowledge (often understood in empirical, scientific terms) from faith (often seen as a private value judgement, alongside morality and aesthetics). Secularization of society reinforced the privatization and subjectivization of faith. Historical study tended to relativize faith by showing its origins, conditioning and successive forms. The most common sceptical opinion was that faith is a projection of human desires, needs or fears.

Responses have tried variously to establish: the inadequacy of reductive explanations; the content of faith as public knowledge; the roots of faith in human nature and experience (in feeling awareness, conscience, freedom, finitude or questioning); the need to understand faith by becoming involved in relating to God; and the dependence of faith in the free initiative of God in communicating himself.

Mainstream Christian consensus has aimed to affirm the following positions. Christian faith is given and shaped by its object, the trinitarian God. As God is one than whom none greater can be thought, there is no more comprehensive standpoint by which faith can be neutrally verified or falsified, but this does not exclude moral and rational discussion of it. It has historical content (especially testimony to Jesus Christ), and involves the social, historical response of discipleship in the Church. It is an act of the whole person, including free discussion, imagination, intellect, feeling, action and suffering, in a giving of self to God and others that responds to God's self-giving in Jesus Christ. Faith is a life-project enabling and calling for repentance, love, trust, courage, hope, joy, obedience and worship. It is worked out in three interrelated dynamics of relationship: with God (most explicit in prayer and worship); with fellow-Christians in the community of faith; and with the world in love, learning, service, evangelism, and dedication to peace, justice and the coming of the Kingdom of God.

4. *Relevant to pastoral care.* If human beings are created for relationship with God, faith is an essential consideration in their care, and each of the above dynamics needs attention. Faith (and its denials or distortions) is intrinsic to issues of fundamental meaning and direction in life, identifying human wholeness and its corruptions, and to recognition of the resources available for dealing with sin (q.v.), misery and other problems. Above all, it gives a horizon in which problems are not ultimate and the response of hope, thanks and praise is most appropriate.

Aquinas, Thomas, *Summa Theologiae* (Blackfriars, 1966). Augustine, *Confessions* (Penguin, 1961). Barth, Karl, *Church Dogmatics* IV.1 (Edinburgh, 1956). Bultmann, R., *Existence and Faith* (Fontana, 1964). Calvin, J., *Institutes of the Christian Religion* (SCM, 1961). Kittel, G., *Theological Dictionary of the New Testament*, vol. VII (Eerdmans, 1965). Lindbeck, G., *The Nature of Doctrine: Religion and Theology in a Postliberal Age* (SPCK, 1984). Rahner, Karl, *Foundations of Christian Faith* (Darton Longman & Todd, 1978). Schleiermacher, F., *The Christian Faith* (Harper, 1963).

DAVID F. FORD

See also: DOUBT; HOPE; TRUST.

FAITH HEALING
See: SPIRITUAL HEALING.

FAMILY COUNSELLING
See: MARRIAGE AND FAMILY: CARE AND COUNSELLING.

FAMILY PLANNING
Fecundity is essential to the survival of any living species. Among animals, natural forces determine the population of any species at any given time in history. Human beings are subject to some of these forces but fertile couples can also control their numbers by choice. They can comply with nature by observing the biblical command, 'Be fruitful, and multiply,' (Gen. 1.28), or plan the size of their families by spacing their children. They can do this, either by preventing conception, or by destroying the products of conception before, or after, birth.

Conception can only be prevented in fertile people by ensuring that ova and spermatazoa do not meet. Total abstinence from sexual intercourse, other than for the express pur-

pose of procreation, is, therefore the safest way of limiting reproduction. Partial abstinence, by refraining from intercourse during the time each month when a woman is fertile because she has ovulated, is used by many couples as a 'rhythm method of natural birth control'. Individual ovulation times are not easy to determine, so this method is far less safe than total abstinence but is widely used by people who have religious, moral or aesthetic objections to other forms of contraception. These are the only two methods of contraception officially permitted by the Roman Catholic Church.

More effective methods of family planning depend on preventing fertilization, either by placing a temporary or permanent barrier between the sperm and the egg, as in the use of spermicides, penile sheaths, cervical caps and sterilization, or by interfering with the function of the generative organs, as in the use of oral or injectible hormones to inhibit the production of ova or spermatazoa. Such methods are acceptable to a great many people including religious couples, and are widely used by those who want to limit their childbearing for health and socio-economic reasons, or because of the problems associated with over-population.

Other modern methods of birth control, such as the use of intra-uterine devices or the 'morning-after-pill', are less acceptable to many people because they rely partly on the destruction of the fertilized ovum, either by preventing its implantation, or by causing an early abortion after implantation. Abortion and infanticide are sometimes used as methods of family planning, but they are not acceptable to most advocates of family planning because of their obviously destructive nature.

Further information is available from the Family Planning Association, 27 Mortimer Street, London W1, or the International Planned Parenthood Federation, 18–20 Lower Regent Street, London SW1Y 4PW, England.

UNA KROLL

See also: ABORTION; GENETIC COUNSELLING; SEXUALITY, THEOLOGY OF.

FANTASY
An activity of the imagination affecting perception of reality.

In ordinary use, the word 'fantasy' has a slightly belittling quality: 'mere fantasy' is trivial, whimsical; or, as in 'fantasy' fiction, it is just 'escapist'. In psychotherapy, it is used as a technical term, and as such has none of this belittling quality. The distinction is hard to maintain but is extremely important. (In British psychoanalysis the word is often spelt phantasy, in an attempt to maintain this distinction.) In this sense, fantasy is used in two ways:

(1) It refers to the whole imaginative life of the mind, conscious or unconscious, which underlies and structures all thinking and all action. According to the analytic picture, all adult motives and interests, however valid in their own right, are built up on primitive and instinctual desires and pleasures, which are present in the form of fantasy in the adult activity. Contrary to the popular caricature, this view does not entail a diminution of the adult motive. 'Hitler was really just a little boy having tantrums', is not something any competent therapist would be likely to say. But it does imply that the child is seen to be still alive in the adult, and the pleasures, fascinations and fears of adult life are continuous with those of childhood.

(2) Fantasy is also used to refer to a particular piece of this imaginative activity, e.g. 'His fantasy in losing the tennis-match was of losing the competition with his sister for his father's love.' Much fantasy of this sort is unconscious. So long as the adult feeling and behaviour are unproblematic, there is no need to inquire into them further; but if people are bewildered by their feelings, or confused or alarmed by their behaviour, then the picture will often remain incomprehensible to them until they discover the unconscious fantasy, that is to say, discover that to another more primitive part of them the situation is being imagined in quite different, and perhaps quite inappropriate, terms. One means of getting access to fantasy is by way of dreams (q.v.).

It should be mentioned that the English psychoanalyst Donald Winnicott has also used the verbal form, 'fantasying', to describe daydreaming, a split-off and unproductive use of the imagination. This is closer to the ordinary-language use of the word.

Isaacs, S., 'The Nature and Function of Phantasy', in M. Klein, *et al.*, *Developments in Psycho-Analysis* (Hogarth, 1952). **Winnicott, D.W.,** *Playing and Reality* (Tavistock, 1971).

DAVID BLACK

See also: DREAMS; IMAGINATION; PLAY.

FEELINGS
See: EMOTION.

FEES
See: PAYMENTS AND GIFTS.

FEMININITY/MASCULINITY
Those personal characteristics which are believed to differentiate one sex from the other, e.g. empathy, tenderness, ambition, objectivity.

While biological, physiological and anatomical differences between men and women are legion and are probably directly genetic in origin, differences of personality and behaviour are much more problematic. They are difficult to define and measure with accuracy, and there is a great overlap between the sexes; apart from menstruation, pregnancy and lactation, there are few behaviours which are exclusively male or female. Indeed meticulous anthropological fieldwork in this century should have done much to end earlier speculation, or even dogma, by teaching us that differences which appear instinctive in Western society may be absent or even reversed in other societies.

The question, 'What is a man/woman?' is at the heart of pastoral care, and it has been of abiding interest to the human race. The fact that there are almost as many 'solutions' as there are cultures does not deter each from claiming natural law as its basis, usually underpinned by concepts of divine will and providence. Such claims have been seriously challenged in the last fifty years or so, starting with a quest for universal and stable differences between the sexes, based of course on the assumption that they existed and were measurable. A central issue was the 'nature' *v.* 'nurture' debate on the importance of a topping-up process in relation to factors already given. While it is now recognized that biological determinants do provide clues as to parameters of behaviour, there is now a much greater awareness of a complex interactionist process whereby each strand of the developmental process – genetics, upbringing, society at large – contributes to and changes the others. It remains an area of complexity and mystery.

What is clear, however, is that one of the most important tasks in the first three years of life is that of establishing a core identity, of which gender is a central element. We also know that men are dominant in every society in terms of preferential access to whatever is valued in that society, so a woman is involved to some extent in internalizing asymmetries of power and esteem. The influence of such asymmetry has been largely unacknowledged but is now being seriously explored.

Sex remains the single most important peg on which to hang prescriptions about character and behaviour. Acknowledging that the content will change from age to age and place to place, self-labelling as a boy or girl is a basic way of organizing experience and may help a child handle anxieties over sexual differences. Shared expectations about gender-linked human behaviour also provides a choreography which makes communication possible. Its pathogenic qualities occur when people feel that some valued aspect of themselves is inappropriate to their gender and must be discarded or denied. Moreover it seems conceptually unsatisfactory to have different criteria for mental health in each sex: self-assertiveness which enables one to persist and work for what s/he believes in, despite anger or criticism, may be essential for mental health or it may have pathological underpinnings – in either sex.

Ardener (1981) has suggested that there should be a search for the true meaning of 'femineity' (OED: 'quality of womanliness') a specifically female model with essential physical, spiritual and moral attributes, instead of a preoccupation with 'femininity' related to secondary sexual characteristics. Perhaps 'masculinity' should be similarly reclaimed. Others would feel that a search for androgyny (q.v.) would be more conducive to mental health.

In conclusion, many gender patterns, which 30 years ago were considered prefigurated, are now seen as culturally biased. Even those who conclude that femininity/masculinity are archetypal structural patterns of the psyche of no less importance than biology in influencing behaviour, realize that in respect of identifying their specific content an open mind still needs to be retained.

Ardener, S. (ed.), *Defining Females: The Nature of Women in Society* (Croom Helm/Oxford University Women's Studies Committee, 1981). Howell, E. and Bayes, M. (eds.), *Women and Mental Health* (Basic Books, 1981). Miller, J. Baker, *Towards a New Psychology of Women* (Penguin, 1978). Ruether, R. Radford, *Sexism and God-talk* (SCM, 1983). Reid, I. and Wormald, E., *Sex Differences in Britain* (Grant McIntyre, 1982). Whitmont, E.C., 'Re-assessing Femininity and Masculinity: a critique of some traditional assumptions', paper presented at International Congress for Analytical Psychology (1980), edited and reprinted in *Quadrant*.

YVONNE CRAIG

See also: BODY, THEOLOGY OF; SEXISM; SEXUALITY AND SEXUAL DEVELOPMENT; WOMEN: ORDINATION.

FIELD EDUCATION
See: PLACEMENTS.

FORGIVENESS
See: RECONCILIATION.

FREEDOM AND DETERMINISM
As ordinary agents in the world we cannot help believing that we freely choose what we do and that we are responsible for it, whereas there also seems to be various good reasons for saying that all events, including our actions, are predetermined. But how can what is already decided still be open to us to decide? This problem can arise in various contexts. In Christian theology it takes the form of a problem about God's omniscience. If God knows everything then he knows already what I shall do next week or ten years from now. In reply to this some theologians argue that from the fact that God already *knows* what I am going to do it does not follow that he is *making* me choose in that way; to know my future is not to determine my future. It is not immediately clear whether or not that answer is satisfactory, and rather similar considerations arise when the problem is posed in the context of science, as it has been by philosophers from the end of the 16th century to the present day.

It is an assumption of science – indeed, of our everyday way of looking at the world – that every event has a cause. Now human actions are events and will therefore be open to causal explanation, but if a cause is 'what makes an event happen' then human actions must be 'made to happen' and therefore cannot be said to be 'freely chosen'. And, if doubt is cast on the reality of free choice, then doubt must also be cast both on the reality of moral responsibility and on our beliefs about ourselves as human beings; for it is fundamental to those beliefs that our actions are in a basic sense 'ours', that we genuinely initiate them.

Philosophers have reacted in various ways

to this type of argument. Some (often called 'libertarians') have rejected the claim that causality, as so described, reigns supreme. They point out that the rise of quantum mechanics casts doubt on the thesis that nature is a rigidly deterministic system, and they assert that our belief that as agents we genuinely initiate action is as well-founded as our belief in universal causality. Other philosophers (hard-line determinists) are willing to accept the implications of determinism and conclude that human freedom and responsibility are illusions.

The most common approach is that of 'soft' determinism. According to 'soft' determinism, what is illusory is not either our choice or causality, but rather the idea that they are mutually exclusive; actions can be truly said to be *both* freely chosen *and* subject to causal law like other events. There are many versions of this attempt at reconciliation. Most of them include the point, made by Hobbes in the 17th and Hume in the 18th centuries, that causal laws do not compel, but simply record what in fact happens, so actions, although 'caused', are not 'made to happen'. (This is like the theological reply described above.) Some philosophers go on to argue that it is our own desires which are the causes of our actions and they analyse 'choice' in terms of desire. This view is popular in the social sciences. Determinism has recently had a boost from work on artificial intelligence and the plausible analogies between the human brain and complex computers. But ordinary moral agents, with no theological views, are resistant to the idea that they are any sort of machine, no matter how complex. The problem remains unresolved.

Pears, D.F. (ed.), *Freedom and the Will* (Macmillan, 1963). **Raphael, D.D.**, *Moral Philosophy* (Oxford UP, 1981).

R.S. DOWNIE

See also: CONSCIENCE: PHILOSOPHICAL ASPECTS; RESPONSIBILITY.

FRIENDSHIP
See: BEFRIENDING.

FUNERALS
All known cultures and religions have a ritual to mark the fact that a death has occurred and which is associated with the reverent disposal of the bodies of the dead, usually by burial or cremation. Funeral rituals may be secular – like the 'Wake' or the funeral rituals developed in the Soviet Union – or religious, involving a specific acknowledgement of a transcendent dimension and normally an affirmation of hope of life beyond death. There is very little evidence about funerals in the early Church, but such as exists suggests that the first Christians adapted pagan or Jewish rituals to express the Christian hope of resurrection. Down the centuries the emphasis in funeral services has changed, sometimes suggesting that the purpose of the rite was to affect the eternal destiny of the departed, sometimes seizing upon the service as an evangelistic opportunity, sometimes concentrating principally on ministering to the mourners. In some contexts Christian funerals have expressed a strong hope and joy which contrasted with the often sombre funeral rituals of classical paganism. In other contexts there has sometimes been a profound uncertainty about the eternal destiny of the departed dominant in the funeral service. Calvinist reformers tended to strongly discourage funeral rituals, as in Scotland in Knox's *Liturgy* and the *Westminster Directory for Publick Worship of God 1645*. This was, however, balanced by a strong insistence on the preparation of the faithful for their dying – pastoral care took priority over ritual, but the position of the mourners was given scant attention. Such efforts to discourage funeral services have been notably unsuccessful.

Funerals may appropriately be regarded as rites of passage in which there is public recognition that a person has died, and that the status of the mourners has changed, together with an interpretation of the significance of what has occurred – in the case of a Christian funeral, an affirmation of the Church's belief about death and hope for eternal life. The funeral service can play a positive role in the grieving process and should be a significant stage in an on-going pastoral care. In rituals such as this, deep feelings may be worked through and expressed. In modern society a funeral is one of the few places where the public expression of intense feelings is acceptable, and thus it plays both a pastoral and a therapeutic role. Mourners also experience social support through sharing the service with a congregation of friends and relatives.

Forrester, D.B. *et al.*, *Encounter with God* (T. & T.

Clark, 1983), pp. 158–61. **Spiegel, Y.,** *The Grief Process* (SCM, 1978). **Speck, Peter** and **Ainsworth-Smith, Ian,** *Letting Go* (SPCK, 1982). **Willimon, William, H.,** *Worship as Pastoral Care* (Abingdon, 1979), ch. 5.

D.B. FORRESTER

See also: BEREAVEMENT; DEATH, MEANING OF; RITES AND RITUALS.

G

GAMBLING

'Gambling consists of an agreement between parties with respect to an unascertained outcome that, depending on the outcome, there will be a redistribution of advantage (usually but not always monetary) among those parties. This redistribution may be achieved directly (as in a game of poker) or through an agent (as in the case of football pools and lotteries). Essential conditions in this definition of gambling are that the participation in the agreement is voluntary and that the agreement not only provides each of the parties to the gamble with the chance of gaining advantage but also involves the risk of loss; failure to participate involves no risk of loss. Those who participate in such activities and risk loss for the chance of gain are termed gamblers.' (Royal Commission on Gambling)

Archaeological evidence supports the view that gambling has existed in various forms in most societies. Ancient Egyptian paintings found in tombs depict men or divinities throwing dice, either for gambling or fortune telling, as long ago as 3500 BC. In the OT, the casting of lots is used to determine God's will: at times of crisis (e.g. 1 Samuel 14.41); and for ritual purposes (e.g. Leviticus 16.8). In the NT, Matthias was assigned a place among the twelve apostles 'by lot' (Acts 1.26) while, in contrast, the Roman soldiers cast lots for Jesus' garments (Mark 15.24).

In modern times 'recreational' gambling includes: gaming (e.g. casino games, bingo, and gaming machines); betting (e.g. betting on horse-races and greyhound-races, on football pools, on the outcome of Miss World competition, or on parliamentary elections); lotteries (e.g. private, society and local authority); and prize competitions (e.g. crossword puzzles, 'spot the ball' competitions).

Speculation on the stock exchange and taking out insurance cover are not usually thought of as gambling, but these activities do exhibit many of the same characteristics.

In some types of gambling the outcome is determined solely by chance (e.g. football pools, bingo, etc.) while in others (e.g. betting on horses and greyhounds) skill has an important influence on the end-result.

The reasons why people gamble are extremely complex: the financial incentive of getting something for nothing; the social attraction of mixing with other like-minded individuals; and the psychological need which some people have to take 'risks'. While occasional gambling is unlikely to produce any harmful effects, regular participation may lead to compulsive or pathological gambling, where the individual finds that he or she has an irresistible urge to gamble regardless of the consequences (see ADDICTION).

Christians hold very different views about gambling. Some regard it as unambiguously evil, a squandering of God-given resources and an encouragement of greed, while others see it as an innocent pastime, or even beneficial. A Christian critique of gambling must take account of the fact that it includes a wide range of activities, some of which can be positively harmful because of their potentially addictive character and the high losses risked (e.g. casino games), while others are merely mildly entertaining (e.g. raffles at a church fête).

Pastoral care of compulsive gamblers should be 'problem-orientated' and not 'sickness-orientated'. The person who experiences difficulties over gambling may have a variety of problems: medical, social, legal, financial, environmental and so on. Counselling should also be available for the families and friends of compulsive gamblers. The only agency in the United Kingdom which offers advice and support is Gamblers Anonymous, and its associate groups Gam Anon (for families) and Gamateen (for young people).

Christians and Gambling, National Council for Social Aid, (Mowbrays, 1983). *Gambling: an Ethical Discussion*. Report of the Social and Industrial Commission of the Church Assembly, CA 972 (1950). *Report of the Royal Commission on Gambling*, vols. 1 & 2, Cmnd 7200 (HMSO, 1978). **Dixey, R.,** and **Talbot, M.,** *Women, Leisure and Bingo* (Trinity & All Saints College, 1982). **Downes, D.M.** *et al.,* *Gambling, Work and Leisure* (Routledge, 1976). **Moran, E.,** 'Pathological Gambling' (*British Journal of Psychiatry,* special publication no. 9, *Contemporary Psychiatry*, 1975).

E.W.F. AGAR

See also: ADDICTION.

GENETIC COUNSELLING

Providing information about the hereditary aspects of a disease in a particular family and indicating the different options members of that family may consider.

Many medical diseases are influenced by genetic factors. In some the presence of a particular gene or pair of genes will be sufficient to cause a condition (e.g. Huntington's disease, haemophilia, cystic fibrosis), and individuals who have inherited such genes will, sooner or later become affected. Other diseases are caused by a mixture of genetic and environmental factors (e.g. coronary artery disease, asthma, eczema). The genetic basis of such conditions is inherited as a susceptibility but individuals with the susceptibility may remain healthy if the 'triggering' factors in the environment (e.g. dusts and pollens in asthma) are avoided.

Although an important part of a genetic counselling interview is to explain what risk there is of a condition recurring in a family, it is not the counsellor's task to decide which option should be taken. For example some diseases (e.g. spina bifida or Down's syndrome) can be diagnosed prenatally, usually by sampling the amniotic fluid at around the 4-month stage of a pregnancy. Some couples will wish the abnormal foetus to be aborted following such a diagnosis, but for others this possibility is unacceptable. Trained counsellors will not influence such decisions their clients must make by using emotionally charged terms – for example, by referring to a Down's syndrome baby as 'a mongol', or by suggesting that the child's abnormality is the 'fault' of the parent known to carry the condition. It is also important to appreciate that the professional who does not ensure that all the available options have been explained, is in a negative manner taking part in 'directive counselling'. Contact with a local genetic counselling service will help to ensure that important, often new, options are not neglected.

Harper, P.S., *Genetic Counselling* (John Wright, 1981).

J.A. RAEBURN

See also: ABORTION; BIRTH.

GESTALT THERAPY

A therapy which focuses on the client's awareness in the 'here and now' to allow the emergence and completion of the client's 'unfinished business' or undealt-with concerns.

Gestalt is a German word meaning configuration or a whole. Fritz Perls, the originator of gestalt therapy, took the name from gestalt psychology, which focused on figure and ground in perception. Perls trained as a psychoanalyst in Germany in the 1930s but was dissatisfied with its emphasis on case histories and interpretation. He maintained that all that is necessary to work with the client is available in the present moment and on the surface, if we are only aware of what is reflected in the body posture, voice, gestures, etc. When clients focus on their own process in the 'here and now', whatever is unfinished will emerge from the background of ongoing concerns and become figure. If clients do not interrupt their processes, but allow the concern to emerge fully and be dealt with, the 'Gestalt' will be completed enabling a new concern to take its place.

Perls regarded neurosis as 'pain phobia'. The therapist frustrates clients' attempts to escape into roles and games in order to avoid their pain or embarrassment, and without this escape they reach an 'impasse'. If clients stay in touch with their experience while remaining in the impasse, they will pass through 'implosion' in which their façade collapses and move into 'explosion' where the energy locked up in the situation will be released into grief, anger, joy, orgasm, etc. Perls said of this process, 'to suffer one's death and be reborn is not easy' (Perls 1969). Clients have lost awareness of the process by which they disown aspects of themselves. Gestalt therapy helps them to identify, explore and integrate the polarities within themselves in the 'safe emergency' of the therapeutic situation.

The goal of gestalt therapy is to enable clients to move from environmental to self-support by increasing their awareness of their own process. This leads to a heightened sense of vitality and more effective functioning. The role of the therapist is to focus on the immediate behaviour of the client in an active, direct way. The gestalt process, with its focus on the 'here and now', affirms the concept of 'the sacrament of the present moment' (De Caussade 1981).

De Caussade, J.-P., *The Sacrament of the Present Moment* (Collins, 1981). Perls, F.S., *Gestalt Therapy Verbatim* (Real People Press, Moab, Utah, 1969). Perls, F.S. *et al.*, *Gestalt Therapy, Excitement and Growth in the Human Personality* (Julian Press, New York, 1951).

JOAN O'LEARY

GIFTS
See: PAYMENTS AND GIFTS.

GLOSSOLALIA
See: TONGUES.

GOD, DOCTRINE OF
The mainstream Christian understanding of God has its classic expression in the Bible and is most explicitly developed in the doctrine of the Trinity – God the Father, Son and Holy Spirit.

1. *Biblical origins.* In the Old Testament the chief names of God are El, Elohim (generic names for God), Yahweh (unique to Israel's covenant God) and Lord. A key passage is Exodus, ch. 3. God, appearing to Moses, is seen to be concerned for justice and the liberation of Israel from slavery, and is identified in two basic ways: as 'the God of Abraham, Isaac and Jacob' (i.e. through particular relationships in history); and as 'Yahweh' ('I am who I am' or 'I will be who I will be' – he is free to show himself in new ways, to do new things). This combination of ethical, historical definiteness and freedom focuses the portrayal of God primarily in personal terms through stories of his action, communication and relationships. Israel came to see history as meaningful and promising in a new way, through relationship to this God, who was creator of all and had committed himself to Israel in a special covenant which included a promise to all peoples.

In line with this identity rendered through narratives of God's speech and action, there was a wide range of rich imagery and metaphors for God drawn from most areas of life: rock, light, husband, father, mother, king, judge, victor in battle, teacher, friend, healer, craftsman, foundation, lion, etc.

A key set of ideas drawn from all this by later doctrine listed God's qualities or attributes: notably holiness, justice, mercy, wisdom, love, patience, omnipotence, omniscience, omnipresence, eternity.

In the NT two major new elements were Jesus as the Messiah and the outpouring of the Holy Spirit, focused in the events of crucifixion, resurrection and Pentecost, which were seen as the climactic expression of God's freedom and historical purpose. There were implications for the content of the images and attributes of God, especially in the light of the 'foolishness' of the cross (cf. 1 Cor. 1). God was now decisively understood through Jesus Christ: e.g. in the words of Paul, 'The God who said "Let light shine out of darkness" has shone in our hearts to give the light of the knowledge of the glory of God in the face of Christ' (2 Cor 4.6); and of John, 'He who has seen me has seen the Father' (John 14.9).

2. *Development.* The beginning of Christianity saw an explosion of ways of speaking about, worshipping and relating to God 'through Jesus Christ' and 'in the power of the Holy Spirit'. As with any language, the attempt to work out its grammar came later. Deciding on the appropriate Christian 'grammar of God' went on for centuries – involving Scripture, tradition, worship, philosophical, cultural and political influences, and much intense debate and conflict – a pivotal decision being for the full divinity of Jesus Christ at the Council of Nicea (AD 325). By the 5th century, the mainstream trinitarian consensus was clear. This was seen best to express the logic of Christian faith: that God is Father and Creator, completely transcendent and free; that he has also given himself in full and frank self-expression in history in Jesus Christ; and that he is powerfully and intimately present among and within people in the Holy Spirit. So Jesus and the Holy Spirit were seen to be intrinsic to the being and identity of God. It was a 'unity with differentiation' going beyond any analogies, all of which tended to overemphasize either the unity (as in the model of memory, intellect and will in one person) or the differentiation (as in the model of love between persons). The most influential theologies of God in Western Christianity have been those of Augustine of Hippo, Thomas Aquinas and John Calvin.

3. *Modernity.* The 18th to 20th centuries have seen many challenges to traditional trinitarianism. Deism affirmed a transcendent creator who has no further involvement with the universe. Pantheism posited an immanent God virtually identified with nature and its dynamics. God was often interiorized or privatized in the form of consciousness or conscience or a higher self. Various atheisms

claimed both to explain reductively the phenomena of religion (in biological, psychological, sociological, economic or philosophical terms) and to offer a more convincing account of reality. Higher criticism of the Bible, contact with other religions, and major developments in society and world history also influenced concepts of God.

The mainstream Christian theological response to this has included major attempts to restate the doctrine of the Trinity while responding to the challenges (e.g. F. Schleiermacher, G.F. Hegel, K. Barth, K. Rahner, H.U. von Balthasar, P. Tillich, T.F. Torrance, J. Moltmann, E. Jüngel). Key tasks have been: to offer an understanding of revelation, of the meaning of history and of the future; to show that divine and human freedom need not be in competition, since deeper involvement with this God capacitates true human freedom; to show the consequences for the being of God of his involvement with suffering, evil and death; to think through the interaction of God and the world in a post-Einsteinian way; to grapple with the cultural relativity of religion and concepts of God; to learn from biblical studies and other disciplines; and, in short, to rethink the whole 'ecology' of reality in relation to a God who is both transcendent and immanent.

Some influential approaches to God have been in a prophetic mode: liberation theology proclaims God on the side of the poor and oppressed; feminist and black theology challenge doctrines and images of God which are biased against women and blacks; Third-World theology offers alternatives to Western cultural confinement of God; inter-religious theology relates the God of Christianity to other religions; process theology relates God to a particular understanding of the universe. Many of these stress the role of 'praxis', active involvement in their struggles, if one is truly to know God.

4. *Implications for pastoral care.* The Trinity offers a fundamental way of relating to reality and conceiving one's own identity: through God the Father as creator, and source of life's truth, goodness and beauty; through God the Son as full participant in the joys, agonies, complexities and ordinariness of human history and the one who has gone to the heart of evil, suffering and death in order to show a way through them; and through God the Holy Spirit as the power of right action,

communication, vocation and personal transformation in relationship with other people in the world. This God takes the problems of life with utmost seriousness, but also shows that life is not ultimately problematic. So thanks, praise and joy in God are the greatest realism, and involve learning who God is, what his purpose is, how to repent and be forgiven, to listen and obey, to trust and hope, to be patient, to resist evil and to be willing to suffer and die for others. 'Loving wisdom' is the quality of God which lies at the heart of pastoral care, and its goal, like God's, is to enable others in turn to be wise lovers.

Aquinas, Thomas, *Summa Theologiae,* part 1 (Blackfriars, 1966). **Augustine,** *On the Trinity* (Eerdmans, 1979). **Barth, Karl,** *Church Dogmatics,* vol. 2. 1, 2 (Edinburgh, 1957). **Calvin, J.,** *Institutes of the Christian Religion,* Book 1 (SCM, 1961). **Newbigin, Lesslie,** *The Open Secret* (Search, 1978). **Moltmann, J.,** *The Crucified God* (SCM, 1974). **Rahner, Karl,** *Foundations of Christian Faith* (Darton Longman & Todd, 1978). **Schleiermacher, F.,** *The Christian Faith* (Harper, 1963). **Tillich, P.,** *Systematic Theology,* vol. 1 (SCM, 1978).

DAVID F. FORD

See also: FAITH; INCARNATION; PRAYER; REVELATION; SPIRIT; TRANSCENDENCE AND IMMANENCE.

GRATITUDE

Gratitude in counselling is an attitude which can have complex significance, and subtle and contradictory meaning. In its usual meaning of appreciation for goods or service received it is unlikely to be experienced in unadulterated form, and therefore needs to be closely studied and understood.

Many people seek counsel on account of a deep personal sense of inferiority, indebtedness and guilt (q.v.), which has been acquired in the experience of former faulty relationships, often parental, where gratitude was required for what was claimed to have been done for them. This experience invariably carries with it the implication of subservience and inequality, and often a response of deep injustice and resentment. To have gratitude expected of one, with its suggestion that one is under an obligation for the receipt of benefits, will often produce rebellion. For such a person it is not possible to offer gratitude, except grudgingly; perhaps by way of placatory appeasement, for fear of retaliation for an imagined offence.

Gratitude should therefore be received with

caution, and met by emphasizing the equal and contractual nature of the counselling relationship, where gratitude, in the sense of obligation, is inappropriate and out of place. The possible demeaning effect of accepting it without further exploration has to be borne in mind. An apologetic and guilty attitude about not offering gratitude is similarly inappropriate.

Some aspects of the counselling process are painful and difficult. Then gratitude may be offered as a denial of the difficulty that is being experienced, and may be gently put aside as irrelevant. This needs a realistic confrontation of the pain being caused.

From a psychological viewpoint, genuine gratitude, which is thankfulness for good received and used, is or may become possible for those who have had the benefit of a sufficiently nurturing and containing emotional environment from birth, and who have therefore not experienced irreparable deprivation. In this case it is possible for the emotion to be recognized and shared, when the initiating distress appears truly to have been overcome. In pastoral care, the same tensions between a defensive and a truly responsive gratitude will be experienced as in all other forms of caring. The meaning of a gift from the person being helped should always be explored by the pastor, at least in his or her own assessment of the situation, and at times it should be discussed with the giver. Gratitude may spring from a gospel of grace, or it may be a sign that the need for reparation of guilt still persists.

Klein, M., *Envy and Gratitude* (Hogarth, 1975).

BARBARA K. FOWLES
See also: PAYMENTS AND GIFTS.

GRIEF
See: BEREAVEMENT.

GROUP PSYCHOTHERAPY AND COUNSELLING
The term 'group psychotherapy' embraces such a wide range of activities within its ambit that an article of this length is inevitably highly condensed and almost telegrammatic. And when it is linked to the cognate, and frequently overlapping, field of counselling (q.v.) its definition and clinical/pastoral relevance can be surveyed only in outline.

Whereas institutions and communities often provide opportunities for group activities (such as clubs, societies and discussion groups) which may be broadly termed 'therapeutic', these are not to be confused with that particular professional undertaking which is the responsibility of a group therapist. Thompson and Kahn (1970) offer a useful distinction between group discussion, group counselling and group psychotherapy. They suggest that these modalities are topic-based, problem-based and personality-based respectively.

There is an almost limitless range of group psychotherapeutic approaches, depending upon the size and purpose of the group, the selection criteria for the group participants, and the setting where the group is conducted. There is an equally variegated spectrum of theoretical approaches which underpin the clinical application and overall therapeutic strategy. Nevertheless, it could be stated as generically true for all the 'group psychotherapies' that the therapist is concerned to structure the therapeutic process in terms of time, depth and mutuality. He will be concerned with the interpersonal and intrapsychic life of each group participant as well as paying attention to those phenomena which arise from the perception of the group-as-a-whole. The interested reader should explore the history of group psychotherapy. This shows how it was originally regarded as 'second best' to individual psychotherapy, but it gave an opportunity for eight individual patients to see one therapist for the time and price of one. This meant that, in the early days of group psychotherapy, each of the eight members of the small group was regarded as having one eighth of the therapist's attention. As a reaction to this original fragmentation there was a swing in the opposite direction which implied that the therapist was only concerned with the group-as-a-whole. The pendulum then swung back to a more central position when the therapist became concerned with the individual, the group matrix and the group-as-a-whole. (*See* Pines (1984) on Group Analysis.)

In the same way that individual psychotherapy can be regarded as a process in which the patients are enabled to do for themselves what they cannot do on their own, though the individual therapist does not do it for them, so it may be said that in group psychotherapy the group is enabled to do for itself what it cannot do without the professional presence of the group therapist, although he or she does not, and cannot, do it for the group. Group psychotherapy may be supportive, in which precarious defences are buttressed and reinforced. It may be confrontational, analytic and interpretive, when an attempt is made to relinquish primitive defences and facilitate more capacious intrapsychic and interpersonal life.

The borderline between group psychotherapy and group counselling is blurred, and its demarcation does little to further an understanding of the complexities of the issues involved. On the whole, it can be said that group psychotherapy is more concerned with the unconscious dynamics of the individual participants and the group-as-a-whole, whereas group counselling is more concerned with the conscious interactional end of the spectrum. But this division is spurious. In the ebb and flow of preoccupation with here-and-now and there-and-then which takes place in any psycho-dynamic group, there is a deep amalgam of support and confrontation which takes place simultaneously. Thompson and Kahn (1970) state 'in a psychotherapeutic group, the very factors that support and sustain the individual member support and sustain him in order to expose him to increasing stress and pain. As his endurance increases, so he is given more to endure.'

By way of summary we may refer to the large reference book of Yalom (1975), which lists the curative factors in group psychotherapy as follows: (1) instillation of hope; (2) universality; (3) imparting of information; (4) altruism; (5) the corrective recapitulation of the primary family group; (6) development of socializing techniques; (7) imitative behaviour; (8) interpersonal learning; (9) group cohesiveness; (10) catharsis; (11) existential factors.

Bion, W.R., *Experiences in Groups and Other Papers* (Tavistock, 1961). **Kaplan, H.I.** and **Sadock, B.J.** (eds.), *Comprehensive Group Psychotherapy* (Williams & Wilkins, Baltimore, 2nd edn 1983). **Pines, M.** *(ed.), The Evolution of Group Analysis* (Routledge, 1984). **Thompson, S.** and **Kahn, J.H.**, *The Group Process as a Helping Technique* (Pergamon, 1970). **Yalom, I.D.**, *The Theory and Practice of Group Psychotherapy* (Basic Books, New York, 2nd edn 1975).

MURRAY COX

See also: COUNSELLING; GROUP THEORY; PSYCHOTHERAPY.

GROUP THEORY

The formulation of concepts and models which seek to further understanding of

100

human experience and behaviour in groups. The focus is on general principles and dynamics underlying group functioning, whatever the particular context or setting in social and organizational life.

There is no single theory which is generally accepted as a paradigm for understanding group behaviour. An important distinction is between theories which interpret group behaviour largely in terms of inter-personal relationships and needs and theories which start from the assumption that the group as a whole is a unified system with its own laws and processes, distinct from the particular motivations, intentions and needs of individual members. Group theory as a distinctive contribution to social understanding refers primarily to this second group of theories.

The idea of the group as a 'social object' has its roots in much of the social and psychological thought of the nineteenth and early twentieth centuries. Marx, Dürkheim, Freud, Macdougall and Jung in different ways all postulated forces or processes operating unconsciously or instinctively to shape, modify and determine the behaviour of individual members or sub-groups within any collectivity.

During this century there have been two main lines of development towards a more systematic formulation and application of group theory. One is associated with what is known as 'group dynamics', a term first coined by the gestalt psychologist Kurt Lewin (1890–1947) in the United States. This term covers a variety of different formulations, each of which views the group as a 'system', a set of bounded relations and activities, and seeks to identify those properties of the system that determine or pattern the relations and interactions that take place. An example is the 'open systems' approach developed by Von Bertalanffy and J.G. Miller in the United States and by Trist, Rice, Miller and their colleagues at the Tavistock Institute of Human Relations in Britain. This approach, which pays particular attention to the interactions between the group or 'system' and its external environment, has been extensively applied in the understanding of organizational and institutional life in different settings: industrial, educational, penal, medical and religious.

System theories emphasize the part played in group life by homeostatic (self-regulating) mechanisms, preservation and management of group boundaries, the tension between resistance to change and the need for change in order to ensure survival in a changing environment. They have thrown light on many pervasive features of group behaviour, including the establishment of rules or norms, factors influencing group cohesiveness, role and task differentiation, the emergence and stability of group leadership, the pressures to conformity, the treatment of 'outsiders' and the phenomena of intra- and inter-group conflict. They have gone some way to demonstrate that what happens in groups is as much determined by the relatedness of members to the group as a whole as by the individual characteristics and relations of the members themselves.

The second main stream of development derives from psychoanalysis. The application of psychoanalytically derived ideas to understanding group behaviour was powerfully stimulated during the Second World War as psychiatrists and psychologists were faced with tackling problems of the selection and deployment of military personnel and the treatment of war neuroses. Experimenting in the use of the group as a diagnostic and therapeutic instrument, British psychiatrists in particular pioneered a variety of approaches which were later to lead to the formulation of new concepts and methods for understanding group behaviour and its practical application within both therapeutic and non-therapeutic settings. These included the idea of the therapeutic community (Maxwell Jones and Tom Mann), the idea of group analysis (S.H. Foulkes) and the radical restructuring of existing conceptions of the relatedness of the individual and the group represented by the work of W.R. Bion.

The influence of Bion's thinking deeply influenced the development of a general theory of group behaviour. Just as Freud had distinguished different processes or systems operating at the level of the individual – conscious and unconscious – so Bion identified analogous processes operating at the level of the group. Consciously, people come together in groups to carry out activities which require co-operation. Unconsciously, group behaviour is simultaneously shaped by powerful emotional drives, related to fears of survival, of the group itself and of the individual as dependent on the group. These emotional drives find expression in unacknowledged 'basic assumptions': that the group's survival depends on the presence of

an all-knowing, all-providing leader, institution or idea (dependence), or on the presence of an enemy, which the group must destroy or take flight from (fight/flight), or on the advent of a new leader born from the group to inaugurate a golden age in which survival will be assured (pairing or expectancy).

Bion sought to show how all behaviour in groups reflects the omnipresence of these two types of mental activity: the culture of work and the culture of basic assumptions. He speculated on the ways in which different social institutions – the Church, the army, the aristocracy or elite – may serve to canalize one or other basic assumption and thereby perhaps liberate energy available for work elsewhere.

Subsequent writers have criticized, extended and sought to apply his insights, both in training courses on group relations and in the practical study of particular organizations and institutions. Attempts have also been made to integrate his insights with those of group dynamics and 'open systems' theory. While no general theory of group behaviour has yet gained acceptance, it seems reasonable to assume that the elements for such a theory have at least been laid.

Andrieu, D., *The Group and the Unconscious* (Routledge, 1984). **Bertalanffy, L. von.,** *General System Theory* (Penguin, 1973). **Bion, W.R.,** *Experiences in Groups* (Tavistock, 1961). **Cartwright, D.** and **Zander, A.,** (eds.), *Group Dynamics: Research and Theory* (Row, Petersen, New York, 1953). **Gibbard, G.S.** *et al.* (eds.), *Analysis of Groups* (Jossey Bass, 1974). **Miller, E.J.** and **Rice, A.K.,** *Systems of Organization* (Tavistock, 1967). **Reed, B.D.,** *The Dynamics of Religion* (Darton Longman and Todd, 1978).

DAVID ARMSTRONG

See also: COMMUNE; ENCOUNTER GROUPS; GROUP PSYCHOTHERAPY AND COUNSELLING; GROUPS IN THE CHURCH; SYSTEMS PASTORAL CARE.

GROUPS IN THE CHURCH

The antipathetical nature of groups is best understood through considering a working definition of a group: 'a plurality of persons, who interact with one another in a given context more than they interact with anyone else' (Klein 1966).

The inherent value of the experience of belonging is here contrasted sharply with a certain exclusiveness, as though belonging 'in a given context' deprives others – as it in fact does – of the company, the presence, of the individual concerned, for however short a time, in some other context – e.g. that of the family. We may also consider two kinds of group: the *primary group*, where the members know one another and are involved in an intimate, face-to-face association and co-operation; and the *secondary group*, a wider association not resting upon immediate personal encounter, but held together by common beliefs and values, by the expression of these in language and symbol, and by a unity of administration. It has been said that 'the weakness of the Church . . . is that its structure of secondary groups has no adequate basis or support in a corresponding structure of primary groups' (Davis 1967).

Many, however, find the anonymity of belonging in a secondary group – a worshipping congregation, for instance – comforting: a sense of belonging is experienced, without any more demanding intimacy than the study of the neck of the worshipper in the pew in front of you. Joining a primary group, on the other hand, makes demands of commitment and possibly self-revelation that are threatening, even if they are accompanied by the promise of closeness to other human beings. It is significant that contemporary forms of eucharistic worship have emphasized the exchange of personal greeting, at the Peace, in an otherwise formal service: an offered bridge between the two kinds of group.

A third antithesis in the phenomenon of the group may be recognized if we consider what groups do when they get together. An impatient church member wrote some years ago: 'We select a dozen kindly Christians, form them into a committee, and find we have begotten a monster which corporately sponsors perfidies to which none of its members, as individuals, would stoop.' Yet contrast with this the warmth, depth and strength of the experience of such an apparently mundane body as a clergy chapter which decides to set aside regular and frequent times for meeting – as recounted by Stephen Verney in his book *Fire in Coventry*: 'Here we seem to be a sort of Fellowship of the Holy Spirit.'

These sets of antitheses – of apparently conflicting loyalties between group and group; of hesitant movement from the safety of belonging in the secondary group to the risky encounters of the primary group; of

participation in activity which, influenced by group membership, seems indeed to take on a life of its own and greater than the sum of its parts – amount to the fundamental conundrum of being a human being. Alone, I am free – to be alone; with others, I am no longer free to be the ultimate authority about myself, who I am, and what I am to do.

The busy pastor and his or her no less busy lay church member, inevitably asks the question: Have I time for groups? and are they worth the trouble? Both might also consider the issue of *dependence* in their questioning – the pastor's dependence on the congregation's support, and their dependence on leadership, finding in that issue some of the contradictions resolved. Consider a group as a circle, and notice one simple aspect of sitting in a circle: 'When groups are used to exchange ideas and to talk freely with one another, then the formation of the circle is nearly always used, and this has come to have significance beyond its essential value [of representing democracy and equality, in that a circle has no definite head or tail] . . . Quite simply, the human vision is very restricted . . . Sitting in a circle makes the absolute most of this 'cone of vision' and allows people to be aware of all the others within the group.' (Douglas 1978).

A circle, then, is both a structure and a space. As a structure it contains and defines, so that its members may say, 'I belong to this group'. Identity is thus accorded to those who belong. Wisely led, the boundary of the group will not be closed to others who wish to join it, or another group like it.

Within its space, there is room for all kinds of activity, as for instance in the so-called task-oriented group (for prayer, for study, for discussion, for painting a room), but also in the so-called unstructured group. It is the nature of groups to abhor vacuum: always the space is filled, either with task and/or with work which leads the members to become more aware of themselves and of one another. In this process, individuals find themselves strangely enhanced. They come to know themselves more, mirrored as they are through the perception of others. In turn, each group member contributes to his or her fellow-members' self-perception. Beyond both of these parameters, something of a common humanity becomes apparent. 'Where two or three are gathered together in my name, there am I in the midst.'

Davis, Charles, *Maurice Lectures*, 1967 (quoted in *Contact*, no. 21). **Douglas, Tom,** *Basic Group Work* (Tavistock, 1978); *Group-Work Practice* (Tavistock, 1976). **Klein, Josephine,** *Working with Groups* (Hutchinson, 1966). **Verney, Stephen,** *Fire in Coventry* (Hodder, 1964).

CHRISTOPHER FENTON

See also: COMMUNE; ENCOUNTER GROUPS; GROUP THEORY.

GROWTH GROUPS
See: ENCOUNTER GROUPS.

GUILT
Objectively: a fact or state attributed to a person who violates the will of God and/or some moral or penal code. Subjectively: moral anxiety accompanying behaviour which contradicts values held by the self to be central to life.

Sigmund Freud spoke of guilt as 'the most important problem in the evolution of culture' (Freud 1951). Much of religious history focuses on the rites and behaviours deemed necessary to remove guilt and to restore the offending person to favour with God, others and self. Guilt is routinely experienced as an alienation from such relationships. A central thesis of Christian faith is that God's saving act in Christ is the overcoming of this alienation. It is through the universal experience of 'fall', of despair and guilty anxiety over the disjunction of essence and existence, that we learn to know our true finitude and our true dependence on the life beyond us. When God, through the life and death of Christ, freely proffers forgiveness, acceptance and love in spite of our alienating wishes and acts, we discover the courage both 'to sin boldly' (because our private 'goodness' is no longer the centre of our anxious living) and 'to believe boldly'. It is on this affirmation that the healing and hopeful power of the Christian ministry to, and therapy of, the guilty person rests.

Oskar Pfister of Zurich and R.S. Lee of Oxford have both documented ways in which the Church over the centuries has distorted its initial pristine affirmations concerning guilt. Eventual exploitation of Christ's forgiveness through authoritarian imposition of conditions of forgiveness, sale of indulgences, manipulation of guilty fear and phobic centring of faith in guilt led to the Protestant Reformation and fuelled much of the Enlightenment rebellion against the Church. R.S. Lee has gone so far as to say that Jesus introduced an 'ego religion' over against the guilt-oriented 'superego religion' of his time (Lee 1948). This means that, in spite of the fact that the Judaeo-Christian tradition has often allied itself with the guilt-oriented superego restraints against impulse life (which become codified and institutionalized in religious structures), this is a violation of the much larger ramifications it should have for humankind. The best in this tradition has never allied itself solely with a code morality ('the letter killeth but the spirit giveth life') or a superego-oriented conception of human relationship with God. (For elaboration of superego dynamics and the origin of guilt, cf. Stein 1968).

Pastoral care of guilt over the centuries has been complicated by what is currently called 'neurotic' or 'false' guilt. This is guilt over the natural constituents of the healthy self: sexuality, self-assertion, self-love (primary healthy narcissism), etc. The kind of oral enthusiasm which goes beyond teaching about how these natural impulses should be expressed or controlled, and which evokes guilt over simply *having* the impulses, produces built-in structural conflict and moral anxiety. This wreaks havoc in the psyche, cripples development and may result in symptoms of dysfunction such as depressions, obsessions, compulsions and self-destructive phenomena. Severe dysfunction, such as is evident in psychosis, is often abetted by guilt-induced repression and dissociation (Menninger 1938).

Freud's contribution to pastoral care is specially clear at this point. He distinguished normal guilt ('remorse') from pathological guilt and opened the way for the pastor and therapist to distinguish guilt that needs *confession* and guilt that needs *therapy*. Often enough, these are intertwined, in which case both theological and psychological expertise are needed by the therapist/pastor. Absence (or failure of function) of guilt is in itself a disturbance, noted in psychiatric nomenclature variously as 'character disorder,' 'sociopathy', 'psychopathy,' etc. Its roots are complex, but it is often related to a developmental failure in identification and/or vicissitudes in the emergence of narcissism and early object relations. This pathology sets in bold relief the continued recognition by both theological and psychological traditions that an authentic existential guilt is a necessary aspect of a healthy human being, an internal warning system that one is at odds with God and with the structures, values and truths which sustain self and world.

Freud, S., *Civilization and Its Discontents* (Hogarth, 1951), p. 123. Lee, R.S., *Freud and Christianity* (J. Clarke, 1948). Menninger, K., *Man Against Himself* (Harcourt Brace, 1938). Pfister, O., *Christianity and Fear* (Allen & Unwin, 1944). Stein, E., *Guilt: Theory and Therapy* (Westminster, Philadelphia, 1968).

EDWARD V. STEIN

See also: ANXIETY; CONFESSION; CONSCIENCE: PSYCHOLOGICAL ASPECTS; RESPONSIBILITY; SIN.

H

HANDICAP
See: DISABLEMENT.

HEALING AND PASTORAL CARE
Patients who receive the right medical treatment, do not necessarily get well (or may fall ill for some other reason); patients expected to succumb, fight their way back to health. Experienced doctors know that they are doing more than treat a disease; they are treating a patient who is suffering from a disease, and who will react to it in a personal way. That is why medicine is an art as well as a science. The great Osler, who led the revolt against too narrow a view of medicine, remarked of the TB patient that what he had in his head mattered more than what he had in his chest. (Osler once described himself as 'an unconscious faith healer'.) Many factors affect the motivation of a particular patient.

From the earliest times this is where religion has played its part. Sick people were carried into the temples of Aesculapius, and into the churches of the first Christians; the titles of many hospitals recall their religious foundation. 'Healers' credited with exceptional powers to heal illness and relieve pain, and 'exorcists', to handle mental disturbance, have always been in demand the world over.

Christ enjoined his disciples to preach the Kingdom and heal the sick; the Church continued the work in which its members had been instructed. 'Anointing with oil' (Mark 6.13; Jas. 5.14) may well have been a simple medical remedy, applied with prayer. The earliest references suggest that the patient was anointed all over or on the affected part; St Hilary of Poitiers, presented with a girl who had lost her voice, poured the oil down her throat (she recovered at once). In modern practice the priest dips his thumb into oil previously consecrated, and makes the sign of the cross on the sufferer's forehead. The sacrament is administered to the baptized, usually in the course of a communion for the sick. The 'laying on of hands' can be given informally to anyone at any time, and by more than one person; hands are laid gently on the patient's head (or on the part affected) with prayer for blessing (q.v.) and healing, or for death to come easily. Exorcism (q.v.), widely practised in Africa in its original form, is the rebuking and expelling of the evil spirit believed to be responsible for the disturbance.

It has been suggested that anointing should now be regarded as the sacrament of God's gifts through medicine, with prayers for doctors, nurses, and supporting professions. It was the custom in the early Church to bless the patient's food, water, and medicine; this should be revived. The laying on of hands (which some think of as an act of adoption) reaffirms the need for 'touch' (q.v.) in our lives, from infancy onwards; the etymology of 'nurse' is significant. 'Healers' often feel as Christ did (Mark 5.30) that 'power' has gone out of them. Exorcism, via Mesmer, has been secularized as hypnosis (q.v.) and psychotherapy (q.v.). The abreaction of a patient suffering from 'battle exhaustion', for example, strongly resembles 'exorcism'; the more gradual release of pent-up emotional drives is the effective basis of modern psychotherapy. It is a pity that we have restricted confession (q.v.) to sin; conflict (q.v.) may well be more damaging.

Revival of interest in the Churches' ministry of healing began with the founding of the Guild of Health in 1904 and of the Divine Healing Mission a year later. It was welcomed by the Lambeth Conference in 1908, and an official commission of doctors and theologians accepted 'healing' for functional disorders but held that it would have no effect on organic disease. The Guild of St Raphael was founded in 1915 to represent the High Anglican point of view, and a further Commission (1924) led to the revision of the Prayer Book service for the 'Visitation of the Sick' in 1928. In 1944 Archbishop William Temple set up the Churches' Council of Healing to co-ordinate the work of existing agencies. A third Commission, reporting in 1958, affirmed that 'this ministry is an integral part of the Church's total work', but failed to resolve the issue of 'organic disease'. Dr Louis Rose examined one hundred cases submitted to him by the spiritualist healer the late Harry

Edwards, but found that in a majority of cases the patient's story and the doctor's record diverged substantially; he thought that there were a few cases in which something significant might have occurred. Although only a very few cases at Lourdes are accepted as 'cured', the spiritual inspiration is obviously deeply felt.

The methodology of medicine is still Cartesian, for it is essential for physiological processes to be studied as such; but this is not the whole story in health and disease. The distinction between 'organic' and 'functional' has gradually been eroded; 'organic diseases' like diabetes and peptic ulcer, for instance, are strongly affected by the patient's own feelings, even more than by his attitude to life. Stress (q.v.) is clearly involved in heart disease, but the degree of involvement is still highly disputed. The latest concept of 'auto-immune' disease, like rheumatoid arthritis (and possibly cancer) may show a similar link between 'mind' and 'body'. One can only suspect that traditional religious teaching, which bases 'love' on 'self-hatred' may have much to answer for. This is the problem which 'healing' has to tackle next, if further progress is to be made.

But it cannot be too strongly urged that the ministry of healing is primarily a ministry of prayer and care. We need the support of our friends who are praying for us, as St Paul did (Phil. 1.19), 'through your supplication and the supply of the Spirit of Christ'. St Paul referred to 'gifts of healing' (in the plural), and these should never be restricted to a single individual or a single gift. Preoccupation with 'miracle' has distorted our approach to the 'healing of the whole man'. We are looking for laws, not for exceptions to laws, and prevention is in any case much better than cure. The personal and social factors in health and ill-health have been much studied in recent years, and the Churches might well give a stronger lead here (the greatest killer of young people is the motor-car).

The doctor relies on the inherent vitality of the body, the psychotherapist on a similar quality in the mind; the religious person believes that 'faith working through love' taps the well of life at a deeper level. But faith must never be a forced belief, or it becomes, as the schoolboy put it, 'believing what isn't really true'. Faith is what St Paul called 'living in the Spirit', and discovering inner resources to meet our need; in which we realize that the

106

body is not an enemy but a friend.

Information about the many guilds and associations concerned with the revival of the healing ministry, and about homes of healing, may be obtained from the Churches' Council of Health and Healing, St Marylebone Parish Church, Marylebone Road, London NW1 5LT (01-486 9644).

Gusmer, Charles W., *The Ministry of Healing in the Church of England* (Alcuin Club, 1974). **Harris, Charles**, articles 'Visitation of the Sick', 'The Communion of the Sick' in *Liturgy and Worship* (SPCK, 1932). **Kelsey, Morton T.**, *Healing and Christianity* (SCM, 1973). **Maddocks, Morris**, *Christian Healing Ministry* (SPCK, 1981). **Rose, Louis**, *Faith Healing* (Gollancz, 1968).

G.C. HARDING

See also: ANOINTING; BLESSING; CHRISTIAN SCIENCE; HEALTH AND ILLNESS: PASTORAL ASPECTS; SPIRITUAL HEALING.

HEALTH AND ILLNESS: ETHICAL AND THEOLOGICAL ASPECTS

Health in Western society is largely shaped by an individualism in medicine and in the Church which concentrates on the relief of illness and the elimination of 'badness'. This results in a largely negative definition of health as the removal of what is wrong and the restoration to a state of normality. By removing the person from the interpersonal environment and applying expert technology to eradicate illness the achievements of medicine are in danger of being cancelled out by the over-medicalization of life — for example, in viewing grief as a sickness, or iatrogenic illness caused by overprescribing drugs (Illich 1975). There are comparable ecclesiogenic illnesses which feed neuroses, obsessions and fantasies. There is rarely a counterbalancing movement outwards from the alienated person into the community. To achieve a more healthy community and to be delivered from illness, various social understandings of health and illness are required, together with an awareness of the untruth that lies in following one model blindly and dogmatically.

1. The extraordinary ability of a community to create health and illness amongst its members was clearly demonstrated by Revens (1966), when he correlated the sickness rates and drop-out rates of student nurses in training at a number of hospitals with the recovery rates of patients from simple surgical

procedures at the same hospitals. He discovered that in hospitals where there was poor communication with an atmosphere of fear and mistrust between staff, student nurses were more often sick and more frequently gave up their training, while patients took up to three times longer to recover compared to those in hospitals where the atmosphere and relationships were better. Health here relates to the quality of life that people achieve together.

2. The Black Report (Townsend and Davidson 1982) found a definite connection between health and the organization of society. Social class 5 members have higher mortality rates among infants, more children in fatal accidents, and higher rates of smoking, strokes and heart disease. They make less use of health services, dental services and immunization services. Children on free school meals tend to eat 'junk food' instead of the balanced diet (q.v.) which was abolished in 1982. Local authority housing stock has declined in quality and quantity. Education services, health services and leisure facilities are less adequate in inner-city-type areas. With the emphasis on high-technology medicine and resistance to learning about primary health care from the developing world, coupled to a lack of involvement of local authorities in the health services, it is hardly surprising that expenditure in the National Health Service (q.v.) has made little impact on the inequalities in health and health care found in the United Kingdom. Health is concerned with social justice.

3. The contrasts in health are even greater in some developing countries, where Western-style hospitals serve the rich, while the urban and rural poor have little access to health-care facilities. Further injustices are caused by transnational corporations who are courted by unscrupulous governments. The latter dispossess the peasant farmers of their land in favour of the big company. The peasants then have no means of livelihood, and their children and women may end up in prostitution (q.v.). The beneficiaries are always the wealthy and powerful countries, who also put limits and quotas on imports from developing countries. Militarism, migrant workers, and the inferior place of women in many societies, are further factors which affect the health of people particularly in developing countries. Concern for health would mean questioning political policies and dogmas such as the free-market economy and the effects of its implementation.

In responding to these systems of injustice the Christian priority would be to serve the poor and and those to whose care no prestige is attached (McGilvray 1981). It would involve becoming aware of the values implicit in their lives – their belonging and caring, their sharing and being on the way. They would then need to participate in the development of basic systems to meet the necessities of life – agriculture, water, sewage, transport, education, health services, prices and incomes. Each system would need rigorous evaluation to see if the aims and objectives were being subtly changed to meet the needs of the wealthy or the staff rather than the poor.

The theological exploration of health goes far beyond the meeting of basic human needs, for the more affluent societies are often afflicted with problems of alcoholism, drug abuse, environmental pollution, unwanted pregnancies and social malaise. This dark side of development reflects the values and disciplines of communal life which is not rooted in God nor accepting of his grace to heal. Corporate reformation is required to develop a worshipping community where God is disclosed within the deepest human suffering. Mutual commitment and sharing can change the stone of affliction into the bread of life. Those at the heart of the suffering situation may find themselves ministering health to others. People create health together through responsibility, sacrifice and discipline. Meaning and fulfilment are discovered in these experiences (Wilson 1975).

The complete and ultimate experience of health lies beyond this life, but insofar as we are in accord with God, neighbour, ourselves and our environment, there is a foretaste of the life to come. Because health involves questions about justice and value, the healing and ultimate health of humanity is bound up with all who are rejected, outcast and marginalized – in particular the poorest of the poor and the powerless.

Illich, I., *Medical Nemesis* (Calder & Boyars, 1975). McGilvray, J., *The Quest for Health and Wholeness* (DIFAM, 1981). Revens, R., *Standards for Morale* (OUP, 1966). Townsend, P. and Davidson, N. (eds.), *Inequalities in Health* (Penguin, 1982). Wilson, M., *Health is for People* (Darton Longman and Todd, 1975).

PETER BELLAMY

See also: HEALTH EDUCATION; JUSTICE AND PASTORAL CARE; NATIONAL HEALTH SERVICE; POVERTY; PRIORITIES IN HEALTH CARE.

HEALTH AND ILLNESS: PASTORAL ASPECTS

Health and illness have to do with relationships. They derive their meaning from the individuals or communities to which they refer. Such relationships, whether considered personally or corporately, can be broadly divided into four: downwards, to things; outwards, to other people; inwards, to themselves; and upwards to God. The divisions must not destroy the recognition that they are interactive and interdependent. Nor must they be thought of as static. Their dynamic is productive of the tension and conflict which are the object, at the personal level, of pastoral care and, at the corporate level, of prophetic vision and political action.

Health and illness must be considered both formally and materially. The formal is the subjective experience and the material the objective reality. They may be at variance with each other. A person may be blissfully unaware of an illness from which he is soon to die or he may be in an agony of pain from a sickness which exists only in his imagination.

Relationship to things. Everyone is related to the things which pertain to his environment, and illness therein may have serious consequences, as would be the case of the surgeon or the engineer with the things with which he has to do. There is a comparable relationship which concerns humankind as a whole and its relationship, for example, with the fossil fuels or the endangered species of the animal world.

Relationship to people. Interpersonal relationships and interpeople relationships are areas of experience of health and illness. In both the individual and corporate dimensions there are widely different norms. The so-called sado-masochistical relationship may be healthier than the situation produced by the healing of the sadism of one partner or the masochism of the other. In international relationships the balance of power may produce a long and lasting state of peace, despite the avowed hostility of the confronting nations.

Relationship to self. The notion of human beings as body, mind and spirit leaves out of account the concept of relationships outside oneself and may do violence to the relation-

ships within the whole person. Body, mind and spirit are inseparable. As a physical unit the body is either enjoying health or suffering illness. The body begins to decay as soon as it is born. Like any machine it is subject to the wearing of its parts. It may suffer accident and be damaged. Paradoxically, it has within it incredible powers of recuperation upon which the work of the doctor depends. He may set the two ends of a broken bone, but he cannot make them join again. Our bodies reflect the sickness of the other parts of our being. Bodily sickness is often the evidence of mental or spiritual disease, just as it is the occasion of distress of mind or loss of faith. The psychosomatic concept is simply that. Heart disease or the duodenal ulcer reflects the stress of mind which may thus find its physical outlet. Stress (q.v.) on the other hand may result in mental sickness, and illness of the body may make us mentally depressed or spiritually rebellious. It is hardly possible to be ill in one part without being ill in all. Nor is the traffic all one way. A buoyant spirit, a lively faith (q.v.), a sure hope (q.v.), such spiritual qualities will help not only the bearing of physical pain but often in the relieving of it; but they are not easily attained. Pastoral counselling is about helping people to work through grief at a bereavement or withdrawal at the removal of alcohol or drugs. The application of spiritual remedies may be conducive to the relief of physical disease, but they ought not to be separated from pastoral care of which they are properly an integral part. The sacraments are closely related to the psychosomatic syndrome. The touch of the minister of healing, the anointing with holy oil, the reception of baptism and holy communion – all these outward signs done to the body seek to induce spiritual health, renew faith and hope, and are the expression of love. That love however also involves the often long and painful accompaniment of counselling or psychotherapy. A person's relationship to himself is healthy only when all his 'parts' work together in harmony. They seldom, if ever, do. Pastoral care co-operates with other therapeutic agencies in seeking such harmony for a person's pilgrimage through life.

Relationship to God. Humanity relates to God individually and corporately. A person is both '*a* member of Christ and *the* child of God' (B.C.P. Catechism), one of a society and a single individual known to God by name.

This relationship with God is part of being human. It is not an optional extra for the religious-minded. There are not 'religious kinds' of people – only people. All human beings are made in the image of God; if God has made them in his likeness, he has so made everyone, not only some persons. The perfection of health in relationship with God we call holiness (q.v.). It is everyone's vocation, the end and object of life's pilgrimage. It is rarely attained in this life but is ever to be sought after, as life's true goal and purpose. Not to know this is itself to be ill. There may be no formal realization of this, no experience of illness. Such ignorance of a person's true destiny may be accompanied by a subjective sense of great well-being. By contrast where that ignorance is recognized, where people realise that they have lost or never had a sense of purpose and direction, they may well experience signs of mental depression. These in turn may produce physical symptoms. The reversal of this process is one of the attributes of Christian healing (q.v.) and counselling (q.v.). When a person is enabled to gain a sense of true destiny he or she can become mentally well and physically rejuvenated. But one's religion, though deeply personal, must never become merely private; it has always a corporate dimension. We must worship as well as pray, belong to the body as well as being part of it. Our membership can find its full corporate expression in that society of Christians which we call the Church. The Church is also in good health or in ill health, or in a combination of both. It is fundamental to its nature to be concerned with its own healing and striving after a more harmonious relationship both within, for its own members, and its dealing with the society in which it is set. Health is its search, its endeavour, its end, and its goal only in heaven (q.v.).

Life is a pilgrimage. It is a pilgrimage to health. It is also a pilgrimage of health. We have it on our journey, always partially, always imperfectly, always with an admixture of that illness which is its opposite or the mark of its imperfection. Health is Heaven. The Kingdom of Heaven is within us. It is also the object of our journey. So is our health. We confess that there is no health in us and in doing so begin to find it. Elusive, intangible, always evading us and escaping us, it is our wholeness and our holiness.

Frost, E., *Christian Healing* (Mowbray, 1946). Lambourne, R.A., *Community, Church and Healing* (Darton Longman & Todd, 1963). **Wilson, M.,** *The Hospital, a Place of Truth* (Univ. of Birmingham Inst. for Study of Rel. Architecture, 1971); *Health is for People* (Darton Longman & Todd, 1975).

C.K. HAMEL COOKE

See also: HEALING; HEALTH: ETHICAL AND THEOLOGICAL ASPECTS; HOSPITAL CHAPLAINCY; HOSPITALS; NATIONAL HEALTH SERVICE; SPIRITUAL HEALING.

HEALTH EDUCATION

A range of educational activities, whether directed at individuals or communities, which are concerned with the prevention of disease or injury, as well as the promotion of positive health.

In a narrow sense it has tended to be confined to attempts to persuade individuals to change harmful behaviours (e.g. smoking, alcohol abuse, bad diet, unprotected sex, etc.) primarily by the provision of medical information about health risks or the need for immunization and screening, leaving it to individuals to decide for themselves. In a broader sense the education of the public about health matters includes (besides individual behaviour modification): attempts to change the life-style of whole communities; public health and community initiatives to improve unhealthy environments; political activity aimed at improving health services and welfare provisions; and the use of legal and fiscal means to control the advertizing and marketing of products damaging to people's health.

Health education in any of its forms is inevitably controversial in both an ethical and political sense. This should not be surprising, since the terms 'health' (*see* HEALTH: ETHICAL AND POLITICAL ASPECTS) and 'education' raise important value questions and often indicate ares of disagreement in society about how we transmit values from one group or generation to another. Approaches to health education can be understood in terms of four different models, namely, the *medical, educational, community development* and *socio-political* models.

1. The *medical model* has historically been the most influential, and in Britain, has its origins in the 19th-century movement to promote public hygiene (by improved sanitation, food and water supplies, and housing standards control), and the introduction of

public health legislation providing for compulsory immunization (small pox, etc.) and notification of certain contagious diseases (e.g. tubercolosis and venereal disease). These methods have been spectacularly successful in controlling and virtually eliminating the major infectious diseases, and in the developed world have completely changed the pattern of morbidity and mortality. Infant mortality rates have been dramatically reduced, and the majority of people live on into old age where premature death from heart attacks, strokes, respiratory disorders, cancers, accidents and suicide (today's big killers) are caused by complex factors which are life-style related.

2. In attempting to change people's lifestyles, other methods are required. A simple reliance on giving people the medical facts and expecting them to change their habits is insufficient, and the traditional public health approach tends to have been negative and authoritarian, more concerned with disease prevention than health promotion. This is where the *educational model* becomes relevant – that is, an approach which is not only informative, but formative. To enable people to resist peer-group pressure, or seductive advertising, means that they have to be positively motivated to be healthy and to accept responsibility for their own health as well as that of their community.

3. What the medical and educational models do not sufficiently emphasize are the social and economic causes of disease, and the political nature of the question of promoting the health and well-being of society. The *community development* and *socio-political models* represent two different but complementary approaches to changing those structural factors which perpetuate unacceptable levels of general morbidity in areas of poverty, high unemployment, poor housing and multiple deprivation. Community development and community education approaches are concerned with mobilizing the social resources within deprived communities to define their own health priorities and to help themselves to health (often by encouraging health professionals to adopt new supportive roles).

4. The *political model* tends to emphasize the need to see health within the context of the total well-being of society and, whether the means chosen are revolutionary or evolutionary, they are concerned with the transformation of society – attempting the more equal distribution of resources for health and welfare, and the control of vested interests which are counter-productive to the health of society.

DHSS, *Prevention and Health: Everyone's Business* (HMSO, 1976). DHSS, *Inequalities in Health: A Report of a Working Group* (Chairman Sir Douglas Black), (1980). Hubley, J., *Health Education and Community Development* (Paisley College of Technology, 1980). Irwin, V. and Spira, M., *Basic Health Education* (Longman, 1977). Kaprio, L., *Primary Health Care in Europe*, The Euro Reports End Studies, 14 (WHO, Geneva, 1979). McGann, B., *Behaviour, Health and Lifestyle* (Villa Books, Dublin, 1980). McKeon, T., *The Role of Medicine* (Nuffield Provincial Hospitals Trust, 1976). Schools Council, *Schools Council Health Education Project, Teachers Guide* (for 5–13 year olds and 13–18 year olds), (Nelson, 1977). WHO, *Regional Programme in Health Education and Lifestyles* EUR/RC31/10, 5469B (WHO, Copenhagen, 1981).

IAN E. THOMPSON

See also: DIET; HEALTH AND ILLNESS; MEDICINE; POLITICAL THEOLOGY AND PASTORAL CARE; PRIORITIES IN HEALTH CARE.

HEAVEN AND HELL

States of being, referring (in the developed theology of the Judaeo-Christian tradition) respectively to eternal participation in the life of God and permanent estrangement from God.

Phrases of ordinary speech, like 'I went through hell', 'It was heavenly', suggest that heaven and hell are merely psychological states but a survey of the development of these concepts reveals that, from a theological point of view, such subjective psychic experiences are derivative from transpersonal reality. We shall consider: (1) the origins and evolution of the concepts; (2) the developed theological polarization of heaven and hell; (3) practical implications.

1. *Origins and evolution.* The two concepts, joined as polar opposites in this entry, did not originate as such in the Judaeo-Christian tradition. For the ancient Hebrew heaven was the upper part of the universe, a hemisphere covering the lower element of the earth, the two together constituting 'heaven and earth' (Gen. 1.1; Matt. 24.35). This firmament was splendid with light by day (Exod. 24.10)· and adorned with innumerable stars by night (Gen. 15.5; Isa. 40.26; Job 38.31ff.). The sky was so marvellous that it was thought of as

the proper dwelling-place and throne of God. And although God who thus reigned in heaven was omnipresent and so could receive the 'supplications of his servant, and of his people Israel' (1 Kings 8.30), he was also infinitely distant (Jer. 23.23ff.; 1 Kings 8.27). Thus 'the heavens are the Lord's heavens, but the earth he has given to the sons of men' (Ps. 115.16), an axiom echoed by St John in his turn: 'No one has ascended into heaven' (John 3.13).

Hell was, in this same early period, envisaged as without any particular relation to the heavens of 'heaven and earth', except in so far as it was the underbelly of the earth, a 'hole' or 'pit' or 'ditch' (Ps. 30.9; Ezek. 28.8) in the deepest depths of the earth (Deut. 32.22; Isa. 14.9). As such it was theoretically a third element in the total topography of the world. But this spatial logic seemed to be as shadowy as this *sheol* itself, the place to which all the living in due course descended and where they met (Gen. 37.35; 1 Sam. 2.6; Job 30.23), good as well as wicked (1 Sam 28.19; Ps. 89.48). From this they would never rise (Ps. 88.10; Job 7.9) and (what was worse for a God-fearing Israelite) they would not praise God (Isa. 38.11ff.; Ps. 6.5), hope in his justice (Ps. 88.11ff.) or in his fidelity (Ps. 30.9). Alongside this notion of *sheol*, however, there was another, more active notion, of *sheol* being like a monster liable to invade the land of the living and to snap people up before their due time (see e.g. Pss. 18.5; 55.15; 88.3ff.; Prov. 27.20; 30.16; Isa. 38.10–11).

It was this latter feature that led to an evolution of Israelite thinking. Hell was thought of in terms of a 'rain of fire' such as had fallen on Sodom and Gomorrah (Gen. 19.24; Amos 4.11; Pss. 11.68; 140.10), and of the worm that would not die and the fire that would not be quenched, such as was symbolized by the incinerator of Tophet, the refuse pit of the valley of Gehenna in Jerusalem (Isa. 66.24; Jer. 7.32). This was gradually seen to be a disorder due somehow to sin and therefore bound up with a differentiated destiny for the good and the wicked. *Sheol* was becoming a hell for sinners. This discrimination was, in its turn, part of the more general evolution of a notion of the resurrection: first of the chosen people as a whole (Hos. 6.1–2; 13.14; Isa. 26.19; 51.17; 60.1; Ezek. 37.1–14; Dan. 7.27), then, in the time of the Maccabean revolt, of just individuals (Dan. 12.2; 2 Macc. 7.9; 11, 23; 14.46).

This evolution was brought to a climax by Jesus. During his earthly life he had worked the precursory signs of raising people from the dead (Matt. 5.21f.; Luke 7.11–17; John 11) and was himself raised from the dead by the Father (Acts 2.24; 3.14; 4.10; 13.33; 17.31; 23.6; 1 Cor. 15.3ff.). Jesus taught that those who kept his commandments would share his ascent into heaven, while those who did not would go to eternal punishment (Matt. 25.31ff.).

2. *The developed theology*. It was thus only with this fulfilment of the evolution of thinking that *heaven* and *hell* were brought into direct relation to each other, and then only as part of the doctrine that human beings could come to share in God's own life (2 Pet. 1.4): heaven is the culmination and manifestation of God's will to save all men (1 Tim. 1.5), and indeed all creation (Eph. 1.9–10), in the wake of Jesus (1 Cor. 15.12ff.); and hell is the refusal of this destiny, the real threat of total isolation (Matt. 5.29–30; 13.42, 50; 22.13; 25.41).

3. *Practical implications*. The conclusion the Church has drawn from this tradition is that there is a 'communion of saints, resurrection of the body, and life everlasting', and that refusal to choose this destiny can result in the definitive torment of permanent estrangement from God (see e.g. Denziger-Schoenmetzer). Thus heaven and hell are not so much projections of certain states of our psyche onto supposed reality but rather projections on to the plane of our psyche of certain transpersonal realities. They are glimpses of objective realities, part of the invisible world that can be apprehended through the visible (Rom. 1.20). But, if this is so, then dealing with 'heavenly' or 'hellish' experiences becomes part of the general pastoral work of helping people to emerge out of their self-enclosure into a shared and objective world, to see their destiny as part of a larger whole and, where possible, to trace their problems to their spiritual root.

Denziger-Schoenmetzer, *Enchiridion Symbolorum Definitionum et Declarationum* 35° (Herder, Freiburg-im-Breisgau, 1973), §§ 72, 76, 411, 858–9. **Léon-Dufour, X.** (ed.), *Dictionary of Biblical Theology* (G. Chapman, 1967), 'Heaven', 'Hell', 'Resurrection'. **Rahner, K.** (ed.), *Sacramentum Mundi* (Burns & Oates, 1969), 'Hell', 'Salvation'.

MARCUS LEFÉBURE

See also: EVIL; FAITH; RECONCILIATION.

HOLINESS

(1) The summit of moral goodness showing itself especially in prayer and self-forgetfulness in the service of God and mankind. Other definitions of holiness presuppose this. (2) A special radiance or beauty of soul in which a human being reflects God's being and presence. (3) (Of places, times, etc.) special relationship with the presence and/or worship of God.

Holiness rises beyond the world of virtue and goodness of life, yet it is founded squarely on the ethical, and if it lacks this foundation it is open to illusion and the abuse of power and privilege. So it is that St Paul, when he is dealing with certain manifestations of 'holiness' among the first Christians, brings his disciples back to earth in his eloquent and uniquely important description of basic and enduring goodness, which is patient, kind, gentle, unassuming, undogmatic, and which he names *agapé*, charity (1 Cor. 13). All religions and all Christian denominations agree on this.

In the Judaeo-Christian tradition the key text in the understanding of holiness is to be found in the first chapter of Genesis, where we are told that: 'God created man in his own image; in the image of God he created him; male and female he created them' (v.27, NEB). The Greek Fathers interpreted the image of God as present in the whole human person, body and soul, so that nature as summed up in man's physical being is part of the image of God, and therefore holy. In Celtic Christianity, as expressed in the 8th-century hymn of St Patrick, in Scotus Eriugena (9th century) and in many blessings and observances, nature is seen as sacred and full of spiritual presences. Connected with this is the cult of holy wells, of which vestiges remain especially in place-names. The more common (Western) interpretation of the Genesis text follows St Augustine (5th century) in limiting the divine image to the *soul* of man and woman. This view tended to emphasize 'the inner light' (pietism) or the inner presence of faith (Protestantism) or 'the salvation of souls' (Catholicism). In our day there has been a partial recovery of the sense of the holiness of the world of nature.

The holiness of the relationship of man and woman is hinted at in the Genesis text, and is expressed with beauty, eloquence and total frankness in the Song of Songs which according to some commentators is at the centre of the Old Testament. St Paul sees this relationship of man and woman as 'a great mystery', that is to say a great mystery of sanctification (Eph. 5.32, RSV). This mystery is bound up with respect and reverence as well as mutual love and tenderness. This acceptance of the special and total holiness of sex has to counter, on the one hand, the puritanical rejection or suspicion of sex (connected with the limiting of the image to the human soul) and, on the other hand, the profanation of sex through consumerism, cheap journalism, and the exploitation of women and children.

The holiness of the relationship between man and woman opens up to the holiness of marriage and birth, and also (in Catholic and Orthodox Christianity) to the holiness of virginity and celibacy as bearing witness to the source of the image in God himself. This is not to be confused with the puritanical rejection or depreciation of sex, rather is it seen as expressing the most profound creativity of this sacred force in prayer and sacrificial love and service. Protestant Christianity tends to see this as at best an unrealizable ideal, and at worst a substitution of works for faith. Both Protestants and Catholics agree in the sacredness of marriage and family life. Here again all the great religions are in agreement.

Finally, there is the holiness of death and of all that leads us to it, of disease and pain of body and mind, and all that follows it for the living, of bereavement and grief. The sense of the holiness of this whole area of dissolution and death is central to the Christian mystical tradition, and is symbolized in the 'kissing of the leper' as a giving and a receiving of the Holy Spirit. A cold, clinical approach to disease and death misses completely this dimension of holiness, and there is in our own day a movement towards affirming the dignity of death and the human aspect of the treatment of diseases such as cancer. From this viewpoint every sickbed is a holy place, and every service of the sick is a kind of prayer, a living into the holiness of God. Here we glimpse what may be called 'the paradox of holiness' according to which what is most broken and forsaken (as Jesus was on the Cross) becomes the source of holiness, beauty and joy.

Chavchavadze, M. (ed.), *Man's Concern with Holiness* (Hodder & Stoughton, n.d.). **O'Donoghue, N.D.,** *Heaven in Ordinaire* (T. & T. Clark, 1979), chs. 4, 5. **Otto, R.**, *The Idea of the Holy*, 2nd edn (Oxford, 1958).

N.D. O'DONOGHUE

See also: HUMAN NATURE; VIRTUES AND VICES.

HOLOCAUST

(1) A sacrifice wholly consumed by fire, a burnt offering. (2) A complete destruction, especially of a large number of people; a great slaughter or massacre (*Shorter Oxford Eng. Dict.*). (3) Contemporary term denoting the murder of 6 million Jews by the Nazis, 1933–1945.

The attempt to understand the mass murder of the Jews in our time exists within various disciplines, notably in history, psychology and religion. The historical approach tends to subsume it under the general definition of genocide, the mass murder of minority groups characteristic of the 20th century. This blots out unique features of the Nazi action: the criminal pattern of a state which made the mass murder of the Jews a national priority over-riding all other considerations (i.e. trains were diverted from supplying troops in order to rush Jewish men, women and children into the extermination camps); the actual technology of murder involving not only death camps, gas chambers, carbon monoxide vans, etc., but a bureaucracy and reorganization of society which made the majority of citizens at least passive participants in the crimes, guided by mass propaganda and re-educational approaches demanding conformity with the state; and a dehumanizing of Jews, Sinti and Roma (gypsies) and other victims of Nazism (homosexuals, etc.). However, historians have been able to present the details of this mass murder with some accuracy, despite attempts by revisionist historians claiming that there was no killing or that the death camps never existed. Attempts to block out this reality are not only the work of apologists for the Hitler regime, but an attempt to escape the dark consequences of our immediate past which also link Auschwitz to Hiroshima; as Robert Lifton points out, much of the world tries 'to dismiss Hiroshima and Auschwitz from human consciousness. To attempt to do so is to deprive us of our own history, of what we are'. (Lifton 1976, p. 132)

In the field of religion, the Holocaust has renewed the discussion of theodicy (q.v.): how could God permit such evil? Radical theology has linked this with the 'death of God', but others have come to a reassertion of faith, even in the camps, and have stressed the 'silence of man' more than the 'silence of God', the right of Jewish survival, and the role of the state of Israel. In psychology, Viktor Frankl's logotherapy, Bettelheim's work, and Eugene Heimler's teachings emerged from the camps. Treatment of post-Holocaust trauma, the survivor syndrome, second-generation anxiety, and guilt feelings within society, indicate a continuing attempt to confront the lasting effects of the Holocaust. The impact on literature, particularly the work of Elie Wiesel, should also be noted.

Cohen, A.A., *The Tremendum* (Crossroad, New York, 1981). **Dawidowicz, L.**, *The Holocaust and the Historians* (Harvard UP, 1981). **Fackenheim, E.**, *God's Presence in History* (New York University Press, 1970). **Friedlander, A.H.**, *Leo Baeck: Teacher of Theresienstadt* (Routledge, 1973). *Out of the Whirlwind: The Literature of the Holocaust* (Schocken, New York, 1968). **Gilbert, M.**, *Atlas of the Holocaust* (M. Joseph, 1982).. **Hilberg, R.**, *The Destruction of the European Jews* (Harper & Row, 1979). **Lifton, R.**, *The Life of the Self* (Simon & Schuster, New York, 1976). **Rubinstein, R.**, *After Auschwitz* (Bobbs-Merrill, New York, 1966); *The Cunning of History* (P. Smith, 1976).

ALBERT H. FRIEDLANDER

See also: EVIL; THEODICY.

HOMOSEXUALITY

The sexual attraction of one person to another of the same sex, which usually, but not necessarily always, leads to various physical activities culminating in orgasm or sexual climax (*Ency. Brit.*) Homosexuality is not a disease, or a disability, but the natural sexual orientation of a human minority, variously estimated at between 4% and 10% of the human race. This estimate is increasingly supported by modern medical knowledge, and by ordinary human experience. It in no way impairs normal physical, creative or spiritual development, and is consistent with the highest attainment in every human profession. Homosexuals are a cross-section of humanity, differing in no perceptible ways, other than sexual orientation, from their fellows (*Homosexual Rights* 1978).

Overt homosexuality is physical sexual contact between members of the same sex. *Latent homosexuality* is having impulses and desires towards a member of the same sex which are unconscious, or if conscious are not sexually expressed. *Inversion* is used as a term equivalent to homosexuality. *Lesbian* or *sappho* are terms often referred to female homosexuality after Sappho, a female homosexual who lived on the Isle of Lesbos in ancient Greece. *Homophobia* is defined as the fear of being in contact with homosexuals and, in the case of homosexuals themselves, self-loathing.

D.J. West (1977, p. 2) reports: 'The use of the word "homosexual" as a label for persons is ambiguous. Few people pass through life without at some stage experiencing homosexual feelings.' Accidental homosexuality, the choice of a man as sexual object when no women are available (*faute de mieux*), indicates that most males are probably capable of a homosexual object choice (Hinsie and Campbell 1970).

In their 1948 and 1953 research Kinsey and his associates, using a 7-point scale to measure whether, and to what degree, their respondents were 'homosexual' or 'heterosexual', determined that nearly half of American males fell somewhere between 'exclusively heterosexual' and 'exclusively homosexual'.

From this and much other research it is clear that sexual orientation is not an either/or proposition. Rather, people can be distinguished on the basis of the degree to which their sexual responsiveness and behaviour are limited to persons of a particular sex (male or female). There are 'homosexualities' and 'heterosexualities', each involving a variety of dimensions. Sexual orientation cannot be referred to by a single noun. The use of such labelling is condemned by Kinsey where he points out that 'the world cannot be divided into sheep and goats so far as sexualities are concerned'.

West distinguishes three types of homosexual: (a) obligatory homosexuals – those who obtain no erotic stimulus whatever from the opposite sex and may experience a positive repulsion at the idea of heterosexual contact; (b) facultative homosexuals – those who indulge only when it suits them and not because they are incapable of enjoying heterosexual outlets; and (c) bisexuals or ambisexuals – those who respond strongly to both sexes.

Inquiries into the origins of human sexuality and homosexuality are dominated by four approaches: (1) the clinical psychoanalytical tradition, represented by Freud, examines emotional development in childhood, focusing on the unconscious. (2) The 'social book-keeping' approach, represented by Kinsey, examines the frequency and social distribution of sexual behaviour. (3) The experimental method, represented by Masters and Johnson, examines the physiology of sexual arousal. (4) The actionist approach, represented by Plummer is concerned with sexual meaning and the way it is socially constructed and socially patterned. Each field of inquiry produces its own perspective, but there is no firm understanding of homosexuality which can make any 'definition' more helpful than misleading.

Homosexuality occurs in virtually every culture and period of history. It is a common human phenomenon. Attitudes to homosexuals and therefore definitions as to its meaning, vary from a serious defect (criminal, moral, psychodynamic) to a harmless variant or even a social asset.

The view of social anthropologists tends to be that homosexual problems are a manifestation of cultural intolerance rather than individual maladjustment, and they question the reasons for labelling a substantial minority of the population psychologically, criminally or medically abnormal.

There is no evidence to show that homosexuals are apt to be weak, immature or neurotic, to lack moral sense, or to be unreliable or unhappy people. West concludes, 'No single predominant cause for all cases of homosexual orientation is ever likely to be found.'

The actual disabilities experienced by many homosexuals are mostly the result of enforced sexual repression, secrecy, fear of honesty, or socially induced shame – all highly destructive forces for any human being to bear. The fact is that far too many homosexuals still endure loneliness and despair, still fear to show love and affection, and occasionally kill themselves. It is also a fact that they may still be discriminated against in employment, unless they conceal their sexual orientation.

Homosexuality is, for many, a minority lifestyle that has been found viable and personally rewarding and that assumes a dynamic of its own. A contented heterosexual has no cause to fret about when or why he repressed his potential homosexuality; some homosexuals feel the same about trying to recover potential for heterosexuality. Similarly, the promiscuous homosexual may lack genuine love and stable friendship, like the promiscuous heterosexual, but condemnation of the former is always greater than that of the equally shallow life-style of the 'swinging' heterosexual.

Psychoanalysts today, as well as Freud himself in later works, emphasize that a homosexual orientation represents a complex psycho-social adaptation, not just a straightforward expression of infantile erotic interests. 'Like other aspects of human behaviour, sexual orientation is the outcome of a complex interplay of different factors, some of them physical, some hereditary . . . most environmental . . . include general cultural habits and expectations as well as . . . the individual's family upbringing and personal circumstances' (West 1977).

The explanations of psychoanalysts, although helpful, tend to be unnecessarily complicated and are likely to apply only to a minority of peculiar neurotic cases. The basic need for homosexuals is to be able to accept themselves with dignity, and then to follow their own moral and spiritual lights. The attempt to bring sexuality and love into harmony is common to all men and women, as is the aspiration to personal wholeness and integrity.

Towards a Charter of Homosexual Rights (Campaign for Reason, 1978). **Freud, S.,** *Introductory Lectures on Pychoanalysis* (Penguin, 1973). **Hinsie, L.** and **Campbell, R.J.,** *Psychiatric Dictionary* (OUP, 4th edn 1970). **Kinsey, A.** *et al., Sexual Behaviour in the Human Male* (Saunders, 1948). **Masters, William H.** and **Johnson, V.E.,** *Homosexuality in Perspective* (Little Brown, Boston, Mass., 1979). **Plummer, Ken,** 'Symbolic Interactionism and Sexual Conduct: an Emergent Perspective', in Mike Brake (ed.), *Human Sexual Relations* (Penguin, 1982). **West, D.J.,** *Homosexuality Re-examined* (Duckworth, 1977).

LESLIE VIRGO

See also: FEMININITY/MASCULINITY;
SEXUALITY AND SEXUAL DEVELOPMENT;
SEXUALITY, THEOLOGY OF.

HOPE

A fundamental condition of human living, expressed in realistic but trusting orientation towards the future.

1. *Universal hope.* Humanity is the only species capable of imagining the future; but because it can only be imagined, and not known, the future is enigmatic, and often more threatening than inviting. When convinced that their future is wholly empty or bleak, human beings may lose their will to endure even the present. Conversely, pain and adversity are regularly tolerated in expectation of a future worth waiting and struggling for. This instinctive ability to transcend the limitations of the immediate environment, and to be open to further possibilities, is 'hope'. Philosophers, anthropologists and doctors have all recognized its universality, and the dignity, courage and creativity with which it equips human beings to deal with negative experience.

2. *Christian hope.* This denotes not a universal human ability but God's gift to believers, and traditionally, at least, it refers less to the future in general as to the particular expectation of 'life beyond death'. Christian thinking about death and the 'hereafter' has been influenced by Plato's concept of the innately immortal soul. But for the Bible, 'God alone has immortality', while human beings are created mortal in their psycho-physical entirety, as well as cursed and enslaved by death, through sin. In raising Jesus from the dead, however, God has overcome the power of sin, and those who believe in Christ share in his victory over the grave, being thus 'reborn to a lively hope'. 'Eternal life' begins now, but faith would be futile 'if for this life only we have hoped in Christ'. The 'hope of glory' is that death cannot terminate the relationship with Christ, but that, like him, the faithful will be raised from the dead with a 'spiritual body' – not physically, that is, but with the personal identities their bodies gave them – and live with him in the presence of his heavenly Father (see especially 1 Cor. 15).

3. *The God of hope.* The essentially personal quality of hopefulness, whose confidence in the future extends to the destiny of individuals, need be neither individualistic nor other-worldly. The OT portrays Israel as a people of hope, brought from bondage into a 'land of promise', who trust that God will deliver them again from situations of hopelessness, and send his liberating Messiah in the last days. Likewise the Christian Church prays, 'Thy Kingdom come,' and celebrates Christ's death 'until he comes', expressing the hope that at the end of history evil selfishness will be judged and destroyed, and the world made new as a community of justice, peace

and love. This cosmic hope evokes patience in present suffering, but also inspires resistance to present evils. That hope has, therefore, a political dimension, is recognized in the present-day 'theology of hope' – closely allied to political theology (q.v.)· – whose call for active opposition to injustice is allied with the Marxist critique of the present order and vision of the future. However, a theological understanding of hope is opposed to 'optimism' (the belief that historical processes will create their own utopia) and to 'planning', which trusts in human progress through science and technology. Such false hopes invite despair and disappointment, while faith trusts in 'the God of hope' (Rom. 15.13), who goes ahead of human history and promises that he will not reach the goal of his own completeness without bringing the hungry and downtrodden to share in his own joy and freedom.

4. *Hope against hope.* Because hope clings unconditionally to a future which may be contradicted by the facts of present experience, it can resemble wishful thinking. Religious hope, especially, has been criticized as illusion (S. Freud). Yet, because 'hoping against hope' (Rom. 4.18) begins by recognizing the inadequacies of the present, it may be judged a realistic assessment of the *status quo* which responds to acknowledged limitations neither with panic nor resignation, but with courage and resolution.

5. *Hope in pastoral practice.* Since all authentic hope begins with this courageous recognition of the way things are, those who seek pastorally to engender hope will be at pains to validate rather than to smother expressions of both hopefulness and hopelessness in a given situation. That counselling which is gounded in faith and religious hope will wish, for example, not to crush but to interpret and expand, any rudiments of 'universal hope', however secular or poorly focused, in the outlook of the client. And all pastoral care will listen with receptivity and solidarity to the articulation of despair. The love thus enacted, the friendship thus extended, may demonstrate more effectively than words, the veracity of hope: the possibility of light amid the darkness, and of new beginnings beyond 'the end of one's tether'.

Barth,, K., 'The Holy Spirit and Christian Hope', *Church Dogmatics*, IV, 3 (T. & T. Clark, Edinburgh, 1962), pp. 902–42. Macquarrie, J., 'Hope', *In Search of Humanity* (SCM, 1982), pp. 243–52. Moltmann, J., *Theology of Hope* (SCM, 1967); *Hope and Planning* (SCM, 1971). Pannenberg, W., *Jesus God and Man* (SCM, 1968), pp. 82ff.

ALAN E. LEWIS

See also: FAITH; PROVIDENCE.

HOSPICE MOVEMENT

A number of homes or hospices which made the care of those dying of cancer and tuberculosis their special concern were founded on both sides of the Atlantic at the turn of this century. Most of them still continue their care today and the modern hospice movement has developed from their work.

Several surveys carried out in the 1950s and 1960s revealed that there was much suffering among dying patients. The need for further provision of special accommodation, skilled home care, concern for families and the spread of appropriate knowledge throughout the general field was the incentive that led to the establishment in 1967 of St Christopher's Hospice in London, the first hospice to apply the academic model of care, research and teaching to this field. This proved to be a major catalyst for a now worldwide movement.

The challenge to such a development began from attention to the nature of terminal pain and the need for its better understanding and therefore more effective treatment. The consideration of its psychological, social and spiritual components, as well as its physical complexities and the need for patients to have as much control as possible, gave great awareness of what they and their families could still achieve. The hospice multidisciplinary team aims, by skilled awareness of patients' symptoms and their feelings, to enable them to live to the limit of their physical, social and spiritual capacity. It works as a complementary local service, integrated into the whole field of medical care.

As this work was developed, initially in the UK, the USA and Canada, a variety of innovations and interpretations under different titles came to be known as 'the hospice movement'. There are now independent units, wards and separate buildings on a hospital campus, and many consulting homecare and hospital teams with no beds of their own. This variety has grown up in response to local initiative and possibilities with the minimum of central organization. One major reason for this has been the aim of every hospice that its experience, research and teaching should be so accepted that those in the general field will approach all dying patients with appropriate attitudes and skills. The special centres and teams continue to be needed for those with particularly intractable problems and to pioneer in a demanding and rewarding branch of care.

Hospice Information Service, St Christopher's Hospice, 51–53 Lawrie Park Road, Sydenham, London SE26 6DZ. The National Hospice Organization, 1311A Dolley Madison Boulevard, McLean, Virginia 22101, USA.

CICELY SAUNDERS

See also: HOSPITALS; PAIN; DYING.

HOSPITAL CHAPLAINCY

(1) The range of specialized non-parochial ministries exercised in hospitals of various kinds. (2) The unit or department in a particular hospital, staffed by a chaplain or chaplains, which provides services of a religious or pastoral nature.

The character of hospital chaplaincy depends upon the type of hospital, the needs of patients, the denomination of the chaplain, and the resources and opportunities available. Its main task is to provide a supportive, pastoral or sacramental ministry to patients. Pastoral ministry in hospital involves forming relationships in which patients can speak openly and with feeling about their illness, injury and hospitalization, as well as about other life experiences, such as recent loss or current conflict, which may be related to their illness. Patients may express feelings of loneliness, anxiety, fear, anger, guilt, doubt, meaninglessness, grief and despair, but also gratitude, relief, security and optimism. Pastoral ministry demands sensitive listening, perceptive observation, careful response, emotional warmth and a capacity to confront ultimate questions of meaning in such a way that patients may be comforted and may come to use their experience of illness positively. The pastoral care of the dying (q.v.) requires special qualities and skills. Sacramental ministry is both relevant and conveniently offered in a hospital context. Baptism, penance, holy communion, the sacrament of the sick and extreme unction address the realities of the human condition and express the love, mercy, renewal, hope and peace which come

from God. The presence of a chaplain in hospital may also have symbolic importance for patients for whom he or she may be seen to represent values, attitudes and beliefs accepted by the faith group to which they belong, which are especially significant for the sick and injured, e.g. the love of God, forgiveness of sins, life after death, the power of prayer, the worth of the individual, the supportive care of the religious community, God's healing and renewing purpose as expressed by Jesus, and his identification with the sick and poor.

In both acute and long-stay wards, chaplaincy is most acceptable and effective when integrated into a programme of treatment and care shared with other health-service professionals, who usually welcome the involvement of chaplains in a supportive role and see them as a useful resource within the hospital, with a valuable contribution to make to the care of patients and relatives. Conflicts may sometimes arise between chaplains and other health-service professionals, because of the different frames of reference with which they work, but these can be illuminating and productive. Increasing specialization in hospital treatment and care has necessitated a corresponding development in chaplaincy expertise.

Requests for visits come from patients themselves, hospital staff, the patients' own clergymen, relatives and friends. Chaplains in the wards also meet patients who have not been directly referred, but the chaplaincy service is available and not imposed. Where any patient wishes to see a representative of his or her own faith-group, the chaplain will normally arrange it and will make himself available to visiting clergymen to provide information, advice and such other consultation as may help to make their ministry in hospital more effective.

Since admission to hospital affects relatives as well as patients, chaplains are frequently expected to minister to them, especially where patients are dying, critically ill or suffering from an illness in which the family is implicated. Increasingly, chaplains are asked to contribute to staff education and counselling. Involvement in programmes of training of nurses and others working in the health service is growing, and members of staff often approach chaplains for help with professional or personal problems.

Chaplains are appointed either by the church with the approval of the hospital authorities or vice versa. Smaller hospitals are usually served by part-time chaplains, who are often local clergymen willing to undertake chaplaincy work in addition to their parochial duties. Chaplaincies in large hospitals are staffed by mixed teams of full-time and part-time chaplains, preferably of different denominations. The advantage of a part-time chaplain is his or her involvement in and knowledge of the local community and ability to call on the help of a local congregation. Advantages of a full-time chaplain are knowledge of the hospital and its staff and continuous availability. Chaplaincy work is maintained financially by hospital authorities, by the churches, or on a shared basis by both. Chaplains are usually accountable for their ministry to church authorities, rather than to secular hospital authorities, but it is important that the chaplain should enjoy the confidence of both.

The chaplain's role may be seen in other ways – ethicist, patients' advocate, psychotherapist, resident theologian, adviser to the ward team, enabler and teacher, an interpreter who functions and communicates at the interface between science and religion, the hospital and the church. Outside the hospital, there may be a prophetic function in recalling the churches to their mission of helping and healing the sick and creating a healthier society. Within the hospital, the chaplain may act prophetically by questioning the system when it violates the humanity of patients or staff.

Faber (1971) maintains that the hospital chaplain, like the clown in the circus, occupies a unique place. There are three tensions: between being a member of a team and being in isolation; of appearing to be and feeling like an amateur among experts; and between the need for study and learning on the one hand and the need to be original and creative on the other. In the face of developing technology the chaplain stands for the common human denominator and, at the same time, he or she identifies the presence and activity of God in the hospital community.

Faber, H., *Pastoral Care in the Modern Hospital* (SCM 1971). Hospital Chaplaincies Council, *The Hospital Chaplain: Report of the Working Party Appointed by the Joint Committee* (Church Information Office, 1973). Wilson, M., *The Hospital: a Place of Truth* (University of Birmingham Institute for the Study of Worship and Religious Architecture, 1971). *Contact* (The Interdisciplinary Journal of Pastoral Studies), no. 16 (Jan. 1966); no. 69 (1980); no. 80 (1983).

T.S. McGregor

See also: HOSPITALS; NATIONAL HEALTH SERVICE.

HOSPITALS

Institutions for: (a) the elimination and cure of illness; (b) the care of the sick and wounded; (c) the training of the caring professions; (d) the learning of healthy responses to illness and death.

1. *Organization and history in the UK.* Four types of hospital existed prior to 1948: the voluntary hospital supported by local donations as a kind of insurance policy for care; the council hospital supported by town and county councils; state hospitals for the armed services and prison service; and private institutions usually of the type and size of small nursing homes. Following the National Health Service Act (1948) hospitals were placed under the control of the Minister of Health. Responsibilities for the service are delegated to regional health authorities and thence to district health authorities. Each district provides a full range of services in hospitals and the community including maternity, paediatrics, psychiatry, general medicine and surgery, and geriatric care. Some hospitals contain units which offer a regional service, e.g. organ transplantation, addiction. Hospitals consume the major amount of the NHS budget, with the running allowances being lowest in the psychiatric and geriatric sectors, e.g. food cost per patient. Priority and prestige are given to the teaching and general hospitals. The local authorities remain responsible for hostels and community homes for the elderly, mentally ill, and mentally handicapped, though voluntary organizations are making up for the lack of provision in these areas. General practitioners are organized independently through the local family practitioner committee. The relationship between hospital and community is changing from the time when the sick were removed to protect society and hospitals were institutions set apart, to a more open contemporary policy with shorter lengths of stay for patients, longer visiting hours, and an emphasis on community care. This shift of policy has not yet seen the same financial shift for the provision of services from hospital to community, without which community care is a meaningless phrase.

2. *Values and beliefs.* Hospitals reflect the cultural values and the strong development of the medical role this century. (1) Curing is

more important than caring; reactions to this can be seen in the hospice movement and in the 'nursing process' (individual patient care). (2) Medicine is an objective science based on research and supported by technology; this carries the danger of a mechanistic view of man, and seeing the individual not as an end in himself but a means to an end in research. (3) Health is seen in terms of problem-solving and ideas of growth are obscured. (4) Materialism permeates the system, emphasizing physical treatments for all illness. Longevity is valued rather than the quality of life. Social, emotional, and spiritual factors are devalued. (5) Treatment focuses on the individual rather than the family or community. (It can still be difficult for a mother to stay in hospital with her sick child.) (6) Professionalism is highly valued. New entrants to medicine and nursing receive training and apprenticeship rather than education. The culture is conservative and lacks critical awareness. Professionalism discounts the role of lay people unless they can conform to the professional pattern under professional control.

3. *Structure and hierarchy.* The early autocracy reflected a mixture of monastic and military styles with a clearly delineated class system, e.g. separate eating and leisure facilities for medical, nursing and domestic staff. The hierarchy today is based on knowledge, with medical knowledge most valued. A strong sense of conformity and obedience to authority remains in the general hospitals as a way of coping with anxiety in the face of illness and death. Psychiatric hospitals have formed more democratic regimes. The 1970s saw the rise of the administrator/manager as a new power in hospitals. Whereas doctors and nurses have values linked to their professions, administrators have bureaucratic and institutional values and loyalties. Administrators/managers have attempted to rationalize services but have brought few new insights to bear on hospital and community priorities. Change requires more consumer involvement on management bodies, and more local accountability through community health councils.

4. *Future perspectives.* Hospitals of the future must embody a changing vision of health and a positive response to disease. Immediate priorities lie in the areas of child poverty and the disabled. Future priorities centre around health as everybody's business

and the challenge to create a healthy community.

Abel-Smith, B., *The Hospitals 1800–1948* (Heinemann, 1964). **Goffman, E.,** *Asylums* (Anchor Books/Doubleday, 1961). **Martin, D.,** *Adventure in Psychiatry* (Cassiver, 1962). **McKeown, T.,** *Role of Medicine, Dream, Mirage, or Nemesis* (Nuffield Provincial Hospitals Trust, 1976). **Townsend, P.** and **Davidson, N.,** *Inequalities in Health* (Penguin, 1982). **Wilson, M.,** *The Hospital: a Place of Truth* (Univ. of Birmingham, 1971).

PETER BELLAMY

See also: HOSPICE MOVEMENT; HOSPITAL CHAPLAINCY; NATIONAL HEALTH SERVICE; NURSING.

HOSTILITY
See: ANGER AND HOSTILITY.

HUMAN DEVELOPMENT
The physical and psychological changes which occur in human life from birth to death.

The various stages of human development have been conceptualized in a great many different ways from Shakespeare's 'seven ages of man' to Erikson's eight stages. These are set out comparatively in the following table. Each stage carries within it possibilities for weal or woe and has to be satisfactorily negotiated before the succeeding stage can be reached. Erikson depends heavily on Freud's psychoanalytic theories for his first five stages, but for the last three he was much influenced by Hindu culture and by Jung who set great store by the wisdom and maturity of old age.

In a rather different framework, Levinson (1978) has mapped out remarkably specific developmental periods from *early adult transition* (ages 17–22), *mid-life transition* (40–45) and *age fifty transition* (50–55), relating the various crises of development to marriage, career choice, and the importance of finding senior mentors to guide and support through each successive stage. He shows how the much discussed mid-life crisis (Jacques 1965) is but one in a series of phases and sub-phases in the adult life. The psychologist Piaget has described intellectual development as starting with a *sensori-motor stage* (0–2) before language is possible, through the stage of *pre-operational thought* (2–7) to *concrete thinking* (7–11) and on to the dawning capacity for *formal abstract thinking* at about 11 years.

Ages	Shakespeare's 'seven ages of man'	Erikson's eight stages of psycho-social development
0–1	at first the infant mewling and puking in the nurse's arms	trust *vs.* mistrust
1–3		autonomy *vs.* shame and doubt
3–5		initiative *vs.* guilt
6–puberty	the whining schoolboy unwillingly to school	industry *vs.* inferiority
adolescence	the lover sighing like a furnace	identity *vs.* identity diffusion
early adulthood	a soldier full of strange oaths	intimacy *vs.* isolation
middle adulthood	the justice full of wise saws	generativity *vs.* self-absorption
later adulthood	lean and slipper'd pantaloon	integrity *vs.* despair
	Sans everything	

Piaget's work has great significance for educationalists who now recognize that the child can be taught only what he is ready for.

The study of human development offers a good deal more than a timetable of the human life-cycle. It offers a new perspective, if we are prepared to consider our own subjective experience as well as that of others.

Out of the work of Freud and his successors it is possible to trace in a new way the continuing influence of early family life. It is useful, perhaps essential, for the pastor nowadays to grasp some of the concepts about mental activity no matter what age is being considered. It is widely agreed that the way we handle our central human needs begins to be determined in infancy by the response of others (mother, siblings, father) to our central needs and drives. The satisfactions and frustrations of these early times continue with us into every stage of the life-cycle, sometimes modified and sometimes persisting unchanged.

In contrast with all of this, the Bible is interested in human growth only in so far as it characterizes the work of God – if boys and girls and old people are mentioned, it is to make the point that the Lord will return to Zion (Zech. 8.5). Just as seed is cast into the ground and leads to the flourishing of a plant, so God's work progresses from the lesser to the greater in regard to the Kingdom, the Church and in the life of the individual believer (Mark 4.26–9). The focus is on growth in grace from spiritual infancy to adult maturity (Heb. 5.12–14).

Brown, D. and **Pedder, J.,** *Introduction to Psychotherapy: an Outline of Psychodynamic Principles and Practice* (Tavistock, 1979). **Erikson, Erik K.,** *Childhood and Society* (Penguin, 1965). **Fowler, J.,** *Stages of Faith* (Harper & Row, New York, 1981). **Jacques, E.,** 'Death and the Mid Life Crisis' (*International Journal of Psychoanalysis*, 46, 1965), pp. 502–14. **Keagan,, J.,** *The Evolving Self* (Harvard UP, 1982). **Levinson, Daniel J.,** *The Seasons of a Man's Life* (Knopf, 1978). **Rayner, Eric,** *Human Development* (Allen & Unwin, 1979).

R.M. LEISHMAN

See also: ADOLESCENCE; AGEING; CHILDREN: PASTORAL CARE; MATURITY; MIDDLE AGE; SELF-ACTUALIZATION.

HUMAN NATURE

'Human' nature is clearly built up out of the same basic building blocks (or quanta of energy) as the rest of 'nature' (genes, DNA, and all the rest of it). The question is, 'What is so special about it (us)?' There is a great variety of philosophical, religious and mythological answers to this, going back to the beginning of recorded history and beyond. (Prehistoric humans went in for special burial arrangements presumably because they felt that 'we are somehow special'). *Human* nature is therefore marked by a capacity for self-consciousness and to wonder about who or what we are, with a hint or longing or faith that we are more than just the natural stuff that rots and is recycled. A main theme in much Western philosophy and religion has been to understand human nature as we experience it, as a 'mix' of spirit-stuff (soul-stuff) and matter-stuff. It is then held that human nature lies 'really' on the spiritual/soul side and various theories or stories explain the current mix and offer various solutions (salvations) for getting out of it. The main religious/philosophical traditions of the East have rejected this (to them) crude dualism and have diagnosed the root of human worries about human nature as lying in self-consciousness itself. The separate self is an illusion, which feeds on its mistaken and illusionary longing. There is no human nature. Rather 'thou art that' and the problems of (human) awareness disappear as one passes beyond all limits and illusions by means of the appropriate psychological, philosophical and religious discipline (e.g. the Buddhist eight-fold path). From the eighteenth century in the West various theories have argued that it is talk about 'otherness' which is the real illusion and human nature must be understood 'scientific-ally' and in no other way. Sometimes this type of view is argued optimistically (e.g. eighteenth century beliefs about the perfectability of man by men through proper education and social organization, and Marxist views about correct understanding of the dialectic leading to the fulfilment of human beings in the classless society), some-times the approach is more neutral or pessim-istic (reductionism – men and women are *nothing but* – e.g, naked apes, determinism, behaviourism, etc.). The optimistic views seem refuted by what actually happens, the 'nothing but' views seem persistently to fail to do justice to some of the things we all experience as human beings (e.g. free will, the glorious value of values, joy, etc.). Historic-ally, Christian views of human nature have been much influenced by the spirit/matter dichotomy, but the belief in creation and incarnation as activities of God seem to tie up with scientific discoveries to make it clear that human beings are *material* creatures who develop as *persons* with spiritual capacities ('in the image of God').

To separate the spiritual from the material in any dualism is to believe in a different story about God, men and women and the world from a Christian one. Human nature, there-fore, must not be *defined* or *confined*. It must always be regarded, and treated, as open, emergent and risky (including the actualized risk of *sin* (q.v.)). Above all it is a matter of *relationships* between men and women, their environment and God. Nothing short of the Kingdom of God is, in the end, good enough for human nature. Meanwhile, if we are committed to a Christian view of humanity we have to wrestle responsibly and in faith with all the information and possibilities science gives us, all the problems we create for ourselves through sin and all the promises God opens to us, including the problems and possibilities pointed to by some aspects of all the other approaches to 'human nature'.

Jenkins, D.E., *What is Man?* (SCM, 1985). Moltmann, J., *Man* (SPCK, 1974). Pannenberg, W., *Human Nature, Election and History* (Westminster Press, Philadelphia, 1977).

DAVID JENKINS

See also: PERSON; SELF; SOUL.

HUMILITY

(1) An attitude of lowliness or submissive-ness. (2) A modest estimate of one's worth. (3) An understanding based on the truth about oneself.

The life of the Spirit within us is meant to lead us towards greater truth and freedom (cf. John 8.32; 16.13). If there are no obstacles to block its way, this same Spirit enables us to recognize our true status as persons before God. The value of our human nature (q.v.) lies in God's love for us; and our weakness lies in our failure to respond to that love. Such self-knowledge as leads directly out of our relationship with God is humility; and in as much as it is a truthful and modest estimate of who we are, it will transform our estimates of and attitudes towards others. If, however, we seek humility for its own sake, we discover the exercise to be self-defeating.

Christians have always considered humility in the context of Christ's example (cf. Phil. 2.5–8). As Christ accepted the limita-tions of the human condition, so his followers demonstrate their humility by accepting the boundaries of their own human condition (*see* NEW TESTAMENT AND PASTORAL CARE). Some elements of these boundaries are fixed; others are open to change.

Today, the concept of humility is often confused with the self-abasement that arises from problems of exaggerated emotional or psychological guilt (q.v.). There is, therefore, a need to explore and refine the feelings that we have about ourselves, so that a more truthful personal assessment may be made. We need to be liberated from neurotic forms of humility, which have their origin in false guilt and lead to self-punishment.

The discernment of our true situation is best achieved with the assistance of an objective witness, who can accept our feelings in a nonjudgemental way and, at the same time, can distinguish between Godward feelings that arise from the truth about ourselves, and feelings that spring from illusions we have, born of guilt and fear. These illusions may have their root in painful experiences in our past life, which need healing.

Ultimately, humility is a sign that we are being freed from illusion, fear and false guilt, and that we are recognizing ourselves in the light of God's knowledge of us. This recognition unfolds in the course of our life and leads to that full realization and self-knowledge that we shall experience in the presence of God (cf. 1 Cor. 13.12). As it is unfolding to us, this self-knowledge issues in an attitude of humility towards God and towards others.

Louf, André, *Humility and Obedience in Monastic Tradition* (Cistercian Studies, vol. 18 1983/84), pp. 261–82.

SIMON HOLDEN, C.R.

HUMOUR

Humour is the human way of coping with difficulty in a playful and pleasurable way. It can be an acceptable expression of normally disguised, unconscious thoughts and impulses. It brings together opposites, highlights contradictions and shows up the absurdity of what is irreconcilable. It is the paradox and absurdity which makes us laugh.

Different kinds of humour belong to different developmental stages, different personality types and different cultures. A very early kind is that enjoyed by the young child who finds signs of weakness, such as lack of control of limbs or a 'rude' noise which he had just mastered, uproariously funny. The practical joke belongs to a slightly later phase, as it involves planned action. Teasing requires

language. Jokes and caricature are more sophisticated still, and humour which enables people to laugh at themselves requires a high degree of maturity.

The practical joke represents a fairly primitive form of humour which can be quite cruel and is generally at the expense of another. Teasing may also contain an element of cruelty, since it frequently makes use of an infirmity or imperfection, but it can also be a gentle and affectionate confrontation of a person's shortcomings. Comedy is a play in which humour is expressed through ludicrous situations, in which the villain tends to become the victim of his or her own villainy. This causes amused superiority in the audience. Jokes are absurdities which gain their verbal hitting-power from condensation and economy of thought. Condensation and brevity are important ingredients for effectiveness. There also has to be an element of pleasurable shock or surprise.

The court jester or fool can turn the world upside down. He is licensed to make fun of authority figures, expressing doubt and aggression in a way that flatters and pleases and helps to see things in a new way. Caricature expresses pictorially what the joke expresses in words. A slight distortion or exaggeraton of a prominent feature makes the 'victim' seem slightly ridiculous and allows us to laugh at seeing a well-known, illustrious figure taken down a peg.

Humour thus provides a strategy for living with hardship. Jokes in the mortuary, for example, help the mortician cope with disturbing feelings about death. It is a safety valve in that it provides an acceptable, even pleasurable outlet for hostile, aggressive or envious feelings. It makes the intolerable bearable by putting it into perspective. The ability to recognize absurdity in our own attitudes and behaviour and to laugh at the antics of the child-self can be very healing. Laughing *with* others creates a feeling of fellowship. Laughing *at* others, on the other hand, is a way of putting the other down and making us feel superior. Mocking laughter is a defence which protects us from fears about ourselves. The new perspective given by humour reconciles opposites and incongruities and helps to transcend what appeared intolerable. Being able to laugh a little at the mighty makes the powerless feel a little less helpless. Humour can thus be used as a balm or a weapon.

Berger, Edmund, *Laughter and the Sense of Humour* (Grune & Stratton, New York, 1956). Freud, Sigmund, *Humour*, Collected Papers, vol. 5 (1928); *Jokes and Their Relation to the Unconscious* standard edn, vol. 8 (1905). Grotjahn, Martin, *Beyond Laughter, Humour and the Sub-conscious* (McGraw-Hill, New York, 1966). Williams, H.A., *Tensions* (Mitchell Beazley, 1979), ch. 7.

IRENE BLOOMFIELD

See also: FANTASY; IMAGINATION; MATURITY; PLAY.

HYMNS

Religious verse suitable for corporate expression when sung in stanzas to a tune.

Musical melodies and rhythms make corporate speech more attractive and decisive. As Routley (1964, p. 18) says, 'Few congregations can speak well in unison, but many can sing very well together.' However, the words, 'take a logical priority over the music'. Music can lift good words, but may also lull singers into acceptance of trivia. Thus a good hymn-text is 'a poem under three monastic vows: clarity, simplicity, and obedience to strict rhythm . . . simple enough to be understood at first sight, yet deep enough to withstand repeated singing' (Wren 1978, p. 22).

Hymn-singing can strengthen a sense of community – important where congregations (q.v.) use repeated spoken utterances, essential where hymns are the congregation's main corporate expression. Thus the choosing of hymns should never be a casual matter; it should neither acquiesce in triviality, nor yet be divorced from congregational preference and familiarity, but should enable people to sing doctrine memorably rather than doggerel lustily; to be moved to wonder, praise and mutual caring; to express real questioning and conviction; and to be unified not merely in warm togetherness (important though this may be) but in openness to God in Christ and in the neighbour.

Good hymns combine refreshing music with powerful imagery (metaphors, similes, etc.) under theological and rational control. Since crisis times prompt people to recall snatches of best-known scripture, prayers and hymns, it is worth teaching good hymns, old and new, and drawing out their meaning. Methods for the former include repetition line by line until the tune is established, repetition of a new hymn several times in a month in different liturgical contexts, and initial use by choir or soloists. Methods for the latter include reading the hymn-text aloud before congregational singing, sometimes with a brief comment on its meaning and authorship, or singing out particular lines or stanzas and asking congregations to meditate silently or discuss them quietly with immediate neighbours before singing (asking, e.g.: What recent events does this bring to mind? What experiences of ours does this express? 'Which lines or stanzas really speak to us, or for us, and why? How would I say this in my own words?).

Since we should no more bow down to poetic images of God than to graven images, pastoral sensitivity means looking for hymns with varied images of God, and explaining their function as pointing to qualities of relationship with God rather than describing the nature of God. Thus God as Father means not a description of a masculine deity but a quality of loving parenting in God's care for us (*see also* SEXISM; SEXUALITY, THEOLOGY OF).

Hymns can deepen, or cheapen, theological awareness. Recent writings bring many fine texts which refresh traditional formulations, of sing to God from the suffering, hope, pain and faith of our century. Pastoral care implies exploration and use of the best new hymnody in preaching, teaching, singing and counselling.

Lovelace, Austin C., *The Anatomy of Hymnody* (GIA Publications, Chicago, 1965/1982). Routley, Erik, *Christian Hymns Observed* (Mowbray, 1983); *Hymns Today and Tomorrow* (Darton Longman and Todd, 1964). Sydnor, James Rawlings, *Hymns and Their Uses, a Guide to Improved Congregational Singing* (Agape, Carol Stream, Illinois, 1982). Wren, Brian, 'Making Your Own Hymn' (*Bulletin of the Hymn Society of Great Britain and Ireland*, 142, May 1978).

BRIAN WREN

See also: WORSHIP AND PASTORAL CARE.

HYPNOSIS

A technique for inducing a trance-like state.

A great deal of argument has been spent on discussion of just what is the hypnotic state or trance. Concepts of the state have included a sham death (on the snake and rabbit analogy), a peculiar change in brain physiology, a form of illness allied to 'hysteria' and plain gullibility. The most convincing theoretical construct of the hypnotic trance has been put forward by the American psychologist, Ernest Hillgard, who conceives of the state as a form of dissociation. Dissociation is a normal state of mind exhibited by anyone preoccupied with profound reverie or concentrating on some matter, such as being 'lost' in a book, to the extent of lack of awareness of other happenings in his environment. A feature of the dissociated state, at least as produced in the setting of hypnosis, is an increased susceptibility to suggestion so that ideas put forward by the therapist or hypnotist take on the appearance of reality.

The techniques of inducing hypnotic states vary from the extremely authoritarian to the gently permissive. Many people will be unable to 'accept' authoritarian statements such as 'your arm is growing lighter and lighter and floating up, up, into the air' and so will be pronounced to be 'poor' hypnotic subjects. However as Braid pointed out, it is really the subject who carries out the procedure and if the therapist confines his role to merely facilitating the procedure by appropriate suggestion, then the majority of people can enter a hypnotic trance and their ability to do so will improve with practice.

In 1974 an American physician and two students (Benson, Beary and Carol, *Psychiatry*, vol. 37, pp. 37–46) undertook a survey of trance states used in religious and therapeutic practice throughout the world and throughout history. They coined a term 'relaxation response' the characteristics of which are: a point of mental fixation, a passive attitude (inviting the experience rather than striving to obtain it), decreased muscle tonus and a quiet environment.

Today there is increasing interest in what are sometimes called 'alternative therapies' and hypnotic techniques are undergoing a revival of interest; sometimes techniques are loosely referred to as 'relaxation therapy', but an essential element of all meditative techniques is intense concentration which is far removed from the state of dozing to a half-sleep implied by the term relaxation. A particular form of self-help programme has been described by the writer under the title 'anxiety control training' (Snaith, *Clinical Neurosis*, OUP, 1981).

A selection of good reading in therapeutic aspects of hypnosis is provided by Snaith, R.P. 'Reading About Hypnosis' (*British Journal of Psychiatry*, no. 144, 1984), pp. 665–6.)

R.P. SNAITH

See also: CONSCIOUSNESS; MEDITATION; RELAXATION; SLEEP.

I

ID
In psychoanalysis (q.v.) that area of the psyche which is unconscious; the locus and source of amoral, instinctual impulses.

Freud, Sigmund, *New Introductory Lectures in Psychoanalysis* (Penguin, 1973), Lecture 31.

IDENTIFIED PATIENT
An individual upon whom the pathology of a group has been projected.

Satir, V., *Conjoint Family Therapy* (Science and Behaviour Books, Palo Alto Calif., 1967).

IDENTITY
(1) Name, status or role; the objective identity of a person in the eyes of others, but see below for the distinction between identity and role. (2) Personal identity, the subjective sense of 'who I am', or the 'real me', which may be different from 'who people think I am'. (3) Psychosocial identity.

Personal identity. Erikson defines identity as 'the ability to express one's self as something that has continuity and sameness, and to act accordingly' (1965, p. 37). He is the main exponent of the term in psychological literature. 'Continuity and sameness' include normal growth and development of identity throughout life (*see* HUMAN DEVELOPMENT), which Erikson spells out in some detail, concentrating upon adolescence (q.v.) as a major time for formulating identity (personal, sexual, occupational and ideological) as preparation for adult life.

In the first few months of life the identity of the baby is intimately related to that of the mother, gradually separating out as a rudimentary sense of self ('I am unique'), although independence is not complete until at least adolescence. Early identity is largely based upon identification with aspects of both parents and significant others. 'What I can do' is built up upon internalizing the 'rules' of the family but also through increasing physical and intellectual mastery. Sexual identity ('I am a boy/girl') also begins in childhood, but is

a major aspect of adolescence when there are physical developments of body identity, with issues about femininity/masculinity (q.v.). Adolescence leads either (a) to a sense of more complete identity, separate from (though not always different from) the values and attitudes of parents, tradition and society (a young person needs to resolve such questions for himself or herself); or (b) to foreclosed identity, where a person acts more to identify with and not offend others than to express self; or (c) to identity confusion, which may result in psychotic, maladaptive or criminal behaviour, and is less amenable to help or change.

Identity remains subject to change throughout life. Identity crises (commonplace in adolescence) can occur at significant points, such as marriage, divorce, birth of children, geographical relocation, changes of occupation or status, redundancy, retirement and bereavement. Often the external role of a person changes, so that the inner sense of identity needs to adjust, but the internal self can also suffer change, particularly when loss occurs. The lost person is 'part of me'. Nevertheless most identity crises are transitory disturbances, enabling the self to change, while at the same time maintaining continuity with the former sense of self. Erikson describes the final stage of life as one of 'integration' of identity, during which life's experiences are re-worked in memory and in reflection towards a sense of wholeness – a parallel term is Jung's 'individuation' (*see* ANALYTICAL PSYCHOLOGY).

Analysts use different terms – such as 'the false self' (Jung's 'persona' is also capable of this meaning) – to describe a feature of identity somewhat different from the social psychologist's distinction between role and identity. Here a person erects a false identity, to mask the unconscious sense of the self as damaged, weak, or felt to be bad. Identity crises may therefore also be triggered by major changes in self-perception, although the false self may also use role and status to disguise the true self.

'Negative identity' occurs where a person's

(or group's) negative self-image is one imposed upon the self by superiors and accepted as true (e.g. 'I am a bad boy because my parents continually say so'; 'We blacks are inferior because white men tell us we are').

Psychosocial identity is a complex interaction between the subjective sense of identity and the objective expectations of others. Goffman describes individual identity as existing somewhere between the virtual self (expectations on a person concerning their place in society, role, status) and the actual self (all that a person is apart from their place in society). There is less tension for both individual and society when the actual self can be expressed in ways available to the virtual self.

Erikson, E.H., 'Identity and the Life Cycle' *Psychological Issues*, 1, no. 1 (1959); *Childhood and Society* (Penguin, 1965); *Identity, Youth and Crisis* (Faber, 1968). **Goffman, E.**, *The Presentation of Self in Everyday Life* (Allen Lane, 1969).

MICHAEL JACOBS

See also: HUMAN DEVELOPMENT; PERSON; SELF.

IMAGINATION
(1) The faculty of creative thought.	(2) Vain or false thinking.

In popular thought, as well as in philosophy, imagination has often been equated with fantasy as either sustained deluded flight from reality or as, in a biblical context, the source of human wrongdoing (Gen. 8.21: 'For the imagination of man's heart is evil from his youth'). Before consideration of other accounts of the term 'imagination', it may be relevant to note that while fantasy as persistent escapism may be psychologically undesirable, in proper dosage and in appropriate applications, it may be eminently commendable. For example, it is an essential feature of the seeing of visions which Joel (2.28) characterizes as one of the gifts of God's spirit, and of the idealism without which both persons and nations spiritually perish. It is endemic to the writing of the romantic sagas which have achieved so much popularity, both in their own right (as in J.R.R. Tolkien's *The Lord of the Rings*) and as religious allegories (as in C.S. Lewis's *Narnia* stories). It is psychologically healthy also as a means of relief in times of stress, but becomes pathologically dangerous when it assumes control of the individual's thought and action, to the exclusion of all realism.

A strong case has been made, however, in recent years for regarding imagination, not as a special faculty of the mind (as was the case in medieval epistemology, reflected recently in Mary Warnock's description of it as 'a power of the mind'), certainly not as agency for evil in the human heart, but as the human mind working in certain specifiable ways, which it is now possible to enumerate.

1. Imagination is the human mind in heightened sensitivity and openness to, and perceptiveness of, features in the world of nature and in persons, which the ordinary observer passes without noticing. Artistic imagination is able to detect in a landscape, in the sky or in the sea, colours and formations, which others notice only when their attention is drawn to them; or in the sitter for a portrait insights into aspects of character which are denied to most casual observers. Such qualities of imagination are seen in Jesus' relationship to persons of his day, and in the Christian ethic they constitute the virtues of care and concern for human need and suffering.

2. Imagination is *selective* from the mass of material with which the human mind is confronted, and out of which it concentrates upon salient, and significant features. The OT prophets seized upon this occasion or that in the past history of the nation, to demonstrate to Israel that God was working out his purpose of salvation for them. From the literature of Israel, Jesus selected such themes as redemptive ransom, the suffering servant, the concept of Kingdom, to be the load-bearing topics of his *kerygma*, or message. In less exalted contexts, ordinary people select parts of their lives as the most meaningful for them, and organize their emotions and their motivation around them.

3. Accordingly, imagination has a special *interpretative* role to play, using the selected topics, points in human existence, as the basis of understanding the rest of life, and even wider spans of history. It does so by establishing analogies, and imagination so employed plays a central part in poetry, and in the enrichment of human experience which poetry achieves.

4. One of the very obvious elements in imagination is its *constructive* and *creative* features. These are in evidence in the arts, but are equally apparent in the scientific constructions of Einstein, in the dogmatic and philo-

sophical works of Tillich or Barth, as in choice of paradigms and models which the expert in any field employs to advance his discipline (Barbour 1974).

5. Imagination has to be recognized further as having a very important *cognitive* role to play in our intellectual lives. There are certain things that we would not know about the world around us, about other persons, about ourselves, about God, the Bible and doctrine, had we – or more precisely, those into whose labours we have entered – not employed the imagination. Mary Warnock's contribution to the study of imagination is to demonstrate that imagination is one imagination, whether perceiving the world about us and the persons in it, or creating artistic works in poetry, painting, music and so on. It has to be affirmed that imagination therefore must not be thought of as adding characteristics to reality which do not actually exist, but rather as cognizing dimensions of reality which are hidden from the unimaginative.

6. It would be wrong to give an unduly intellectualistic account of imagination, for it also has an *empathetic* role to play. It is the medium whereby we project ourselves into a situation, not only cognitively, but affectively and emotionally, so that the plight and suffering of others is not only understood but, being understood, also moves us to effective action. 'Identification', now a key concept in much philosophy of counselling and caring requires imagination as its enabling condition.

7. Imagination is not intended solely to further personal emotion, motivation or ambition, however laudable. It has a specifically *communicative* role to fulfil. It is the responsibility of the artist, the poet, or the dramatist, to make others feel as they do about a certain subject, and, to achieve this end, they must not only have the experience themselves: they have to create the media for this appreciation of it, which will place others where they are, so that these others see with their eyes, hear with their ears, and feel with their hearts. The differentia between the genius and the commonplace lies at the points not just of experiental depth, but also of communicative capacity.

8. There is a function of imagination in relation to time which is worth noting, namely, its *contemporanizing* function, treating the past as present. R.G. Collingwood noted it in relation to history (*The Idea of History*, 1946) when he said that historical knowledge is the imaginative re-enactment of the past, rethinking the thoughts of historical agents. The notion might equally have been applied to Kierkegaard's theme that all Christians are contemporary disciples of Jesus Christ. Imagination is the medium through which the events of the gospels are, for faith, regarded as happening in the category of past-as-present.

9. A not dissimilar role which imagination plays is its *conspatializing* function, making the absent-as-present. J.P. Sartre often discussed the way in which, through imagination, a portait of an absent friend creates his presence for me. In the 'global village' of the modern world, peoples 5,000 miles absent are, through imagination, present in their hunger and deprivation. Our neighbour, however distantly absent, is as near as our next-door neighbour.

10. Finally, Iris Murdoch says that the imagination creates what she calls 'our-world' wherein appear our system of values, our principles, our prejudices, or religious commitments, as well as our fantasies and delusions. Some of this world we create for ourselves, actively or by re-action; some of it, we might wish to say, through the incoming of the grace of God; but, on the human side, the structure is formed and the tone set by our imagination. It is the framework within which our decisions are made, our ambitions defined, our friendships formed, our courses of action determined and in most general terms, our lives are 'lived'.

Barbour, Ian G., *Myths, Models and Paradigms* (SCM, 1974). **Warnock, Mary**, *Imagination* (Faber, 1976).

J. McIntyre

See also: FANTASY; SYMBOLS.

IMMANENCE
See: TRANSCENDENCE AND IMMANENCE.

IMMIGRANTS
See: RACE RELATIONS.

INCARNATION
A theological term for the belief that a divine 'person' or 'word' or 'spirit' took human form.

The belief occurs in many religions and is in itself usually compatible with monotheism. Its Christian occurrence is therefore not unique, but it is different from the others, and this difference is indicative of the specificity of the Christian faith. The principal scriptural source of the Christian doctrine of incarnation is to be found in the Johannine writings: 'the Word became flesh and dwelt among us' (John 1.14); 'That which was from the beginning, which we have heard, which we have seen with our eyes, which we have looked upon and touched with our hands, concerning the Word of Life' (1 John 1.1). And although there are many other ways of formulating the status and function of Jesus of Nazareth in relation both to God and the human world, although many other christologies are possible and others have in fact emerged, the formula that God's Word became flesh in Jesus together with the more elaborate theology to which this formulation gave rise has been historically and unreservedly dominant to this day. This predominance is due in great part to the fact that the Greek religious culture of the Roman Empire, to which Christian missionary endeavour was first directed, was already familiar with the idea of the immanence of the creative and dynamic Word of God in the world, and to the inherent conservatism of Christian doctrinal endeavour.

The incarnation of the Word of God is, like any other symbol, a lure to the mind and, because symbols are centripetal in their dynamism rather than linear in their logic, it can lure the mind back into pre-existence in search of clarity about the discarnate Word and the ensuing immanent binities or trinities, or it can lure the mind forward into the way of all flesh, into history, the life, death and destiny of Jesus of Nazareth, in the conviction which the symbol seeks to convey that in this crucified Jew God's original creative intent is finally being achieved. These directions are not forever mutually exclusive, but persistent preference for one over the other can have profound pastoral consequences.

Partly as a result of the intrinsic theological necessity of saying something about immanent self-differentiation in God as a result of the incarnation of the divine Word, and partly because of the natural proclivity of minds formed in ancient Greek religious culture, the main thrust of early speculation about God's Word took a pre-existence or heavenly direction. The widespread failure of the formative centuries of Christian theology to reckon with the fully human condition of

the founder was not unconnected with such direction of thought; the doctrinal correctives of the 5th century were correctives rather than consistent developments; hence there is something to be said for contemporary complaints that traditional incarnation theology often conveys impressions of the intrusion of a fully-fledged divine person into history, de-personalizes Jesus, and hence diminishes his pastoral relevance to the predicaments in which those who unequivocally share the human condition find themselves.

However, the discovery of history in modern times and the rise of humanism has resulted in modern biblical criticism and the quest for the historical, i.e. the human Jesus; and though this has seemed to some to render incarnation theology obsolete, it has enabled others to read incarnation symbolism in the direction of history. If God's Word is believed to have taken the human condition as Jesus of Nazareth, and that symbol lures the mind in quest of Jesus, then the life he lived in solidarity with the most marginalized of people, the stories he told and lived, the death he died at the hands of legitimate powers, the meals he ate with sinner and outcast, in which he symbolized his death and in which he became present or 'appeared' after his death as the new power or spirit in the world . . . all that, and more, becomes part of the necessary analysing of the incarnation symbol in contemporary theology, and all of it is of the most immediate practical or pastoral relevance to the twin tasks of celebrating the Lord's liturgy and living life in the spirit of Jesus. When the incarnation symbol is read in the direction of history and analysed in such practical detail, the fear of admitting that it is a common creation in comparative religion will decline, because its ability to uncover the uniqueness of Christian faith as a very specific praxis will have already emerged. It is in humanity that God is to be found – hope indeed for pastoral care.

Hick, J. (ed.), *The Myth of God Incarnate* (SCM, 1977). Puntel, L.B., 'Spirit', in *Sacramentum Mundi*, vol. 6 (Burns & Oates, 1970).

J.P. MACKEY

See also: GOD, DOCTRINE OF; SPIRIT; TRANSCENDENCE AND IMMANENCE.

INCEST: MEDICAL AND LEGAL ASPECTS
The present British legal definitions of incest are as follows: (1) 'Incest by a man – it is an

indictable offence for a man to have sexual intercourse with a woman whom he knows to be his grand-daughter, daughter, sister or mother. It is immaterial that sexual intercourse took place with the consent of the woman.' (2) 'Incest by a woman – it is an indictable offence for a woman of the age of sixteen or over, to permit a man whom she knows to be her grandfather, father, brother or son, to have sexual intercourse with her, by her consent.' (Sexual Offences Act 1956). In these definitions 'sister' includes 'half-sister' and 'brother' includes 'half-brother'.

Although such legal definitions state clearly that incest is a crime, it has not always been so. The early Christian concept of 'childhood innocence' with its notions of childhood as a period free from all sexual impulses or interests persisted until the Roman Catholic Church took a stand against incest in the 17th century (Beezley-Mrazek 1981). In England ecclesiastical courts continued to intervene in cases of incest until it became a criminal offence in 1908.

A dramatic increase in the reporting of child abuse in the 1960s followed the work of Henry Kempe and others in Denver on the battered child (Kempe 1978), and it soon became apparent that child sexual abuse and incest were phenomena also characterized by secrecy and taboo, both within and outside the family.

Whilst the legal definitions quoted refer solely to incest, a more generally used term is *child sexual abuse*. This has been defined as follows by Henry Kempe: 'The involvement of dependent, developmentally immature children and adolescents in sexual activities that they do not fully comprehend, are unable to give informed consent to, and which violate the social taboos of family roles. It includes paedophilia (an adult's preference for, or addiction to, sexual relations with children), rape and incest.'

In this way, incest is seen as part of a spectrum of sexually abusive and exploitative relationships, which can occur between an adult and a child, usually within a family context, but occasionally including sexual contacts outside the family, as with child rape and stranger abuse of children. The cardinal feature of an incestuous relationship is the presence of a blood tie as defined in the Sexual Offences Act. Without the presence of these itemized degrees of relatedness, the sexual activity cannot strictly be defined as incest.

For the crime of incest to be proven, sexual intercourse, i.e. intercourse 'per vaginum' between a male and a female, must have occurred. However a range of other sexual activities between a related adult and child may also be loosely described as incestuous: for instance, buggery between father and son or father and daughter, fellatio between father and son or father and daughter, cunnilingus between father and daughter or mother and son; and all of these activities between brothers and sisters, half-brothers and half-sisters, grandparents and grandchildren, as well as all forms of sexual play and fondling between adult and child.

With an ever increasing number of families containing a stepfather or stepmother, there are correspondingly increased opportunities for inappropriate adult/child contact of the type outlined above. These activities should be seen as child sexual abuse rather than incest.

An analysis of the commonest perpetrators of incestuous and child-sexually-abusive crimes shows the following pattern: natural father, 20%; step-parent, 12%; natural mother, 2%; family acquaintance, 31%; other relative, 8.5%; stranger, 26%. This means that in 75.5% of cases the perpetrator is known to the child. Adding the percentages of crimes committed by natural parents we arrive at a total of 22% being truly incestuous according to the strict definition. A further 8.5% occur within the family but, depending on the degree of relatedness, are not necessarily incestuous. About 31% are perpetrated outside the blood tie of incest, but still within the general and extended family/friends network.

A great deal of pioneering work has been done in America with the families of sexually abused children. In England treatment programmes for these children and their families have recently started and the preliminary results of treatment are encouraging (Bentovim *et al.*). However, there is still much we need to learn about the nature of incestuous family functioning in order to know how best to help rehabilitate the unhappy child victims.

At present, both the legal definitions of incest and the legal perception of sexual abuse describe the adult perpetrator as a criminal and the child as a victim, whilst at the same time ignoring the implied need for therapeutic intervention and treatment conveyed by such a view.

Since stepchildren and adoptive children are not included in the definition of incest, and yet their sexual abuse can be correctly described as incestuous, it is clear that aspects of this legislation need reviewing. This work is currently being undertaken by the Criminal Law Revision Working Party, and it is to be hoped that future changes in the law will build in some kind of treatment provision for incestuous families.

Sexual Offences Act 1956. **Beezley-Mrazek, P.** and **Kempe, H.** (eds.), *Sexually Abused Children and their Families* (Pergamon Press, 1981). **Bentovim, A.** *et al.*, *A Treatment Programme for Families Where Sexual Abuse has Occurred*; work currently being undertaken in the Hospital for Sick Children, Great Ormond Street, London. **Kempe, R.S.** and **Kempe, C.H.**, *Child Abuse* (Open Books/Fontana, 1978).

EILEEN VIZARD

See also: MARRIAGE AND FAMILY; SEXUAL COUNSELLING AND THERAPY; SEXUAL DEVIATION; SEXUALITY AND SEXUAL DEVELOPMENT.

INCEST: PASTORAL CARE

It is generally accepted nowadays that incest is rarely only one individual's offence but happens as a result of collusive dynamics within the family arising from shared incestuous fantasies, conscious and unconscious. Those involved in the pastoral care of such families need therefore to view the family as a whole as well as focusing on the problems arising for particular individuals.

In offering pastoral care, points to bear in mind and questions to ask include: (1) *Source of referral.* The decision whether or not to make an approach to the family (and if so, how) will be influenced by whether the knowledge came from inside or outside the family. Was it a cry of help from inside? What might have been the motives of the informer? (2) *Accuracy.* It is important not to take things at face value without verification, but we must also recognize that helpers' own feelings sometimes prevent them entertaining the possibility of its truth. So the pastoral carer must ask: 'What are my feelings about the possibility of incest and the reality if it happens?' (3) *Person to be helped.* Who is going to be seen – an individual, the whole family, or a part of the family? If certain individuals are being excluded, at least initially, what are the reasons for this? (4) *Police involvement.* What are the pros and

cons of calling in the police? This can be a way of avoiding responsibility, but not calling them in could be a way of protecting the family and it might not be in their best interests in the long term. Fostering a relationship with the family first might be important, or sometimes visiting simultaneously with the police (each with different tasks) could be the thing to do. (5) *Appropriateness as helper.* The previous relationship with the family needs consideration. Ask: 'Am I the most appropriate person to be dealing with the pastoral care of this family in this situation? How will this affect my future relationship with them?' (6) *Consultation.* Allegations of incest are both serious and very delicate. Pastoral carers do not have all the answers. Consulting with an appropriate person will ensure that any subsequent action taken is considered action, but confidentiality (q.v.) must be safeguarded.

Incest is a crime, and a very strong taboo operates against it. Yet it is natural for a father to find his daughter sexually attractive just as he might find one of her friends attractive. It is natural for a mother to find she has sexual feelings about other males. Moreover, it is important that daughters feel that their sexuality and femininity is accepted by their fathers, not ignored or experienced as a threat or as something which can't be coped with. The same applies to mothers and sons. Sadly, the incest taboo and the fear of incest are so powerful that all too often, in families, all the natural sexual feelings are repressed, as they are experienced as part of the taboo. In some families this is taken even further into the ordinary relationships, and may mean that fathers never make real relationships with daughters or mothers with sons, so great is the threat of the sexual area.

In the father/daughter dyad the mother also has an important function. If she is for some reason threatened by the father/daughter relationship (maybe because the marital relationship is uncertain), or if she somehow encourages the father/daughter relationship (possibly to keep pressure from the husband away from herself), then she is also influencing the nature of the father/daughter relationship. Fathers also similarly influence the mother/son relationship.

Incest need not be the end of the world, particularly if one result is that the family and individuals in it have help to talk about and explore what is happening between them, move towards acceptance of sexual feelings and as a result make more open relationships. Because of the way a taboo operates, guilt may be one of the predominant feelings. To talk about what has happened, and to be helped to see the way the whole family is involved, can go a long way towards alleviating the paralysing effect of such guilt. Often cases of incest are not talked about either in the family or outside it. For the individuals involved, it becomes a traumatic memory or the incident is totally repressed and forgotten. In either situation emotional development and freedom is stifled. Encouragement to talk, explore and discover could well mean that people are set free for future emotional functioning.

Forward, S. and Buck, C., *Betrayal of Innocence* (Penguin, 1979). Pincus, L. and Dare, C., *Secrets in the Family* (Faber, 1978). Stein, R., *Incest and Human Love* (Spring Publications, 1984).

MOIRA DUCKWORTH

See also: INCEST: MEDICAL AND LEGAL ASPECTS.

INDIVIDUATION
A term coined by Carl Gustav Jung to denote the orientation and end of the individual. It involves the emergence of the self (q.v.) resulting in wholeness, self-realization, self-centredness (not in the moral sense of selfishness) and a balancing of the different parts of psyche.

Jung, C.F., *Memories, Dreams, Reflections* (Collins and Routledge, 1963); recent editions include a glossary and a list of the Collected Works of C.G. Jung.

See also: ANALYTICAL PSYCHOLOGY.

INDOCTRINATION
Literally, the word 'indoctrinate' means 'teach, instruct, imbue with a doctrine, idea or opinion' (*Concise Oxf. Dict.*).

When such cognitive elements represent a consensus within the relevant society or community, the process carries no sinister overtones; but in the modern pluralistic context, the case is very different. The issue of indoctrination thus 'has to do with the social status of beliefs' (Hull 1984) and with 'the frontier between what is permissible, and what is not, in education' (Rodger 1982, p. 28). Nevertheless, much confusion attends the discussion of this subject, and religious education has often been unfairly singled out

in this respect. Indeed, some argue that all teaching involves an element of indocrination, and that one must try to distinguish between good indoctrination and bad (Loukes 1973, p. 99). 'Everyone has to be deeply and significantly indoctrinated from very early in life if he is going really to be a member of any community or nation' (Niblett 1967, p. 54). Others, unconvinced by this argument, distinguish sharply between the kind of teaching which attempts illegitimately to secure cognitive conformity in controversial matters, and processes such as conditioning and socialization. But it is not clear that the latter processes are free from controversial cognitive element, nor do they necessarily avoid the problems of pluralism. Liberal and authoritarian attitudes to education are philosophies which are highly debatable and controversial, yet educators act on them (Mitchell 1970). And what of moral values, which certainly possess a cognitive aspect? It is not enough to say that pupils are simply encouraged to debate them. Certain values are also commended, in 'secular' as in 'relgious' education. Neutrality is not a viable life-stance. 'We must not be afraid of educating for commitment' (Niblett 1967, p. 60). How then can we avoid the culpable type of indoctrination?

The pejorative use of the term 'indoctrination' has several different roots. Sometimes the *methods* used to communicate ideas are faulted: e.g., when a pupil is unfairly induced to accept conclusions approved by the teacher but not demanded by the subject matter (Smart 1973, p. 37). Others (e.g. J. Wilson) take *content* as the principal criterion; yet others find it in *aim* (e.g. R.M. Hare). Frequently, appeal is made to both content and intention (e.g. I.A. Snook): the indoctrinator intends 'to cause his subjects to accept his controversial doctrines as if they were uncontroversial assertions, and to adhere to them with an unquestioning emotional and intellectual loyalty' (Hull 1984). The operation is an assault on the integrity of the receiver, who is programmed to suspend independent critical judgement. In a media-conscious age, reservations of a similar kind are felt about certain types of advertising and propaganda, and some form of monitoring or control is usually exercised.

To avoid falling into culpable indoctrination, the communicator requires to develop self-knowledge, to recognize the nature and requirements of the context in which he or she is operating, to have profound respect for the personal worth and dignity of the receivers, and to develop to the full the possibilities of communication and dialogue. The teaching of religious education in schools must give priority to such characteristics, and they are relevant also to education in the believing community, where the aim is to promote 'growth in grace', which entails the development and flourishing of the whole person. Nor should evangelism (q.v.), with its call for personal decision and renewal, fail to respect the integrity of the hearer. All communicators who are confident in their material will feel free to discuss it openly and learn from the difficulties others have about their interpretation of life. Through such exploration and sharing, pupils are helped towards 'becoming autonomous agents in the spiritual realm of life' (Holley 1978, p. 166).

Cox, E., *Problems and Possibilities for Religious Education* (Hodder, 1983), pp. 101–12. Elliott, J., 'Problems of R.E. Syllabus Construction in a Democracy', in J.M. Hull (ed.), *New Directions in Religious Education* (Falmer Press, 1982). Holley, R., *Religious Education and Religious Understanding* (Routledge, 1978), pp. 163–66. Hull, J.M., 'Indoctrination', in J.M. Sutcliffe, *A Dictionary of Religious Education* (SCM, 1984). Loukes, H., *Teenage Morality* (SCM, 1973), pp. 96–100. Mitchell, B.G., 'Indoctrination', in I.T. Ramsey (ed.), *The Fourth R* (SPCK, 1970), pp. 353–58. Niblett, W.R., *Education and the Modern Mind* (Faber, 1954, 1967), pp. 51–74. Rodger, A.R., *Education and Faith in an Open Society* (Handsell Press 1982), pp. 26–32. Smart, P., 'The Concept of Indoctrination', in G. Langford and D.J. O'Connor (eds.), *New Essays in the Philosophy of Education* (Routledge, 1973). Snook, I.A., *Indoctrination and Education* (Routledge, 1972).

J.I.H. McDONALD

See also: LEARNING; NURTURE, CHRISTIAN; PASTORAL CARE IN SCHOOLS.

INDUSTRIAL CHAPLAINCY

Ministry to occupational rather than residential or confessional groups.

1. Origin and aims. Industrial chaplaincy in its present form dates from the Second World War. A number of quite separate influences have shaped its present diversity and breadth of aim, but it has generally been seen as an arm of the 'social responsibility' of the churches, seeking to contribute in the particularly important sphere of economic life to the strengthening of individual freedom in

a world increasingly threatened by concentration of economic power or by state corporation on the political right or left. Primary among all other motives has been this aim of promoting changes in the relationships enjoyed by people in employment. Industrial chaplaincy has also shared the aim of tincturing the de-Christianized or unevangelized 'working-class' with the presence of the Christian priesthood. The 'servant' model of the Christian life is exemplified in this ministry to the 'poorest' in society, identified at first with the manual industrial workers and more recently with the unemployed and the low-paid, who are predominantly women.

2. *Methods*. Industrial chaplaincy works by building up a general acquaintance with the patterns of employment in an area, partly by as broad contacts as possible across the total work-force in selected key companies and partly by selective contacts with key individuals at all levels. A massive base of individual friendships is supplemented by a variety of shorter or longer courses and alliances in professional and labour organizations or around *ad hoc* campaigns.

3. *Issues*. Most of the major issues of industrial life as they have emerged over the past 40 years have been the concern of industrial chaplaincy – the emergence of professional management and the retreat of managerial ownership, the increased demand for training and personnel services, redundancy and unemployment, hours, shift-work and overtime, rewards, incentives and differentials in payment, investment ethics, labour law, etc.

4. *Qualifications and training*. Most industrial chaplains have an initial qualification in theological studies and most are clergy or ministers of their churches. In addition, many individual chaplains have made themselves industrially and economically knowledgeable by 'learning on the job' and by following degree or diploma courses in personnel or general management, industrial and social psychology or general sociology.

5. *Organization*. The importance of industrial chaplaincy has not been grasped by the churches, and its development and even its continuity is a matter of local conviction on the part of practitioners and patrons (both ecclesiastical and industrial). There is a voluntary Industrial Mission Association which combines most of the chaplains and is open to

other interested persons. It publishes a monthly newsletter and holds regular regional and occasional national conferences. At national level the main churches unite with the Association in the Churches' Consortium on Industrial Mission which recommends basic theory and practice as it has emerged. The major denominations (with the exception of the Roman Catholic Church) have national committees or officers to serve this work, and national councils of churches also carry some responsibility in the field.

The Consortium on Industrial Mission publishes a number of helpful pamphlets, as do the various central denominational committees. *Theology and Politics* (1978), *The End of Work?* (1980) and *Thinking in Practice* (1981) are three Working Papers from Industrial Mission, available from the IMA Theology Development Group, c/o the William Temple Foundation.
Kane, M., *Gospel in Industrial Society* (SCM, 1980); *Theology in an Industrial Society* (SCM, 1975). Paradise, S.L., *Detroit Industrial Mission: a Personal Narrative* (Harper & Row, New York, 1968). Phipps, S., *God on Monday* (Hodder, 1966). Wickham, E.R., *Church and People in an Industrial City* (Lutterworth, 1957). Wilkie, G., *Christian Thinking about Industrial Life* (St Andrew Press, 1980).

M.H. ATKINSON

See also: UNEMPLOYMENT; WORK; WORK-RELATED MINISTRIES.

INSIGHT

Knowledge or awareness of oneself or others which penetrates beneath superficial appearances or conventional assumptions. It may further refer to the ability to understand the symbolic meaning of things or events.

Much of Jesus' teaching and conversation may be regarded as being concerned to challenge conventional ways of looking at things and to help people to face deeper insight into themselves in order to bring about change. Ascetic and mystical writers have always insisted on the need for self-knowledge, both as a way of overcoming temptation and sin and as an essential step in coming to the knowledge of God (e.g. *The Cloud of Unknowing*, ch. 14). Prayer (q.v.), meditation (q.v.), self-examination and retreat (q.v.) can all be used for this purpose. The difficulty of achieving insight on one's own is acknowledged in the tradition which emphasizes the importance of using a confessor or spiritual director (*see* SPIRITUAL DIRECTION).

In analytical psychology (q.v.), psycho-analysis (q.v.) and those forms of psychotherapy (q.v.) and counselling (q.v.) which are based on them, the achievement of insight is regarded as an important factor in effecting personality change and constitutes a vital goal of such therapies. To bring about real change, insight must be experienced at the level of feeling and not merely known about intellectually. Such 'intellectual insight' will usually be seen as a defence against experiencing true self-knowledge which may seem too painful to tolerate. Analytical therapy aims at providing the conditions in which resistance to insight may be overcome. Personal insight is regarded as an essential condition of being able to understand other people and, following Jung, all training institutes in the analytical tradition insist on trainees undergoing therapy themselves in order to develop this.

The cultural resources of drama, literature, art and music all have an important contribution to make to the development of both personal and social insight.

The development of insight, both personal and corporate, may be regarded as part of the pastoral task of any Christian community in nourishing the development of its life and that of its members. It should be borne in mind however that individuals vary widely in their ability to accept new insight into themselves. A pastor may need to acquaint himself with counselling methods which do not depend on achieving insight (Clinebell 1984). Furthermore the offering of insight may be experienced by the recipient as very threatening and even as an attack, so that it may succeed only in mobilizing his resistance. Careful attention needs therefore to be paid to providing favourable conditions for the acquisition of insight, e.g. trust (q.v.), acceptance (q.v.) and understanding. The pastor's ability to understand and to help others in this respect will depend on the degree of his or her own insight. Growth in self-understanding and awareness should be an essential feature of all pastoral training.

Clinebell, H.J., *Basic Types of Pastoral Care and Counselling* (SCM, 1984). Jacobs, M., *Still Small Voice* (SPCK 1982). Webb, J. and Walker, A., *The School of Self Knowledge: a Symposium from Medieval Sources* (Mowbray, 1956).

DEREK BLOWS

See also: INTUITION; SELF-ACTUALIZATION.

INSOMNIA
See: SLEEP.

INSTITUTIONALIZATION
The current use of the term 'institutionalization' refers to effects good or bad on the members of organizations such as prisons, hospitals, homes for children, monasteries, boarding education establishments, etc.

Over the centuries the words institute and institution have covered a wide variety of meanings but mostly they refer to organizations rather than writings or systems of thought. The word 'institute' rather than 'institution' tends to imply scholarly activities, whereas the latter covers a wider variety of organizations. For good reasons related to their functions many of them have residential requirements, in communities that may be more or less separate from the general society in which they are placed. In most such places there are two categories of person – the staff who usually have some particular training or expertise; and the clients whom the staff exist to serve in some way through the exercise of their special knowledge. However, in the case of some closed religious communities all members are joined together in one common aim, though even here as in many other institutions there are some in a learning or novice category.

The effects of institutionalization are usually cumulative, and they may not appear for a number of years. They are also usually more marked in institutions which are rigorously closed and/or have been in existence for long periods of time so that their ways of working have become settled, perhaps fossilized. Before enlarging on the bad effects of institutionalization it is worth remarking that good effects can be seen, such as the containment of anti-social behaviour, the development of altruistic feelings and the ability to work and think for common ends and common good rather than personal gain and satisfaction. These good effects can be seen in both staff and clients, as can the bad effects. The latter have been described in a number of different sorts of institution with remarkably similar results. There is a loss of initiative, uniformity is encouraged, and the dependency of clients on staff. Within the staff there is increasing dependency of those lower in the hierarchy on those who are higher. Activities are unnecessarily routinized and apathy sets in.

Many types of clients (e.g. the mentally ill, or emotionally disturbed children) may have personality difficulties that make them particularly prone to suffer these ill-effects by, for example, lacking drive or craving dependency. Even staff members may have been attracted to work in such places by reason of feeling more secure in a rigidly ordered and relatively impersonal environment. The rewards of conforming to the 'system' such as the earning of privileges may outweigh the disadvantages of comparative freedom achieved only by rebellion and inevitable sanctions.

Many institutions deal with very intense emotional problems, e.g. care of the seriously ill and dying by nurses and of emotionally disturbed children in many residential homes. Varying the conditions and hours of work, especially the use of shorter shifts, and many different staff members, are methods of protecting staff against intolerable personal emotional involvement. Carried too far, such procedures dehumanize the caring relationships. There are special problems in one-sex establishments which are to do not so much with tolerance (or intolerance) of homosexuality, covert or overt, as with the use of more or less overt sexual attractions or liaisons to manipulate the proper power and authority structure of the organization.

Many of the bad effects of institutionalization can be summed up by saying that such institutions tend to be run for the benefit of the staff and not the clients whom they exist to serve. Staff privileges can then make reform difficult if not impossible. A particular form of institutionalization problem is seen when the founder/leader of a community or group of communities becomes too old or infirm, or the organization too large for him or her to control it. As there is usually then no obvious successor and the founder's own particular leadership qualities do not usually translate into clear rules and regulations, 'the routinization of the charisma', in Max Weber's famous phrase does not occur, and the institutions either close or degenerate and become fossilised.

To prevent the bad effects of institutionalization, staff training is the first essential. Staff should understand their roles as fully as possible and be alive to the possible ill-effects that may occur. With few exceptions, staff and clients should not expect to be in a more or less closed institution, especially involuntarily, for a lifetime or some other long period of years. Institutions should always be as open to the society in which they exist as is compatible with their functions. Clients must be encouraged to assume as much personal responsibility as their physical or mental infirmities allow, and treatment or management plans individualized as far as possible. Regular supervisions by someone quite external to the institution, with power to modify its ways of behaviour, can sometimes anticipate trouble and lead to much needed reforms, which rarely come from inside only. The episcopal visitor to monasteries and nunneries undoubtably had and has to exert such authority from time to time.

Once the bad effects of institutionalization have reached a certain point, there is usually little that can be done about them except close the organization. The clients (and sometimes staff too) may need considerable rehabilitation before they are fit to resume living in open society or sheltered but less malignant environments.

Menzies, I.E.P., *The Functioning of Social Systems as a Defence Against Anxiety*, Tavistock Pamphlet, no. 3 (Tavistock, 1961). Tizard, J. and Tizard, B., 'The Institution as an Environment for Social Development', in M.P.M. Richards, *The Integration of the Child into a Social World* (CUP, 1974).

DESMOND POND

See also: HOSPITALS; MENTAL HEALTH.

INTERCULTURAL PASTORAL CARE

All churches are influenced by the cultures in which they emerged. This was already evident in the struggles between Jewish and Hellenistic Christians. It is also evident in the fact that what one church considers as a normal expression of its spirituality (e.g. the presence of the Holy Spirit (*see* SPIRIT) in ancestors, including non-Christian ancestors; the veneration of saints; the tombs of political and religious leaders in churches) is considered by another church as pure superstition. What one church considers to be an expression of her trust in God (e.g. the belief that prayer and worship foster success, health and wealth) is considered by another church as remnants of paganism. What many Christians in the tradition of the Reformation consider to be the heart of the Gospel, namely that trust in God's friendship does not depend on our religious experience, is considered by others as pure theory.

The differences do not lie only in outward questions of liturgical language, architectural forms and church music; they concern the heart of Christian commitment. As, however, the gospel is not identical with celebrating our own contextual and cultural tradition, ecumenical and intercultural encounters are necessary in order to remind churches and their members of their inevitable cultural and social limitations and of the otherness of other churches. Intercultural pastoral care is therefore, in the first instance, the application of the catholicity and ecumenicity of the church on the local and personal level.

Models of this intercultural pastoral care can be seen in two typical NT situations: (1) In the inconsistent attitude of Jesus and his followers to power and wealth; amongst his disciples there were revolutionaries (Luke 6.15) and collaborators (Matt. 9.9ff.); and he accepted both. (2) It can be seen in the early Christian churches, e.g. in Corinth where there were slaves and free people of wealth and influence (Theissen 1982); they were not brought together in one church by one consistent ideology, theology or ethics, but by their belief that in their diversity they formed the body of Christ.

This diversity of cultures, values and ideologies has to be respected in intercultural pastoral care. The criterion of whether a morality or a theological position is valid from a Christian point of view is not that people agree with the counsellor or his church. The criterion lies in the willingness to accept one's antagonists as belonging equally to the body of Christ. This does not hinder but enables strong convictions both for clergy and laypeople. But it disallows a cultural or ideological hegemony.

Where is the limit? The limit is where my own convictions (or the traditions of my church and culture) take precedent over the loyalty to the body of Christ (which is not identical with my church). The practical application of this position is evident in matters of racism, also exploitation of the poor, educational and cultural imperialism. To take an example: it is not the fact that somebody considers foot-washing (or observing the sabbath on a Saturday) as important that makes him a 'sectarian', but the fact that he wants to impose his belief on everybody else. The contrary is also true: To prohibit foot-washing (or sabbath-keeping on a Saturday) under all circumstances is a sign of cultural imperialism (or sectarianism). The same applies to the important experiences and convictions in the area of dreams and visions (q.v.), spiritual healing (q.v.), speaking in tongues (q.v.), polygamy, pacifism, military chaplains, episcopal succession, liturgical forms, church music, dancing and specific interpretations of the Eucharist (see COMMUNION), christology and pneumatology.

An intercultural approach which is based on one's cultural and traditional convictions but is at the same time open to other positions within the body of Christ, leads to a pastoral care which is neither authoritarian nor relativistic.

Hollenweger, W.J., *Evangelism Today: Good News or Bone of Contention?* (Christian Journals, Belfast, 1978). Theissen, G., *The First Followers of Jesus* (SCM, 1978); American edition: *Sociology of Early Palestinian Christianity* (Philadelphia, 1978); *Essays on Corinth: the Social Setting of Pauline Christianity* (T. & T. Clark, Edinburgh, 1982).

WALTER J. HOLLENWEGER

See also: MIXED MARRIAGE; MULTI-FAITH MINISTRIES; RACE RELATIONS.

INTERFAITH MARRIAGE
See: MIXED MARRIAGE.

INTERNATIONAL ORGANIZATIONS
See: ORGANISATIONS FOR PASTORAL CARE.

INTERPROFESSIONAL RELATIONSHIPS
A profession (see PROFESSIONALISM) draws on a number of related academic disciplines, some of which may have originated in the profession, and combines them with a body of received practice, serving the public. Interprofessional relationships therefore involve interdisciplinary study and an understanding of the practice. Interdisciplinary study at any depth is difficult, because it undermines the conservatism necessary to hold the discipline together, and also because there is little financial support or institutional encouragement. Some universities offer degrees in combined subjects, but there is little interaction between them. Philosophical self-examination would reveal some of the assumptions and reductions necessarily but unconsciously made. Professional practice involves customs, standards of legality, confidentiality (q.v.), status, organization, payment, stance and style. Learning about another profession and revealing the secrets of one's own is a difficult and costly process.

Clergy differ from other professionals in having to lead, administer and finance a congregation and parish. Their authority, as well as deriving from technical expertise, derives from a more diffuse religious and moral authority and from charisma. This raises particular problems for them and for others who relate with them professionally. Clergy vary, according to their tradition, in the extent to which they can acknowledge God's activity within the professions as such. They do not all have the same standards of confidentiality (q.v.), nor the same focuses of loyalty. It is very important to recognize this. The result is that most professionals relate to clergy as individuals whom they trust rather than as members of a profession with recognized norms of practice.

This is the background against which interprofessional relationships take place. A discipline other than our own requires us to learn a new language, see through different spectacles. Another profession involves a culture shock. Therefore we should listen carefully, and explain clearly and honestly. We should seek to understand the nature of the other's integrity and effectiveness. The main motive, however, is concern that the person or group being helped should have the fullest range of support available. This involves the assumption that our own profession is not omni-competent *and* that co-operation is in itself beneficial to all concerned.

Co-operation takes place through case conferences, referrals (q.v.), consultation and mutual study. Regular meetings, often over lunch, bring professionals in an area together to share insights and friendship. Such meetings can include a wide range of professions – teachers, bank managers, youth leaders, race relations officers, as well as the normal voluntary and statutory bodies. Clergy can often act as initiators. At national level a few bodies promote conferences and field groups, arrange explanatory lectures or seminars. The Institute of Religion and Medicine includes other helping professions within its membership.

N.H. TODD

See also: PROFESSIONALISM; REFERRAL.

INTIMACY
The state of being closely familiar with

another person not necessarily of the opposite sex.

Intimacy with at least one other person is widely regarded as an essential ingredient of a happy and satisfactory life, whilst the absence of intimacy is a significant cause of mental and even physical distress (*see* LONELINESS). Research on friendship indicates that the capacity for intimacy creates a sense of worth, a feeling of belonging, important chances to compare oneself, one's emotions and one's beliefs with other persons, and a significant sense of one's contribution to the social life of a community. These several products of intimacy are universally regarded as essential for a healthy life.

Women seem to be generally more intimate in conversations with other people than do men, but it is not yet entirely clear why this should be. Women are generally more willing to make personal statements about themselves and to display greater warmth and openness than men do. However, it appears that men may simply define intimacy differently and do so in terms of shared activities. Thus, for men, playing sport together may be taken to indicate familiarity and intimacy, whilst for women it would not count. It may simply be that men are less willing to admit to intimate feelings or that they are more selective about the partners with whom they are willing to be intimate. However, several pieces of research now indicate that it is more likely that men and women actually differ in their relative capacities to make intimate statements, men being relatively incapable of intimate socializing even when it is desirable to do so. Such differences are sometimes explained in terms of the early experiences of the two sexes during infancy and childhood, but it is not entirely clear what could account for such experiences nor why they should differ nor what exact experiences would produce the long-term effects. What is clear, however, is that all persons, regardless of their own sex, prefer to speak openly to women rather than to men and that they feel more relaxed and at ease in so doing.

Intimacy develops as relationships develop, although not all lengthy relationships are intimate or vice versa. Both physical and informational intimacy increase systematically in developing relationships in a process known as 'self-disclosures'. Individuals self-disclose to other people according to established social rules or norms, in a process that

has been likened to the peeling of an onion. Sophisticated systems have been developed for measuring such growth of intimacy and they depend on assessment of the verbal content of interactions taken together with subtle measures of bodily change, such as eye-movements, postural changes, gestures and inflexions to the voice. Using such methods it has proved possible to index the intimacy of pairs of persons and to make assessments of the reasons why some people fail to become intimate with other persons at all. This work on 'social skills' has had a major effect on counsellors dealing with persons who describe themselves as lonely, unhappy and dissatisfied with life.

Duck, S.W., *Friends, for Life* (Harvester Press, 1983). **Hinde, R.A.,** *Towards Understanding Relationships* (Academic Press, 1979).

STEVE DUCK

See also: COMMUNICATION; FEMININITY/ MASCULINITY; LONELINESS.

INTUITION
In popular usage intuition signifies an awareness which arises from within or beneath consciousness (q.v.) rather than by imposition from outside by teaching or logical argument. It indicates general subjective awareness and hence includes the possibility or probability of self-deception. Often associated with the feminine element of personality (the yin) it is welcomed by those who advocate a more even balance of the two principles (e.g. F. Capra in *The Turning Point*).

Most psychological schools have a way of describing intuition: lateral thinking, creativity, core construct, gut reaction. In Jung's analytical psychology (q.v.) it has a more precise usage, being one of the four functions of psychic activity, 'beyond which nothing fundamental remains to be said'. Sensation ascertains that something is there. Thinking establishes what it is. Feeling states whether it is pleasant or not. Intuition indicates where it came from and where it is going, its potentiality. For most people in Western culture it is a function which is partly conscious but mostly unconscious. It is not often integrated with feeling or with the superior (Western) function, thinking.

It has an even more precise usage in the phenomenology developed by and from Husserl. By intuition we have a direct knowledge of the thing in itself, its essences, and

137

also of its significance. Thus, in addition to individual intuition there is *eidetic*, which provides a shared thematized awareness of the sense of meaning of things (Natanson 1973). Scholastic philosophy gave this name to the direct knowledge available to spiritual beings for whom vision and knowledge are not separated. Although the word is little used in theology, the notion of an inner awareness is, of course, common to all understandings of the ways we receive revelation (Ephesians 1.18, 3.16; Colossians 1.19 1 Peter 3.4). Many of these depend upon the notion of the 'heart', the inner core of personhood, as the source of such understanding. It is the special concern of ascetical theology (q.v.), mystical theology and spiritual direction (q.v.).

In pastoral care and counselling careful attention should be paid to the intuitions of both client and counsellor within the particular methods used. This will involve a method of working with the intutions and seeking to understand them in terms of the person having them rather than someone else on to whom they are projected. The counsellor should be particularly suspicious of collusion (q.v.) with the client in shared intuitions. If we feel a 'spiritual' closeness to our client we should discuss it with our supervisor or director. However, the main emphasis must be positive, valuing the intuitions, testing them, learning and teaching how to use them.

Capra, F., *The Turning Point* (Fontana, 1983). **Jung, C.G.**, *Complete Works*, vol. 5 (Routledge, 1978), p. 164. **Natanson, M.** (ed.), *Phenomenology of the Social Sciences* (Northwest UP, 1973).

N.H. Todd

See also: IMAGINATION; INSIGHT.

J

JUDAISM
See: PASTORAL CARE IN JUDAISM.

JUDGEMENT
The quality of discernment and wisdom; discretion. (1) Also the declaration of a moral evaluation. (2) In 'divine judgement', the ultimate determination of the value of human actions by God expected, in Christian tradition, at the end of the age.

Generally, in the pastoral sphere, discernment and discretion have been valued as qualities to be sought, while moral judgement has been thought of as an obstruction to the client's ability to achieve insight and self-understanding. In earlier centuries this was not so; those who heard confessions (q.v.) were generally expected to have a grasp of moral theology and therefore to be in a position to give an evaluation of the penitent's life. The sense of guilt (q.v.) was not of as much concern to the confessor as objective judgement according to theological criteria.

However, since the advent of psychoanalysis (q.v.) the pastoral function has been seen to have more to do with enabling understanding and an honest facing of realities which had previously lain concealed. With this have developed non-directive counselling techniques which rely on the suspension of the counsellor's own value stand in order to allow the client to take personal responsibility for feelings and choices. This gave rise to the notion of the counsellor as a morally neutral person to whom the values of the client were of no personal interest provided that they were self-chosen.

More recently the values inherent in the non-directive approach itself have been recognized, and with that recognition has come the sense that judgement cannot in fact be suspended in pastoral situations. It is possible for the suspension of moral judgement to be itself a form of manipulation (q.v.) in which the counsellor's own aims remain covert, and that the very declaration of the counsellor's own values can liberate the client to make personal judgements.

With this recognition has come the awareness that pastoral care takes place in a social and political context and therefore either supports or resists judgements being made by society at large. It is also doubtful whether Christian pastoral care can ever take place without some recognition of values, norms and commandments by which God will judge the world, since that judgement already impinges on the lives of human beings.

Browning, D., *The Moral Context of Pastoral Care* (Westminster Press, 1976). Rogers, C., *A Way of Being* (Houghton Mifflin, Boston, 1980). Selby, P., *Liberating God* (SPCK, 1983).

PETER SELBY

See also: ACCEPTANCE; RESPONSIBILITY.

JUNGIAN PSYCHOLOGY
See: ANALYTICAL PSYCHOLOGY.

JUSTICE AND PASTORAL CARE
In the New Testament, pastoralia and politics are never far apart. Caring for people is seldom, if ever, seen in an individualistic context. The image of the good shepherd is a social one, but no less personal on account of that. The idea that the gospel has social implications is mistaken. The Good News of the Kingdom *is* social, as the very word Kingdom implies. It is in relationship with God and with each other that we become persons. Baptism and Eucharist *incorporate* us, make us part of the Body of Christ. The warfare of the spirit to which Christians are committed by their baptism is the struggle for righteousness, for justice, at every level of human existence. This comes out most clearly in the prophetic tradition to which Jesus was heir. Only once in the New Testament do we hear Jesus preaching a sermon in a synagogue; his text is from Isaiah: 'I have come to liberate captives . . . to let the oppressed go free . . . to proclaim the year that finds favour with God.' The reference is to the year of jubilee when, in ancient Israel debts were remitted, offences forgiven,

relationships put right. The sermon itself pointed to the fact that 'being right with God' was not a possession of the chosen people but open to all. Those outside the true faith were often closer to God than those who rejoiced in their orthodoxy. God's justice is universal. He is not a tribal or a national deity. This was clearly deeply offensive to Jesus' congregation in Nazareth.

A single ministry. Priestly, pastoral and prophetic ministry are – in the Judaeo-Christian tradition – not three different ministries; they are three essential elements of the one ministry, a ministry expressing God's self-sacrificing love for his creation. That love is inevitably in conflict with injustice, with everything that impedes 'abundant living'. The pastor – as Jesus did – both reconciles (the priestly role) and divides (the prophetic role). Until sin is finally defeated there can be no escape from the tension between these two. In the Kingdom (to quote the psalmist) 'justice and peace will kiss each other'; in the struggle for the Kingdom there is no such harmony. There is torture, crucifixion, death.

Critical solidarity. There is a widespread assumption that a pastor's task is to minister to his flock, his congregation, *on their terms.* A great deal of chaplaincy work is wrongly based on this principle, with the effect that the pastor adopts the social attributes and attitudes of the group to which he or she ministers. If it is to soldiers, the chaplain will raise no hard questions on the ethics of killing. If it is to trade unionists, the pastor will 'side with the workers'. The possibilities are endless. If it is to a mixed congregation in a complex class-ridden society the pastor had better refuse to take sides for fear of 'dividing the people' – even though Jesus did precisely that. For the sake of the people. 'I have come', he said, 'not to bring peace, but a sword. To divide father from son . . .' The conservative church for conservatives, the radical church for radicals, the guerilla church for freedom fighters, the peacemaking church for pacifists: that is to deny the God who stands in judgement on every human structure and is at the same time in solidarity with all people. The pastor, then, is called to identify with those in his or her care, but they are owed more than that, they are owed *critical* solidarity. In the pursuit of justice the pastor is constantly challenged to take sides, to make difficult choices, to opt for the poor and oppressed and therefore to be vulnerable

alongside those to whom he or she ministers. When Jesus challenged the rich young ruler to abandon wealth and power, that was an act of pastoral care. The pastor may make wrong choices. But not to choose is also to choose. The pastor is not God, is not justified by his or her own wisdom or goodness, but by God's grace.

Equipping the people of God. Pastoral care is the equipping of the people of God with the weapons of the spirit to be an effective resistance movement to all that dehumanizes, to all that obscures God's presence in every person. 'The curses of prisoners are also prayers, and the prayers of the rest of us have to be judged in relation to the attention we give to what our society's outcasts are experiencing. That concern needs to take a variety of forms, including attention to the immediate needs they have as individuals, but not excluding the battery of forces and circumstances that have put them where they are . . . If we look not at others but at our own interior landscape, we shall also find clues about where we stand in the public issues of our day. We shall discover to what extent we are either surrendering or offering resistance to the oppressive powers at work in the world outside.' (Selby 1983, pp. 22–3) A prophetically pastoral Church is not called to wield power or to be subservient to power but to speak the truth to power, in love.

Martyrdom. The Good Shepherd is a gentle image. But Jesus, the pastor, was not lacking in anger. When, the common people at his heels, he staged a demonstration against the corruption of the Temple, that was dangerously political. The only fatal casualty – soon thereafter – was the pastor. The pastor may indeed be loved. But if faithful to the standards of the Kingdom, just as likely to be rejected, as Jesus was: 'his own knew him not'. Archbishop Oscar Romero's compassion for the oppressed of El Salvador was also his death warrant. As injustice, to greater or lesser degree, is part of every society and as the victims of injustice are invariably human beings, to side with those human beings will always be costly. That is why the nexus between justice and pastoral care is martyrdom. Such dying to self is a classical description of life in and with Christ. Quite clearly – though in the Church not self-evidently – the costly pastoral caring demanded by the Gospel is not just a vocation for the clergy, the professional carers. It is of the essence of all Christian living, indeed of all living that is truly human.

Selby, P., *Liberating God* (SPCK, 1983).

PAUL OESTREICHER

See also: LIFE STYLE MOVEMENT; MORAL ISSUES IN PASTORAL CARE; POLITICAL THEOLOGY AND PASTORAL CARE; SOCIAL STRUCTURES AND PASTORAL CARE; SYSTEMS PASTORAL CARE.

L

LAY PASTORAL CARE

Lay pastoral care is part of the personal response that every Christian makes to the experience of God's unconditional love; the Christian's caring reflects and extends that love to other people. Institutionally, it is part of the Church's response to God's love, as it gives itself away of the sake for those who do not belong to it. Lay pastoral care includes a diversity of activities ranging from shopping for a house-bound pensioner to the organization of a drop-in centre for unemployed teenagers. It has assumed more importance recently because of the greater seriousness with which the ministry of the laity has been taken; and because of the increasing recognition that laity are involved in areas of human life which ministers often fail to reach, at a time when clerical manpower is shrinking.

Sometimes haphazard, often unnoticed, always diffuse, lay pastoral care naturally and quite properly resists classification; but four strands can be identified: (1) The individual's *spontaneous response* to a neighbour's need. (2) Still a personal, but a more *integrated response*, when the carer has been made aware of the insights about caring and human experience which are available as a result of the development of the human sciences. Carers can be helped through courses run by churches in an area in collaboration with the social services and other educational agencies. These courses would include topics such as the ambiguities and paradoxes involved in helping and caring, the making, breaking and restoring of relationships and the exploration of areas of human distress like loneliness (q.v.) and emptiness. (3) The use of *voluntary organizations*. Leisure-time and talents may be used in attempting to reduce human suffering and promote well-being through membership of some social organization which exists for this purpose: Family Service Units, the Samaritans, Marriage Guidance Councils are ready illustrations. This entails working humbly alongside others of different religious faith, without looking for ways, because of that faith, to feel superior or distinctive. The Christian will, nevertheless,

be sustained by the hope which is not destroyed by any depths of sin, and he or she will always see beyond human defilement the image of God in every human being. (4) Mobilizing a *local congregation* to come together, under *lay*-leadership, to work out imaginatively the pressing needs of the community (q.v.) in which its church is set. This entails examining the resources it possesses in responding to those needs, and then working out a strategy as to how it may most profitably do so. The response of the Church amidst inner-city deprivations will obviously differ from its subtler and more complex response in prosperous suburbs.

If these strands of lay pastoral care are to be sustained, there must be ministerial encouragement to a service which is seen to be of the essence of, and not an optional extra to, Church life. Mutuality in ministry is a prerequisite of lay pastoral care, an opportunity for carers to share honestly together their joys and weaknesses, frustrations and perplexities in caring, and which relates their experiences both to the corporate worship of the church and to forms of spirituality which are taught and practised. What is most obviously lacking in lay pastoral care is the supportive structure of a professional identity. Substitutes for this must be found, without jeopardizing the spontaneity of such caring.

Campbell, A.V., *Paid to Care?: The Limits of Professionalism in Pastoral Care* (SPCK, 1985). Taylor, M., *Learning to Care* (SPCK, 1983). Wright, F., *Pastoral Care for Lay People* (SCM, 1982).

FRANK WRIGHT

LEADERSHIP

Leadership combines three functions: (a) satisfactory identification and effective pursuit of the task to be accomplished; (b) maintaining the cohesion of the group or community; (c) acknowledgment and handling of the individual needs of the various members. How this balance of interests should be maintained, will depend upon priorities dictated by the circumstances. The functions of leadership have therefore been labelled 'task', 'maintenance' and 'individual needs'.

Four styles of leadership can be identified: (1) *Classical leadership* is vested in the individual whose authority derives from either inheritance or due appointment. Loyalty is commanded by virtue of the office. Energies are canalized towards a mutually agreed task. This kind of leadership is most appropriate in a stable society operating in a stable environment where leadership can call upon a store of established wisdom.

(2) *Bureaucratic leadership* emerges in a more complex environment which needs to draw upon wider resources of information and skill. More people share responsibility. It lacks flexibility in adapting to new conditions, because it operates through carefully planned structures. Once set up these become a force for conservatism, e.g. a well organized committee structure in one denomination can operate as a barrier in ecumenical experiment.

(3) *Charismatic leadership* is the most appropriate to the crisis situation. It is vested in one person who is apparently thrown up by the needs of the moment. The personal qualities which are appropriate at that point can become a liability in changed circumstances. The self-assurance required to cope in a crisis may become a dogmatism that refuses to learn in more normal situations. The organization may therefore need to overthrow the leader; this will be done only at considerable cost in terms of human relations.

(4) *Systemic leadership* derives its name from the understanding of society or any part of it as a series of interlocking systems. The need for flexibility increases with the complexity of the situation, therefore leadership is not vested in one person but shared so that the most appropriate person or group can take over. Those who lead must know to whom they are accountable. Without this, there is the danger of a continual struggle for power, resulting in a paralysis of decision-making.

No one pattern of leadership is universally right or theologically acceptable. Ideally the whole membership of a group should accept the appropriate model required by its environment which will then help it relate to other institutions. A maladaptive group may however produce a leadership which enters into a collusion (q.v.) with the membership to avoid growth and development.

A unique quality of pastoral leadership will be the inclusion of *diakonia* as an integral part of its nature.

Adair, J., *The Skills of Leadership* (Gower, 1984); also a contributor to *The Becoming Church* (SPCK, 1977). Küng, H., *The Church Section E: The Offices of the Church* (Burns & Oates, 1968). Rudge, P., *Ministry and Management* (Tavistock, 1968).

MICHAEL HARE DUKE

LEARNING

The process by which we assimilate and acquire knowledge, understanding and skills, and by which we are personally enriched and enabled to cope more adequately with living.

The theoretical basis of learning is problematic. Prominent views include *stimulus-response* theories, which emphasize reinforcement and/or conditioning. Conditioning is, of course, a factor in learning and nurture, and the pastor may well reinforce positive responses made by the impaired or immature personality; but a reflex system is inadequate to account for learning in all its aspects, not least in a Christian perspective (cf. Boehlke, p. 156f.). On the other hand, *cognitive* theories of learning place emphasis on the active role of the intellect as people respond to the totality of the field they perceive and the dynamic relationships of the factors within it (e.g., Gestalt). The fact that one's view of the situation may be modified is important for counselling (cf. Rogers, p. 4). A mediating theory is that of *purposive* learning, which emphasizes the learner's goal as inner stimulus. In views such as *functionalism*, attention is focused on the problems of adjustment to the human situation.

To understand learning, one requires to focus on the learner. Here, three points relevant to pastoral care may be briefly noted: (1) Psychotherapy and depth psychology (q.v.) afford important insights, particularly into guilt, failure and the whole range of human disturbance which directly affects learning. (2) The social dimension is of central importance; learning takes place through social interaction, and socialization and acculturation are important aspects of the process. (3) The learner, of whatever age, is a developing, maturing being: hence an understanding of human development (q.v.) is essential to an appreciation of learning. Relevant areas include the cognitive (Piaget), the emotions (Erikson), moral learning (Kohlberg) and growth in faith or trust (Fowler). The development of religious thinking has been studied by Goldman, and Bruner's 'spiral curriculum' has applied developmental insights to curriculum construction. Such studies are relevant to the pastor not only as general background but also because pastoral discussion, itself a learning experience, may focus on the next step in personal learning and the problems which inhibit one from taking it

Boehlke, R.R., *Theories of Learning in Christian Education* (Westminster Press, 1962). **Bruner, J.S.**, *Toward a Theory of Instruction* (Harvard, 1966). **Elkind D.** (ed.), *Jean Piaget, Six Psychological Studies* (Harvester, 1980). **Erikson, E.H.**, *Childhood and Society* (Paladin, rev. edn 1982). **Fowler, J.W.**, *Stages of Faith* (Harper & Row, 1981). **Goldman, R.**, *Religious Thinking from Childhood to Adolescence* (Routledge, 1964). **Hargreaves, D.H.**, *Interpersonal Relations and Education* (Routledge, 1972). **Kohlberg, L.**, *The Philosophy of Moral Development* (San Fransisco, 1981). **Little, S.**, 'Learning, Theories of', in *Westminster Dictionary of Christian Education* (ed. K.B. Cully, 1963), *in loc.* **Rogers, C.**, *Client-centred Therapy* (Houghton-Mifflin, Boston, 1951).

J.I.H. McDONALD

See also: INDOCTRINATION; NURTURE, CHRISTIAN; PASTORAL CARE IN SCHOOLS.

LESBIANISM
See: HOMOSEXUALITY.

LETTER-WRITING AND PASTORAL CARE
Written communications between pastor and others about or to those in his or her care.

As a means of communication the letter is more detached and less direct than personal conversation, and nowadays it tends to be second to the telephone (q.v.). Letters are better not written if they are to avoid personal conversation, or as a replacement for proper communication between colleagues, but they may provide a means of contact when all else has failed.

Letters are especially useful: for communication between persons divided by distance; when some visible record is required of the exchange; when time is needed to reflect on a question before reply; as a way of working through some difficult intellectual or spiritual block; or for working out and clarifying complicated issues in a compact way.

Writing and replying to letters requires a disciplined use of time to enable prompt response. Usually replies form in the mind as the pastor reads, so the quicker the reply, the less the struggle.

To begin a letter, there are those who

favour the warmer 'My dear' for pastoral or spiritual letters, but when in doubt write 'Dear'. If you cannot write legibly, then type; content, however well expressed, is quite lost, if the letter cannot be read.

The great letter-writers tend to be brief, focusing on and developing one major theme, and finishing with personal messages and an ending. Simple warm endings flow from the subject matter, and only jar if they are forced, or artificially religious. 'Yours sincerely' is perfectly all right.

Help is to be found by reading examples of letters, e.g. Catherine of Siena, Archbishop Fénelon, the Abé de Tourville, Bishop Edward King, Dom John Chapman, Baron F. von Hügel, Evelyn Underhill and many others.
The Amnesty Letter Writing Guide (Amnesty International). **Autton, Norman**, *The Pastoral Care of the Bereaved* (SPCK, 1967), part 3. **Foster, K.**, and **Ronayne, M.J.** (eds.), *I Catherine* (Collins, 1980).

DAVID GOODACRE

LIBERATION THEOLOGY
See: POLITICAL THEOLOGY.

LIFE CYCLE
See: HUMAN DEVELOPMENT.

LIFE STYLE MOVEMENT
A movement, mainly within the developed nations, in favour of simplicity of life, solidarity with the poor and the oppressed, and the conservation of the Earth's resources.

Since the Second World War, but particularly in the Nineteen Seventies, more and more people have been realizing that the future of the human family depends on a more equitable distribution of the Earth's resources and their conservation for our own and future generations. People have been asking what they personally can do to promote justice and peace in the world and have been looking for an appropriate life-style which combines space for reflection, sharing of ideas, political action and personal moderation. The resulting movement is secular but with a strong Christian component. In the United States in 1978 a professional survey indicated that some five million people were fully committed to voluntary simplicity of life and twice that number partially committed. In Norway the 'Future in Our Hands' recruited six thousand members in its first year and continues to grow, having an appreciable influence on national attitudes and policies.

FIOH is a secular movement, but in the Netherlands 'New Life Styles' and in Sweden 'Life is More than Affluence' have been church-based, though open to all.

Britain's 'Life Style Movement', founded in 1972, is also open to all, whatever their creed or lack of it, but has found that many of its members have a Christian motivation. 'Life Style', as it is often called, co-operates with other agencies such as Christian Aid, Future in Our Hands, One for Christian Renewal, the National Association of Christian Communities and Networks, and the Little Gidding Community. Central organization is minimal as Life Style operates through a network of local cells. But there are an elected council, a national co-ordinator, regional co-ordinators, residential and one-day conferences, a quarterly newsletter and other publications. Membership is worldwide but most members are from the United Kingdom. Life Style provides 'Guidelines' and a 'Commitment' for those who are looking for mutual support and a disciplined life in their personal adherence to the cause of justice and peace. The commitment and one of the four guidelines (by way of example) are as follows.

The Life Style Commitment. 'Recognising that the peaceful development and perhaps the survival of the Human Family are threatened by: (1) The injustice of extremes of poverty and wealth; (2) The widespread pollution of natural resources; (3) The Arms Race; (4) The wasteful consumption of all our resources; I therefore intend to: Live more simply that all of us may simply live, understanding that my greed may already be denying another's need or damaging the environment. Change my own life style as may be necessary, before challenging others to change theirs. Give more freely, that all of us may be free to give. Learn from those who are poorer than I how to live cheerfully and well. Support political action and economic policies leading to a fairer distribution of the earth's resources and to their conservation and development for the benefit of all. Enjoy such good things as are compatible with this Commitment and the freedom from the tyranny of possessions. Encourage others to join me in this Commitment.'

The Life Style Guideline, no. 3. 'Those of us who accept the Life Style Commitment are invited to be generous without ostentation and hospitable without extravagance; neither to eat nor to drink to excess, nor to consume what in our judgement depends for its production on the deprivation or the exploitation of the poor. To make time in our lives for reflection; for the deepening of our understanding of the world in which we live and of the people in it; for recreation and for the sharing of simple pleasures with others; and for sufficient sleep for good health and good temper. In our proper concern for the whole Human Family, not to neglect those near and dear to us or any others towards whom we have particular obligations.'

Dammann, E., *The Future in Our Hands* (Pergamon, 1979). **Dammers, A.H.,** *Life Style – a Parable of Sharing* (Turnstone, 1982). **Mallison, J.,** *Christian Lifestyle – Discovery through Small Groups* (Renewal Publications, 1977). **Patey, E.,** *Christian Life Style* (Mowbrays, 1976). **Rivers, P.,** *Living Better on Less* (Turnstone, 1977). **Schumacher, E.F.,** *Small is Beautiful* (Blond and Briggs, 1973; Sphere, 1974). **Sider, R.J.,** *Rich Christians in an Age of Hunger* (Hodder, 1977). **Taylor, J.V.,** *Enough is Enough* (SCM, 1975). **Ward, B.** and **Dubos, R.,** *Only One Earth* (Penguin Books, 1972).

A.H. DAMMERS
See also: JUSTICE AND PASTORAL CARE.

LIMIT-SETTING
See: STRUCTURE.

LISTENING
Making an effort to hear something, hearing with attention.

Pastoral listening is, ideally, hearing focused by a genuine desire to understand. The human mind listens selectively according to personal considerations. We do not invariably listen to others with total attention to the significance *for them* of what they are saying. It is natural to defend ourselves from talk, either by 'summing up' the situation or the speaker prejudicially or by preparing an answer before the communication is complete.

Pastoral care begins with learning to be aware of our defences (*see* DEFENCE MECHANISMS) against communication (which will vary from person to person) so that we can achieve an accurate and empathic understanding of what is being communicated, verbally and non-verbally. Noting the effect on ourselves of what we hear, we can avoid over-identifying with the speaker, or over-reacting to the message, or being seduced by curiosity. We can also allow for the speaker's defences which block the full expression of his or her troubles. Tone of voice, posture, facial expression and other non-verbal hints may modify or even contradict the verbal message. Techniques, like reflecting back what you hear, can deepen the feeling awareness of both speaker and listener, enabling as much as can be borne at the time to be shared and clarified.

At least half of an initial pastoral interview will probably need to be devoted to listening. The temptation is to move into questioning, interpretation or the exploring of solutions before rapport (q.v.) has been achieved through listening thoroughly. If our work involves having to make pronouncements, we may forget the value of silence when someone is talking out what is on his or her mind and adjusting to it in the process. But, although always receptive, pastoral listening is not merely passive. A flood of words may be used to conceal pain, and may need to be checked before it drowns the listener or arouses the speaker's emotions so acutely that he or she hardly dare risk further communication at depth.

Often what we hear has the character of a saga, or 'story', with several layers of significance. 'In effective therapy the response that is most helpful cuts through the story material, to its origins in the personality of the other' (Kennedy 1977). What is 'real', in one sense, is also *symbolic* of the speaker's underlying conflicts. In beginning to listen to his or her innermost self, the counsellee may see: how the effect of the story upon his or her life depends upon its interpretation; or how self-image may be reassessed; or how ways of handling life may be changed.

Clinebell, H.J., *Basic Types of Pastoral Counselling* (Abingdon, Nashville, 1966), pp. 59–62. **Jacobs, Michael,** *Still Small Voice* (SPCK, 1982), pp. 29–32. **Kennedy, Eugene,** *On Becoming a Counsellor* (Gill & Macmillan, Dublin, 1977).

RONALD SMYTHE

See also: COMMUNICATION; EMPATHY; RAPPORT.

LITERATURE: PASTORAL USE

The use of literature in the maintenance or restoration of mental and spiritual well-being.

The selection of literature for this purpose must be adapted to the need, ability and, at least to some extent, the taste of the person cared for. Poetry which would bring healing

to some would be meaningless to many. For some, almost anything worthy of the name of literature would be ineffective. In this matter, each person may to some degree be his or her own physician and little purpose is served by struggling to imbibe medicine which is uncongenial. Nor is there any need to feel guilty if Augustine, Dante, or T.S. Eliot fails to register.

Three general areas of need and types of remedy may be recognized: (1) the tension which results from prolonged overwork or the mental lassitude which can follow illness may be relieved by escapist or humorous literature; (2) the maintenance of general mental and spiritual balance may be aided by prose or poetry which, while serious, does not seek to expose the extremes of complexity and anguish in human experience; (3) the literature which depicts and anlayses the gravest moral problems and the most intense forms of suffering may meet the need of those involved in such experience.

1. The literature in this class is abundant and varied. It may, however, be difficult to persuade one who is dedicated to work and the slave of duty to recognize his need and take his medicine. Wesley's advice to his helpers, 'never be triflingly employed' is not of universal application. To escape from work to the literature of humour, adventure or fantasy may be the best way to return to it with fresh enthusiasm. Similarly, the jaded condition of mind which often accompanies physical weakness may be alleviated by the kindling of fresh interest.

2. Here the varieties of taste make specific suggestions seem almost pointless. The sanity and humane quality of Scott's novels and the robust quality of much of Browning's poetry may well meet the need of some. Biography may serve to enlarge the reader's vision and understanding of human experience. For some, the great essayists may achieve the same end.

3. In much of the poetry, drama, and novels of our time there is presented the experience of malaise, frustration, insecurity, and anguish which is the lot of many. For the comfortable and secure it may make painful and unpalatable reading. For those who are baffled by the complexity and pain of their own experience it may bring its own comfort. With such literature we may link the angry and bitter outcries of Job, Jeremiah, and some of the psalmists. Such rebellious candour,

expressed towards God, prepares the way for restoration.

Anderson, D., *The Tragic Protest* (SCM, 1969).

G.W. ANDERSON

See also: IMAGINATION; SYMBOLS.

LITURGY AND RITUAL

(1) *Liturgy*: 'the form of public worship', worship itself being 'reverent homage or service paid to God'. (2) *Ritual*: the prescribed order of performing religious service' (*Oxford Eng. Dict.*)

Both words denote the performance of particular actions of a symbolic kind, with or without the use of words, as a means of communication between persons, divine and human. In contrast with private devotion and faithful daily living, liturgy and ritual are essentially corporate ways of talking and listening to God. In Christian worship the conversation is between the Body of Christ and the Persons of the Trinity. This is the organizing principle of all Christian liturgy, although it stands out most clearly of all in the sacraments.

In religions throughout the world, men and women use artistic form to express a well-made wish to enter God's presence. In ritual, special actions and words, in some cases a particular spatial location, signify the awareness of the unique quality of this kind of event. The link between two spheres of being, the divine and the human, is provided by the religious symbol, which is the conscious remembrance or actual physical re-presentation of a historical event or an incident held to have taken place in a pretemporal era, when the circumstances of mortality were definitively transcended and humanity met God face to face. Thus, art (q.v.) is used within the present moment to invoke a timeless setting for encounters that take place in eternity, and the presence of the symbol actualizes the entire salvation-history of the community.

The rite's *shape* is fundamental to its effect, because the ritual scenario provides the aesthetic distance essential for the emotional involvement of those taking part, but a special *language* is also used to mediate a symbolic reality, a meeting of persons which under any other circumstances would be impossible. This language need not be archaic; but it must, in the nature of human discourse about God, be metaphorical. For Christian believers, the name of Christ, however it may be signified, recapitulates the entire gospel, making every act of Christian worship the actualization of Christ's passion and resurrection. Imagery and metaphor lie at the heart of worship, but they are used for purposes of encounter rather than of evasion. Liturgy is a confrontation with the fundamental realities of human being. In the rite men and women are brought face to face with the basic issues of living and dying, protected by a mediating symbolism, but exposed to the other by the same symbol's ability to induce in us an intense imaginative involvement, a revelation of identity-in-separation impelling us towards personal relationship and giving us strength for the crossing of existential thresholds.

In rites of passage, the rituals which mark out the psychologically critical stages of our journey through life, we communicate with the source of our inner unity, the divine life which is able to 'defeat' death, so that we are strengthened and refreshed for our daily existence. According to C.G. Jung, 'ritual since time immemorial has been a safe way of dealing with the unaccountable forces of the unconscious mind', as the vehicle for dogma which 'expresses aptly the living process of the unconscious in the form of the drama of repentance, sacrifice and redemption'. Like theatre, ritual and liturgy exist primarily in the act itself; they forestall argument and postpone reflection while having a profound influence upon all subsequent thought. This is the reason for their appropriateness in situations where ordinary human dialogue is impractical or impossible because people are too frightened, too depressed, or simply too ill, to be reached in any other way. Christian liturgy is robust and flexible, and can be used anywhere, so long as the intention is appropriate.

The significance of the rite is often very striking in social settings which are most unchurchlike, where the oddness of the setting increases the impact of the service, and the liturgy is able to 'speak for itself'.

Crichton, J.D., 'A Theology of Worship' in C. Jones *et al.* (eds.), *The Study of Liturgy* (SPCK, 1978). **Douglas, M.**, *Purity and Danger* (Routledge, 1966). **Eliade, M.**, *Patterns of Comparative Religion* (Sheed & Ward, 1958). **Gennep, A. van**, *The Rites of Passage* (Routledge, 1960). **Jung, C.G.**, *Psychology and Religion* (Yale UP, 1938).

ROGER GRAINGER

See also: RITES AND RITUALS; SYMBOLS; WORSHIP AND PASTORAL CARE.

LONELINESS

The pain of a felt inability to satisfy the basic human need for intimate relations with other persons.

That broad definition covers many different meanings which have been proposed by writers with varying theoretical standpoints. In the diffuse and sparse literature there are three areas of agreement: loneliness is felt as a deficiency in personal relationships; it is unpleasant, distressing and often desperately painful; it is a subjective experience.

The last point is of great importance: the distinction between the *experience* of loneliness and the *conditions* which precipitate or perpetuate it. Old people in high-rise tenements, prisoners in solitary confinement, politicians making world-shaking decisions and middle-aged single women are likely to be lonely, but they may not be. Loneliness is a personal, felt experience.

The many definitions which have been proposed focus upon particular aspects, or methods of investigation, of the experience and associated behaviour. Three are important: (1) Loneliness arises from the lack or distortion of an inborn drive for intimacy, 'attachment' or 'bonding' (Bowlby) which persists and develops as a need for a mutual, personal, I–Thou dialogue (Buber). (2) Everyone has an ideal notion, an optimum, of relations with others. If the optimum is exceeded, if it is 'all too much', then a person is distressed by the invasion of his or her personal space, feeling 'crowded'. If, however, the person perceives and construes a wide gap between desired and perceived degrees of interaction then he or she will adopt the label 'lonely'. (3) Behaviourists (*see* BEHAVIOUR THERAPY) regard loneliness as a defect of (potentially measurable) quantity and type of 'social reinforcement'.

Living with loneliness. Loneliness is a fact of life for many and perhaps most of us. Acknowledged or unacknowledged, it is intimately related to such disorders as alcoholism, behaviour problems in adolescence, serious depression, and a multitude of psychological symptoms such as headaches, lack of appetite and insomnia. It is a factor in serious physical illness and in suicide. But it is also an agony for millions who never gain the attention of doctors, psychiatrists, counsellors or clergy. Perhaps it lies at the root of religion. Yet only in recent years has loneliness begun to be seriously investigated by psychologists and sociologists.

Between 1932 and 1977 there were only 208 (mainly anecdotal) publications on the subject. Perhaps this is because of the stigma. It is shameful to say 'I am lonely', and even psychotherapists and researchers avoid being confronted by their own loneliness. During the last decade the situation has changed somewhat, but a comprehensive review of the topic (Peplau and Perlman) reveals a paucity of hard data.

Experience of loneliness. The experiences of loneliness are legion. They range from a frightening, gnawing distress or restless, bored hostility to a frozen emptiness. The agony is that there are no words. Loneliness in lesser degrees can motivate and drive a person to seek out others but, as it mounts, there is only worn-out, helpless, futile paralysis. In general there is a heightened self-focus, an increased self-centredness, and a lessened ability to attend and concentrate. Oversensitivity results in misinterpretation and exaggeration of slight cues of hostile or positive feelings in others. It leads either to further silent withdrawal or to dependent, demanding heart-pouring.

Precipitating factor. (1) Changes in social situations. The loss of a close personal relationship such as by death, divorce, physical separation (e.g. children going away to school) can precipitate extreme loneliness. But, so too, can loss of more superficial contacts such as movement to a new area. (2) Changes in social needs or desires. As we grow up, our needs for personal relationships change. Desires and capacities vary during a life-cycle. In pre-adolescence there is a quest for a different mode of intimacy (q.v.). In middle-life a successful professional man has a renewed interest in intimate friendships apart from work. Retirement (q.v.) brings stresses with a search for new modes of companionship.

Predisposing and maintaining factors. (1) Certain *personality characteristics* predispose to loneliness. Shy, self-deprecating people with low self-esteem take less social risks. They are slow to learn social skills, and hence have difficulty in dealing with environmental

and/or class changes. (2) A competitive–
acquisitive *culture* inculcates values of independence and uninvolvement. Town-
planning and architecture promote physical
isolation in home-life and in work. At the
same time the mass media vividly portray an
idealized picture of blissful intimacy. We are
put in a double-bind (q.v.) situation.

Coping with loneliness. Loneliness is often
denied and indeed banished from awareness
– for a time. Social relations may be devalued,
and a person may escape into work or a
round of superficial social activities. Conforming to 'bleak reality' (Weiss), he or she may
find satisfaction in solitary activities, in adoration of TV personalities or in the solace of
pets.

More effective methods of coping involve a
re-examination and re-evaluation of standards
of social relating. With the help of social
agencies, church bodies, self-help groups,
psychotherapy and counselling, a lonely
person might seek and find rewarding
relationships. But it is important that the
psychotherapist, counsellor, spiritual director,
or enthusiastic member of the Men's Society
or the Women's Guild, should not indulge his
or her own fear of loneliness by offering
patronizing advice. In the view of many
humanistic psychologists (Yalom), it is important to live with the deep loneliness which lies
at the heart of existence.

Existential loneliness. Two modes of loneliness may be distinguished which are
associated with two kinds of anxiety (q.v.). A
state of *cut-offness* is related to the fear of
separation from, and loss of, a loved person.
Existential loneliness embodies basic anxiety, a
terror of ceasing to be. In infancy it seems that
the sense of 'I am' comes and goes. The fear
of losing 'I' persists throughout life. In the
deepest loneliness we are confronted with
'non-being' or 'no-being', an abyss of
nothingness. Experienced by me, and only by
me, it can at best be dimly apprehended by
another in an imaginative act within and
beyond a relationship.

A personal relationship may be conceived
as a state of *aloneness-togetherness*. The hyphen
is important. I can only be alone in so far as I
can be together with another. I can only be
together in so far as I can be alone (Hobson).
When I am able to be alone (as distinct from
being isolated and lonely), I can stay with, and
perhaps rest in, solitude where, in
Wordsworth's words, 'all stand single'

(Whitehead), in existential loneliness. Yet
aloneness is inseparable from expanding
personal relationships. With the word
'expanding', we move into religion.

Loneliness is a crucial problem for our time.
It calls for disciplined psychological and
sociological investigation. Pastoral care means
developing social networks, self-help groups
and counselling skills which are grounded on
a sound theory of intimate relationships. But
ultimately we are faced with
A.N. Whitehead's statement: 'Religion is
what the individual does with his own
solitariness . . .'.

Bowlby, J., *The Making and Breaking of Affectional
Bonds* (Tavistock, 1979). Buber, M., *I and Thou*
(T. and T. Clark, Edinburgh, 1971). Hobson, R.F.,
'Loneliness' (*Journal of Analytical Psychology* 19, 1974),
pp. 71–89. Peplau, L.A. and Perlman, D., *Lone-
liness* (John Wiley, 1982). Weiss, R.S., *Loneliness:
the Experience of Emotional and Social Isolation* (MIT,
Cambridge, Mass., 1973). Whitehead, A.N.,
Religion in the Making (CUP, 1926), p. 16f. Yalom,
I.D., *Existential Psychotherapy* (Basic Books, New
York, 1980).

BOB HOBSON

See also: BEREAVEMENT; INTIMACY; SINGLE
PERSONS; SOLITUDE.

LOSS
See: BEREAVEMENT.

LOVE
A liking, fondness, concern, affection; it also
describes sexual desire.

Love has meant many different things in
different cultures, but it usually has these two
basic, often overlapping meanings. Different
words have indicated particular aspects of the
notion of love, such as the familiar and much
criticized contrast in Christian and non-
Christian writing between *eros* and *agape*.

God in the Christian tradition, though sometimes defined as the absolute or the ground of
being, is often characterized as being, in his
essential nature, love. Love is not simply
another attribute such as power, wisdom or
holiness, but is *the* central characteristic of
God in himself and in relation to the created
order. The grounds for this affirmation lie in
reflection throughout the Christian tradition
that the biblical teaching about God is a
narrative best understood as a witness to
love. Love is a notion which enables us to
deepen our appreciation of the divine nature.

God in the Old Testament, conceived of in a

149

variety of ways, remains always the sustainer of his creation, looking after his people. All our human experience helps us to recognize the character of God's concern. The reference to God as creator suggests dimensions in God which go beyond our own experience. The basis of Christian understanding of God's love has been an interpretation of the New Testament in terms of God's self-giving in the sacrifice of his son, and in Jesus' self-giving to God and mankind. God is identified with his creation through his presence in Jesus Christ, suffering, sharing in life and death, bringing life and reconciliation out of death and disaster.

Jesus of Nazareth identified himself through his actions and teaching with the lives of people around him. His love for others was expressed in specific teaching about the nature of God and his relation to mankind. It was expressed in concern for particular individuals, with a distinct bias towards the poor and the disadvantaged. It brought him into conflict with the religious and political authorities of the day. He was crucified. Central to classical Christianity is the affirmation that death, identification in suffering, was not God's last word. Through the resurrection of Christ, God's love has in a profound and mysterious way overcome evil. Hence Paul's comment that nothing can now separate us from God's love.

The understanding of God as love, of God's purpose for the created order as leading to fulfilment in love, has sweeping implications for individual and social ethics. Love is to be the informing principle, not just in special cases but in all human social life. Here is the perennial relevance of an impossible ideal.

Christian reflection on love has developed over the centuries in dialogue with philosophical ideas derived from ancient Greece. Eros is a powerful god, the source of unquenchable sexual desire, driving men and women to distraction. For Plato there is a close assimilation between eros, including sexual attraction to one or both sexes, and philia, friendship. Eros is created initially by attraction to the beauty of the form of the human body. From this attraction friendship and philosophical dialogue in the joint love of wisdom may grow. Beauty becomes the means of transition between the material and the ideal world. The spiritualization of love, with its attendant advantages and disadvantages, reached a climax in the neo-Platonic ideal of the highest love as a purely spiritual contemplation of a perfectly incorporeal God. This tradition had deep influence on Christianity, emphasizing ascetic and monastic love of God at the expense of love between the sexes.

Augustine emphasized the polarization between love with a sexual dimension and love for God, *amor Dei*. The Middle Ages saw the development of mystical piety, the search of the soul in love for God, and a wide literature on courtly love, centred on the selfless devotion of the lover to his beloved. In the writings of the mystics sexual symbolism was transformed to describe the mystical marriage between the believer and God; in Dante earthly love leads on to union with the divine love. Modern literature and philosophy have explored the psychological and moral dimensions of love. Psychology and psychiatry have brought fundamental changes to our perception of the springs of all human feeling and action. It would be hard to overestimate the importance of Freud, even though many of his theories are no longer widely held. Freud understood the libido, or sexual instinct, as the driving force behind much human action.

Christianity is concerned for loving relationships between people at every level. As a religion of incarnation it resists devaluation of the material world in favour of ideas. Love between persons is often expressed appropriately in sexual terms. Love for society means feeding the hungry with real food rather than benevolent sentiment. Yet Christianity also has a truly spiritual dimension and does not regard perfect union as always quasi-substantial physicality. Love includes allowing space to the other, letting be, encouraging independence. The clue remains the self-giving love of God in Jesus Christ.

Lewis, C.S., *The Four Loves* (Fontana, 1963). **McIntyre, J.,** *On the Love of God* (Collins, 1961). **Newlands, G.M.,** *Theology of the Love of God* (Collins, 1980). **Outka, G.,** *Agape* (Yale UP, 1972). **Pittenger, N.,** *Love is the Clue* (Mowbray, 1967). **Stafford-Clark, D.,** *Five Questions in Search of an Answer* (Fontana, 1970). **Vanstone, V.H.,** *Love's Endeavour, Love's Expense* (Darton Longman & Todd, 1977). **Williams, D.D.,** *The Spirit and Forms of Love* (Nisbet, 1968).

G.M. NEWLANDS

See also: INTIMACY; SEXUALITY, THEOLOGY OF.

M

MAGIC

Magic has been defined as 'the science of causing changes in consciousness in conformity with the will'. It presupposes and depends upon the limitless power of the disciplined human will, and it seeks to operate in that realm best described as the 'universal unconscious'. Claiming to be a science it has religious connotations, manifests a monistic theology, and draws its philosophical background from the whole corpus of esoteric teaching and tradition, including the Hebrew kabbala and hermetics.

The aim of magic has been described as 'seeking to know in order to serve'. The knowledge in question is esoteric and includes the mastery of techniques for the futherance of its ends. It is essentially a manipulative operation, and its integrity is always under threat. Magic also seeks 'contact on the inner planes' with discarnate consciousness in order to work in a common (or supposedly common) cause. Evelyn Underhill comments that 'it is an individualistic and acquisitive science: in all its forms an activity of the intellect, seeking reality for its own purposes, or for those of humanity at large' (*Mysticism*, p. 71).

Magic is encountered in many forms and is mostly a group activity. Most magicians claim to be practising 'white' magic, but magic is a fragmenting occupation and there is much mutual suspicion between serious groups. There are a great many groups who are overtly 'black', and some satanist. Witch covens of several kinds are also to be met with. There is much human degradation and some criminal activity in these groups which are abhorred by the 'white' fraternity.

Undisciplined magical activities which are widespread include Ouija and a number of spiritualist techniques, such as table-tapping, etc. Involvement in these, as in any 'shady' magical activity, can cause serious psychological disturbance and, in some cases, an inability to break away from the group, obsessions of many kinds, sometimes insanity and occasionally suicide. Pastoral care of those disturbed involves careful counselling (q.v.), and not infrequently the laying on of hands or anointing (q.v.), and sometimes exorcism (q.v.). The mind can be disturbed at several levels and made vulnerable to stresses with which it cannot cope. Not infrequently psychiatric as well as sacramental ministry is called for.

Magic is essentially a matter of technique, and activities which are magical by definition include ritual of any kind and lodge rituals in particular, meditational techniques of any kind, a number of psychotherapeutic methods which involve group work, and public prayer for rain or similar changes in environmental circumstance. There are to be found a number of magical groups who would claim the practice of magic to be a part of their own Christian vocations. While some activities (e.g. Ouija) would seem to be questionable in any circumstances, in the main it is the intention and the integrity of the magical practice which indicates the health or morbidity of the exercise. It is certain that magic, combined with dubious intention and the loss of personal integrity, is potent for the destruction of the personalities of those involved and the disturbance of others.

Duncan, A.D., *The Christ, Psychotherapy and Magic* (Allen & Unwin, 1979); *The Fourth Dimension* (Mowbray, 1975). **Fortune, D.**, *The Mystical Qabalah* (Benn, 1935). **Koch, K.E.**, *Christian Counselling and Occultism* (Kregel, 1965). **Knight, G.**, *Experience of the Inner Worlds* (Helios, 1975); *A History of White Magic* (Mowbray, 1978); *Practical Guide to Kabbalistic Symbolism* (Helios, 1965). **Underhill, E.**, *Mysticism* (Methuen, 1911).

ANTHONY B. DUNCAN

See also: EXORCISM; SPIRITUALISM/SPIRITISM; SUPERSTITION.

MANIPULATION

So handling a situation as to bring about certain ends.

The ends are generally undeclared and the process usually covert. The term generally carries a negative evaluation, especially when those prone to the use of such processes are described as 'manipulative'.

Since it is unusual for human beings to be fully aware of their motives, a component of manipulation is likely to be present in all pastoral situations and counselling settings. It is, for example, unlikely that any request for advice will not contain some element of a quest for approval of actions already taken or contemplated, and the client is likely to present the situation so as to manipulate the counsellor into offering that approval. Failure on the counsellor's part to be aware of the manipulation can lead to collusion (q.v.) on his part with it, and therefore to a failure to offer to the client the opportunity to recognize the manipulative component in the way in which needs have been presented; awareness of the manipulative component can lead to a clearer grasp of real needs and the options available for meeting them.

While the notion of manipulation generally carries with it a negative evaluation, it is in fact a highly appropriate response to situations where demands are unlikely to be met or satisfaction of needs denied. The child–parent relationship is therefore an ideal school in manipulative techniques; the child is powerless against a refusal by parents to meet a demand, and therefore seeks, and quickly learns, forms of behaviour, or ways of voicing demands which can circumvent that refusal. Where this means of obtaining satisfaction is not replaced in later years by processes of negotiation and compromise, the manipulative pattern becomes set and reappears in any situation where it appears that the straightforward voicing of a demand will not produce the desired end. Hence its appearance in the pastoral situation: the client knows that certain ends will not be acceptable and therefore does not bring them to expression or even to consciousness. This is particularly likely where the pastor has some other role, such as responsibility for a local church; the client can use the confidentiality (q.v.) of the pastoral relationship as a means of securing an alliance, or the willingness of the pastor to take responsibility for aims which in fact belong to the client.

Harms, E. and **Schreiber, P.** (eds.), *Handbook of Counselling Techniques* (Pergamon, 1964).

PETER SELBY

See also: COLLUSION.

MARRIAGE AND FAMILY: CARE AND COUNSELLING

Family, in this context, is defined as two or more people in a relationship of kinship involving some commitment over time. The kinship relationships provide the framework and structure within which those involved develop both emotionally and spiritually.

Kinship may be: biological–brothers, sisters, grandparents, parents, children; formally and legally established – marriage, adoption (q.v.), fostering; established by religious confirmation – marriage vows, vows of religious communities; self-established with some level of social recognition – common-law marriages, homosexual (q.v.) couples and other forms of commitment over time. The family may be nuclear, divorced, separated, single-parent (q.v.) or blended and remarried.

Two main areas of theory are used to provide a framework for the exercise of family pastoral care: *family life-cycles* and *family systems theory*.

The family life-cycle: a cluster of ideas which focuses on the development of the family through the different stages of life. This is conceptualized as providing a 'major context and determinant of the development of individual family members'. The development of each family is understood within the context of any particular culture's expectations of appropriate behaviour from each family member moving through life's phases. When exercising pastoral care, the individual expectations, structure and organization of a particular family are to be attended to and respected. Every family is seen as having its own set of ways of behaving which are a collection of responses of that family to the demands of the present in the light of its own history.

Central points in the family life-cycle relate to the changes in a family's pattern of living at times of joining or leaving, such as birth, death, marriage or adoption. Allied to these points are those specific experiences which require adjustments in the balance of family relationships: children going to school or reaching adolescence, or retirement of grandparents, etc. Each phase of the cycle has the goal of enabling major changes to take place, so that each family member can go from one sphere of activity or role to another enriched, secure and flourishing. The way in which each family manages these times of transition is to be seen in the context of geographical moves, historical and social events such as war or unemployment.

Writers divide the stages up in the following manner. (1) The courtship period and the developing young adult. (2) Marriage and the beginnings of the new family. (3) The family with young children: (a) childbirth and rearing; (b) going to school and exploring the world. (4) The family with adolescents (q.v.). (5) Launching children and moving on. (6) The family with grandparents. (7) Retirement (q.v.) and later life.

In addition to these developments family life stages are deeply affected at other times. Major events include: (a) the family with sudden death or a major disabling illness; (b) the family in which divorce or separation takes place; (c) families formed by further marriages or alliances; (d) families affected by major political, social or economic changes.

Family systems theory is used to provide a model for understanding family organization. The family is seen as a system that, in time, comes to have patterns of routine behaviour. These patterns make up the stability of the family and consist of those routine actions and reactions to each other which family members have come to expect over a number of years.

As family members live, during the passage of time, the patterns of action and reaction can be watched and listed as sequences or moves as in a game of chess or as a series of dance steps as in the choreography of a ballet. The family behaviour patterns, in time, take on the nature of prescriptive rules to which family members become subject. These rules also describe the balance whereby family members act and react in such a way that order and organization are maintained whilst change can also take place. In the literature this is described as family 'homeostasis', or self-balancing steady state, and family capacity for transformation. Thus the family system is seen as greater than the sum of its parts and is viewed as providing the limits and possibilities for change and development in the parts of the system.

Family systems theory views all family behaviour in a circular fashion. 'All parts of the organism form a circle. Therefore every part is both a beginning and an end' (Hippocrates). A sequence of interaction between family members can be described from a variety of perspectives. 'A' can be said

to initiate and 'B' to respond; 'B' can be said to cue 'A' in to initiate something to which 'B' responds. Thus 'A' and 'B' can be said to initiate and respond simultaneously. To be able to plot such sequences all interactions are classed as communications and responses. A communication can be verbal, 'Do as I ask'. Then the meaning of the verbal communication is partly content, but is also to be found in the non-verbal accompaniments as well as the response of those who are part of the sequence. All behaviour is communication.

Practice of pastoral care. At times of *transition* the focus needs to be on the family *as a whole*. The task is facilitation of adjustments in roles for family members appropriate to the particular life-cycle phase, supporting the letting go of previously appropriate behaviour and encouraging adoption of new ways of relating. Religious rituals (*see* RITES AND RITUAL) are an integral part of the work, and the pastor relates these to those ritual customs specific to each family at such times. Methods used include meetings with the whole family or parts of the family. Open communication is fostered, participation by all family members ensured. Appropriate boundaries between generations are drawn and supported. The pastor/counsellor employs a neutral stance, supporting every family member whilst avoiding siding with one family member against another. Tasks are set for problems to be solved; conflicts are openly expressed and resolution sought.

It is believed that problems and symptoms are indications of tangles in communication and of difficulties at times of transition. Severe psychiatric symptoms are treated by specialists. At such times pastors and counsellors provide important support as families undergo major, and at times painful, reorientation in treatment. Further understanding of the issues can be gained from referring to the literature.

General and comprehensive works: **Hoffman, L.,** *Foundations of Family Therapy* (Basic Books, New York, 1981). **Minuchin, S.,** *et al., Family Therapy Techniques* (Harvard UP, 1981). *Problem Solving Therapy* (Josey Bass, San Francisco/London, 1976). **Satir, V.,** *Conjoint Family Therapy: a Guide to Theory and Technique* (Science and Behaviour Books, Palo Alto, Calif., rev. edn 1967).

Family structure and organization: **Carter, E.A.** and **McGoldrick, M.** (eds.), *The Family Life Cycle: a Framework for Family Therapy* (Gardner Press, New

York, 1980). **Haley, J.**, *Uncommon Therapy* (W.W. Norton, New York, 1973), ch. 3, 'The Family Life Cycle'. **Satir, V.**, *Peoplemaking* (Science and Behaviour Books, Palo Alto, Calif., 1972). **Skynner, R. and Cleese, J.**, *Families and How to Survive Them* (Methuen, 1983).

Journals: Journal of Family Therapy (published quarterly, Academic Press, London). *Family Process* (published quarterly, 149 East 78th St., New York).

PETER LANG

See also: ADOLESCENCE; BIRTH; CHILDREN: PASTORAL CARE; DIVORCE: PASTORAL ASPECTS; HUMAN DEVELOPMENT; MARRIAGE, THEOLOGY OF; PARENTING; PREMARITAL COUNSELLING.

MARRIAGE: NULLITY

1. Civil law. The Nullity of Marriage Act 1971 indicates three grounds on which a marriage is *void* (that is, not a lawful marriage at all): (a) that it is not a valid marriage under the provision of the Marriage Acts of 1949 and 1970 (that is to say, the parties are within the prohibited degrees of consanguinity or affinity, or either party is under the age of consent, or the parties intermarried in disregard of certain necessary formalities such as the need to publish banns or obtain a licence); (b) that at the time of marriage either party was already lawfully married; (c) that the parties are not respectively male and female (in terms of biological sex).

The Act also indicates six grounds on which defects in the making or performance of the marriage contract can enable courts to recognize that there is no marriage and declare it null. This is a *voidable* marriage: a marriage made with lack of consent or lack of capacity, but which remains legally binding on the parties until a declaration of nullity is obtained. The six grounds are: non-consummation through incapacity; wilful refusal to consummate; lack of valid consent; mental disorder at the time of marriage; venereal disease at the time of marriage; pregnancy by another at the time of the marriage.

Christians of all churches have hitherto recognized the grounds for marriage annulment admitted by the civil law, and have had no objection to either party contracting another marriage.

2. Catholic Canon Law. In addition to the above civil-law provisions, the Church of Rome has its own marriage tribunals which

are empowered by the Church to review certain decisions of the civil courts. Such tribunals may seek to establish on what grounds, if any, some marriages which have been legally terminated in a divorce court can be considered in terms of Canon Law never to have existed.

The Church of Rome stresses the three elements of an indissoluble marriage union: validity, consummation and sacramentality, and teaches that a 'union which does not possess these three qualities may be, in some sense of the word, dissoluble; or may be said not to exist' (R. Brown). The Code of Canon Law indicates that a non-consummated marriage between baptized persons can be dissolved by the Roman Pontiff (Canon 1142); that a marriage entered into by two unbaptized persons may be dissolved 'in favour of the faith' of one of the parties who receives baptism, provided the unbaptized party departs (the so-called 'pauline privilege') (Canon 1143). Canon Law also indicates various diriment impediments which render a person incapable of validly contracting a marriage. These include regulations about age of consent, impotence, the existence of a previous marriage, lack of baptism in the Catholic Church, those under sacred orders or vows of chastity, affinity and consanguinity.

Canon Law is also concerned with the nature of valid consent, noting that consent may not be valid (a) for those who 'lack sufficient use of reason', or whose psychological state renders them incapable of understanding or assuming the essential obligations of marriage; (b) if there is error about a person; (c) if consent is not free and voluntary.

The Catholic Canon Law (at least in its outworkings in the United Kingdom) thus has a much wider concept of nullity than that admitted in civil law. Other Christian denominations do not follow the Church of Rome in this respect.

The Church and the Law of Nullity of Marriage (SPCK, 1955). **Brown, R.**, *Marriage Annulment in the Catholic Church* (Kevin Mayhew, 1977).

DAVID ATKINSON

See also: DIVORCE: DOCTRINAL AND LEGAL ASPECTS.

MARRIAGE, THEOLOGY OF
Christian theology has developed and defined the human institution of marriage as the union of one woman with one man, mutually

undertaken as a life-long commitment. This is based on the biblical affirmation that husband and wife belong together as 'one flesh' (Gen. 2.20, Mark 10.7). The nature of this union includes a biological function in the procreation and nurturing of children, but more importantly it stresses the relationship between the partners and the hope of mutual growth in love (q.v.). The belief that such union is good and is part of God's creation is central to the theology of marriage.

Marriage as sacrament (i.e. 'something sacred') has been responded to with varying degrees of commitment by Christians and theologians. Protestant reformers of the 16th century led the reaction against scholastic ritualism and magical usages of sacraments. Such reaction led to the rejection of the concept of marriage as a sacrament mediated by a priest (a view still held in Catholic churches) and movement towards a more contractual declaration which yet retains its sacramental character. This is now held to be affirmed by the couple themselves, and mediated by the exchanges of life-long vows made voluntarily each to each in church before the congregation and confirmed by the priest in his statement, 'Those whom God hath joined together, let no man put asunder.' Other and varying views are held about the nature of Christian marriage, and these can be seen ranged across a broad spectrum: at one end the indissolubilists hold that marriage by definition cannot be ended except by the death of a partner; at the other, that marriage itself as a relationship can 'die' (*see* DIVORCE; MARRIAGE: NULLITY).

Theological changes in the Church's teaching on marriage need to be seen in the context of social, historical and psychological developments. The Industrial Revolution, with its growth of urban living and mobility of labour, helped to highlight changes in marital status. These changes were manifest especially in the loss of the extended family which provided that supporting network of relationships from which parents and children drew resilience and help, tacit or acknowledged. The emergent pattern of the nuclear family had both positive and negative features. Greater mobility of labour gave more freedom of choice to individual partners, in comparison with arranged marriages. On the other hand it created an increased loneliness which was experienced (though mainly unexpressed) by women. Their partnership

role was laid down by the domestic requirements of work within the home and overfrequent child-bearing. Health hazards were high, infant mortality was commonplace and life expectation for both men and women was much shorter than at the present time. Thus, partnership in marriage was largely distinguished by clearly marked roles. The expectation that a wife would obey, submit to and care for her husband, would keep the home clean and bring up children, was matched by the expectation that men would concern themselves with wage-earning, often in hard conditions and for long hours, in order to provide for and to protect his family. Sexual partnership tended to be equally divided by role: desire and enjoyment for men; acquiescence and pregnancy for women.

This seeming stereotype is powerfully illustrated in the marriage service of the Book of Common Prayer, until in 1928 a revision took place. In the early version Christian marriage is offered as a remedy for sin, and ordained to avoid fornication 'for such persons as have not the gift of continency'. The echo of St Paul's teaching on sex and marriage, its emphasis laid on women as the submissive partner, enjoined to obey and depend on her husband, is unmistakable. The contrast between this and newer concepts of marital partnership is marked in the marriage service of the Alternative Service Book (Church of England, 1980). Here the stress is on mutual comfort and help, upon tenderness in love, and the joy of bodily union. Secondary emphasis is upon the procreation of children, and here too the partnership and mutuality of caring is underlined.

The most potent sociological influence in contemporary marriage is (a) greatly increased longevity and (b) the widespread availability and use of contraceptives. The requirement in Christian marriage of life-long commitment and faithfulness is likely to meet with stresses that are especially felt in social areas: (1) Women are increasingly engaged in paid work of all kinds, and find new stimulus and new friendships outside the home. (2) Since female sex need not now be linked with pregnancy, sexual freedom becomes a new option within the social climate. (3) With the increase in longevity, couples (as children move out from home) may face each other with the challenge of a seemingly 'new' relationship together, stretching ahead over many years. Changes that have happened to each individual within the shared experience of bringing up children may have been largely unrecognized or unexamined. (4) Though the legal ceremony of marriage embodies the state recognition of its function as a social institution and the one best suited to affirm and protect human growth, yet recent trends in legislation may be thought to run counter to this (e.g. permitting application for divorce after one year of marriage – Matrimonial and Family Proceedings Act, July 1984).

In all these ways marriages may be subjected to stress and anxiety of a kind previously unknown. The task of theology in Christian marriage today is to affirm the claim that God's grace can be experienced in the sustaining of these tensions, leading to growth and development, and can also be found within its failures.

Marriage and the Church's Task: the Report of the Church of England General Synod Marriage Commission (1978). *Marriage Matters: Report of the Marriage Guidance Working Party*, DHSS & Home Office (HMSO, 1979). **Thielicke, H.,** *Ethics of Sex* (J. Clarke, 1964).

MARY WELCH

See also: DIVORCE; MARRIAGE AND FAMILY; MIXED MARRIAGE.

MASCULINITY
See: FEMININITY/MASCULINITY.

MATERNAL DEPRIVATION
Inadequate mothering in childhood especially, in the first two or three years, is generally agreed to have possible bad effects on subsequent mental health, with impaired capacity for emotional relationships, low IQ and language ability, and anti-social behaviour.

The term covers in fact a variety of conditions each of which may affect the child in different ways: (1) *Insufficiency*, as for instance in an institution where there may be no stable and continuous close relationship with a mother figure for a child to interact adequately with. (2) *Discontinuity*, either through prolonged separation from or loss of a mother figure or a succession of changing mother figures. (3) *Distortion*, in which the quality of relationship given by the mother figure is ill-adapted to the needs of the child.

Since the work of John Bowlby in the 1950s, institutions concerned with child care, including hospitals, have become increasingly aware that the emotional needs of the child deserve

156

as much attention as their physical needs.

Bowlby, J., *Child Care and the Growth of Love* (Penguin, 1965); *Attachment and Loss* (Penguin, 1973). **Rutter, M.,** *Maternal Deprivation Reassessed* (Penguin, 1972).

MATURITY
In physical terms, the completion of growth. More generally, 'a state that promotes physical and psychological well being' (Turner and Helms 1979).

Physical maturity can be said to have been reached when the anatomical and physiological changes associated with puberty are complete. The timing of these changes varies considerably between individuals and appears to be largely under genetic control (though the trend observed during the last 100 years towards earlier maturation is probably attributable to improved nutrition, health care and the like). Girls, on average, mature earlier than boys. Early maturation (within the normal range) seems to be an advantage socially and psychologically, particularly for boys. However, *extremely* early or extremely late development may have negative psychological consequences.

Psychological maturity is a more nebulous concept. Various criteria of maturity have been suggested including: the ability to reason abstractly and to think about hypothetical situations in a logical way (Piaget); the ability to enter into sexually gratifying love relationships with members of the opposite sex; productive use of one's talents and relative freedom from the conflicts and anxiety that result in personal anguish and behavioural symptoms (Freud); the successful resolution of various developmental 'crises' (Erikson); the ability to cope successfully with life's problems (White).

Allport (1961) considered the following attributes to be characteristic of the healthy, mature adult: the capacity for 'extension of the self' (which requires active participation in a variety of interests and planning for the future); the capacity for warm relationships with others; a fundamental 'emotional security' and acceptance of self; realistic perception; 'self-objectification' (self-insight coupled with a sense of humour, i.e. the ability to laugh at the things one loves, including oneself); and, perhaps most important of all, 'a unifying philosophy of life', a value-system or guiding purpose that gives meaning to everything one does. Allport viewed religion as the search for a value underlying *all* things and as such the most comprehensive of all philosophies of life.

Allport, G.W., *Pattern and Growth in Personality* (Holt Rinehart & Winston, New York, 1961), ch. 12. **Conger, J.J.**, *Adolescence and Youth: Psychological Development in a Changing World* (Harper & Row, New York, 1973), ch. 4. **Erikson, E.H.**, *Childhood and Society* (Norton, New York, 1963). **Freud, S.**, *Introductory Lectures on Psychoanalysis*, vols. 15, 16 (Hogarth, 1965). **Piaget, J.**, 'Piaget's theory', in P.H. Mussen (ed.), *Carmichael's Manual of Child Psychology* (Wiley, New York, 3rd edn 1970). **Turner, J.S.** and **Helms, D.B.**, *Life Span Development* (W.B. Saunders, 1979), pp. 339–45.. **White, R.W.**, *Lives in Progress: a Study of the Natural Growth of Personality* (Holt Rinehart & Winston, New York, 1966).

S. HENLEY

See also: HUMAN DEVELOPMENT.

MEDIA

Modern forms of communication: print, radio, television, video, film.

Sociologically, mass media are the institutions and techniques by which specialized social groups employ technological devices (press, radio, television, etc.) to disseminate symbolic content to numerically very large, heterogeneous, widely dispersed and often relatively isolated members of audiences. Mass media perform essential functions in a society based on complex technology.

The techniques of mass media make for a loss of direct personal communication between the communicators and their public, and so is quite different from folk culture, from the elitist 'high culture' of the traditional arts and from church worship. Mass media content tends to be pegged at a level that appeals to the largest number of people and so tends to be inoffensive and uncritical of established order. This effect is emphasized where there is a commercial interest involved.

Television, among all media, is likely to have the highest proportion of those characteristics which feature in any definition of *media*. Of all forms of communication it has by far the largest audience, it is not dependent on language, and it can reach audiences all over the world at virtually the same time.

Issues of public concern: (1) *Persuasion*. Media's effects on attitudes and behaviours are not as important as is commonly thought. Media cannot change taste radically or upset deep-seated assumptions; where programmes follow the grain of personal or social group predisposition it can reinforce them, produce immunity to counter-propaganda and bring stray sheep back into the fold. The audience is better informed, but the media support the *status quo* and the dominant ideology. (2) *Violence on TV* only encourages acts of violence in the psychotic or mentally disturbed, and repeated acts of violence have no effects at the deepest levels of the psyche on the millions of normal viewers. (a) *Taste* is neither raised nor lowered, but whatever levels of aesthetic taste the audience member brings is reinforced. (4) *Trivialization* (Pilkington Report, HMSO 1960) is a tendency in television. This can occur in any type of programme, whether frivolous or prestigious, through a trivial grasp or treatment of its subject. Nevertheless, serious subjects like religion, science and art get the least broadcast time. (5) *Passivity* is facilitated by television only in passive children. Children who are naturally curious and active find it a source of new interests and activity. (6) *Effect on events being recorded*. The presence of television cameras at political conventions, rallies or demonstrations brings in a new self-consciousness and often determines the 'staging' of the event. Access TV has developed to allow the public some unedited use of television communication.

Pastoral considerations (of non-religious media). Symbols (q.v.), myths, inter-personal relationships and individual scenarios are the substance of both psychological counselling and of media. Soap operas, short stories, drama and film are explorations of human character, situations and story. Serious science programmes, science-fiction and music programmes often invoke transcendence and peak experiences; natural history programmes are perhaps expressions of natural theology; horror films, pornographic videos, endless TV violence and comedy symbolize the unredeemed and unintegrated 'shadow', and shock or amuse us. Westerns have been described as 'a secular redemption myth', and symbols of all kinds are forever on our screens. As Nietzsche said, 'You yourself are riding on many a symbol towards many a truth.' There are also an increasing number of obviously psychological programmes exploring issues and problems, often with a 'helpline' phone-in facility.

Despite their comprehensiveness and

excitement, mass media are no substitute for personal counselling, fellowship with other human beings and ritual enactments invoking the presence of God in our hearts. New developments in 'Air-Care' (see below) have been attempting to bring impersonal media together with personal communication.

Specifically religious media. On the whole, religious media are conventional in their approach. Specialized newspapers and journals and broadcast media convey information and news, discuss ethical and theological questions, witness and explore religious quests, present religious worship and music (hot-Gospel to oratorio) and introduce world religions. They can also be pastorally caring through the presentation of psychological, social or health subjects – with or without a phone-in facility. Producers need to be aware that the media audience includes the committed, the uncommitted, people on the fringes and people of other religious convictions.

Of the BBC's television programmes produced in 1984, only 1.3% were specifically religious (contrasting with 23.4% on current affairs; 13.1% sport; 3.8% drama. Radio had slightly more religious broadcasts (1.4%). In Britain there are approximately 26 million television sets with 40 million people watching at some time during the week. There are some 562.5 million television sets in the world.

There is much debate as to how far the churches should attempt to include radio and television in their pastoral strategy. However, the 'electronic church' seems to be underway, with the first of three Christian satellites starting transmission to North and South America in 1985; the second will transmit to Europe and Africa, and the third to Asia and the Pacific. In America religious channels have been started with computerized mailing lists and fund-raising schemes. The Good News Broadcasting Association transmits in 80 different languages.

In the UK more modest technological innovation has been used: 'care-Line' phone-ins; the Freephone system; Ceefax and Oracle have carried religious texts, and research is being done in the use of Prestel. Granada and Yorkshire Television have transmitted special services followed by an invitation to write or phone-in with questions and problems. Besides telephone-manning staff there has been

a support group of clergy and counsellors for follow-up work, thus linking media to personal communication.

Organizations. Both the National Catholic Radio and Television Centre and the CCTV Foundation for Christian Communication offer training programmes in radio and television in their studios for religious bodies. CCTV has a large film, video and sound cassette library on Christian, social and psychological themes; and its own production team. The Central Religious Advisory Committee (CRAC) advises both the BBC and the IBA (Independent Broadcasting Authority) who have their own religious broadcasting officers. Among various international bodies is the Vatican's 'Pontifical Commission for Social Communication and the World Association for Christian Communication (London) which works for the improvement of Christian communication through consultation and co-operation between organizations throughout the world. It publishes books and reports, including 'Air-Care' which stimulated the Granada experiment (above), and proposed a nationwide locally based pastoral care support system linked to radio and television programmes.

Bakewell, J. and Garnham, N., *The New Priesthood: British Television Today* (A. Lane/Penguin, 1970). Heinze, Peter, *Air-Care* (World Association for Christian Communication, 1982). McQuail, Denis, *Mass Communication Theory* (Sage, 1983). Robertson, Edwin, *The Local Radio Handbook* (Mowbray, 1974). Wolfe, Kenneth M., *The Churches and the British Broadcasting Corporation 1922–1956* (SCM, 1984).

ROGER COWARD

MEDICINE

1. In the broadest sense medicine refers to all those human activities and branches of knowledge which relate to the prevention, cure and management of states of disease and illness. In the more limited connotation in which the word is frequently used, however, it relates to activities carried out by people who have undergone a distinctive kind of formal training, as contrasted with all the caring carried out by lay people, nurses, chaplains and others.

2. Medicine as an institution can be grouped alongside the law and organized religion, since they all function as agents of social control, determining the limits of

acceptable behaviour. With the decline in religious observance it seems as if medicine has taken on an increasing role as the arbiter of life-styles or of the 'good life', and its practitioners frequently pronounce upon many details of our day-to-day existence. Thus doctors may not only prescribe treatment regimens, define healthy diets and recommend ways of keeping fit but also counsel people regarding sexual and reproductive matters and personal relationships. Doctors make momentous judgements regarding the point at which a life may end. Such mortal powers paradoxically derive from the greatly increased ability of modern medicine to maintain the life of embryos, frail elderly people and unconscious patients.

3. Medicine may refer to the medical profession. Membership of this profession is difficult to attain, necessitating an arduous and protracted apprenticeship for a selected group of students and culminating in a series of examinations designed to ensure that they have learned enough to make them fit to practise. Since doctors are permitted uniquely privileged access to the bodies and minds of patients, they are also expected to maintain high ethical standards in order to merit such trust. The precise expression of medical ethics varies from time to time and from place to place, but a respect for the value of human life, concern for the welfare of individual patients and insistence upon confidentiality are common elements in many codes (see ETHICS, PROFESSIONAL). The profession of medicine affects public policy as well as private lives. Doctors acting together can obstruct governmental plans with which they disagree, and they frequently comprise a formidable pressure group in regard to the detailed organization of medical care in any country where they earn high salaries or are allowed to make much money. In this context it may be noted that doctors' powers are considerably less in communist states.

4. Medicine, as one area of expertise within the wider medical profession, may be distinguished from surgery. The separation is in part historical. Surgeons practise invasive techniques, they perform operations, whereas specialists in any of a wide number of different branches of medicine restrict themselves, by and large, to investigation and treatments (by drugs or other means) which do not involve opening up the body. Some examples are renal, respiratory, psychiatric

and geriatric medicine, as well as community, occupational, rehabilitative and sports medicine.

5. Medicine, as one area of expertise within the Third World has a wider connotation than in Western Europe and North America, since modern high technology medicine is available only to the minority of the population who live in large towns. Others continue to depend on traditional forms of medicine, practised by locally recognized healers or experts who, although technically illiterate, may have considerable knowledge and experience of psychotherapeutic techniques and of herbal medicines. Elements of folk medicine also persist in developed countries.

6. This leads to the other use of the word medicine, namely a substance used to treat symptoms and illnesses. It relates generally, but not exclusively, to medicaments for internal use. Formerly medicines were noxious mixtures of ingredients, and suggestions that someone should, metaphorically, 'take their medicine' implied a thoroughly unpleasant experience. Nowadays this is not the case and patients expect and are often given 'a pill for every ill'. Medicines are ubiquitous and only a small fraction of them are prescribed by doctors, the rest being patent, proprietary preparations easily obtainable from chemists and general stores.

7. Finally, veterinary medicine should not be forgotten, if only because animals have so many uses for men and women, including companionship.

Bannerman, Robert H. et al. (eds.), Traditional Medicine and Health Care Coverage (WHO, Geneva, 1983). Dunlop, Sir Derrick, Medicines in Our Time (Nuffield Provincial Hospitals Trust, 1973). McKeown, Thomas, The Role of Medicine: Dream, Mirage or Nemesis? (Nuffield Provincial Hospitals Trust, 1976).

UNA MACLEAN

See also: ETHICS, PROFESSIONAL; HOSPITALS; NATIONAL HEALTH SERVICE; NURSING.

MEDITATION
An exercise of the mind designed to awaken the sense of God's presence and strengthen the grasp of unseen realities. It might further be described as thinking with a view to prayer.

The adherents of many religions meditate, e.g. Hindus, Buddhists, Muslims, Jews, as well as Christians. In this article Christian meditation will be taken as the model.

Traditionally Christian meditation has been closely associated with the slow, devout reading of Scripture, with the listening to the voice of the Spirit in the reading and the turning of heart and mind to God in prayer. This traditional meditation was free and unstructured. Later developments systematized meditation by introducing methods designed to involve the whole person – reason, imagination, feeling, intuition, the body – in the approach to God. Christians, believing that God has uniquely revealed himself in Jesus Christ, give the Bible and especially the New Testament an important place in the reflection that enhances the awareness of God.

Meditation can be active or passive. We can analyse a passage, ask ourselves questions about it, relate it to our daily lives and our other knowledge, we can let our imagination form pictures about it; we can meditate actively. But we can also make ourselves receptive, we can open ourselves to impressions, we can look and listen to what the vast sea of the unconscious throws up onto the beach of consciousness; we can meditate passively. This passive meditation, commonly known as contemplation, is of especial value and normally active meditation prepares for it. Meditation of any kind demands concentration, one of the conditions for which is a certain inner stillness. Two common obstacles to this tranquillity of mind are anxiety (q.v.) and anger (q.v.) or resentment. It is necessary to let go of both these disturbing emotions in order to become inwardly still. Our greatest resource here is faith in God's presence and active, caring love. Further, in the often difficult task of stilling the mind we have a powerful ally in the body. Body and soul intimately interact. Fear or anger causes adrenalin to be secreted into the blood-stream and the body automatically to tense up. But, equally, if the body relaxes, fear and anger tend to weaken and fade. For this reason many find some method of relaxing the body an indispensable preparation for meditation. There are many methods of relaxation (q.v.). A simple but effective one is to sit in a comfortable position and, with eyes shut, quietly become aware of the sensations in the body, beginning perhaps at the head and moving slowly down to the feet.

Meditation, especially the passive type, requires some point of focus to enable concentration. This could be a visual symbol (q.v.), such as a picture, a crucifix or a lighted candle, or it might be an imagined picture or symbol, perhaps a scene from one of the gospels. Not all are helped by visual or imagined symbols, but practically everyone needs verbal symbols – a sentence, a phrase, a single word pregnant with meaning. The repetition of the word or words helps to focus the attention. In the active kind of meditation the individual repeats the words from time to time trying to enter deeply into their meaning. But in the passive type the words have a different function. They help to awaken a deep yearning for God, a kind of inner flame of aspiration which life's pressures tend to keep suppressed. This inner yearning, sometimes accompanied by a vivid sense of God's presence, becomes the focus of meditation. The words act as a kind of windscreen to protect the flame of aspiration from being extinguished by the winds of distracting trains of thought.

One of the effects of regular meditation is a sense of inner peace and a release of energy for commitment to God and to life. There are schools of meditation which seek to enable a fuller commitment to life without any religious commitment. The best known of these is Transcendental Meditation, an ancient Hindu meditation method, adapted for the West by the Maharishi Mahesh Yogi.

De Mello, Anthony, *Sadhana, a Way to God* (Gujarat Sahitya Prakash, Anand, India, 1978). Merton, T., *Contemplative Prayer* (Darton Longman & Todd, 1973). Ward, J.N., *The Use of Praying* (Epworth Press, 1967).

CHRISTOPHER BRYANT

See also: PRAYER; RELAXATION; SILENCE.

MEMBERSHIP OF CHURCH: PREPARATION

To be a member of the Church is to be a member of the body of Christ with all that this implies by way of belonging to a faith community distinguished by its beliefs, values and code of behaviour. Although there is no conclusive evidence that Jesus established or even anticipated an institutional body such as the Church, he was from the beginning and remains the inspiration of all that the Church is as an agency of worship, evangelism and servanthood. Church members are both called and pledged to engage in Christian discipleship and to share in the ministry of the

Church in the fullest possible sense. Membership is therefore a distinctive commitment to a prescribed cause and a particularized lifestyle. It is the nature of this commitment and the seriousness with which it is pursued which requires that there be full and adequate preparation of all potential members.

Incorporation into membership of the Church involves the individual in a pilgrimage characterized by participation, reflection, education and expressed commitment, and facilitated by the Church through a series of programmes, rites and sacraments. Admission to membership requires both induction and initiation; process and event.

Division and disruption within the Church throughout the Christian era have led to diversity of understanding concerning the nature of, and entry into, membership. In this respect the polarization both of theological positions and pastoral oversight brought about by the Reformation has been axiomatic. Despite the legacy of confusion which has left many fundamental questions in sacramental theology unresolved in our time, a definite convergence of theory and experience is clearly discernible. Behind the difficulties of the baptism/confirmation controversy, the renewal of the debate over child versus believer's baptism and the question of the precise moment of the reception of the Spirit, there is considerable consensus on how the individual may be prepared for active and responsible discipleship within the membership of the Church. The application of the insights of sociology, psychology and modern educational theory to the practice of Christian nurture has been of particular significance. The acknowledgement of the learning process as continuing beyond adolescence and throughout the entire lifespan of the individual, the importance of the emotions in the formation of attitudes and beliefs, the application of developmental theories of Erikson, Piaget and Kohlberg towards the formulation of models of faith development (see Fowler 1981), and the challenge to the traditional 'banking' theory of education by the experiential approaches of writers such as Freire and Groome have, taken together, led to a more open system of nurturing for personal growth throughout the lifelong pilgrimage in faith.

Modern catechesis stresses the importance of shared experience, story-telling, celebration and all the interactions in community between 'faithing' selves. Westerhoff has called this process *enculturation* and has described experience in the group as being 'foundational to faith'. At the intrapersonal level Westerhoff has also suggested that faith expands through the interaction of four distinctive *styles* of faith which he has named as *experienced faith, affiliative faith, searching faith* and *owned faith*. Many Christian educators see the future of Christian nurture in terms of designing and creating opportunities for growth within the whole worship/learning community as a single entity and regard Sunday schools and other stratified groups as being counter-productive.

The failure of the Western Church to incorporate children into congregational life has received considerable attention. This has resulted in the call to take seriously the membership rights of the child by virtue of its baptism, and the obligations of the Church toward all children within its sphere of influence. In recent times the Church's failure to retain young people within its ranks has called in question the whole ministry to children and called for a fundamental reorientation of the thinking of Christians with regard to parenting, formal instruction, shared experiences, and the place of the child in the worship service. Without an adequate policy and practice of child-rearing within the Christian community, initiation into the Church must remain in a state of crisis characterized by the admission of fewer young people and a greater dependence on the evangelization of adults, where in all too many instances the provision made for preparing and sustaining adults in faithful membership leaves much to be desired.

The Child in the Church, British Council of Churches Report on Ministry among Children, 1976. *Understanding Christian Nurture*, British Council of Churches Report, 1981. **Astley, J.**, 'The Role of Worship in Christian Learning' (*Religious Education*, vol. 79, no. 2, Spring 1984), pp. 243–51. **Bushnell, H.**, *Christian Nurture* (Baker, 1979 – reprint of 1961 edn). *A Dictionary of Religious Education*, ed. J.M. Sutcliffe, (SCM, 1984) articles on 'Confirmation' and 'Nurture'. **Forrester, D.** *et al.*, *Encounter with God* (Clark, 1983), ch. 6. **Fowler, J.W.**, *Stages of Faith* (Harper & Row, New York, 1981). **Groome, T.H.**, *Christian Religious Education: Sharing Our Story and Vision* (Harper & Row, New York, 1980). **Hamilton, D.G.**, 'The Place of the Child in the Church: Historical Perspectives', in *Children at the Table*, ed. D.G. Hamilton and F.A.J. Macdonald (Church of Scotland Education, 1982), pp. 22–7. **Holeton, D.R.**, 'Confirmation in the 1980s', in

Ecumenical Perspectives on Baptism, Eucharist and Ministry, ed. M. Thurien (WCC, 1983), pp. 68–89. **Martos, J.**, *Doors to the Sacred* (SCM, 1981). **Moran, G.**, *Education toward Adulthood* (Gill & Macmillan, 1979)**Westerhoff, J.W.**, *Will Our Children Have Faith?* (Seabury, New York, 1976). **Westerhoff, J.W.** and **Willimon, W.M.**, *Liturgy and Learning Through The Life Cycle* (Seabury, New York, 1980).

DAVID HAMILTON

See also: CHILDREN: PASTORAL CARE; FAITH; INDOCTRINATION; LEARNING; NURTURE, CHRISTIAN.

MENTAL HANDICAP
See: DISABLEMENT.

MENTAL HEALTH
The mental health of an individual or a community depends upon the environment or context in which it is being considered, so its definition should include a specification of that context. This is rarely made explicit and mental health (like health itself) remains an ill-defined concept. Yet in any community what is thought to be 'healthy, normal and ordinary' (Dingwall 1976) provides the implicit criterion by which its members decide whether they are well or ill. It is quite precisely understood by them, if rarely verbalised, and can vary between one family and another as well as between regions. If physical health is understood to mean the harmonious working together of the partial structures and functions of a body in a particular context, then mental health refers to the behaviour and experience of the body acting less as a collection of parts and rather as a whole. It is a concept of a more comprehensive logical category than physical health. While the brain's nutrition and appropriate energy transformations are necessary to mental function, it is transformations of information which are peculiar to the activities of mind, and in particular exchanges of information between people. Interpersonal relationships are thus a basic component of mental health, which is itself a component of community or social health. Although at different levels, physical, mental and community health are as intimately connected and interdependent as are the biological cell, organ and body system. The requirements for bodily health are largely material, e.g. food, oxygen and protection from injury – materials which are consumed in use. The requirements for mental and social health, by contrast, are

largely psychological, e.g. affection, courage, courtesy, patience and curiosity – virtues which become more abundant with use (compare the 'fruits of the Spirit', Gal. 5.22). Where these are lacking, and mental health poor, excessive demands are commonly made for material things. Improvements in mental health will then make for material economy.

In practice, mental health may be viewed from three perspectives:

(1) The assumption that it depends upon the *absence of mental ill-health* governs the work of professional care-givers such as psychiatrists and counsellors. The approach is of value when therapist and client have a common understanding of what is 'healthy, normal and ordinary', but often professionals are trained in settings which foster their unconscious allegiance to a set of norms which are not shared by their clients. Doctors and counsellors are prone to believe they know best what is good for people, and seek compliance rather than co-operaton in treatment regimes. This approach focuses attention narrowly on the sufferer and usually pays too little attention to his/her social context. It tends to be satisfied with a restoration of the client's *status quo ante* – which is often mental health of only a mediocre level.

(2) A more comprehensive approach seeks to *prevent mental ill-health*. It involves taking interpersonal factors into account among people who do not see themsleves as ill; so it lies in the hands of non-clinicians who include parents, schoolteachers, factory managers, community leaders and others. This does not free the clinician from responsibility for offering appropriate preventive advice – e.g. anticipatory guidance for those likely to be exposed to stress. Training may also be offered to those who are likely to encounter people at times of crisis (*see* CRISIS THEORY AND INTERVENTION), when changes in behaviour and attitude are evoked which may either be turned to good account as learning experiences, or else may lead to neurotic defensive manoeuvres.

(3) A third approach to mental health is to find ways of *enhancing the current mental health* status of a community. This requires an understanding of the sense of direction and purpose along which it is appropriate for a particular community to grow. It is a prophetic task for educationists and visionaries who may find themselves painfully involved

in a creative tension with the community's leaders. Pastoral care should of course concern itself with all three of these approaches, and not with counselling only.

Caplan, G., *An Approach to Community Mental Health* (Tavistock, 1961). Dingwall, R., *Aspects of Illness* (M. Robertson, 1976), p. 63. Lambourne, R.A., 'Mental Health, Christian Medical Mission and the Future Concept of Comprehensive Health Care', *Religion and Medicine 2*, ed. M.A.J. Melinsky (SCM, 1973). Wilson, M., *Health is for People* (Darton Longman & Todd, 1975).

J. MATHERS

See also: PSYCHIATRY AND MENTAL ILLNESS.

MIDDLE AGE

Middle age is the middle period of life, between youth and old age. It comprises the years around or after the mid-point of the life-span (about 35 years of age in men, nearer to 40 in women). According to the context it may be an arbitrary number of years between the limits of 30 and 65 years of age.

Middle age may be seen as a time of consolidation after maturation before senescence. After the struggles and strivings of youth it is typically a time of responsibility, authority and stability, even sagacity and relative affluence. It may also be a time of complacency, materialism and conservatism. Whereas the young look forward and the old look back, the middle-aged tend to live very much in the present, as pragmatic realists. Yet the middle-aged too may look back nostalgically, to their youthful vitality, idealism, lack of commitment and range of choices, and look forward in apprehension to the decline in old age. To paraphrase Victor Hugo – 'Middle age is the youth of old age and the old age of youth'.

Physically there is in both sexes a diminution of energy and activity while, as the appetite may if anything be enhanced, there is a tendency to obesity – the middle-aged spread. Serious illnesses – cancer, hypertension and ischaemic heart disease – start to become relatively common, giving intimations of mortality when peers succumb. Anxiety occasioned by the special stresses of ageing may produce symptoms which resemble those of some physical disorders, promoting hypochondria. Depressive illness becomes more common with advancing years and alcoholism reaches a peak in middle life.

The major physiological event in middle-aged women is, of course, the menopause, climacteric or (eloquent phrase!) 'change of life'. This is an endocrine event with psychological implications – the end of fertility and perhaps femininity, freedom from the 'curse' of menstruation, a milestone on the journey to old age and death. With the decline in function of the ovaries and a lower level of oestrogen hormones in the blood, many women suffer hot flushes (or flashes) which make them excessively 'hot and bothered', while dryness of the vagina can make sexual intercourse painful. These symptoms may be relieved by hormone replacement therapy (HRT). Other common complaints in menopausal women are depression, fatigue, nervousness, headaches, insomnia, irritability, palpitations, tingling and poor concentration, but their relationship to the physiological changes is less certain. They are almost as common in middle-aged men (and by no means limited to the middle-aged), and are probably the consequence of psychological stress and emotional disorder.

There is very little evidence of any physiological event in men which substantiates the concept of a male menopause, often invoked to account for the occasional vagaries of middle-aged men which are better explained by the mid-life identity crisis (see below).

Once accepted, middle age can usually be enjoyed, but there may be special stresses at this time. Work worries (mainly in men) include fears of redundancy, being overtaken by younger people, being in a dead end or promotion beyond one's competence (the 'Peter principle'). At home there can be concern about the children who have yet to establish themselves and aged parents in decline. In marriage one partner may have outgrown or grown away from the other, and either may feel bored, disillusioned and restive.

The term 'mid-life crisis' was probably coined by the psychoanalyst Elliott Jacques (1965) who sought to explain his observation that, after the age of 35, many artists of genius changed significantly, becoming much more or much less creative, altering the direction of their work or simply dying. Jacques' view was that in youth there is a lyrical, optimistic, creative idealism in which good is split from bad, which can then be disowned and fought, whereas in mid-life this gives way to a more thoughtful realistic recognition of limitation and of the shades of grey between black and white. There is, in the language of Melanie Klein, a reworking of the depressive position, a realization that what had been seen as bad and hateful is part of what is good and prized.

The 'mid-life crisis' generally arises in a sense of panic and futility and regret after passing a significant age (40, say, or 50) or mid-life milestone (the menopause, the last child's departure, becoming a grandparent). There is a feeling of being past the prime, over the hill, on a downward slope towards death, with little or no time to do those things which ought to have been done. There is an anguished review of past achievements and failures, of hopes deferred now probably beyond realization, and of the quality of current existence.

These feelings may lead to clinical depression and anxiety, or to attempts to recapture youth by crash programmes of diet and exercise, more youthful dress and seeking younger company in a frantic denial of aging. Accidie, a heedless torpor, may lead to cynicism, disillusion, 'burning out' ruthlessness and corruption. C.S. Lewis has said that 'the long dull monotonous years of middle-aged prosperity or middle-aged adversity are excellent campaigning weather for the devil'. Sometimes there is a dramatic change – of career, abode, partner (one divorce in five in the UK occurs after 20 years or more of marriage), even sexual direction, religious conversion or total loss of faith. Conducive to such a change are the loss of parental authority, guidance and disapproval once the parents are dead; freedom from the responsibilities of parenthood; a sense of having too prematurely and precipitably chosen a career and a spouse when young; a strong need to feel still lovable and loved or belated growing up and 'putting away childish things', having the chance and means to break away – e.g. the offer of a new job or love, money for a new home – and a powerful feeling of 'now or never'.

The Jungian view (see ANALYTICAL PSYCHOLOGY) is that various unconscious aspects of personality, neglected and forgotten in the course of development or repressed because at the time they were too difficult, painful or threatening to be acknowledged, may take over in middle life, sometimes harmoniously, sometimes dramatically disrupting. Thus the 'shadow' comprises not only the dark, destructive side of the person-

ality but also that which was overshadowed by the preoccupations and pressures of youth. The mid-life crisis may then mean, through the acceptance and understanding of what was hidden, the realization of potential rather than a catastrophic upheaval.

Jacques views Dante's *Divine Comedy* as a working through of mid-life depression and Shakespeare's late plays *The Winter's Tale* and *The Tempest* may be seen somewhat similarly. The task may be accomplished by loving reparation. Conflict is tolerated, work accepted though imperfect and incomplete, and the approach of death met with appropriate grief, not denial. Contemplation, detachment, resignation and serenity characterize the successful resolution of the mid-life crisis.

Cooper, Wendy, *No Change* (Arrow Books, 1976). Jacques, Elliott, 'Death and the Mid-life Crisis' (*Int. J. Psychoanalysis* 46, 1965), pp. 502–14. Jung, C.G., *Collected Works* (Routledge, 1978). Pitt, Brice, *Mid-life Crisis* (Sheldon Press, 1980).

BRICE PITT

See also: HUMAN DEVELOPMENT.

MINISTRY, DOCTRINE OF

The practical exercise of Christian vocation towards others.

There are several words denoting ministry in the NT, e.g. 'helpers, administrators' (RSV) at 1 Cor. 12.28, 'service' at Rom. 12.6; at Rom. 12.8 Christ is called 'a servant to the circumcised' and at Rom. 16.1 Phoebe is described as 'a deaconess of the church at Cenchreae'. This does not, however, mean that the NT is preoccupied with an official ministry. Its earliest references to ministering (1 Cor. 12 and Romans, chs. 12–13) use language incompatible with the existence of an official ministry or with a distinction between clergy and laity, even though the NT as a whole witnesses to the beginnings of an (inevitable and proper) permanent ministry. The concept of ministry in the NT in fact covers a much vaster scope than could be undertaken in any consideration of the official ministry or its form. At Rom. 15.16 Paul says that he is 'a minister of Jesus Christ to the Gentiles in the priestly service of the gospel of God, so that the offering of the Gentiles may be acceptable, sanctified by the Holy Spirit', and at 2 Cor. 9.12 he describes the giving of support by the Corinthian church to the needy Christians in Jerusalem as 'the rendering of this service'. Indeed most of 2 Corinthians is preoccupied with Christian ministry. Its basic meaning is the handing on or inculcation of the gospel. But this is much more than a mere dinning of words into people's ears. It means an imparting of the grace and the love of God revealed in Christ in every possible dimension, spiritual, pastoral and material. And its administration cannot be confined to official ministers. Ministry is incumbent upon the whole of Christ's people, because where one suffers or rejoices all suffer or rejoice, and all are bound together in the Body of Christ (Rom. 12; 1 Cor. 12) of which the bond is love (John 15.1–17; 1 Cor. 13; Eph. 4.2–7). The charter for Christian ministry is therefore not to be found in John 20.21–3 nor in the pastoral epistles but at Mark 10.45 and Matt. 25.31–46. Christ's self-giving ministry to the sinful, the crippled, the sick, the mentally disturbed and the outcast is the pattern ministry for all Christians; Christians are being judged, and will be judged, not primarily by the validity of their official ministries nor the catholicity of their doctrine nor the Scriptural nature of their belief or preaching, but by the extent of their caring for the sick, the naked, the hungry and the oppressed. To minister to these is to minister to Christ. Indeed this is one way to impart Christ, the true gift of the Christian ministry.

In spite of some movements during the Middle Ages and some serious attempts at the Reformation to reach a deeper conception of ministry, it is only in very recent years that this all-embracing idea of ministry has been widely accepted by Christian churches. It has inevitably entailed a lessening of the distinction between clergy and lay people, a reformation of worship and liturgy to make them express the action not merely of the minister but of the whole congregation, and an increased stress upon the necessity of Christian belief, doctrine and worship being complemented by and leading to Christian action at several different levels. On one side it has led to the formation of Christian political groups and the whole movement called 'liberation theology', and on another the increased employment of lay folk in various forms of pastoral care, preaching, visiting, teaching the Bible, healing, leading prayer groups (see LAY PASTORAL CARE). Ministry is no longer the exclusive prerequisite of the official (minister, priest, pastor). It is the ongoing activity of all Christians in the task of building up the common life in the Body of Christ.

Ayres, F.O., *The Ministry of the Laity, a Biblical Exposition* (Westminster, USA, and Ryerson, 1962). Campenhausen, H. von, *Ecclesiastical Authority and Spiritual Power in the Church of the First Three Centuries* (Black, 1969). Dunn, J.G., *Unity and Diversity in the New Testament* (SCM,. 1977). Hanson, A.T., *The Pioneer Ministry* (SPCK, new edn 1975). Kraemer, H., *A Theology of the Laity* (Lutterworth, 1958). Küng, Hans, *The Church* (Search Press, 1969). Newbigin, J.E.L., *The Household of God, Lectures on the Nature of the Church* (SCM, 1950). Power, David N., *Gifts That Differ: Lay Ministries Established and Unestablished* (Pueblo, USA, 1980). Thornton, L.S., *The Common Life in the Body of Christ* (Black, 1943).

R.P.C. HANSON

See also: CHURCH, DOCTRINES OF; ORDINATION; WOMEN: ORDINATION.

MISCARRIAGE
See: STILLBIRTH AND MISCARRIAGE.

MIXED MARRIAGE
Marriage across faith or cultural boundaries.

The growing pluralism of modern society has led to an increasing number of mixed marriages. It is said that where different groups in society live side by side they either intermarry or oppress one another or fight. The term 'mixed' includes marriages between people of different races, different religious faiths and different Christian churches. This article focuses primarily on the last two.

Interfaith marriage. Most religious leaders oppose unions between partners of different religious faiths (Christian–Muslim, Hindu–Sikh, etc). This is particularly true in the Jewish community, which suffers severe erosion through intermarriage. Muslims allow a Muslim man to marry a Jewish or a Christian woman, but if a Muslim woman marries a non-Muslim her marriage is invalid according to Islam. Hindus traditionally marry only within the same caste. In contemporary Europe the most common mixed-faith marriage is between a Muslim man and a Christian woman.

The Old Testament shows that several of Israel's leaders (e.g. Joseph and Solomon) had mixed-faith marriages; but there was considerable opposition at certain periods to marriage outside the faith, because of the consequent corruption of the Jewish home (e.g. Deut. 7.3–4). In the NT Paul alone deals with this subject, when he counsels Christians already married to unbelieving partners at the time of their baptism (1 Cor. 7.12–16). He recommends persistence in the marriage where possible, but advises that a future marriage should be 'in the Lord'. 2 Cor. 6.14 may also prohibit marriage with a non-Christian.

In counselling couples who propose to marry across religious frontiers (and therefore often across racial and cultural ones as well), pastors should care for the spiritual integrity of all concerned. They will not wish to conduct a ceremony, for example, in which a Muslim or a Jew makes promises in the name of the Trinity. They will satisfy themselves that the couple have discussed their understanding of marriage, the religious upbringing of their children, their future place of residence (if the husband is a Muslim, Muslim laws of divorce, custody and inheritance may apply), and their legal status, and consequently that of the marriage, in the country where it is to be solemnized.

Interchurch marriage. Until the second half of this century the term 'mixed marriage' was normally used in the British Isles of marriages between Christians (whether practising or not) of different church allegiances. These marriages have tended to be seen as a threat, especially by minority churches, and therefore to be discouraged. The problem has been acute for Protestant Churches in southern Ireland, where Roman Catholics form 95% of the population. In England and Wales two-thirds of weddings performed in Roman Catholic churches are 'mixed', but only in a minority of these is the non-Catholic partner likely to be a practising Christian.

The primary cause of difficulty for these marriages has been the divisions between the churches, and as these have grown less sharp, so the problems have eased. A secondary cause of difficulty is the ecclesiastical regulations with which certain churches have tried to protect their own membership.

In this century the greatest difficulties have existed in marriages between Roman Catholics and other Christians. Roman Catholic regulations eased considerably with the publication by the Vatican of *Matrimonia Mixta* in 1970. A Roman Catholic requires permission from the Church to marry someone who is not a Roman Catholic, and has to

undertake to do all in his or her power to bring up any children of the marriage in the Catholic faith. The non-Catholic partner is no longer required to give such an undertaking. This change shows that the Roman Catholic Church recognizes the upbringing of the children to be the *joint* responsibility of the parents, each of whom has equal rights of conscience. The Irish *Directory* on Mixed Marriages (1983) and the English and Welsh *Directory* (1977) both recognize that this could mean in effect that some children will not be brought up as Roman Catholics. In certain circumstances the Roman Catholic Church will now also give permission for an inter-church wedding to take place in the church of the non-Catholic partner.

All the major Churches have recognized their responsibility for the *joint* pastoral care of interchurch families, and in 1971 a joint working group of the English, Scottish and Welsh Churches published recommendations on the subject. However such joint care depends largely on the mutual trust of local priests and ministers, and it is not yet common.

Associations of Interchurch Families exist in England, Ireland (south and north) and Scotland, as well as in many other countries. Their primary purpose is the mutual support of their members, and help for those entering an interchurch marriage.

Two-Church Families (Association of Interchurch Families 1983, The Old Bakery, Danehill, Sussex, RH17 7ET). **Heron, A.,** *Two Churches – One Love* (APCK, Dublin, 1977). **Hurley, M.** (ed.), *Beyond Tolerance: the Challenge of Mixed Marriage* (G. Chapman, 1975). **Lamb, C.,** *Mixed-Faith Marriage: a Case for Care* (BCC, 1982).

CHRISTOPHER LAMB and MARTIN REARDON

See also: MULTI-FAITH MINISTRIES.

MORAL ISSUES IN PASTORAL CARE

Pastoral care raises moral issues because it involves personal relationships. All pastoral actions arise from the intentions of the pastoral agent and from an assessment by him or her of the likely consequences of them being acted upon. These are the positive or practical results of pastoral attention and arise because that attention is selective. The distinction between right and wrong is inherent in such action, which is why pastors must always ask how can I do what is right?

This interpersonal nature of pastoral care

raises a fundamental question with moral implications; how are persons (q.v.) understood? Unless this is answered, it is not possible to act pastorally in their interest. Before effective pastoral care can take place a moral context has to be created which gives persons an identity which is more specific than that derived from the abstract concept of 'mankind'. Whether or not any particular pastoral act is considered to be morally right, will depend largely upon whether or not it accords with this identity or anthropology, providing that it takes account of claims about the rights and needs which are often held to be fundamental to all human flourishing.

A common example of a moral disagreement which can arise in pastoral care from a confusion about anthropology, occurs whenever pastors who are governed by the teachings and requirements of institutions, such as churches, care for individuals who are either not so governed or are only tenuously so. The pastor sees what the church requires as being what is morally right, whereas the individual or individuals in receipt of his or her care might consider that what is morally right is what is strictly in their own interest. An example of this would be a Roman Catholic lay person who chose to use artificial forms of contraception against the advice of a priest who accepted that church's teaching that it is wrong to do this.

In practice, such disagreements are often resolved; either by the pastor distinguishing between pastoral theology (q.v.) and pastoral care (q.v.) and by permitting in the latter what the former prohibits, or by the pastor allowing for dissent in order to encourage spiritual growth towards practices which are more orthodox than those temporarily condoned. A related moral issue arises whenever pastors who are also ministers tolerate even gross immoral conduct for this reason and who, if it becomes public knowledge, come under pressure from their congregations not to do so, out of fear that the toleration will be more widely misconstrued as approval. Although many Christian churches have disciplinary procedures which can be followed in such circumstances, they are seldom used (see DISCIPLINE AS PASTORAL CARE).

A further way in which pastoral care raises moral issues arises from the fact that it may be held to be immoral to minister to individual need without ministering also to its causes, be they social, political or economic ones.

Morally sensitive individual pastoral care ineluctably leads to forms of social, political and economic action. Political theology (q.v.) is the study of this.

There are five other ways in which moral issues commonly arise in pastoral care:
1. It is often claimed that pastoral care should be non-directive and that it is immoral for pastors to direct the lives of those in their care. Behind such a view lies a markedly existential approach to psychotherapy which claims not just that pastors ought not to give ethical or other advice, but that it is futile for them to do so, because every individual must create his or her own well-being. Although this view has its value as a preventative to overweening directiveness, it overlooks the sense, which has always been present in Christian pastoral care, in which individuals have to bear one another's burdens and even, at times, face the awesome responsibility of being directively involved in doing so. This is especially acute when the cared-for are incapable of acting in their own interest, as when they are severely mentally handicapped (see DISABLEMENT: PASTORAL CARE OF MENTALLY DISABLED PEOPLE) or similarly debilitated.
2. The termination (q.v.)· of pastoral care can involve moral issues in two ways: (1) Whenever the cared-for has to be referred (see REFERRAL) to someone else. An example would be a pastor who relied upon faith-healing to cure a severe physical disorder and who, in so doing, discouraged the cared-for from seeking orthodox medical treatment, or who suggested that any previous failure of such treatment was due solely to a lack of faith. Such an approach clearly raises moral issues about who should be responsible for the welfare of certain individuals and about how they should exercise that custody in co-operation with others. (2) Whenever pastoral care becomes interminable, self-perpetuating and an end in itself rather than a means to an end. Some forms of psychotherapy (q.v.) have been thought guilty of this whenever the absence of any improvement has been held to be the sole reason for the continuation of the therapy. The moral problem here is that it might not have the means of assessing its own efficacy and thereby continue against the best interest of the patient. More generally, the question of the morality of terminating pastoral care arises whenever, in continuing, it does not serve the best interest of the cared-for. An

uncomfortable truth is that pastoral care can sometimes be exercised as much for the benefit of the pastor as for those in his or her care. As a form of dependency (q.v.) it can be immoral.

3. The problem of confidentiality (q.v.) raises moral issues when pastors have to obtain intimate information about their charges. In Christian pastoral care this is often solved by the seal of the confessional which extends to quite informal exchanges in which such information is gathered, but the inviolability of this is often challenged. The question of confidentiality is also raised whenever pastoral responsibilities are shared. Professional etiquette often helps, as between ministers and medical practitioners, but the area is a morally sensitive one. It is also often exacerbated whenever confidential information is written down or stored electronically.

4. The extent to which pastors become emotionally or physically involved with their charges also raises moral issues. Traditional Christian pastoral care has prohibited any but the most formal of physical contact, but this has been challenged; most extremely by some sexual counselling (q.v.) which has claimed that even sexual intercourse can be a morally legitimate form of pastoral therapy.

5. Moral issues are also raised whenever it is thought necessary to act pastorally in the interests of another person without his or her consent (q.v.). This is most common in the pastoral care of the very young, the chronically sick and the senile demented (*see* DEMENTIA).

Browning, D., *The Moral Context of Pastoral Care* (Westminster, 1976). **Halmos, P.,** *The Faith of the Counsellors* (Constable, 1965), pp. 176–200. **Macmurray, J.,** *The Self as Agent* (Faber, 1957); *Persons in Relation* (Faber, 1961).

R. JOHN ELFORD

See also: ETHICS, PROFESSIONAL; JUDGEMENT.

MORAL THEOLOGY

The theological discipline concerned with Christian conduct.

Theology is the systematic study of God, the creator and saviour of mankind and his activity and purposes for humanity. Moral theology studies humankind's response to the gift of divine life offered and granted through Jesus Christ in the Spirit, a gift which is accompanied by a call to repent and follow

Christ, to witness to him, to take up the cross and be faithful to him in the Christian fellowship and the sacramental life until he comes.

Moral theology is usually divided into two parts: fundamental or general and special moral theology. The former deals with the foundations of Christian morality: Scriptural ethics; the sources of moral theology; Christian anthropology; the nature and goals of Christian choice; freedom and responsibility; conscience; the nature and discernment of moral norms; sin; conversion and sanctification; and authority in morals. The latter deals with particular aspects of Christian living: social, political and economic morality; medical ethics; sexual and conjugal ethics; theological and moral virtues; and so on. Within special moral theology one can distinguish speculative moral theology from casuistry. The former looks for principles, guidelines and orientations, the latter seeks to apply them to particular types of case. One can also distinguish moral theology from pastoral care; the former is general and universal, the latter is concerned with guiding an individual.

Moral theology draws on several sources. Its ultimate norm is the wisdom and will of God. The revealed Word of God in Scripture is normative for moral theology. The difficulty is to know how to use Scripture. What in it is revelation and how should we use it to derive moral norms? Christian tradition, the living stream of Christian practice since apostolic times also witnesses to God's moral claims. Discernment is required to sift the essential from the changeable and the divine from the human. The Church too teaches authoritatively; how is debated. God is Lord of creation and history. So human experience and reflection is a source of moral knowledge. There is debate about how far human beings can trust their powers of discernment, about methods of ethical inquiry, and the relationship of human wisdom and revelation.

Moral theology today has an ecumenical dimension. Various traditions have developed in the different communions and they can be mutually enriching.

The related discipline of Christian ethics provides a different perspective on Christian norms through the application of categories derived, in part, from philosophical ethics.

Dunstan, G.R. (ed.), *Duty and Discernment* (SCM, 1975). **Gustafson, J.,** *Dictionary of Christian Ethics*

(SCM, 2nd edn 1985). **Haring, B.**, *Free and Faithful in Christ*, 3 vols. (St Paul, 1978–81).

BRENDAN SOANE

See also: ASCETICAL THEOLOGY; MORAL ISSUES IN PASTORAL CARE; PASTORAL THEOLOGY; PRACTICAL THEOLOGY.

MORALE

A term used to describe the social health of a group or community.

Although it tends to receive attention only when a group is facing hardship or risk (as in a coal mine, or military or exploratory adventure) morale has a wide relevance to pastoral concern: when a group's morale is low, the incidence of sickness, accident, delinquency and interpersonal conflict tends to rise. Conversely, attention to morale will make a community healthier. Morale is primarily a matter of *shared subjectivity* and its two essential factors are a *shared sense of purpose* and a *shared sense of security* among group members. In practice, good morale requires: (1) that free communication (q.v.), both verbal and non-verbal, be fostered between all members of the group, whatever their role or status within it. Therefore there needs to be regular and frequent face-to-face contact between them: written, telephonic and televisual links are of secondary value only and are inadequate on their own. (2) that the leadership (q.v.) function be adequately exercised. People in groups have an innate tendency to pay attention to a central figure, so at any one time it is important that there should be one person recognized as leader, and that he or she should maintain face-to-face communication with the constituency. But it is a mark of maturity in a community or group that it is more concerned to ensure that the leadership *function* is well exercised than that one person is maintained in the role indefinitely. The function needs to be exercised so as to provide the group with a vision of a desired future in which all can share, and a goal towards which all can work in harmony with one another.

One common misunderstanding is to assume that attention to the material security of the group will necessarily enhance the *sense of* security. Material provision is important, but on anything greater than a subsistence scale is mainly of symbolic value as indicating that 'somebody cares'; while 'conspicuous consumption' is a sign of a defective sense of purpose and consequent low morale.

A similar misunderstanding is to assume that the morale requirement is satisfied if all component parts of an organization are moving toward the same objective. This is only true if good lateral communication exists between the components; otherwise they will be as likely to compete destructively in their progress as to co-operate.

An important element in the pastoral care of a parish, community or institution is to discern and monitor the way the leadership function is being exercised in it, especially when morale is low.

Mathers, J., 'The Pastoral Role: a Psychiatrist's View', in *Religion and Medicine*, 2, ed. M.A.H. Melinsky (SCM, 1973); 'Man, Medicine and Morale' (*Contact*, no. 52, Edinburgh, 1976). **Revans, R.W.**, *Standards for Morale: Cause and Effect in Hospitals* (OUP, 1964).

J. MATHERS

See also: LEADERSHIP; SYSTEMS PASTORAL CARE; SUPPORT GROUPS.

MOURNING
See: BEREAVEMENT.

MULTI-FAITH MINISTRIES
Work towards and with those of fundamentally different religious belief.

This may take place at a number of levels: (1) Christian ministry to member(s) of a non-Christian religion in the form of pastoral or social care, shared prayer, worship, inter-marriage, education. (2) Relationship between different non-Christian faiths, e.g. Sikh–Muslim, Buddhist–Hindu, Jewish–Sufi. (2) Intellectual dialogue on biblical and theological themes by experts. (4) Practical living and working together by ordinary people, discovering belief, moral code, customs and way of life, recognizing each other rather than repudiating; acceptance as servants of 'God', of the 'one', of 'Allah'.

Since the Emperor Constantine (*c*.274–337), Christianity has been the common religion of Europe. For centuries 'pagans' invaded Europe. European emphasis was on defending the (Christian) faith and destroying the infidel. As Europeans ventured to new worlds by land and sea, territories conquered and subjugated were 'converted', even by force, to Christianity. The Christian attitude was uncompromisingly evangelistic, finding it difficult even to allow the existence of non-

Christian religions in conquered territories. Christian missionaries accompanied military invasions or trading expeditions, attempting wholesale conversion and totally rejecting non-Christian faith or worship.

With a few exceptions, this European attitude prevailed in all Christian denominations. Some countries were more religiously resistant – Muslim, Sikh, Chinese and Japanese. Others were less susceptible to penetration – Hindu, Buddhist.

There has been a radical change of attitude in the 20th century. Emigration and immigration have spread, individual national states have emerged, theological insights and pastoral considerations among Christians have changed. In many areas society has become pluralist.

The Roman Catholic Church's attitude modified dramatically at Vatican Council II. In October 1965 the Vatican issued *Nostra Aetate: Declaration on the relation of the Church to non-Christian religions*. The emphasis was new working and thinking with Hindus, Muslims, Jews and others, pleading for forgetting the past, urgency for new understanding, rejection of nothing true and holy in these religions, and a prudent and charitable entry into discussion and collaboration with members of other religions. The common heritage of Jew and Christian, and even with Muslims the fatherhood of Abraham, are suggested by the Council of biblical and theological inquiry in a spirit of mutual appreciation. The World Council of Churches and the British Council of Churches have been working for years on the basis and background for dialogue with people other than Christian who belong to living faiths and ideologies. The BCC has a committee for relations with other faiths, the Church of England has a Board for Mission and Unity, and the Vatican a secretariat for non-Christians.

Ministries vary. Small numbers of scholars are engaged in biblical and theological study and dialogue. Many ordinary pastors and people have found themselves suddenly living in multi-racial and multi-faith surroundings. This is true of most cities in England. The sphere of practical living among people of other faiths has often been dominated by immediate needs – accommodation, teaching English as a second language, initiating newcomers to customs in England, clothing, money, cuts of meat, admission of children to school and so on. The number of refugees has highlighted need and presented 'welfare' problems, among Buddhists from Tibet and Vietnam, or Muslims from Iran.

Christians have concentrated on 'welfare' work, helping to settle people in, etc. Dialogue and collaboration are much more difficult. The use of church buildings for non-Christian worship has been strongly condemned, but is now occurring and redundant church buildings are being sold; the climate is changing. Many Christian church people continue with a completely evangelistic approach, not admitting pluralism and preaching hard for conversion. Others admit pluralism, while maintaining the uniqueness of Christ. Inter-faith marriages are the most difficult meeting points from both sides. Schools are much involved in inter-faith relations and this is an area for intense work. Such initiatives as the Week of Prayer for World Peace, One World Week, etc. are attempting to build foundations among ordinary people for admitting each other and tolerating different forms of faith and worship, while using all that is good in each other's convictions.

Anderson, G.H. and **Stransky, T.F.** (eds.), *Christ's Lordship and Religious Pluralism* (Orbis Press, New York, 1981). **Board of Mission and Unity,** *Towards a Theology for Inter-Faith Dialogue* (CIO, 1984); *Our Ministry and Other Faiths* (CIO, 1983). **Camps, A.,** *Partners in Dialogue* (Orbis, 1983). **Cole, Owen** (ed.), *Religion in the Multi-Faith School* (Hulton, 1983). **Hick, J.,** *God Has Many Names* (Macmillan, 1980). **Senior, H.** and **Stuhlmueller, C.,** *Biblical Foundations in Mission* (SCM, 1983).

MICHAEL HOLLINGS

See also: INTERCULTURAL PASTORAL CARE; MIXED MARRIAGE; RACE RELATIONS.

NARCISSISM

A condition described by Freud (*see* PSYCHO-ANALYSIS) where the ego (q.v.) takes itself as object and behaves as though it were in love with itself.

NATIONAL HEALTH SERVICE

The British system of health care services.

The National Health Service (NHS) was created in 1946, to secure improvement, for the British people, both in their physical and mental health, and in the prevention, diagnosis and treatment of illness. While there had long been voluntary and local government hospitals, together with a variety of insurance and mutual aid health schemes, the NHS was to provide almost all forms of care for the whole population. Under parliamentary control and paid for from public funds, it was to make its services available at the time of need, equitably, without means-testing and with only minor charges for a limited number of services; doctors who wished and patients who could afford it, however, were still free to choose private practice. These provisions were made at a time when improvements in housing, hygiene and nutrition were helping to reduce maternal and infant mortality and the impact of many formerly fatal infectious diseases; it was also a time when many new and effective forms of diagnosis and treatment were becoming available. As a major plank in Britain's post-war reconstruction, the NHS embodied ideals not only of both democracy and benevolent paternalism, but also of medical excellence and patient-satisfaction alike. The subsequent considerable expansion of its services, over three decades, created not only many large new buildings, but also a whole climate of opinion, in which its benefits came to be seen, by many patients, doctors and other health workers, as a matter of reasonable entitlement. At the same time, the financial cost both of pursuing excellence and of ensuring an expanding but equitable provision of services, made governments of different political complexions undertake a variety of schemes designed either to reorganize the NHS more efficiently, or to limit its growth by, *inter alia*, encouraging expansion of private practice. Despite these difficulties, a Royal Commission in 1979 reasserted the traditional ideals of the NHS and, while arguing that it could make better use of its existing resources, found it 'difficult to argue that there is widespread inadequacy; or to point to substantial improvements which could be made readily'. (*See also* PRIORITIES IN HEALTH CARE.)

For most purposes, the individual's initial contact with the NHS is through a general practitioner (GP), who is not an employee of the NHS but a doctor who contracts with the NHS to give 'personal, primary and continuing care to individuals, families and a practice population, irrespective of age, sex and illness'. Everyone in Britain is entitled to be on the list of a GP, whom they may choose, and change, although the GP also is entitled not to accept or to have removed from his or her list any patient. Subject to appointments systems, patients are entitled to consult their own GP or a colleague during surgery hours, and the GP should provide a telephone number for messages at all times. When necessary, a GP will visit a patient at home, and in emergencies a hospital casualty department will give treatment; individuals may also directly consult hospital special clinics for the treatment of sexually-transmitted diseases. Otherwise, most hospital services are available only through referral by a GP or clinic (e.g. family planning clinic). Patients are not entitled to choose (but may be asked by the GP) which hospital or consultant they wish to be referred to; subject to mental capacity, however, they are free to refuse any particular treatment, to seek a second opinion, and to request a limited number of alternative forms of treatment (e.g. homeopathy, acupuncture and hypnotherapy). Patients who are seriously dissatisfied with GP or hospital services are free to complain (to the relevant administrative or professional disciplinary body or to the Health Service Commissioner), and may occasionally take legal action against health authorities. If such potentially complex questions of patient-choice or dissatisfaction arise, it is always advisable to consult a Community Health Council, the local body set up to represent and provide information to NHS consumers.

The majority of the NHS's employees are not doctors (6.7%, including GPs), but nurses (43%) and various ancillary staff (21.9%); much NHS effort is now expended on preventive medicine and health education as well as cure and care; and the majority of patients, according to the 1979 Royal Commission, have, if anything, 'too rosy a picture of the state of the NHS'.

Report of the Royal Commission on the National Health Service (HMSO, 1979). **National Consumer Council,** *Patients' Rights* (NCC, 1983). **Willocks, A.J.,** *The Creation of the National Health Service* (Routledge, 1967).

K.M. BOYD

See also: HEALTH EDUCATION; HOSPITALS; MEDICINE; NURSING; PRIORITIES IN HEALTH CARE.

NEUROSIS
See: PSYCHIATRY AND MENTAL ILLNESS.

THE NEW TESTAMENT AND PASTORAL CARE

The books of the NT reflect a variety of forms, purposes and milieux, and were written by different authors at different times and with contrasting theologies; yet there is remarkable unity about the fundamental message, which relates to the faith and expectation of Israel and has its focus in the life, death and resurrection of Jesus, the Christ. It is thus possible to pursue a recurring theme such as pastoral care, although the limits of this article confine our discussion to a sample of the material. We will therefore: (1) focus on Mark's account of the ministry of Jesus; (2) very briefly note interpretative emphases in Matthew and Luke; (3) highlight some emphases in Paul; (4) consider the shepherd theme in John and elsewhere; and (5) offer a few concluding observations.

1. *The Markan account of Jesus' ministry.* The story Mark tells is of a *caring ministry.* Jesus' ministry is understood as the work of the Spirit (1.10, 12), as messianic (1.11a) cf. Ps. 2.7), as expressing servanthood (1.11b; cf. Is. 42.1), and as locked in battle with evil (1.12f.). He proclaims God's good news

(1.14), *viz.,* that God's reign is 'at hand', and summons to repentance (Heb. *shuv* = turn back). His teaching is said to be embodied in his healing work and characterized by authority and effectiveness (1.27; cf. 1.22). Specific issues emerge: the demons recognize that their destruction is imminent (1.24); Jesus is deeply moved (1.41 – compassion? anger?) at the plight of the leper; he speaks to the paralytic of the forgiveness of sins (2.5), a reminder that healing comes as one turns to God. Healing comes also through personal and social relationships: the calling of a tax-gatherer (2.14), and table fellowship with 'many tax-collectors and sinners' (2.15). Like a doctor, Jesus' ministry is directed to those in need of health and wholeness (2.17); it is a time for joy, not fasting (2.18ff.), a new event (2.21) that transforms life but disconcerts those who are bound to conventions. Hence Jesus is criticized for his attitude to the sabbath, which he relates directly to the health of man (6.3ff., 7.1ff.). The unforgivable sin is to confound the work of the Spirit with that of 'the prince of demons' (3.22ff., 28–30); the right response is trust in or openness to the power and mercy of God, with whom lies our peace or salvation (cf. 4.39f., 5.19, 34, 36); and this involves coming to terms with oneself (7.14–23). Those who developed this trust or openness found Jesus to be their *shepherd* (6.34; Gk. *poimēn*; Lat. *pastor*), but in the momentous messianic conflict with evil the shepherd is struck down and the sheep scattered (14.27; cf. Zech. 13.7). Jesus' messianic vocation is fulfilled through suffering and rejection (8.27—9.31, 10.33f.), self-giving (8.34ff.) rather than self-seeking (10.43). The disciples, Jesus' team of 'learners' from an early period (1.16–20, 6.7–13), are now imperceptive and resistant. The way of the cross involves a new order of values that exalts servanthood, radical obedience to God's will, and the care and acceptance of the lowly; its symbols are the cup and baptism (10.38f.), and a life given as a ransom for many (10.45: a martyr motif here). For Mark, God negates Israel's rejection of the rightful heir (12.1–9) and makes the rejected rock the keystone of the new structure (12.10f.). But this is accomplished only through a personal ministry in which the messianic servant-healer is himself wounded and killed: his is 'the blood of the covenant poured out for many' (14.24). The cost to Jesus is total. At the extremity of his human resources, he asks for the support of his friends (14.34) and prays that the cup might be taken away (14.36). Then, having brought his fears into the open, he faces the terrible climax with courage and faith. The words of the dying Christ – 'Why hast thou forsaken me?' (Ps. 22.1) – rule out any sentimentalizing of cross and resurrection. The resurrection is not a 'happy ever after' ending, but an expression of faith that through Christ, the broken healer, we ourselves – like the disciples – are made whole. In Galilee, the disciples will 'see him, as he told you' (16.7): i.e. they will discern in the risen Christ 'the reign of God come with power' (cf. 9.1). 'God's good news' is complete.

2. *Emphases in Matthew and Luke.* Briefly, four points are to be noted: (1) The Sermon on the Mount ('Q') emphasizes the importance of non-violent and loving relationships, integrity in worship and devotion, complete trust in the Father and the need to decide about priorities in life (Matt. 5—7). Such teaching is divine wisdom, fundamental for living (Matt. 7.24–27; cf. Luke 6.47ff.). (2) Matthew emphasizes the suffering servant (Matt. 8.17 = Is. 53.4; Matt. 12.18–21 = Is. 42.1–4): the OT symbol includes the notion of bringing justice to the poor, being non-violent yet strong, and suffering for others. (3) Luke applies the Isaianic concept of the 'healing liberator' to Jesus' ministry (Luke 4.18f. = Is. 61.1f., 58.6; cf. Luke 7.22/Matt. 11.4f.('Q') = Is. 29.18f., 35.5f., 61.1). (4) Pastoral motifs can also be found in many parables (e.g. Luke 10.25–37, 15.3–32).

3. *Paul and pastoral care.* Paul does not set out a theology of pastoral care, but his pastoral concern shows through his understanding of ministry. He is the servant (*doulos*) of Jesus Christ (Rom. 1.1, Phil. 1.1), who himself took 'the form of a servant . . . obedient unto death' (Phil. 2.7f.). Apostles and church leaders should embody Christ's self-giving and thus set an example to the church (cf. 1 Cor. 4.1, 9f.). Indeed, as all believers share in the death and resurrection of Christ (Rom. 6.4, Col. 2.12), the Christian way is characterized as 'coming alive', 'being raised with Christ through faith in the working of God', or 'new life'. In his pastoral counselling, authority is located in 'commands of the Lord' or dominical tradition and in apostolic teaching, his own included; but he also speaks as a 'father in Christ Jesus' who guides and admonishes his beloved

children (1 Cor. 4.14f.; cf. Gal. 4.19). He can show patience and understanding of others' difficulties and presents reasoned arguments to help Christians take informed decisions of faith (cf. 1 Cor. 7 and 8). He looks for growth in faith and love (cf. 2 Thess. 1.3) towards Christian maturity (cf. Eph. 4.13f.) in and through the *koinonia* of faith (cf. 1 Cor. 11 and 12). Though some are particularly gifted as pastors (*poimenes*) and teachers (cf. Eph. 4.11) and others have 'gifts of healing by the one Spirit' (1 Cor. 12.9), the whole community must develop a sensitivity to the needs of its members. To 'bear one another's burdens' is to fulfil the law of Christ (Gal. 6.2); the aim being that, supported by the community, each is able to bear his own load (Gal. 6.5). Paul as pastor feels 'the daily pressure upon me of my anxiety for all the churches' (2 Cor. 11.28). But he is able to go on in the faith that 'as we share abundantly in Christ's sufferings, so through Christ we share abundantly in comfort (consolation) too' (2 Cor. 1.5). Paul's work and inner life, like that of the churches themselves, are sustained by prayer (e.g. Rom. 1.9f., 2 Cor. 1.3ff., Phil. 1.3–11, 1 Thess. 1.2f.).

4. *The shepherd symbol.* A prominent biblical symbol is that of shepherd. It is applied to Yahweh and his anointed king (cf. Ps. 23, Is. 40.11, Ezek. 37.24; and so to messianic expectation (cf. Matt. 2.6). The good shepherd seeks the lost, brings back the strayed, binds up the crippled, strengthens the weak, watches over the strong and 'will feed them in justice' (cf. Ezek. 34.16). A sharp contrast is drawn between good and bad shepherds (cf. Ezek. 34, Zech. 11, John 10). Jesus is the true shepherd who wins response from the flock (they 'hear his voice': 10.3, 27); he knows them personally, exercises leadership, nourishes and enhances their life (10.9f., 28), and lays down his life for his sheep (10.11, 15). The bond of trust between shepherd and sheep reflects that between Father and Son. The self-giving of the shepherd, even to death, is an expression of the Father's love; hence he lays down his life in order to take it again (10.17). When he does take it again, he gives to his disciples his blessing ('Peace be with you') and their commission (20.21). His command to Peter is, 'Feed my sheep' (21.17; cf. 21.15f.). In Heb. 13.20, Jesus is called 'the great shepherd of the sheep' (cf. 1 Pet. 5.4), because by his death he sealed the eternal covenant, with all its life-giving power. Made

perfect through suffering, he is able to help us when tested (Heb. 2.18, 4.15f.). The Christ who ministered as the suffering servant and left an example of patient endurance remains 'the shepherd and guardian' of our souls (1 Pet. 2.25). In Rev. 7.17, the 'Lamb in the midst of the throne' will shepherd the martyrs and lead them to springs of life-giving water. Thus, the glorified Christ who suffered is the archetypal shepherd who exercises his ministry for and through the church.

Concluding observations. Pastoral images in the NT encompass the servant (with many variations, including a hint of 'the fool' in 1 Cor. 4.10), the wisdom teacher, the father and the shepherd. Certain offices in the Church are inseparable from pastoral ministry: e.g. *episkopos* or bishop (1 Pet. 2.25, Acts 20.28, 1 Tim. 2.5), presbyter (cf. 1 Pet. 5), and 'pastor and teacher' (Eph. 4.11). But 'feeding the sheep' does not imply authoritarianism on the part of the pastor nor unthinking passivity on the part of the flock. The *koinonia* is an inter-active, caring fellowship, providing the conditions for spiritual growth and development. Since all Christians are called to discipleship, all are charged to 'feed my sheep'. 'We must learn to speak of the *pastorhood of all believers* and to explore the idea that *each* person has a call to lead in that special way characteristic of the Good Shepherd' (Campbell).

Campbell, A.V., *Rediscovering Pastoral Care* (Darton Longman & Todd, 1981). Hiltner, S., *The Christian Shepherd* (Abingdon Press, Nashville, 1959); *Theological Dynamics* (Abingdon, 1972). Jeremias, J., 'Poimēn', article in G. Friedrich (ed.), *Theological Dictionary of the New Testament*, tr. G.W. Bromiley, vol. VI, (SCM, 1969), pp. 485–99. Virgo, L., 'First Aid in Pastoral Care: the Biblical Basis' (*Expository Times*, 95, 7, April 1984), pp. 196–200).

J.I.H. McDONALD

See also: BIBLE: PASTORAL USE; CROSS AND RESURRECTION.

NULLITY
See: MARRIAGE: NULLITY.

NURSING
Nursing is a helping and sustaining activity which is concerned primarily with assisting the sick person in accomplishing those everyday tasks which in his or her culture would be normally performed unaided by a competent adult. In all cultures and at all times nursing

has been recognized as the individual care given to a sick person.

If sickness diminishes a person's strength or will to fulfil individual and fundamental physical, emotional, intellectual, spiritual or social needs, or if he or she lacks the knowledge to do so, nursing aids the individual in appropriate ways. Nursing activities are therefore at times as simple as providing a refreshing drink or as complex as helping a person to regain trust in other people.

The ultimate aim of nursing is to help the individual toward recovery or to his or her highest level of independence. If this is not possible, nursing should assist the person toward a peaceful and dignified death (q.v.).

The constant objective of nursing is to sustain the sick person and those who are important to him or her through the experience of illness, pain and distress. Nursing is the most intimate service, both physically and emotionally, which an adult will accept from a caring professional worker. It is also a unique service in that it responds to the immediate and spontaneously expressed needs of the sick person, who normally does not make a time-limited appointment in order to be nursed. Its often continuous availability puts nursing in the privileged position of having the closest and most personal relationship with the sick individual. It therefore has important mediating functions to other members of the caring professions including doctors, all paramedical services, social workers and ministers of religion.

Depending on the seriousness and complexity of the health problems suffered by the individual, nursing has extensive technical and specific therapeutic functions, including the prevention of ill-health and health education (q.v.).

Professional nursing services in the United Kingdom are provided by registered general nurses, registered mental nurses, registered nurses for the mentally handicapped, and registered sick children's nurses as well as by enrolled nurses. The title 'nurse' is legally protected by statute. Persons misusing it can be prosecuted.

Most nurses prepare for registration in three-year programmes in colleges of nursing and midwifery or in schools of nursing. A small but increasing number of undergraduate nursing students are studying in integrated degree nursing programmes in institutions of higher education such as universities and colleges. These students complete their basic (usually four and a half years) preparation as a graduate with a bachelor degree and registration as a nurse.

Nurses work with physically and mentally ill as well as with physically and mentally disabled people (see DISABLEMENT) of all ages both in hospitals and in the community. Midwives and health visitors are registered nurses who specialize after further training in their respective fields of work. Health visitors engage entirely in the promotion of health and prevention of ill-health in the community and have considerable statutory duties, especially in relation to babies and children.

The education and standards of practice of all nurses, midwives and health visitors are under the control of statutory bodies. The United Kingdom Central Council for Nursing, Midwifery and Health Visiting can institute disciplinary proceedings and remove a nurse, midwife or health visitor from the professional register in cases of professional misconduct.

In recent decades, nursing in the United Kingdom has been developing from a highly routinized and strongly disease-orientated paramedical occupation into a patient-orientated caring profession which can base its activities on an ever-increasing body of nursing research. The methodical assessment of patients' individual needs and an increasing awareness of a person's social and cultural identity have also raised nurses' awareness of patients' spiritual needs. Although routinized and stereotyped confirmation of a person's 'religion' have by no means disappeared, especially in hospitals, more nurses have now the knowledge and interpersonal skills to assist a patient and his or her family in expressing and exploring spiritual needs and in identifying in a much more comprehensive way appropriate sources of pastoral care. Developments especially in the care of the terminally ill patient and the disabled person have enriched nurses' understanding of people's spiritual and pastoral care needs.

Auld, M.E., *The Challenge of Nursing: a Book of Readings* (C.V. Mosby, Saint Louis, 1973). Duncan, A.S. *et al.* (eds.), *Dictionary of Medical Ethics* (Darton Longman & Todd, 1981), pp. 308–12. Henderson V., *The Nature of Nursing: a Definition and its Implications for Practice, Research and Education* (Macmillan, New York, 1966).

RUTH A. SCHRÖCK

See also: HOSPITALS; INTER-PERSONAL RELATIONSHIPS; MEDICINE; NATIONAL HEALTH SERVICE; REHABILITATION; SOCIAL WORK.

NURTURE, CHRISTIAN

The processes whereby the growth and development of individuals, groups or institutions are fostered. These processes may occur formally or informally and may proceed from individuals or institutions. In its widest sense, as in the expression 'nurture or nature', nurture may refer to all of the environmental influences which promote the maturation of an organism. Christian nurture is the process whereby the Christian faith and life of individuals or communities are strengthened. Similarly one could speak of Islamic nurture, Humanist nurture, etc., although the expression is only common in the Christian context.

1. *History.* The modern usage of the term derives from the American theologian Horace Bushnell (1802–78) who taught that the uninterrupted spiritual development of the baptized child in the Christian family should be regarded as the normal pattern of Christian growth, and that in cases of such Christian children experiences of conscious conversion need not be sought. Christian nurture thus became a characteristic emphasis of liberal Protestantism and is associated with what today is often known as the socialization theory of Christian upbringing. In Catholic Christianity 'Christian formation' would be a roughly equivalent expression.

2. *Current British usage.* The expression has been used in Britain since the middle 1970s to distinguish the situation in which the religious (e.g. Christian) faith of a child or adult is deliberately fostered from that in which religious education of a more descriptive, critical and open-ended type is offered. Christian nurture is thus often thought of as being appropriate for the Christian home and church, whereas religious education without any particular faith outcome is thought of as being more appropriate for the county school curriculum. Although the validity of this distinction is generally maintained by county school religious educators, it remains controversial (especially among the Muslim, Sikh and Hindu communities and some of the smaller Christian movements), and the distinction is often obscured by the continued use in both church and school of the more ambiguous expression 'Christian education'.

3. *Main problems.* (1) It is important to develop a deeper understanding of a process which is neither a closed authoritarian instruction or indoctrination nor merely a general education into world religions, however valuable the latter process may be in county school contexts. The expression 'Christian nurture' is ideally suited to describe a process which is freedom-enhancing, exploratory and critical and yet seeks to develop these qualities as a result of specific Christian commitment and as an expression of continued Christian spirituality. The word 'nurture', with its suggestion of a fostered growth, is compatible with the view that Christianity itself is in process of development, and this in turn is compatible with the idea that Christianity (along with other world faiths) is to be studied in county schools because it is the outstanding resource provided by our culture for the stimulation of personal growth. Any over-protective suggestions which the word 'nurture' might convey can be met by emphasizing the need for Christian nurture to draw its inspiration from the self-critical and exploratory aspects of the Christian faith. (2) The theoretical and practical difficulties encountered in the attempt to maintain this kind of process in the contemporary context of modernity and plurality are considerable. The various ways in which different kinds of Christian families and communities might become more effective agents of Christian nurture are being actively explored today, and the increased interest in questions relating to baptism (q.v.) and the child's reception of communion may also be seen as aspects of this concern. The possibilities of a constructive relationship between religious educators in the schools and faith nurturers in the religious communities are also being actively pursued, it being increasingly thought that this relationship may be a mutually helpful one, in which different but related activities come to respect and to support each other.

The Child in the Church (British Council of Churches, 1976). *Understanding Christian Nurture* (British Council of Churches, 1981). **Bushnell, Horace,** *Christian Nurture* (first pub. 1861, Yale UP, 1979). **Fowler, James W.,** *Stages of Faith* (Harper & Row, New York, 1981). **Hull, John M.,** 'From Christian Nurture to Religious Education: the British Experience' and 'Christian Nurture and Critical Openness', in *Studies in Religion and Education* (Falmer Press, 1984), pp. 27–44 and pp. 207–25. **Westerhoff, John H.,** *Will Our Children Have Faith?* (Seabury Press, New York, 1976).

JOHN M. HULL

See also: INDOCTRINATION; LEARNING; MEMBERSHIP OF THE CHURCH: PREPARATION.

O

OBEDIENCE

(1) The living response of one being to the words of another. (2) Submission to the rule or authority of another.

In the Jewish tradition, to 'obey' is most often expressed by the verb to 'hear'. In the same tradition, the spoken word of God is the very act of creation (cf. Gen. 1; Heb. 11.3). Linking these two strands of tradition together, it could be said that we continue to receive our meaning as persons by hearing the word of God and acting upon it, thus making the principle of our relationship with our creator one of obedience. This creative word of God is mediated through the people and conditions which make up our daily life. In some situations it might involve submission to the authority or rule of another.

Christians claim that a major breakdown in this principle has been restored or healed, once and for all, by the obedience of Jesus Christ to his Father. His followers, sharing in the benefits of this healing obedience, seek to imitate the pattern of it, as a community and as individuals.

The example of Jesus requires that our response to life break out from the limited area of our personal preferences, in order to obey the immediate claims of God upon us. Such self-transcendence frees us from the burdens imposed upon us by the desire to control our future (cf. Matt. 6.25–33), and opens us towards the future that God is addressing to us in the details of everyday experience.

Such obedience demands certain qualities, among them discernment and courage. From among the various claims made upon us, we need to discern what God is asking from us, as well as have the courage to act upon it.

One of the persistent obstacles to a straight answer to the claims of God is the conditioned nature of our response to life. Anxieties and fears left over from past experiences can distort our hearing, so that we either become deaf or we manipulate what we hear because we are afraid.

In these circumstances, we need to share our task of obedience with a friend or guide who can bring a more experienced and objective ear to our situation. Such a guide will both help us to discern what God is asking, as well as supplying support and encouragement when a costly response has to be made (cf. Heb. 5.8).

Louf, André, 'Humility and Obedience in Monastic Tradition' (*Cistercian Studies*, vol. 18 no. 4, 1983), pp. 261–82.

SIMON HOLDEN, C.R.

See also: DISCIPLINE; SPIRITUAL DIRECTION.

OBESITY
See: DIET.

ORDINATION

Ordination is the commonest term for the rite of admission into the official ministry of the Church, sometimes understood as the conferring of Holy Orders, a special grace, or an 'indelible character'. The ordination of bishops is often called consecration, and in Presbyterian churches elders are ordained but remain lay, not being charged with the ministry of word and sacrament. The process of which the ordination service is a culmination starts with a call from God which is tested by the Church, and after appropriate preparation and training a candidate is ordained to a specific ministry and is given responsibilities within a particular fellowship. The essentials of the rite are usually stated to be prayer (most notably an invocation of the Spirit), the laying on of hands by a bishop or other authorized persons, as a sign of apostolic continuity and of the passing on of responsibility. As is common in ritual, additional elements cluster around this core, and divergent theologies and varied rites (q.v.) develop.

Ordination has always been understood as a rite of entry into the pastoral office, and all the functions and responsibilities entailed by ordination have a bearing on pastoral care. Ordination places the ordained person in a representative capacity, in two senses. In the first place, there is representation of Christ to the church which in its turn represents Christ to the world. Christ is the Good Shepherd, who tends the sheep and gives his life for them. The ordained ministry should model itself on this pattern of pastoral care because it represents Christ. In the second place, the ordained represent the whole Church to the specific local fellowship, reminding them that they are not alone but are part of a Church which spans the ages and exists in every land. The ordained ministry, then, is a living sign that the congregation should not become domesticated within any culture or situation, that it is 'a colony of heaven'.

Ordination is to leadership (q.v.) within the church. Despite the tendency down the ages to over-emphasize the significance of leadership in the cult to the neglect of leadership within the life of the community, the two properly belong together. Leadership in pastoral care involves enabling and encouraging mutuality of pastoral care and outreach into the broader society rather than the ordained monopolizing pastoral care. A pastoral fellowship needs leadership that is itself pastoral. It is a function of the whole church rather than of a few.

Ordination has frequently been seen as the conferring of authority and the making of rulers in the Church. Vatican II and equivalent developments in most other denominations have shifted the emphasis from ruling to pastoring. This, of course, does not dispose of the question of authority but invites us to view the authority conferred in ordination in the light of the authority of Jesus, who came 'not to be served but to serve and to give his life as a ransom for many' (Mark 10.45) and drew a sharp distinction between the authority appropriate to 'the kings of the gentiles' and the servant or pastoral authority which should characterize ministry within the Church.

Cooke, Bernard, *Ministry to Word and Sacraments* (Fortress, 1976). Fransen, Piet, 'Orders and Ordination', in *Sacramentum Mundi*, vol. 4 (Burns & Oates, 1969). Jones, C.P.M. *et al.* (eds.), *The Study of Liturgy* (SPCK, 1978), article on 'Ordination'. Martos, Joseph, *Doors to the Sacred* (SCM, 1981), ch. 12. Schillebeeckx, Edward, *Ministry: A Case for Change* (SCM, 1981).

D.B. FORRESTER

See also: LEADERSHIP; MINISTRY, DOCTRINE OF; VOCATION; WOMEN: ORDINATION.

ORGANIZATIONS FOR PASTORAL CARE

Bodies set up with the specific purpose of facilitating the practice of, and education for, pastoral care.

Since 1960 there have come into being in Britain, several groups representing different interests and emphases in this field. Among the most important are the Clinical Theology Association, the Richmond Fellowship, the Westminster Pastoral Foundation, and the Dympna Centre. Parallel developments have been the establishment of courses in pastoral studies in some British universities and theological colleges, the appointment of advisers on pastoral care and counselling in certain dioceses of the Church of England, and the opening of several pastoral counselling centres throughout the country. The interfaith, as well as the interdenominational nature of this movement is shown by the more recent opening of the Raphael Centre, a Jewish counselling centre in London.

In 1972, the main British groups formed the *Association for Pastoral Care and Counselling* (APCC), itself a division of the newly established *British Association for Counselling*. APCC has seen its role, not as a training organization, but as enabling the various organizations concerned with pastoral training to identify appropriate concepts, goals, standards and methods. Though part of a larger counselling organization, APCC has always insisted upon its own wider understanding of pastoral *care*.

These developments in the United Kingdom have been part of a wider international movement. Gatherings were held at Arholdshain (1973), Zurich (1975) and Eisenach (1977), the last named marking the full participation of East Europeans in the pastoral care movement. An international congress was held in Edinburgh in 1979, bringing together three hundred persons, including good representations from Asia, Africa and Latin America. At Edinburgh the International Committee on Pastoral Care and Counselling came into being, but by the time of the second congress held in San Francisco in 1983, this structure could not contain the pressure for representation from other new national organizations and the committee was reconstituted as a larger International Council. Meanwhile autonomous continental committees have been formed in Europe (which held a conference in Lublin, Poland, in 1981), Asia (the first Asian Conference being held in the Philippines in 1982) and Africa.

The growth of the pastoral care movement has not been without controversy regarding the function of the various organizations established, and indeed regarding the nature of pastoral care itself. While in the United States, organizations such as the Association for Clinical Pastoral Education and the American Association of Pastoral Counselors have seen one of their main functions to be the accreditation (q.v.) of individuals and institutions. This has not so far happened in Britain, APCC serving mainly as a vehicle of communication between different interest groups. There have also been tensions, (a) between the advocates of pastoral counselling as an autonomous discipline practised by specially trained professionals and those who see it as part of the ongoing pastoral care ministry of the whole church, (b) between a medical model of pastoral counselling based upon the 'elimination of defect' and a growth-in-community model of pastoral care (for a fuller discussion of these issues see the papers by Hiltner and Clinebell in *Pastoral Psychology* and those by Lambourne and Clinebell in *Contact*), and (c) between the affirmation of pastoral care as a specifically Christian activity and the recognition that carers from other faiths might appropriately be represented on pastoral organizations.

Useful addresses: Association for Pastoral Care and Counselling, 37a Sheep Street, Rugby CV21 3BX. Clinical Theology Association, St Mary's House, Church Westcote, Oxford, OX7 6SF. Dympna Centre, 24 Blandford Street, London W1H 3HA. Raphael Centre, 100 Ashmill Street, London NW1. Westminster Pastoral Foundation, 23 Kensington Square, London W8 5HN. American Association of Pastoral Counselors, 9508a Lee Highway, Fairfax, VA 22031, USA. Association for Clinical Pastoral Education, 475 Riverside Drive, Suite 450, New York, NY 10115, USA. For European and international committees, write c/o APCC.

Becher, W., 'International Conferences on Pastoral Care and Counselling' (*Contact*, no. 75, 1982). **Hiltner, S.**, 'The American Association of Pastoral Counselors: a Critique' (*Pastoral Psychology*, vol. 15, no. 143, 1964), pp. 8–16; **Clinebell, H.J.**, 'The Challenge of the Speciality of Pastoral Counseling' (*ibid.*), pp. 17–28. **Lambourne, R.A.**, 'Objections to a National Pastoral Organisation' (*Contact*, no. 35, June 1971), pp. 24–31; **Clinebell, H.J.**, 'Response to Lambourne' (*Contact*, no. 36, Oct. 1971), pp. 26–9.

DAVID LYALL

P

PAIN

Suffering which can be physical, emotional or both.

The Greek root *poinē*, meaning penalty, from which the word pain is derived, implies that pain was seen as a consequence of wrong doing. This idea still lingers on among some groups, but acceptance of pain has sharply diminished in the Western world and endurance of it has become a less respected virtue since the development of chloroform and other pain-relieving drugs.

For Christians pain has always presented a dilemma. 'If God is good and all-powerful, why does he allow his creatures to suffer pain?' The response to that question can only be individual. Pain has caused some to reject the idea of God and others to turn to it. Literature is full of examples, but the Book of Job is unsurpassed for a statement of the problem.

Physical pain is not yet clearly understood. It has sensory components but these are linked to, and may be sharpened or relieved by, emotions and motives. It is usually caused by damage being inflicted on the body but may occur without obvious cause. Sometimes there is no pain despite obvious damage; at other times pain continues long after the injured areas have healed and remains a constant problem for the sufferer and a puzzle for friends and family.

Until recently most people accepted Descartes' view, published in 1664, that pain is like a bell ringing an alarm system in order to warn that the body is injured or diseased in some way. But in the 1960s research led to a more dynamic conception. Pain is determined by many factors besides injury – personality, culture, and other activities in the nervous system play their parts. Then Melzack and Wall put forward the gate-control theory which is now widely accepted, showing that injury signals can be blocked or modified at the earliest stages of their transmission in the nervous system. This work and that of others has led to the view that chronic, severe pain is a problem in its own right, and which justifies

attention and research into pain control. Much has been learned. There is a journal devoted to pain, pain clinics have been set up in major cities where appropriate pain-control techniques are offered on an individual basis, and for the terminally ill the hospice offers an entirely new approach for the chronic pain of illnesses such as cancer.

Pain has some value. It teaches us to avoid injury and thus improves our chances of survival. Pain can force us to rest and give our body the opportunity to use its powerful capacity to heal itself. Some pain, however, can be excruciating, e.g. post-operative pain and neuralgia, and serves no biological purpose. It may be so exhausting that it leads to suicide. A variety of physical and psychological techniques – including massage, relaxation and autohypnosis – are now being tried to relieve this distress. It may only be possible to reduce it to bearable levels, but an important factor is to enable the sufferer to gain some control over the pain rather than feel helpless and afraid. Within tolerable levels personal dignity, courage and even heroism can be maintained. Those levels vary for each of us.

Emotional pain, or pain of the heart, mind and spirit, is as real and powerful as any physical pain. It may express itself in physical, sensory experiences, like the ache of bereavement. Suppression of emotional pain can lead to physical disorders, and we are seeing new forms of therapies for illness like cancer which involve the expression of repressed emotional states through techniques like visualization of the tumour and the use of dreams.

Serious physical pain may for many years be avoided, but emotional pain is part of the experience of being human. It begins when we are cast into the world as separate persons. The course of our pain lies in our need and our capacity to relate to other human beings and the constant threat to those experiences in a world where loss and change are inevitable. We may suffer a more general loss of self-respect or of meaning and purpose in our lives through unemployment,

poverty, bereavement, divorce, imprisonment, migration, the growing up of our
children and so on. Helplessness, loneliness,
guilt, fear, frustration . . . each cause pain.
The list is not complete: each person has to
make their own. There is another pain –
perhaps the greatest of all – the discovery of
the self as a separate person.

Common features of many of these pains
are helplessness and vulnerability. For some
this comes early in life through desperate
experiences in childhood; for others it comes
later. Both as children and as adults our
natural response to pain is to protest. But
many people are trained to suppress that
reaction and be ashamed of it. This drives the
energy of their pain deeper into minds and
bodies and makes healing harder. Chemical
changes may take place which create physical
symptoms of distress or chronic states of
tension or depression or anxiety. Each
person's circumstances and genetic make-up
will shape their responses. Just as in physical
pain, so also in emotional pain people seem to
have differing levels of toleration: an event
which might cause one person moderate
distress, may seem to another like a death
blow.

A special kind of pain can be aroused by
seeing another human being suffer, particularly if the suffering person is deeply loved.
Like all other pain it has a component of
anger (q.v.) in it, and this is more easily expressed for another person than for oneself. No
matter how often we are taught that life is not
'fair', we still seek fairness to give ourselves a
sense of meaning. If we can express our anger
– to ourselves, to a friend, even to a stranger
we meet on a train – infantile and pitiable
though that may seem, we have a better
chance of releasing energy, which would
otherwise be blocked, and using it to give
meaning to the experience. If energy is locked
into denying anger, pain alternates with
exhaustion. But the experience of anger
should open a path to the creative use of the
pain. We have many examples of this from
the genius of Beethoven struggling, enraged,
with the pain of his deafness to the simpler
but no less heroic daily care given by parents
to their mentally handicapped children.

Therapies for emotional pain were until the
1960s sharply divided between psychotherapy
and chemotherapy. Now the picture is very
different. There has been a great expansion in
techniques which do not rely on relating
present distress to early-life experience but
which concentrate on helping people come to
terms with the here and now. Some of these
are based on individual self-help: rational
emotive therapy is an example. Others
depend on groups of sufferers who come
together to gain and share understanding of
their difficulties and offer each other mutual
support in overcoming them: an agoraphobic
group is such an example. In each case people
are creatively using their own pain to help
themselves and others. Different styles of
therapy will suit different kinds of people,
and some will prefer to find more personal
solutions. If a real choice has been offered we
have to respect the right of people who
choose to stay with their pain.

One of the oldest forms of therapy which
fell into disrepute and is now being revived is
spiritual healing through prayer, the laying
on of hands or distance healing. There is a
developing view that each of us has this
power to heal if we choose to use it. Certainly
each of us can be with a person in pain and
quietly share their experience. If we are at
ease with ourselves and our own pain that
will often help them.

Camus, A., *The Myth of Sisyphus* (Penguin, 1975).
Descartes, R., *L'homme* (1664), trans. M. Foster
(CUP, 1901). **Huxley, A.,** *The Devils of Loudun*
(Chatto, 1952). **Lewis, C.S.,** *The Problem of Pain*
(Fontana, 1957). **Melzack, R.** and **Wall, P.,** *The
Challenge of Pain* (Penguin, 1982).

K. CARMICHAEL

See also: EVIL; HEALTH AND ILLNESS;
LONELINESS; THEODICY.

PARAPSYCHOLOGY
The scientific study of paranormal
phenomena.

The word 'paranormal' is deliberately non-
committal with respect to the ultimate explanation or interpretation of the phenomena and,
as such, may be compared with the word
'supernatural' which usually carries a religious connotation. A given phenomenon is
said to be paranormal only if it cannot be
explained, even in principle, on any accepted
scientific basis. The two principal phenomena
that concern the parapsychologist are
(1) extra-sensory perception (ESP) where the
individual acquires information about the
external world otherwise than by any known
sensory channels and (2) psychokinesis (PK)

where the individual influences events in the external world otherwise than through any known motor mechanism. Collectively these two categories are known as 'psi phenomena' or, separately, as 'psi gamma' and 'psi kappa' respectively. Familiar examples of (1) include: telepathy, i.e. the non-inferential awareness of what is in another person's mind; clairvoyance, i.e. the non-inferential awareness of concealed or remote objects or events; and precognition, i.e. the non-inferential awareness of future events. Familiar examples of (2) include: influencing mentally the fall of dice or, more recently, the output of an electronic random-number generator; influencing mentally other organisms, e.g. the growth of plants or, as in psychic healing, organic processes in another person's body; and, a recent phenomenon, paranormal metal-bending.

Despite these negative definitions of the basic phenomena, many parapsychologists believe that we are dealing here with fundamental properties of mind conceived independently of the brain and having the power to transcend the world of space, time and matter. This is speculation, however, and in our present state of ignorance no positive definition of the phenomena could command a consensus. The serious study of paranormal phenomena may be said to have commenced with the founding of the Society for Psychical Research in London in 1882. The word 'parapsychology' was given currency in the English-speaking world by J.B. Rhine of Duke University, North Carolina, and at first it was used to indicate the strict experimental approach associated with Rhine, but gradually it has come to supplant the older expression 'psychical research', especially in the USA. At the present time the scientific community is still reluctant to acknowledge the reality of the phenomena and hence the legitimacy of parapsychology as a science. Three reasons may be suggested for this state of affairs: (1) the phenomena are extraordinarily elusive and difficult to produce to order; (b) a great many spurious claims have been made which tend to obscure what may be genuine; and (c) the nature of the phenomena are such as to strike many scientists as being more akin to magic.

Eysenck, H.J. and Sargent, Carl, *Explaining the Unexplained* (Weidenfeld & Nicolson, 1982). Grattan-Guinness, I. (ed.), *Psychical Research: a Guide to its History, Principles and Practices* (Aquarian Press,

182

1982). Wolman, B.B. (ed.), *Handbook of Parapsychology* (Van Nostrand Reinhold, 1977).

JOHN BELOFF

See also: MAGIC; SPIRITUALISM/SPIRITISM.

PARENTING
The structure of living together as a family, in which parents execute the task of helping their children to become adults.

Ethology shows that parenting is a fundamental structure in the life of animals, which guarantees the continuation of a species. In human society parenting is, besides this, one of the means by which children find their place in society and culture. This includes finding their place as adults, and as independent people with their own freedom and responsibility. It includes also an independent relation to God.

Parenting is a way of living together in which children will get enough 'basic trust' to have the courage to become adults, enough insight to find their own way in society, enough ideals to make their own life-project and enough faith and belief to enter upon an independent relation to God. It must be seen as a process in which constraint gradually gives way to freedom, nearness to distance, closeness of the family to openness, and property-feelings to willingness to abdicate.

Parenting contains a set of special problems which often occur in pastoral care situations: (1) Parents may use their children in open or in subtle and hidden ways to serve their own egoistic ends, e.g. children are expected to secure a safe living for their parents, they are loved by their parents in so far as they contribute to their 'good name', they are not allowed to leave their parents 'alone'. In this way they do not get an opportunity to become adults. (2) Parents may see their children as a personal property. They therefore do not get enough stimulus to try out the adventurous and unsafe aspects of life nor do they get enough encouragement to enter into deeper relations with other people. They may feel uncertain and guilty, when they grow up. (3) Parents may be over-anxious and may always want to be sure about what their children are doing or thinking. In this way they do not get enough opportunity to develop 'basic trust'. (4) In consequence of these patterns of education and behaviour the right balance between dependence and independence, which in the process of growing up gradually must shift towards independence, is not found. Children then become either too rebellious or too submissive. (5) These problems often come to the surface, when parents get involved in the crisis of a divorce. Very often the (infantile) emotions of the parents in relation to their children, mentioned above, hinder a healthy 'working through' of the problems, which the children in consequence of the divorce have to face, such as guilt, separation-anxiety, loneliness, and constitute in this way a serious strain on their emotional development. (6) Adopted children often have special problems with their 'parents'. Parenting in this case must be aware that the 'mystery' around the 'real' parents may haunt the child and that therefore the balance of nearness and distance is often fragile (see ADOPTION).

In pastoral care, problems of parenting are often put before the pastor. In order to be able to help, some knowledge of family therapy is advisable. This also helps to identify which problems must be referred. The minister should always be aware of the temptation of taking sides. Some insight into the problems of modern family-life and of modern youth-culture helps to gain more objectivity.

Behind all this must stand a 'theology of parenting', a conviction concerning parenting in the light of God. Three things seem essential: (1) Parents receive their children as a gift and as a responsibility; they may enjoy having children and must see it as a task. (1) The thrust of parenting is towards the future, for which the children must be educated. (3) In being a family in this way a community is built, in which the light of God's parenting becomes visible.

Hoffman, L.W., *Parenting* (LEA Publishers, Hillsdale, New Jersey, 1982).

HEIJE FABER

See also: ADOLESCENCE; CHILDREN: PASTORAL CARE; MARRIAGE AND FAMILY: PASTORAL CARE.

PARISH: PASTORAL CARE

The word 'parish' comes from a Greek word meaning 'district'. Originally it described an ecclesiastical area under a bishop (the modern 'diocese'), but after the 4th century it was increasingly used of the subdivisions of a diocese. Since the word defines an area rather than a congregation, the minister of the parish is often charged with pastoral responsibility for most or all of the inhabitants. (This

is particularly true of 'established' churches.) In the 20th century there has been a renewed interest in the development of pastoral ministry by lay members of the congregation, both among church members and in the wider community.

Nevertheless the minister or priest remains the focus of pastoral care in the parish. 'It is not too much to say that the parish parson . . . is the last remaining genus of the general-practitioner-at-helping people' (Clebsch and Jaekle 1967, p. xv). But whereas in earlier centuries the pastor would usually be alone, now he or she is often surrounded by specialists from other caring professions. This calls for new skills in learning effective co-operation, while retaining confidence in a ministry (rooted in faith) which addresses itself to the whole person.

Pastoral care in the parish should not be seen as synonymous with all the tasks usually assigned to the pastor. Its primary concern, as with teaching, is that of 'building up the body of Christ, until we attain to the unity of the faith and of the knowledge of the Son of God, to mature manhood, to the measure of the stature of the fullness of Christ' (Eph. 4.12–13). It reaches out to all the members of the church and beyond (and not just to those in evident need), and the emphasis is on growth and maturity in Christ for each one. The parish pastor seeks to help men and women of all ages to recognize how they may grow in personal faith, and also find that healing and guidance which they may need along the way.

The *practical exercise* of pastoral care in the parish may be described in various ways. Pre-eminent, perhaps, is the task of conveying a *vision* of God's glory in ways which can come alive for this individual or that. In the pastor himself or herself there is an abiding sense of Jesus as the Word made flesh, the true or 'proper' Man, who invites us to 'come and see' (John 1.39,46). Indeed the whole work of the parish centres on this task, which provides a common foundation for worship, teaching, evangelism, service and pastoral care.

Pastoral care involves a ministry of *reconciliation* (q.v.) with both God and neighbour. This may be practised sacramentally, as commended in the first exhortation in Holy Communion in the Book of Common Prayer, or informally through prayer and counselling (q.v.). It is naturally associated with *guidance* in recognizing and making moral decisions, and the training of parish pastors should include an introduction to the accumulated wisdom of the past. In both these tasks the modern pastor also draws on the knowledge now available to him or her in understanding some of the dynamics of human behaviour, both individually and in groups.

Healing is prominent in the ministry of Jesus to individuals. For long periods it has figured little in most parishes apart from intercessions for the sick and occasional prayer with them. Nowadays there will often be a more developed ministry, in which others may be involved besides the parish pastor. This will include visiting (q.v.), laying-on of hands, anointing with oil and regular prayer (q.v), as well as making the Sacrament of Holy Communion available to the housebound. There may be occasional services of healing in the parish church.

Healing is primarily concerned with the renewal of faith and the recovery of 'wholeness' in union with Christ. It may or may not be accompanied by physical well-being. The parish pastor therefore ministers also to those who may find themselves called to endure *suffering* and learn how to use it in faith (see Rom. 5.3, Heb. 5.8, 2 Cor. 17.7–9, etc.). He or she stands also with the *dying*, a fellow-pilgrim facing the last enemy, turning together with confidence to the promises of Christ.

Finally, pastoral care in the parish cannot ignore those issues which are raised 'at the other end of the commuting line'. Failure to recognize that there is a *social and work context* to individual pastoral care is a diminution of the gospel. 'Kingdom' theology also requires pastoral perspective in the parish and its pastor.

Campbell, Alastair V., *Rediscovering Pastoral Care* (Darton Longman & Todd, 1981). Clebsch, William A. and Jaekle, Charles R., *Pastoral Care in Historical Perspective* (Harper, New York, 1967). Hollings, Michael, *Living Priesthood* (Mayhew-McCrimmon, 1977). Newbigin, Lesslie, *The Good Shepherd* (Faith Press, 1977). Selby, Peter, *Liberating God* (SPCK, 1983). Wright, Frank, *The Pastoral Nature of the Ministry* (SCM, 1980).

RONALD BOWLBY

See also: COUNSELLING; HEALING; JUSTICE AND PASTORAL CARE; LETTER-WRITING; RECORD-KEEPING; TELEPHONE USE; VISITING.

PASTOR: IDENTITY AND ROLE

In neither church nor society is there one view of who a pastor is or what he, or she, does. Traditionally the title was applied to the ordained ministry, particularly by churches of the Reformed tradition. This looked to the model of Jesus as the Good Shepherd and led on to an understanding of the priestly or ministerial role as 'being Christ to the people'. Contemporary theology, as in the World Council of Churches' statement, *Baptism, Eucharist and Ministry*, sees all activities of ministry as charisms derived from and dependent upon the Holy Spirit at work in the Church. Pastoral care, therefore, belongs to the Christian community in general and is not necessarily linked with the task of the ordained ministry. If pastoral care is defined as 'meeting people at a point of need', then it can be exercised by a wide variety of groups or individuals. This is accepted in the documents of Vatican II, where pastoral functions are acknowledged to be part of the apostolate of the laity.

In most denominations this view is still at variance with popular expectation. In any survey respondents continue to equate 'pastor' with 'priest' or 'minister'. Many forms of ministerial training also foster the expectation that pastoral care will be a task specific to the ordained ministry. Yet even in Victorian times this expectation was breaking down in practice, and the clergy in town parishes organized visiting societies to undertake a range of pastoral contacts. Some denominations, e.g. the Church of Scotland, have a tradition of eldership which in principle should militate against the popular expectation.

As the church is struggling with a redefinition, popular usage applies the term 'pastoral' to a number of forms of secular care, e.g. that exercised by teachers with a specific caring role in the school community. The common ground shared by those in the religious tradition and those in the new counselling professions has been explored by Halmos in *The Faith of the Counsellors*.

The pastor, whether lay or ordained, may perceive care in different ways. Using a model derived from crisis-management he or she will seek to help at a specific point of need. This may involve an attempt to change the outer circumstances which are pressing upon a person or to produce an inner ability to cope. In either case the emphasis will be upon the particular complaint which has led to a person's appeal for help. The satisfactory resolution of that crisis may be a relatively short-term piece of work. Pastoral care may, however, be understood as concerned with growth not simply through a crisis but in the normal development stages, and then an educational model is more appropriate. A pastoral relationship can be expected to extend over years with its aim of building up an individual or a community in the Christian life.

The understanding of the pastor's role has been profoundly affected by the insights arising from psychology and sociology. It has become apparent that personality needs were often disguised under theological attitudes and that the way that the clergy exercised their pastoral office in particular periods was an amalgam of social perceptions and Christian obedience. In the course of counselling or dealing with experiences of high emotional content, such as bereavement, the pastor will be subject to the same mechanisms of transference (q.v.) and projection as a psychotherapist. Within a community, expectations may put pressure on him or her to enter into a collusion (q.v.) that avoids the appropriate pastoral tasks.

For such reasons there is an increasing awareness that pastoral care should not be exercised in isolation but be the function of a team where members are able to call upon skills of supervision (q.v.). In this way the individual pastor would be helped to understand something of the inner working of his or her own personality as those impinge on the needs of the client or parishioner. Such a development would bring the skills of other disciplines into the church's pastoral care and, in the long term, break down the sense of the minister as the lonely successor of the 'Good Shepherd'.

Campbell, A.V., *Rediscovering Pastoral Care* (Darton Longman & Todd, 1981). Halmos, P., *The Faith of the Counsellors* (Constable, 1965). Pickering, W., *A Search for New Approaches to the Sociological Study of the Priesthood*, Downside symposium on 'The Christian Priesthood' (Darton Longman & Todd, 1970). Russell, A., *The Clerical Profession* (SPCK, 1980). Tiller, J., *A Strategy for the Church's Ministry* (CIO, 1983).

MICHAEL HARE DUKE

See also: LAY PASTORAL CARE; PASTORAL CARE, NATURE OF; PROFESSIONALISM.

PASTOR: PERSONAL AND FAMILY LIFE

Since pastoral care entails personal relationships with those in need, the pastor's own personal life, including his or her family life, can have a positive or negative effect on the quality of care offered.

The author of the First Epistle to Timothy, in referring to the office of bishop, outlines the personal qualities required of pastors and their families: 'A bishop must be above reproach, the husband of one wife, temperate, sensible, dignified, hospitable, an apt teacher, no drunkard, not violent but gentle, not quarrelsome and no lover of money. He must manage his own household well, keeping his children submissive and respectful in every way; for if a man does not know how to manage his own household, how can he care for God's church?' (1 Tim. 3.2–5). Generations of pastors have aspired to this ideal, just as their congregations have assumed it of them, the more so as traditional values and standards have been threatened. But little attention has been paid to the difficulties created by such high expectations. The following problems may be identified: (1) decreasing congregational support; (2) the effect on the pastor's family of social changes; (3) lack of boundaries on pastoral involvement; (4) conflicts created by the nature of pastoral work.

1. *Decreasing congregational support.* Despite theological encouragement to seek and value quality rather than quantity and to beware 'worldly' success, clergy and congregations are adversely affected by the declining numbers of those committed to churches. Clergy are prone to blame themselves and to absorb the demoralizing effect of diminishing congregations.

2. *The effect upon the pastor's family of social changes.* The general tendency to level out classes in society, combining with the movement for co-operative ministry between clergy and laity has exposed both to a greater and more intimate knowledge of one another. Pastors and families are exposed to greater scrutiny at a time when they are less and less likely to conform to a traditional pattern. More spouses have careers of their own and a pastor's children may have little to do with their parents' occupation or interests. The openness of many pastors' homes exposes tensions and strains of an often 'idealized' family for all to see. Increasingly it may be the female partner who is a pastor and this will add different tensions.

3. *Lack of boundaries on pastoral involvement.* The majority of professions closely involved with those in distress or need have developed systems which, in part, protect them from too personal involvement in their clients' lives and problems (e.g. by appointment systems, limited case-load, working closely with colleagues and team and by regular supervision). A pastor's traditional availability, combining with the fundamental initiative-taking of pastoral care, provides little structure (q.v.) to enable pastors to protect themselves from over and unhelpful involvement with others. They can easily create a dependency (q.v.) which is unhealthy for them and those they seek to serve.

4. *Conflicts created by the nature of pastoral work.* The tension between an 'idealistic' versus a 'realistic' approach to life and its problems is at the heart of all pastoral work, e.g. the debate about the remarriage of divorcees in church. As the number and complexity of moral issues grows, pastors are continually confronted with the request to help people resolve confusing and overwhelming moral issues. The more that is discovered and understood about individuals and society as a whole, the harder it is for individuals to reconcile their beliefs with their knowledge and to give proper value to each. The intellectual and academic ability required of pastors can often separate them from those they serve in a way which makes it difficult for them to help intuitively or empathetically (*see*: MORAL ISSUES IN PASTORAL CARE).

The pastoring of pastors and their families is often ignored or taken for granted and, insofar as this happens, their work is undermined. The effective pastoring of pastors and the families requires the following:
1. All who are accepted for training need to learn to understand and care for themselves and those closest to them. Learning of this kind includes both intellectual and experiential elements. (1) *Intellectual*: Appropriate knowledge of the behavioural sciences, their application to the work and role of the pastor in a changing society, and its relationship to theology and spirituality. (2) *Experiential*: Self-knowledge and understanding obtained through individual or group counselling and sensitivity training. Practice in the art and skill of caring, and counselling, learned first through the experience of being cared for and counselled, and then applied through the

practice of supervised pastoral work.
2. All pastors need to pursue their own personal and professional development, including care of themselves, their spouses and families. This can best be achieved by receiving regular personal counselling, supervision of work and spiritual direction (q.v.). Occasional career reviews, easy access to career guidance, and active encouragement to seek opportunities for training, further education, recreation and retreat will all enhance a pastor's personal and family life.
3. Pastors cannot simply pastor themselves. Those responsible for a pastor's work and well-being, and also the recipients of a pastor's ministry, are often well placed to encourage the self-understanding and self-care essential to effective pastoral work. At selection and appointment, and then at regular intervals, pastors can be encouraged to account for their own care and recreation and that of their spouses and families. The latter should be personally involved in the process of selection, appointment and review. And pastors need not to be responsible for seeing that their work is covered while they are involved in their own or their family's care, development and recreation. To have to choose between themselves or their family and their work places impossible burdens upon a pastor. The devaluing of either produces an unrealistic and unethical conflict which church authorities and congregations have a responsibility to help resolve.

Constitutional Papers of the Association for Pastoral Care and Counselling, 1973 (APCC, c/o 37a Sheep Street, Rugby, Warwickshire) pp. 3–5. **Argyle, M.,** *Religious Behaviour* (Routledge, 1961). **A'Brook, M.F.** *et al.,* 'Psychiatric Illness in the Clergy', (*British Journal of Psychiatry*, 1969). **Bier, S.J.** (ed.), *Psychological Testing for Ministerial Selection* (Fordham UP, 1970). **Eadie, H.A.,** 'Health of Scottish Clergymen' (*Contact*, no. 42, 1972); 'They're Human Too' (*Contact*, no. 45, 1974); 'The Helping Personality' (*Contact*, no. 49, 1975). **Foskett, J.,** *Meaning in Madness* (SPCK, 1984), pp. 99–104. **Menges, R.J.** and **Dittes, J.E.,** *Psychological Studies of Clergymen* (Nelson, 1965). **Oates, W.E.,** *The Minister's Own Mental Health* (Channell Press, 1961). **Phipps, M.,** 'The Clergy Marriage' (*Westminster Pastoral Foundation Quarterly*, no. 19 1982).

JOHN FOSKETT

See also: PASTOR: PERSONALITY;
SUPERVISION, PASTORAL; SUPPORT GROUPS.

PASTOR: PERSONALITY

Psychotherapeutic literature gives much attention to the function of the therapist's personality in the process of therapy. Similarly, the importance of the pastor's personality and typical interaction with others within a pastoral relationship is well recognized. The pastor, as in any caring role, is in a position to enhance or damage the well-being of others, and his or her personality is a central factor in this process. Therefore, a high degree of self-awareness and insight into the dynamics of his or her own personality is essential.

Investigations reveal that effective pastors and counsellors possess common personal attributes: empathy and perception; authentic respect and concern for others; a quality of firmness and self-assurance; an ability to respond with openness and genuineness; a sense of immediacy and a focus on the present; and natural spontaneity. Others have emphasized the importance of the pastor's self-respect and confidence founded on the fulfilment of basic needs for satisfaction and security: 'One can respect others only to the extent that one respects oneself' (Sullivan 1955). It is crucial that pastors intentionally work to satisfy needs for sleep, recreation, food, sex, affection, intimacy and recognition in their personal life, so that unfulfilled needs do not intrude into pastoral relationships.

But pastors are human too and just as vulnerable to inner conflicts, unresolved needs and emotional disturbances as any other. A pastor may, wittingly or unwittingly, utilize pastoral relationships for personal gratification and to meet unfulfilled needs. When such counter-transference occurs, then it may cause disturbances for the client, thus provoking 'diakonogenic illnesses' (in medicine, 'iatrogenic' refers to emotional and personal difficulties stimulated by a doctor, or doctor-caused illnesses). Studies suggest that religious counsellors share some common personality attributes and intrapersonal conflicts which may be reflected in typical patterns of interacting with others.

Rollo May (1939) observed that religious counsellors seemed to display some common characteristics which deserved attention: a tendency to experience higher tension and to relax less than others; an excessive sense of responsibility and dread of failure; an ambitious striving for success and a sense of indispensability; compulsive concern for detail, perfectionism and driving sense of

duty; and common feelings of insecurity and inferiority sometimes masked by authoritarian and judgemental attributes. These tendencies, he observed, could reduce the pastor's effectiveness and interfere wth counselling relationships if not adequately resolved.

Subsequent research, despite inconsistent results on some measures, generally indicates that May probably came close to the mark in observing a typical guilt–neurosis syndrome among religious counsellors. A growing body of research suggests a distinctive 'helping personality' commonly found within the caring professions, including the ministry. More research is needed to validate this hypothesis. But available evidence is persuasive.

The 'helping personality' is usually motivated by high self-expectations and an altruistic desire to be helpful and to care for others accompanied by a strong sense of responsibility. The helping person possesses well developed capacities for intuition, empathy, sensitivity, and co-operativeness as well as genuine respect and affection for others. These may be constructive attributes in pastoral relationships.

The profile of the helping personality suggests other characteristics which may cause some conflict, anxiety and dissatisfaction: perfectionist expectations to be loving, caring and affectionate reflected in ambitious striving for success and admiration; low self-esteem accompanied by excessive self-criticism and guilt; fears of isolation, failure and rejection, together with efforts to inhibit sexuality and to repress aggression; and tendencies to conformity and passivity which may appear as compliance. Helping persons, driven by idealistic expectations, also may deprive themselves of opportunities for pleasure and relaxation. These tendencies may be a source of tension unless they are resolved in the pastor's personal and professional development. The pastor must struggle with such unresolved conflicts and unfulfilled needs. But there is no evidence to suggest that pastors or clergy generally are unusually vulnerable to neuroses, emotional disturbances or mental ill-health. Indeed, they may be *less* prone to depression and self-destructive behaviour than other occupational groups.

It is a truism that only those who care for themselves can genuinely care for others. Personal development and self-awareness

187

training, therefore, is considered an essential aspect of a pastor's preparation.

Aden, L., 'Ministers' Struggle with Professional Adequacy' (*Pastoral Psychology*, 20, March 1969). Barry, W.A. and Bordin, E.S., 'Personality development and the Vocational Choice of the Ministry', (*J. of Counselling Psychology*, 14, 1967). Dittes, J.E., 'Psychological Characteristics of Religious Professionals' in M.P. Strommer (ed.), *Research on Religious Development: a Comprehensive Hand Book* (Hawthorn Books, 1971). Eadie, H.A., 'Psychological Health of Clergymen' (*Contact*, 42, 1973; 'They're Human Too' (*Contact*, 45, 1974); 'The Helping Personality' (*Contact*, 49, 1975). Hulme, W.E., 'Pastoral Care of the Pastor' (*Pastoral Psychology*, 14 (136), 1963). Jansen, D.G. *et al.*, 'Personality Characteristics of Clergymen Entering a Clinical Training Program at a State Hospital' (*Psychological Reports*, 31, 1972). May, R., *The Art of Counselling* (Abingdon, Nashville, 1939). Menges, R.J. and Dittes, J.E., 'Psychological Studies of Clergymen' (Nelson, 1965). Mitchell, K.R., 'Dealing with Ministers' Defences' (*J. of Pastoral Care*, 22, 1968). Nauss, A., 'The Ministerial Personality: Myth or Reality?' (*Religion and Health*, 12, 1, 1973). Schurman, P.G., 'On Being Professionally Religious' (*J. of Religion and Health*, 15, 1976). Sullivan, H.S., *The Interpersonal Theory of Psychiatry* (Tavistock, 1955).

HUGH A. EADIE

See also: PASTOR: IDENTITY AND ROLE; PASTOR: PERSONAL AND FAMILY LIFE; VOCATION.

PASTORAL CARE, NATURE OF

Pastoral care is that aspect of the ministry of the Church which is concerned with the well-being of individuals and of communities.

Pastoral care is to be distinguished from pastoral counselling (q.v.), although it may include it, and from pastoral theology (q.v.) or practical theology (q.v.), which are its theoretical counterparts. Clebsch and Jaekle (1967), in their study of pastoral care through the ages, have identified four main pastoral functions – *healing, guiding, sustaining* and *reconciling* – and have suggested that pastoral care gains its distinctive quality by being offered by 'representative' (not necessarily ordained) 'Christian persons' and by dealing with problems 'within the context of ultimate meanings and concerns'. These descriptions appear to do justice to the complexity and subtleties of pastoral care, but suffer from abstractness and from a lack of clear theological identity. This article will expand them in the following four respects: (1) the

providers of care; (2) the recipients of care; (3) the aim of care; (4) the limits of care.

1. *Providers.* A theological understanding of pastoral care must begin with a full account of the ministry (q.v.) of the whole church (q.v.). The basic discipleship of *all* Christians entails caring for others as though they were Christ (Matt. 25.31–46). The great commandment (Luke 10.27) requires love of both God and neighbour and (as the parable of the Good Samaritan makes plain) the neighbour is whoever is in need. These considerations throw into question a distinction sometimes drawn between 'works of charity' and pastoral care, the latter being understood as a 'tending of the flock' by the 'shepherd', i.e. ordained minister. This view of pastorhood derives from a misunderstanding of the normative image of shepherd in the OT and NT. There is, in the biblical understanding, only one true shepherd, God or God's chosen one. Leadership in the church, although it may sometimes be described in pastoral imagery (e.g. 1 Peter 5.2f.) is functional in character, its purpose being to equip the whole people of God for their ministry in the world. Thus pastoral care, when defined narrowly as a professional function of the clerical minority in the Church, loses sight of its main purpose which is the arduous and lifelong task of loving one's neighbour in need. Thus the term 'lay pastoral care' (q.v.) is perhaps misleading, if it implies two classes of caring, one by the clerical professional, the other by the 'ordinary' Christian. Faced with love's impossible ideal, there are no acknowledged experts, only those who recognize their inadequacy and those who, like the proud Pharisee in another parable (Luke 18.9–14), do not. Moreover, an important implication of the good Samaritan parable is that the love which God requires is often found *outside* the group of those who believe themselves to be his faithful people.

2. *Recipients.* The corollary of this account of the providers of care, is that the recipients are not defined by religious boundaries. Jesus rejected the company of the religiously respectable in favour of those who were not so secure in their social status and religious faith. The 'ultimate meanings and concerns' referred to by Clebsch and Jaekle are a common human experience, impinging equally on those within and those outside the membership of churches. Thus, in place of a

chaplaincy to the religious, there is required a pastoral care which responds to human distress wherever it is found, especially when that distress leads to a loss of hope in the power of love.

The identification of areas of general human need can be aided by paying attention to two dimensions, neglected in some traditional forms of pastoral care: (a) the *developmental* and (b) the *communal*. (a) The developmental approach (*see* HUMAN DEVELOPMENT) recognizes that different needs arise and different questions must be faced according to the stage of a person's life. It has long been recognized that adolescence (q.v.) raises specific problems, often related to faith (q.v.) and doubt (q.v.), but equally now attention is being paid to the special needs of children (q.v.), of families (q.v.), of the ageing (q.v.) and bereaved (q.v.) and of those in 'mid-life crisis' (*see* MIDDLE AGE). It is no accident that many of these critical times are often marked by religious rituals (*see* BAPTISM; FUNERALS; MEMBERSHIP OF THE CHURCH; MARRIAGE, THEOLOGY OF), since the issues which every human being, irrespective of church affiliation, will face at such times raise fundamental religious questions of faith, hope and love. Increasingly those who offer pastoral care are learning that help can be received only when the different places in life's pilgrimage are properly understood.

(b) Equally the recipients of pastoral care cannot be properly understood outside their social context (*see* JUSTICE; POLITICAL THEOLOGY; SOCIAL STRUCTURES; SYSTEMS PASTORAL CARE). Many of the sources of human distress are institutional or socio-political in character. A pastoral care which deals only with the distressed individual but ignores or condones social forces which cause the distress can be regarded as worse than useless, a tacit acceptance of injustices inimical to love. Thus the prophetic and the pastoral must be viewed as two aspects of a single ministry of love, and caring must include a critique of the structures of both church and society. Lambourne (see Wilson 1983) has suggested that, in place of its flirtation with psychotherapy and counselling, pastoral care should regard as its prime task the formation of a supportive and responsible community. Unfortunately, there is a dearth of literature following Lambourne's early, but undeveloped, ideas (but see Selby 1983).

3. *Aim.* The individual and communal well-being which pastoral care aims at needs to be given proper theological grounding. There has, in the past, been a polarization between pastoral theologies stressing proclamation, conversion and spiritual discipline. (Thurneysen (1962) provides an important example from the Reformed tradition) and views stressing practical acts of caring and counselling, the 'tender, solicitous concern' of the shepherding perspective (see Hiltner, 1958), but recent writing by Capps (1984), Nouwen (1977), Browning (1976) and the present author (Campbell 1981), has redefined the theological agenda. Pastoral acts are now seen to have a moral and a symbolic dimension, making them forms of proclamation or of moral guidance and support without the necessity for a translation into some special religious language. In Capps' terms, there is a *hermeneutic* of pastoral acts which reveals their religious significance, even when the agents themselves do not fully realize it (cf. the important element of surprise in the parable of the sheep and the goats, in Matt. 25).

Thus the theological grounding of pastoral care is seen in the symbolic significance as well as the practical usefulness of its practical acts of helping. For example, in experiencing the frustration and anger of young people, pressing them to undertake responsibility for their own future, but also challenging a society which permits high levels of unemployment (q.v.), a provider of pastoral care is proclaiming the love of God, which supports, comforts, challenges, but also seeks justice for the oppressed. Similarly, a prophetic pastoral care of the dementing elderly, will, as well as witnessing to the love which treasures all human life, also question the low priority given to research, support services and appropriate institutional care for this group of people. Thus pastoral care is revealed as the furtherance of a true humanism, proclaiming in action what is symbolized in belief by doctrines of incarnation (q.v.) and cross and resurrection (q.v.).

4. *Limits.* Finally, the high aim of pastoral care for human well-being must be qualified by an awareness of its limits. The pastoral ministry of Christians is carried out in a complex world in which numerous agencies are operating for good and for ill. A confidence in the omni-competence of pastoral care must be avoided. Often the most caring

pastoral act is referral (q.v.) to other persons or agencies better qualified to act. In many other situations there is a sense of hopelessness not easily overcome, either because people seem incapable of genuinely receiving help (see COLLUSION; MANIPULATION) or because their social circumstances seem irremediable. The hope for human well-being of pastoral action is qualified by an awareness of the 'not yet', of the Kingdom yet to come, and the realization that the kingdoms of this world pay little heed to the vulnerable plea of love for all humankind. Often those offering pastoral care will feel wholly lacking in the knowledge, leadership and courage of the shepherd, knowing more of Good Friday than of Easter Day, feeling themselves to be wounded healers, more vulnerable than victorious, of no account in the company of the successful and self-confident, knowing only the unpopular, and seemingly irrelevant, wisdom of the fool (see Campbell 1981).

Browning, D., *The Moral Context of Pastoral Care* (Fortress, Philadelphia, 1976). Campbell, A.V., *Rediscovering Pastoral Care* (Darton Longman & Todd 1981); *Paid to Care? the Limits of Professionalism in Pastoral Care* (SPCK 1985). Capps, D., *Pastoral Care and Hermeneutics* (Fortress, Philadelphia, 1984). Clebsch, W.A. and Jaekle, C.R., *Pastoral Care in Historical Perspective* (Harper, New York, 1967). Hiltner, S., *Preface to Pastoral Theology* (Abingdon, New York, 1958). Nouwen, H.J., *The Living Reminder* (Seabury, New York, 1977). Selby, P., *Liberating God: Private Care and Public Struggle* (SPCK, 1983). Thurneysen, E., *A Theology of Pastoral Care* (John Knox, 1962). Wilson, M. (ed.), *Explorations in Health and Salvation: Selected Papers of R.A. Lambourne* (Birmingham Univ., 1983).

ALASTAIR V. CAMPBELL

See also: PASTORAL CARE: HISTORY; PASTORAL COUNSELLING; PASTORAL STUDIES; PASTORAL THEOLOGY; PRACTICAL THEOLOGY.

PASTORAL CARE: ASPECTS
See: CHILDREN; DISCIPLINE; EVANGELISM; JUSTICE; LETTER-WRITING; MORAL ISSUES; NEW TESTAMENT; ORGANIZATIONS; PARISH; POLITICAL THEOLOGY; PREACHING; SALVATION; SOCIAL STRUCTURES; SYSTEMS.

PASTORAL CARE: HISTORY – THE EARLY CHURCH
Pastoral care as an expression either of a mutual bond of love or as a means of inculcating the ideals and discipline of the

Church among its members has characterized Christianity since its origins. The Lord's commands recorded in the New Testament laid on the Christian the duties of hospitality, feeding the hungry, compassion towards the destitute, and visiting the sick and prisoners (Matt. 25.34–7), to which were added others, inherited from the Pharisaic morality of much of the inter-testamental literature, such as almsgiving and securing a decent burial for the dead (Tobit 1.3, 1.18, 2.7 and compare 1.16–17, feeding the hungry and destitute).

These duties remained individual. Believing in the approaching Coming, there was no attempt to change society – slavery, for instance, was accepted as an institution (see Paul's Letter to Philemon, and Ignatius of Antioch, *Polycarp*, IV.5). Pastoral care concentrated on the maintenance of those moral and ethical prescriptions that would safeguard the Christian's holiness and so ensure his salvation.

Thus, the guidance of Christians in day-to-day living is a prominent feature in Pauline and other New Testament letters. Apart from the Apostle's admonition to live worthily, accepting that 'your body is a temple of the Holy Spirit . . . So glorify God in your body' (1 Cor. 6.19–20), there was the practice of mutual correction and edification. 'Encourage one another and build one another up' (1 Thess. 5.11). An offender under discipline should be warned as a brother, not treated as an enemy (2 Thess. 3.15). A generation later, the writer of the Letter to the Hebrews wrote with equal firmness, 'But exhort one another every day, as long as it is called "today", that none of you be hardened by the deceitfulness of sin' (Heb. 3.13).

The first decades of the 2nd century saw the emergence of the bishop, or presbyter-bishop, as the leader of each Christian community. Pastoral care as well as the administration of the sacraments became increasingly his responsibility. 'Do you follow the bishop as Jesus Christ follows the Father and the presbytery as the apostles: and reverence the deacons as the command of God. No one is to do any church business without the bishop' (Ignatius, *To the Smyrnaeans* 4). This may be an extreme statement but it indicates how, in Antioch at least, pastoral care was devolving on to the bishop and clergy.

One can, however, point to the two other tendencies at this time. First, at Rome the prophet Hermas shows that 'bishops' were in charge of dispensing hospitality and sheltering the destitute and widows (*Similitudes* IX, 27.2). It is not sure who these *'episcopoi'* were, and even whether they were clergy. Moreover, the general duties expected of the Christian included pastoral work, 'ministering to widows, looking after orphans and destitute, redeeming from distress the servants of God' (*Mandates* VIII.10). Duties towards widows and orphans were also stressed in *Barnabas* (*c.* 130), almsgiving in *2 Clement* (*c.* 100) and emphasis is placed in the *Apology* of Aristides (*c.* 145), as in Tobit, on securing a proper burial for the poor. It would seem that whether under episcopal supervision or not, down to the mid-2nd century pastoral care was considered as among the duties of every Christian towards his neighbour.

So far as discipline was concerned, confessors, being men and women specially favoured by Christ and partakers of the Spirit, were regarded as being empowered to 'bind and loose' on earth. The martyrs of Lyons, for instance, were praised in 177, for having 'bound none and loosed all' (Eusebius, *Hist. Eccl.* V.2.7) and, indeed, had restored some Christians who had lapsed under intolerable pressure.

Nonetheless, during the 2nd century, a rudimentary system of penitential discipline was growing up, which it was becoming the responsibility of the bishop to administer. Hermas narrates that the Angel of Repentance permitted the restoration of his adulterous wife with the statement, 'There is but one repentance to the servants of God' (*Mandates* IV.1.3). This was an act of divine mercy in recognition of human weakness. Repentance, too, was to be a public act: 'in church' and 'on the Lord's Day, gather yourselves together and give thanks, having first confessed your transgressions' (*Didaché* 14.1, written *c.* 100); and from Irenaeus, *c.* 185 (*Against Heresies* 1.13) confessions would be made 'openly', and no doubt in front of the bishop or his representative. In the *Didascalia*, a Syrian document reflecting the situation *c.* 200, the bishop is described as 'the high priest who loosed you from your sins and repentance regenerated you by water' (*Didasc.*, ed. R.H. Connolly, ch. 7).

By the beginning of the 3rd century, however, one may detect early signs of a difference of outlook regarding pastoral discipline in the Latin-speaking and Greek-speaking churches respectively. In the West, Tertullian, writing (*c.* 200) *De Paenitentia* (*On Repentance*), describes the ordeal of exomologesis or public penance. Derived from practices prescribed in the Pentateuch such as Num. 19.7 (the use of ashes of a heifer to purify uncleanliness) – and reinforced by references to prophecies relating to the last times (Joel 2.12) as to rending garments, fasting and weeping – penitents would be dressed in sackcloth and, after undergoing stringent fasts, would confess their faults in public, weeping and 'rolling at the feet of presbyters imploring forgiveness'. Even then, the three deadly sins, inherited from Judaism, adultery, apostasy or idolatry, and bloodshed, could be forgiven by God alone. No 'human satisfaction' could avail.

If Carthage was to maintain the rigorist tradition, Rome under Pope Callistus (218–22) adopted a more lenient view. Whatever the exact intention may have been, the effect of Callistus's 'edict' was to allow the reconciliation of adulterers, even if they were clergy. Hippolytus and Tertullian, writing *De Pudicitia* (*On Modesty and Purity*), protested in vain.

In the East, a less legalistic and more ethical view of penance and the responsibilities of the bishop towards the penitent was emerging. Clement of Alexandra, *c.* 190, not only followed Hermas in admitting one post-baptismal sin and repentance, but allowed for the grading of sins as between the less and the more deliberate. Moreover, gross sins, such as adultery, were interpreted in terms of allegory, as 'vain opinion', while theft was 'plagiarism', 'the imitation of true philosophy' (*Miscellanies* VI, 142 and 143). Origen (*Homil. V on Leviticus* 4), while maintaining that sins should be confessed first in private and then publicly, strips the process of retribution. The priest is one who 'knows the discipline of compassion and sympathy . . . a learned and merciful physician'. The role of the priest was to admonish, exhort and instruct the sinner.

Penitential discipline was therefore well established as part of the responsibilities of the bishop and his clergy by the first half of the 3rd century. In Cyprian's Carthage (*c.* 250) there seems to have been a formalized system of steps which the sinner had to take before his 'rehabilitation at the hands of the bishop and clergy' (Cyprian, *Letters* XV.1. and XVI.2). *Exomologesis* with its attendant humiliation was reserved for graver sins, such as

191

adultery (*Letter* 4.4). In addition, members of certain professions, such as actors and circus performers, were excluded from the Church on moral grounds (*Letter* 2).

The Decian persecution in 250 shattered this carefully constructed system. What was workable for individual sinners was impossible in face of mass apostasies. Cyprian's Councils of 251 and 252 restored episcopal control over the Christian community as a whole, deciding that the lapsed should not be denied reconciliation for all time, but should be eligible for readmission after shorter or longer terms of penance. Even apostates, if penitent, could be readmitted on their deathbeds. The North African Church was not notably more severe in its discipline than some other churches in the west. Soon after the end of the Great Persecution there, in 305, the Council of Elvira in south-eastern Spain, castigated sexual offences and many of its canons finished inexorably 'it is decreed that he cannot be reconciled even at the end'.

In the East, greater emphasis was placed on denial to the sinner of the sacraments. In 255, Gregory the Wonderworker, was confronted with the fact of Christians in Pontus siding in various ways with the invading barbarians against their fellow-provincials. The canonical letter that he circulated to the churches under his control divided the penitents into 'weepers' and 'mourners' who were condemned to standing outside the church beseeching the faithful to intercede for them, the 'hearers' and 'kneelers' who were assimilated to catechumens, and the 'co-standers' who might join in the services but were still denied the communion. None, indeed, was denied hope of restoration. At the Council of Nicaea in 325 this viewpoint was confirmed; apostates even being eligible for restoration after two years among the 'hearers', seven years among the 'kneelers' and two years among the 'co-standers' (Canon XI).

During the almost-three centuries of the Church's existence, practices and attitudes that had started as the mutual pastoral concern of Christians for the maintenance of conduct worthy of the Spirit within them, had developed into an elaborate penitential system supervised by the bishop or his representatives. In this, eastern and western Christendom reflected different approaches to the problem of pastoral care. The canons of Elvira and Nicaea respectively illustrate the pattern of the pastoral ministry in the two

halves of the Roman world at the moment of the Church's triumph.

Frend, W.H.C., *The Rise of Christianity* (Fortress, Philadelphia, 1984), ch. 12. **Greenslade, S.L.,** *Shepherding the Flock* (SCM, London, 1967); 'The Unit of Pastoral Care in the Early Church', *Studies in Church History* II, ed. G. Cuming (Nelson, 1963). **Kirk, K.E.,** *Conscience and its Problems* (Longmans, 1933). **McNeill, J.T.,** *A History of the Cure of Souls* (SCM, 1952), especially chs. 4 and 5. **Porchmann, B.,** *Penance and the Anointing of the Sick,* Eng. tr. by F. Courtney (Burns & Oates, 1964). **Telfer, W.,** *The Office of a Bishop* (Darton Longman & Todd, 1962).

W.H.C. FREND

See also: NEW TESTAMENT AND PASTORAL CARE.

PASTORAL CARE: HISTORY – THE ANGLICAN TRADITION

'Anglican' is here generally taken to mean the post-Reformation period in the English Church, but with the important proviso that Anglicanism always claims continuity with past ages, and back to the New Testament. 'Pastoral care' is an ambiguous phrase, comprising several distinct, if inter-related areas. Those treated here are: (1) love, care and concern for the individual; (2) responsibility for groupings within society; (3) spiritual direction.

1. Love of neighbour is a dominical injunction universally applicable within any Christian society, but within the Anglican pastoral tradition it takes on two specific characteristics: (a) There is a pronounced *domestic* emphasis as compared with a more clerical and authoritarian stress seen elsewhere, and traceable to the central Benedictine influence on English religion. It is well illustrated by George Herbert in the early 17th century and by John Keble in the 19th. There is a pronounced doctrinal stress on the unity of the Church in opposition to clerical-lay gulf of the pre-Reformation period. (b) It follows that overall pastoral care of the sick, poor and distressed is seen as the concern of the Church, with the laity taking a leading part. Although co-operation between clergy and nobility is universal in Christian countries, from the 17th to the 19th centuries Anglicanism produced a unique partnership between parson and squire. Their usually large families freely accepted care for their dependants as God-given duty, not only in almsgiving and relief of need but also in teaching, support

and moral guidance. The pre-industrial village was a Christian family in much the same way as a Benedectine abbey.

2. The late 18th and early 19th centuries, socially transformed by the Industrial Revolution, witnessed a sad decline in Christian, and especially clerical responsibility; the laxity of the age has been treated often enough. Reaction arose from two sources: the evangelical stress on the need for individual piety and that of the Oxford Reform on the corporate Church as a redemptive organism. The two inter-acted in the advent of Christian Socialism led by such men as Wilberforce, Maurice and Kingsley. The interpretation of pastoral care moved from direct alleviation of personal need and poverty – assumed to be of the natural order – to reform of social conditions that created those needs. Latterly, and up to the present day, the psychological work of Freud, Jung and others again changed the emphasis to what is now called pastoral counselling (q.v.). To summarize, pastoral care in the 17th century was interpreted as personal care and almsgiving, in the 18th and 19th centuries this was supplemented by a more general attack on prevalent social evils, and today by psychological techniques concerned with mental aberration and emotional stress. Plainly the stages are not mutually exclusive.

3. Throughout the whole period, and for centuries before, Anglican–English pastoral care contains a prominent emphasis on spiritual direction; the positive attempt to draw out and nurture the faith, piety, gifts and graces of individual Christians of all types and social strata. Manuals of direction such as the *Ancrene Riwle* from the late 12th century and Hilton's *Scale of Perfection* in the 14th century exerted influence long after the Reformation period. The Anglican divines of the 17th century, notably Taylor, Sanderson, Cosin and Ken, continued the tradition, supported by numerous laywomen such as Margaret Godolphin, Suzanna Hopton and Mary Caning. A large number of devotional manuals such as *The Whole Duty of Man* also appeared at this time. After the inevitable late-18th-century lapse, spiritual direction returned to prominence with the Oxford Reform. This century has produced those who have made this pastoral ministry their central concern, such as Somerset Ward, Evelyn Underhill and Eric Abbott. This trend continues.

These three facets of pastoral care are common to all Christian traditions, yet their particular interaction and emphases here combine to give the Anglican interpretation its particular orginality.

Holloway, R. (ed.), *The Anglican Tradition* (Morehouse-Barlow, 1984). McAdoo, H.R., *The Spirit of Anglicanism* (A. & C. Black, 1965). Moorman, J.R.H., *The Anglican Spiritual Tradition* (Darton Longman & Todd, 1983). Wand, J.W.C., *Anglicanism in History and Today* (Weidenfeld & Nicolson, 1961).

MARTIN THORNTON

See also: SPIRITUAL DIRECTION.

PASTORAL CARE: HISTORY – THE REFORMED TRADITION

By 'the Reformed tradition' we understand that branch of the Reformation originating in Switzerland, associated chiefly with John Calvin (1509–64).

The ideal of a Reformed church, towards which ministry tended, was a believing, disciplined community gathered round the Lord's table. The marks of the true Church were the pure preaching of the Word of God and the right administration of the sacraments (Calvin, *Institutes*, IV,i,9) and to these was added 'ecclesiastical discipline uprightly ministered' (*Scots Confession*, 1560, Art. XVIII). Preaching has a pastoral function, breaking the bread of life to hungry souls, and the Lord's Supper itself is 'a singuler medicine for all poore sicke creatures' (Knox, *Liturgy*).

The assurance of forgiveness comes not through auricular confession and priestly absolution, but through preaching. 'We must always beware of dreaming of any power apart from the preaching of the gospel.' But the person whose conscience is not relieved by public preaching may go 'to his pastor and hear these words of the gospel specially addressed to him, "Son, be of good cheer: thy sins be forgiven thee" (Matt. 9.2)' (Calvin, *Inst.*, III,iv,14). Pastoral care is thus preaching in private.

Ecclesiastical discipline, like preaching, has a public and private aspect. Discipline ('discipling') may be held to include both catechizing and correction. Catechizing might be in public exercises, as with the children each Sunday afternoon, or in private, as with households in preparation for the sacrament. In private exercises the pastor could deal not only with ignorance, but with doubts and difficulties.

As regards correction, the Reformed churches dealt only with outward offences, leaving it to God to try the heart; but they maintained the ancient distinction of public repentance for public and scandalous offences and private repentance for secret offences. 'The principal use of public discipline is not for the offender himself, but for the church' (Richard Baxter, *Reformed Pastor*, 1656). Nevertheless, the orders for public repentance show considerable pastoral concern. In Knox's *Form*, the penitent is assured and encouraged and the congregation is admonished, remembering their own sins, to forgive and forget. 'Accept and embrace him as ane member of Christ's body; let none tak upon him to reproche or accuse him for any offences that before this hour he hath committed.' (cf. Baxter, *op. cit.*). The same spirit is required for private discipline 'that our admonitions procede of a godly zeale and conscience, rather seeking to wynne our brother then to slaunder him'.

Pastoral care in the Reformed tradition develops from these sources: (1) private dealing with those whose conscience is not eased by public preaching; (2) catechizing of households; (3) discipline of offenders.

(1) From this there developed, in 17th-century Puritanism, a considerable and intricate dealing with cases of conscience, and, in the later evangelical revivals, a wrestling with souls; modern 'crisis-counselling' may be seen as a descendant of this. The Reformed pastor did not aim to be a continuing 'spiritual director'. 'He is a physician for a crisis' (McNeill 1951, p. 200). Visitation of the sick was given a high priority in Reformed churches. The pastor went, not to perform ritual acts, but to speak with the afflicted and pray with them. The conversation and the prayer were adapted to the particular needs of the sick person, the pastor 'like a skilfull phisition, framyng his medicine accordyng as the disease requireth' (Knox, *op. cit.*). Sickness, as sent by God, was seen as a call to penitence and resignation; and since the outcome was not infrequently death, a call to prepare for that eventuality. But the practical needs of the sick were not neglected.

(2) From the catechizing of households there developed one characteristic pastoral practice of Reformed churches – systematic parish visitation. In all the later manuals for pastors,

the faithful discharge of this duty is commended. By it, pastoral care is seen as for the strong and happy as well as for the sick and troubled.

(3) The stern but loving discipline seen in the earliest documents of the Reformation is still to be found in Richard Baxter a century later. However, the tendency for discipline to become legalistic and judicial rather than gracious and pastoral was irresistible, and there is ample evidence for this not least in 18th-century Scotland. The decay of public discipline was partly because of social change and partly in revulsion against a loveless discipline, and the treatment of offenders began to be left to the pastoral admonition of the minister.

The involvement of church courts, both in catechizing and in discipline, points to another characteristic of Reformed churches – the eldership. In the Church of Scotland, for example, ruling elders, together with the minister, form the Kirk Session, which is responsible for discipline, and which admits new members to the Lord's table. Since 1648 each elder has had the oversight of a district, and reports on it to the Kirk Session. The sharing of authority between minister and elders helps to counterbalance a tendency towards clericalism in the Reformed churches, arising from their stress on preaching. But the elder's pastoral function is limited – it is no part of his office to pray with the sick.

Letter-writing (q.v.) was used pastorally by the Reformers (especially Calvin and Knox) and their successors, dealing, with much tenderness and sensitivity, with friends in sickness or grief, or exhorting steadfastness in persecution. Yet along with the brotherliness, there is found in all the literature a strong note of authority: the authority not of the priest, but of the preacher, who speaks from God. The church tends to be seen as 'the flock' which is dependent entirely on the pastor. In the many books which give pastoral advice there is little sense of a reciprocal relationship between pastor and flock.

The 20th century has seen a crisis of authority in the ministry. The confident authority of former centuries crumbled before the modern world, and, for many, neither biblical theology nor fundamentalism can revive it. Writers like J.G. McKenzie and Harry Guntrip in Britain, and Anton Boisen in the United States, performed a great service in helping pastors to see depth psychology as a friend and not a foe. But by mid-century pastoral care had lost its nerve and its theological base, and was becoming amateur psychotherapy. It is a welcome development that begins to recover a theology of pastoral care through a discovery of genuine authority – that not of the master but of the servant, the authority of vulnerability.

Baxter, Richard, *The Reformed Pastor* (1656) is the greatest book on its theme. Hiltner, S., *A Preface to Pastoral Theology* (Abingdon, 1958) sought to use theology constructively. McNeill, J.T., *A History of the Cure of Souls* (Harper, 1951) is indispensable. Thureysen, E., *A Theology of Pastoral Care* (E.T. 1962) gives a Barthian view. Vinet, Alexandre, *Pastoral Theology* (Neuchatel, 1850) and van Oosterzee, J.J., *Practical Theology* (Utrecht, 1978) were both widely used and translated. Watson, John, *The Cure of Souls* (1898) deserves mention for the rare virtue of wit. Campbell, A.V., *Rediscovering Pastoral Care* (Darton Longman & Todd, 1981) points a way to a new view of authority and integrity in Pastoral Care.

JAMES A. WHYTE

See also: BIBLE: PASTORAL USE; DISCIPLINE AS PASTORAL CARE; PREACHING AND PASTORAL CARE.

PASTORAL CARE: HISTORY – THE ROMAN CATHOLIC TRADITION

In the early Middle Ages pastoral care remained much the same as it had been in previous centuries. Centred on the liturgy (q.v.) it necessarily involved bishops, presbyters and deacons who celebrated the liturgy or had certain roles to perform in it, for instance in the sacraments of initiation. Instruction and preaching were given in this context though not exclusively. The care of the sick received expression in the sacrament of anointing (q.v.), and the dying were given Holy Communion. Each diocese also undertook a large-scale work of welfare: caring for widows, dedicated virgins, orphans and the poor, for all of whom a portion of the people's offerings at the Eucharist was set aside.

Towards the end of the 5th century, as the Church began to move into rural areas, a presbyter – still a member of the episcopal household and usually accompanied by lesser ministers – would set up a chapel for the celebration of the liturgy. Gradually such clergy acquired a certain independence and with it the full care of the people.

With the rise of monasticism, monks, who normally settled in undeveloped areas, took on the pastoral care of the people around them. Benedictines were by rule obliged to welcome guests, pilgrims and the distressed. As in the course of time they appropriated parishes, the care of the people attached to them devolved on the monks.

In the 8th and 9th centuries Charlemagne, with the assistance of the English monk Alcuin and others, did much to improve the education of the clergy and by legislation over many years endeavoured to secure adequate pastoral care of the people committed to their charge. With the collapse of the Carolingian empire all had to begin again. Pastoral renewal came only with Gregory VII (d. 1085), whose work was carried forward by synods and councils, reaching a climax in the strongly pastoral Fourth Council of the Lateran in 1215.

The foundation of the Dominican and Franciscan Orders in the first decades of the 13th century brought a new and important element to the pastoral care of the people. The ministry of preaching (q.v.), much neglected by the secular clergy, received a new emphasis, though the friars' sacramental ministrations were regarded by parish priests as an invasion of their rights.

Though much concerned with doctrine, the Council of Trent (1545–63) inaugurated a new era. It redressed the moral decline of the later Middle Ages, reminded bishops that they were first and foremost pastors and imposed on them the duty of preaching and instructing their people regularly. Its insistence that bishops should set up seminaries for the pastoral training of the clergy eventually produced a body of priests who in the centuries to come would be very active in the service of the people. Examples of pastoral care were St Charles Borromeo in northern Italy, Jean Jacques Olier in 17th-century France, and above all St Vincent de Paul whose work was all-embracing, reaching from pastoral formation of priests to the care of the sick, the poor and the orphan. The 'internal missions' of St John Eudes and others revived the faith and moral life of thousands who had been much neglected. Yet others undertook the Christian education of both boys and girls. The Jesuits were prominent in the sphere of spiritual direction (q.v.). Redemptorists and Passionists were active especially in Italy in the 18th century.

The 19th century was marked by a proliferation of new religious communities of both men and women who undertook, usually in collaboration with the parish clergy, every kind of task, from education to the care of the blind and the deaf, the sick and the dying. This work continues. In the latter half of the century the Church showed an increasing concern for working-people and their rights, as witness the encyclical letter of Leo XIII, *Rerum Novarum* (1891).

The main feature of the 20th century has been the increasing part taken by the laity in pastoral work which has embraced the old, the poor, the handicapped and alcoholics, as well as the cause of peace and justice. Their role in the life of the Church as promoted by successive popes, and their status and apostolate were endorsed by the Second Vatican Council, all of whose findings are marked by a strong pastoral emphasis. The clergy are at the service of the people, the people must give loving service to each other, and the whole Church is a servant church that seeks to care for all who are willing to receive its service.

The New Catholic Encyclopedia (McGraw-Hill, New York, 1967), vol. 10, pp. 1081–2, s.v. 'Pastoral Theology'; other articles under 'Pastor', 'Pastoral', etc. For the Council of Trent see E. Outram Evenett, *The Spirit of the Counter-Reformation*, (CUP, 1968). *Concilium*, vol. 3, no.1, (Burns Oates/T. & T. Clark, 1965); there is one issue every year on pastoral matters. **Delummeau, J.**, *Catholicism between Luther and Voltaire* (Darton Longman & Todd, 1982). **Flannery, A.** (ed.), The Conciliar and Post Conciliar Documents – Vatican II (Dominican Pubs., Dublin, 1983). **Rahner, K.**, *et al.* (eds.), *Sacramentum Mundi* (Burns Oates, 1969), vol. 4, pp. 359–64, s.v. 'Pastoral Ministry' and other articles. **Rogier, L.J.,.** *et al.* (eds.), *The Christian Centuries*, vol. 1 (Darton Longman & Todd, 1964), vol. 2 (1969), vol. 5 (1978); 3 and 4 not yet in English translation.

J.D. Crichton

See also: ANOINTING; CONFESSION; RITES AND RITUALS; SPIRITUAL DIRECTION.

PASTORAL CARE IN JUDAISM

In Judaism counselling is done by laypersons as well as rabbis. Incumbent upon all Jews is the responsibility for counselling the sick and comforting the bereaved. In addition to the commandment or *mitzvah*, Jews are enjoined to emulate God who practises loving-kindness and cares for the individual soul. Although Jews lack the tradition of pastoral care familiar to the Christian clergy, recent years have seen the rise of a counselling emphasis among

rabbis. To be sure, there were models of rabbinical counselling in history, the most representative being the master in the Hasidic tradition, beginning in Eastern Europe in the 18th century. Rabbis have always taken the role of masters or teachers and were expected to instruct communities and individuals in the application of the Torah to the issues of everyday life and to ethical and personal dilemmas. Much of this counselling was done via correspondence in the form of 'questions and answers' and the more learned the rabbi, the more authoritative his counsel. The work of the late Rabbi Joshua Loth Liebman and the examples of counselling done by contemporaries like Harold Kushner and Earl Grollman can be taken as indications of the growing popularity of rabbis in the field of counselling and religious psychotherapy.

Nearly all Jewish seminaries offer training programmes in counselling, and currently the volume by Robert L. Katz documents the theological basis for rabbinical counselling. Some rabbis function as chaplains in the armed forces and in hospitals and homes for the aged. Counselling is largely assumed to be part of the general master role of the rabbi, and only a few take advanced training and allocate a significant part of their time to it. Jews have been active in the field of psychiatry and social work, and of late efforts are being made to determine the possibilities and limitations of the clergy offering religio-psychological assistance in the framework of Judaism and the synagogue.

More traditional rabbis will draw more extensively from the body of religious law in counselling individuals, seeking to harmonize the teachings of Judaism with the insights of the social sciences as far as possible. Most rabbis, traditional or otherwise, attempt to practise empathy (q.v.) and to individualize their approach. It is likely that the model of the Christian pastor has had its effect on the Jewish clergy. There is a growing concern with personal salvation and with the psychological significance of religious processes like repentance and prayer. The problem most commonly brought to rabbis is in the area of marital adjustment. Spousal adjustment and parent–child conflicts are typically considered the concern of the rabbis who generally are capable of suspending moralistic judgements and of providing insight as well as alternatives for more fulfilling relationships. Other areas of rabbinical concern are problems in the life-cycle such as ageing (q.v.), bereavement (q.v.), and loneliness (q.v.). In recent years the increase of marriages out of the faith as well as marriages among born Jews and Jews by choice have led to increased consultation with rabbis (*see*: MIXED MARRIAGES). Depending on their variety of interpretation of Judaism, rabbis approach these problems differently, although nearly all concern themselves with balancing the mandates of Judaism with the particular needs and problems of individual Jews.

Katz, R.L., *Pastoral Care in the Jewish Tradition* (Fortress, Philadelphia, 1985). **Kushner, H.S.,** *When Bad Things Happen to Good People* (Pan, 1982).

ROBERT L. KATZ

PASTORAL CARE IN SCHOOLS
The welfare dimension of schooling.

The usage is of recent origin. Ribbins and Lang (1985) were unable to trace any such use of the term in a published document before 1954. The religious antecedents of the use of the concept of 'pastoral care' in schools and colleges are widely acknowledged in educational circles, but few attempts have been made to explore its theological origins. Of those who have undertaken this task both Dooley and Hughes (see Best *et al.* 1980) question whether the heavily paternalistic connotations that the term carries from its original religious context makes it an appropriate one to use in educational settings. These reservations are widely shared amongst educationalists, but this has not prevented the term 'pastoral care' from becoming a part of the normal vocabulary of teachers today.

Despite this wide usage, and despite the fact that pastoral care is found in some institutionalized form in almost every secondary school in England and Wales, it still lacks a truly authoritative definition. The HMI (1979) suggest a set of tasks which they found the majority of secondary schools expect their pastoral systems to perform: '(a) attempt to co-ordinate consideration of pupils' personal, social and academic development; (b) facilitate the development of good relations between teachers and pupils; (c) try to ensure that each pupil knows and is known by a particular adult; (d) make available relevant information through the development of effective communication and reward systems; (e) involve parents and outside agencies in the work of the school where appropriate; (f) enable someone to respond quickly and appro-

priately to pupils' problems or indeed to anticipate a problem which might arise; (g) by these means to improve the learning of pupils' (p. 219). More recently, the Welsh HMI (1982) have distinguished two further tasks which involve 'applying disciplinary sanctions [and] providing educational and careers guidance' (p. 1). Finally, during the 1980s the idea of a 'pastoral curriculum' designed to facilitate the personal and social development of pupils has received a good deal of support (Marland in Best, *et al.* 1980).

To undertake this formidable catalogue of tasks most secondary schools have set up pastoral systems described by the HMI (1982) as 'generally substantial administrative structures involving many teachers . . .' (p. 1). The ramifications of this provision are enormous. Almost every teacher in secondary schools will have some kind of tutorial responsibility for a designated group of pupils, and it has been estimated that 'some 35,000 responsibility-holders [carry] allowances [for pastoral care] in schools throughout the country, being heads of year, heads of house, [and] as people responsible for personal, educational and vocational guidance' (Marland 1983, p. 6) at a cost of 'some 178 million pounds . . . on pastoral responsibility post salaries above their scale-one equivalent' (*ibid.*).

Much of this development took place, largely unaccompanied by any research or even a published literature (see Ribbins and Best 1985), in the wake of comprehensive secondary reorganization in the 1960s and early 1970s. The first book which deals explicitly with pastoral care was not published until 1974 (Marland). Thus the year 1982 represents something of a landmark, with the setting up of a National Association of Pastoral Care in Education and with the publication of the first journal, *Pastoral Care in Education*, dealing specifically with this topic.

However, various attempts have been made to clarify the concept of 'pastoral care' and to relate it to the 'academic', 'disciplinary' and other dimensions of schooling. In one such attempt, Best and Ribbins (1983) argue that 'pastoral care' should be understood as one expression of the commitment of schools to the 'good' of the child, through the development of autonomy, rationality, sensitivity, morality and the like. As such, it is certain to share areas of concern in common with both the academic and disciplinary activities of the school. But such a commitment to the 'good' may be expressed in many ways, and there are characteristics of pastoral care which make it quite distinctive. In fact, the differences in the grounds upon which academic, pastoral and disciplinary activities are justified, in the nature of the relationships between the child and the teacher as instructor, carer and disciplinarian, and in the practices appropriate to each, provide a basis for claiming a distinctiveness for each of these teacher roles.

In the case of pastoral care, the 'good' of the pupil is conceived of as his or her personal (physical, social, moral, and emotional) welfare. The aim is not so much with the development of the educated person, as the facilitation of the secure and happy child. The fundamental principle which underlies this part of a school's provision is the recognition of the child as a person whose individual happiness, personal integrity and social development can be enhanced only by the school actively engaging in something more than just teaching the academic curriculum and maintaining order.

The set of activities which this entails may be further differentiated as one or more of three kinds depending upon the part they also play in the academic or disciplinary dimensions of the work of the school. (1) Some activities are aimed exclusively at the personal welfare of the individual child and are justified on the principle that people matter regardless of their educational pursuits. (2) Other aspects of the pastoral work of the school may be executed by activities which serve in common its academic and/or its disciplinary purposes. An example of an activity which is both instructional in an academic sense which may yet be pastoral insofar as it is aimed at resolving the problems of individual pupils might be a lesson in careers education which is also aimed at helping the student to make a wise vocational choice. (3) There are other activities which, whilst they are clearly located within the pastoral dimension, may yet perform a servicing or facilitating function for the academic or disciplinary purposes of the school. A case in point would be helping children to resolve or contain worrying personal problems which might otherwise preoccupy them and inhibit their performance during lessons.

Our understanding of 'pastoral care' and of its practice within all kinds of educational settings, has undergone a number of changes

over time (Ribbins and Best 1984, identify five main, overlapping phases). Should it survive in some institutionalized form till the end of this century, and this is by no means certain (see Best and Ribbins 1983) then it is not hard to predict that further changes will take place.

Best, R. et al., Perspectives on Pastoral Care (Heinemann, 1980); includes chapters by Dooley, Hughes and Marland. Best, R. and Ribbins, P., 'Rethinking the Pastoral–Academic Split' (Pastoral Care in Education, 1(1), 1983), pp. 11–18. Best, R. et al., Education and Care (Heinemann, 1983). HMI, Aspects of Secondary Education (HMSO, 1979); Pastoral Care in the Comprehensive Schools of Wales (HMSO, Cardiff, 1982). Marland, M., Information Skills and the Whole-School Curriculum, paper presented to the British Library Conference, 12 Oct. 1983 (mimeo); Pastoral Care (Heinemann, 1973). Ribbins, P. and Best, R., 'Pastoral Care: Theory, Practice and the Growth of Research' in P. Land and M. Marland (eds.), New Directions in Pastoral Care in Educaton (Blackwell, 1983). Ribbins, P. and Land, P., 'Pastoral Care in Education', entry in The International Encyclopedia of Education (Pergamon, 1985).

PETER RIBBINS

See also: SCHOOL CHAPLAINCY.

PASTORAL COUNSELLING
The utilization by clergy of counselling and psychotherapeutic methods to enable individuals, couples and families to handle their personal crises and problems in living constructively.

This modern expression of the ancient ministry of pastoral care draws on insights and techniques from three primary sources—contemporary understandings of human personality and interpersonal relationships from the human sciences (especially psychology); therapeutic methods from one or more of a variety of current counselling and psychotherapeutic approaches; and biblical, theological, and historical resources from the Judaeo-Christian heritage.

Each of the five traditional pastoral care functions is expressed in contemporary pastoral counselling: (1) The healing function is expressed in depth pastoral counselling (also called pastoral psychotherapy) aimed at helping those with major psychological and spiritual problems. (2) The sustaining function is expressed in supportive, crisis, and bereavement counselling. (3) The guiding function is expressed in educative counselling (such as preparation for marriage), ethical guidance and spiritual direction. (4) The *reconciling* function is expressed in approaches such as marriage and family counselling designed to help people resolve interpersonal conflicts and increase the quality of their relationship. (5) The growth *nurturing* function is expressed in a variety of individual and small-group methods aimed at helping people enhance their lives and deal creatively with their developmental crises.

Pastoral counselling is unique (compared with counselling by secular professionals) in the ministerial identity (*see* PASTOR: IDENTITY AND ROLE), theological training, and ethical and faith orientation of its practitioners; the context in which it most often occurs – the pastoral care ministry of a gathered community of faith (*see* CHURCH, DOCTRINES OF); its use of religious resources (e.g. prayer, scripture, sacraments); and its underlying premise that spiritual growth is the ultimate and essential goal of all pastoral counselling, whatever the particular problems which brought persons for help.

Although clergy have offered guidance and support for people in crisis throughout the centuries of the Judaeo-Christian tradition (utilizing the particular psychology of each historical period), psychotherapeutically oriented pastoral counselling is a comparatively modern development. The antecedents of this movement include the growing interest since about 1870 in applying psychology to the work of ministry; the flowering of psychology of religion in the early decades of this century; the increasing use of psychological and counselling approaches by persons in religious education during the post-World War I surge of interest in psychology; the use of psychological resources by such prominent pastor-authors as Leslie D. Weatherhead in Britain and Harry Emerson Fosdick, John Sutherland Bonnell and Norman Vincent Peale in America; and the clinical pastoral education movement (q.v.) (beginning in America in the mid-1920s and developing somewhat later in other countries including Germany, the Netherlands, Switzerland and Britain). The pressure on chaplains during World War II to provide counselling help, and the surge of interest in psychological approaches to human problems following that war, provided a fertile social context within which the rapid development of pastoral counselling occurred during the late 1940s and in the 1950s and 1960s in America and in other countries.

'Pastoral counselling' describes both an essential function of clergy in parish and other general ministries, and also a growing speciality within the ministry. Specialization has been most prominent in America, but it is an increasing development in many other countries including Britain, where institutional chaplaincies, church-related counselling centres, and post-seminary clinical and academic training programmes in pastoral psychology and counselling are proliferating. The burgeoning international pastoral care and counselling movement has been both a response to and a stimulus to this world-wide development of pastoral counselling.

The field of pastoral counselling currently is in lively ferment. Among the trends which may point toward directions in which the movement will continue to evolve in the years ahead are these: increasing inter-cultural and international communication and cross-fertilization; determined efforts to transcend the middle-class, Protestant, North-American/European origins of the movement; a growing emphasis on the theological, ethical and ecclesiological dimension of pastoral counselling, including the integration of spiritual direction (q.v.) and spiritual healing (q.v.) with the psychotherapeutically oriented approaches; the utilization of more systems-oriented, 'right brain', non-analytical, and body-therapy methods; efforts to integrate the prophetic, social-change dimension of ministry with pastoral care and counselling (*see* POLITICAL THEOLOGY AND PASTORAL CARE); increasing training of lay pastoral care (q.v.) and crisis counselling teams; the increasing influence of feminist theologians and therapists, and women pastoral counsellors, on the movement.

Clinebell, Howard J., *Basic Types of Pastoral Care and Counselling* (SCM, 1984). **Dicks, Russel,** *Pastoral Work and Personal Counselling* (Macmillan, New York, 1944). **Hiltner, Seward,** *Pastoral Counselling* (Abingdon-Cokesbury, New York, 1949). **Johnson, Paul,** *Psychology of Pastoral Care* (Abingdon, New York, 1953). **Lake, Frank,** *Clinical Theology* (Darton Longman & Todd, 1966). **Oates, Wayne E.,** *The Christian Pastor* (Westminster, Philadelphia, 1951). **Weatherhead, Leslie,** *Psychology, Religion and Healing* (Hodder, 1951). **Wise, Caroll,** *Pastoral Counselling: Theory and Practice* (Harper, New York, 1951).

HOWARD CLINEBELL

See also: CLINICAL PASTORAL EDUCATION; COUNSELLING; PASTORAL CARE, NATURE OF; PRACTICAL THEOLOGY; PSYCHOTHERAPY.

PASTORAL EDUCATION

See: CLINICAL PASTORAL EDUCATION;
PLACEMENTS; TRAINING METHODS.

PASTORAL STUDIES

(1) Formally: (a) a group of post-graduate university courses; (b) some courses in applied theology in some degree courses; (c) professional courses in some theological colleges; (d) the related academic structures and associated teaching. (2) More generally: (a) areas of study related to ministry, clerical or lay; (b) a synonym for (e.g.) practical or pastoral theology. (3) Perhaps secularly for training for other 'pastoral' work.

Pastoral studies in British universities started in Birmingham (1963) under the guidance of R.A. Lambourne, followed by Cardiff and Manchester and within the Scottish departments of Practical Theology, notably at Edinburgh and St Andrews. These developments reflected the local opportunities but certain common ground can be discerned: (1) Courses are open, not specifically for clergy, reflecting the recognition that all Christians are engaged in mission. (2) Ministry is conceived as including the communal, the political, the educational, etc. as well as the more usual areas of casework and counselling. (3) The aim is to provide a context for training in pastoral skills within a critical understanding of ministry and the social sciences. (4) The inter-disciplinary context is crucial, demanding critical dialogue as well as mutual learning. (5) There has to be a loyalty to academic demands for critical conceptual awareness. (6) Supervised field education (*see* PLACEMENTS) is an essential academic teaching medium. (7) There is a proper theological task which relates both to the traditional disciplines and the discernment of theological reality in the reflection on praxis.

The emergence of pastoral studies reflects the theological concerns of the time and is part of the widespread interest in different aspects of applied theology. It is not always easy to distinguish from and is clearly dependent on, for example, doctrine, ethics, pastoral theology (q.v.). Time may bring gradual clarification.

Within the theological colleges pastoral studies expanded in the late 1970s, so that almost every denomination expects provision of some kind. In part it is a response to the need for professional training for clergy

comparable to that elsewhere. This was influenced by a series of reports, notably *Pastoral Care and Training of Ministers* (BCC 1969). Generally this has meant a new unit, with its own appointments, alongside the older subject areas, without too much success at cross-fertilization. There have, however, been valuable attempts to make theological reflection the core of unified training. In terms of curriculum it is increasingly normal, alongside or incorporating traditional topics (e.g. preaching, liturgy, ascetics), to introduce a study of (e.g.) society, human socialization, communication, administration. Also there is initiation into (e.g.) community work, youth work, counselling, teaching and management. At the same time the structuring and supervision (q.v.) of placements (q.v.), ecclesiastical and secular, is important. Some have found, especially for part-time students, reflection on experience the basis for learning. There are difficulties in holding in balance the pressures to equip students with skills, the demands, especially from special-interest groups, to try to be comprehensive, and the necessity to develop adequate, critical foundations to provide a basis for sustained practice. There is gradually emerging an awareness of the dangers of uncritical reliance on models taken from elsewhere and the need to create theologically adequate models.

Since 1970 teachers in the subject have come together regularly in the Universities Conference on Pastoral Studies, which has been instrumental in its development.

Pastoral Care and Training of Ministers (British Council of Churches, 1969). **Dyson, A.O.,** 'Pastoral Theology: towards a new discipline' (*Contact*, no. 78, 1983), pp. 2–8. **Elford, John,** 'Pastoral Theology at Manchester University' (*Contact*, no. 80, 1983), pp. 27–30. **Lambourne, R.A.,** *Explorations in Health and Salvation*, ed. M. Wilson (Institute for the Study of Worship and Religious Architecture, 1983), section III. **Pattison, Stephen,** 'Pastoral Studies: Dust Bin or Discipline?' (*Contact*, no. 80, 1983), pp. 22–6. **Wharton, Martin,** 'Pastoral Studies in an Anglican Theological College' (*Contact*, no. 78, 1983), pp. 9–13.

PAUL H. BALLARD

See also: CLINICAL PASTORAL EDUCATION; CLINICAL THEOLOGY; PASTORAL CARE, NATURE OF; PASTORAL THEOLOGY; PLACEMENTS; PRACTICAL THEOLOGY; SUPERVISION.

PASTORAL THEOLOGY

The theological study of the Church's action in its own life and towards society, in response to the activity of God.

Pastoral theology is at present an unstable concept, reflecting a variety of churchly traditions, theological movements and secular influences. Under this name or sometimes, ambiguously, as 'practical theology' (q.v.), a discipline is pursued which is less explicit in method and less defined in subject-matter than, say, biblical studies or church history. Partly this arises because of pastoral theology's oscillation between a status as an autonomous academic field and a status dictated by the demands of vocational practice and venerable tradition in the domestic life of the Church. In earlier times what are now called doctrinal, moral (q.v.), ascetical (q.v.) and pastoral theology were not carefully distinguished. Since the 18th century pastoral theology has been more and more treated as a separate sector with its own criteria of truthfulness. This development reflects the characteristic tendencies of the Enlightenment, with the growing professionalization of theology and of the clergy's work.

Six detectable uses of the term 'pastoral theology' indicate the wide range of theory and practice: (1) The theoretical and practical training of the clergy for their task, including preaching (q.v.), teaching, evangelism, sacramental ministry, counselling (q.v.), social action, visitation and church-extension. (2) More narrowly, the study of the priest's office, in relation to sacramental and juridical functions, especially penance (see CONFESSION). (3) Again more narrowly the theology of spiritual direction (q.v.) or guiding of souls, normally by the ordained minister, on the premise that ascetical theology, with moral theology as its correlate, is the true core of pastoral practice. (4) Again narrowly, the study and practice of Christian face-to-face counselling, normally by the ordained minister, e.g., Anton T. Boisen and the clinical pastoral education (q.v.) movement. (5) Socio-theological analysis, leading to principles which can promote the church's distinctive but relevant internal life and social action.   (6) An enterprise within systematic theology in which the study of human nature (q.v.) is pursued in conscious interaction with the behavioural and human sciences.

All six positions find dedicated theoreti-cians and practitioners. (Some theologians have exhibited coolness towards all forms of pastoral theology except that which concerns preaching, on the grounds that they elevate human effort above faith). Attention must be drawn to some major problems in all these positions, especially when one is commended in isolation.

Much recent pastoral theology, especially (4) above, has been unduly controlled by types of psychotherapeutic theory and practice to the relative exclusion of theological, ethical and prophetic considerations which represent the constant negative judgement and positive challenge of the Christian message. The frequent absence of such considerations in 1, 2 and 3 above should also be noted. In consequence, pastoral practice can easily be determined by secular fashion, obsolete church tradition, and parrot-like imitation of teacher by apprentice.

These types of pastoral theology (1–4 above) have also been notably individualistic, both in the sense that they have seen the individual, rather than the collectivity in relation with the individual, as the primary object of pastoral care, and in the sense that they have neglected the social setting of the individual. This weakness is now more and more recognized. Nevertheless new schemes of thought are required; collectivities are more than aggregates of individuals.

In many Christian traditions the clergy function as the chief agents of pastoral care and, since most clergy and theologians are male, pastoral theology has been shaped in no small measure by a male clerical culture. This clericalism has obscured questions about the whole church, the congregation and the 'lay' person in pastoral theology. The male-centredness has in turn obscured questions about differences between male and female religious quests, moral outlooks and personal resources. Thus the probings of feminist theology serve as a necessary irritant to the inherited pastoral theology. (See FEMININITY/ MASCULINITY; SEXISM; WOMEN: ORDINATION).

While most types of pastoral theology (see 1–4 above) can be criticized for their excessive pragmatism and theological superficiality, some writers remark on the possibly pivotal character of a revised pastoral theology as that theological discipline which could uniquely mediate theology to practice *and* practice to theology (cf., Schleiermacher's treatment of practical theology). If theology is to be a living science, not simply involved in the transmission and rehearsal of earlier formulae, it must be put to the test by that body of human experience with which pastoral theology has to deal. Hence pastoral theology cannot avoid a complex and shifting relationship with theology and the secular sciences.

Clearly, pastoral theology must have in view the foundational human experiences of birth (q.v.), love (q.v.), loss and death (q.v.). It must also pay attention to the communal character of life in respect of social, political, economic and other conditions (*see* JUSTICE AND PASTORAL CARE). But it should avoid a one-sided concentration, in either case, on casualty, crisis and misfortune. Pastoral theology explores the criteria of humanhood implied by the person and work of Christ. These criteria can be referred to the quality and nature of the *routine* patterns of individual, group, and institutional living. Furthermore, a pastoral theology too preoccupied with abnormality and crisis will be, and often has been, rendered intellectually and practically marginal in processes of secularization as the secular arm takes over the management of specialized pastoral care, and pastoral theology has nothing to say about general patterns of human living.

Pastoral theology as socio-theological analysis (5 above) overcomes many of the objections here levelled at received understandings of the discipline. However this usage is strongly influenced by political-liberation theology (*see* POLITICAL THEOLOGY AND PASTORAL CARE) and is open to many of the criticisms directed at this development. Is a Marxist analysis of society to dominate a new pastoral theology, analogous to the domination of pastoral theology by psychological theory with, in both cases, a reduction and domestication of detailed ethical and doctrinal Christian content? Again, if much received pastoral theology has suffered from accommodation to sentimental versions of kindness and care, compassion and forgiveness, how far would a new pastoral theology be justified in adopting a more conflictual approach to its subject-matter? But a truly responsive pastoral theology may not explore only symptoms, ignoring causes.

In a 'post-industrial' era of uncertainty and disorientation in value systems, social policy, and individual experience, there is a significant opportunity to wrest pastoral theology

from servitude to alien norms, and to venture new forms of expression and practice, in which an integration of Christ-centred vision, critical analysis of the conditions of life, and churchly freedom for women and men, can interact, not uncritically, with new stirrings about the meaning and quality of life in society at large.

New Schaff-Herzog Religious Encyclopedia, vol. 8, pp. 373–80 (strong on earlier bibliography). *Sacramentum Mundi*, vol. 4, pp. 365–8. **Balmforth, Henry,** et al., *An Introduction to Pastoral Theology* (Hodder, 1937). **Browning, D.,** *The Moral Context of Pastoral Care* (Westminster, 1976). **McNeill, J.T.,** *A History of the Cure of Souls* (Harper, 1951). **Oglesby, William, B., Jr.** (ed.), *The New Shape of Pastoral Theology* (Abingdon, 1969). **Ruether, Rosemary R.,** *Sexism and God-Talk* (SCM, 1983), chs. 4, 7, 8. **Wright, Frank,** *The Pastoral Nature of the Ministry* (SCM, 1980).

A.O. DYSON

See also: PASTORAL CARE, NATURE OF; PASTORAL STUDIES; PRACTICAL THEOLOGY.

PAYMENTS AND GIFTS

Payments. Payments from the person to the counsellor are important aspects of a counselling contract, and have significance which is to be noted. A contract constitutes an agreement for regular time and skill from the counsellor in return for realistic payments. This committed structure enables the process for the distressed person to be contained whilst he or she grows towards some resolution.

It is sometimes felt by the person that payment is inappropriate to a relationship which has come to be important and intimate; personal rather than professional. This attitude has within it the transference (q.v.) element, and can be met by showing that the feeling belongs to former relationships of a different nature, which now need to be re-examined in this specific setting; this being the purpose of the process. Payments can be used to conform, always being made conscientiously on time or in advance; or to rebel, being delayed, questioned, used for attempted negotiation, and so on. All such indications need to be mutually understood, clarified and accepted.

Gifts. Gifts offered to the counsellor also indicate aspects of the counselling relationship which require recognition and attention.

They can indicate a person's wish to be bought off, to have nothing more required of him or her, or a wish to place the relationship on to a different and a closer footing, a wish to be loved; they can convey an embarrassing sense of not knowing what is appropriate in this relationship at such times as Christmas, or a sense of social obligation, or a sign of competitive struggle.

Gifts may also be used to make a statement about the self, particularly if the gift is a self-created piece such as a painting, carving or poem, to be recognized and accepted in what it states. It may also be an expression of true thankfulness, particularly when therapeutic work is successfully and creatively ending.

The meaning of gifts should always, in each case, be carefully considered and discussed. When the significance of the gift is clear to both parties they can mutually decide whether the healing process will be enhanced or hindered by the acceptance of the gift. The person often identifies with the gift he or she is making. If a gift is rarely made and the gesture has been mutually understood, it is probably in most cases appropriate to accept it so that the person will also feel acceptable.

Cox, Murray, *Structuring the Therapeutic Process* (Pergamon, 1978). Storr, Anthony, *The Art of Psychotherapy* (Secker & Warburg, 1979).

BARBARA K. FOWLES

PEAK EXPERIENCES
A term coined by A.J. Maslow to describe ecstatic life-events which are overwhelmingly intense, positively valued and said by those who experience them to have long-term effects on their lives.

Maslow argues that we spend most of life in a chronic state of deficit because our basic needs for love, attention, security, etc. are never completely met. We perceive things primarily in terms of what they will do for us in our search for fulfilment and avoidance of pain, and neurosis ties up our energy in a rickety pattern of adjustment to the world. But a more mature person, with needs reasonably well-fulfilled, may have a certain 'permeability', an openness to what is, to paying total attention to an object or person regardless of use or purpose.

This total attention is the hall-mark of a peak experience, when self is forgotten, time and space dissolve and language· other than poetic or mythical is inadequate. Accompany-

ing feelings are of humility and gratitude at being singled out for such a gift, for the experience can be neither earned nor manipulated. Whereas we are all predictably similar in our neurotic patterns, in a peak experience we are most our unique selves. Our creativity is released, our sense of purpose renewed and our life-style may be altered to pursue beauty, truth, justice, etc., which have just been made manifest.

Maslow also identifies the Jonah complex, whereby we are ambivalent about such joy and try to 'evade our destiny'. The dangers are well understood: a fear of being overwhelmed, becoming self-indulgent, fatalistic, undiscriminating, lacking responsibility for others. The harder task is to recognize the value of such experiences and to put ourselves in the way of them. Maslow has two practical suggestions: we should transmute 'our nastiness and petty meanness' into 'humble admiration, gratitude, appreciation, adoration even worship', although he explicitly denies the supernatural in the transcendent. And, since with the people Maslow studied, music and sex were the two most likely paths to peak experiences, he places art, music and dance at the centre of a healthy educational process designed to give people a glimpse into eternal values.

It would be in the spirit of Maslow's work if the reader paused to list the peak experiences of his or her life, and reflect how at the moment one is a different person because of them.

Maslow, A., *Towards a Psychology of Being* (Van Nostrand, Princeton, 1962); *The Farther Reaches of Human Nature* (Penguin, 1971).

YVONNE CRAIG

See also: SELF-ACTUALIZATION; TRANSCENDENCE AND IMMANENCE.

PENANCE
See: CONFESSION.

PERSON
A human individual in relationship with other humans. The personal is that which distinguishes the human from the non-human, i.e. from animals, and from machines which may perform some of the same functions as humans.

Person and role. The origins of the word 'person' seem to lie in the actor's mask of the

Greek theatre, a physical symbol of role. Human behaviour can be analysed in terms of our social roles. The danger of this is in thinking that that is all there is to a person. Persons may choose between various roles or make decisions about how to act when roles conflict. Persons can stand back from their roles and monitor their performance. The integrity of the person as distinct from performance of roles, such as pastor, counsellor, etc., is an important issue in our understanding of pastoral relations.

Rationality. Philosophy from Descartes down to this century has seen the thinking subject as the starting point for our thought about human beings, to see the defining characteristics of the personal as being rationality. This is a false starting point, since persons are the basic reality we know and the concept of a mind or consciousness is an abstraction from this. To focus on rationality alone is to separate thinking from emotion and from the springs of action.

A peculiarity about the language we apply only to persons is that we learn to understand and use correctly words like 'fear', 'in pain' and so on concerning states of mind by learning to apply them *both* to our own experience *and* to the experience of others. I apply them to myself through direct awareness of myself, and I learn to ascribe the same language to others without that direct awareness of their states of mind but on the basis of their behaviour. So built into the structure of the language we use of persons is the presupposition that we have to know how to ascribe the same states of mind to others as well as to ourselves even though by different criteria. 'Person' is therefore essentially a social concept.

Causality and agency. In early theoretical formulations, social scientists, noting what we have in common with the animals have sought to give a *complete* account of human behaviour in terms of causal laws.

While we do describe our behaviour in language which we also use of animals or of material bodies, we also use another range of language which we apply only to persons. Some of what we do may be explained causally, but there are some actions we do regularly which are the result of a decision to follow a particular rule of action. Thus persons have intentions and purposes, make choices and solve problems. They perceive the world in a way which is interpreted by the concepts and beliefs they hold. They have emotions which they can name, and form attitudes to things in the world around them which they may reflect upon and perhaps change. A person is an agent, and therefore to give an account of how a person may form an intention and act upon it we need to use both material body language and person language.

Related terms. The word 'self' (q.v.) is used in its most fundamental sense as 'myself' or 'yourself' to mean the person. It is also used in other senses to mean only a part of the person. 'Respect for persons' has been seen as the basic principle of morality, since other important principles such as utility, liberty, equality presuppose it. 'Individual' is an analytical concept. We become persons through our relations with other persons, that is, through our participation in community. An individual is therefore a person viewed in isolation from the relationships which have enabled him to become a person.

The foregoing conceptual exploration of what we mean by persons has emphasized the basic importance of the concept.

Biblical approaches. The word 'person' does not figure in biblical anthropology, but the Hebrew tendency to view man as a whole is fundamental to biblical thinking. In contrast, the Hellenistic tendency has been to analyse human nature and separate the constituent elements, giving special emphasis to the rational and this has heavily marked the cultural forms of the West. In this respect the philosophical rediscovery of the concept of person takes us closer to the assumptions of biblical thinking.

The biblical story is throughout about the relationship of God to a community, to a family, tribe or nation, but certain individual persons have a special place in it. The story is about such matters as God's choice of them, his covenant relationship with them, their response in action and how God respects their personhood by holding them responsible for the choices and decisions they make, corporately and individually. God is seen as a living God, who is in the business of forming and deepening community and enabling persons to grow through the encounter with him in their history and experience.

Personal life of individuals or communities is constituted in the biblical perspective by the address of the divine Word, the Word is finally and fully revealed as a person. 'It means that God is so personal that we see what He is only in a personal life. God can become man because man is person and because God is personal. And, on the other hand, when God appears in a person, it becomes manifest what person should be.' (Tillich 1955, p. 38).

Thus Christ becomes an image of the ideal of personhood which is God's purpose for humanity. The Epistle to the Ephesians well represents the creative interplay between person and community which runs through Old and New Testaments. 'Until we all attain to mature manhood, to the measure of the stature of the fullness of Christ . . . we are to grow up in every way into him who is the head, into Christ, from whom the whole body . . . makes bodily growth and upbuilds itself in love' (Eph. 4.13, 15, 16).

In reflecting on their encounter with the personal God, the early Church found that a holy community of persons expressed best what they had known. God himself is a trinity of persons whose nature is ever proceeding to create other persons and form communities in love. Thus the concept of person holds together insights from linguistic analysis, ethics, theology, and the social sciences. That some measure of convergence between these various disciplines may be detected in their beliefs and assumptions related to persons, offers one point from which Christian faith may be interpreted to our age. It is a necessary part of the framework of concepts within which pastoral care and pastoral theology must be discussed.

Downie, R.S., and Telfer, E., *Respect for Persons* (Allen & Unwin, 1969). Ecclestone, A., *Yes to God* (Darton Longman & Todd, 1975), ch. 7. Hollis, M., *Models of Man* (CUP, 1977). Strawson, P.F., *Individuals* (Methuen, 1964). Tillich, P., *Biblical Religion and the Search for Ultimate Reality* (Nisbett, 1955).

BRIAN PETTIFER

See also: COMMUNITY; HUMAN NATURE; SELF.

PERSONALITY DISORDER
Personality disorder needs to be distinguished from mental illness. The latter is characterized by *discontinuities* of personal functioning whereas personality disorders are deeply ingrained maladaptive patterns of thought and behaviour, generally recognizable during adolescence or earlier and usually continuing throughout adult life. A patient with a personality disorder may also suffer from a mental illness.

The following description and classification is based on the World Health Organisation International Classification of Disease. (Although it describes individual categories of personality disorder, commonly an individual will have personality traits from more than one category):

Paranoid Personality Disorder
Excessive sensitiveness to setbacks or to humiliations and rebuffs, a tendency to distort experience by misconstruing the neutral or friendly actions of others as hostile or contemptuous, and a combative and tenacious sense of personal rights.

Cyclothymic Personality
Lifelong predominance of a pronounced mood which may be persistently depressive, persistently elated, or alternatively one then the other.

Schizoid Personality Disorder
Withdrawal from affectional, social and other contacts with preference for fantasy and introspective reserve; behaviour may be slightly eccentric or indicate avoidance of competitive situations. Apparent coolness and detachment may mask an incapacity to express feeling.

Explosive Personality Disorder
Instability of mood with liability to intemperate outbursts of anger, hate, violence or affection.

Obsessional Personality Disorder
Feelings of personal insecurity, doubt and incompleteness leading to excessive conscientiousness. There may be insistent and unwelcome thoughts or impulses which do not attain the severity of an obsessional neurosis. Rigidity and excessive doubt may be conspicuous.

Hysterical Personality Disorder
A shallow and labile emotional state, characterized by dependence on others, craving for appreciation and attention, suggestibility and theatricality. There is often sexual immaturity, e.g. frigidity and over-responsiveness to stimuli.

Dependent Personality
Passive compliance with the wishes of elders and others, and an inadequate response to the demands of daily life.

Sociopathic Personality Disorder
A disregard for social obligations, lack of feeling for others and impetuous violence, or callous unconcern. People with this personality are often emotionally cold and may be abnormally aggressive or irresponsible. Their tolerance to frustration is low; they blame others or offer plausible rationalizations for the behaviour which brings them into conflict with society.

JOHN COX

See also: PSYCHIATRY AND MENTAL ILLNESS.

PHYSICAL HANDICAP
See: DISABLEMENT.

PLACEMENTS
Negotiated arrangements between academic institutions and arenas of professional practice. Learners on placement, under competent supervision (q.v.), are enabled to engage in and reflect upon a limited involvement in professional practice.

A typical example of a placement is when a theological college arranges for a student to be attached to a local congregation (q.v.) or hospital chaplaincy (q.v.) under the supervision of the minister or chaplain. This enterprise, in which students are enabled to reflect upon their initial experiences of the practice of ministry, with consequent personal and professional growth, is sometimes referred to as *field education*. The term replaces an older one, fieldwork, the change in nomenclature reflecting a contemporary emphasis upon the educational benefits to the student rather than the service offered in the placement setting (though of course these factors are not mutually exclusive).

Two broad categories of placements are found in theological education: (1) *In-role placements* in which the student functions with a definite but limited responsibility for ministry. Thus, if attached to a congregation, a student may share in its worship and occasionally preach or engage in pastoral visiting or exercise some leadership role within the educational work of the church, under the supervision of, and acceptable to, the minister (and possibly a group of lay people); if attached to a chaplaincy, the student will have some similar limited responsibility for its work within the institution served. (2) *Out-of-role placements* in which the student exercises a quite definite non-ministerial role, e.g. as an unqualified member of a social work team or as an auxiliary nurse in a hospital, the aim being to help the student gain an understanding of an area of human need or potential service from a non-ministerial perspective. Until recently, most placements in theological education had a pastoral emphasis, but there is a growing interest in 'social action' placements where students share in the prophetic and political dimensions of the church's ministry within society.

Placements may be *block* (i.e. full-time) or *concurrent* (i.e. coterminous with an academic course). The former has the advantage that the student can give a total commitment of time and energy to the placement, the latter that there exists the possibility of interaction between issues raised by the placement and concurrent academic studies.

A placement normally has a number of distinct phases:
(1) The academic institution initiates negotiations with the area of professional practice, the choice of placement site depending upon various factors such as the availability of appropriate tasks in which the student may engage, the quality of supervision which the learner is likely to receive and the willingness of the placement situation to welcome (and sometimes provide financial assistance for) a student.
(2) The student and the supervisor having met to ascertain that they can work together, further negotiations take place between the academic institution, the placement setting and the student, which may be formalised in a 'Learning Agreement' or 'Covenant of Learning'. This may take the form of a written document and will embody the compromise arrived at between the requirements of the academic institution, the goals and expectations of the student, the needs and resources of the placement setting and the expectations of the supervisor. It will contain a statement of the tasks which the student has agreed to undertake, the hours to be worked and the arrangements for supervision, etc. While setting guidelines for the placement, the Learning Agreement may, with the concurrence of all parties, be renegotiated at some

appropriate point, e.g. the half-way stage of the placement.

(3) Throughout the placement the student will engage in meaningful tasks and receive regular supervision either individually or in a group of peers. The value of the placement depends upon the quality of the supervision provided, for the student must be enabled to learn by reflecting both personally and theologically upon the practice of ministry.

(4) The placement will end with an evaluation process. It is important however that the form of evaluation used should be integral to the student's learning rather than a simple judgement upon performance.

Fielding, C.R., *Education for Ministry* (American Association of Theological Schools, Dayton, Ohio, 1966), especially chs. 6 and 7. Hunter, G.I., *Theological Field Education* (Boston Theological Institute, 1977). Lyall, D., 'Field Education and Ministerial Formation', in *Theology and Practice*, ed. D.B. Forrester (Hesketh, 1986).

DAVID LYALL

See also: CLINICAL PASTORAL EDUCATION; SUPERVISION, PASTORAL.

PLAY

By its very nature, play eludes reductive definition. It occupies an 'in-between' state in human affairs – in between reality and fantasy; it overlaps the areas of dreaming, creative thought, scientific invention, the arts and sport.

Margaret Lowenfeld, in her comprehensive study, *Play in Childhood*, points out that play serves four main purposes: (1) It serves as the child's means of making contact with the environment and fulfills much the same social purpose as work in adult life. (2) It makes the bridge between the child's consciousness and emotional experience, and fulfills the role that conversation, introspection, philosophy and religion fill for the adult. (3) It represents the externalized expression of a child's emotional life, and in this aspect serves the function taken by art in adult life. (4) It serves as relaxation and amusement, enjoyment and rest.

Further than this, it can be argued that the function of play is to help establish the foundations of mental development, just as it also helps establish and maintain bodily development. The mental activities of thinking, imagination, intuition and language depend upon the capacity to symbolize, to make mental representations and transformations between and within the worlds of, so-called, internal and external reality. In infancy this latent human facility is brought to life and brought *into* life by the natural process of play. The symbolic process is activated in play. It is sustained, throughout life, by play.

Play in learning and therapy. It may be necessary to distinguish between play, as such, and play in learning and therapy. In learning, the influential work of Froebel, Piaget and Montessori must not be ignored, and there is now a whole edifice of research and published material, including that overseen by Jerome Bruner. In therapy one should look to the seminal work of Margaret Lowenfeld, Melanie Klein, Anna Freud, Virginia Axline, D.W. Winnicott and Michael Fordham.

Montaigne noted long ago that 'the play of children must be counted . . . as their most serious activity'. It is clear, within therapy and counselling, that play is being recognized as having a valuable and valid place, not only in work with children but also among adults. Winnicott, among others, reiterates that 'to arrange for children to be able to play is itself a psychotherapy that has immediate and universal application'.

The significance of this seriousness is revealed if we grasp that the capacity to play is a sign of sanity and that disturbed children can be returned to sanity by the process of playing in the presence of a receptive and attentive adult. (Interpretation in the conventional sense may not be at all necessary.) Playing is the state within which most children 'work things out'. Playing is thinking, in action. It is the natural medium of transition between psychic reality and the realities of the child's physical and human environment: between conscious and unconscious. Where there are disturbances in any of these areas then play becomes the immediate and useful tool with which the child can be helped to 'sort things out'.

Play in adult life. Winnicott takes things one step further, applying the concept of play to therapy with both children and adults: 'Psychotherapy is done in the overlap of the two play areas, that of the patient and that of the therapist. If the therapist cannot play, then he is not suitable for the work. If the patient (child or adult) cannot play, then something needs to be done to enable the patient to become able to play, after which psychotherapy may begin. The reason why playing is essential is that it is in playing that the patient is being creative. (Winnicott, 1971, ch. 4)

Thus we could suggest that, if dreams and the use of dreams is 'the royal road to the unconscious' as Freud showed, then so, too, is play. There is little written on this as yet, but for deeper study one could start to look into the connections between play, the symbolic process, symbol formation and the transcendent function in the work of Jungians (e.g. Rosemary Gordon 1978), and tie this to the work of Marion Milner (1971) and Charles Rycroft (1979).

Axline, Virginia, *Dibs in Search of Self* (Penguin, 1971). **Berg, Leila,** *Look at Kids* (Penguin, 1972). **Bruner, Jerome,** *et al.,* *The Developing Child* [series] (Fontana, 1977–). **Gordon, Rosemary,** *Dying and Creating* (Society of Analytical Psychology, 1978). **Hodgson, John** (ed.), *The Uses of Drama* (Eyre Methuen, 1977). **Kalff, Dora M.,** *Sandplay* (Sigo Press, Calif., 1981). **Lambert, Jack,** and **Pearson, Jenny,** *Adventure Playgrounds* (Penguin, 1974). **Lorca, Federico Garcia** (the poet), *Deep Song and Other Prose* (M. Boyars, 1980). **Milner, Marion,** *On Not Being Able to Paint* (Heinemann, Educ., 1971). **Rycroft, Charles,** *The Innocence of Dreams* (Hogarth, 1979). **Winnicott, D.W.,** *Playing and Reality* (Penguin, 1974).

CRAIG SAN ROQUE

See also: DREAMS; FANTASY; HUMOUR.

POLICE CHAPLAINCY

The organization and structure of chaplaincies to the police has, at the time of writing, yet to be developed in Western Europe. There are however situations where local police forces have non-stipendary chaplains attached to them. The role of police chaplains can not be easily compared with other chaplaincies connected with institutions, e.g. hospital, prison, airport and school.

The chaplain to a closed institution identifies closely with the life and occupants of the institution, whether they are inmates, patients, pupils or staff. The ministry is to the total membership, and is regarded as the 'church' presence within its structure. The terminology and title given to the chaplain defines and determines the role as in 'padre', to the regiment, chaplain to the hospital.

The police role in society differs from the organizations mentioned above because it is not clearly institutionalized like the regiments

or hospitals. The police, in Western society, generally reflect the social ethics of the society in which they serve. The police are the agents of the civil power. They do not make the law, but along with others they have the responsibility for its operation in society; they are concerned with civil order and with the welfare of the community. As one executive arm of the civil authority the police are essentially engaged in assisting the community to live a good and full life. The negative and restrictive aspects of their duties are minimal and exist only because of the positive side of their work.

The Church then has a positive helping role to play in relation to the police. The Church can: (a) assert the importance of the police in the community as an instrument of the civil power, and encourage better working conditions and higher standards within the police force; (b) help to break down the isolation which many policemen feel from the community; (c) act as a reconciling agent between a multiplicity of agencies, and indicate the positive contributions they all make towards the maintenance of law and order; (d) give guidance to the police in matters which affect law and morality.

The role of police chaplains falls into three areas of concern: (1) *Their responsibility to the police.* Here their role will be to confirm the role of the police and support individual officers in their duties of upholding the law and order. (2) *Their responsibility to the victim of crime.* Here chaplains will meet people who are feeling violated and insecure, because they have suffered an invasion of their person or property. (3) *Their responsibility to accused persons.* This may be the most difficult role for chaplains because they will encounter accused persons in situations of conflict. They may feel anxious about coming into contact with law breakers but the role is to show compassion and mercy.

Chaplains often are faced with the dilemma of ministering to the instrument of law and order, the law-breaker and the victim, all within the same situation. It is within this complex role that the concepts of grace and forgiveness are given a new meaning. The redemptive power of the 'good news' is witnessed on the cross as Jesus is crucified between two robbers. Grace and forgiveness are for all. Police chaplains have a creative role to play within the community, and by their understanding and compassion they are able to assist the civil power in its maintenance of law and order. They have a missionary role, also, for they come in contact with those who are often on the fringe of society and who are in trouble. By their presence, police chaplains should be agents of reconciliation, proclaimers of forgiveness and heralds of the opportunity of renewal.

Grubb, G.W., 'The Role of the Police in Society' (unpublished Dissertation, New College, 1971).

G.W. GRUBB

See also: CRIME; PRISON CHAPLAINCY.

POLITICAL THEOLOGY AND PASTORAL CARE

Throughout its history Christianity has held together the concepts of love and justice, of concern for individuals and concern for whole communities. Acknowledgement of the importance of, and tension between, the demands of communally orientated justice and individually orientated love is a necessary backdrop for a discussion of the relationship between political theology and contemporary pastoral care.

Pastoral care in Western countries has all but ignored the socio-political context and implications for justice of its theory and practice. Building upon 19th-century, individualistic pietism in Protestantism, the modern pastoral care movement has been reinforced in its almost exclusive concern for troubled individuals by its encounter, in the present century, with dynamic and humanistic psychology. This has provided many new insights and tools for understanding and improved care of the distressed person. The techniques of counselling, married to the existentialist and personalist themes of much modern Western theology, have ensured the growth, particularly in the USA but also latterly in this country, of a flourishing psychologically informed and equipped pastoral care movement. This has probably raised the standard of pastoral ministry to individuals considerably but has failed to place that ministry in its proper socio-political context. Political theology can provide a much needed critique and correction in this situation. If the purpose of pastoral care is the alleviation of suffering and the facilitation of growth for all people there must be consideration of wider factors which impinge on that goal.

Contemporary political theology is, like psychologically influenced pastoral care, a product of the 20th century. There are some interesting similarities between political theology and the theology which has emerged from the pastoral care movement. For example, both focus on the need to improve and alleviate the contemporary human condition in practical ways and they are both anthropocentric. Thereafter the similarity ends, because political theology – or, more accurately, political theologies – reject psychological and personalistic categories, insights and methods in order to give primacy to the political dimension of existence. All political theology is practical, public and critical and it uses political categories to mediate the truth of the gospel in the world. There are several types of political theology presently extant, e.g. black theology, the theology of revolution, and the theologies associated with the names of Metz and Moltmann. Most have been developed in the light of situations of great, overt injustice. The most striking, complete, fully articulated and influential of the political theologies presently available is the so-called liberation theology of Latin America. It is from the theology of liberation that a critique of the theory, theology and practice of modern Western pastoral care can be outlined.

Latin America is a continent racked by extreme and overt social injustice, exploitation and oppression. The concept of liberation came into theological and ecclesiastical usage there in the late 1960s. It denotes freedom from all that inhibits and oppresses, and freedom for the growth and development of whole peoples who have hitherto been oppressed to the point of annihilation. Liberation is not an abstract or metaphysical concept but rather an active, corporate, human, social and political struggle. It has no connotation of being an intra-psychic or individual process, as it might be portrayed in the Western practice of pastoral care.

Possibly the most important insight so far provided by liberation theology has been its emphasis on the socially influenced nature of all human institutions and ideas, including the Church and theology. Churches and theologies reflect their social context and serve the interests of human groups. Where there is conflict and division between groups, theology and ecclesiastical practices will not be characterized by a divine neutrality but will, willy-nilly, serve the interests of one group or another. Where neutrality is impossible and bias is inevitable, it is vital, according to the tenets of liberation theology, that theology and the Church should make an active option for the struggle of the oppressed against their oppressors and should not collude either knowingly or inadvertently with the forces of injustice.

Liberation theology is itself a secondary activity, following on from a concrete option for the liberation struggle. It is reflection on that struggle in the light of the Christian tradition. From the standpoint of practical commitment to liberation, it is possible to reconstruct theology in a new way which no longer serves the interests of the powerful against those of the powerless.

An important corollary of the concern of liberation theology for contemporary social reality is its use of the insights and methods of the social sciences. Disciplines like sociology and economics (usually of a Marxist type as this fits the Latin American situation particularly well) expose the nature of Latin American society and the place of the Church and theology within it before any attempt is made to try and produce theological insights relevant to the liberation struggle. Segundo has expounded the method of liberation theology using a 'hermeneutic circle', which connects practical involvement and the theological tradition in a dynamic, progressive, dialectical relationship. There are four stages in this: (1) The experience of reality in practical action for liberation leads to a profound suspicion that there is unacknowledged bias in all ideologies including theology. (2) This suspicion is explored using the insights of the social sciences. (3) The experience of new theological realities emerging from liberating praxis is allowed to modify and reinterpret exegesis of the Christian tradition. (4) New theological insights and interpretations which have been arrived at are now allowed to influence praxis, thus completing the circle.

Liberation theology is socio-culturally specific and does not seek to be universalizable. Nonetheless, it is possible to adopt some of its methods and insights for heuristic purposes in trying to formulate a critique of Western pastoral care. A methodological circle can be outlined which permits the integration of pastoral care and some insights and methods of liberation theology, without com-

promising either. The circle has five stages, commencing with (a) the theoretical insights and methods of liberation theology which (b) arouse suspicion that the practice, theory and theology of British pastoral care may have covert socio-political effects and implications. This leads to (c) analysis, using social scientific insights, of the context of pastoral care and particularly matters of injustice and inequality. Thereafter (d) pastoral care is analysed and, if found to be colluding with forces of oppression, is reorientated towards the oppressed and powerless. This in turn (e) produces new insights and questions and thus the process starts again, though from a different point.

The insights and methods of liberation theology offer many challenges to pastoral care. They highlight the need to see all ecclesiastical practice and thought in its broadest socio-political and ethical context and require the integration of social justice with love and care for the individual. They question whether pastoral care is politically neutral and suggest that, if not, it should be biased towards the oppressed and not against them. Social and political causes of suffering and stunting of growth are highlighted, and pastors are confronted with the possibility of socio-political commitment and action as well as personal care. This critique thus comes as a timely and necessary corrective to potentially harmful trends in pastoral care.

Campbell, A.V., 'The Politics of Pastoral Care' (Contact, no. 62, 1979), pp. 2–15. Fierro, A., The Militant Gospel (SCM, 1977). Gutierrez, G., A Theology of Liberation (SCM, 1974). Halmos, P., The Personal and the Political (Hutchinson, 1978). Kee, A. (ed.), A Reader in Political Theology (SCM, 1974). Pattison, S., 'Pastoral Care in Psychiatric Hospitals: an Approach Based on Some of the Insights and Methods of Liberation Theology' (unpublished Ph.D. diss., Univ. of Edinburgh, 1982). Segundo, J.L., The Liberation of Theology (Gill & Macmillan, 1977). Selby, P., Liberating God (SPCK, 1983).

STEPHEN PATTISON

See also: JUSTICE AND PASTORAL CARE; PASTORAL THEOLOGY; POVERTY; SOCIAL STRUCTURES; SYSTEMS PASTORAL CARE.

PORNOGRAPHY

The word literally means 'the writings of prostitutes', which sets it in a context, although definitions of pornography may vary. The General Synod Board for Social Responsibility, in its evidence to the Williams Committee on obscenity and film censorship in 1979, described pornography as 'the representation of sexual relations or substitutes for them, where the stimulation of sexual desires in the readers or viewers are an integral part of the representation . . . and where by contrast a context of personal caring or affection is either missing or insignificant.' An American Court decision is more concise. 'Pornography is material which deals with sex appealing to prurient interest.'

Pornography needs to be distinguished from two other things. It needs to be distinguished from eroticism which reflects, celebrates and affirms the sexual nature and life of men and women. It needs also to be distinguished from obscenity which is more aggressive and contains a fundamental assault on what it means to be human combined with a desire to offend existing beliefs about human sexuality.

Any consideration about pornography raises three main issues. The first is the moral difficulty entailed in affirming pornography when on reflection it depicts sexual behaviour in terms of impersonal relationships and in the case of 'hard' pornography of deviant relationships (see SEXUAL DEVIATION).

The second issue is concerned 'with whether pornography actually corrupts and depraves. It is important to distinguish between the creation of an undesirable climate of thinking and individual experiences of corruption. It is inevitable that reaction to this problem is subjective. For example, Court (1977) has argued that pornography has powerfully corrupting effects, while the Williams Committee (Cmnd 7772) concluded that pornography could be offensive but in fact did little harm.

It is a consideration of this problem which raises the third issue, about the control of pornographic material. Most pornographic material is of little artistic value and is produced mainly for gain. There is, however, a strong and vocal resistance to any legal controls on the grounds of censorship. The recommendations of the Williams Committee were mainly in terms of limited prohibition and restriction to those over 18, with no restriction on the written word. The Courts' power to confiscate material was to be removed, and private prosecution in this field was to be abolished.

In the field of sexual therapy (q.v.), pornographic material has been used in various techniques to ameliorate some sexual dysfunctions.

Obscenity and Community Standards (St Andrew's Press, Edinburgh, 1979). *The Report of the Committee on Obscenity and Film Censorship* (Cmnd 7772, Nov. 1979). *Submission to the Home Office Committee on Obscenity and Film Censorship* (General Synod Board for Social Responsibility, Feb. 1978). **Court, J.,** 'Pornography and Sex Crimes' (*International Journal of Criminology and Penology*, vol. 15, 1977), pp. 129–57.

DAVID WAINWRIGHT

See also: BODY, THEOLOGY OF; SEXUAL COUNSELLING AND THERAPY; SEXUAL DEVIATION; SEXUALITY AND SEXUAL DEVELOPMENT; SEXUALITY, THEOLOGY OF.

POVERTY
The state of indigence or want.

When unqualified, the reference is usually to material poverty, the lack of sufficient resources to sustain an adequate standard of life. By extension, however, the word is also used to refer to spiritual poverty, usually understood as a lack of a sense of purpose, or of adequate stimulation to the capacity for imagination or for the formation of relationships.

In the more common, material, sense the specific definition of what constitutes poverty is a matter of intense debate, not least because upon the type of definition chosen depend both the diagnosis of the causes of poverty and the type of pastoral care and remedial action thought to be appropriate. Definitions generally fall into one of two types, *absolute* and *relative*.

Defined in an *absolute* sense, poverty is the lack of sufficient resources to maintain life, measured in terms of such items as food, clothing or housing. On the basis of such absolute definitions poverty is a finite problem, and caring for the poor consists in lifting the standard of those who are poor to the point where they are no longer poor. Statements such as, 'There is not the kind of poverty around that you used to see in the 1930s,' are based on such absolute definitions.

Relative definitions of poverty take account of the fact that the perception of poverty, and the experience of the poor, changes according to social context. If the standard of living generally is rising, so is likely to be the level below which people are perceived to be in poverty. Further, the experience of being poor is changed if the situation of a person ceases to be in the midst of a community in which poverty is general to one in which people are generally better off and expectations are rising. It is because of this relative element in the definition of poverty that the list of those necessities without which a person is poor is constantly revised to take account of general changes in the general standard of life, and therefore of expectations.

Parallel to the debate of definition in relation to poverty is the debate about causes, and these are directly related to suggested means of caring for the poor. Such definitions may broadly be categorized as *natural, individual* and *structural.*

The *natural* causes of poverty are differences in the resources of the land or of the country, harvest failures and natural disasters. It may also be claimed that there are natural differences in individual endowment and inheritance which make it inevitable that there will be differences in attainment and therefore in the rewards gained. Those who see such natural, or inevitable, differences as the chief cause of poverty would see care for the poor first in terms of alleviation – by means of charity or social provision – of a problem which, like the poor, will always be with us. They would secondly seek to bring the poor to an understanding and acceptance of the inevitable.

Those who see the causes of poverty lying primarily in the individuals who are poor focus on the higher incidence of crime, idleness and bad financial management among the poor, and see care for the poor principally as an educational task concerned with the reform of the individual. On that understanding, welfare provision can be seen as often counter-productive, since it lowers the sense of personal responsibility among the poor and therefore their motivation to improve their own lot.

Those who see poverty as structural, originating in the way society is ordered, focus on the injustices of which the poor are the victims, and regard the crime and the apathy found among the poor as the results rather than the causes of poverty. The right means of pastoral care for the poor is, therefore, political action with or on behalf of them, so that those with power, those who are not poor, may take responsibility for their part in bringing poverty into being. Such pastoral

care finds theological support in liberation or political theology (q.v.).

Atherton, John, *Scandal of Poverty* (Mowbray, 1983). **Boerma, Conrad,** *Rich Man, Poor Man and the Bible* (SCM, 1979). **Gutierrez, Gustavo,** *The Power of the Poor in History* (SCM, 1982). **Paget-Wilkes, Michael,** *Poverty, Revolution and the Church* (Paternoster, 1981). **de Santa Ana, Julio,** *Good News to the Poor* (World Council of Churches, 1977). **Selby, Peter,** *Liberating God* (SPCK, 1983). **Sheppard, David,** *Bias to the Poor* (Hodder, 1982). **Sider, R.J.,** *Rich Christians in an Age of Hunger* (Hodder, 1978). **Townsend, Peter,** *Poverty in the United Kingdom* (Penguin, 1979).

PETER SELBY

See also: JUSTICE AND PASTORAL CARE; POLITICAL THEOLOGY AND PASTORAL CARE; SOCIAL STRUCTURES.

PRACTICAL THEOLOGY
The theology of practice.

'That may be all right in theory', it is said, 'but it doesn't work in practice.' In which case, one may answer, the theory must be wrong. If our theories are not pure fantasy their relationship to reality is tested, in some way, by practice. But if this is true, theory directs practice, but practice also corrects theory.

Schleiermacher was the first to present a systematic account of the relationship of the theological disciplines. For him, theology is a function of the Church (though strictly of an elite within the Church); its goal is the guidance of the Church and practical theology is its crown. In effect, this led to a view of practical theology as applied theology, 'the doctrine of how the truth, once it is recognized, is to be applied and appropriated' (Häring). Tillich called it 'the technical theory' through which historical and systematic theology are applied to the life of the Church.

This view is unsatisfactory in many ways. It assumes a simple, one-way relationship between theory and practice. Theology is formulated by the systematic theologian and applied by the practical theologian. The danger is that the theological content of practical theology diminishes to vanishing-point. It becomes, in the older European models, the communication of sound advice by an experienced practitioner to the apprentices, or, in the American model, the communication of highly sophisticated skills borrowed from other professions, in counselling, educating, communicating, managing, etc. Practical theology, thus seen, concerns the training of clergy for their work. It answers the question 'How?', but does not raise the question 'What?'.

When, however, the theological task itself is understood to be more critical than prescriptive, practical theology takes its place as a critical theological discipline. It is the theology of practice. The systematic theologian asks critical questions about the way faith expresses itself in language; the practical theologian asks critical questions about the way faith expresses itself in practice, and about the relation between the practice and the language. Since the Church's life and action is related not only to its own self-understanding and comprehension of its faith, but also to the changing society in which it functions, practical theology is triadic, concerned with the interrelationships of faith, practice and social reality, and is aware that the lines of force flow in both directions. Practical theology must therefore listen to the social sciences, but in itself it is not primarily descriptive but critical, not primarily technical but normative. It is concerned 'with the Church's self-actualization here and now – both that which is and that which ought to be' (Rahner).

On this view, the relation of practical theology to the other theological disciplines becomes mutual rather than one-sided. 'It can put new questions before the systematic theologian, questions arising out of the cultural life of the period' (Tillich). 'It exercises a critical function in respect of the other theological disciplines' (Rahner).

Practical theology was traditionally concerned with ministerial function, and the subject was divided accordingly: homiletics, liturgics, catechetics, poimenics. The scope of a critical discipline is broader than the functions of the clergy, and concerns the whole life and practice of the Church. Christian ethics finds its place most naturally within practical theology. Indeed, there is no reason in principle why a theology of practice should be limited to the practice of the Church. A theological critique of the practice of social work, or of education, or of politics is quite feasible, for there are hidden theologies in much human activity. In a concern for the human, practical theology may merit Gollwitzer's claim that it is 'the heart of theology.'

Campbell, A.V., 'Is Practical Theology Possible?' (*Scottish Journal of Theology*, vol. 25, no. 2, May 1972), pp. 217–27. Gollwitzer, H., *An Introduction to Protestant Theology* (Westminster, 1982), ch. 2. Pannenberg, W., *Theology and the Philosophy of Science* (Darton Longman & Todd, 1976), pp. 231–41, 423–40. Rahner, K., *Theological Investigations*, vol. 9 (Darton Longman & Todd, 1972), pp. 101–14. Whyte, J.A., 'New Directions in Practical Theology' (*Theology*, vol. 76, no. 635, May 1973), pp. 228–38.

JAMES A. WHYTE

See also: PASTORAL STUDIES; PASTORAL THEOLOGY.

PRAYER

Communication between the creature and the Creator.

Like all human communication, it begins with words but can be sustained non-verbally by gestures and, especially, by silence (q.v.). Prayer can be either communal or personal. Communal prayer is both liturgical (that is, the official prayer of the Church), and spontaneous and free. In this article we deal only with personal, individual prayer: (1) the theology of it; (2) its point of departure; (3) its growth; (4) its relationship to the rest of Christian life; (5) its relationship to the Bible; (6) mystical prayer; (7) prayer to the saints.

1. Two things can be said theologically about prayer. Firstly, it is always a response to the prior initiative of God. God first approaches us and we respond. Prayer is our response to the revelation of God. The initiative is on God's side. This has to be remembered, because often the 'feel' of prayer is that we are chasing an elusive God and never quite catching up with him. The opposite is, in fact, true. God is chasing us and has found us and dwells with us. Francis Thompson's 'Hound of Heaven' is the correct picture. God does not run away from us, but we sometimes run away from him. The apparent elusiveness of God is due to his transcendence, not his absence. Secondly, our response to God in prayer is entirely God-given, not an achievement on our part. We pray in the power of the Spirit, through Jesus Christ the one mediator, to the Father. The Spirit prays in us, enabling us to call God 'abba' (Rom. 8.14–27; Gal. 4.6). Thus even our response to God in prayer is due to God's initiative, i.e. grace.

2. The point of departure for prayer is human need. Freud said that the experience of human need, in particular for a super-

adequate Father, created the idea of God. Believers say that God implants in his creatures certain needs which enable us to discern his existence. For both schools, human needs point to God, the contingent to the Absolute. For Freudians, however, the existence of God is not real, but merely 'created' by the psychological need for him, whereas for believers the needs are implanted in many by the truly existing God. Prayer begins when (a) we ask for things from God. This is the prayer of intercession and petition. This leads on to (b) the prayer of thanksgiving, when we thank God for granting our requests. A third stage is reached when we recognize that God is concerned for our good behaviour and watches over our consciences. This leads to (c) the prayer of sorrow or repentance when we have done wrong. Lastly we notice that implicitly we have been recognizing God as Sovereign Lord in (a), (b) and (c), so we turn to him explicitly to give him (d) praise and adoration. All four forms of prayer: petition, thanksgiving, repentance and adoration are to be found in the OT and NT, especially the psalms, and were practised by Jesus during his life on earth.

3. Growth in prayer comes when the prayers of petition, thanks, sorrow and praise coalesce into one single relationship to God. Instead of there being an agenda between the soul and God to be prayed about, e.g. a request, God himself becomes the agenda. The person praying dwells upon the reality of God himself, present to the one who prays. At this stage one is content to dwell on God without moving on to any 'business'. One finds oneself caught up in a personal, I–Thou relationship of love and wonder. This simple, often wordless, prayer is called contemplation. It is intuitive rather than discursive, loving rather than thinking. It can be expressed in short words like *Love, Abba, God, Mercy, Sin*. It grows towards silence.

4. Unless prayer is an expression of the Christian life of the one who prays it is useless and harmful. In prayer we express ourselves towards God; that prayer is meant to be an expression of the endeavour of our whole lives, not just an 'honouring God with our lips'. The relationship between prayer and living is that they are reciprocal. Good living makes for good prayer. Good prayer makes for good living. They build each other up. When the connection is broken, prayer becomes a dishonest hobby, an escape from

Christian commitment instead of a springboard for commitment. When the connection is maintained one grows simultaneously in Christian discipleship and in prayer, so that eventually the whole of life may be said to become a prayer.

5. Because prayer is a response to the Word of God, it is intimately connected with the Bible. By reading the Bible, Christians open themselves to the influence of God's creative and redemptive Word. The Bible is a privileged place for receiving the saving love of God. This happens first in the liturgy where God's Word is read publicly, and this gives rise to the public prayer of the Church in response. Secondly, Christians can read the Bible privately, which in turn gives rise to the private prayer of individuals. The OT and NT are rich in examples of prayers which Christians can make their own in the privacy of their hearts. The Lord's prayer is the best known of many such examples.

6. The human mind proceeds to understand objects by encapsulating them in finite concepts. It 'comprehends' them. Faced with the infinite nature of God the human mind cannot encapsulate him in finite concepts. It cannot comprehend God. Before God it is baffled. It enters into a 'cloud of unknowing' rather than the light of comprehension and knowledge. It knows that its vocabulary, which is culled from human experience, is inadequate and to that extent untrue. For instance the use of the word 'him' above with regard to God is inadequate and strictly untrue. The human mind, therefore, is faced with a breakdown in concepts and vocabulary when dealing with God. It can only reach an infinitely inadequate approximation to truth. The mystic is one who not only recognizes this as theologically true, but experiences it in prayer, with pain. All prayer grows towards mystical prayer, towards the cloud of unknowing. This truth was recognized in the OT by the repeated phrase 'no man can see God and live', exemplified, for instance, by the story of Moses being able to see only the back parts of God (Exod. 33.18–32). In the NT Paul said, 'For now we see in a mirror dimly, but then face to face (1 Cor. 13,12). Mystical prayer teaches humility because it brings one face to face with the truth about God's transcendence and one's own incompetence.

7. In the Catholic and Orthodox traditions there is prayer to the saints. Two things are involved in this. The first is to ask the saints

to join their prayers to ours for a special intention. Just as members of a family will gather round to pray for a sick relative in this world, so we ask our brothers and sisters in the Communion of Saints to join their prayers to ours for the things we pray for. The saints are asked to pray to God alongside us, through Christ the one Mediator. The saints in heaven are considered well placed before the throne of God to join with us in petition. The second element in praying to the saints is that of honouring them as examples of Christian living who have led the way before us. The saints act as inspirations to us on our pilgrim way. An example of this is the way Oscar Romero's martyrdom in 1980 in El Salvador inspired the whole Latin American continent in their struggle to follow the gospel. Some places in the world are particularly associated with certain saints and become numinous centres of intercession: Lourdes, Czestachowa, Assisi, Lisieux for instance.

Anon. *The Cloud of Unknowing,* tr. C. Wolters (Penguin, 1961). **Chapman, J.** *Spiritual Letters* (Sheed & Ward, rev. edn 1976). **Dalrymple, J.,** *Simple Prayer* (Darton Longman & Todd, 1984). **St John of the Cross,** *Ascent of Mount Carmel* and *Dark Night of the Soul,* tr. Allison Peers (Burns & Oates, rev. edn 1976). **Kelly, T.,** *A Testament of Devotion* (Quaker Home Service, 1941). **Merton, T.,** *Seeds of Contemplation* (A. Clarke, new edn 1972).

JOHN DALRYMPLE

See also: SILENCE; WORSHIP AND PASTORAL CARE.

PREACHING AND PASTORAL CARE

Preaching is the activity of communicating, in the context of worship, the message contained in the Bible, and witnessed in the Church that God in Christ is reconciling the world to himself.

Proclamation of the word about God holds up the ideals and goals of the Kingdom of God. While some listeners may receive encouragement, others find that the distance between their present experience and the high ideal leads to despair. The preacher cares pastorally when both groups feel understood. The affinities between preaching and pastoral care, and the contrasts between them, may be considered in relation to: (1) the listeners; (2) the message; (3) the preacher; and (4) the context.

1. For preaching to be more than oratory,

those addressed need to feel that their situation is understood by the preacher. Pastorally shaped preaching comes from the hearts and minds of those who know the temptations and motivations, pastimes and pleasures, work and homes of those to whom they speak. Such preaching communicates to a congregation (q.v.) that the preacher and the God whose word is proclaimed are no strangers to human nature.

2. The message is pastorally effective when healing is initiated or invited. The central affirmations of the Christian faith are more helpful for this than novel, obscure or startling ideas. Moreover, the building up of trust (q.v.) to enable further pastoral encounter comes more from sincerity than involved argument. The message needs to meet people where they are and be illustrated by examples from a life known by them. Use of modern methods and expressions helps this aim.

3. The preacher himself or herself is addressed by the sermon. The ability of preachers to handle their own brokenness with integrity, to demonstrate honest endeavour as well as unashamed repentance, enables the hearers to share as fellow-travellers in a pilgrimage rather than to see themselves as inferior Christians chastised by an infallible external authority.

4. Preaching takes place in a context of worship (q.v.) whose whole liturgy (q.v.) reflects and is in sympathy with pastoral concern. Preaching the reconciliation to God in Christ in such worship sustains, nurtures and heals those gathered and gives opportunity for response.

Despite their close affinities, preaching and pastoral care are to be distinguished in that one is more clearly a public affair whilst the other is ordinarily more personal. (A pastor who is a preacher will be very careful not to allow worshippers to identify themselves in sermon illustrations.) There may also be a contrast between the portrayal of ideals in preaching and the understanding and acceptance of human failure entailed in pastoral work. On the other hand the two are similar in the establishment of a relationship of trust and dependable love. Caring preaching provides a time during which defences and suspicions may be relaxed. The spoken words and attitudes of both caring preaching and pastoral care invite further encounter, reflecting and interpreting the receiver's life situations in the light of Christian truth, and encouraging faith in God and participation in the community of Christ's people.

Oates, W., *The Christian Pastor* (Westminster, New York, 1951). Oglesby, W.B., *Biblical Themes for Pastoral Care* (Abingdon, Nashville, 1981). Willimon, W.H. *Worship as Pastoral Care* (Abingdon, 1979).

PETER BOWES

See also: BIBLE: PASTORAL USE; EVANGELISM AND PASTORAL CARE; PASTORAL CARE: HISTORY – REFORMED TRADITION; WORSHIP AND PASTORAL CARE.

PREJUDICE

A strongly held attitude, belief or judgement which is not based on knowledge, but rather on biased and emotionally coloured information.

Prejudice is essentially irrational. It has powerful negative and positive connotations and is directed towards specific groups of people, objects, situations or doctrines. It leads either to denigration or to idealization, such as, 'French people are only interested in food or sex' (denigration), or, 'Only the British know how to keep a stiff upper lip' (idealization). Prejudices are generally held on to with great tenacity, and there is strong resistance to anything which might bring about a change of attitude, e.g. southern Whites were unwilling to meet black people as individuals until integration was forced on them by law.

Prejudices are frequently instilled in us early on in life before the age of reasoning. They can also be evoked in any highly charged, emotional atmosphere, such as a political rally, a call to arms, a revivalist meeting or a football match. Recent examples have been: Nazi rallies; wars in Vietnam and Argentina; conflict in Northern Ireland; and Jihad or Holy War in Iran, Iraq and Lebanon.

Clever orators and the media can whip up primitive feelings of hatred and fury or of worship and adoration by using emotive language or pictorial material. They play on the human wish to divide the world into good and bad, and black and white. Prejudice is thus a tribal defence which enables us to maintain a sense of worth by projecting our unacknowledged, undesirable characteristics on to those we label as inferior or evil, or as

superior and saintly. This mechanism enables people to see all the badness in the 'enemy' or 'heretic' and to fight it out there, rather than in themselves. Prejudice distorts perception, for we do not see the mote in our own eye.

Meeting the so-called enemy face to face, seeing him or her as human rather than as the stereotyped 'evil one' helps to reduce prejudice. Encounter and dialogue can lead to a recognition that our neighbour, whether black or white, red or yellow, Catholic, Protestant, Buddhist or Jew, is very like us. Encouragement of real meeting diminishes prejudice and hatred and is thus a very important aspect of pastoral care.

Adorno, Theodor et al., *'The Authoritarian Personality: Studies in Prejudice* (Social Studies Series 3, Westpont, Conn., 1954). Allport, G.W., *The Nature of Prejudice* (Addison-Wesley, 1954). Dollard, John, et al, *Frustration and Aggression: the Scapegoat Theory of Prejudice* (Yale UP, 1939), ch. 2.

IRENE BLOOMFIELD

See also: RACE RELATIONS; SEXISM.

PREMARITAL COUNSELLING

Premarital counselling is a widespread practice amongst ministers who help to prepare couples for marriage by offering teaching, advice and relationship training. It is also practised on a more limited scale by agencies, especially Marriage Guidance Councils, and in schools, notably in Roman Catholic schools, drawing on resources such as those of the Catholic Marriage Advisory Council.

The aims and methods of premarital counselling are diverse, particularly amongst ministers. This is partly because it is an area of counselling which is as yet poorly supplied with resources, and partly because the scope of the work is so vast. Indeed, one option for ministers, recognizing the short time available to them and the immensity of the task, is to limit their activity to preparing the couple for the wedding service, in the course of which some counselling may occur fortuitously on an *ad hoc* basis. This is not properly premarital counselling. Where it is directly approached, an important generalization about the nature of premarital counselling is that the motivation and initiative for counselling comes primarily from ministers and agencies and is offered gratuitously. Couples are generally agreeable to the teaching and advice offered, however, for at such a point of social transition their readiness for learning is high.

It is perhaps more an exercise in adult education than in counselling. Three broad groups of approach may be distinguished. They can be called the *socialization*, the *problem avoidance*, and the *enrichment* approaches. They are not exclusive, and although one emphasis may predominate, they are used in all combinations.

Socialization. It is apparent that many couples intending marriage have not acquired essential social skills for embarking on married life, particularly in relationships and managing oneself in society. Couples may lack ability to discern what constitutes a healthy relationship, be inexperienced in sustaining person-to-person communication, be poor financial managers, lack access to family planning advice, and so on. The socialization approach attempts to provide the necessary teaching and advice. Schools particularly focus on this area. Ministers also often attempt to provide some basic social education, but within the constraints of limited time, may resort to some kind of checklist to indicate where attention is needed. In some cases ministers may attempt to persuade couples to delay or abandon their plans for marriage when they consider a couple is inadequately equipped.

Problem avoidance. The churches and agencies recognize certain crises and developments in marriage which they believe should be avoided. In this approach the counselling process becomes one of making the couple aware of potential marital problems disapproved by the counsellor, and encouraging skills to avoid them. For example, an agency may show that physical conflict is socially unacceptable, and demonstrate how it may be avoided. A minister usually sets an agenda conditioned by the ideals of the church. If he or she considers marriage breakdown to be theologically unacceptable, a minister may attempt so to prepare a couple for marriage as to minimize the possibility of breakdown. It is not uncommon for there to be difficulties in this second counselling approach where it predominates. Couples often find difficulty both in accepting the relevance of the imposed agenda of the counsellor, and in facing the reality of potential problems.

Enrichment. The third broad approach is not problem-centred, as in the first two approaches, but considers marriage as an opportunity for fulfilment which should be maximized. It is usually characterized by offering a process of individual and mutual development rather than a set body of advice. It may, for example, facilitate a couple in evaluating their hopes and fears so as to set mutually satisfying objectives, or help a couple develop a fully sexual understanding of each other. Some counsellors vary in the aspects of marriage enrichment they encourage, such as, communication, sex, or spirituality; others allow couples to define the areas where they desire enrichment.

British Council of Churches (Division of Community Affairs), folder: *Preparing for Marriage* (BCC, 1980). **Chave-Jones, M.,** and **Howarth, S.,** *Preparation for Marriage* (Scripture Union, 1983) **Dominian, J.,** *Make or Break* (SPCK, 1984), ch. 19. **Foley, M.,** *Marriage: a Relationship* (DLT, 1981). **Melinsky, M.A.H.,** *Forward to Marriage* (Church Information Office, 1984). **Mitman, J.L.C.,** *Premarital Counselling* (Seabury, New York, 1982).

W.H. HOPKINSON

See also: MARRIAGE AND FAMILY; MARRIAGE, THEOLOGY OF; SEXUALITY, THEOLOGY OF.

PRIORITIES IN HEALTH CARE
Decisions about allocating scarce resources efficiently and fairly.

Priorities in health care, traditionally determined by market forces or charitable impulses, are today commonly the subject of political and clinical decision-making. Such decisions generally take into account not only broad demographic and epidemiological trends, but also needs and demands generated by the existing provision of health-care services. Public provision of an ever-increasing range of medical and caring possibilities has contributed to widespread rising expectations of health care. But the financial and human resources needed to meet these expectations are limited, ultimately by other purposes and activities on which individuals and society wish to spend their time and money. This limitation may be less apparent in times of economic growth, but even then choices are made which imply that some needs and demands are not given priority; and in health care this always carries the risk of harmful or even fatal consequences for someone. The difficulty of making such choices, whether political or clinical, is compounded by a growing demand for accountability to a society which, nevertheless, lacks any clear or firm consensus about the values and principles on which these choices should be based. In recent years however, increasing public and professional emphasis has been laid on the need for priority decisions to uphold the values of efficiency and fairness.

Efficiency in determining priorities has its classical medical expression in 'triage', a concept developed from the screening of battlefield casualties to determine who should be saved when all cannot be. In triage, priority is given to those who need treatment in order to survive, over both those likely to survive without treatment, and those unlikely to survive even with it: if two or more in the first group can be saved with the same effort as for one, they receive priority over the one; priority may also be given to any in the second group whom treatment can make of immediate usefulness to the other casualties (e.g. a medical attendant with minor injuries). In emergency priority choices between individual lives, triage criteria, while rough-and-ready, may be medically and morally defensible. They also seem to have played a part, historically, in justifying priority given to life-saving medical specialties (e.g. coronary care units, renal dialysis, intensive neonatal care). Where patients are acutely ill, but with good prospects of recovery, this priority too may be defensible. Much health care today, however, is of the chronically ill elderly, middle-aged victims of diseases often precipitated by behavioural or environmental factors, and the mentally ill or handicapped. It thus may be more efficient to give priority to services concerned with care and prevention rather than cure; the effective benefits of the former, however, are more difficult to demonstrate than those of services which can point to specific lives saved.

The value of fairness can be expressed in either non-comparative or comparative terms. Many doctors and other professionals express it primarily in the former, focusing attention on what would be fair or unfair to a particular patient or group of patients in their own care. The doctor's relationship of trust with individuals may make this morally defensible. Others, including administrators and politicians, emphasize the comparison of needs, costs and benefits in arriving at priorities. This may be defensible in terms of the principle of equity, which assigns priority in proportion to differing need or merit. What different individuals or groups merit is always contestable however, as may be comparative needs, costs and benefits: costs, for example,

may be social as well as monetary; while needs and benefits are often radically incommensurable (e.g. expensive infertility treatment for a childless couple, compared with relatively cheap hip-replacement surgery for an old man). The infinitely complex calculus of the greatest happiness of the greatest number ultimately founders on the subjective nature of happiness. In political and administrative practice, priorities are normally determined in relation to broad epidemiological, demographic and socio-economic trends, pragmatically considered; while at the clinical level, longer waiting times may obscure choices implicitly made, and private medicine may seem (non-comparatively) fairer to those who can afford it. The practical difficulty of determining priorities which are both efficient and fair has led some to claim that the choices involved are ultimately 'tragic', and thus a problem as much for theodicy (q.v.) as political economy.

Boyd, K.M., *The Ethics of Resource Allocation in Health Care* (Edinburgh UP, 1979). Calabresi, G. and Bobbitt, P., *Tragic Choices* (W.W. Norton, New York, 1978). Campbell, A.V., *Medicine, Health and Justice* (Churchill Livingstone, 1978). Winslow, G.R., *Triage and Justice* (Univ. California, 1982).

K.M. BOYD

See also: HEALTH: ETHICAL AND THEOLOGICAL ASPECTS; NATIONAL HEALTH SERVICE.

PRISON CHAPLAINCY

Prison chaplaincy refers to ministry authorized by church and state and directed towards spiritual needs within custodial environments.

This sphere of chaplaincy has social justification. Suspension of civil rights should not include loss of religious rights. UN resolutions uphold religious freedom in captivity and advocate employing chaplains (cf. Minimum Standard Rules 41 and 42). Prisons evince violence and can be barometers of suppression in society; spiritual values in their midst can be a moderating influence. Religions themselves offer identity and are often connected with independent, cross-cultural, cohesive organizations able to help inmates bridge home and prison.

On a theological level chaplains can relate the dignity of people in prison to the image of God and help them identify with Jesus' death among prisoners and his mandate to visit prisoners (Matt. 25.36). Chaplains proclaim the gospel depicted in metaphors apposite to imprisonment, like darkness and bondage, and offer reconciliation at many levels – so creating spiritual fellowship through pastoral care.

Chaplains survive amid tensions. Ideally their detached, informed maturity and sensitivity to humour (q.v.) give versatility among parties manifesting rigid attitudes. They can share guilt (q.v.)·, anger (q.v.) and depression (q.v.); they might unravel intricacies of attachments, separations and loss; they may enter the depths with those facing truth, justice, or their deserts. Many want chaplains to make sense of life and give hope (q.v.) – especially staff who are often under stress.

A chaplain relates to organizational structures and other professional disciplines. He or she promotes worship, converses with prisoners, plans introductions with befriending (q.v.) prison visitors, institutes discussion groups and integrates outside church contributions. Prisons are unconventional parishes; consequently ecumenism can be promoted, although religious prisoners are often conservative. Ministerial visits from home parishes and assistance for minority faiths can be fostered.

In the UK, 84 people in 100,000 are imprisoned. This is high by European but not by US standards (e.g. 34 in Holland, but 250 in the USA). Three prison services function in the UK. In England and Wales centrally organized chaplaincy services cover 125 establishments and include 80 full-time Anglican and 13 full-time RC chaplains. Every prison has Anglican, RC, and Methodist chaplains, sometimes part-time. In Scotland all 19 prisons have part-time RC and Presbyterian chaplains. In Northern Ireland all 5 prisons have part-time chaplains from four main denominations.

Architecture, security and staffing cause establishments to differ. Prisons constitute a young man's world; impetus to commit crime diminishes after the age of 30, and in the UK female prisoners number only 1,600 among a total 50,000. Inmates cross social strata, but most come from the less endowed. The largest group are burglars. Mental health (q.v.) and alcoholism are often significant. The average sentence is one year; it was one month in 1900. Most prisoners serve their sentence in two establishments.

Prisons purvey moral values and are designed to inculcate remorse. Their model, for which no widely applicable alternative exists, emerged from monastic life and is now suggested by reference to penitentiaries, cellular life, routines by bells and enforced 'poverty, chastity and obedience'. With associated roots chaplains face popular expectations, lightheartedly expressed but seriously believed, that they should be deununciatory. The humour inevitably inherent in 'prison religion', can be an ice-breaker and endearment if a chaplain can balance formality with informality, judgementalism with acceptance (q.v.) and intermittent burlesque with indiscriminate compassion. This heritage is unique.

Victorian prisons were built around chapels. Formerly newsreader, librarian, teacher, almoner and assistant at executions, the chaplain has now lost these jobs. Nevertheless, essential justification remains, enhanced by contemporary recognition of lay pastoral care (q.v.).

Chaplaincy work is conducted in a cloistered and condemned environment. Criticisms include taking state pay, colluding with official secrecy, deserting parishes and specializing in allegedly futile endeavours. Conversely, wider commentators say chaplains portray to prisoners regenerative possibilities for any suppressed human spirit – possibilities supremely articulated from prison by Bunyan, Bonhoeffer and Solzhenitzyn. Moreover, to 'respectable' outsiders chaplains can convey from prison the potential for liberation and re-creation within every 'inner man' whilst otherwise stripped and stigmatized. Prisons expose the grotesqueness and grandeur of 'everyman'.

ALAN R. DUCE

See also: CRIME; POLICE CHAPLAINCY.

PRIVATE MEDICINE
See: NATIONAL HEALTH SERVICE.

PROFESSIONALISM
In pre-industrial Europe, the term 'profession' denoted a limited number of vocations – divinity, medicine, the law and commissioned status in the armed services – which enabled people without an unearned income to make a living outside commerce or manual work. A more contemporary view would exclude the military, probably accord divinity an uncertain standing along with some 'aspiring'

occupations, and see professions as socially prestigious avocations that control their own training, recruitment and practice, and which apply specialized knowledge, under the guidance of an ethical code, to individual and social problems. For example, Talcott Parsons (1964) sees professions as related to the growth of knowledge. As knowledge expands, so do specialisms develop which allow social needs to be more effectively met; but this also raises questions as to what knowledge is most relevant for dealing with particular types of problem, and how the uses of such knowledge may be controlled. Professional associations oversee training and practice-standards, thus guaranteeing technical competence; and enforce a code of ethics which ensure that the client's interests remain paramount. Parsons therefore sees professions as necessary – in the sense that they arise inevitably from the division of labour in industrial societies – and desirable, in that they ensure that knowledge and the power it endows are used for collective, rather than personal ends.

As against this, various authors have claimed that such interpretations are ahistorical and too readily inclined to take professionals at their own valuation. Berlant suggests that Parsons' account is more of a prescription than an explanation of professionals' behaviour. It discounts the possibility that professionals will not always conform to the prescriptions implied in Parsons' analysis – less because transgressions *do* not than because they *should* not occur. More recent historical analyses of the processes leading to professional recognition suggest that professionalism may be better understood as a particular kind of occupational control than as reflecting the 'intrinsic' nature of certain occupations. Such authors have concentrated on power relationships and the structures which permit an occupation to control its own work. Freidson (1970) argues that medicine has achieved its dominant position by establishing claims to specialist knowledge ('expertise') and a concern for the service of humanity ('ethicality'). The same author further distinguishes between the *content* and the *terms* of work: the former comprising the tasks the professional performs; the latter, the conditions and sanctions governing the conduct of those tasks. Expertise is the major justification advanced by professionals to support the claim that they should be per-

mitted to practise without interference by other groups. Ethicality is claimed to demonstrate their commitment to service. With its implicit promise to regulate members' behaviour in the public interest, it is presented as the main justification for allowing professionals autonomous control over the *terms* of their work. Through an analysis of medical organization and practice in various countries, Freidson and other writers conclude that effective control of members' behaviour is in fact almost entirely restricted to preliminary (technical) training, with rather weak formal mechanisms for the subsequent enforcement of standards or rectification of abuses.

The only significant attribute distinguishing professions from other occupations is therefore the legal right – granted through negotiation with the politically powerful – to control the content of their own work. Expertise and ethicality are resources used to justify monopoly control and self-regulation. Professions may be seen as groups which have attained dominance within an occupational area, protecting their members from competition and external direction, and dictating the terms on which other groups may enter their 'territory'.

The relationship between knowledge and ethics is thus crucial in understanding professionalism. Are ethics simply the prime among a set of largely specious bargaining counters advanced to justify a privileged self-regulating status, or the moral core which guarantees the public interest at all times? In attempting to shift the balance towards the latter alternative, part of the answer perhaps lies in a greater concentration on the ethical component in professional training. To make professionals more publicly accountable for transgressions would provide a more definite assurance, but one for which the attainment would demand the reversal of arrangements that in themselves constitute the very stuff of modern professionalism.

Berlant, J.L., *Profession and Monopoly* (Univ. California, 1975). Campbell, A.V., *Paid to Care? The Limits of Professionalism in Pastoral Care* (SPCK, 1985). Freidson, E., *Profession of Medicine* (Dodd Mead, New York, 1970). Johnson, T., *Professions and Power* (Macmillan, 1972). Larkin, G., *Occupational Monopoly and Modern Medicine* (Tavistock, 1983). Parsons, T., 'The Professions and Social Structure' in *Essays in Sociological Theory* (Free Press of Glencoe, new edn 1964).

A. ROBERTSON

See also: ETHICS, PROFESSIONAL;
INTERPROFESSIONAL RELATIONSHIPS;
PASTOR: IDENTITY AND ROLE.

PROSTITUTION

The use of sexual activities for material gain.

A prostitute may be male or female; although the vast majority are female. There are no established reasons for a person to become involved in prostitution. However, common factors can be deduced which affect the needs of the individual person regardless of age or social status. These include a need for money, for a sense of identity, purpose and security; sometimes gained from working for a pimp (male who controls the finances) or for a 'madam' (female who organizes a group of prostitutes). However recent trends seem to indicate a more independent spirit amongst working women controlling their own affairs. Prostitutes work in a variety of venues: hotels, saunas, massage parlours, escort agencies, with regular clients, through telephone and contact magazines as well as the traditional street activities in red-light areas of major towns and cities.

There are a number of different attitudes to prostitutes and to prostitution. The legal system of each country determines the overall state attitude, e.g. West Germany has legalized brothels with strict controls on the women who work there, whereas in Britain prostitution is seen as a criminal offence. The Josephine Butler Society and other interested groups seek to change the relevant laws. Where there is a known red-light area in a town or city of Great Britain there is also a high police presence to try to control the nuisance, noise and disturbance factors of street prostitutes and their clients driving around making contacts (kerb crawling). This obviously affects the attitude of local residents. A number of extreme political feminist groups have been established to try to speak out on behalf of prostitutes e.g. English Collective of Prostitutes, U S PROS (USA), Collective of Australian Prostitutes.

The attitude of the Church is generally one of indifference or judgement, often based on a lack of understanding of the complexities of prostitution. Throughout the world there are very few church groups or charities actually grappling with the ethical problems of child prostitution, or with the reasons why prostitutes are needed as well as with the practical problems of helping a prostitute leave the addictive life (or the 'game'). In Britain there is one Christian charity: the Wellclose Square Fund which has two homes, in Birmingham and London for young women at risk of becoming involved in prostitution. The charity also has a field-work team based in London trying to help prostitutes as well as trying to stimulate the Church to look afresh at its attitude to prostitutes in the light of a detailed study of the compassion of Christ for people such as prostitutes as found in the New Testament.

Prostitution will always be here. There is a great deal to be done if alternative life-styles are to be offered and the sexual needs of those who use prostitutes are to be confronted, counselled and channelled into more constructive relationships.

McLeod, E., *Women Working: Prostitution Now* (Croom Helm, 1982). Williamson, J., *Josephine Butler: the Forgotten Saint* (Faith Press, 1977). Research documents of the Wellclose Square Fund senior field-work officer, 5 Cosway Street, London NW1.

BARBARA HARROP

See also: BODY, THEOLOGY OF;
PORNOGRAPHY; SEXUALITY, THEOLOGY OF.

PROVIDENCE, DOCTRINE OF

As the Christian doctrine of creation affirms that the world is originally and continuously dependent on the creative will of God, so the docrine of providence affirms that the course of history, at the level both of nations and of individuals, is ordered and governed by God's providential control and care.

The faithful may point to this or that occurrence as a clear example of God's providential activity. For example, they have prayed for deliverance from evil and they have been delivered. God has 'answered' their prayers. If the answer has been within the ordinary pattern of events, then it is an instance of God's *particular* providence; if outside the ordinary pattern, then it is an instance of God's *miraculous* providence. Over and in everything that occurs is God's *general* providence.

Belief in divine providence is grounded in an understanding of the character of God rather than in observation of the way the world goes. Progress may or may not occur in this or that area of human life, but it is certainly neither universal nor automatic. Nor is it obvious that the lives of the faithful are less vulnerable to the ills and accidents of chance than the lives of unbelievers. Believers may be convinced that they have been the recipients of God's providential care, but there can be no objectively compelling proof that they are correctly so convinced.

God is a God who calls individuals and peoples, guides them and guards them. He is not a distant and uninterested God: he comes to his world and works out his purposes in his world. Because he is that sort of God, a God who can be confidently addressed as 'Father', whose being is fully expressed in the person and character of Jesus Christ, then clearly he is a God who cares for his creatures. Creation and providence may be distinguished the one from the other, but they cannot be separated.

The question, pastoral as well as theological, now is: *How* are we to understand God's providential activity in the world? Because God is not part of the world, and because his activity is not simply alongside and parallel to other centres of activity in the world, we cannot observe him at work. We have to use models and analogies to express the manner of his activity. There are a number of such models and analogies, but for our purposes we can group them in two classes. On the one hand there are the models which emphasize the *commanding power* of God; on the other hand there are those which emphasize the *persuasive love* of God.

If God is creator – it may be argued – if the very existence of the world derives from his word of command, if past, present and future are all open to him together in his eternity, then surely everything that happens in the world is part of his providential ordering. There is nothing that happens which does not in one way or another fulfil his good purposes. It may be impossible in some circumstances to discern what these good purposes are, but faith must hang on to the conviction that they are according to God's will and therefore all for the best. An interesting literary exploration of a view such as this is to be found in Thornton Wilder's classic novel, *The Bridge of San Luis Rey*.

The difficulty with this approach is that so much that happens in the world does not seem to express the providential care of God. If, in spite of all appearances, faith demands that nonetheless we affirm that it is part and parcel of God's providential care, are we not endangering our whole idea of God as Father?

If, however, we begin with a model of God as loving Father, then we may explore the idea that in creating the world God wills to let it go and gives it an independence of its own. Thus it creates itself through experiment, failure and achievement. There is built into it an element of chance and risk. Evil does occur. God exercises his providential care, not by preventing evil, but by bringing good out of evil. He picks up and mends the broken pieces.

If we may so understand God's way with his world, then faith in God's providence becomes a practical and powerful support to Christian discipleship. It is the faith that nothing in this world can separate us from the sustaining and recreating love of God (cf. Rom. 8.37f.).

Berkouwer, G., *The Providence of God* (Studies in Dogmatics, 2, Eerdmans, USA, 1952). Harkness, G., *The Providence of God* (Abingdon, USA, 1960). Hazelton, R., *Providence* (SCM, 1958). Niermann, E., 'Providence', *Sacramentum Mundi* (Search Press, 1970). Pontifex, M., *Providence and Freedom* (Burns and Oates, 1960). Sutcliffe, E., *Providence and Suffering* (Nelson, 1955). Wright, J.H., 'The Eternal Plan of Divine Providence' (*Theological Studies*, 27, 1966), pp. 27–57.

PETER BAELZ

See also: CREATION; EVIL; FAITH; GOD, DOCTRINE OF; THEODICY.

PSYCHIATRY AND MENTAL ILLNESS
1. Psychiatry is a medical speciality concerned with the prevention, diagnosis and treatment of mental illness; a psychiatrist is a doctor trained to recognize disturbance of mood, behaviour and intellect. A psychiatrist may also treat individuals with personality disorder (q.v.), drug abuse and situational crises (such as marital problems or bereavement reactions).

Most psychiatrists are employed by the National Health Service or by a university department; some work in private practice. A Consultant Psychiatrist has full responsibility for referred patients. (The training grades are Senior House Officer, Registrar and Senior Registrar.) Only a minority of psychiatrists are psychoanalysts (*see* PSYCHOANALYSIS), and a psychoanalyst is not always medically qualified. A clinical psychologist may treat individuals with mental illness but is not usually a qualified doctor of medicine. The sub-specialities are child psychiatry, forensic psychiatry, psychotherapy (q.v.), mental disability (*see* DISABLEMENT) and the psychiatry of old age (*see* AGEING; DEMENTIA).

2. Mental illness has conventionally been classified into (a) psychoses and (b) neuroses. The neuroses occur in up to 15% of the population and are generally characterized by the absence of delusions or hallucinations; the patient also usually retains insight into the disturbance. The distinction between neuroses and psychoses however is at times indistinct.

(a) *The psychoses*: (1) *Depressive psychoses* are characterized by slowness of movement and speech, persistently low mood and early morning wakening, weight loss and lack of interest. Delusions of guilt and self-blame also occur; self-esteem may be so low that suicide (q.v.) is contemplated or attempted. (2) *Mania*: a major psychosis that may alternate with depression and is characterized by excessive activity, lack of sleep, pressure of speech, words being linked by rhyme or sound, and the mood is usally elated. Irritability may also be a prominent feature. (3) *Schizophrenia* is a chronic mental disorder usually associated with deterioration of the personality and characterized by particular forms of abnormal mental experience, such as certain types of auditory hallucination when several voices are heard talking together describing the individual in the third person. Delusions of control may occur, as when a patient feels his or her mind or will is taken over by an outside force which controls thinking and behaviour. Religious language is sometimes used to describe the abnormal experience. Delusions of reference and somatic delusions are often present but are not regarded as specific for this illness. Thinking is often disordered and illogical; in some instances it is almost unintelligible. (4) *Organic psychoses* are caused by physical disturbances to brain function and may be acute, as following alcohol withdrawal, or chronic as in senile dementia (q.v.).

(b) *The neuroses*: (1) Anxiety neuroses are characterized by fear, worry, agitation and physical symptoms caused by excessive activity of the autonomic nervous system, e.g. frequency of micturition, restlessness, headache, abdominal pain, sweating and palpitations. (2) Obsessive-compulsive neuroses are less common neuroses and are characterized by repetitive ritual (e.g. hand-washing or

checking) carried out more frequently than necessary. Such rituals are usually regarded as unreasonable and are often resisted. Obsessional aggressive or sexual thoughts can cause much distress. (3) Hysteria: a physical symptom may be complained of which does not conform to the pattern of symptoms associated with a specific physical illness. These symptoms can be understood as a way of solving a repressed psychological conflict or achieving an advantage for the patient (secondary gain). Such a patient for example may lose his voice and so avoid a choir practice taken by a disliked choir master. (*See also* PSYCHOSOMATIC PROBLEMS). (4) Phobias are characterized by anxiety when confronted with a particular situation, e.g. claustrophobia or agoraphobia, which is common especially amongst middle-aged women and is characterized by fear and panic when leaving the house or when going to a crowded place such as a supermarket, church or theatre. Agoraphobia is often exacerbated by a co-existing depression.

3. *Causes*. Recent research has shown the substantial contribution of 'life events' (usually losses) to the causation of many mental illnesses and especially depression. When 'loss' events occur to an individual already vulnerable through personality difficulties or inheritance, then a mental illness is more likely to occur. A depressive illness is a common sequal to bereavement (q.v.) and may require urgent psychiatric treatment. Schizophrenia may be caused by abnormalities of the transmission of nervous impulses in the brain as well as by stressful life events.

Physical treatments such as electroconvulsive therapy (ECT), anti-depressant medication and major tranquillizers have an established and proven place in the treatment of some mental illnesses. ECT is especially useful in the treatment of a severe depression.

The psychotherapies include psychodynamic psychotherapy, as well as behaviour therapy. Behaviour therapy (q.v.) is particularly useful in the treatment of obsessive-compulsive neuroses and in phobic disorders. Cognitive therapy (where the therapist attempts to change the client's negative thoughts which are regarded as the primary disorder leading to the development of a depressed mood) is effective in some forms of depression as well as for patients with eating disorders.

Most general psychiatrists consider the contribution of three different aetiological models to the understanding of mental illness: (a) a developmental model when the contribution of personality and early experience to understanding the presenting problems is considered; (b) a social model which involves understanding the relevance of personal, family and social events; and (c) a biological model in which the contribution of genetic and physical factors to the illness is considered.

4. *Conclusions*. A psychiatrist may want assistance from a theologian or priest in understanding a patient's unfamiliar religious ideas. Access to the community resources of a church is helpful for some patients who require rehabilitation. A few psychiatrists may welcome a theological reflection on their work and discussion of ethical issues.

Clergy may want assistance with a disturbed parishioner and sometimes seek advice about their own difficulties. The previous hostility between psychiatry and theology is less evident, and increasingly psychiatrists work in multi-professional teams (*see* INTER-PROFESSIONAL RELATIONSHPS) that include clinical psychologists, social workers, psychiatric nurses and occupational therapists. The contribution of a religious counsellor to such a team may also be most valuable.

Clare, A., *Psychiatry in Dissent* (Tavistock, 1976).
Stafford Clark, D. and Smith, A.C., *Psychiatry for Students* (Allen & Unwin, 1964).

JOHN L. COX

See also: MENTAL HEALTH; PERSONALITY DISORDER.

PSYCHOANALYSIS

The term 'psychoanalysis' has two quite distinct connotations; it is both a technique for investigation and a treatment of emotional and mental disorders, founded by Freud and added to by subsequent psychoanalytical theorists and practitioners.

The basic assumption is that the conflict and the defences secondary to it are in the 'unconscious' and therefore inaccessible to the patient and are the result of repressions (*see* DEFENCE MECHANISMS). The psychoanalytic technique is therefore basically concerned in providing a setting in which the patient is enabled to experience and appraise

himself or herself without constant need to make excessive use of defensive mechanisms such as repression, denial, projection and sublimation.

Psychoanalytical therapy involves among other psychological principles such important ones as: unconscious content, free association, resistance, transference/countertransference, interpretation and analysis of dreams. The permissive trusting and secure relationship between the analyst and patient facilitate free association; opinions and feelings are expressed by the patient with minimum guidance from the analyst irrespective of its logical content. The patient is asked to express 'anything that comes into mind'; this facilitates the emergence of symbolic material from inaccessible portions of the mind, and what has been unconscious becomes conscious and understandable and its meaning can be recognized and accepted. Free association may be regarded as a method of recovering the history of a symptom and its defensive function. Perhaps the most significant concept in psychoanalytical therapy is what is called the transference (q.v.); this is the emotional reaction of the patient towards the analyst. The ingredients of this reaction are usually manifested as a repetition in the patient's present life of unconscious emotional attitudes developed during childhood within the family group and especially towards his or her parents. It represents a carrying over and attaching to the therapist of friendly, possessive, dependent, as well as hostile and ambivalent attitudes and feelings that the patient previously experienced towards the parent or a meaningful person in early childhood.

The analyst becomes symbolically the parent or parent-substitute within this scenario, and important unconscious repressed factors are revealed which, in conjunction with dream material and free association, can be analysed, interpreted and made understandable to the patient. The analyst, through interpretation and understanding of the patient's communication (q.v.), both verbal as well as behavioural, attempts to penetrate the patient's personality defences and bring the underlying conflicts into consciousness so that they may be dealt with rationally.

Psychoanalytical treatment can be conducted only by a suitably trained analyst, who apart from didactic training has also had a personal analysis and during training had extensive experience of treating patients analytically under supervision of a senior training analyst.

The selection of suitable patients for a psychoanalytic treatment is a matter of considerable importance. Many factors relating to the severity of disturbance, capacity for insight, motivation and feasibility of such a commitment within the individual's life-style have to be carefully considered. This again can only be done by an experienced psychoanalyst.

Psychoanalysis is an intensive treatment which necessitates the patient attending regularly for 4 or 5 sessions weekly, each lasting 50 minutes. The duration of the treatment varies, depending on the severity of underlying problems, but usually extends to several years. The patient is encouraged to recline on the couch during the session, while the analyst is seated behind and to one side, the reason being that this setting enables the patient to relax and develop free association, and to be observed by the analyst without being able to look constantly for signs of the analyst's responses. This procedure has been found to be most suitable for exploration of the patient's unconscious.

Psychoanalysis has elucidated many aspects of human behaviour, it has produced insights which broadened our understanding of human relations, creativity, destructiveness. It has influenced methods of child-rearing, our education system, and also given a degree of understanding of the meanings of religion, works of art, literature and politics. The contribution of psychoanalysis to the understanding and treatment of mental illness has had a profound influence on the various reforms and has resulted in a more liberal, compassionate and accepting social attitude to those conditions.

Abraham, K., *Selected Papers on Psychoanalysis* (Hogarth, 1922). Freud, S., *Selected Papers* (International Psychoanalytical Library, 1924–1950). Glover, E., 'The Indications for Psychoanalysis' (*J. Ment. SC.*, 100, 1954), pp. 393–401. Karush, A. and Ovesey, L., 'Unconscious Mechanisms of Magical Repair' (*Arch. Gen. Psych.*, 5, 55–69, 1961), pp. 55–69. Kubie, L.S., *Practical and Theoretical Aspects of Psychoanalysis* (Internat. Univ. Press, New York, 1960). Nunberg, H., *Principles of Psychoanalysis; their Application to the Neuroses*. Internat. Univ. Press, 1955.

ANDREW SKARBEK

See also: ANALYTICAL PSYCHOLOGY; COUNSELLING; PSYCHIATRY AND MENTAL ILLNESS; PSYCHOTHERAPY.

PSYCHOLOGY
See: ANALYTICAL PSYCHOLOGY; DEPTH PSYCHOLOGY; PARAPSYCHOLOGY.

PSYCHOLOGY OF RELIGION
The question, 'What is the psychology of religion?' has no straightforward answer. There are almost as many definitions of 'religion' as investigators, and there are many different 'psychologies', each with its own interpretative framework and experimental method. In the most general sense, the various psychologies of religion are efforts to identify and understand psychological factors in human experiences of what is believed to be divine. Their concerns are not only with the major world faiths, but also with the newer cults and sects, some of which show distinctive behaviour patterns.

For psychologists, religion is an area of human experience and behaviour interesting both in its own right and for the illumination it can provide for study of other fields, e.g. superstition and myth. For Christian pastors, the psychologies of religion can offer insights into aspects of the development and maintenance of religious attitudes and behaviour. One issue for pastors is the relationship between Christian theology and psychology, and the interpretative framework by which psychological theories and experimental results are evaluated. Although some psychologists seek to interpret religious phenomena in a reductionistic way, most acknowledge that their concern is with psychological accounts – for example, of the development of religious faith, and of the functions which beliefs serve – and not with the truth claims of religion (which are not open to psychological investigation). From the standpoint of Christian theology, therefore, psychology can be seen to serve an important though limited function as one among several levels of understanding of the human person.

Many religious thinkers have reflected on their inner experiences: Jeremiah, Augustine, John Bunyan, Jonathan Edwards, Søren Kierkegaard, to name a few. But it was the birth of psychology as an experimental science at the end of the nineteenth century which encouraged systematic studies of religious processes. In 1881 G.S. Hall published his research on conversion. In 1899,

E.D. Starbuck wrote the first 'Psychology of Religion'. It was William James, whose Gifford Lectures of 1901–2 (*The Varieties of Religious Experience*) brought the psychology of religion into the centre of academic interest, who set the agenda for much subsequent work. There was a decline in scientific psychology of religion between 1910 and 1940, but a revival of interest in the 1950s led to the establishment of the *Journal for the Scientific Study of Religion* in 1962.

Psychologists of religion have had difficulty in defining appropriate methods of study. James based his work on biographies and personal descriptions. More recent scientific investigators have used questionnaires and statistical surveys. The problem is that true religious experience includes an intensely personal, mysterious and other-worldly element which cannot be the object of empirical investigation. Psychologists have therefore tended to choose between a *phenomenological* approach, based on the phenomena of religious experience as reported, and an *empirical* approach limited to what can be observed and measured, namely religious *behaviour*, or 'religiosity'.

During the period of decline in psychology of religion, some interest was kept alive by the analytical psychologies, notably of Freud and Jung. Freud offered two main theories of the psychological roots of religion, both of which had considerable influence. In *Totem and Taboo* he proposed that religion represents an elaborate projection of the need to cope with guilt, shame and remorse arising from primitive jealousies. Later in *The Future of an Illusion*, he saw religion as a compensation for frustration and stress, provided by a fantasy protective parent figure. Jung was much more positive towards religion than Freud, believing that a religious attitude was natural to human beings, and associating experiences of 'God' with the unconscious levels of mind which Jung believed all people share. (*See* ANALYTICAL PSYCHOLOGY; PSYCHOANALYSIS.)

Current research focuses on the following areas of specific interest to pastors:
(1) Definition and measurement. What constitutes the 'religiously committed' person? What is religious behaviour? And what methods are appropriate to measure 'religiosity'? Some writers have distinguished between 'intrinsic' religion (religion as an end in itself: such persons *live* their religion); and 'extrinsic' religion (a means to another end, e.g. security, solace or status; such persons *use* their religion). What is the significance of 'folk religion'?
(2) Developmental psychology. What are the psychological roots of religion? What psychological factors are relevant to conversion? What correspondence is there between emotional and cognitive development and spiritual maturing?
(3) Social psychology. What are the social factors which underlie religion? Why, for example, is there much more religious activity in the USA than in Britain? What effects do parental attitudes, social influences, sex, age, class, life-crises, have on a person's religious experiences? What light does the psychology of group behaviour throw on the nature of the church as a group, and of the priest as a leader?
(4) Personality. Can links be made between temperament-type and e.g. denominational allegiance; modes of worship and prayer, attitudes to dogma?
(5) Mysticism and altered states of consciousness. What are the points of comparison and contrast between true religious experiences and other similar mystical or drug-induced states?
(6) Religion, psychopathology and mental health. Which sorts of religious experiences are associated with good or poor personal adjustment and what is their relationship to mental health and stability?

All these questions are being explored. Some recent Christian writers have also sought to develop a pastoral psychology of religion, drawing on the findings of psychologists, the primary purpose of which is to guide the Christian counsellor and spiritual director.

Argyle, M. and **Beit-Hallahmi, R.**, *The Social Psychology of Religion* (Routledge, 1975). **Batson, C.D.**, and **Ventis, W.L.**, *The Religious Experience* (OUP, 1982). **Faber, H.**, *The Psychology of Religion* (SCM, 1972). **Hardy, A.**, *The Spiritual Nature of Man* (Clarendon, 1979). **Hay, D.**, *Exploring Inner Space* (Penguin, 1982). **Newton Malony, H.** (ed.), *Current Perspectives in the Psychology of Religion* (Eerdmans, 1977). **Oates, Wayne E.**, *The Psychology of Religion* (Word Books, Texas, 1973). **Tisdale, J.R.** (ed.), *Growing Edges in the Psychology of Religion* (Nelson Hall, 1980).

DAVID ATKINSON

PSYCHOSIS
See: PSYCHIATRY AND MENTAL ILLNESS.

PSYCHOSOMATIC PROBLEMS
'Psychosomatic' is a vague term applicable to two groups of actual or supposed relations between bodily and psychological (mental) events.

1. *Causation*. Certain diseases with obvious physical manifestations – bronchial asthma, rheumatoid arthritis, and ulcerative colitis, for instance – have sometimes been said to be caused, in a fundamental sense, by psychological disturbances often formulated in psychoanalytical terms such as 'unconscious conflict' or 'repressed anger'. It is now recognized that, in these illnesses, emotions play relatively little part in initial causation, while often affecting established disease.

Many ailments other than these so-called 'psychosomatic diseases' occur in relation to environmental events which are either generally stressful (i.e. make demands on the person) or signify important individual meaning. These are the same kinds of circumstances which tend to provoke psychiatric disorders such as depression; it seems to be a matter of individual predisposition and vulnerability which determines whether a person develops a psychiatric or a bodily disorder in response to stress.

So psychosomatic problems concern the occurrence of bodily illness, or the worsening of established disease, in response to emotional events.

2. *Experience*. Bodily and psychological experiences often coexist. (a) normally, e.g. in behaviours involving bodily functions, such as sexual intercourse or eating a meal; (b) when there is malfunction in some mechanism required for such an experience, as for instance in erectile impotence or when abdominal pain follows a fatty meal; (c) in normal emotions.

The fact that emotions ordinarily have bodily and psychological components draws attention to problems which may arise when bodily or psychological experiences fail to occur when they should. Add to this the normal tendency of feelings to be evoked by events and we can distinguish several sorts of problems. Firstly, experience of bodily emotion without the psychological aspect: this may lead to fruitless searching for serious bodily disease. Secondly, experience of psychic distress without bodily distress; suffering may be misunderstood, underestimated, and inappropriately ascribed to personal (moral) failure. Thirdly, emotional experiences, which create a sense of helplessness because the environmental participants are not perceived.

Help for all these problems is based upon spending time listening to, and trying to understand, the distressed person's account of bodily, psychological, and environmental aspects of their troubles. The pastoral carer need not be over-concerned about 'missing' serious bodily disease if medical help is advised for a client who looks 'ill' or who reports symptoms which sound serious.

Stafford-Clark, D. and **Smith, A.C.**, *Psychiatry for Students* (Allen & Unwin, 7th edn 1964).

J.P. WATSON

See also: BODY, THEOLOGY OF; MENTAL HEALTH.

PSYCHOTHERAPY
A psychological method of treatment which aims at bringing about changes in the patient through direct, mainly verbal, communications.

Psychotherapy has as its basis a psychodynamic approach to the situation, in that the individual's past life, especially childhood, is seen to have an emotional influence on present adult relationships. This influence may arise from emotional traumas which were experienced in childhood and remain not only unresolved but also have been banished from memory.

The process of psychotherapy may be seen to have three facets: (1) *Insight* – the discernment of those factors in childhood which have created patterns of emotional reaction. These may result in the individual unconsciously setting up situations which are symbolic of the past either in the hope of resolving or preventing the basic hurt. Insight is the process of interpreting these symbolic patterns gradually working towards uncovering the prime events. (2) *Emotional discharge* – the emotions requiring discharge are those which relate to the primary events. These are often distorted by covering emotions set up as a method of coping, i.e. a secondary emotion which acts as a resolution to or a prevention of the primary emotion. (3) *Behavioural modification* – while insight may be gained and

227

emotions discharged, there may remain an habitual reaction to symbolic patterns of the past. This now requires modification.

Psychotherapy exists in a variety of forms. These variations may be considered as dependent upon which of the above processes is taken as the major focus of treatment and the relationship of this major process to the other two.

Since the emotional problems are seen as flowing from childhood experience, the methodology will always take this into account in some way. In classical analysis this is achieved through the transference in which the therapist becomes, emotionally, the parent and the client relives the childhood relationship. This process may be seen to take place more symbolically in other therapies, which would rely on the therapeutic alliance in which to help the client reclaim the 'hurt child' within while still retaining their adult relationship with the therapist.

Research shows that three elements are required for a good outcome: (1) Empathetic relationship, which may vary from the full use of transference to a therapeutic alliance. (2) The methodology employed is one in which both therapist and client concur. The methodology itself appears to be secondary to its mutual acceptance, and no doubt also as to its effective use. (3) A safe place in which the therapy is undergone. The client needs to feel secure. While this comes primarily from the relationship with the therapist, there is now good evidence to demonstrate that the place itself plays a vital role.

Brown, D. and **Pedder, J.**, *Introduction to Psychotherapy* (Tavistock, 1979). **Malan, D.**, *Individual Psychotherapy and the Science of Psychodynamics* (Butterworth, 1979). **Marteau, L.**, *Encounter and the New Therapies: Practical Psychiatry*, ed. S. Crown (Northwood, 1981), pp.111–14. **Meltzoff, J.** and **Kornreich, M.**, *Research in Psychotherapy* (Aldine, 1970). **Varma, V.**, *Psychotherapy Today* (Constable, 1974). **Wills, T.**, (ed.), *Basic Processes in Helping Relationships*, (Academic Press, 1982).

LOUIS MARTEAU

See also: ANALYTICAL PSYCHOLOGY; COUNSELLING; GROUP PSYCHOTHERAPY AND COUNSELLING; PSYCHOANALYSIS.

R

RACE RELATIONS

(1) The attitude of one ethnic group to another ethnic group or groups, or of individuals within such groups to neighbours of different origin and/or colour. (2) The new growth of awareness of tension in society between races, leading to the establishment of bodies to encourage good social mixing and acceptance between races. (3) Central and local government legislation and rules governing the expression of antagonism based on race, colour, discrimination at work, in housing, etc. (4) Educational provision, syllabus content and teacher attitude in school and college. (5) Attitudes of churches to colour, common Christian worship, inter-faith relationship (*see* MULTI-FAITH MINISTRIES).

Fundamentally, there is only one race – the human race. Within this race, differences of attitude arise from origin, social, cultural and religious background, giving rise to pluralizing and blurring the use of 'race' to ethnic origins and colour. Prejudice (q.v.) is not necessarily inherent in human nature. It springs from the instinct of self-preservation and self-development. Nature breeds association and national preferences, standards, moral and religious principles with loyalties to be held and defended. Some philosophies, psychological writings and political systems teach the superiority of one race over another.

Old Testament revelation seems to give the chosen people a superior status with a divine right over other peoples, with laws against inter-marriage (cf. relationship to the Samaritans). This is used by those sponsoring apartheid etc. Jesus Christ broke this tradition (cf. Samaritan woman, John 4.7–42; centurion, Luke 7.2–10; Good Samaritan, Luke 10.29–37). Early Christian church controversy centred on circumcision. Peter's racial views were broadened after having a personal vision and meeting Cornelius (Acts 10.9–48).

Throughout history, religion has been deeply inter-woven with enmity between races (e.g. the Crusades). The idea of racial and religious superiority was frequently expressed by European powers extending into Africa, India, and the Americas (cf. the slave trade, American Indians, Spain and the Incas). This was also true of Chinese and Japanese attitudes to Europeans. Twentieth-century thinking on and working through relationship between races has advanced radically. In the USA Martin Luther King's leadership helped to change American attitudes, and then spread worldwide. World War 2 led to the break up of the British Empire and emergence of new independent nations, together with widespread immigration from Third-World countries.

Immigration dented established patterns of thought and racial mixture in church and society in many Northern and Western countries. Britain responded to its new status and role with Race Relations Acts (1960s and 1970s) and Immigration and Nationality Laws. Community Relations Councils and Officers were set up locally. Central government worked through to the present Commission for Racial Equality. Churches established their own bodies in the British Council of Churches and in different denominations.

The new social mixture in Britain led to polarization between those working for racial harmony and those opposing any black presence (the 'National Front' etc.). Efforts towards racial harmony began with the theory of *assimilation*, by which immigrants gradually lose separate identity among the indigenous population. Then came *integration* – not total absorption but a welding together of differences. Today the key theory and policy is *pluralism* – the acceptance of differences between cultures, races and religions, knowledge of which should be shared, while assuming a basic living by all according to the rule of law.

Education has come under close scrutiny, with demands to eliminate racially biased textbooks, and for accommodation of dietary rules and customs, and acceptance of some religious requirements (e.g. the Sikh turban, Muslim rules on mixed PE and swimming).

Teacher training and teacher attitudes have recently been reviewed by the Swann Committee. Racial tension and rioting have led to new regulations on stopping and searching, and to police returning to the beat – community policing. Churches, especially in the inner city, have played a useful part in bettering relations between races and between 'blacks' and the police. The Scarman Report following the Brixton riots in 1981 has made sweeping suggestions, many still to be implemented.

The Scarman Report (HMSO, 1981). *Select Committee on Race Relations and Immigration* (HMSO, 1977). **Centre for Contemporary Cultural Studies,** *The Empire Strikes Back: Race and Racism in 70s Britain* (Hutchinson, 1982). **Eysenck, H.J.,** *Race, Intelligence and Education* (Temple Smith, 1971). **Fryer, Peter,** *Staying Power: the History of the Black People in Britain* (Pluto Press, 1984). **Milner, David,** *Children and Race: Ten Years On* (Ward Lock Educ., 1983). **Rex, John,** *Race, Colonialism and the City* (Routledge, 1973).

MICHAEL HOLLINGS

See also: INTERCULTURAL PASTORAL CARE; MIXED MARRIAGE; MULTI-FAITH MINISTRIES; PREJUDICE.

RAPE AND RAPE COUNSELLING

In the context of this article rape describes a crime in which a man over the age of fourteen years forces a woman or girl to have sexual intercourse against her will.

The man may achieve this by the actual use of, or threat of, physical violence, or he may render her incapable of resistance with alcohol or other drugs. A man can be guilty of rape if he takes advantage of a woman by false pretences, for instance, by impersonating her husband and approaching her just as she wakes from sleep. A woman may be considered to have been raped if she allows a doctor to put his penis into her vagina because she thought that he was carrying out a medical operation and so does not offer initial resistance. Legally, rape has occurred as soon as forcible penetration of a woman's body has been effected. The sex act does not have to be completed.

Rape is a serious crime. Women who have been raped commonly report the event with horror and disgust. They suffer fear, pain, humiliation and degradation. If they resist they know that they may lose their lives or be maimed. If they are overpowered physically, or surrender through fear, they are likely to feel polluted. They may even regret having survived. They are often distraught, restless and incoherent immediately after the attack,

although some women remain unnaturally calm and over-controlled. Later, their present or future personal relationships may suffer because the memory of the rape can interfere with their ability to experience sexual pleasure or orgasm. Rape victims often feel guilty, and their guilt is sometimes reinforced by police officers, doctors or lawyers who suggest that they may have contributed to their plight by provocative behaviour, or accuse them of lying. Experience in rape counselling suggests that many victims never report the crime because they, their relatives and counsellors hesitate to expose them to the ordeal of trial by innuendo and public exposure.

Rape victims and rapists need skilled help. The victims need immediate help and support after an attack. They need the catharsis of describing the rape in detail, but this is only helpful if they can pour out their feelings uninhibitedly to a sympathetic, objective and experienced listener. Rape is such a terrible experience that the shock itself can distort a person's memory in the immediate period after the attack. The help of experienced counsellors is valuable at this stage, especially if the listener is not connected with anyone who might be concerned with asking necessary questions and making examinations for legal reasons. In some countries like Britain, rape crisis centres exist to give this kind of help, and their addresses are known to local police officers and social workers. Continued counselling is usually necessary, although some people mistakenly advise a raped person to forget the experience as soon as possible. Long-term counselling is often wise because of the frequency of delayed psychological effects which can cripple a woman years after the original event.

In recent years it has been recognized that rapists need skilled help as well as their victims. They may be appropriately punished, and some men deserve the life-sentences they are given. Sometimes custodial sentences are necessary for the protection of society, but in general rapists need more help than they have commonly received in the past. One recently tried form of treatment has involved the setting up of special meetings between convicted rapists and their victims at which the feelings of both parties can be ventilated in the presence of skilled counsellors. The effectiveness of this kind of treatment has yet to be fully evaluated, but some initial reports have been encouraging.

This article has confined itself to women who have been raped by men. It should be remembered that men and boys who are sexually assaulted by members of their own sex, and women who are forcibly attacked by other women, can suffer very similar traumata, and similar careful counselling is helpful to them and their attackers as well.

Brownmiller, Susan, *Against Our Will* (Secker & Warburg, 1975). Coote, Anna, and Gill, Tess, *Women's Rights* (Penguin, 1974).

UNA KROLL

See also: PROSTITUTION; SEXUAL DEVIATION; SEXUALITY, THEOLOGY OF.

RAPPORT

Used generally to describe accord or harmony between people. In psychotherapy and allied work, a state of relatedness, or the process that leads to it, which can promote healing.

Rapport was adopted by hypnotists of the second half of the 19th century to describe the basic relation with their subjects. Janet (1896) elaborated a theory of rapport in psychological medicine, distinguishing a two-fold progressive function: it expressed a creative dependence arising between doctor and patient in which the latter could begin to face psychic pain, and it could enable the doctor to engender movement towards maturity and independence. Its effect on the doctor was not examined until Freud used these researches to fill out his theory of transference (q.v.) and counter-transference. Freud also observed that a deepened rapport revived in patients their earlier attitudes towards parents and significant others, which could be used therapeutically.

Today rapport has been defined as 'the foundation . . . for any growing therapeutic relationship' and 'the psychic environment in which healing, growth and successful coping can occur' (Clinebell). It is considered to arise through disciplined listening (q.v.) and the reflecting back of a client's feelings, which promotes empathy in the counsellor and catharsis (q.v.) in the client. Research quoted by Rogers (1967) suggests an *intellectual* attempt to grasp a person's trouble is less effective than a whole-hearted *desire to understand* and to be present emotionally with the sufferer. Using intuition and sensitivity to pick up 'resonance' between his or her own humanity and the client's, the counsellor eschews curiosity and intrusive attempts to solve troubles, allowing rapport to grow through genuine respect for and accurate awareness of the sufferer's condition.

Rapport can be lost through premature interpretation and blocked by a counsellor's unawareness of interaction with the client. It is increased by empathic focus on presenting problems, underlying feelings or hidden agenda and by well-timed interpretation. In work with couples, some 'gate-keeping' may also be required to let the less articulate partner in. In group counselling (q.v.) and groups in the church (q.v.), rapport can arise creatively through the leader's attention to group process, and may promote a high degree of self-understanding and acceptance (q.v.) in members, so that attitudes and ways of functioning can change for the better. Rapport is always under threat from ambivalence (q.v.) and especially in closing sessions, where strong affirmation of the client's feelings has to be joined with equally firm insistence on the realities of termination.

Clinebell, H.J., *Basic Types of Pastoral Counselling* (Abingdon, Nashville, 1966), p. 49ff. Ellenberger, H.F., *The Discovery of the Unconscious* (Harper, New York, 1970). Rogers, C.R., *On Becoming a Person* (Constable, 1967), p. 44.

R.M. SMYTHE

See also: EMPATHY; LISTENING; TRANSFERENCE.

REASSURANCE

The attempt to relieve anxiety by interventions designed to show that things are not as bad as had been thought.

At first sight this seems an obviously desirable activity and particularly appropriate for the pastor as a representative of the Christian gospel (*see* CONSOLATION). There are, however, certain considerations from the discipline of counselling which should be born in mind: (1) It may be important for a troubled person to experience fully their painful feelings such as grief, depression, anger, doubt or despair in order to work through these feelings in a healthy manner. Premature reassurance or comfort may deprive them of the space needed for doing this. (2) The attempt to reassure may in fact succeed only in communicating the pastor's own anxiety. Recipients may feel that their bad feelings are too frightening for the pastor to tolerate and their worst fears about them will thus be confirmed. (3) Reassurance that

231

may be most needed by people in distress is that conveyed indirectly by experiencing the warm, attentive, understanding presence of another as they face the worst, without any distraction of attempts to reassure.

This may make considerable demands on the resources of the helper. Anxieties may be stirred up both by those unresolved problems in the counsellor that resonate to those in the sufferer, e.g. anger, grief, fear of dying, and also by the particular experience of helplessness. It is difficult for a would-be helper in an activist, technological culture to realize that to allow oneself to feel helpless may be an important condition of actually being helpful.

Moreover, there is often a particular pressure on pastors to promote positive attitudes by exhortation. These factors, together with a widespread confusion of optimism and hope (q.v.) may lead to a misplaced attempt to reassure. There are of course occasions when direct reassurance is entirely appropriate, especially where simple factual information is needed. The crucial question is whether the pastoral counsellor, in offering direct reassurance, is doing so to meet his or her own needs or that of the sufferer.

Clinebell, H., *Basic Types of Pastoral Counselling* (Abingdon, Nashville, 1966;. Foskett, J., *Meaning in Madness* (SPCK, 1984). Jacobs, M., *Still Small Voice* (SPCK, 1982).

DEREK BLOWS

See also: CONSOLATION; EMPATHY; LISTENING.

REBELLION

Open resistance against established authority.

A person, or group of people can respond to an intolerable situation, either personal or institutional, by openly fighting to achieve change. It can be a healthy and brave act to do this and can lead to a genuine improvement in circumstances to the good of society as a whole or the individual concerned. At times, however, the rebellious act can, of itself, cause great damage on both sides, increase aggression (q.v.) and replace one repressive situation with a worse one: the ideological impetus being lost, and brutality and counter aggression replacing the old order. Individuals, faced with repressive situations at home, at work, or in the larger society, have the capacity to grow and mature by acts of rebellion, or, if these are improperly focused, can become violent either to the self or others,

call up increased repression upon themselves or relapse into apathy (q.v.) and depression (q.v.) by being unable to free themselves from their circumstances.

Working for change does not necessarily involve rebellion. In a healthy society, individuals and groups should be able to enable change to occur by negotiation rather than confrontation. There may be anger (q.v.), but not despair. There is the element of mutual trust and hope.

All human beings need sufficient freedom to be able to establish their own identity, to express their point of view, to create and to give and take affection and caring. People who have experienced a basically caring home environment can be trusted to have sufficient internal controls so that they neither need harsh outer controlling systems nor to be destructive toward others. Good parenting involves allowing for dependency and for offering of sufficient external controls, so that the children know where they stand, but sufficient freedom to enable them to learn to take responsibility for themselves and their own actions.

The severely deprived child will have little sense of personal value and few internal controls, and will not be capable of coping with necessary external ones. The over-repressed child may either withdraw into helpless dependency, never reaching mature autonomy, or become destructively rebellious. All small children and adolescents test the love and strength of their parents and the outside environment; it gives them hope that the world is safe and that they can have some personal power without being destructive. The over-repressed individual or society may explode into destructive acts against others or the self which are unfocused and purely negative and aggressive. A genuine rebellion has the seeds of an ideal and creative effort, in effect, hope for a betterment of the situation and liberalization of the individual or the institution. Such changes have taken place throughout the history of humanity. Social groupings have given way to repressive systems and these in turn have had to give way to more liberal systems. This can be said to be true of any institution be it the State, the Church, or even the family.

In repressive systems the problem is that those people struggling to emerge from repression, seeking an ideal of liberality may, and frequently do, after the early, idealistic battle, themselves create structures as rigid as the very institution they have fought to eradicate. They often fear that the new institution is so fragile that they must fight to protect it. While rebellion, therefore, can be healthy and morally sound and necessary, what has to be constantly guarded against is that the brave members of a rebellious force, excellent in battle, are unable when in power to enable freedom to flourish, for so often the seeds of anger and hostility are within the very people who fight so bravely.

To return to the family, the child can rebel against parents in order to achieve independence, safe in the knowledge that this can be done constructively. That is to say that the parents will be able to learn from the child that such efforts are necessary, but they will be capable of seeing that the child does not go too far, by not giving freedom to endanger emotional or physical safety, or to become a little dictator who not only causes anguish in the family, but is harmful to himself or herself. A really angry and rebellious child can create a situation where he or she is thoroughly disliked and can cause such disruption as to be finally excluded from love.

Negotiation is not always possible, and people caught in an attitude of mind cannot always be reasoned with and frequently are not prepared to change, but one should beware, if rebellion is necessary, that counter-aggression does not recreate the very system that has been fought against. One should work toward understanding a deepening of trust that new ideas, new ideologies are not necessarily undermining of the old order, but are as likely to enhance the old order, refresh it and give it greater stability.

Skynner, Robin, and Cleese, John, *Families and How to Survive Them* (Methuen, 1983). Storr, Anthony, *Human Aggression* (Penguin, 1971)

FAITH SPICER

See also: ADOLESCENCE; AGGRESSION; ANGER; CONFLICT; PARENTING.

RECONCILIATION
The superseding of estrangement between persons, or groups of persons, by their coming willingly to accept, and in some degree to love, one another; reconciliation can be an action, a process, or an accomplished fact.

In the Bible, an initiating agent of reconciliation is sometimes the offended party, as when God reconciled the world to himself (2 Cor. 5.19); sometimes the offender, as when 'at the altar' we remember that our brother 'has something against us' and, in accordance with Christ's command (Matt. 5.24), we go at once to be reconciled to our brother; and sometimes a third party, as when those who have a 'ministry of reconciliation' urge others to 'be reconciled' (2 Cor. 5.18, 20). Since people who are reconciled to one another are only willingly reconciled, a person, a third party, who wishes to act as reconciler has limited power, succeeding only if those whose estrangement he or she wishes to see ended are, or come to be, willing that it should be ended. Accordingly, those who believe in human freedom (q.v.) will not expect that a third party who aims at the reconciliation of two estranged people can guarantee success for his or her efforts, however resourceful, purposeful, or sensitive these may be. In our world, reconciliation is at least an important part of that peace whose makers are said to be 'blessed' . . . sons of God' (Matt. 5.9), and so, although it is of uncertain outcome, reconciling peacemaking belongs to all Christians.

The superseding of estrangement need not require that justice be satisfied; forgiveness or forgiving mercy can and often does enable reconciliation to happen in circumstances where justice cannot be done, either because the offender does not possess that of which forfeiture would or could be just, or because no one can say what justice might consist of in the case in question. It might be thought that the importance of forgiveness in the prime case of New Testament reconciliation, namely God's loving acceptance of sinners, would make this point inescapably. But in Western Christianity the Pauline assertion that God's righteousness has been established by the justifying and redeeming work of Jesus Christ (Rom. 3.21ff.) has been widely taken, since St Anselm, to mean that retributive justice (according to which every offence must be balanced and cancelled by a fitting *quid pro quo*) has been satisfied. On this view, God's *kindness* is seen, in that God provided that which has to be paid for man's salvation; but this kindness is not, properly, forgiveness; because the debt is paid, the Evangelists' note of forgiving mercy is lost, St Paul's understanding of righteousness is distorted, and a false paradigm of reconciliation as requiring retributive justice is set up.

While, therefore, just reparation or punishment is not a necessary condition of reconciliation, a readiness on the part of an offender to make good, so far as possible, the wrong done is nevertheless an important mark of his or her willingness to enter into a genuine reconciliation. Otherwise the costly grace extended by God or neighbour is cheapened (see Rom. 6 and Bonhoeffer 1959).

The reconciliation which God effects in Christ involves the kindling of love (2 Cor. 5.14), and the peace of God's rule which the blessed peacemaker brings is more than the absence of hostility. Mere absence of animosity to, or resigned acceptance of, another is not therefore a sufficient aim of the reconciler.

There are other kinds of reconciliation, such as reconciliation between viewpoints, which are of secondary interest here; but one further species of reconciliation does call for particular notice, that in which a person is reconciled to himself or herself (see ACCEPTANCE). To the extent that a person may be regarded as two people (as in some psychoses (see PSYCHIATRY AND MENTAL ILLNESS) or in self-deception), to that extent the foregoing may helpfully apply to the process of integration, though when integration has come about and the person is, as we might say, whole and self-loving, talk of plurality of selves has ceased to be so obviously appropriate. The interpretation of such talk in any context is a continuing matter of controversy in psychoanalytic and philosophical literature.

Anselm of Canterbury, *Cur Deus Homo*. **Bonhoeffer, D.**, *The Cost of Discipleship*, tr. R.H. Fuller (SCM, 1959), pp. 33–47, 95–103. **Haight, M.R.**, *A Study of Self-Deception* (Harvester, Brighton, 1980). **Kittle, G.** (ed.), *Theological Dictionary of the New Testament*, vol. 1, tr. G.W. Bromiley (Eerdmans, Michigan, 1964), pp. 254–59. **Taylor, V.**, *Forgiveness and Reconciliation* (Macmillan, 1941).

J. HOUSTON

See also: CONFESSION; FAITH.

RECORD-KEEPING

Record-keeping covers the recording and storing of written information required for present use and/or future reference. Clergy and other Christian pastoral workers, as a mark of their love for others, and in obedience to God, will want to give of their best to those they seek to help. Good record-keeping

is a practical and an important reflection of this concern. Much time can be saved, serious mistakes avoided, and help and support more quickly and effectively given where good records are available and properly used.

Broadly speaking such records need to cover personal circumstances, details of discussions and correspondence, records of visits made, together with other relevant material. Any tendency to think that such records can be dispensed with because less important than other aspects of the work should be resisted. To be even moderately effective pastoral workers, whether working on their own or as a team, pastors must be able to rely on accurate and sufficient written records. A good memory is a poor alternative. When pastoral workers are involved together as a team, an efficient system is essential so that information is available and accessible to all in an agreed and understandable form.

Careful thought should be given as to exactly what such records will be for and what form they should take. It is possible to keep too many records; too much time is taken up in maintaining them. The rule should be to have a system which is as simple as possible yet adequate, keeping only what is important. A second rule is to keep records completely up-to-date with changes made as and when they occur. Inaccurate records can be worse than no records at all. This is particularly so where records may be used by several workers, for example in a counselling or chaplaincy centre.

Basic information to be recorded covers an outline of people's circumstances and history: name, address, telephone number, age, family details, employment history, church relationship, health, etc. Index cards are ideal for this, the reverse of the card allowing for dates of visits and brief comments to be recorded. Or an alphabetically indexed, loose-leaf notebook can do the same work. Both methods are easy and quick to keep up-to-date and are portable. Correspondence, notes on meetings, discussions and visits can be filed along with other relevant papers in an ordinary filing system.

Most records can be kept in a short, annotated form: personal 'shorthand' or abbreviation usefully reduces time spent on records. But when other workers in the team require to use these records such information must be readily understood.

Confidentiality is important, because good

pastoral work can be spoilt by a breach of trust, or the fear of such. Records containing private information should be kept secure at home, or locked in offices and files, with access restricted to those properly authorized.

Computers are increasingly being used for keeping records. Speed of retrieval is an advantage, but they can be time-consuming to maintain. For a small and simple system the cost and effort involved are probably not worth it.

Bacon, Fred, *Church Administration, A Guide for Baptist Ministers and Church Officers* (Bristol and District Assoc. of Baptist Churches, 1981). Clinebell, Howard J., *Basic Types of Pastoral Counseling* (Abingdon, 1966), pp. 75–6.

ANDREW F. ANDERSON

See also: CONFIDENTIALITY; VISITING.

REFERRAL

The practice of referring a person to another more qualified individual or agency.

In pastoral care it is the practice of referring a parishioner or counsellee to a more appropriate resource. Important to the practice of referral is a knowledge of whom to refer, where to refer, and how to refer. Ministers should look for help through referral in cases: (a) where the counsellee can receive more effective help from someone else; (b) where medical or institutional care is needed; (c) where there are severe and chronic financial needs; (d) where there is doubt about the nature of the problem; (e) where there is obviously psychopathology; (f) where there is a need for long-term psychotherapy; (g) where there are specialized agencies available in the community (e.g. with alcoholics, blind people, single parents, handicapped people, etc.).

Ministers and pastors should know where to refer persons for appropriate help. A minister should develop an extensive file of referral resources within his or her community and develop relationships with doctors, psychiatrists, solicitors, psychotherapists, and all helping agencies within the community. If located in a small village or rural parish, it is important to know where the nearest resources are and how they can be obtained. The best way to evaluate these resources is to become personally acquainted with them where possible.

It is important to know how to refer effectively. Proper referral requires the follow-ing: (1) Creating an awareness in the counsellee's mind of the limitation of the pastor's skills and the possibility of referral. This should happen in the first contact. (2) Working towards integrating the counsellee's perception of his or her problem with his need for specialized help. (3) Helping the person understand why referral is indicated, what kind of help may be expected and how it may be given. (4) Using rapport (q.v.) to help serve as a bridge to the new relationship and as a continuing resource if further guidance is wanted.

In summary, the pastor needs to be aware of his or her abilities and limitations; being aware of tendencies to refer too quickly, as well as tendencies not to refer at all. Access to resources is essential, also knowledge of how to integrate the needs of counsellees with the resources available.

Clinebell, H.J., *Basic Types of Pastoral Counseling* (Abingdon, New York, 1966); see in particular ch. 10, pp. 176–88). Jacobs, M., *Still Small Voice* (SPCK, 1982). Kennedy, E., *On Becoming a Counsellor* (Gill & MacMillan, Dublin, 1977); ch. 16, pp. 115–21.

JOHN P. MILLER

See also: INTERPROFESSIONAL RELATIONSHIPS.

REHABILITATION

Rehabilitation implies the restoration of patients to their fullest physical, mental and social capability (Mair 1972). This formal definition has been widely accepted, particularly its appreciation that psychosocial factors are as relevant as physical ones. Other descriptions have been used to convey other implications, e.g. 'planned withdrawal of help'. This emphasizes the dynamic nature whereby there is change from a state of dependency.

Terminology. When considering rehabilitation, new terms are coming into use. The World Health Organization has distinguished between three aspects, rehabilitation being necessary to minimize the effects of one upon another. *Impairment* is 'any loss or abnormality of psychological, physiological, or anatomical structure or function'. *Disablement* (q.v.) (disability) is 'any restriction or lack (resulting from an impairment) of ability to perform an activity in the manner or within the range considered normal for a human being'. *Handicap* is 'a disadvantage for a given indi-

235

vidual, resulting from an impairment or a disability, that limits or prevents the fulfilment of a role that is normal (depending on age, sex, and social and cultural factors) for that individual. (WHO 1980). These terms can be applied to psychiatric disorders, mental handicap (syn. subnormality or deficiency) or physical illness/injury (congenital or acquired).

Assessment. The key to effective rehabilitation is adequate assessment. This can be likened to diagnosis, which should be a logical process occurring as information becomes available. Facts must be ascertained about medical, psychological and social matters, preferably from several sources including the patient and his family and the various staff providing the care. Functional capability should be established, usually by direct observation. The emphasis will be determined by the nature of the patient's condition, but the spectrum should always be reviewed, even if in some parts only superficially. The aim is to establish a list of all the patient's problems so that help can be applied for each, hopefully in an integrated manner. Rehabilitation is a dynamic process, and so assessment may require to be repeated in order to provide longitudinal information about change.

Management of disability. Rehabilitation generally lies close to treatment, but when there is residual reduction of function the endeavour moves more toward maintenance, encouraging maximal independence and minimal requirement for support services. Just as improvement of function means less disability, so there is a need to encourage less social disadvantage. Services from several agencies may be required in addition to health, such as social work, employment, social security, housing and voluntary organizations. The complexity of their arrangements may be considerable, a feature that is well recognized as a difficulty against sustaining an integrated approach (Blaxter 1976).

Important disorders for rehabilitation. In theory, every patient requires rehabilitation. Nevertheless, there are certain disorders which require special attention of rehabilitation services, different ones being prominent at different ages. In childhood, congenital disorders like cerebral palsy predominate. In young adults, spinal cord injury producing para/tetraplegia produces special problems such as for bladder control, transport (wheelchair), sport, just to mention a few. Rheuma-

toid arthritis and multiple sclerosis are common in middle life. In the elderly, who are by far the largest group, degenerative disorders are common, whether of joints or blood vessels (peripheral artery disease leading to amputation, coronary to heart attacks, or cerebral to strokes). The most severely disabled patients in hospital most commonly have neurological disorders. Less precise diagnoses, as in many patients with chronic low back pain, may present a considerable challenge for rehabilitation, having much handicap (prolonged unemployment, poverty, social isolation and misery).

Rehabilitation can involve wide breadth of application; it is not a precise activity, but rather all else that needs to be done in addition to the specific treatment aimed to restore well-being to patients and their families.

International Classification of Impairments, Disabilities, and Handicaps (WHO, 1980). *Medical Rehabilitation: the Pattern for the Future* (Mair Report), Scottish Home and Health Department (HMSO, Edinburgh. 1972). **Blaxter, M.,** *The Meaning of Disability* (Heinemann, 1976).

CAIRNS AITKEN

See also: DISABLEMENT.

RELAXATION

Adjustment of muscle 'set' to alleviate tension, both physical and mental.

The will controls the voluntary muscles; it controls nothing else (any other influence of 'mind' on 'body' is indirect). The direct linkage with the skeletal musculature is supplemented by innervation of the muscle spindles ('gamma efferent innervation') which facilitates muscular contraction or inhibits it. The habitual 'set' of the muscles can thus be adjusted. This is what 'relaxation' is about.

The autonomic ('involuntary') nervous system carries the messages which bring into play the mechanisms of self-defence. The active (sympathetic) reaction mobilizes all the resources of mind and body when danger threatens; aptly nicknamed the 'angry cat', with its implied picture of tense muscles, claws out, spitting (which have their human counterparts), ready for 'fight or flight'. The passive (parasympathetic) reaction is the 'paralysed rabbit', freezing into the landscape, hoping to escape detection; in this case the muscles of neck and shoulders are tense, the rest flaccid. The autonomic nerves are efferent nerves; that is to say, responses can be modified by rethinking and reconditioning, thus altering long-term attitudes of anger and fear.

The skeletal muscles (or muscle groups) are organized in opposed pairs; when one is contracted, its opposite is relaxed. Systematic relaxation can reduce tension all over the body. It promotes a parasympathetic reaction ('rest and digest'), which improves rest and assists circulation. The modern athlete is trained to relax; if any muscle is used unnecessarily, this is a waste of energy and a brake on activity. (I once heard a Test-Match commentator say of a fast bowler, 'He is not yet bowling his fastest, he is not yet relaxed'.)

That is physical relaxation; the second level of relaxation depends on suggestion. Thoughts which pass through the speech centre of the brain bring about changes in the physiological pattern, affecting muscular contraction, heart rate, secretions of the endocrine glands, and so on. Floating on water, lying on a sunny beach, or any other thought of happy inactivity induces a pleasant laziness. It helps if one talks to the different limbs in turn, suggesting that there is no need to be tense: 'I am not carrying a heavy load, I am not defending myself against anybody at the moment, I am coming into life with an open hand and not with a clenched fist.' This may well reveal why one is on the defensive and enable one to be easier about it.

The third level is the level of meditation, which this leads into; most systems of meditation (q.v.) depend on the link between the speech centre in the brain and physiological changes in the body. Contemplative meditation is based on repeating gently to oneself some appropriate word or phrase like 'peace' or 'God is love'. If one's brain reacts primarily to auditory stimulation (if one is a hearer, that is), this can work like a charm; if one is a visualizer, it will be less effective, and some other method of 'turning cares into prayers' should be tried instead. The Eastern Church, following the lead given to it by St Gregory Palamas, pays great attention to relaxation in the spiritual life. Relaxation enables us to pause, to repent, and to trust; it is invaluable in the improvement of personal relations and in the relief of 'dis-ease'.

Benson, Herbert, *The Relaxation Response* (Collins, 1976). **Harding, Geoffrey,** *How to Relax* (pamphlet from St Mary Woolnoth Church, London EC3, 1974). **Keers, Walter, A.** *et al.,* *Yoga, Art of Relaxation* (Watkins, 1979). **Meares, Ainslie,** *Relief without Drugs* (Souvenir Press, 1968). **Mitchell, Laura,** *Simple Relaxation* (J. Murray, 1977).

G.C. HARDING

RELIGION
See: PSYCHOLOGY OF RELIGION; SOCIOLOGY OF RELIGION.

REPENTANCE
See: CONFESSION.

RESPONSIBILITY
The idea of responsibility faces two ways, backwards and forwards. On the one hand there is the notion of being *answerable* for one's past actions; on the other hand there is the notion of being *responsive* to the claims and opportunities of the future.

Normally speaking, we hold people *answerable for their actions*. They are the authors of their own actions. So fundamental is our conviction that people are morally responsible for their actions that we are not prepared to allow any theory of scientific or theological determinism to dislodge it. When, at the end of John Braine's novel *Room at the Top*, Joe Lampton's friends try to console him with the remark, 'Nobody blames you,' he reaffirms his basic humanity with his reply, 'Oh my God, that's the trouble.'

In some cases we also hold a person *answerable for things not done*; there are sins of omission as well as sins of commission. However, not everything that we fail to do is to be laid to our charge: we are responsible for those omissions which we could and should have done something about. We are also, to some extent, *answerable for what we are*. We are not prepared to accept as a legitimate excuse for some morally reprehensible action the disclaimer, 'I'm afraid that is just the sort of person I am.' Our character is our responsibility. Within limits, we are free to make of ourselves the sort of person we choose to be. Granted that our genes determine the colour of our eyes and even our temperament and predispositions, it is nevertheless within our own power to make these building-blocks into this or that kind of character. And if such an endeavour is too much for us as isolated individuals, we can associate and identify ourselves with a community whose life and history we wish to shape our own self-understanding.

There are circumstances in which we recognize that people's responsibility for their actions is *diminished*. In what they did or failed to do they may have been victims of forces over which they had little or no control. Subnormality of development and some forms of mental illness may provide grounds for asserting that a person's responsibility has in this way been diminished.

Responsibility for an action may be *shared*. More than one person may have taken an active part in the planning and preparation of the action. In that case they all share in the responsibility for that action, even though the parts they played were of varying significance and culpabililty. Care must be taken, however, about the way in which we speak of a *corporate* responsibility. I am in no way morally responsible for what has been done by other members of my group without my knowledge and consent, simply because I belong to that group, unless it can be shown that I ought to have known about it and ought then to have taken steps to prevent its being done. On the other hand, if there is a wrong to be righted, and if that wrong has been committed by members of a group to which I belong, although I am not, strictly speaking, morally responsible for the wrong, I may nevertheless feel a special claim upon me to *make myself responsible* for doing what I can to right that wrong. The question of who is to blame here gives way to the question of who is prepared to do something about it. Responsiveness takes over from answerability.

It is a sign of maturity when a person is willing to acknowledge responsibility and does not try to find a scape-goat. However, it is also a sign of maturity for a person to recognize that there are *limits* to his or her responsibility. For example, even if as a parent I am responsible for the way in which I have brought up my children, I am not therefore responsible for all that they do or are. They too have a responsibility of their own.

It is a sign of even greater maturity when, having come to terms with the past, a person becomes responsive to the potentialities of the future. Christianly speaking, confession of sin is only a preface to growth in grace.

Classroom Teachers Speak on the Opportunity for Responsibility (National Educational Association, USA, 1966). **Adkins, A.**, *Merit and Responsibility* (Univ. of Chicago Press, 1975). **Molinski, W.**, 'Responsibility', *Sacramentum Mundi* (Search Press,

1970). **Morris, H.** (ed.), *Freedom and Responsibility* (Stanford UP, 1961).

PETER BAELZ

See also: CONSCIENCE; FREEDOM AND DETERMINISM.

RESURRECTION
See: CROSS AND RESURRECTION.

RETIREMENT
The obligatory and abrupt cessation of work, regardless of one's fitness to do it but simply because one has reached a certain age, is a modern phenomenon. It began in 1917 with the introduction of old-age pensions for everyone too old or too infirm to continue working, and moved from a simple eligibility for retirement pension at a fixed age, to obligatory retirement. More recently the concept of voluntary retirement has returned with numbers of people in certain occupations being encouraged to take an early retirement for largely economic reasons.

Loss of work. Retirement brings important problems of readjustment for many people. In addition to the practical issues of money and housing, which may be the ones most paramount in their minds, there may be difficult emotional adjustments to make through the loss of work.

(1) Work may have been relied on for a sense of identity, enabling one to decide who one *is* in terms of what one *does*. Its loss may expose a basic anxiety about identity (q.v.).

(2) The social status offered by work, with a defined position in the world of people and a predictable pattern of mutual expectation, provides people with an external source of value and of guidance on how they should conduct themselves in order to be valued. Loss of this framework may give rise to anxieties about personal worth.

(3) Work may be relied upon as a source of meaning for life, particularly perhaps for people whose personal relationships have been unrewarding. Without it they may be exposed to feelings of meaninglessness and futility.

(4) Work may provide people with a range of relationships, particularly with members of the opposite sex, in a way quite diffrent from those shared with a spouse at home. Some people, like clergy and doctors for instance, may enjoy through their work access to and intimacy with a variety of people whom they might otherwise know only superficially. Loss

of these work and professional relationships may be experienced as a real impoverishment. (5) Many depend on their work to provide them with a regular routine to protect them from having to make too many choices. Loss of these external constraints may cause considerable anxiety.

(6) People may gain from work a sense of potency and of power to influence or control people, things or events. Without it there may be feelings of hopelessness or inferiority and perhaps a need to be over-assertive in compensation.

Effects on marriage. Partners in a marriage may differ in their feelings about the retirement of one of them. The man, for instance, may look forward to it as emancipation from servitude, and a long-awaited opportunity to enjoy being at home. His wife, however, may dread this invasion of her domain. Separate work situations may have provided the couple with individual space where they can be separate from each other and enjoy their own territory and responsibility. The loss of this separate space on retirement may bring to the surface conflicts, such as competitiveness and envy, which have been successfully contained in the former balance. At the same time, the interest and stimulus brought into a marriage from work outside will now be missing and may leave partners feeling deprived or disappointed. Reduced income and, if they have moved to a new area on retirement, the loss of friends, may add to the stress on the marriage.

Pastoral care. Many people's reaction to the above problems may be understood as 'bereavement' (q.v.). Depression or anxiety may be experienced with varying degrees of intensity, and physical illnesses are common. Retired people often report that they 'have never been so busy'. While this may be a genuinely satisfying state for many, the pastor should not be blind to the possibility that for others it may be a frantic attempt to escape from inner distress.

Retirement is one of those transitional stages of life where people are at risk and may need help if they are to cope with it successfully. The pastor may be well placed to play an important part in providing this help through pastoral care, both in preparing people for it, and in helping them adjust to it when it comes.

1. *Preparation for Retirement.* (1) The pastor may help people to overcome their resistance to facing retirement until it happens, by enlisting the aid of specialists in the field of finance, insurance and housing to help people tackle the material aspects of retirement. It is on these aspects that most people focus their anxiety and, until they are dealt with, other areas of difficulty may not be faced. (2) People may be helped to explore and share the emotional issues involved. The more these can be anticipated before retirement, the easier the transition may be. People may also be encouraged to develop friendships apart from their professional role or work. Some may need encouragement and even help to find the space for 'play' in their lives as a source of satisfying personal creativity and renewal for them that can exist apart from work. (3) While affirming the reality of the 'dark' or loss aspect of retirement, the pastor may also help people to see it as not just the end of the road, but as a precious opportunity for further growth and development.

2. *The Newly Retired.* The pastor may help people integrate into a new community if they have moved house, find new social roles, make friends, and discover the contribution they can make to the people around them. They should be helped with any feelings of loss, resentment or anxiety which might otherwise keep them in isolation. The pastor may further be able to help couples renegotiate their relationship, and adapt to the new situation. He or she will be able to encourage them to seek specialist help should their problems require it and, for those problems which are intractable, provide them with encouragement and support.

Consumer Association, *Approaching Retirement* (Hodder, 1983). **Kay, I. and Kay, E.,** *Your Hopeful Future* (Macdonald, 1982). **Kemp, F.** and **Buttle, B.,** *Focus on Retirement* (Kogan Page, 1979).

DEREK BLOWS

See also: AGEING; BEREAVEMENT; IDENTITY; WORK.

RETREATS
To spend a day, a week or a month in some quiet place to reflect, to intensify attention in prayer, to examine the direction of one's life has been a permanent feature of Christian discipline. It has its inspiration in the days and nights Christ spent alone on the hillside. Retreats can be made singly or in groups. They are best made in a a place away from familiar surroundings. Most people prefer

someone to conduct them, i.e. to give them a daily aid to reflection, and also to be available for advice on personal problems. A yearly retreat provides a time of reassessment and rededication. Many renewal centres, monasteries and convents accommodate retreatants as part of their service to the churches.

The standard form of a retreat consists of daily addresses, provided or suggested reading, and times of corporate prayer punctuating the days of silence. This form emerged with the Counter Reformation in the 16th century, and a similar pattern was adopted on occasion by Reformed churches. Today there is a greater flexibility in conducted retreats, e.g. quiet instead of silence, more variety of participatory exercises. There is, however, a tendency to return to the familiar tried pattern of the last four centuries and an increase in the number of people requiring a private retreat, of those who retire for a day or more to a house of prayer, a caravan or a cottage.

Retreats are not intended to be a time of great tension or strenuous effort but rather a chance for the body, the mind and the spirit to relax and receive rather than give. It is there to be a space which is free of fuss and bother, and of the usual complexities of life, so that the often suppressed and unnoticed realities of life can come to the surface and God can receive undivided attention as we read the Scriptures or reveal our own heart's longings. Such a time is particularly important when a person is faced with a major decision. The Ignatian Retreat provides for a thirty-day retreat, and there is a growing number of places where such long retreats can be made. Married couples who periodically make a retreat together are helped to review their marriages and renew their vows. Retreats are also advisable before a change of work, or at a time when a specific vocation to ministry has to be tested. One does not need any more reason for retreat than Christ's own invitation: 'Come into a place apart and rest awhile for there are many coming and going' (Mark 6.31; cf. Luke 9.10).

Baldwin, Joanna, *Learning about Retreats* (APR Publication, 1983). Holliday, Mary, *What is a Retreat?* (MRG, 1983).

ROLAND WALLS

See also: PRAYER; SILENCE; SPIRITUAL DIRECTION.

REVELATION

The unveiling or making known of that which

was previously hidden or obscure.

In a theological context, revelation refers particularly to the making known, usually by God, of matters of religious or human importance. A wide range of content has at different times been claimed to have been revealed: God, his purpose, will, promises, etc.; truths about God, the world and humanity; credal or doctrinal statements. Some have doubted whether revelation is a biblical concept at all, but most authorities hold that the word denotes the content of a number of biblical expressions.

With some simplification, it can be said that historically there have been three phases in which different conceptions have predominated. In biblical times revelation was understood dynamically and personally, with God making himself and his purposes known through the natural world (Ps. 19), but predominantly through people and historical events. For the New Testament, such revelation centres on Jesus Christ (e.g. John 1.18; Heb. 1.1ff.), but concerns also more generally the purposes of God in salvation (Eph. 1.9f.). It is seen as a past and present reality, but also – perhaps predominantly – as eschatological, in the sense that the fullness of revelation has yet to come.

The Middle Ages saw the heyday of what has come to be called the propositional view of revelation, seeing as its content primarily truths about God and the Christian religion divinely communicated to mankind. Truths of revelation were understood to fall into two classes, those knowable by reason alone and those for which faith is required. Correlative to this view is a tendency to conceive religious belief in terms of intellectual assent and the Bible as a source of propositional truths. The propositional view came under attack at the Reformation and during the Enlightenment, although it survived during Protestant scholasticism and more particularly within Roman Catholic theology. In more recent times it has had few exponents and has been replaced by conceptions more like those of the biblical period, with a greater stress on God's historical self-revelation and on personal encounter and appropriation.

There is, however, little agreement about the way in which historical revelation is understood. Broadly, a spectrum of views can be discerned, with, at one end, conceptions stressing the objective historical character of the event of revelation and, at the other, a calling of attention to the personal appropriation of such disclosure. Four examples give some impression of the range of views. For Barth, revelation is the historical self-unveiling of God, the temporal event in which he makes himself known. The centre of the conception is christological, but the overall structure austerely trinitarian. By contrast, for Tillich revelation ('the manifestation of what concerns us ultimately') has to be both subjective and objective if it is to count as revelation. Rahner takes a dialectical approach, juxtaposing human openness to transcendence and God's historical self-presentation. Another distinctive concept is that of Wolfhart Pannenberg, for whom revelation is indirect: it is a function of history as a whole and is known only at its end, though it is anticipated in the resurrection of Jesus. All of these theologians see God as the source of revelation; differences concern the manner in which he is conceived to operate.

Two aspects of revelation are of particular pastoral interest. First, God may be understood to reveal in the Gospel the ends to which human life is directed, as they are expressed in such concepts as forgiveness, reconciliation, healing and the redemption of the whole created order. Second is the conception, found in Barth among others, of the life, death and resurrection of Jesus as the revelation of true humanity, the image of God, the model for ethics and the bearer of promise.

Baillie, John, *The Idea of Revelation in Recent Thought* (Columbia UP, 1956). Barth, Karl, *Church Dogmatics* I/1 (T. & T. Clark, 1975), section 8. Niebuhr, H. Richard, *The Meaning of Revelation* (Collier-Macmillan, 1941). Pannenberg, Wolfhart (ed.), *Revelation as History* (Collier-Macmillan, 1968). Rahner, Karl, *Hearers of the Word* (Seabury Press, 1969). Tillich, Paul, *Systematic Theology*, vol. I (Nisbet, 1968), chs. 5 & 6.

COLIN GUNTON

See also: GOD, DOCTRINE OF; VISIONS.

RITES AND RITUAL

The Oxford English Dictionary defines both 'rite' and 'ritual' in various ways. Here 'rite' is defined as 'a religious ceremony', and 'ritual' as 'the way in which religious ceremonies are performed'.

In three realms of human experience (personal relationships, art and religion) the only means of communication is the living metaphor or symbol (q.v.) – word, form, action, gesture or posture. Living symbols open up new dimensions of thought, feeling and understanding. Symbols are born in and for an encounter: they demand commitment to what they reveal. In worship, a 'rite' is a combination of symbols. Even in its simplest form, a rite is composed of word and gesture. Words alone fail to engage the dimension of the body and may therefore lack the power to convince. By itself, a gesture (action or posture, or a combination of the three) may fail to engage the intellect and therefore lack the necessary clarity of expression. Together, word and gesture may become not only a skilful instrument of communication but also a moment of disclosure. Yet a rite will be as good as the symbols it employs. Symbols live and die. When a rite is composed of dead symbols it becomes a form of idolatry which demands commitment only to itself.

Since ritual is composed of individual rites, what happens to the latter will happen to the former. Ritual may decay and turn into meaningless routine. It may become a mere aesthetic experience, a form of escapism, or both. Having ceased to point to the Other, it may assume a demonic power of its own. In the hands of a demagogue, it may turn into a tool of manipulation by the simple means of incessant repetition of key actions and words. In the hands of a leader intent on self-glorification it will turn into an instrument of domination over one's fellow beings. In certain cases, it may turn into the means by which one expresses and keeps in check one's obsessional neuroses. Yet when it makes use of living symbols, ritual may turn into an instrument of growth which contributes to the successful maintenance of psychological balance in both individuals and groups.

Grainger, R., *The Language of the Rite* (Darton Longman & Todd, 1974). Kennedy, E. 'The Contribution of Ritual to Psychological Balance' (*Concilium* 2, no. 7, 1971), pp. 53–6. Shaughnessy, J.D. (ed.), *The Roots of Ritual* (Michigan, 1973). Vergote, A., 'Symbolic Gestures and Actions in the Liturgy' (*Concilium* 2, no. 7, 1971), pp. 40–52.

G. TELLINI

See also: LITURGY AND RITUAL; SYMBOLS.

ROLE PLAY

An educational method designed to promote learning by experience rather than by teaching.

Role play is an attempt to enter into someone else's situation, to feel what it is like to be there, to react spontaneously to the other characters in the play and, by reflection on the experience with the other members and with observers, to deepen understanding. Children use it in coming to terms with the strange and unknown world around them, e.g. playing at being parents (*see* PLAY). In the context of pastoral care, its specific use is to increase awareness, sensitivity and understanding, particularly about relationships and communication (q.v.).

For effective use a number of conditions pertain: (1) A continuing group, small enough for personal relationships to exist or develop. (2) Clarity about the objective. (3) Adequate time for: preparing the brief or scenario (outline of characters, their situation and immediate purpose of meeting); enabling the members to enter into their roles; briefing the observers; the actual play to take place (10–20 minutes); and reflecting on the experience (one to two hours at least). (4) Experienced leadership (q.v.) to control the boundaries of time, depth of involvement and pressure on individuals.

Certain constraints must also apply: (1) Participants must *not* be asked to take roles which are their own. Transference (q.v.) of deep-seated feelings can take place and lead to unhelpful identification with the role, and confusion of issues. (2) The scenario should be sufficiently unlike the members' own to allow some objectivity. Projection of 'back-home' factors, conditions and personalities can also be confusing and destructive of learning. (3) Role playing is *not* acting out a preconceived plot before an audience. In that sense there are no actors and no audience, only participants. Some may be observers, but all are working together to understand what is going on in the human interactions emerging in the play. (4) Undue pressure on the members, by criticism or questioning, without their willingness to be open should be prevented by the leader as it feels threatening, leads to the erection of stronger defences (*see* DEFENCE MECHANISMS), and inhibits learning.

Role play is widely used in industry and management, in education and voluntary organizations, for training and the development of skills, for the dissemination of information and problem-solving. Groups vary in size from three (consultant, client, observer) to possibly hundreds in a simulation game (a complicated structured exercise incorporating detailed information).

van Ments, Morry, *The Effective Use of Role Play* (Kogan Page, 1983).
'Simulation/Games for Learning', Journal of SAGSET, Society for the Advancement of Games and Simulation, Loughborough.

LAURENCE READING

See also: TRAINING, METHODS OF

S

SACRAMENTS
See: ANOINTING; BAPTISM; ETC.

SALVATION AND PASTORAL CARE
Salvation refers to being removed from a predicament. Theologically the predicament is estrangement from God and the consequences thereof.

When people cry, 'Save me', they are likely to be in danger – for example, of drowning. So to offer salvation is at least to respond to people's perceived need, as when Jesus healed blindness or cast out demons. Pastoral care has to do with helping people, with meeting their needs. We might expect then that pastoral care and the offer of salvation are closely related; for both are to do with discerning need and meeting it.

In the history of the Church there have been many different understandings of salvation and, alongside that, different perceptions of what the job of the pastor is. If the perceived need is rescue from purgatorial trials, the pastor's function will be offering masses for the dead. If the need is deliverance from guilt, the pastor's role will be found in receiving confession (q.v.). If it is to find and follow the right way of life for fear of hell (q.v.), the pastor will concentrate on purveying the right teaching; whereas if assurance of life after death is the perceived need and the Eucharist is understood as the medicine of immortality, the pastor's chief activity will be celebration at the altar (see RITES AND RITUAL). Each of these perceptions and practices, and many others also, could be documented from church history. And this inter-relationship still occurs: liberation-theology perceives the needs of the oppressed, and the pastor takes on a political role (see POLITICAL THEOLOGY AND PASTORAL CARE); the counsellor perceives the problems of individuals in terms of modern psychology and interprets his role in a way analogous to clinical consultation (see COUNSELLING).

There is a close parallel between the practice of pastoral care, which clearly cannot be limited to the clergy, and the theory of salvation which informs it. Under these circumstances, agreement as to where a pastor should concentrate energies is bound to be elusive. Evangelicals will be trying to save souls, while political activists are trying to change society, etc. Each different approach may be open to criticism for an underlying concept of salvation which is inadequate, but every approach has a contribution to make, however limited, and deserves respect. The claims of here and hereafter are not mutually exclusive, nor are the claims of the individual and the claims of the community. All are embraced in the Christian vision of God's kingdom. A particular pastor cannot realistically play all roles at once, and each should be regarded as developing a particular emphasis as part of a larger whole to which many different pastors make different contributions.

There are two things, however, which should inform this diversity:
(1) Perceived need is not necessarily the real need. This is not simply a truism of depth psychology but a profound note in the New Testament. Paul is not best understood as finding at the moment of his conversion a solution to already perceived guilt and frustration with the Law, for he describes himself as a Pharisee 'as to righteousness under the Law, blameless' (Phil. 3.6); rather Paul perceived the inadequacy of the Law and the depth of human sin in the light of increased awareness given in Christ. Often, like Paul, people do not recognize their need. They contrive to avoid facing up to reality, particularly the reality of sin. The worst sins are a kind of blindness in which one takes a pride (e.g. racism, nationalism); it is others who see them as sins, not oneself, and without a profound conversion, one is incapable of doing other than produce aguments of self-justification. The pastor's job surely includes the discernment of the deeper need that goes unrecognized, so as to startle people into seeing it themselves and crying out, 'What must I do to be saved?' For the Christian gospel is not simply about meeting perceived need, but about *change*. In the Orthodox East

it would be characterized as 'divinization', in the modern West as 'humanization'.

(2) Salvation is dynamic, not the achievement of a static perfection. Christianity is not the revolution to end all revolutions which establishes utopia, nor is it the creation of a spiritual elite. It is a vision of God re-creating a world which is somehow corrupted. The pastor's job is never the imposition of ready-made solutions to the world's ills. It is being on a pilgrimage under God, facilitating God's activity in a process of discernment and change in the self, others and society. The Christian tradition would affirm that worship is the essential context for such creative change.

A New Dictionary of Christian Theology (SCM, 1983); articles (with bibliographies) on Atonement, Redemption, Sacrifice, Salvation and Soteriology. **Lambourne, R.A.**, Community, Church and Healing (Darton Longman & Todd, 1963). **Wilson, M.** (ed.), Explorations in Health and Salvation (Institute for the Study of Worship and Religious Architecture, Univ. of Birmingham, 1983).

FRANCES YOUNG

See also: RECONCILIATION; SIN.

SCHOOL CHAPLAINCY

This article is concerned with full-time appointments (to residential or non-residential independent schools) of clergy or other pastoral workers. The practice arose out of clergymen founding schools to inculcate the Christian faith to the young and to foster vocations, rather than from a desire on the part of some ministers to be pastors to educational foundations. Until the middle of this century most public schools employed several clergymen or were run by religious orders, and all the members of staff considered themselves to be in a pastoral as well as an educational role. Sometimes one priest was made responsible for the conduct of worship in chapel, but more usually this was the responsibility of the headmaster himself who was invariably in orders, and he delegated this task as he saw fit. In some cases the chaplain was more the headmaster's chaplain than one appointed to minister directly to the pupils.

It would perhaps be more realistic to think of schoolmasters in holy orders than of chaplains when looking at former times, but this is no longer the case. Part of the great burst of philanthropic endeavour of

Christians in the last century was to found or refound public schools for the education of Christian gentlemen who would serve and manage the British Empire. While most of these schools were Anglican (due to such men as Arnold of Rugby and Nathaniel Woodard and his corporation of schools to educate the middle classes) others were founded by Roman Catholic orders and Nonconformist churches, and later still a few by free thinkers.

Many of these institutions founded as Christian schools remain faithful to their original ethos, but increasingly it is the headmaster, the chaplain and a few other members of staff who foster it, rather than the whole community of governors, teachers, pupils and parents. The school chaplain is therefore a link with the founders' aspirations, and the Christian way of life, in an institution which is often becoming a reflection of the secular nature of society as a whole. One consequence of this juxtaposition is the controversy (which may now be past its peak) as to whether such schools should continue the practice of compulsory worship on a daily or weekly basis. Worship must essentially be voluntary, but schools are institutions which make compulsory the activities they believe to be important and believe there is a duty to expose the young to the Christian faith. Most schools appear to have weathered the storm of the previous decade and, despite a general post-Christian climate, they have retained their basic pattern of worship, but probably with a smaller compulsory element.

A person might be a school chaplain for but a short period of his or her ministry. Not being dependent upon the school for a career, chaplains can be more prophetic, remaining over and against the system and acting as the institution's conscience; this gives the chaplain a special relationship with the headmaster and his colleagues. This independence can also allow chaplains to be seen as people less identified with the authorities and thus aid them as counsellor and confidant to pupils and staff alike.

Though some schools are experimenting with non-teaching chaplains, this is still rarer and the reverse is more usual. Many find their pastoral role hampered by excessive teaching loads and extra-curricular activities. There often is a tension between the role in the classroom and that as a pastor and befriender (q.v.). Most chaplains would argue that school life can only be penetrated by being involved in what schools are about and by doing a professional teaching job. They are usually, therefore, responsible for the teaching of religious education and often head that department in a school; for this reason chaplains are increasingly expected to be professionally qualified to teach and to play a full part in the life of the school. They are often responsible for counselling (q.v.) of individuals, but this they do in co-operation with the school's doctors, counsellors and tutors.

School chaplains have their own organization, the Association of School Chaplains and Schoolmasters in Holy Orders. It does not have a permanent address, but its officers can be contacted through the National Society, Church House, Westminster. Its membership is predominantly clerical and Anglican, but there is a trend towards new members both from other denominations and those described as 'lay chaplains'. Women are entering this field both in clerical and lay capacities. The Association holds an annual residential conference and provides training days for those newly taking up school chaplaincy work. School chaplaincies still tend, almost exclusively, to be in the independent sector of education. However, there are a number of ordained teachers working in the maintained sector, but rarely are they described, or overtly functioning, as school chaplains. More commonly in this sector a parish minister or priest acts as part-time chaplain to the school, conducting worship and offering some pastoral care where possible.

The role of a school chaplain varies from school to school, but generally he or she will be expected to be a living reminder of the Christian foundation and ethos, responsible for worship and initiation into the Christian faith, a prophet and conscience, and a competent teacher in the classroom normally in religious studies but not necessarily so. He or she is also appointed by the head, or the governors, and paid by the school, though in the Anglican Church this will be in consultation with the diocesan bishop whose licence he must hold.

ROGER MARSH

See also: PASTORAL CARE IN SCHOOLS.

SCRUPULOSITY
See: CONSCIENCE: PSYCHOLOGICAL ASPECTS.

SELF
A term used to describe the subject of personal experience and behaviour.

Confusion arises over the scope of the term. What was once the province of theologians and called the soul (q.v.) has also become the interest of psychologists and called the self – the 'summit of the soul' of Christian mysticism. Subjective notions of the self follow the apprehension of external objects, and self is seen separate from these and in relation to them.

Differing views of self cannot be reconciled into any universal perspective. Some major contributions are here considered:

(1) *Kierkegaard* described 'being' as *aesthetic* and *ethical*. Real existence involves decisions to commitment, and only in such decisions is the self constituted. Since such choices are necessarily made with the recognition of limitations, the constitution of the self includes a sense of dependence on God (religious being). The self is freedom, but it is freedom to be self-constituting yet dependent.

(2) *William James* saw the self as the sum of all that any individual can call his own – body, abilities, mannerisms, possessions, etc. These were divisible into material, social and spiritual self, and also 'pure ego' which is that aspect of consciousness which enables a sense of identity. James thus combines the ideas of 'self as object' and 'self as process'. Latterly, the self as process has been the main area of discussion.

(3) *Freud's* id, ego and superego made up the personality which he saw as synonymous with the self. Self-knowledge by way of insight, intellectually and affectively, underlies Freud's theories of psychoanalysis (q.v.).

(4) The self is an archetype in *Jung's* understanding. It is the centre of the whole personality (as opposed to the ego which is said to be the centre of consciousness). All other aspects of an individual's being are dependent on and centred on the self which holds them in equilibrium. Being an archetype, the self motivates and directs the inner quest for wholeness.

(5) The 'creative self' was described by *Adler* as an abstract entity discernible only by its effects. It takes the raw material of heredity and environment and creates meaning for life. This is the key to the human mastery over fate, rather being a mere victim of it.

(6) *Allport's* thinking of self was similar to that of James. He postulates a 'proprium' which,

maturing with time, becomes the sum of the many facets of human existence which are uniquely one's own – self-esteem, rational thought, self-identity, etc. The self consists of this proprium and all those adjunctive activities which enable others to see one as unique.

(7) The views of *Rogers*, subsequent to his client-centred therapy (q.v.), are arguably the most influential views of self for current counselling practice. In client-centred therapy Rogers stresses the client's own responsibility (q.v.) in the perception of problems and the enhancement of self. The self is a part of the phenomenal field (the totality of experience) and develops out of the individual's interaction with the environment. It has a homeostatic thrust, in that the subject usually acts in accord with the self, and experiences inconsistent with the self are perceived as threatening. The self consists of conscious perceptions and relates to the 'I' or 'me' of the phenomenal field.

(8) *Erich Fromm* holds that certain needs must be met in the inherent contradiction that is human being (i.e. we are a part of nature yet are separated from nature). One of these needs is for a sense of personal identity, the living in acceptance of our unique and individual self.

Thus these interlocking views of the nature of 'the self' provide a central value for pastoral care, that each has a unique quality we call the self, and that its realization (life lived in accord with it) is one of the goals of individual human existence and one of the ways in which life is given meaning.

Allport, Gordon, *Becoming* (Yale UP, New Haven, 1951). **Ansbacker, H.L.** and **Rowena, R.,** *The Individual Psychology of Alfred Adler* (Basic Books, New York, 1956). **Fromm, Erich,** *Psychoanalysis and Religion,* (Yale UP, New Haven, 1950). **James, William,** *Principles of Psychology* (New York, 1890). **Jung, C.G.,** *Modern Man in Search of a Soul* (Harcourt, New York, 1933). **Rogers, Carl,** *Client-Centred Therapy* (Houghton, Boston, 1951).

WARWICK D. ROSS

See also: ANALYTICAL PSYCHOLOGY; INDIVIDUATION; MATURITY; PERSON; SELF-ACTUALIZATION.

SELF-ACTUALIZATION

A conception, developed by humanistic psychologists, of optimal individual psychological health.

246

Originating in the United States, this concept was developed in its most thorough form by Abraham Maslow; the self-actualizing person being the individual who has realized his or her inborn potential in full measure. The achieving of self-actualization is said to constitute the ultimate motivational principle inherent in human life and to be the aim of counselling and psychotherapy. Self-actualization as a concept may be compared to Jung's 'individuation' and Frankl's 'will to meaning'; the self-actualizing person to Freud's 'genital man' and Rogers' 'fully-functioning person' (*see also* CLIENT-CENTRED THERAPY).

A prime mover in the development of humanistic psychology in America after World War II, Abraham Maslow attempted to develop a science of the person which took account of the highest of human qualities and thus transcended the 'reduced' conception of Freudians and behaviourists that the human being is a mere 'reactor' to deep instinctual or environmental forces respectively.

Maslow's conception of self-actualization began with informal musings concerning the personal traits of two admired college teachers. Later, having progressed to the use of a more systematic investigative method and applied it to a wider range of individuals – namely, other contemporaries, college students, and well-known figures like Beethoven, Einstein and Freud – Maslow laid claim to the discovery of a common cross-cultural pattern expressive of the 'perfect' person, a pattern exhibited by his subjects to varying degrees. In describing the restorative capacity of the human organism Kurt Goldstein had coined the term 'self-actualization'. It was this epithet which Maslow took over to describe 'full-humanness'.

As depicted by Maslow, self-actualizing people see life clearly for what it is; show acceptance of what they see in themselves, others, and nature; covet privacy; have a spontaneous manner; possess a sense of vocation; are independent-minded, not culture-bound; continually experience profound appreciation of mundane reality; regularly undergo mystical or 'peak' experiences (q.v.); feel deeply for people in general; enjoy deep relations with select others; display a non-malicious sense of humour; are unpretentious, highly ethical and creative.

Maslow hypothesized that the 'drive to self-actualization' came into play after deficiency needs had been met (*e.g.* hunger, love, sex). Other humanistic psychologists adopt the more plausible view of a single drive concerned with both the enhancement *and* preservation of self.

Maslow, A.H., *Motivation and Personality* (Harper, 1954); *Toward a Psychology of Being* (Van Nostrand, 1962); *The Farther Reaches of Human Nature* (Viking, 1971)

IVAN H. ELLINGHAM

See also: ANALYTICAL PSYCHOLOGY; CLIENT-CENTRED THERAPY; INDIVIDUATION; MATURITY; PERSON; SELF.

SENILE DEMENTIA
See: DEMENTIA.

SEXISM
Discrimination on the basis of sex.

In practice 'sexism' usually describes discrimination against women. A sexist assumes that a person's abilities and roles in society are predetermined by his or her sex; this assumption is often seen to be justified on (1) religious, (2) psychological, (3) physical and (4) social grounds.

1. *Religious justifications.* It is suggested that the biblical creation narratives, as traditionally interpreted, must remain normative for our understanding of the roles of the sexes: God made man to oversee creation, to organize and cultivate it; God made women to be companions and helpers for men, and to bear children. The Pauline and Deutero-Pauline writings take this up and suggest that the relationship between men and women, husbands and wives, must be that between Christ and the Christian (1 Cor. 11.3–4; Eph. 5.21–25). The wife must look to the husband as the Christian looks to Christ (1 Tim. 3.15 may even suggest that a woman only gains salvation through her role as wife and mother).

This reading of Scripture at worst makes women subordinate to men and at best defines their Christian discipleship in terms of their relationship to men. Much modern feminist theology has questioned whether this is a true interpretation of the gospel. No human being can claim any innate status in the eyes of God; all are equally indebted to God in Christ for their salvation; in the new community of those who acknowledge their dependence upon Christ, the only recognized authority is the authority of service; so any arguments about 'natural' hierarchy becomes irrelevant. Christian discipleship lays the same claims on and makes the same promises to all.

2. *Psychological justifications.* Sexism also tries to justify itself on the grounds that men and women are psychologically equipped for different roles. The founders of modern psychology, Freud and Jung, both in different ways reinforced this belief. Many modern studies also suggest real differences between the sexes: women are less outgoing and achievement-orientated, and tend to under-achieve in relation to their apparent intellectual abilities; they value achievement in relationships and in areas traditionally designated 'feminine' more highly than in jobs, examinations, etc.

However, this cannot be assumed to be a 'natural' psychological difference. From earliest childhood women and men face different expectations and receive different treatment, so that psychological differences are as much learned as they are innate (*see* FEMININITY/ MASCULINITY).

3. *Physical justifications.* Here, at least, it would seem that sexism is on safe ground – men and women *are* different physically, and therefore must have different roles. Women *have* to be the child-bearers; they are physically less strong, and so more suited to making the home and rearing the children. Luther went even further, and said that women ought to be the home-makers because 'they have broad hips and a wide fundament to sit upon, keep house and bear and raise children' (*Table Talk*, 1531).

But even this argument is no longer very convincing. Women have fewer children than in the past, so that not so much of their lives are taken up with child-bearing, and it is increasingly thought beneficial for parents and for children if child-rearing is shared between mother and father more equally. At the same time, fewer jobs nowadays require the kind of strength that women on the whole lack, so that division of labour between the sexes on the grounds of physical suitability is no longer straightforward.

4. *Social justifications.* The justification for sexism on social grounds is obviously closely connected with the three foregoing points –

all go to reinforce our society's belief that women and men have significantly different roles and capacities. It is assumed, for example, that most full-time workers are men, and that their work is serviced by women in the home, cooking, cleaning, shopping and rearing the children. Thus advertisements assume that women are the main consumers of household goods, men of cars, etc. If advertisers succeed by being good at taking the social pulse, it is probably instructive that this pattern is changing slightly, showing more women competing at work, etc.

Although many of the major grounds for sexism are now seriously questioned, it should not be taken for granted that there are *no* differences between men and women, apart from the biological. However, a much more sensitive approach to these differences is essential; definitions of the characteristics and abilities of either sex are always as false as they are true, and they become damaging both to those who try to confine themselves to fit the definition, and so fail to achieve their own personal potential, and to those who try to live outside the definition but feel that they lack approval and support. Sexism is not merely an academic question: it is also a pastoral one.

Feminist Anthology Collective (ed.), *No Turning Back* (The Women's Press, 1981). **Frieze, Irene H.** et al., *Women and Sex Roles* (Norton, New York, 1978). **Furlong, Monica** (ed.), *Feminine in the Church* (SPCK, 1984). **Ruether, Rosemary** (ed.), *Religion and Sexism* (Simon & Schuster, New York, 1974). **Young, Kate** et al. (ed.), *Of Marriage and the Market* (CSE Books, 1981).

JANE WILLIAMS

See also: BODY, THEOLOGY OF; FEMININITY/ MASCULINITY; PREJUDICE; SEXUALITY, THEOLOGY OF.

SEXUAL COUNSELLING AND THERAPY

(1) Sexual counselling is a way of helping people with sexual problems to explore the nature of their difficulties, to find solutions to their problems, or to come to terms with their continuing existence. (2) Sexual therapy often includes counselling, but the therapist also offers specific treatments which are directed towards the removal of disabilities which are interfering with sexual function and personal fulfilment.

The distinction between counselling (q.v.) and therapy is important to some profes-

sionals, less so to others, but clients seldom worry overmuch about the difference. Some of them have considerable difficulty in asking for help from anyone for they are often shy about their sexual problems, sometimes ashamed of them, occasionally convinced that they are incurable, or even feel that they are damned. Their prime need is to find someone to talk to who is accessible, approachable and able to listen to them sympathetically as they endeavour to disclose intimate facts about themselves.

A very wide range of disorders is presented for treatment. Many sexual problems are relatively simple ones, such as those stemming from people's ignorance about their own bodily functions or mistaken ideas about what is normal between people who enjoy loving sexual relationships. Others are the result of comparatively mild malfunctioning of physical functions, such as may occur in some forms of frigidity, impotence or premature ejaculation. These kinds of problems often yield to counselling or simple therapies which involve training in good techniques for enjoying sexual intimacy. The greatest number of problems presented to a counsellor or therapist are of this kind.

Some personal problems, however, are of a more complex kind. Ingrained narcissism, habitual loss of self-confidence leading to near permanent impotence, compulsive rituals such as bondage, fetishism, transvestism, sado-masochistic practices and excessive dependence on pornographic material as a stimulus to sexual activity, need prolonged counselling and other appropriate forms of treatment before they can be corrected. Some sexual problems, such as those caused by exhibitionism, paedophilia and some forms of trans-sexualism cause misery to the individuals affected and anxiety to the community at large. Sometimes people find themselves in trouble with the law through sexual activities which are legally forbidden, such as incest, rape, bestiality, sodomy, sexual intercourse with children, or gross indecency.

Each community and each society has its own ideas about norms of sexual behaviour and sets its own limits. These limits, whether customary or legal, vary widely according to the cultural norms of the community, the prevailing mores and religious attitudes which dominate individual and communal behaviour. Counsellors and therapists can only do their work within the context of the community in which they live, and many of them find themselves at some time or other at variance with the customs and laws of the communities they serve. A serious study of social and religious attitudes towards homosexuality (q.v.) will show just how difficult it is to define normative behaviour which is acceptable to every section of any community and, thus, how difficult it is for clients and counsellors to decide on the right course of advice or treatment for a particular individual. Similar difficulties are encountered in relation to prostitution (q.v.), sex shops, nude revues and group sex. People tend to have fixed ideas and prejudices about sexual activity and behaviour, and their ideas can be contagious so that sexual counselling and therapy is a field of work which requires of its professionals skill, tact and considerable self-knowledge as well as a deep understanding of human nature.

Clients who know that they need help for a sexual problem have, in fact, access to a wide variety of help but they do not always find it easy at the outset to know whether the help that they are being offered is the kind they really want or need, so it may be helpful for them to ask their intended counsellor or therapist how he or she works before embarking on a definite course of treatment.

All caring professionals in this field of work will begin by listening (q.v.) and helping their clients to identify the problem, its causes and effects, before suggesting how that problem could be resolved. It is at that point that attitudes vary widely among counsellors and therapists. At one end of the spectrum there are those who are totally non-directive in their approach. They invite clients to find their own solutions. They will often prefer to work wholly within the moral framework adopted by the client rather than advancing a different view. At the other end of the spectrum are counsellors and therapists who are much more directive. Some of these are pragmatists, others would acknowledge that they subscribe to moral standards which consciously or unconsciously govern their attitudes towards their work. Thus, for instance, some devoutly religious counsellors might rule out masturbation as a way of relieving sexual tension; others might refuse to treat homosexuals unless they agreed to try to change their orientation to enable them to relate in a heterosexual way. Some of the people at this end of the spectrum would not describe themselves as moralists or religious in the ordinary sense; feminists, for instance, often see pornography and prostitution as exploitative of women and would not advise either, even as the lesser of two evils.

Between these extremes are the majority of professional counsellors, who try to help their clients to use their sexuality as an expression of a loving and responsible relationship between sexual partners who are committed to each other. Some would describe themselves as Freudian, some Jungian, some behaviourist in approach: others would acknowledge openly that they make use of the best of all approaches and will happily marry psychotherapy to a behaviourist technique like the Masters and Johnson sensitivity training programmes. Some will use sex aids and surrogate sexual partners to help their clients; others will not. Some will use drugs and hormones; others will eschew them. Some will see pleasure as a proper goal at all times and orgasm as the proper fulfilment of pleasure: others will accept celibacy and friendship as a proper goal for some people even if that means the renunciation of orgasmic sexual pleasure. Clients who are fortunate enough to find counsellors and therapists who treat their sexuality as an integral and important part of their humanity will usually build up enough trust for the relationship to be truly therapeutic.

Some sexual counsellors and therapists are medically qualified doctors, many are practising psychologists or psychotherapists and many are specially trained counsellors. Training for this type of work is still in its infancy. Specialized courses are offered under the auspices of the Family Planning Association and the Institute of Psychosexual Medicine, and training in these skills are offered as part of wider courses by the Westminster Pastoral Foundation and the National Marriage Guidance Council among others. Steps are being taken to provide recognized training courses which could lead to approved registration at national level in due course.

Dominian, J., *Proposals for a New Sexual Ethic* (Darton Longman & Todd, 1977). **Kaplan, H.**, *Illustrated Manual of Sex Therapy* (Souvenir Press, 1968). **Kroll, Una**, *Sexual Counselling* (SPCK, 1980). **McNeil, J.J.**, *The Church and the Homosexual* (Darton Longman & Todd, 1977). **Masters, W.H.** and **Johnson, V.E.**, *Human Sexual Inadequacy* (Little Brown, 1970). **Trimmer, E.**, *Basic Sexual Medicine* (Heinemann, 1978).

Una Kroll

See also: SEXUALITY AND SEXUAL
DEVELOPMENT; SEXUAL DEVIATION.

SEXUAL DEVIATION

To define normality in sexual behaviour, and thereby to provide a yardstick for the definition of deviations, is not a straightforward task. Cross-cultural and historical evidence suggest widespread sexual variations. However, frequency of incidence neither proves nor disproves normality, in the sense of a positive ethical evaluation. More significant are criteria such as emotional maturity, and respect for the sexual partner. Here our working definition of normative sexuality will be heterosexual intercourse within a stable adult partnership, which is traditionally sanctioned by the form of marriage (q.v.).

Many alternative forms of sexual behaviour are to be found. Some persons seek partners of both sexes (bisexuality), of the same sex (homosexuality, q.v.), children (paedophilia), or close blood relatives (incest, q.v.). More rarely, sexual contact may be sought with animals (bestiality) or even dead persons (necrophilia). Genital intercourse may be replaced by anal intercourse (sodomy or buggery, whether homosexual or heterosexual), oral-genital contact (fellatio, cunnilingus), or solitary or mutual masturbation. Sexual satisfaction may be gained by exposing the self (exhibitionism) or by observing the sexual activities of others (voyeurism). Erotic pleasure may be linked with the infliction of pain (sadism) or the reception of pain (masochism). The fetishist is particularly attracted by one part of the body, or by an inanimate object such as a shoe, or silk or rubber. The transvestite – whose physical contact is most often heterosexual – derives erotic excitement from dressing in clothing of the opposite sex. The sexual partner may be paid (prostitution, q.v.), or taken without consent (rape, q.v.). However, it should be borne in mind that much alternative sexual behaviour is between consenting adults. The role of the law in relation to sexual ethics is a complex and delicate matter, but it is generally considered that legal intervention should be largely restricted to non-consenting sexual behaviour.

Much sexual deviation may stem from an insecure sexual identity or from some form of emotional immaturity. In any case, pastoral responses should be compassionate and sensitive to the needs of the given individual, who may well require some form of therapeutic help. Pastoral care may also be required for relatives and other persons concerned; and for victims and their relatives, in cases of non-consenting behaviour.

Homosexuality (q.v.), whether male or female, tends to be regarded either as pathological (the traditional viewpoint), or as a legitimate variation. A third perspective can obviate this dichotomy. Moberly (1983) speaks of same-sex love as a legitimate developmental need – in its origin, the need for attachment to the parent of the same sex. As such, this need should be met, and not left unmet. However, precisely because this need pertains to the pre-adult developmental process, it is regarded as inappropriate to fulfil it sexually.

This viewpoint has major implications for the understanding and treatment of homosexuality, and also of the analogous condition of trans-sexualism. Heterosexuality is seen as the ultimate goal of development, but it presupposes the fulfilment of these developmental needs for same-sex love. There are no short-cuts to heterosexuality, and it is both mistaken and irrelevant to promote increased contact with the opposite sex. To attempt this is to ignore the legitimacy of the developmental process. Much traditional therapy has been misdirected in this way, and has therefore had relatively little success in 'changing' homosexuals. Pastoral care should focus on same-sex relational needs, with a counsellor or therapist of the same sex as the homosexual. The aim is to meet legitimate developmental needs, and also to resolve an underlying ambivalence towards members of the same sex. To see fulfilment as sexual, or conversely to regard healing as merely the suppression of sexual activity, is to miss the main point at issue. The main point is that the same-sex developmental process was checked early in life, and that it is desirable to resume its fulfilment, which can take place without sexual activity.

'Symposium on Sexual Deviation' (British Journal of Psychiatry, no. 143, 1983), pp. 215ff. **Allen, Clifford,** A Textbook of Psychosexual Disorders (OUP, 1962). **Moberly, Elizabeth R.,** Psychogenesis (Routledge, 1983); Homosexuality: A New Christian Ethic (J. Clarke, 1983). **Storr, Anthony,** Sexual Deviation (Penguin, 1964)

ELIZABETH R. MOBERLY

See also: RAPE AND RAPE COUNSELLING;

SEXUAL COUNSELLING AND THERAPY;
SEXUALITY AND SEXUAL DEVELOPMENT.

SEXUAL THERAPY
See: SEXUAL COUNSELLING AND THERAPY.

SEXUALITY AND SEXUAL DEVELOPMENT

Sexuality. Adult sexuality is complex and variable. It may involve any individual human experience from the physical over-stimulation that may be induced by a brain tumour causing hypersexuality to the spiritual relinquishment of sex as with a celibate priest or nun. Sexuality also involves interpersonal factors – thus the close communication (q.v.) of an emotionally committed couple, both verbal and non-verbal, through to the destructive non-communication of a couple, whose maladjusted relationship spills over into their sexuality leading perhaps to male erectile impotency or to female sexual coldness and withdrawal ('frigidity'). Environmental forces, family, social and cultural, also exert pressure and reward or punish selected aspects of sexual expression such as fidelity versus extra-marital sex. Individual psychological sexual needs are extremely variable and intensely personal. Any component of sexuality, talking, looking, touching, kissing, smelling, may lead to sexual arousal. Although major aspects of sexual fantasy may be fairly universal, as with the generalization that most men become sexually aroused by looking, the combination of looking is individual and unique. Thus some may be aroused by nudity; others by certain combinations of dress or undress. The range of normal, in the sense of usual, sexual expression is extraordinarily wide, and it behoves sexual counsellors to recognize this. Arbitary limitation on what is 'normal' sexuality, based on one person's personal life experience, will lead to therapeutic disappointment, sometimes to disaster (e.g. persuading a life-long, obligatory homosexual that change in sexual orientation is the only acceptable goal).

In both sexes the act itself involves a sequence. The individual components of the sequence may become disordered (as in male premature ejaculation) or the rhythm and timing. This latter point is often forgotten. It seems likely that a universal aspect of the expression of human emotion is that it should wax and wane before leading finally to release. In this sense the sex act resembles the basic structure of any work of art such as a novel, a symphony, an opera or a play.

Sexuality begins prior to the sex act and ends after it. Initially sexual drive and the communication system with a particular partner are involved. After this follows a period of sexual arousal signified in the male by penile erection, in the female by vaginal lubrication. This state of sexual readiness is followed by penile insertion into the vagina, by thrusting movements by both partners and to the sexual climax (orgasm). Orgasm has two components, physical and psychic. Physical orgasm consists in the ejaculation of sperm in the male. Psychic orgasm, often of greater importance in sexual fulfilment, consists in both partners giving to the other so that there is an altered state of conscious awareness, the body images seeming to merge. After this psychic joining and release of tension there comes a post-sexual intercourse phase. With a good relationship this is characterized by contentment and fulfilment, by feelings of tenderness and relaxation, of closer communication. In the sexually dysfunctional couple, however, the sex act itself may be incomplete or clumsy for one or both partners, or the psychological attitude is such as to lead to post-coital rejection, to hatred or withdrawal, or to behaviour such as cleansing rituals which offend the partner; there also may be a resumption of the non-communication and quarrelling that existed prior to sexual intercourse.

Sexual Development. Knowledge of sexual development has not been rigorously established. It rests on a combination of scientific and clinical, especially psychotherapeutic, experience. This, however, all points to the relevance of inborn and acquired factors and to a long and complex learning history that begins before birth and continues throughout life.

Inborn components relate principally to the intra-uterine period, especially the establishment of the sex of the foetus through the action of male sex hormones. To the pastoral counsellor, while an appreciation of the relevance of genetic factors is important, it is to environmental and cultural factors that their interest and counselling skills will inevitably turn.

There are two major psychological approaches to sexual development; behavioural and psychoanalytical. The behavioural approach emphasizes a person's continuing history of learning by conditioning. Thus the physical and psychological fulfilment of normal sexuality within a good relationship will constantly be rewarded, and these patterns will be perpetuated. Negative incidents such as a girl's early experience with a clumsy sexual partner or even with attempted rape may permanently condition her to negative feelings towards men or towards sexual expression as such. A chance occurrence of sexual excitement in a male child while exposed to his sister's clothes may lead to a transvestite (cross-dressing) tendency. The constant interaction of a male child with a domineering, bullying mother may condition him to regard all women as a threat and to making sexual arousal with a woman difficult or impossible (heterophobia), and possibly predispose him to homosexuality.

The major criticism of the behaviouristic approach to sexual development is that it rests too heavily on apparently chance factors of experience, whereas there appears to be consistency and regularity about sexual development which the majority share.

Psychoanalysis (q.v.) accounts for both the preliminary component of the sex act (kissing, touching, etc.) and the act itself by postulating an infantile (pre-genital) component and a more adult (genital) component to sexual development. The infantile component, up to the age of 5 years, includes the oral component (sucking, biting, kissing) and the so-called anal or holding-back component, coinciding with the waxing and waning of the sex act. The more mature (genital) components (age 5 years to adolescence) relate to how the child has worked through and resolved the oedipus complex. This consists of the attraction to the opposite-sex parent and rivalry and competitiveness with the same-sex parent (see ADOLESCENCE). The relatively emotionally mature child is involved in a model or paradigm of relationships, including sexual relationships, that will repeat itself in adulthood. Thus envy, jealousy, possessiveness, difficulty in sharing, competitiveness and hostility, all adult emotions, are involved. All of these may be incorporated later into the expression of normal sexuality. Conflicts not worked through may intrude unduly in later life and lead to sexual dysfunction or even to sexual deviance (q.v.).

The limitation of the psychoanalytic view is that it is based on purely clinical experience derived from the psychotherapeutic treatment of patients. There are profound methodological problems to the proof of psychoanalytic theory.

The social and cultural environment is also relevant in developing and shaping sexuality in childhood, adolescence and adult life. This is seen most clearly in comparing the sexual expression and sexual problems of persons from different cultural backgrounds. Extremes may be the free-for-all sexual experimentation of sophisticated, white middle-class urban people compared to the explicit controls in a family of Asiatic background. Similarly, in presenting sex as a problem to a counsellor the former group is disinhibited and direct; the latter shy and controlled and may need to disguise the sexual problem by embedding it in a legitimized 'medical' problem such as a headache or stomach-ache. Within our own culture too there are age, social-class and sex differences in the enculturation of sexual codes and practices, also in the conception of a sexual problem should this arise.

'Symposium on Sexual Dysfunction' (*British Journal of Psychiatry*, no. 140, 1983), pp. 70ff. **Brown, P.** and **Faulder, C.**, *Treat Yourself to Sex* (Penguin, 1980); a helpful text for patients' reading. **Belliveau, F.** and **Richter, L.**, *Understanding Human Sexual Inadequacy* (Hodder, 1971); a straightforward account of Masters and Johnson's classic text. **Crown, S.**, *Psychosexual Problems* (Academic Press, 1976); an introduction to sex problems in medicine, surgery — chapter on sexual problems with religious background. **Gillan, P.** and **Gillan, R.**, *Sex Therapy Today* (Open Books, 1976); a simple account of behavioural approaches to sex problems. **Kaplan, H.S.**, *The New Sex Therapy* (Penguin, 1978); a good general reference book.

SIDNEY CROWN

See also: FEMININITY/MASCULINITY; SEXUAL COUNSELLING AND THERAPY; SEXUAL DEVIATION.

SEXUALITY, THEOLOGY OF

Some unexpected side-effects have followed from recent disputes as to whether God is essentially not just masculine but male; or whether, on the contrary, God in essence transcends all human distinctions between male and female, masculinity and femininity. For the reactions to these arguments, both rational and emotional, have demonstrated just how deeply our sexuality pervades our own sense of personhood – the Me-ness of me. Clearly the sense of our personal identity, as in some way allied to our sexuality, goes far beyond occasions when we are sexually aroused. It seems to permeate every facet of human experience.

This pervasive characteristic of sexuality accords well with the biological understanding of what distinguishes sexual reproduction from a-sexual replication. Sexual reproduction introduces an infinity of permutation and combination in the genetic make-up of new individuals. Thus human sexuality can be held to undergird the uniqueness of the individual's personality, and so the theological wonder of the value of every human being in the eyes of God, our creator. Sexual reproduction also necessitates mutual attraction between individuals, and, where the newborn are as helpless as are human children, a further community-forming impetus to ensure their protection and upbringing. It is arguable that these necessities underlie all that complexity of human association which we name religion, culture, civilization. We are here confronted with the theological mystery that we are by nature 'members one of another'; that our physical, mental and emotional needs as human sexual beings are all of a piece with our spiritual needs.

For many centuries Christian thinking was dominated by a dualism linked to the doctrine of the fall. This set the bodily element in human beings, over against their divine soul, as a source of corruption and sinfulness. A tendency to sin was thought to be communicated physically from one generation to another in the act of conception. In addition, since the only known part played by women in procreation was the provision of shelter and nourishment for the child growing in the womb, women could be regarded as essentially inferior to men; imperfect human beings who could only find wholeness through the 'headship' of a male.

The Church has often spoken with an ambivalent voice about sexual behaviour: exalting virginity above the married state, yet using marriage as a symbol of the unity between Christ and the Church; urging the married to procreate as many children as possible, yet denying any dignity to the act of intercourse in itself. An obsessive attention has then been paid to restraint in the effort to remedy sin, to the neglect of such human relationships as enhance companionship and loving concern.

In recent times, many contemporary secular disciplines have drawn our attention to the interdependence of our mental, physical, emotional, social and spiritual well-being both within and between individuals. This has made possible a renewed appreciation of the biblical understanding of human nature (q.v.) as a body/spirit unity. There is also fresh recognition that in both old and new dispensations God establishes his covenant (his relationship) with individuals-in-community (see CONTRACT AND COVENANT). We are born in, not reared into, relatedness. In addition we have become aware that in human beings the correlation between biological maleness and femaleness and what is perceived as masculinity and femininity, is neither direct nor simple, but varies in different cultures.

Our sexuality can now be regarded, not as an isolated component of our human make-up, but as the basic energy of psychosomatic human nature. It plays a part, whether creative or destructive, in all our human relationships and in all our imaging of the Godhead. Both as a source of diversity and individual identity, and also as an impetus towards all kinds of relatedness, this energy can become potent in the drama of restoring, reconciling and renewing the world-wide community of women and men. It calls out to be used creatively at all the stages and in all the contexts of our lives, not just at times when we are sexually active. Otherwise it may fuel the fires of jealousy and hatred.

In early years we need the sense of belonging to a stable family group, if our sense of personal identity is to be both strong and responsive to others. But the Christian is called to transcend that closed family circle, and be neighbour to all. The pastoral task of the Christian community is not only to nurture its youngest members in the fellowship of the congregation. It must also foster a readiness to welcome strangers and to reach out in empathy towards all humanity, accepting the vulnerability to others which ensues. It is for this universal fellowship in the Spirit that we are called to offer our human sexual energy in Christ's service.

Davis, Charles, *Body as Spirit* (Hodder, 1977). **Dominian, Jack,** *Proposals for a New Sexual Ethic* (Darton Longman & Todd, 1977). **Goergen, Donald,** *The Sexual Celibate* (SPCK, 1976). **Haughton, Rosemary,** *The Knife Edge of Experience* (Darton Longman & Todd, 1972); *The Mystery of*

Sexuality (Darton Longman & Todd, 1973). **Koznik, X.** (ed.), *Human Sexuality* (Search Press, 1976). **Moss, Rachel** (ed.), *God's Yes to Sexuality* (BCC/ Fount, 1981). **Nelson, James B.**, *Embodiment: an Approach to Sexuality and Christian Theology* (SPCK, 1979). **Thielicke, H.**, *The Ethics of Sex* (J. Clarke, 1964).

RACHEL MOSS

See also: BODY, THEOLOGY OF; FEMININITY/ MASCULINITY; HUMAN NATURE; MARRIAGE, THEOLOGY OF; SEXISM.

SHALOM

Shalom is a word that appears frequently in the Hebrew OT and is usually translated in the English versions as 'peace'. However 'peace' does not convey adequately the richness and complexity of its fundamental meaning, which is that of 'totality'. 'Totality' includes the idea of harmonious community, and so *shalom* denotes a relationship rather than a state. It is a gift of God (Ps. 85.8ff.) and refers not to the absence of conflict but to wholeness; indeed it sums up the blessings of the messianic age (Isa. 52.7) and is the equivalent of salvation (q.v.) (Isa. 45.7). It is therefore a social concept and is neither an inward feeling nor an individual possession. *Shalom* is applicable to the in-between of persons; it includes unity, solidarity, the exercise of mutual responsibility and confidence; it expresses all forms of well-being and happiness, as long as these stem from community with others. So it involves neighbourliness, reconciliation, responsible faith and hope.

In the LXX *shalom* is rendered by *eirene*, which in classical Greek does refer to a state, and in particular to one that constitutes an interlude in hostilities. But within the Bible *eirene* takes on the depth of meaning of the Hebrew word, and this is so whether one considers either the Old or the New Testament.

The gospel is itself the good news of *shalom* (Eph. 6.15), which refers not to spiritual prosperity but to the salvation of the whole person (1 Thess. 5.23), and peace has come as an historical event through Jesus Christ who is our peace (Eph. 2.14). *Shalom* or *eirene* is then a gift not of inner peace in the soul but of righteousness, trust and fellowship. It is a keynote of the Kingdom of God (Rom. 14.17), its eschatological character emphasizing its positive aspect. Just as salvation is not to be confined within freedom *from* something but

is rather to be comprehended as freedom *for* something, so positive peace is not a condition but a process of continuing interaction between human beings and between them and God. The promotion of *shalom* is to be regarded as one aspect of pastoral care, devoted as it should be to furthering personal integration, which is not a simple one-to-one exercise but has an essential communal reference. To be a mediator of the divine gift of *shalom* is to foster relationships in love (q.v.), and this has its ritual counterparts both in greetings and blessings ('Peace be with you'), and in the *pax* or kiss of peace at the Eucharist (2. Cor. 13.12). This is intended to be a prophetic symbol or effective sign of the *shalom* that should animate the Body of Christ, and it reaches its climax in the act of communion.

Davies, J.G., *New Perpectives on Worship Today* (SCM, 1978), pp. 51–6, 73–5. 'Eirene' in G. Kittel, (ed.), *Theological Dictionary of the Bible*, tr. G.W. Bromiley, (Eerdmans, 1964), vol. 2, pp. 400–17. **Pedersen, J.**, *Israel* (OUP, 1946), I–II, pp. 264, 313.

J.G. DAVIES

See also: HOPE; RECONCILIATION; SALVATION AND PASTORAL CARE.

SILENCE
The absence of noise.

Although we sometimes speak of silence among inanimate objects as tangible – for instance the silence over a highland loch at evening time – nevertheless it is entirely negative: an absence of sound. This is not so when silence exists between persons. Between persons silence is never merely negative. It has degrees of the positive. It can be comparatively empty, for instance between two strangers sitting beside each other in a bus, or comparatively full, for instance between two lovers alone together.

Because silence between persons can be rich and meaningful, it has spiritual pastoral significance. There is an inverse proportion between the amount of talking which takes place between persons and the amount of deep communication. At a certain stage of intimacy, the more talk, the less communication; the less talk, i.e. more silence, the more communication. When two strangers meet they are compelled to keep talking to each other, because silence between strangers is a breakdown in communication. Even when they talk the communication is minimal. If the two strangers become friends they are able to remain silent with each other and begin to communicate at a deep level. Friends on a walk together or sitting by the fireside often communicate better when not speaking than when speaking. Finally, lovers find themselves in situations when they cannot speak because to use words would actually prevent adequate communication; words fail them; they find themselves speechless, with wonder and love. At this level silence is not just a form of communication, but the only way to communicate. Such silence is deep, rich, positive, replete with meaning, far from empty. It is the opposite to silence between strangers.

This rich silence (as opposed to the empty silence between strangers) has at least four pastoral and spiritual uses:
1. In counselling, silence plays an essential part, provided it is the silence explained above, which is not empty but full of communication. By remaining silent, but in touch, a counsellor gives the person room to speak about his or her problems, room to express emotions, room to reach his or her own conclusions. Of course, such silence is interspersed with words, even whole sentences, which enable the client to have a direction and to feel approved, but the majority of the time, during a counselling session, is filled with empathetic silence. This absence of words on the counsellor's part enables him or her to be more effective in what may be said when eventually the time comes for speech. A chattering, seldom silent, counsellor gets nowhere in therapeutic listening and fails to draw out the other person. A skilled counsellor also recognizes the range of silences from the person being helped. Sometimes the silence indicates trust, acceptance or restfulness, but often it indicates hostility, anxiety, withdrawal or bewilderment. Silence is rarely simple or unambiguous, and the pastor must rely heavily on an understanding of non-verbal communication (q.v.).
2. In preaching and teaching, silence is invaluable. It enables the speaker to establish a rapport with the audience. It gives the audience time to think. Above all, it enables the speaker to relate not primarily to his or her theme, but to his or her audience, the human beings addressed. In the first case the speaker never actually relates to the other persons but remains in a closed circle relating to his subject (Buber's 'I-it' relationship). In

the second case the speaker relates through words and silence to the real person being addressed (Buber's 'I-Thou' relationship). He speaks to the hearts of the audience. Silence is essential for this. Without silence we speak *multa, sed non multum* (many things but not much).
3. The communication (q.v.) of the sacraments is often enhanced by silence. What is said in words appeals to the rational mind. What is said without words in symbols appeals to the unconscious in us (*see* RITES AND RITUALS; SYMBOLS). Catholic liturgy is replete with this latter kind of communication, by lights, coloured vestments, statues, crucifixes, genuflections and bows, etc. The churches of the Reformation impoverished themselves of this deeper form of preaching and teaching. Sacramental communication is itself derived from the Incarnation of the Word as man, God's non-verbal communication to mankind. Edwin Muir said of the Calvinist preachers he heard as a youth: 'The Word made flesh has here been made word again.' By too much talk they diminished the impact of the Incarnation.
4. Silence is the major factor in contemplative prayer. All that was said above about the growth of communication between strangers, friends, lovers, which is itself a growth into silence, applies to growth in prayer. As we approach God in prayer we increasingly experience the need for silence. As prayer expands in our souls, words fail us and silence takes over. This fourth use of silence (in prayer) is the best foundation for the other three uses of silence in counselling, in teaching, in sacramental worship. One who has experienced the supreme value of silence in prayer will actively allow it to spill over in the other activities of life.

Biestek, F., *The Casework Relationship* (Allen & Unwin, 1961). **Buber, M.,** *I and Thou* (T. & T. Clark, 1971).

JOHN DALRYMPLE

See also: EMPATHY; LISTENING; PRAYER; RETREATS; SOLITUDE.

SIN
Most profoundly, estrangement from God, but also the moral wrongdoing of which it is a consequence.

This concept arises because human persons characteristically make moral distinctions between good and evil and between right and wrong; and know that they should follow what they judge to be good or right and shun what they judge to be evil and wrong. But they certainly disobey their own moral judgements and do what they know they ought not to do and leave undone what they know they ought to do. This is vividly analysed by St Paul in Rom. 7.15–23, and in the succinct line of the Latin poet Ovid, 'I see the better and approve of it: I follow the worse'. The Judaeo-Christian faith links (but does not identify) the holiness of God with the realization that he must require goodness of those who worship him; so acts of thought, word and deed judged to deserve moral blame are seen as sins against God.

There is much about sin in the Bible. In the OT it arrives at realizing that every action affects the character of the person who acts, so that sin poisons the person from within unless some atonement is made. The OT came to see that the sacrificial system could not put the sinner right with God, only a broken and contrite heart could do that (Ps. 51.17). It left unresolved how that was to be achieved. However a key element in early Christian preaching was the forgiveness of sins; that Christ had done for us what we could not do for ourselves (and the various doctrines of the Atonement have been attempts to give a rationale of this) (see RECONCILIATION; SALVATION AND PASTORAL CARE). Jesus himself assumed the reality of sin, and associated particularly with those who were thought of as sinners by those who thought themselves righteous (cf. Luke 18.9ff.). Theology came later to maintain that Jesus was sinless and, while it is impossible to prove a negative, it is noteworthy that while he seems to have had no sense of conscious sin, he aroused a sense of it in others. St Paul writes dramatically (e.g. in Romans) of humankind as being enslaved to sin through a kind of mystical union with Adam and freed by a mystical unity with Christ.

This raised issues which were to be much discussed. Should a Christian incorporated in Christ ever sin again? There are indications in the later NT writings that the Church was beginning to exclude grave sinners at least from earthly forgiveness. 1 John 5.16 refers to a 'sin unto death' which, if anyone commits, others are forbidden to pray for him (cf. also 1 John 3.9 and 1 John 1.8; commentaries

explain that these passages have to be understood against the struggle with Gnosticism). Soon a rigorist penal discipline was widely adopted, which allowed either no, or perhaps one, grave sin after baptism, a harshness which produced its own reaction in laxity (see PASTORAL CARE: HISTORY – EARLY CHURCH). However a doctrine which calls all Christians to perfection, and maintains the possibility of it, has never died out, its most notable protagonist in the United Kingdom has been John Wesley. It founders on the fact that the most subtle sins are not the dramatic ones but those that corrupt virtues, e.g. the taint of vanity in the virtues of the 'saints'.

The traditional distinction between mortal and venial sin grew out of such passages as 1 John 5.16. It became too formalized, though it is evident that not all sins are equally serious. Recent moral theology (q.v.) has tended to relate the distinction to the person rather than the action, and ask how far for the person the sin was a 'fundamental option'. The term 'mortal' is unfortunate; it suggests something incurable. 'Grave' is a better term. Grave sins came to be listed using the favourite number, seven – pride (the most deadly), avarice, lust, gluttony, anger, envy and sloth. St Augustine produced some of the most profound analyses of sin, and of pride as the root one. Pride is a tendency to overestimate our virtues and achievements (sometimes disguised in humility), and to use our reason not to master our selfish interests and passions but as instruments of them.

This discussion presupposes actions for which one is responsible, i.e. that they are free and not coerced. There have been extensive discussions of freedom and determinism (q.v.); suffice it to say that (leaving certain pathological states aside) we are sure that to some extent we are originators of our own actions and therefore rightly open to praise or blame. Traditionally a distinction was made between formal (or culpable) sin and material sin (objectively sinful but due to invincible ignorance or coercion). Both terms are unfortunate, because easily misunderstood. The discussion also raises the question of the entail of sin which we each inherit by being born into structures of life from the family outwards, which are partially corrupt and influence us from infancy before we are able to take responsibility for our lives. This is how to understand another misleading term, 'original sin'. It appears archaic, although it refers to one of the most attested facts of human experience. The archaism is due to the associations of the term with the view that it was literally inherited from the 'fall' of Adam, and St Augustine's view that it is transmitted through sexual intercourse. However, there is no need to be tied to St Augustine, and the reality is important against the utopianism which holds *either* that sin is a diminishing relic of a more primitive stage of evolution *or* that human history is on the way to the elimination of all unjust structures after which human virtue will be unconstricted. (Marxism is the outstanding instance of this latter belief.) Nevertheless 'original sin' should not be stressed to the neglect of positive human qualities, or 'original righteousness'.

A further issue raised by these discussions is corporate sin, in which we are involved because of the structures of life in which we are placed, and, practically speaking, cannot extricate ourselves. Sometimes we have to act representatively; and in any case we are caught up on the entails of the past and the actions of others in the present, e.g. how far were, or are, all Germans involved in war guilt? Or the British as 'exploiters' of primary producers in the Third World? There are many questions here involving basic issues in Christian social ethics.

Such issues need to be wrestled with in the corporate life of the Church at every level, from the local congregation upwards, if Christians are to live boldly, confident that they will not fall out of God's care. As to personal sins, strength can also be drawn from the corporate life of the Church as a company of forgiven sinners (though it often seems to be made up of the 'unco guid'). In pastoral care the aim will be to help the penitent to avoid occasions of sin and to fill his life with more worthwhile activities. Traditionally, occasions of sin have been classified as remote (where temptation is unlikely), proximate (where it is likely), free (where the circumstances are easily avoided), and necessary (when they are not); it is a roughly useful guide in pastoral care.

Imaginatively, the close connection between the deepest capabilities of both freedom and sin, and the impossibility of drawing a sharp line between the sheep and the goats, is powerfully exposed in the novels of Dostoyevsky, with his pictures of 'holy sinners'.

A New Catechism: Catholic Faith for Adults (Search Press, 1970), pp. 258–92, 449–56. **Coates, J.R.** (tr. and ed.), *Sin* (Biblical Key Words), (Black, 1951). **Telfer, W.,** *The Forgiveness of Sins* (SCM, 1959). **Temple, W.,** *Christianity and Social Order* (SPCK, 1976), ch. 4.

RONALD PRESTON

See also: DISCIPLINE, PASTORAL CARE AS; GUILT; RECONCILIATION; RESPONSIBILITY; VIRTUES AND VICES.

SINGLE PARENTS

Single parents are fathers or, more commonly, mothers bringing up their child or children alone. One in eight families in Britain are one-parent families.

Single parents may be unmarried mothers, separated or divorced parents, widows or widowers. Between 1971 and 1981 the number of single parents increased from 570,000 to 975,000, an increase of more than 70%. The number of children under the age of 16 in single-parent families increased by 62%. The largest group of single parents is the divorced and separated who make up 62% of the total. Now 1 in 5 children will experience their parents going through a divorce. Unsupported fathers account for 12.6%.

Single parents are one of the fastest-growing disadvantaged groups in Great Britain. In 1981, 11.9% of all families were single-parent families, yet they make up almost 50% of families with children claiming supplementary benefit; almost 50% of all families rehoused under the Housing (Homeless Persons) Act; over 50% of all children in care come from single-parent families, and almost 50% of children on child-abuse registers are from single-parent families.

The quality of life for single parents is determined not only by low income and poor housing. Stress is a major problem shared by most single parents. The task of raising children, running a home and providing financially, single-handed, demands considerable personal resources as well as boundless energy. In addition, most single parents experience specifically stressful events, such as bereavement (q.v.) and loss, the trauma of a long and bitter divorce settlement (*see* DIVORCE: PASTORAL ASPECTS), or the rejection of family and friends due to an unplanned pregnancy. Fortunately these emotional difficulties do not last for ever (nor indeed does the 'single' state of many single parents) but while in existence they can lead to profound mental-health problems or a break-down in parent-child relationships which can have long-lasting effects if there is not adequate support and understanding available to the parent.

Isolation is another common problem. Time-out from family responsibilities is essential for mental well-being yet baby-sitting, for example, can be expensive or, if reciprocity is demanded, impossible. Community support is essential both for local initiatives, such as after-school schemes or child-care relief, and for national movements such as conciliation schemes or improvements in welfare benefits.

Addresses:
National Council for One Parent Families, 255 Kentish Town Road, London, NW5.
Scottish Council for Single Parents, 13 Gayfield Square, Edinburgh, EH1 3NX.
Gingerbread, 39 Hope Street, Glasgow, G2 6AE.

FIONA RAFFAELLI

See also: LONELINESS; PARENTING.

SINGLE PERSONS

The single person is, by convention, defined as an unmarried adult, but such an individual may be living in intimacy with someone of the other or the same sex, in which case the single state is essentially a legal fiction. A more realistic concept of single persons includes those who are obliged to live alone, whether unmarried or deprived of their partner through death or legal separation; in a pastoral context the single person would include the widowed and the divorced.

The person living alone may have adopted this life-style because of physical or mental incapacity. For instance,, progressive loco-motor disability may so cripple a person quite early on in life that he or she becomes housebound, as is seen in rheumatoid arthritis and multiple sclerosis, both of which sometimes show themselves in youth. A psychosis may likewise blight the life of a promising young person so as to cause progressive isolation from society; schizophrenia is a common example. But the less destructive anxiety states can have a similar effect; agoraphobia, the morbid fear of public places, can be so crippling that a person dares not venture out, and home becomes a prison. More frequently, however, people remain single because of personality defects; the timid, emotionally inadequate person, for example, cannot face the demands of total self-exposure in a permanent relationship with someone else. Not infrequently there are undertones of homosexuality (q.v.) that are dimly felt but cannot be faced directly. Finally there is the person who has voluntarily adopted the celibate life in order to be dedicated to God and fellow-beings.

These various categories of single persons share in common a call to a life alone, whether it has been thrust upon them by external circumstances or willingly assumed on behalf of others. They may have never known an intimate relationship with another person, and so have, to greater or lesser extent, learnt to cope with their own solitude. By contrast the bereaved and the divorced have been deprived of a previous intimacy, however unsatisfactory it might have been, on which they depended for fellowship and support, and now find themselves floundering in an ocean of emptiness apparently devoid of hope or meaning. Their desolation is especially severe if the previous union was barren of offspring.

The pastoral care of the single person is determined primarily by the cause of the situation. Those who are ill physically need specialized medical attention, and those with mental disease require all the help that modern psychiatric practice can offer. Nevertheless, devoted pastoral care can complement the prescribed therapy with concern and moral support. Those with personality problems should receive appropriate counselling (q.v.), with psychotherapy (q.v.) according to the severity of the circumstance. At the same time social workers can be of great assistance in discussing the client's problems so that he or she can face the future with its difficulties in an atmosphere of trust and calm hope. The overwhelming problem of the single person is, however, loneliness (q.v.), and it is here that pastoral care is particularly valuable by befriending (q.v.), so that the deeper wounds of the isolated person can be gently brought to light, discussed, and eased by mutual sharing. Loneliness can, of course, be alleviated to some extent by fostering the interests and hobbies of the client so that links may be made with groups of people of similar tastes, whether artistic, educational or political. But in the end, the single person has to make the journey inwards to find a place of peace and security within from which it is possible to issue forth as a more authentic individual, able to bestow his or her own essence on the world around. As a more complete, balanced person, free self-giving to the community in service becomes ever more devoted as the process of inner growth becomes established. The dedicated celibate has trodden this path in the way of self-giving service, and often lives in a community of like-minded people. The single life should eventually move along this path, except that the community the person enlists may embrace the whole world. One who is single-minded in approach to life by being centred in his or her own being, is eventually at home in diverse situations even in totally alien groups. The work of acceptance (q.v.) accelerates this growth in adversity, and the practice of meditation (q.v.) and prayer (q.v.) help immeasurably by quickening the inner life of the single person.

Evening, Margaret, *Who Walks Alone* (Hodder, 1974). **Israel, Martin,** *Living Alone* (SPCK, 1982).

MARTIN ISRAEL

See also: BEREAVEMENT; CELIBACY; DIVORCE: PASTORAL ASPECTS; LONELINESS; SOLITUDE.

SLEEP
Sleep is a healthy, recurrent state of inertia, of unresponsiveness to the environment, and of rest for the brain and the body. Mental life continues but is poorly in contact with reality during drowsiness and sleep, and memories of these times are quickly lost. Drowsiness is accompanied by brief dreamlets (hypnagogic hallucinations), including visions and voices, such as hearing one's name called. Dreams can occur at any time during sleep (*see also* DREAMS).

The sleep-wakefulness rhythm represents the most powerful amongst our *biological rhythms*. If we fly east or west round the world, we are sleepy when our hosts are alert, and wakeful while they sleep. Shift workers, seeking to retain normal social life, never fully adjust their own rhythms; consequently many experience tiredness, irritability, moodiness and indigestion, and their relationships suffer.

There is also a 100-minute rhythm which manifests itself during the night by periods of paradoxical (REM) sleep. This is a time rich in dreaming, with flaccidity of muscles, jerking

eye-movements and penile erections. The proportion of paradoxical sleep is greatest in the morning, and so morning erections are normal. During paradoxical sleep there occur the 'wet dreams' of normal young men.

Insomnia, or dissatisfaction with sleep, is common, especially among older women of nervous temperament. Some aver that they hardly sleep at all; electrical brain wave studies show that they sleep more than they believe, but tell us nothing about the restorative quality of their sleep. Sometimes uncharacteristic insomnia appears as a feature of depressive illness (*see* DEPRESSION), a treatable mental condition: in other cases, the complaint becomes part of a life-style, a reason for sympathy and occasionally the prescription of drugs. Today's sleeping drugs are safe and can help at times of bereavement or other distress; they should be only temporary aids, and should not be used to prevent the normal course of grief.

Daytime life is reflected in sleep; although nightmares are normal for everyone, they are more frequent at times of waking stress. Predisposition to sudden night terrors and sleep walking is inherited, but these occurrences become commoner when daytime anxiety is enhanced. Good sleep is helped by regularity of habits, including regular meals, by healthy exercise, avoidance of smoking, abstention from evening coffee or tea, low alcohol intake and a willingness to forgive others and to accept ourselves as we are.

Cohen, D.B., *Sleep and Dreaming* (Pergamon, 1979). **Oswald, I.,** *Sleep* (Penguin, 1966). **Oswald, I. and Adam, K.,** *Get a Better Night's Sleep* (Martin Dunitz, 1983).

IAN OSWALD

See also: DREAMS; RELAXATION.

SOCIAL STRUCTURES AND PASTORAL CARE
Activity which is concerned with changing social structures in order to facilitate the pastoral care of individuals living within those structures.

Although there is as yet no unified approach to pastoral care of social structures, there is a shared assumption that the adequate pastoral care of individuals must give some attention to the social structures within which they live. At its most extreme, it is contended that the pastoral care of individuals is valueless if it does nothing to change the economic and political structures responsible for oppressing those individuals. In a weaker form, it is contended that even *ad hoc* actions of pastoral care are actions within specific social contexts, raising specific social expectations and requiring specific social communities to make them thoroughly effective.

The stronger form of this contention is to be found in much 'liberation theology' (*see* POLITICAL THEOLOGY AND PASTORAL CARE). Its exponents share a common critique of society in its capitalist forms and a common conviction that theology must side consciously with the poor and oppressed in an attempt to bring about social and political change. It is the latter which can be identified as a form of pastoral care or alternatively as an essential prerequisite to the pastoral care of individuals. On this understanding, the pastoral care of the oppressed, and even of the oppressors themselves, requires a sociopolitical perspective. There is, however, considerable debate within liberation theology itself about whether or not it is legitimate to use violence as a means to change violent and oppressive socio-political structures and about how far liberation theology is to be explicitly identified with Marxist ideology. Marx and Engel's *The German Ideology* of 1848 is often regarded as providing the seminal insights for this approach, with its insistence that 'liberation is an historical and not a mental act, and it is brought about by historical conditions, the development of industry, commerce, agriculture' (p. 61).

The weaker form of the contention is evident in those who have attempted to use insights from the sociology of organizations, or from studies in the nature of communities, within pastoral care. R.A. Lambourne's work in pastoral care came increasingly to stress the largely ignored communal and political aspects of pastoral care. He argued that psychotherapy, in particularly, was practised in an 'artificial situation' of professional and middle-class seclusion, and that churches would be mistaken to model pastoral care too closely on it. E. Mansel Pattison (in America) and Mady Thung (in Holland) have both attempted to use the social sciences to construct more communal models of pastoral care. Thung combines insights into the nature of religious institutions from the sociology of religion (q.v.) with more general organization theory to produce a blue-print of a future church which is better able to combine

pastoral and prophetic functions. Once it is observed empirically that differing ecclesiastical structures have differing effects upon the priority given to pastoral care, the force of Thung's position becomes evident.

Support for a systems pastoral care approach can also be found in some comparatively conservative theological approaches. Eduard Thurneysen (1962) for example, argues that 'pastoral care occurs within the realm of the church. It proceeds from the Word and leads back to the Word. It presupposes membership in the body of Christ, or it has this membership as its purpose' (p. 53). On this understanding, preaching and even services themselves (particularly the pastoral offices), can be seen as forms of pastoral care. Pastoral care is identified as an activity done for and by the religious community.

Bonino, J.M., *Revolutionary Theology Comes of Age* (SPCK, 1975). **Campbell, A.V.,** 'The Politics of Pastoral Care' (*Contact*, no. 62, 1979) pp. 2–15. **Fierro, A.,** *The Militant Gospel* (SCM, 1977). **Lambourne, R.A.,** 'With Love to the USA', in *Religion and Medicine*, vol. 1, ed. M.A.H. Melinsky (SCM, 1970). **Pattison, E.M.,** *Pastor and Parish: a Systems Approach* (Fortress, 1977). **Thung, M.,** *The Precarious Organization* (Mouton, 1976). **Thurneysen, E.,** *A Theology of Pastoral Care* (John Knox Press, 1962).

ROBIN GILL

See also: JUSTICE AND PASTORAL CARE; POLITICAL THEOLOGY AND PASTORAL CARE; SYSTEMS PASTORAL CARE.

SOCIAL WORK

Social work is carried out by persons qualified to assess and help with social, emotional and practical problems which individuals, families or groups cannot resolve for themselves. Help is given in improving poor relationships, and providing information about available financial resources and practical aids.

Many of the tasks undertaken by social workers are statutory duties, for example, the care of children neglected by their parents, the admission of some patients to psychiatric hospitals and the control of offenders in the community (Barclay Report 1982; Davies 1981).

Most social workers are employed by local authority Social Services Departments (in England, Wales and Northern Ireland) and Social Work Departments in Scotland (Mays *et al.* 1983; Sainsbury 1977); it is unfortunate that the former are so named, since they are often confused with the Department of Health and Social Security. In England, Wales and Northern Ireland there is a separate Probation Service for adult offenders and couples facing separation and divorce. Some social workers are employed in voluntary organizations catering, for example, for chronic illness, bereavement and child abuse (Wolfenden Committee 1978).

Various methods are used according to the nature of the problem and the circumstances in which it arose. A widow might find difficulty in feeding and clothing her young children and may also be very lonely. Social workers ensure that all appropriate financial benefits are being claimed and they offer grief counselling if time allows, or refer the person for such help.

Parents may be accused of physically abusing their children. The social worker prepares an independent report for the court about the family's circumstances and subsequently, if the case is proved, carries out the order of the court. This could be a supervision order for up to three years while the children remain at home, or an order requiring care for the children in a residential unit or a foster home. Assessment of the family might reveal that the parents need help in their mutual relationship as well as with the children and that additional stress has been placed on them by sudden unemployment. The social worker may be able to do little more than listen, but even this could improve communication within the family.

A court might decide that an adolescent offender would benefit from Intermediate Treatment (participation in evening and weekend group activities supervised by social workers) instead of admission to residential care. The decision would be made so that the offender would learn better use of free time. A physically or mentally disabled person (see DISABLEMENT) living at home would need a social worker to co-ordinate for example, the home-help service, occupational therapy, aids to independence and adaptation of housing, as well as helping him or her and the relatives and neighbours to understand and live with each stage of disability.

An elderly person may be referred to a hospital social worker after treatment for bronchitis. If the social worker's assessment shows, for example, that the person's home is in a damp, deteriorating block of flats, action would then need to be taken with the housing

authority, which, if successful, would benefit other tenants as well as the client.

Talking to people in confidence about their personal problems is known as *casework*, and when intensive, *counselling* (q.v.). The theoretical base is psychotherapy (Roberts and Nee 1970). Acting on behalf of clients to obtain, for example, welfare rights, housing repairs or to rectify some of the injustices which many disadvantaged people suffer, is known as *social work advocacy*. Supervision of offenders in day or residential care, or on Community Service Orders (unpaid work in the community) is using methods of *group work*. Working with a number of tenants on a run-down housing estate in order to improve general living conditions is known as *community work*.

Since 1970 most social workers have been 'generic'; they have worked with clients of all ages and with every kind of problem. The exceptions in England, Wales and Northern Ireland are probation officers and, in some towns, social workers specializing in the Child Guidance Service which works in conjunction with local education authorities and the National Health Service. Generic social work has not suited many clients, social workers or referring agencies, particularly the medical profession. Specialization is returning. As yet the form is not clear. There are some indications that the pre-1970 pattern may re-emerge, particularly in mental health and child care.

The Future of Voluntary Organisations, Report of the Wolfendon Committee (Croom Helm, 1978). *Social Workers: their Roles and Tasks*, the Barclay Report, for the National Institute for Social Work (Bedford Square Press, 1982). **Davies, M.**, *The Essential Social Worker: a Guide to Positive Practice* (Heinemann Educational, 1981). **Douglas, T.**, *Groups: Understanding People Gathered Together* (Tavistock, 1983). **Leighton, N.** *et al.*, *Rights and Responsibilities* (Heinemann Educ., 1982). **Mays, J.**, *et al.* (eds.), *Penelope Hall's Social Services of England and Wales* (Routledge, 10th edn 1983; 1st edn by M. Penelope Hall 1952). **Roberts, R.E.** and **Nee, R.H.** (eds.), *Theories of Social Casework* (Univ. of Chicago Press, 1970). **Sainsbury, E.**, *The Personal Social Services* (Pitman, 1977). **Thomas, D.N.**, *The Making of Community Work* (Allen & Unwin, 1983).

JOYCE RIMMER

SOCIOLOGY OF PASTORAL CARE
The attempt to analyse pastoral care, and those connected with pastoral care, as social phenomena.

Such analysis would, like that in the

sociology of religion (q.v.), be concerned with the social factors of both determination and influence. That is, pastoral care and those connected with pastoral care could be analysed in terms of the social factors that have shaped and conditioned the discipline. But pastoral care could also be analysed in terms of the influence that it may have upon society at large and upon people's perceptions within that society. A study of the social determinants of pastoral care might focus upon the ideas, models and symbols operative at any point in the discipline, knowing that these change from one generation to another and suggesting that such change may owe something to changes already taking place in society at large. Alternatively it might focus upon the agents or agencies of pastoral care, analysing them in terms of social class, organizational types or professional role expectations. The major resource for the first approach would be the sociology of knowledge and that for the second would be the sociology of professions (see PROFESSIONALISM) or the sociology of organizations. It is not necessary to assume from such study that pastoral care is 'nothing but' a social product; it is only necessary to assume that social factors have some influence upon it. But, of course, it is possible that pastoral care itself may be influential in present-day society. Allowing for such a possibility, it might be shown, for example, that notions of 'care' and pastoral concern have had a profound influence upon the social services and upon the assumptions on which the Welfare State in post-war Britain was founded (see NATIONAL HEALTH SERVICE; SOCIAL WORK). If a social or political notion of pastoral care is adopted the question of the wider social influence of the discipline becomes crucial.

A background to the various sociological approaches suggested here can be found in **R. Gill**, *The Social Context of Theology* and *Theology and Social Structure* (Mowbray 1975 and 1977).

ROBIN GILL

SOCIOLOGY OF RELIGION
The academic discipline concerned with analysing religion in so far as it is a social phenomenon.

Recent exponents of this discipline have tended to focus upon two broad areas of interest; the social function of religion and the social typology of religious institutions. However, in principle any aspect of religion, in so far as it is a social phenomenon, can be analysed sociologically, Such analysis does not necessarily make assumptions about the validity of religious phenomena, nor does it seek to discredit them as 'mere social products'. But it does assume that religion, in common with any other element of human behaviour or culture, is subject to social factors, and that it can be analysed in terms of either society's influence upon it or even its influence upon society.

Studies of the *social function* of religion still owe much to the pioneer works of Dürkheim and Weber. For Dürkheim, religion was a crucial element in the stability and integration of a society. Within a traditional society it provided rituals and values which served to unite that society into a single moral community. For Weber, religion could sometimes have a more radical function and even be instrumental in social change. He argued specifically that certain values, such as thrift, hard work and honesty, derived from popular Calvinism and played a key role in providing the appropriate climate for the rise of Western capitalism. Both sociologists tended to believe that religion, however critical it might have been in traditional society, is declining in modern society. A number of recent sociologists, such as Wilson and Berger, have followed them in this belief and have advanced thoroughgoing theories of secularization. Others, however, such as Martin and Bellah, have pointed instead to the persistence of private and even 'civil' forms of religion, even in situations of considerable institutional decline, to the comparative resilience of some religious institutions, and to the large variations in religious practice in Europe and North America.

Studies of the *social typology* of religious institutions owe much to the work of Weber and Troeltsch. Weber distinguished between the church and the sect, regarding the former as inclusive in both doctrine and membership and the latter as exclusive in both. For Troeltsch, the church emphasized grace, attempted to cater for the masses, adjusted itself to the world and was characterized by objective sacramentalism. The sect, on the other hand, was a voluntary society, consisting of strict and definite believers, who had experienced new birth and who were living apart from the world in small groups, were eschatologically inclined, and emphasized law rather than grace. A third type consisted of informal and unstructured groups of 'mystics' (or 'cults' as they would be termed today). Considerable energy has been spent refining these differing types and particularly on distinguishing between differing types of sect. Under the considerable influence of Wilson a number of sociologists of religion have made detailed and illuminating studies of specific sects, such as those of Scientology, the Unification Church and Jehovah's Witness movement. In addition, there is a growing understanding of how new religious movements develop and cope with a hostile world.

As an autonomous academic discipline, the sociology of religion is only of indirect relevance to pastoral care. Nonetheless, an adequate understanding of systems pastoral care (q.v.) clearly cannot ignore it, as Mady Thung's *The Precarious Organization* (Mouton 1976) demonstrates. If attention is given either to the specific type of religious institution to be involved in pastoral care or to the overall values and social integration upon which successful pastoral care depends, the analytic work of sociologists of religion assumes a greater importance.

Classic Works: **Dürkheim, E.,** *The Elementary Forms of the Religious Life* (Allen & Unwin, 1976). **Troeltsch, E.,** *The Social Teaching of the Christian Churches* (Harper, 1960). **Weber, M.,** *The Protestant Ethic and the 'Spirit' of Capitalism* (Scribner, 1958); *The Sociology of Religion* (Methuen, 1965).
Modern introductions: **Mill, M.,** *A Sociology of Religion* (Heinemann, 1973). **Scharf, B.,** *The Sociological Study of Religion* (Hutchinson, 1970). **Wilson B.,** *Religion in Sociological Perspective* (OUP, 1982). **Yinger, J.M.,** *The Scientific Study of Religion* (Macmillan, 1970).

ROBIN GILL

SOLITUDE

A little known feature of contemporary Christian life is the growth of the number of people of all traditions who are being called to the solitary life, either permanently, or for an extended length of time. This century in which the corporate understanding of the Church has received so much attention has also seen the growth of interest and theological assessment of the solitary way of life in the West. Eastern Christendom has always had a continuous history of such a vocation fostered by its monastic tradition. In the West

the solitary vocation flowered in the Celtic church in the 7th century, in the Church of the high Middle Ages, and it had another spring-time in the 16th century under the influence of men such as Paul Giustiniani. The present appearance of this rare calling has turned attention on the Christian use of enforced solitude or loneliness due to old age, chronic infirmity, or social marginalization. The principles underlying voluntary solitude throw light on the possible conversion of loneliness into solitude.

Tradition saw the prophetic mission of John the Baptist as a type of the Christian solitary. His detachment from earthly society and religion was a prophetic prelude to the coming of the Messiah. So the solitary person proclaims by his or her reclusion the preparation for the second coming of the Messiah with a kingdom not of this world, transcending all our religion. Solitude is not a retraction into privacy. It is essentially a churchly vocation undertaken for the Church and traditionally under the direction of the Church. It engages those called to it in the task of profound intercession, and involvement in the final struggle of good and evil. It is inspired by the same spirit that drove Christ into the desert to face the temptations. It involves the slow stripping of self as the solitary works out in his or her own vocation the baptismal calling to be dead and buried with Christ as a sign of everyone's final stripping and silence in death, when there is no future but in God and all is focused on the resurrection. The feast day of the solitary is Holy Saturday.

This strange vocation is renewing our understanding of the need of solitude as a part of human experience, especially in present-day urbanized collective society which creates its own sterile loneliness. The health of close relationships, and the need of the artist and scientist for creative solitude, are related to the need of the spirit for times of disciplined solitude. Then, God and oneself can be faced and the real relation with the human scene can be allowed to surface free from the distractions of speech and company.

Le Clercq, J., *Alone with God* (Hodder & Stoughton, 1962). **Allchin, A.M.** (eds.), *Solitude and Communion* (Fairacres Publications, 1977). **Progzato, Allesandro,** *Meditations on the Sands* (St Paul's Publications, 1981).

ROLAND WALLS

See also: LONELINESS; MEDITATION; PRAYER; RETREATS; SILENCE; SINGLE PERSONS.

SOUL

(1) The self as enduring and as related to God (OT and NT). (2) The life-principle (psyche, anima) in plants, animals and humans, seen as having an intellectual, spiritual, immortal part (Plato and Platonism, from the 5th century BC up to the present day). (3) The thought-principle in the human as against the material or body principle, thinking being, *res cogitans*, as against extended being, *res extensa* (Descartes in the 16th century).

Two main questions concerning the soul have divided philosophers and the philosophically minded all through the centuries, and today as much as at any time in the past: (a) the question of the unity of soul and body, and (b) the question of the immortality of the soul.

On the first question Cartesian dualism makes a sharp distinction between soul and body seen in terms of the third definition given above. Platonic dualism places almost everything on the side of the soul, which lives on after death while the body is shed like a garment: in this tradition Shakespeare has Hamlet asking what the soul or self experiences 'when we have shuffled off this mortal coil'. Monism refuses to make any distinction between soul and body as separate entities, and either sees the soul in its consciousness as the whole person (idealism, close to Platonic dualism), or sees the body as the whole person and the soul as merely an expression of the body's behaviour (materialism, behaviourism, logical positivism).

On the second question the Platonic and Christian traditions say that the soul, however defined, is of its nature immortal, though some Christian theologians nowadays say that the human is naturally mortal but can rise again in Christ. The materialist tradition rejects immortality, and this philosophy has found eloquent voices in recent times in behaviouristic philosophers such as Gilbert Ryle ('the ghost in the machine') and B.F. Skinner (Man is no more than his reactions and responses).

It is to be noted that none of these positions has been either fully proved or totally disproved, and that Christian theologians (with some marginal exceptions) defend the survival of the soul after death in a region or sphere of fullness of life where it expresses itself (immediately or after the Last Judgement, variously understood) through the body restored and transformed. These affirmations are nevertheless understood as no more than images 'seen in a glass darkly' (1 Cor. 13.12) of the glory that shall be revealed when the soul returns to the God of love and mercy.

Badham, Paul, *Christian Beliefs about Life After Death* (Macmillan, 1976). Hick, John, *Death and Eternal Life* (Collins, 1976). O'Donoghue, N.D., 'Body and Soul' (*Journal of Medical Ethics*, vol. 5, 1979), pp. 203–4. Plato's *Phaedo* in *The Last Days of Socrates* (Penguin). Leeuw, G. van der, *Religion in Essence and Manifestation*, tr. Turner (Allen & Unwin, 1938), pp. 275–323.

N. O'DONOGHUE

See also: HUMAN NATURE; PERSON; SELF.

SPIRIT

All Western doctrines interpret the Holy Spirit as an actualization of the *Christus praesens*. Eastern doctrines of the Spirit, and African, Asian and OT understandings of the Spirit, see primarily the *Spiritus Creator*, the source and ground of *all* life, not just Christian or religious life. That is the reason why ancestral spirits and pre- or extra-Christian religious phenomena can be seen in the latter traditions as belonging to the realm of the Spirit. The distinction between spirits and Spirit is for them not absolute.

This raises some important questions for pastoral care when dealing with clients whose understanding of the Spirit is different from the Western. Amongst such clients are Christians from non-Western cultures and also Europeans who have been influenced by spiritism, theosophy and modern natural sciences. For all of them the Spirit is not only, and perhaps not even, primarily to be understood in personalistic categories but much more in categories of energy and power. The implications of this for the doctrine of the Trinity cannot be discussed here. It may be supposed that they would lead to a revision of the hegemony of the *filioque* and a recognition of the female aspects in God (N. Zinzendorf advocated the mother-ministry of the Spirit; the Spirit is female in the OT).

If the Spirit is understood as also operating outside the influence of Christian tradition and outside the categories of christology, this opens the way for a dialogue with non-

Christians without having to give up the belief in the decisiveness of the Christ event. It makes possible a cautious appreciation of religious forms outside our ethical and theological plausibility structures without falling into mere relativism.

Hollenweger, W.J., 'All Creatures Great and Small: Towards a Pneumatology of Life', in D. Martin and P. Mullen (eds.), *Strange Gifts?: a Guide to Charismatic Renewal* (Blackwell, 1984).

WALTER J. HOLLENWEGER

SPIRITUAL DIRECTION
The name given to a personal relationship between two people in which one assists the other to grow in the spiritual life.

The concept is not specifically Christian, and parallels have been drawn with the shaman, the Zen master, the guru, and the therapist, among others. In the Christian tradition, the practice began in 4th-century desert monasticism, and was associated with *diakrisis*, discernment or spiritual insight. The director, often called *pneumatikos pater* (spiritual father) was seen primarily as a person of experience, insight and holiness of life, the ministry of direction being a by-product. Direction became associated, especially in the West, with sacramental confession (*see* CONFESSION) and has often taken place within that framework. However, as the practice of confession in the Western church became more mechanical, direction ceased to be a major part of it, though the *Ordo Poenitentiae* of 1974 has sought to restore it. In Anglicanism, confession and direction have been more closely related. In recent years interest in spiritual direction has revived within many Protestant traditions, though there has been a tendency, especially in the USA, to see it as a technique which can be acquired by training, and as related to counselling (q.v.) and psychotherapy (q.v.). There are dangers in the professional model, and it is certainly alien to the main tradition in which direction is a charisma which overflows from a life of serious prayer (q.v.) and discipleship.

Spiritual direction is not a ministry restricted to priests and pastors, and is often exercised by lay persons. Many of the great Christians of the past exercised ministries of personal guidance, some of it preserved in books and collected letters. A central element in direction is enabling people to see themselves against the background of the spiritual tradition. So an acquaintance with the tradition is important. Key influences include the Desert Fathers, the mystical writers of the 14th century, St Ignatius Loyola (in whom the directed retreat (q.v.) assumes a central place), St John of the Cross (who is concerned particularly with the movement of contemplative prayer), Jean Grou, and many others.

Spiritual direction is different from pastoral counselling (q.v.) and from psychotherapy (q.v.), though these areas overlap. Direction is less problem-centred, less concerned with crises, more located in the Christian community, and with discerning the will of God. It is part of ordinary growth in Christian maturity. It is not necessary for all Christians, and it can be abused. Excessive reliance on a director is not part of Christian tradition.

Spiritual direction is concerned with nourishment of the life of prayer, the inner life. It seeks to help a person interpret the movements of the Spirit (q.v.), and to distinguish the voice of God from other voices within the person. Since St John of the Cross, a major focus of direction has been the transition to contemplative prayer, and the spiritual crisis known as the 'dark night'. In general, it may be said that the need for direction becomes articulated as people make progress in contemplative inwardness (*see* MEDITATION).

The qualities sought in a director will include: experience; spiritual insight and perception; a self-effacing manner; prayerfulness and interior silence. St Catherine of Siena (1347–80) described the three principles of spiritual direction as: (a) a non-judgmental approach; (b) prayer for those under one's care leading to a deepening sensitivity to their condition; (c) the recognition that everyone is led by a unique path. Much recent writing has emphasized friendship (cf. the Celtic term *anmchara*, soul friend) more than professional skills. The relationship of direction is one that is freely chosen and freely ended. It is a temporary relationship, non-authoritarian, concerned with the whole of life.

Spiritual direction is increasingly seen to have a prophetic and even political dimension, since it seeks to enable people to attain clarity of vision in their response to reality, and to see more clearly their responses. Direction is particularly necessary for those Christians who are in situations where they are called to resistance to structures of injustice and oppression (*see* JUSTICE AND PASTORAL

265

CARE). It is no part of spiritual direction to enable people to adjust to unjust situations, but to help them build up inner resources to enable them to struggle against evil.

Barry, W.A. and Connolly, W.J., *The Practice of Spiritual Direction* (Seabury Press, 1982). English, J., *Spiritual Freedom* (Loyola House, Guelph, Ontario, 1974). Gratton, C., *Guidelines for Spiritual Direction* (Dimension, Denville, 1980). Jones, A.W., *Exploring Spiritual Direction (Seabury Press, 1982).* Kopp, S.B., *Guru* (Science and Behavior Books, Palo Alto, 1971). Laplace, J., *The Direction of Conscience* (G. Chapman,, 1967). Leech, K., *Soul Friend* (Sheldon, 1977). Merton, T., *Spiritual Direction and Meditation* (A. Clarke, 1975). Thornton, M., *Spiritual Direction* (SPCK, 1984).

KENNETH LEECH

SPIRITUAL HEALING

The enabling of a person to function as a whole in accordance with God's will for him (Gusmer 1974). Other terms also used: (1) Divine healing, the original term of reference given to the Archbishops' Commission (1958) who preferred to use – (2) The Church's ministry of healing, chosen to emphasize the redemption of the whole man, the cure of bodily ailments being only one element in this ministry. (3) Christian healing, preferred in ecumenical dialogue. (4) Faith healing, the shorthand term used in the secular world, but largely rejected by Christians because it has led to a belief in the healer's powers rather than Christ's.

Spiritual healing must not be confused with spiritualist healing or spiritualism (q.v.). Rather it conveys the important truth that the restoration to health is the work of the Spirit (q.v.). Nor should the Church's ministry be confused with the work of various spiritual healers' associations, now being brought together under the Confederation of Healing Organizations.

This is not to say that some healing is unspiritual: there is a spiritual element in all healing, even in physical healing. Doctors and nurses are also engaged in a spiritual task. The purpose of all true healing is the restoration of the person to wholeness in which the spirit, mind, body, bio-energy and emotions are in perfect balance. Physical and psychological healings received as an answer to prayer frequently include as a predominant element a deeper conversion of heart and commitment to the doing of God's will, i.e. a spiritual healing. The double grace of receiving God's forgiveness and at the same time his power to live in a more Christian way is a spiritual healing of the soul.

The revival of spiritual healing within the churches is a significant phenomenon of our times. It marks a recovery of obedience to the commission given by Christ to his apostles to preach the Kingdom and heal the sick. It is increasingly common to find spiritual healing offered during the course of public worship as well as in private in one of the following ways: (a) prayer (q.v.) with or without the laying-on-of-hands; (b) anointing (q.v.) see Jas. 5.13–16; (c) penance or confession (q.v.) before a priest; (d) counselling (q.v.). (Note: The laying-on-of-hands has therapeutic implications through touch and theological significance as an act of adoption, commissioning and blessing. Baptism (q.v.) and communion (q.v.), the two 'gospel' sacraments, are also sacraments of healing.)

Formative influences in this revival have been:
1. The Guilds and Fellowships, e.g. the Guild of Health (1904), the Divine Healing Mission (1905), the Guild of St Raphael (1915), the Dorothy Kerin Trust at Burrswood, the Institute of Religion and Medicine.
2. The Lambeth Conferences of Anglican bishops during this century (see Lambeth Conference Report 1978, resolution 8).
3. The Churches' Council for Health and Healing, founded by William Temple in 1944 to co-ordinate all Christian healing movements in Britain, to promote co-operation between doctors and clergy and to bring the work of spiritual healing into closer relation with the regular work of the churches.
4. Individual pioneers who gave their lives to this ministry, e.g. James Moore Hickson, Dorothy Kerin, Dr Leslie Weatherhead, Rev. George Bennett, etc.

With the re-emergence of the holistic approach in modern medicine, the spiritual element in healing is gaining in emphasis, thereby establishing more common ground between the healing professions in which the hospice movement (q.v.) has also assisted.

Frost, Evelyn, *Christian Healing* (Mowbray, 1940). Gusmer, C.W., *The Ministry of Healing in the Church of England* (SPCK for Alcuin Club, 1974). Maddocks, Morris, *The Christian Healing Ministry* (SPCK, 1981). Pearce, Ian, *The Gate of Healing* (Neville Spearman, Jersey, 1983). Wilkinson, John, *Health and Healing* (Handsel Press, 1980).

Also the following, now out of print: **Kelsey, Morton,** *Healing and Christianity* (SCM, 1973). **Weatherhead, Leslie,** *Psychology, Religion and Healing* (Hodder, 1951).

MORRIS MADDOCKS

See also: HEALING; HEALTH AND ILLNESS: PASTORAL ASPECTS.

SPIRITUALISM/SPIRITISM

Spiritualism (often called spiritism by its denigrators) is a religious system, originating in the USA in 1848.

It is based upon acceptance of the data scientifically studied in parapsychology (q.v.) and involving the belief that death (q.v.) has in itself no significance except as a transition to another state in which the dead survive and from which they can communicate in various ways with those remaining behind on earth. Some spiritualists are Christians, but most would not accept the doctrines of the Incarnation or Atonement (and thus fail the test given in 1 John 4.1–3). Some spiritualists meet in churches for regular worship, but many hold their beliefs without congregating together to do so.

A person capable of receiving communications from discarnate spirits is termed a medium or sensitive. He or she (most are females) may receive them either in trance or in a normal state of consciousness, as verbal messages or in automatic writing through a pen lightly held in the hand which appears to move of its own volition. Messages can come by direct voice or direct writing or through the medium's personal 'control' spirit, who acts as a go-between. Planchette is a pencil on wheels which enables automatic writing to come more easily, but is more often used by amateurs than by serious mediums. The ouija board is a similar device whereby letters or words are indicated so that messages may be spelt out, generally in answer to questions. Unsupervised use of planchette or ouija can be dangerous, and is not to be recommended. Materialization of spirits and physical phenomena seem almost completely to have come to an end nowadays.

The interpretation of phenomena is hotly disputed. Spiritualists accept them at face value (though many recognize the possibility of conscious or unconscious fraud and of symbolic rather than literal interpretation of the messages). Many people regard them as messages originating in the medium's subconscious, with the trance or the paraphernalia enabling the normal censorship between conscious and subconscious to be circumvented; others hold that there is a large element of telepathy between the living agents involved in communication, and little or no commerce across the divide of death. It seems more likely that there is an element of truth in all these views, which are complementary rather than contradictory. Some Christians, particularly evangelicals and those affected by the charismatic movement (q.v.) see the whole business as a manifestation of the demonic and as warranting exorcism (q.v.), since it is akin to, but not identical with, the incident at Endor (1 Sam. 28) and to necromantic practices condemned in the OT. Others see the phenomenon as morally neutral in itself and capable of being used for good as well as for ill.

Spiritualists are frequently practitioners of faith healing, which they often interpret as being effected through the assistance of discarnate former doctors, surgeons or 'natural healers'. Healing may be carried out by touch or, as 'absent healing', on patients not physically present.

Those suffering bereavement (q.v.) may initially be helped over their trauma by a spiritualistic or psychic assurance that their loved one lives on, though it is sometimes possible for people to be fixated on this phase, or even to become monomaniac about spiritualistic or psychic practices. Pastoral care should aim to prevent spiritualistic phenomena becoming a be-all and end-all in themselves, but should set them firmly and in a subordinate position within a Christian context, affirming the reality and presence of Jesus as the Christ, the conqueror of death and Satan in the power of the Holy Spirit.

Discriminating and responsible advice and help can be obtained from the College of Psychic Studies, 6 Queensberry Place, London SW7 2EB, or from the Churches' Fellowship for Psychical and Spiritual Studies, St Mary Abchurch, Abchurch Lane, London EC4N 7BA.

Beard, Paul, *Living On* (Allen & Unwin, 1980). **Fryer, C.E.J.,** *A Hand in Dialogue* (J. Clarke, 1982). **Wellman, J. Dover,** *A Priest's Psychic Diary* (SPCK, 1977).

MICHAEL PERRY

See also: EXORCISM; MAGIC; PARAPSYCHOLOGY.

STILLBIRTH AND MISCARRIAGE

Stillbirth: a baby born dead after 28 weeks gestation. *Miscarriage*: a baby born dead after less than 28 weeks gestation.

There are blurrings and incongruities, e.g. a child born alive before 28 weeks gestation is registered as a live birth even though it may soon die. These incongruities may lead to a change in the legal definition of stillbirth, to that of a baby born dead of over 500 grams.

Mourning a stillbirth (most of what follows also applies to miscarriage and the death of very young babies) is difficult and commonly fails or is interrupted by a subsequent pregnancy. As a result, difficulties may become chronic or there is a latent vulnerability to subsequent traumas. Stillbirth is complicated by extraordinary sensations of confusion and unreality, as birth and death are fused. After months of hopes and growing fullness there is a sudden emptiness with nothing to show, an incomprehensible non-event. Bereaved women are avoided or expected to go on as if nothing has happened, left alone with their shame, blame and a sense of failure as a woman (Bourne 1968). Although feelings about stillbirth are intense, the thoughts are intangible and confused, and this impedes the thinking necessary for mourning. It is hard for parents, but even more so for surviving siblings who need special help with their bewilderment and reality-testing to try and avoid scars which can endanger their future marriage and child-rearing.

To facilitate mourning all the family require a tangible experience of the stillborn, especially if malformed, to help make memories, test reality and negate magic thinking (Lewis 1976). The baby should be seen and held; photographs kept; a proper name registered and a stillbirth certificate kept; an autopsy is advisable; there should be a form of christening, a funeral service and a decent marked grave and an individual rather than a mass grave (Lewis 1979; Klaus and Kennel 1982). There is no present satisfactory method of disposal of a miscarriage – the Church could well make suggestions. Holding a live baby can help bereaved mothers overcome phobic ideas about babies. Talk and counselling help, as may visits to the grave and a memorial service on anniversaries. Parents should be given the booklet *The Loss of Your Baby* and put in touch with SANDS or the Miscarriage Association. Obstetric and genetic counselling (q.v.) are necessary.

The desire of parents and professionals for a quick replacement pregnancy should be resisted. Especially to be avoided is a birth on or around the first anniversary. Children born after any bereavement are at risk of becoming 'replacement children' (Poznanski 1972); their childhood is affected by the parents' anxieties and sadness, together with the confused hopes carried over from incomplete mourning. There can be confused identity, gender uncertainty, disturbances of ambition and achievement, and sometimes a life-long sense of ill-understood guilt about 'living in someone else's shoes'. The next baby should not be saddled with the name intended for the dead baby, so as to avoid confusion between the live and the dead baby and to counter ideas of reincarnation. The parents should be warned to expect to have some difficulties with the mothering of the new baby, including experiencing confusion between the live and dead babies and reawakened griefs and grievances.

Bourne, S., 'The Psychological Effects of Stillbirth on Women and their Doctors' (*J. Roy. Coll. Gen. Pract.*, 1968, 16:103). **Bourne, S.** and **Lewis, E.**, 'Pregnancy After Stillbirth or Neonatal Death' (*Lancet*, July 1984), pp. 31–3. **Klaus M.H., Kennel J.**, 'Caring for the Parents of a Stillborn or an Infant who Dies', in *Parent-Infant Bonding* (Mosby, St Louis, 1982), p. 259. **Lewis, E.**, 'The Management of Stillbirth – Coping with an Unreality' (*Lancet*, Sept. 1976), pp. 619–20. **Lewis, E.**, 'Mourning by the Family After a Stillbirth or Neonatal Death' (*Arch. Dis. Child*, 1979,. 54:303). *Loss of Your Baby*, obtainable from Mind and Health Education Council. **Oakley, A., McPherson, A.** and **Roberts, H.**, *Miscarriage* (Fontana, 1984). **Peppers, L.G.** and **Knapp, R.J.**, *Motherhood and Mourning* (Praeger, New York, 1980). **Poznanski, E.O.**, 'The "Replacement Child": a Saga of Unresolved Parental Grief' (*J. Pediatr.*, 1972, 81:1190).

The Miscarriage Association, Dolphin Cottage, 4 Ashfield Terrace, Thorpe, Wakefield, Yorks; tel: Leeds 828946. SANDS (Stillbirth and Neonatal Death Association), Argyle House, 29/31 Euston Road, London NW1 2SD; tel: 01-833 2851.

EMMANUEL LEWIS

See also: BEREAVEMENT; BIRTH; GENETIC COUNSELLING.

STRESS

Stress is a psychological and physiological phenomenon which is the product of internal and external factors. Internal factors include the biological, mental, psychological and emotional, forming together a network of cause and effect. External factors are work, family, community, and the wider world round about us. Stress is increased or decreased by an individual's personality and its 'fit' with the internal and external factors. It is caused by a real or perceived overload in one of the internal or external factors. If people say they are stressed or exhibit stress symptoms, they should be believed. What *feels* real has a basis in reality.

Stress tends to slow efficiency and bring personal ability to a halt. It certainly affects creativity, for the creative self is freed by a positive energy flow, and symptoms of sustained stress tend to consume personal energy. The effect of stress forces one to keep going and block recognition of stress feelings (thus creating additional problems), and can nurture despondency in which nothing seems worthwhile and everything grinds to a halt.

Chronic stress comes from the release of adrenalin into the bloodstream nearly continually over a long period of time. It may cause adrenalin burn-out as well as other biochemical changes in the human system.

If people are placed in situations where undue pressure is put on them and maintained over a period of time, the system begins to show effects. Needing to have the adrenalin flow may become habitual for some people; they feel they cannot perform without it. For example, procrastinators may wait until the last possible minute before doing something, so that the fear of not getting it done or the challenge of pushing a deadline causes the adrenalin to flow.

Symptoms of stress include tiredness, disturbed sleep pattern, loss of interest and ability at work, reduced sex drive and irritability. Those who are liable to be subject to stress should take precautions to prevent its pathological debilitating effects. For example, having a support group (q.v.) who can alert one to signs before they become chronic; regular time for recreation; time to be alone; saying 'no' to unnecessary tasks; focusing on priorities and on realizable goals. In short, the aim should be to develop a balance in the system of internal and external factors with the individual personality.

For the counsellor it is critical to see the person suffering from stress as one who has lost the ability to make choices or to see alternatives, and feels not only powerless, but drained of energy to do anything about it. Since there are some external factors that will

not change in people's lives, counsellors help their clients by enabling them to discover an area where, if supported, they can begin to behave differently and find inner control again. 'Bearing one another's burdens' means, in the context of helping people with stress, that practitioners encourage people into altered behaviour. It does not mean that the practitioner takes on additional stress on behalf of the client.

Finally, stress has positive as well as negative effects. Life would be dull indeed without some of the drive that stress brings to it.

Levinson, Harry, 'When Executives Burn Out' (*Harvard Business Review*, Cambridge, Mass., May-June 1981). **McQuade, Walter**, and **Aikman, Ann**, *Stress* (Bantam Books, New York, 1974). **Pelliter, Kenneth**, *Mind as Healer, Mind as Slayer* (Dell, New York, 1977). **Rogers, T.G.P.**, in J.L. Kearns (ed.), *Stress in Industry* (Priory, 1973). **Selye, H.**, *The Stress of Life* (McGraw Hill, New York, 1965).

BARBARA THAIN MCNEEL

See also: PSYCHOSOMATIC PROBLEMS; RELAXATION.

STRUCTURE

A concept, important in counselling (q.v.) and psychotherapy (q.v.), referring to the framework and discipline within which therapy is conducted.

Structure includes the practical arrangements negotiated between counsellor and client about such things as fees, time, duration, frequency and place of sessions. It will include acceptable procedures of work usually determined by the professional preferences of the counsellor. There will be a clear differentiation of roles between the client who seeks help and the counsellor who gives it, in a relationship which is asymmetric and in which mutuality and reciprocity may be excluded at a functional level, though not of course at the level of feeling and value. The relationship between counsellor and client will be limited to the counselling sessions for the duration of the counselling. Where this is not possible the counsellor would normally refer the client to someone else. Finally, there is usually an agreement about goals to be pursued, though this itself may be open to review.

While the establishment of such a structure arises out of an explicit request for help by the client, it is the particular responsibility of the counsellor to establish and maintain it to ensure that as far as possible changes are only made after adequate consultation.

The benefits of structure. A clear differentiation of roles helps the counsellor to keep his own problems from obtruding. The firm boundaries that structure provides, marking it off for instance from social relationships, may make the counselling a safe place for dangerous feelings such as envy, hatred or greed, to be explored particularly in relation to the counsellor. By setting limits to what the client and counsellor may realistically expect from each other, the structure may protect both of them from any tendency to act out collusive fantasies such as that of the omnipotent parent/counsellor with the helpless infant/client.

Structure defines the space that belongs to the client, who is thus enabled to take responsibility for the use made of it, and for his or her own progress. It carries the purpose of counselling so that whatever happens, be it silence, play, interaction or introspection it can be understood in the light of that purpose, and not with the meaning which it might have on a social occasion.

What is withheld in counselling may be as important for the client as what is given. Structure may enable the experience of both frustration and gratification to be regulated in a consistent and reliable non-arbitrary manner, comparable to good parenting, so that both experiences can be integrated positively by the client. Finally, it represents the counsellor's 'holding' of the client after the model of a 'good enough' parent, which over a period of time, may provide enough support for dependency needs to enable difficulties to be overcome.

Structure in pastoral care. Apart from occasions of formal ministry or counselling, pastoral care is typically characterized by informal encounters where needs may be real but not made explicit, where there is often no clear boundary between pastoral and social aspects of the occasion and where there may be need for spontaneity and self-disclosure on the part of the pastor. There are unique advantages in terms of accessibility and immediacy in all this which would be lost by any simplistic attempt to impose a counselling type structure. There are, however, disadvantages, which may be obscured by a common tendency to idealize informality, mutuality and lack of structure as marks of

'real' or 'Christian' caring, and to regard the limitations of structure as contrary to the biblical injunction to be ready to go the second mile and therefore to true Christian loving. Among these disadvantages may be a tendency to lose a sense of pastoral purpose so that visiting, for instance, may seem pointless; a tendency to superficiality in relationships, due to the inhibition of dangerous feelings; and finally the possibility that the relationships may develop in ways which become inappropriate or unmanageable, usually leading to an abrupt and unhelpful termination.

The concept of structure needs to be very flexibly applied to pastoral care if the distinctive features of the latter are to be preserved. It will arise out of the fact that, to the extent that a relationship is pastoral and not simply personal, it will have (1) a purpose, however unclear, and (2) a sense of the symbolic meaning of the pastor's role.

(1) The pastor needs to develop clear goals, and where appropriate share them with the parishioner, so that some simple negotiation of appropriate conditions can be made. 'I have called to see how things are with you,' is a statement of pastoral purpose which, if accepted, can enable the pastor to suggest that the television be turned off, for example, or that it might be more convenient to return at another time. Where appropriate, the pastor may wish to suggest a more formal structure for counselling, or religious ministry. Often the pastoral purpose, however, will be left unstated, and the structure implicit. Someone who is housebound, for example, may gain important support by regular visits for 'a cup of tea'. The pastor will then need to keep a clear pastoral purpose if the disciplines of good listening (q.v.) and supportive counselling that might be required are to be maintained.

(2) The symbolic and transference (q.v.) significance of the pastor's role for the parishioner (as representative of God, the Church or parental figures) may endow the pastor's presence (or absence) with powerful meaning. In the light of this there is a need to be aware of the implications for the parishioner of the behaviour of the pastor, e.g. regularity/irregularity, consistence/arbitrariness, giving/withholding, and to structure behaviour accordingly.

Structure in pastoral care may be likened to the rules of harmony in music. The performer needs to know and understand them, especially when improvising but the less they intrude on the listener, the better. The technical considerations referred to above need to be sufficiently assimilated by the pastor so that there is freedom to be spontaneous and natural in ways which are pastorally effective.

Bion, W., *Learning from Experience* (Heinemann, 1962). **Clebsch, W.** and **Jaekle, C.**, *Pastoral Care in Historical Perspective* (Harper, New York, 1967). **Jacobs, M.**, *Still Small Voice* (SPCK, 1982). **Saltzburger-Wittenberg, I.**, *Psychoanalytic Insight and Relationship* (Routledge, 1973). **Winnicott, D.**, *The Maturational Process and the Facilitating Environment* (Hogarth, 1972).

DEREK BLOWS

See also: COUNSELLING; PSYCHOTHERAPY; TRANSFERENCE; TERMINATION OF COUNSELLING.

SUFFERING
See: PAIN.

SUICIDE
A deliberate act of self-injury resulting (and to some degree intended at the time of commission to result) in death.

Acts of self-injury in which there is little or no intention that death should result are properly termed *parasuicide*. The widely (but improperly) used expression 'attempted suicide' should not be used for parasuicide, as it begs the question of what was being attempted. The only accurate use of 'attempted suicide' would be for those cases where the preponderant intention of the act of self-injury was to die but that outcome was prevented by faulty planning or unexpected intervention. In the pre-suicidal state almost all human beings are ambivalent (*see* AMBIVALENCE), wanting both to die and to be saved, both to escape from an intolerable situation and to experience some transformation of the situation which would enable them to continue living. Suicide prevention by crisis intervention (q.v.) is possible in most cases because of this ambivalence: when the desire to die is temporarily outweighed by the instinct of self-preservation, an appeal for help may be made if the availability and acceptability of such help are known and making (as well as breaking) contact is easy. In the first instance the best form of help in such cases is befriending (q.v.) as given, for example, by the

Samaritans, so that the desire to find some alternative to death may be strengthened and facilitated, and the way found to some form of professional treatment in those cases where this is indicated and desired.

Prevention of parasuicide is a more complicated matter, because of the greater variety of intentions. In those cases where there is marked ambivalence, and the only thing which distinguishes the act from (fatal) suicide is that there is little or no intention that the act should be fatal (though through ignorance or mismanagement death may in fact result from it), the method of crisis intervention by befriending is likely to be as effective as in cases of preparation of suicide. But parasuicide, particularly in the immature, is often without ambivalence: there is a clear desire to 'cry for help' by an act of self-injury calculated to require emergency medical attention but without much risk of death, and thus the offer of crisis intervention, substituting discussion of problems for a dramatic and cathartic contriving of helplessness, has little appeal. That seems to be the reason why in the only country blanketed by branches of the Samaritans the deaths by suicide have decreased from their 1963 peak but parasuicides continue to rise. The chief cause of suicide is depression (q.v.) which may be endogenous or situational. The former responds only to medical treatment (chemotherapy or electroplexy). The latter (also a cause of parasuicide) can be helped by befriending, supplemented if necessary by counselling (q.v.) or psychotherapy (q.v.). Loneliness (q.v.) exacerbates the problems that lead to situational depression, but on the other hand relationship difficulties are a common cause of suicide and parasuicide.

In many cultures suicide is condemned, and survivors of a suicidal act punished. It was decriminalized in England in 1961, some twenty years after the practice of burying the bodies of suicides in unconsecrated ground had begun to die out.

The Bible does not plainly condemn suicide as do Buddhism and Mohammedanism, but the OT records the suicide by hanging of Ahitophel, a traitor (2 Sam. 17.23), and the NT the same fate and description for Judas (Matt. 27.5). Patristic writers discuss suicide, and Augustine notes that it is a form of homicide which by its nature precludes the possibility of repentance. Present-day theologians would apply the mitigating consideration of 'diminished responsibility' to suicide as well as to homicide and consider that human despair would arouse God's compassion rather than his wrath.

CHAD VARAH

See also: BEFRIENDING; CRISIS THEORY AND INTERVENTION; DEATH: MEANING.

SUPEREGO
See: CONSCIENCE: PSYCHOLOGICAL ASPECTS.

SUPERSTITION
'Credulity regarding the supernatural, irrational fear of the unknown or mysterious, misdirected reverence; a religion or practice or particular opinion based on such tendencies' (Concise Oxford Dictionary). The two main distinguishing features are (1) the irrational nature of the particular belief or practice, and (b) an irrational fear which attends it. It follows that superstition has a diminishing and inhibiting effect upon human dignity and freedom of action. It is therefore a morbid phenomenon.

It is necessary to recognize that the non-rational is not the same as the irrational. It is easy for a number of beliefs, practices and opinions to be arbitrarily labelled as superstitious when in themselves they may not be. Thus it has frequently been the case that the great corpus of intuitively perceived insight and understanding, often appearing to lack any immediately discernable rational foundation, and expressed in terms at once imprecise and alienating, has been dismissed as 'mere superstition'. The work of the psychoanalytical schools, and in particular that of C.G. Jung, aimed to reveal how superficial such a judgement can be.

A great many insights and practices of folk-wisdom and folk-religion appear in superstitious guise and, however irrational in a particular context, derive from beliefs and practices of a more considered – though often dubious – nature. Thus the widespread carrying of 'lucky' objects is an unconscious carry-over from the practice of talismanic magic. Other seemingly irrational activities have divinatory or ritual origins.

The connection between superstitious behaviour and matters of an esoteric or occult nature is close but not always obvious. Superficial judgements should be avoided; the origins are not necessarily morbid in themselves; it is the irrational behaviour and the

irrational fears that are morbid.

An understanding of, and a proper respect for, the deep-seated and usually unconscious origins of superstitious practice is an important first step in pastoral care. The reconciliation with reason, of that which is non-rationally perceived, is also of the greatest importance, but often far from easy. Superstition is a manifestation of ignorance and irrationality, attended by fear. Understanding is the first step to be taken in its healing.

Duncan, A., The Fourth Dimension (Mowbray, 1975). Frazer, J.G., The Golden Bough (Macmillan, 1922). Richards, J., But Deliver Us from Evil (Darton Longman & Todd, 1974).

ANTHONY DUNCAN

See also: MAGIC; PARAPSYCHOLOGY; SPIRITUALISM/SPIRITISM.

SUPERVISION, PASTORAL
The practice of overseeing, guiding and assessing the relationship between the helper (in this case the pastor or counsellor) and the client (parishioner or counsellor).

The practice of supervision involves a supervisor (one who has special training and expertise in the counselling relationship) and the supervised or student (one who seeks guidance and oversight in his or her care and counselling). In supervision, the supervisor stands at the centre of a triangle which involves the needs and demands of (a) the agency (counselling centre or church, etc.), (b) the student (counsellor, therapist), and (c) the client. The supervisor must have the requisite relationship skills to understand, and stay equidistant from, the needs of the agency, the student, and the client.

Pastoral supervision is normally conducted in groups, usually consisting of a supervisor and three to six students. Peer supervision, a group of pastors supervising each other, is done out of necessities of time and expense. Individuals involved in full-time counselling work may seek individual supervision.

Supervision takes place on a regular weekly or bi-weekly basis for a set period of time, usually between one and two hours. During this time the student may present work in various forms: verbatims (word-for-word accounts of the counselling sessions); video-tape or tape-recordings of the session; notes taken following the session. (Pastors doing family or marital counselling may have live supervision, i.e. be supervised during the actual counselling session.)

An on-going and necessary part of supervision is the assessment by the supervisor of the student. The supervisor must continually assess the work the student is doing and be able to confront the student about unsatisfactory quality of work. Because supervisors are not only teachers but judges of their student's work, there is considerable anxiety on the part of most students in supervision. It is important that supervisors be aware of this inequity and the way it works itself out in supervision. The supervisor is the only person with access to what is going on between the student-counsellor and the client and, therefore, must have the necessary information to assess what is going on. The supervisor should also be ready to help the student-counsellor set the appropriate boundaries in his or her work and to facilitate referrals (q.v.) if the work is beyond the student's capabilities as a counsellor.

Supervision is not psychotherapy (q.v.) and the supervisor should not be counselling the student nor, through the student, the client. The supervisor is primarily a teacher, who by previous knowledge and experience facilitates the student's development as a counsellor. The supervisor teaches through modelling, instruction and by suggestion.

The supervisor shows by doing, being a model to students, and teaching by example such things as boundaries (see STRUCTURE), contracts, confidentiality (q.v.), respect, and trust. The supervisor instructs by examining, framing and exploring different explanations and possibilities of what is taking place between student and the client. It is, therefore, important for the supervisor to have experience with and knowledge of different types of counselling (q.v.). The supervisor suggests – through reference materials, books, tapes, articles, films – ways in which the student's understanding of a particular problem or situation may be enlarged.

Research has shown that a parallel process of interpersonal dynamics operates in supervision. The interaction between the student and client is reflected in a similar way in the interaction between the supervisor and the student. Thus, the student's problems with the supervisor are related to the client's problems with the counsellor and vice versa. It is crucial that the supervisor be aware of

this process and be prepared to interpret and work through the problems and possibilities which arise because of it.

Finally, in group supervision, the supervisor must be aware of group process and understand how the dynamics of the supervision group can block or facilitate the development of the individual student's work with clients. In this regard, it is important to be able to use the contributions and abilities of various group members within the supervision session.

Doehrman, M.J.G., 'Parallel Processes in Supervision and Psychotherapy' (*Bulletin of the Menninger Clinic*, 40, 1, Jan. 1976), pp. 1–105. Ekstein, R. and Wallerstein, R., *The Teaching and Learning of Psychotherapy* (Basic Books, New York, 1958); the classic reference book in the field of supervision. Foskett, J., *Meaning in Madness* (SPCK, 1985). Kent, Bessie, *Social Work Supervision in Practice* (Pergamon, 1969). Langs, R., *The Supervisory Experience* (Jason Aronson, New York, 1979). Young, Priscilla, *A Student and Supervision in Social Work* (Routledge, 1967).

JOHN P. MILLAR

See also: CLINICAL PASTORAL EDUCATION; PLACEMENTS; SUPPORT GROUPS.

SUPPORT GROUPS
Small groups providing support for clergy and laypersons with pastoral roles and tasks.

Support group schemes have been pioneered in several Anglican dioceses as one way of making available adequate and regular pastoral care to clergy. They are not confined to clergy but they are an extension of the bishop's care for clergy, a structure within the Church for 'caring for the carers'. The first scheme began in Southwark in 1970, co-ordinated by the diocesan Director of Pastoral Care and Counselling and using group leaders who already had relevant training. Other dioceses followed; some schemes are officially sponsored and accountable in some degree through diocesan structures, others are more informal developments meeting local needs.

The London diocese set up an officially sponsored scheme in 1977, now with a part-time director. Experienced psychotherapists were seconded as part of the NHS commitment to community medicine. They conduct training groups whose members are normally proposed through their area bishops as potentially suitable for support group leadership. After two years' training there is an accreditation process, after which they set up a local support group, co-leading it in a male/female pair. They recruit clergy and others who work with people, not necessarily Anglicans or avowed Christians. They continue with their original training group, whose task changes to supervision.

Support Groups in this scheme aim for a balance of men and women, and an average complement of eight plus the leaders. They may continue for several years, meeting weekly or fortnightly; other members can be brought in by agreement to fill leavers' places. Their task is to explore issues arising at work, to look at the way these are handled, and to help in the search for better ways. Members assist each other to understand their own blind spots and how these affect their work. The 'here and now' of the group's interaction is found to reflect the relationship patterns at work or in the parish. Away from usual responsibilities and established roles the safety of the group allows members to see themselves in a new light and to give and receive the truth about each other. The mixture of clergy and laity, and of a variety of disciplines, churchmanship and experience, makes for a widening of understanding and sympathy, and so for growth towards greater wholeness. In a mature group the mutual trust may allow personal and family matters to surface.

These schemes are in an early stage of development and are small in comparison with the needs which they could be meeting if they were able to expand. The 'take-up' rate among clergy is low, and leaders face disappointments as they set about recruitment.

A parallel in the Roman Catholic Westminster Diocese is the 'Ministry to Priests' programme. Membership of a group is obligatory and confined to clergy. Each group decides on its activity, which may be of a recreational nature. The trained leadership of the previously described scheme is not a feature; the aim is to provide companionship for a celibate clergy.

HEWLETT and JOY THOMPSON

See also: ENCOUNTER GROUPS; PASTOR: PERSONAL AND FAMILY LIFE; SUPERVISION, PASTORAL.

SUSTAINING

Ongoing pastoral care and support.

Sickness confronts us with an experience of

dis-ease, for the wholeness of life has been disrupted. A sick person inevitably feels frustrated not only as a result of physical, mental or emotional disability, but also because of a sense of loneliness and apartness. The housebound and chronically sick need a sustaining ministry, and one of the prime tasks of pastoral care is to offer companionship, with regular calls to help keep the parishioner in contact with as much normal life and affairs as possible. They will need a strong supportive and caring community. The mentally ill need to be nurtured, motivated and guided within an atmosphere of trust and goodwill, and nothing helps to reintegrate a disturbed personality more than acceptance (q.v.) and an assurance of an on-going relationship. Such love, compassion and understanding foster and encourage recovery and growth. Continuity of pastoral care is also an essential function of the ministry to the dying (q.v.). There may possibly be one person with whom the terminally ill patient may wish to talk and relate, and it is extremely important that that individual should not at any stage have to withdraw. There can be no substitute for a continual sustaining 'presence', a readiness to 'watch and wait', to stay, to be silent in an atmosphere of spontaneous love and support; the presence of one who can talk calmly and unemotionally, and who can listen (see LISTENING) quietly and assuredly.

Groups of caring lay people are able to provide a most worthwhile and valuable service by their readiness to be available and accessible. Unfortunately the bereaved often find themselves cut off from those about them. There is a tendency on the part of those eager to help to want those who grieve to recover quickly, for so easily can the bereaved become a threat, as it were, to the local community and to its emotional stability. There is much need, therefore, for an on-going relationship and companionship by means of both priestly and lay pastoral care (q.v.), particularly during the initial months following the bereavement. When the community, as part of the living Church, the body of Christ, learns to care, to sustain, to become present to the other, to listen, hear, and to receive, a new vitality and power is to be found, a spirituality attained, and a wholeness discovered to confront the strains and stresses of life.

NORMAN AUTTON

See also: BEFRIENDING; PASTORAL CARE, NATURE OF; VISITING.

SYMBOLS

A symbol, in the widest sense, is anything that mediates some other reality. Where the referent is precisely delineated it is more appropriate to talk of a 'signal' or 'sign', because the symbol always communicates with a 'penumbra of indefinable suggestion'. Some writers make an absolute distinction between symbol and sign; others see a spectrum of usage.

Symbols are not chosen arbitrarily, but are seen to be appropriate or suggestive. The sign must usually be as simple or economical as possible and may be quite arbitrary. It serves to indicate the referent without ambiguity. The symbol may be complex, attract attention to itself and suggest meanings that are not clearly articulated. This is true both of discursive symbolism (language, music) and presentational symbolism (art, q.v.). Signs may or may not be related to what they signify, but symbols must have some intrinsic relation to their referents. In this sense they 'participate' in that which is signified.

The diagnostician and the clinician deal in signs; the pastor deals in symbols, for it is the symbol that is specifically human. 'Man' has been described by Ernst Cassirer as *homo symbolicus*, the symbol-using animal. Study of symbolism transcends the normal boundaries of the human sciences, because it is the study of human expression or communication in all its modes. Understanding the symbolic world of humanity is a central concern of hermeneutics (the study of meaning).

Important contributions to the study of symbols have been made by thinkers in a number of fields: philosophy (Cassirer, Langer, Ricoeur), psychology (Freud, Jung, Jaspers), anthropology (Mary Douglas), theology (Tillich). In each field writers may be found who look for 'scientific' precision by the elimination of symbolic ambiguity or by demythologization, and writers who are prepared to recognise and work with a fundamental level of ambiguity or mystery in all human communication. Ricoeur speaks of a 'hermeneutics of suspicion', which looks for the supposed meaning behind symbols, seeking to decode them as do Marx, Nietzsche and Freud in their respective critiques of the religious symbol-system, and a 'hermeneutics of recollection', which continues to attend expectantly to traditional symbols. What is needed in a 'post-critical' age, when symbolic communication is constantly subjected to a rationalist critique, is a 'second naivety' whereby the pastor or interpreter, who has rightly rejected a literal or dogmatic understanding of symbols, remains properly attentive to their continuing 'testimony'. 'Beyond the desert of criticism', says Ricoeur, 'we wish to be called again.' If any of Tillich's students spoke of a 'mere symbol', their teacher was infuriated.

Reflection on symbols raises a number of important issues for pastoral care: (1) The recognition that human existence is a mystery which remains and will always remain unplumbed, expressed in, but not explained by, symbols. (2) The importance of the concrete, the physical world, of objects, and of the body, in human interaction. (3) The need for attention, to be able to 'hear' the resonances of symbols presented in words, actions, objects, dreams, etc. (4) The place of imagination (q.v.) in promoting facility with symbols. For the Christian these points must be linked with alertness to the symbols of the Bible and tradition, which are the vehicle of God's self-expression, Christ being the fundamental symbol; hence the importance of the sacraments, in which physical objects are used as effectual symbols of divine grace.

Dillistone, F.W., *Christianity and Symbolism* (Collins, 1955); *Traditional Symbols and the Contemporary World* (Epworth, 1973). **Langer, S.K.**, *Philosophy in a New Key* (Harvard, 1941). **Ricoeur, P.**, *The Symbolism of Evil* (Beacon, 1969). **Tillich, P.**, *Dynamics of Faith* (Allen & Unwin, 1957).

NICHOLAS SAGOVSKY

See also: ART; IMAGINATION; LITURGY AND RITUAL; RITES AND RITUALS.

SYSTEMS PASTORAL CARE

An area of pastoral care identified and expounded by the North American psychiatrist and pastor E. Mansell Pattison, who asserts the importance of the social system of the local church as the primary sphere for pastoral activity in the quest for individual and communal health, identity and well-being.

Living systems theory was formulated in the 1940s in an attempt to understand better the interactions between living organisms. It rests on three principles: (1) Holism – the whole system is greater than the sum of its parts. (2) Open synergy – the parts of the system work together to produce equilibrium but the system is open because it is always having to take into account new factors. (3) Isomorphism – the purpose, character, direction and goals of the whole system are shared by each of its parts.

Applied to human social systems this theoretical framework has proved of great value, for it has shown how much individual behaviour is the product of systematic interaction. It has been recognized in secular helping modes, e.g. family therapy, that the behaviour of individuals is heavily influenced, for good or ill, by the social systems of which they form a part. Pattison applies this thinking and congruent elements from psychotherapy and social psychiatry to the church. He argues that it too is a social system. In order that its members will live more fully, it could and should be orientated towards health, well-being and identity in the wider community of which it is a part. The local church and its sub-system of symbolizing, moralizing, learning-growth, sustaining-maintaining and repairing must therefore develop the characteristics of a healthy system. These are leadership, common commitment, precise expectations and behavioural sanctions, well-established organization, shared goals and tasks, opportunities for members to associate and be together, behavioural taboos in the areas of sex and aggression (to facilitate intimacy without social disruption resulting), and semi-permeability to the wider community.

The parish pastor should function principally as shepherd of systems in the church and exercises a crucial leadership role by virtue of office held rather than skills possessed. The pastor's task is to act as a symbol of the system, recalling it to its purpose, to affirm the individual integrity of those who participate in the system, to share responsibility, authority and control with other system members, to act intentionally and deliberately in interactions with the system, to model desirable behaviour and take necessary risks, to set limits which enable the system to serve a beneficial function, and to act as facilitator, catalyst, mediator and connector between the different sub-systems which comprise the whole. These functions enable the church system to be healthy, growing and full of love so that it becomes a vehicle for the health and growth of its individual members.

Pastoral care of systems as outlined here has three main attractive features. Firstly, it broadens the concern of pastoral care beyond the bounds of the individual psyche. Secondly, it is positive and preventive in orientation rather than being clinically or pathologically focused. Finally, it capitalizes on the position and strengths of the parish and its pastor and not on the acquisition of elaborate professional skills or a setting divorced from the main life of the congregation.

Pattison, E.M., *Pastor and Parish – a Systems Approach* (Fortress 1977); 'Systems Pastoral Care' (*J. of Pastoral Care*, 26, 1972), pp. 2–14. Walrond-Skinner, S., *Family Therapy* (Routledge, 1976).

STEPHEN PATTISON

See also: CONGREGATION; LEADERSHIP; PASTOR: IDENTITY AND ROLE; SOCIAL STRUCTURES AND PASTORAL CARE.

T

TELEPHONE USE

The telephone is an efficient tool for rapid and informal contact between people spread even worldwide. Arrangements can be made, and problems aired and solved without needing to move. It is an advantage that calls are not usually recorded.

The major difference between face-to-face encounter and telephone conversation is that cues to assist listening are all concentrated in the voice. It is not difficult to mishear what is said and the absence of non-verbal communication exacerbates the problem of dealing with silence.

In recent years, a wide range of telephone counselling services have been inaugurated, using two benefits of the telephone – easy contact and possible anonymity – in a world where people are often isolated and cut off from traditional sources of help. The caller can ring from home, and can more easily control what information is given. 'The Samaritans' (*see* BEFRIENDING), which began in 1953, now have almost 200 branches around the country. From the start they found it necessary to offer a specific service, clearly stating that they were beside a telephone 'to befriend the suicidal and despairing'. They offer a befriending service, while some other services confine themselves to telephone counselling.

With discipline and full attention a caller can be encouraged to present and ventilate a problem, and be helped in much the same way as in any pastoral dialogue. The pastor may prefer to encourage a one-to-one meeting if that can be achieved.

Obscene and angry calls are a hazard to agencies, and procedures have been developed for dealing with these.

It is prudent, when about to answer the telephone, to compose yourself before picking up the receiver, allowing it to ring about three times, and state calmly and naturally who you are. If under pressure, say so. People are becoming more used to the answer-phone, and some will value being able to leave a message rather than wonder when they will get through. But the subsequent personal contact by the person receiving the message is an important counterbalance to the distancing effect of a machine.

Brown, Loraine, *Person to Person* (Manchester Council for Voluntary Service, Gaddum Centre, 274 Deansgate, Manchester M3 4FT, 1983); a training manual for telephone counselling services. **Varah, Chad,** *The Samaritans in the '80s* (Constable, 1980); describes the history of the movement and its befriending work.

DAVID GOODACRE

TEMPTATION

The possibility of being tempted, of being allured and seduced, belongs to the dignity of the human person endowed with free will and committed to a struggle in a world of good and evil, of light and darkness, of reality and lies. Temptation is not possible where the freedom of the will has been removed by psychic disorder. It is reduced by the force of habit when actions are more and more determined by a habitual giving way to temptation. To be tempted therefore is a human condition. The more a person is truly human the more he or she will be tempted. Christ *par excellence* is the tempted one.

Temptation is not primarily an individual matter. It is primarily social. Humans are social beings and as such are tempted, for it is human society that is the object of temptation. It is human society that has been set on a course and has a history and a future to be aimed at and attained. The Church is above all a tempted society and all the more so as it freely undertakes a faithfulness to its vocation. The experience of Israel, pre-eminently of Christ and of his company, is the privilege of being tempted, of being allured into leaving the path – to go after power, influence, security, status and anything else that would relieve the necessity of the way of the cross, and succumb to the worship of the penultimate, or of plausible lies. Temptation can rightly be perceived in all the tragedy and grandeur of its possible outcome in the light of the primal conflict of good and evil. It is trivialized if it is reduced to the individual's possibility of lapses. Nevertheless, it is in the complexity of the temptation experience of persons that the corporate outcome of the temptations of the people of God and of human society is determined. Temptation assumes the reality of responsibility, personal and corporate.

In the Christian story the two temptations of Adam, who succumbed, and of Christ, who stood firm, are the two primary experiences into which we are drawn for defeat or victory. In each case there is an allurement of self-satisfaction, self-security and the avoidance of the limitation of the human condition. To resist temptation is to maintain direction, to keep to the path, and the more one is concerned with doing so the more one is aware of temptation. Self-justification presents itself with most temptations. As in the classic stories of the original temptation and that of Christ's, there are always at hand excellent reasons why we should give way. They keep their strength even though often they are contradictory.

Much talk about temptation in traditional religious instruction is more an expression of the neurotic fears and anxieties of the teacher than a genuine help to self-acceptance and realistic self-criticism. There may be a danger at the present time (in Western cultures at least) that moral boundaries have become so ill-defined and self-justifying excuses so common, that temptation is no longer properly recognized. On the other hand, an obsession with temptation which encourages neurotic scrupulosity and a fear and rejection of the body (see BODY, THEOLOGY OF) is equally unhelpful morally, and its passing need not be regretted.

Much has been said of the moral purpose of temptation as a testing ground for the soul (q.v.), but an undue emphasis on this aspect can lead to a pursuit of spiritual perfection which obscures the corporate nature of the struggle. Certainly the awareness of the power and subtlety of temptation throws one back on God, and the first stages of dealing with temptation involve an awareness sometimes painfully acute of our own lack of resources and of our defencelessness against the assault. There is also the common condition of leaving ourselves open to being overcome through lack of attention and loss of purpose in unguarded moments.

We are tempted and we can also tempt, both other people and God. To tempt God means to put him to the test by asking for a

manifestation of his presence to supply our needs and desires. This is due to a failure of faith to endure the seeming absence of God, and to trust in God on the basis of past care. It can also take the form, as in the temptation of Christ, of presumptuously acting in the belief that God must always be at hand to save us from our own follies.

Christians find in the experience of temptation the only recourse is to the victory of Christ over temptation and to the belief that 'God will not allow us to be tempted above that which we are able, but will with the temptation provide a means of escape'.

Dictionary of Biblical Theology, 'Temptation', Xavier Leon du Four (Chapman, 1967). **Bonhoeffer, D.,** *Ethics* (SCM, 1955). **Lewis, C.S.,** *Screwtape Letters* (Fontana, 1955).

ROLAND WALLS

See also: CONSCIENCE: PSYCHOLOGICAL ASPECTS; EVIL; SIN.

TERMINATION OF COUNSELLING
The completion of counselling (and breaks for holidays, which provide a rehearsal for the ultimate break) is more than a practical necessity, and the arrangements made for ending are more than etiquette. Breaks and endings are opportunities for: (1) Reviewing the progress (or lack of it), especially as felt by the client; and sometimes for clarifying issues which merit continued reflection by the client. (2) Preparing the client for the absence of regular counselling and of ongoing support, encouraging development of autonomy and continued self-understanding. (3) Seeing how far termination of counselling might mirror feelings experienced (consciously or unconsciously) about previous endings (e.g. death of a parent), or earlier breaks in the continuity of relationships (e.g. hospitalization of a child or parent in infancy).

Termination may evoke feelings such as rejection, grief, fear of autonomy, anger at being let down, etc; which (providing the termination of counselling is appropriate) are probably associated with earlier experiences (see BEREAVEMENT). Intense reactions are less likely when: (a) counselling has been concerned with a short-term problem which has been resolved, and where strong transference (q.v.) has not developed; or (b) long-term counselling has enabled transference feelings to be worked through. Even then the counsellor should expect to work with the normal sadness associated with the end of positive relationships. Where there are problems with endings (such as clients who need to perpetuate contact), either the limitations of counselling, or the transference, have probably not been satisfactorily resolved.

To use termination in these ways it is necessary for all breaks and the final sessions of counselling to be agreed in advance, allowing sufficient time to work on the different tasks. It is usual to give a few weeks notice of temporary breaks; notice of the final break (unless agreed at the outset) will depend upon the length of counselling and the degree of importance attached to counselling by the client. Some counsellors make contracts and discourage either premature termination (which may indicate resistance to uncovering painful feelings or to experiencing feelings associated with termination); or extension of the contract (likewise sometimes a way of avoiding endings), unless obviously necessary. If a counsellor has to terminate unilaterally before the completion of counselling, referral (q.v.) to another counsellor is normally suggested, and, as far as possible, is discussed with the client beforehand so that reactions can be explored and expressed.

Similar problems arise within a parish setting, although the nature of the relationships may be less intense and so the phenomenon of grief, etc., less obvious. It is unfortunate that so little attention is paid at present to the psychological effects on parishioners of the loss of a pastor, through retirement or a move to another parish. Part of the minister's pastoral care should be careful preparation for a move, especially amongst those who have been closely involved in his or her particular ministry.

Jacobs, M., *Still Small Voice* (SPCK, 1982), ch. 11. Malan, D.H., *Individual Psychotherapy and the Science of Psychodynamics* (Butterworth, 1979), ch. 16.

MICHAEL JACOBS

See also: STRUCTURE; TRANSFERENCE.

THEODICY

The attempt to show by reason that the existence of suffering and evil is compatible with the existence of a loving and omnipotent God.

In pastoral care, it is rare for people to ask for a full-scale rational argument. The existence of the Book of Job is a standing rebuke to those who inflict rational arguments on the suffering. It is also a reminder that rational theories are so partial and limited that they are unlikely to present the truth in its fullness. Indeed, they can be offensive and perverse. Yet it is necessary to find some way of understanding one's own suffering and that of others in relation to the loving providence of God.

The natural question, 'Why should I suffer?' must be clearly answered by denying that God specifically chose to inflict suffering on me, either as a punishment for my sin or as a test of my faith. Though these theories have been held by Christians, they can lead sufferers to despair at their own sinfulness or, if penitent and suffering continues, these theories may undermine assurance of forgiveness. They also give an odd idea of a loving God, who thus punishes his children to see if they are good. And they accord strangely with the healing ministry of Jesus, who seemed to regard sickness as a work of Satan. At Luke 13.1–5, Jesus seems specifically to reject the view that suffering is the result of particular sins.

God's will is always for health; the ministry of Jesus shows that unequivocally. His death on the cross also shows that suffering is not adequately accounted for as punishment or trial. It shows that God does not obliterate suffering, but uses it for good: 'All things work together for good, to those who love God' (Rom. 8.28). God shares in our suffering, and will bring good from it, if we are faithful to him in love. Further, suffering can provide a time to reassess our lives; it may compel us to re-order our priorities and hopes and give God a higher priority, and give submission to his will in all things a deeper meaning for us. And there is point in saying that it may enable us to offer our suffering with Christ's self-offering, to be used by God to help others, in ways we cannot know. Above all, Christians believe that our present suffering will be taken up and used by God to forge a vastly greater good, as we develop to the fullness of the unique life God has created in us.

But how can suffering exist at all, if God does not will it? One response is to say that we can only exist, as the individuals we are, in a world like this – a relatively independent universe, operating in accordance with general laws, in which rational, free beings develop and interact. If God willed to create

279

us, rather than some other, more perfect beings, he had to create a world in which suffering often occurs by chance or misfortune. Suffering is a foreseen consequence of what God wills. But he does not will the suffering itself; and, when it occurs, he acts to redeem it and use it for good. On lines such as these, it may perhaps be suggested that, though we cannot see just why suffering exists, it is compatible with the existence of a loving God. It is necessarily true that it may come to exist in a world of free, rational creatures like us; and, if it does, God will certainly use it to produce a great good, which could not otherwise have existed.

Elphinstone, Andrew, *Freedom, Suffering and Love* (SCM, 1976). **Hebblethwaite, Brian,** *Evil, Suffering and Religion* (Sheldon, 1976). **Moberly, Elizabeth,** *Suffering, Innocent and Guilty* (SPCK, 1978).

KEITH WARD

See also: EVIL; PAIN; PROVIDENCE.

THEOLOGY
See: ASCETICAL THEOLOGY; BODY, THEOLOGY OF; CLINICAL THEOLOGY; MORAL THEOLOGY; PASTORAL THEOLOGY; POLITICAL THEOLOGY; PRACTICAL THEOLOGY; SEXUALITY, THEOLOGY OF.

THERAPY
See: BEHAVIOUR THERAPY; CLIENT-CENTRED THERAPY; GESTALT THERAPY; PSYCHOTHERAPY.

TONGUES (GLOSSOLALIA)
Speaking in tongues (or glossolalia) is a religious practice which is known inside and outside Christianity. To the observer it appears like a language which he does not understand. Adherents of pentecostal and charismatic movements (q.v.) see in glossolalia a gift of the Spirit (q.v.). The claim that glossolalics speak actual foreign languages which they have never learned has so far not been adequately documented.

Two questions are of special importance in the area of pastoral care. Firstly, who are the glossolalics? And secondly, what is the function of glossolalia?

(1) The medical researcher Vivier, the linguist Samarin, the theologians Christie-Murray and Williams have clearly established that glossolalics are not abnormal or especially excitable persons. Due to our social and cultural climate they may be considered as such, but this says more about the observer than about the observed. That which we consider to be inarticulate is not identical with absence of meaning. The function of language is not restricted to conveying information, for it can be used to express a relationship or to create ties of union. The nearest parallel to glossolalia is dreaming, singing or dancing; although they do not convey exact semantic meanings (if they are not interpreted into semantic language) they are not useless or even abnormal.

(2) The function of glossolalia is to remind us of that important and deep dimension of language which we tend to suppress in our discussion on language and without which language ceases to exist. Glossolalia is 'yet another kind of communication' (Christie-Murray). In its private form it is a kind of prayer on a level which borders on the preconscious – an experience with which Paul was familiar (1 Cor. 14.8). In its public form it creates a kind of socio-acoustic sanctuary, a cathedral of sound for people who have no cathedrals of stones or who do not feel at home in them. The criteria for its genuineness are not phenomenological but functional. Genuine glossolalia edifies the glossolalic (by opening up a new dimension of prayer, 1 Cor. 14.4) and in its public form accepts the judgement 'of the others', both Christian and non-Christian (1 Cor. 14.23–5).

Christie-Murray, D., *Voices from the Gods: Speaking with Tongues* (Routledge, 1978). **Kildahl, J.P.,** *The Psychology of Speaking in Tongues* (Hodder & Stoughton, 1972). **Samarin, W.J.,** *Tongues of Men and Angels: the Religious Language of Pentecostalism* (Collier-Macmillan, 1972). **Williams, C.G.,** *Tongues of the Spirit: a Study of Pentecostal Glossolalia and Related Phenomena* (Univ. of Wales Press, 1981).

WALTER J. HOLLENWEGER

See also: INTERCULTURAL PASTORAL CARE.

TOUCH
Physical contact between people with such intentions as to communicate non-verbally, to stimulate sexually or emotionally, to comfort or support, to bless or consecrate, to heal sacramentally or through the transmission of healing energies, to authorize, set apart and commission as in ordination.

Many developmental psychologists and paediatricians believe that the touch of significant other people, especially the mother, or a mother substitute, but including the father and siblings, plays an important part in the growth of a secure and lively child. It is through the sensory pathways that the baby and child learns that it is loved and develops a confident personality. A parent may have a high spiritual and theoretical motivation, but unless her or his ideas and feelings find physical expression the baby is largely unaware of them. Without sufficient experience of touch from a consistent mothering person, the child suffers varying degrees of deprivation which, in turn, can give rise to neurotic or psychotic behaviour in later life, including 'touch-hunger' or 'touch-revulsion'.

The naive response of some pastoral carers to people who have experienced touch deprivation is an attempt to give them what they have lacked. This response is almost always destined to failure, (a) because you cannot give to someone the fulfilment the deprived child within yearns for, and (b) because you will become quite frequently the object of insatiable expectations, or erotic demands with which you will not be able to cope. Moreover, touch often by-passes emotional pain which, far from being avoided needs to be experienced and worked through.

Is touch ever to be used in pastoral care and counselling? Opinions differ. The analytical tradition operates a non-touch rule in order that clients are offered no escape from what has to be faced both within themselves and between themselves and the therapist. It also frees the therapist from certain possible levels of collusion and self-gratification. Other approaches vary in their attitude to the therapeutic value of touch. Particular forms of massage, for instance, are seen as a form of psychotherapy, not simply as an exercise in physical relief. The body/mind/spirit interaction is taken very seriously, and it is believed that appropriate massage of the body can affect or contribute towards psychical wholeness. Such therapists also assert that they can maintain a therapeutic contract which guards against the 'acting-out' of the client's or therapist's problems.

In some forms of pastoral counselling, physical contact is thought to be appropriate at times of crisis, such as bereavement or in order to encourage a parishioner to relax or express emotion. The usual rider is that the counsellor is not 'touch-hungry' or seductive, and that he or she is aware that the parishioner is not avoiding inner reality

through such physical contact.

Touch also has an important part to play in the Christian ministry of healing (*see* SPIRITUAL HEALING), in blessing (q.v.) and the sacralization of life and in ordination (q.v.). Such acts of touching undoubtedly derive some of their power from the reverberation of memories of parental approval and care, but this does not necessarily mean that they do not communicate supernatural energies.

Lowen, A., *The Language of the Body* (Collier Books, 1971). Kaplan, L., *Oneness and Separateness* (Jonathan Cape, 1979).

JOHN GRAVELLE

See also: ANOINTING; BLESSING; COUNSELLING; TRANSFERENCE.

TRAINING METHODS

Pastoral care is about relationships which often have to bear the extremes of human experience, and make heavy demands on the personal resources of the pastor. Training therefore must help learners develop awareness of self, others and inter-personal dynamics; an ability to handle transference (q.v.), collusion (q.v.) and projection; an understanding of theoretical models; and an insight into ideological implications. These areas of learning are dealt with most satisfactorily within an experiential approach. The learning cycle of experiential education is Activity – Examination – Interpretation – Integration.

1. *Activity*. The specific learning goal will usually determine the choice of activity from an enormous range. *Structured exercises* highlight specific areas of learning such as listening, communication, empathy (q.v.), etc. These can be exercises for individuals, pairs or groups of differing sizes. *Simulation and games* are more highly developed exercises usually based on simplified 'real life' situations, which allow learners to try out one or more courses of action. Simulations often involve role play (q.v.). *Training groups* focus on intra- and inter-personal awareness in the setting of group experience. Groups vary according to the declared learning goal and the style of the trainer. Goals can be personal growth (e.g. group psychotherapy) or interpersonal (encounter groups) or group process learning (T-groups). The trainer style may be as a fully involved group member, an intro-

ducer of group exercises, an interpreter, or as a therapist. *Placements (q.v.) and fieldwork* provide an opportunity for learners to practise skills in 'real life' situations and to develop a deeper understanding of different contexts.

2. *Examination.* The activity is always followed by an opportunity to examine it (often called de-briefing). Those who have been involved in the activity, in whatever role, talk about what has happened and how they felt about it. In some cases a record is kept of the activity either by participants using a diary, or by observers taking notes, or with video or audio equipment. Examination will focus at *what* actually happened (the content) and *how* it happened, with an emphasis on the participants' feelings (process). The use of positive and negative *feedback* allows learners to find out what effect their behaviour has. Feedback needs to be specific, direct, non-interpretive and non-judgemental, and above all the learner needs to be motivated to receive it. A structure for feedback requires separating the experience into: what happened? what effect did it have on others? what feelings did I have? Questionnaire and personality profile instruments are often used to provide outside reference points, so that learners can come to greater self-understanding, either about themselves as human beings or in the tasks they might undertake (e.g. as group leaders, chairpersons, counsellors, etc.).

3. *Interpretation.* Examination of experience leads to research and the development of practical and theoretical models of human development, normal and pathological behaviour, group theory (q.v.), and the role of the pastor (q.v.). These models will need to take account of developments in clinical and social psychology, biblical studies and pastoral theology. Interpretation also needs to set the pastoral relationship within the wider context of social, political and ideological considerations, so that the full implications of any pastoral behaviour can be understood.

4. *Integration.* If learning has been integrated then it will lead to decisions about more effective behaviour, which can be evaluated by new activity which may simply be a repeat of the previous one, or practise in some similar activity. In terms of a placement, it may mean continuing doing the same thing but in a new way. This doing gain is the beginning of a new learning cycle.

The experiential approach implies that pre-

paratory training needs to be supplemented with regular in-service training. Conferences are used to extend the range of understandings and competence. Case-conference groups allow discussion on cases and the effect they are having on the learner. Thirdly, learners who are often the givers of pastoral care need to ensure that they are also the recipients of pastoral care, through either spiritual direction (q.v.), counselling (q.v.) or psychoanalysis (q.v.) for themselves.

Miles, N.M., *Learning to Work in Groups* (Teachers College, 2nd edn 1981). **Pfeiffer, J.W.,** and **Jones, J.E.,** *Annual Handbook for Group Facilitators* (University Associates Inc., 45/47 Victoria Street, Mansfield, 1972–1984). **Smith, P.,** *Group Processes and Personal Change* (Harper & Row, 1980). **Taylor, M.H.,** *Learning to Care: Christian Reflection on Pastoral Practice* (SPCK, 1983).

KEITH LAMDIN

See also: CLINICAL PASTORAL EDUCATION; PLACEMENTS; ROLE PLAY; SUPERVISION.

TRANSACTIONAL ANALYSIS
Transactional Analysis (TA) is a body of theory and practice (developed by Eric Berne, a psychoanalyst) which uses an *ego state* model to examine internal mental processes.

An ego-state is a coherent set of feelings, thoughts and actions. Each ego-state is distinct and discrete, therefore identifiable: (a) the *Parent* – our experience of others internalized; (b) the *Child* – our self experience of childhood; and (c) the *Adult* – our reality-testing function. All combine for healthy functioning. When one or other is inactive, or the boundaries lax, our responses may be out of balance and potentially dysfunctional. While psychotherapy (q.v.) focuses on Child/Parent distortions, pastoral counselling (q.v.) may more commonly use the TA model for clarifying thinking, testing reality and self-awareness.

Ego-states provide a way of analysing communication (transactions). By analysing the interactions among the six discrete ego-states shared by two people, (each having a Parent, Adult and Child), open, blocked and hidden communication can be identified with their consequences. This offers some precision in dealing more effectively with communication. Another focus of TA concerns repetitive unconstructive interpersonal behaviour patterns (psychological *games*). The motivation lies in the basic need for stimulus, constructive attention (positive 'strokes') and in the person's self-image (life position). If a child is not given constructive attention, it will settle early in life for unconstructive attention (negative 'strokes'). The reaction becomes compulsive, so that as an adult, if adequate attention is not forthcoming, behaviour is initiated to provide negative 'strokes'. When this becomes a characteristic pattern it is a psychological game. TA provides models and theoretical bases for analysing psychological games and for dealing with them constructively at the level of psychotherapy or counselling.

In addition to these other concepts, TA offers the notion of a *Life Script*. The Script consists of the major negative impressions (*injunctions*) communicated by the words, behaviours and feelings of grown-ups towards the little child, which have the impact of inhibiting growth as a person. The child's reception and interpretation of these impressions become early life-decisions. As an adult everyday life is then lived without sufficiently up-dating these childhood techniques. Exploring injunctions, life-decisions and self-perceptions, and enabling new permissions and re-decisions to emerge is part of the focus of TA therapy. Understanding the nature of Script will be fundamental information for the practice of counselling.

The significance of Transactional Analysis for pastoral counselling is that its theories are in the mainstream of post-Freudian social psychology, that its principles are easily grasped, that it is neutral in relation to theology and that it provides a rationale and a tool-kit for counselling.

Barnes, G. (ed.), *Transactional Analysis After Eric Berne* (Harper, 1977). Berne, E., *Transactional Analysis in Psychotherapy* (Souvenir Press, 1961). Goulding, R. and Goulding, M., *Changing Lives Through Redecision Therapy* (Brunner/Mazel, 1979). Schiff, J. et al., *The Cathexis Reader* (Harper & Row, 1975). Woolams, S. and Brown, M., *Transactional Analysis* (Huron Valley Inst. Press, 1978).

ARCHIE MILLS

TRANSCENDENCE AND IMMANENCE

Transcendence is the state or action of exceeding limitation. Immanence is the indwelling of creation by God.

Transcendence may be affirmed of people who rise above their given conditions, in achievement, for instance, or in memory and hope. Such human transcendence is a positive though finite analogue for God's state of existence beyond all external limitation (although he may voluntarily limit himself). Since God (q.v.) is transcendent he cannot be contained in space-time, nor in any human concept. God is therefore said to transcend all particular occasions and expressions, yet to be discerned and related to through the value and significance of finite experience in ways which cannot be adequately expressed (*see also* REVELATION). Since the 1960s there has been a move to express human transcendence in religious terminology, often without belief in God but retaining Jesus as exemplar (Kee 1971), or insisting that over-emphasis on divine transcendence drains the world of its own reality (Robinson 1963; for criticism, Cairns 1967).

Immanence has been expressed, often with neo-Platonic or Hegelian philosophical backing, in sacramental views of nature disclosing spirit. Since the 19th century God's immanence has frequently been interpreted as the intelligent, creative principle working in and through evolution and history. Yet immanence has been largely distrusted in the history of theology because of its apparent connection with *pantheism*, a doctrine which calls the whole world divine and thus endangers the distinction between Creator and creature. Yet modern views of *panentheism* (Tillich's God as Ground of Being; Hartshorne's Divine Relativity) which hold that God is *in*, but is not to be *equated with* creation obviate the difficulty of pantheism while maintaining God's necessary involvement in all-that-is. Panentheists, however, rarely stress the personal nature of God. Helen Oppenheimer has developed a model of human immanence in the relation of love between two persons who remain distinct and has applied it to the divine immanence of 'Christ in us'.

Transcendence as a single concept is essential to a doctrine of God since it reflects the quality of religious experience which goes beyond the visible and expressible, and thus provides the human perspective on divine infinity. Yet, in the practice of relating to God in theology and devotion, transcendence has also acquired connotations of place. It is spatially 'up' while immanence is spatially 'in'. Ideally the two terms together express God's omnipresence, but because they have overtones of location they tend to be competing or alternating orientations for the presence of God. Each term, moreover, has its own difficulties as well as its benefits. A transcendent God may seem uncaring and remote from everyday life. Further the above/below paradigm, especially when echoed in Church structures, is currently experienced as oppressive. Conversely immanence runs the danger of losing sight of God's otherness by domesticating him within the thought forms or social processes of the time, which themselves are ambiguous and vulnerable to upset. It seems that when the difficulties in either location are felt there is a swing to the opposite affirmation.

The connotations of place, however, are not accidental, undesirable accretions. For a relationship to take shape and be lived with imaginatively and responsively there has to be some definition and quasi-location of God. One possible way out of the alternatives of transcendence and immanence is to change the emphatic preposition form 'up' or 'in' to 'with'. God's presence *with* us is not remote, yet remains independent; it expresses solidarity without removing human responsibility. The horizontal relationship would not deny God's limitless transcendence since that too may be conceptualized horizontally, radiating out from every particular 'here' rather than descending vertically from above to below. Theologians as different as Moltmann and Sallie McFague explore the theme of God with us, using the model of friendship.

Cairns, D., *God Up There?* (Saint Andrew Press, 1967). Hartshorne, C., *The Divine Relativity* (Yale UP, 1948). Kee, A., *The Way of Transcendence* (Penguin, 1971). McFague, S., *Metaphorical Theology* (SCM, 1983), pp. 177–94. Moltmann, J., *The Church in the Power of the Spirit* (SCM, 1977), pp. 114–20. Oppenheimer, H., *Incarnation and Immanence* (Hodder & Stoughton, 1973). Robinson, J.A.T., *Honest to God* (SCM, 1963). Tillich, P., *Systematic Theology*, vol. 1 (Nisbet, 1953).

RUTH PAGE

See also: GOD, DOCTRINES OF; INCARNATION; SYMBOLS.

TRANSFERENCE

A feature of psychoanalysis (q.v.) in which the patient, mainly unconsciously, displaces on to the analyst emotions which were earlier felt in relation to some other significant figure in the patient's life, such as a parent. The analyst is felt about, and in some sense perceived, as if he or she were this other figure in a form which had become lost in the unconscious.

More broadly, transference is the whole of the special relationship which develops between analyst and patient, but especially referring to the unconscious aspects of the relationship. The broader concept includes the *countertransference*, the reciprocal part of the process in which the analyst feels towards the patient in a way which is shaped, again largely unconsciously, by experiences outside the professional relationship. The unconscious interaction between analyst and patient is emphasized in the use of the term 'transference–countertransference'.

In 'classical' psychoanalytic method the analyst aims to identify significant elements in the transference and help the patient become aware of them, i.e. 'interpret the transference'. Since the unawareness of these elements can be a major factor in mental illness (*see* PSYCHIATRY AND MENTAL ILLNESS), the analysis of them may be healing.

While the theoretical notion of transference comes from psychoanalysis, it refers to psychological processes which can occur in any important relationships, including pastoral relationships and non-professional relationships such as marriage.

Underlying the transferred feelings are unconscious mental representations, unrecognized ideas or images, e.g. of a parent. But what is transferred is never simply a realistic idea of an actual person. It may be a primitive representation of a 'part-object' originating from a rudimentary perception, in very early infancy, of the mother as a sort of nourishing and comforting organ. This may be treated as a thing, having no feelings of its own. A more complex kind of primitive, mysteriously or magically powerful quality in the transferred image may come from the collective unconscious (*see* ANALYTICAL PSYCHOLOGY).

Transference feelings tend to polarize into good ('positive transference') or bad ('negative transference'), and sometimes swing from one extreme to another. The recipient of the transference may experience being treated as a parent, a bit of a parent, a thing, a saviour or a demon. Transference generates illusions; these are not necessarily expressions of neurosis but may be natural, e.g. the temporary idealization of a minister or priest. (But the process of disillusion calls for supportive understanding.) Transference may be a vehicle for the profound process of psychological development described by C.G. Jung as individuation (q.v.). Although this is a natural and healthy process it involves disturbing movements in the transference–countertransference, for instance when dark, undesired parts of the personality are being explored or when the unknown regions of the psyche are approached and sensed as vast and threatening.

In later analytical studies countertransference has been understood in new ways. The analyst will inevitably have areas of unconscious feelings which will sometimes be displaced onto the patient; he or she should be practised in becoming aware of them. As this is done, some of the feelings will be recognized as belonging simply to the analyst but others may reflect parts of the patient's psychology and enhance understanding of problems or developments. (Clearly skill and rigorous honesty are required in order to distinguish what belongs to the analyst and what to the patient.)

Relevance to pastoral care. Pastoral care and counselling often evoke responses which seem inappropriate and may be confusing, alarming or provoking, especially if they are sexual or aggressive. A general understanding of transference theory and manifestations can help to maintain the degree of detachment and emotional containment needed in such circumstances. A more technical application, such as offering transference interpretations, generally needs specific training of the kind sometimes included in counselling courses.

Freud, S., *Complete Psychological Works,* vol. 16 (Hogarth, standard edn 1963), ch. on 'Transference'. **Jung, C.G.,** *Collected Works,* vol. 16 (Routledge, 1954), 'Introduction to Psychology of the Transference'. **Racker, H.,** *Transference and Countertransference* (Hogarth, 1968).

D.D. HOWELL

See also: PSYCHOANALYSIS; ANALYTICAL PSYCHOLOGY.

TRUST

A sense of reliance upon and belief in the efficacy (passive or active) of an outside entity.

Religious trust. A fundamental aspect of nearly all religions is trust in an outside agent, usually supernatural, upon which the subject feels a degree of reliance and dependence. This is a very wide description, and different religions have their own particular expressions of it. Trust is essentially a psychological concept (see below), having a particular focus in a religious context where it is clearly related to faith (q.v.). However, religious faith need not necessarily mean that trust is present; indeed, the very lack of trust in life and in fellow humans can be the source not only of 'faith in' (focused religion) but also 'faith against' (i.e. emphasis against perceived evil). Ideally, faith and trust are coterminous in religious practice and are expressed as trust not only in God but also in self, life and humanity.

Psychological trust. This aspect of development and being is alluded to by many writers, but Erikson and Bowlby develop the idea more fully.

(1) Erikson coined the term 'basic trust', which means 'to have confidence in' and carries a sense of hope. For him it is the primary requirement of a healthy personality, being a positive attitude towards oneself and the world which is shaped in the first year of life. The word 'basic' implies that this trust is fundamental to health, but that it is not a fully conscious trait – it is part of the total personality. Since the first year of life involves factors which tend to break down trust, the later sense of basic trust depends on the balance of trust and distrust being in favour of trust. The oral phase is particularly important because of the relationship between the mother and the child. This is a giving/receiving relationship which is essential for the survival of the child, but is relatively optional for the mother. It is necessary for the pair to establish a mutual rhythm to enable the relationship to develop. A breakdown of this rhythm is, according to Erikson, the model in sensitive individuals for later disrupted relationships with the world and with people, especially people who might otherwise be loved and respected.

(2) Bowlby's theories centre on attachment and separation. Attachment is set in the scheme of attachment, trust, reliance and self reliance, and separation is the breaking of these bonds which arouses anxiety. Attachment is personal and specific and does not imply any sort of dependence, so it is not initiated only in infancy. Because 'dependence' and 'independence' are terms which suggest successive developmental stages, to talk of any sort of dependent behaviour in the putatively independent individual implies regression. Bowlby recognizes this and rejects the use of these terms, because his attach-

ment theory involves trusting behaviours of the sort which might otherwise be seen as regressive or infantile, but which are really part of an emerging attachment. Particularly, he challenges the idea that trust and attachment are defined in the oral stage (see above). Self-reliance appears to be related to the ability to seek assistance and to the trusting knowledge that such is available, if needed, from a significant other or others. Attachment behaviour (including trust) involves ever-widening circles of movement from such persons and is most evident between the ages of one and three. Self-reliance arises out of a steady growth to maturity during which the trustworthiness and encouragement of significant others enables the child to develop trust in self and trust in others. This trust is what self-reliance depends on.

The pastor is interested in eliciting and fostering trust in God, self and others.

Incarnational theology demands a close identification of these. Trustworthiness must also be encouraged as a correlate, with the aim of establishing a trusting community. In this task, failure to develop mature trust will be encountered. Counselling may help, or, where basic trust is absent through an experience in infancy, psychotherapy may be indicated.

Bowlby, John, *Child Care and the Growth of Love* (Penguin, 1953); *Attachment* (vol. 1 of *Attachment and Loss*) (Hogarth, 1969); *The Making and Breaking of Affectional Bonds* (Tavistock, 1979). Erikson, E.H., 'Growth and Issues of the Healthy Personality' in *Psychological Issues*, vol. 1 (1959), pp. 50–100; *Childhood and Society* (Hogarth, 1964).

WARWICK ROSS

See also: FAITH; HUMAN DEVELOPMENT; INTIMACY; MATERNAL DEPRIVATOIN.

UNCONSCIOUS, THE
See: ANALYTICAL PSYCHOLOGY;
PSYCHOANALYSIS.

UNCONSCIOUS PATIENTS
Unconsciousness is a state of unawareness of oneself and one's environment, of greater or less depth and duration.

Sleep (q.v.) is the normal state of unconsciousness, in that the person can usually be roused from the physical and mental inactivity by stimulation such as physical disturbance, pain or unaccustomed noise. Other forms of unconsciousness range from *confusion* (where the person may be disorientated and not conscious of surroundings); *stupor* (requiring vigorous and often continuous stimulation to maintain an aroused state); *light coma* (in which the person cannot be aroused but will react to painful stimulation); and *deep coma* (where there is no arousal to any stimulation and may lead to involvement of the vital centres of the brain with the possibility of consequent death).

Research into people's sleep-patterns indicate that the brain passes progressively into a state of unconsciousness and that hearing is the last sense to 'close down'. For example, although the mother of a new-born baby may appear to be in a deep sleep, she will immediately awaken if her baby stirs or cries; though asleep her hearing is still alert and tuned to the child's movements. Therefore it is wise to assume in the case of unconscious people, that *they may still be able to hear* even though unable to respond. Familiar voices and sounds may well be able to 'speak' to the unconscious person; therefore, never discuss the patient's condition in his or her presence however unresponsive he or she may be. Similarly it is important that clear and concise explanations should be given before anything is done to or for the unconscious person. This applies to physical care – 'I am just going to wash you, or turn you'; and also to spiritual care – 'I am going to anoint you, lay hands on you, bless you, . . . etc.'

It is not uncommon for a seemingly unresponsive and unconscious person to make the sign of the cross at the time of being anointed (q.v.), which again indicates that communication may still be possible. Those pastorally involved should introduce themselves to the patient and explain what they are about to do and why. Preferably speak in a clear voice and close to the patient's ear – loud noises may jar. People are often embarrassed about holding a one-sided conversation with an unconscious patient, but using the patient's name, talking quietly, and the use of touch (q.v.) can be very important. Relatives should be encouraged to have physical contact, especially in high technology units such as an intensive-care unit, where they may be afraid to touch anything. Communication problems and feelings of inadequacy are common, and relatives find it difficult to hand over someone they love to the care of others. It helps, therefore if they can still continue to care in some way – if they wish to.

There are many instances of relatives using tape-recordings to stimulate the patient to respond, whether to human voices, or music, or the sound of a family pet. Other relatives might find it helpful to read a book to the patient, especially a child, or the daily newspaper in order to keep the patient up to date with the world outside.

Pastoral care of the patient should also include the relatives and, as appropriate, the staff. The acknowledgement of fears and the maintenance of hope (q.v.) are all important aspects of pastoral care. The physical care of the relatives who are sitting by the bedside for long periods is also important, in that they may not be eating, exercising or sleeping properly. They may be afraid to leave the bedside, but may do so if the pastor agrees to stay with the patient while the relative has a break.

In those instances where the death of the unconscious person is a likely outcome (*see* DEATH: DEFINITIONS), then the pastor may need to support the relatives whilst they cope with their grief and any discussion of possible organ donation or request for a post-mortem.

Commendatory prayers, the reading of appropriate portions of Scripture, dealing with negative feelings about God may all feature at this point in the patient's life (see also DYING).

The long-term care of unconscious people can create stresses in the hospital staff, and providing an opportunity to share some of their feelings and reactions may be an important pastoral function.

Shafer, K.N. et al., *Medical-Surgical Nursing* (Mosby, 6th edn 1979). **Speck, P.W.,** 'The Relative Nuisance', in *Religion and Medicine*, vol. 3, ed. D. Millard (SCM, 1976), pp. 30–44. **Walton, J.N.,** *Brain's Diseases of the Nervous System* (OUP, 8th edn 1977).

PETER W. SPECK

See also: CONSCIOUSNESS; DEATH: DEFINITIONS; SLEEP.

UNCTION
See: ANOINTING.

UNEMPLOYMENT
The lack of paid employment, reflecting the job gap between those seeking work and the amount of work available.

The contemporary experience of and ideas about unemployment, like experiences and views of work (q.v.) are linked with the emergence of capitalism and industrialization. The creation of a labour force dependent on wage-work ensures that when high unemployment occurs it has a damaging effect on families and communities. The high moral valuation of work has often meant that it is accompanied by an equally hard attitude against those without work, the unemployed and 'the idle'.

Unemployment is of current concern in the UK (although also a European and world problem) because of its large-scale (over 3 million registered unemployed in 1986) and long-term nature (over 1 million unemployed for over one year), and because of the importance of work in contemporary society. Heralding the end of full employment, it threatens the viability of a Welfare State built by Beveridge on the assumption of full employment. The structural nature of current unemployment is related to a radically changing economy. It has disproportionate effects on younger and older age-groups, the unskilled, inner cities, peripheral regions and black people (see RACE RELATIONS; INTERCULTURAL

PASTORAL CARE). Because it is concerned with the vulnerability of individuals, families and communities to economic and social change, it has consistently aroused Christian concern, and makes demands of pastoral care, including the need to understand the effects of unemployment and their implications for Christian ministry.

Being unemployed is the obverse of what it means to be employed. It often involves poverty (q.v.), the loss of status and identity (q.v.), isolation, boredom and purposelessness, and lack of time structure. The resulting withdrawal into the home ensures that that is where the main stresses are felt, fuelled by over-proximity and financial worries. There is an important correlation between unemployment and health (cardiovascular disease and cirrhosis of the liver), high death rates (including suicides and homicides), and admissions to mental and penal institutions (especially of young people). The effects of long-term unemployment on communities and society is equally damaging and include a general apathy (q.v.) and a deteriorating environment (vandalism). Its cumulative cost, through its effects on human aspirations, and on caring, educational and penal provision, has never been fully measured.

Unemployment has three implications for ministry:

(1) The most common response of the State, voluntary agencies and the churches is to seek to change the unemployed individual. First, by supporting individuals and families to manage the stress of unemployment and to enhance their self-esteem. This requires understanding psychological perspectives on the phases through which unemployed people pass (similar to bereavement (q.v.)). These include the minimization of the initial shock of redundancy (taking a holiday, painting the house), the move from optimism to pessimism when 'the holiday is over' and the debilitating job-search begins, and then finally a fatalism when it is realized that employment is totally outside one's control. Secondly, the unemployed can be helped to develop job-search skills (interviewing techniques) and new work skills (through retraining). Many long-term unemployed need help to acquire a new identity and purpose unrelated to employment.

(2) Increasing numbers of community-based small groups and organizations can analyse local unemployment, provide mutual support

for the unemployed (drop-in centres), and develop work-creation schemes. Churches are involved in such ventures.

(3) Pastoral care, because it is associated with individuals, is likely to minister to symptoms rather than causes (but *see* JUSTICE AND PASTORAL CARE; SOCIAL STRUCTURES AND PASTORAL CARE). Adequate responses to unemployment must recognize its origin in economic change rather than personal misfortune. They need to address the defective attitudes which blame the unemployed for their idleness and enshrine such hostility in the social security system (the long-term unemployed are on the lowest rate of supplementary benefit). In particular, they have to decide whether governments should give the highest priority to reducing the job gap or inflation (they need not be mutually exclusive). The former requires reducing the work force and working life (work-sharing measures) and creating work opportunities, especially for manual workers.

Hayes, J. and **Nutman, P.,** *Understanding the Unemployed* (Tavistock, 1981). **Seabrook, J.,** *Unemployment* (Quartet Books, 1982). **Sinfield, A.,** *What Unemployment Means* (Martin Robertson, 1981).

JOHN R. ATHERTON

See also: POVERTY; WORK.

UNIVERSITY CHAPLAINCY
See: COLLEGE/UNIVERSITY CHAPLAINCY.

V

VICES

See: VIRTUES AND VICES.

VIOLENCE

'Unnecessary, excessive, hurtful and unlawful use of force' (Adam Curle), whether against people or property.

This definition draws out the complexity of the concept and the wide range of issues involved. Fundamentally it is about the misuse of power and strength. This makes it a moral issue, about relations between persons or groups. All power has to be responsibly exercised, especially where force is used to restrain or compel or change. Thus violence relates to the principles involved, e.g. in war, revolution, human rights, law and order, the nature of persons and property and the ethical perspectives lying behind them.

Violence takes many forms: armed conflict; terrorism; riot; social, institutional or racial oppression; vandalism; murder; domestic or self-inflicted violence, etc. Violence can be deliberate or spontaneous; pro-active (seeking an end such as social change) or reactive (in defence) or expressing social tensions. Cultures and sub-cultures vary as to the form, level and function of violence that is acceptable. There is anxiety as to whether our society is becoming more violent and too readily accepting it as normal.

Liberal democracy regards violence as dangerous and destabilizing in a society based on consensus and conciliation. Some ideologies, of left and right, regard violence as a tool of change or even as intrinsically good.

The reasons for violence are proving elusive despite considerable investigation. Social factors must include: the need for groups and individuals to react to suppression, frustration, fear, extreme circumstantial pressures, threat to life or possessions, victimization or alienation.

Psychologically, violence is variously perceived as: instinctive; aggression rooted in evolution; faulty ego development and lack of self control; defective socialization, etc. Therapeutic practice will depend on the understanding of the social and personal factors.

Theologically, violence is contrasted with *shalom*, peace. But in a fallen world violence is endemic. The classic Western, Augustinian, approach is to recognize that human violence has to be restrained, including the controlled use of force, while at the same time the gospel offers the possibility of human renewal. The Christian pacifist position is that violence can only be overcome by redemptive, sacrificial love.

Ballard, Paul A., *A Christian Perspective on Violence* (British Council of Churches, 1979). Ellul, Jaques, *Violence: Reflections from a Christian Perspective* (Mowbray, 1978). Tournier, Paul, *The Violence Within* (SCM, 1978). Tutt, Norman, *Violence* (HMSO, 1976). Wilkinson, Paul, *Terrorism and the Liberal State* (Macmillan, 1977).

PAUL H. BALLARD

See also: AGGRESSION; ANGER AND HOSTILITY; CONFLICT; RECONCILIATION; SHALOM.

VIRTUES AND VICES

Medieval thought classified the virtues as 'cardinal', from a Latin word meaning 'hinge' or 'pivot', and 'theological'. Cardinal virtues were four: prudence, temperance, justice and fortitude. These were regarded as the 'natural' virtues, or what C.S. Lewis called the 'virtues of all civilized people'. 'Prudence' was used very much in the sense with which we would use 'common-sense', 'temperance' had not acquired its later meaning of teetotalism, but was used in the sense of 'moderation', 'justice' had its modern meaning of 'fairness', and 'fortitude' meant courage and endurance.

Theological virtues were three: faith, hope and charity. These were the virtues specially cultivated by Christians. *Faith* (q.v.) was often taken to mean doctrinal correctness, but the underlying and more important meaning was about sticking with, and growing in, Christian belief even at times when, for personal or social reasons, this was painful and difficult. Faith was commitment, perseverance, developing insight and language to enable an individual or a community to reach a new level of understanding. *Hope* (q.v.) was used by many writers to suggest that Christians could look forward to a happy release from this world into a trouble-free heaven. This seems to appeal less to modern Christians who may prefer to regard hope as a tool for this life – a way of living with a sense of joy, whatever our particular circumstances. *Charity* (*caritas* did not have the Lady Bountiful overtones that the word has for us, but meant a generous, open-hearted love (q.v.) for others. From the time of Acts, when non-believers exclaimed in astonishment, 'How these Christians love one another!' love was the hallmark of a Christian.

Just as the medieval writers believed there were seven virtues, so they had the same schematic approach to vices, or sins. Sins were divided up into 'venial' (those which would not cut one off completely from the source of grace) and 'mortal' (those which, unless repented of, would condemn one to hell (q.v.). There were seven mortal, or deadly, sins and these were often graphically shown in paintings of hell, as in the 'Garden of Delights' by Hieronymus Bosch. The deadly sins were anger, lust, greed, sloth, envy, covetousness and pride.

It will be seen that these are fairly generalized words – not as specific as, say, 'telling a lie' – which suggests that they are about a 'state', a continued habit of living, or as we should say now a 'mind set', which was inimical to spiritual growth. Everybody is angry, lustful, greedy, slothful, envious, covetous or proud sometimes – this is part of our human condition – but if these states 'run away' with us, become obsessional, then we are likely to destroy ourselves and contribute to the destruction of others.

Anger, lust, greed, envy and covetousness were used with much the same meanings as they have now. 'Sloth' (accidie) was used in a context where we might use such words as 'bored', 'depressed' or even 'masochistic'. (Bosch depicted it as somebody being savagely beaten.) For whatever reason, slothful people refuse to change a situation which is intolerable, will not or cannot 'act'. 'Pride' is used in the sense of 'self-conceit', an illusory sense of one's own importance in the scheme of things, and a refusal to submit one's will to the will of God. This was regarded as the worst of the sins.

Flew, R.N., *The Idea of Perfection in Christian Theology*

(OUP, 1934). **Forsyth, P.T.,** *Christian Perfection* (Hodder & Stoughton, 1899). **Kirk, K.E.,** *Conscience and its Problems* (Longmans, Green, 1927). **Lewis, C.S.,** *Christian Behaviour* (G. Bles, 1943). **Mortimer, R.C.,** *Elements of Moral Theology* (Black, 1947). **Wallace, J.D.,** *Virtues and Vices* (Cornel UP, 1978). **Williams, H.A.,** 'Theology and Self Awareness', in A.R. Vidler (ed.), *Soundings* (CUP, 1966).

MONICA FURLONG

See also: RESPONSIBILITY; SIN; TEMPTATION.

VISIONS

The word 'visions' is used in various ways, and overlaps with dreams (q.v.) and fantasy (q.v.). The following uses are relevant here: (1) Visual hallucinations, seen when the person is awake, and seeming bizarre to others. (2) Visual experiences of a non-ordinary kind, had when the person is awake, but recognized by others as of great significance. An example would be Moses before the burning bush. (3) 'Big dreams', of great emotional power for the dreamer, and recognized by others as of great significance. Examples would be Jacob's dream in Bethel (Gen. 28.10–15), or the great dream described by the American Indian healer, Black Elk.

The first of these belongs in psychopathology, and is a sign of serious and often psychotic disturbance. It is sometimes described as 'dreaming when awake', as if the dream process somehow breaks through into waking consciousness (imaged by one schizophrenic patient as 'the stars being visible in the daytime').

Categories (2) and (3) are mysteries. There can be no doubt that they occur, and are often of immense importance for the person who sees them and sometimes for others also. The visions of Moses, or of St Paul at his conversion, have altered the course of world history. The visionary dream of Black Elk is moving precisely because, for all its 'big-ness', it seems to have been ineffective, or effective only on a far smaller scale than Black Elk himself anticipated.

In the early history of psychoanalysis, when there was a desire to use the new tools to explain everything, visions tended to be interpreted as if they were personal dreams. Nowadays there is probably more willingness among psychotherapists to acknowledge that some visions, at least, remain mysterious events. C.G. Jung attempted to understand them in terms of the 'collective unconscious', an unconscious stratum of the mind at which the differentiation between individuals ceases to exist, and from which imagery can emerge that is relevant to other people besides the visionary. Other mystical thinkers have used similar notions, such as the *anima mundi*, *spiritus mundi*, or world-soul. More scientific thinkers find these notions embarrassing, as founded on too little, and uncontrollable, evidence, and as tending to lead to an excessive respect for irrational processes.

James, W., *The Varieties of Religious Experience* (Random House, New York, 1936). Jung, C.G., *The Archetypes and the Collective Unconscious* (Routledge, 1959); *Memories, Dreams, Reflections* (Collins, 1963). Moltmann, J., *The Crucified God* (SCM, 1973), pp. 166ff. Neihardt, John G., *Black Elk Speaks* (Barrie & Jenkins, 1974)

DAVID BLACK

See also: DREAMS; REVELATION.

VISITING

Going in Christian faith and love to where people are, whether at home, alone or with their families, at their place of work, when sick in hospital, when elderly and frail in a nursing home, or when, for some other reason, committed to institutional care.

It is visiting both where there is an obvious need, and where there is no apparent need. It should be more than merely social, and different from (say) a doctor's visit; a visit from the clergy or other Christian pastoral worker is a tangible expression of the ministry of the Church at large for healing and wholeness. Jesus taught his disciples to visit and care for the needy in that by serving them they were serving him. Today the Church continues that ministry, and regular and effective pastoral visiting remains an important means by which such service is given and Christian love expressed.

There are always those who are in various stages of need and for whom care and counselling can best be offered by a visit to them at home or in hospital. Amongst such are the dying, the bereaved, the sick, the 'shut-in', the aged, those suffering a sudden misfortune or facing a particular problem.

But there are other groups of people with different needs: newcomers into a district or parish, young people considering church membership and confirmation or wanting to get married in church, young members needing spiritual nurture and encouragement,

parents asking for baptism for their children. Or there could be visiting at a school or hospital or nursing home where staff would welcome the interest of the local congregation. In addition there could be visiting to meet pastoral opportunities at nearby industrial or commercial premises. Or there could be a local prison to visit. Specialized chaplaincies (q.v.) serve some of these needs, but not always, and pastoral help, if kindly offered, can be welcomed.

To this wide range of visiting the clergy and church visitors should bring a particular and distinctively Christian element. Their ministry is a unique one, and they should think carefully about, and define, the purpose of their visiting. The first purpose is to get to know people and to establish a link of mutual trust and friendship. There is a symbolic significance to the visit which should not be overlooked, for a visit by someone 'from the church' brings with it its own importance and implications. A visit will not be forgotten, but failure to make it can be a source of criticism. Secondly, the minister or priest or pastor or church visitor has a distinctly spiritual authority, insight and experience to bring and share and conversation during the visit should move from initial social chat and pleasantries on to the more difficult but more fruitful ground of spiritual welfare and Christian concern. The purpose here is gently to bring out the fears and anxieties, the guilt, misconceptions and problems so that they may be met with comfort and encouragement, with advice, or with challenge as circumstances dictate. This is the important ground of pastoral care, and it may take several visits to get there. Here is the real object of the work, and during visiting and afterwards some assessment should be made as to whether this object is being or has been met, and if so how successfully.

Regular and systematic visiting is time-consuming. A few minutes is not usually sufficient; twenty minutes or half-an-hour can be, and it is worth some effort to keep to this target, though a few visits must be longer. Good visiting is also emotionally exhausting for the visitor. It is demanding to listen to the problems and detailed concerns of others, particularly others in need, and to be expected to give out of oneself all the time. There is, therefore, a limit to the amount of visiting that can be efficiently accomplished in any given period. However conscientious a visitor may be, there must always be some visiting left undone, for visiting is a never-ending pastoral duty which cannot be fully discharged. It follows from this that some system of priority must be devised. The dying (q.v.) and the bereaved (q.v.) should come at the top of any list, with the sick and the 'shut-in' thereafter. Lower down the list opinions as to the importance of one group over another will vary. But priorities must be carefully assessed and kept to if visiting is not to become unmanageable and unbalanced.

Some visiting can be unnecessary, and adequate pastoral contact can sometimes be made by letter-writing (q.v.) or telephone (q.v.). Also ministers, priests or pastors can make themselves available at a stated time and place to be consulted by those with particular needs; such arrangements can greatly increase the number of people seen at a given time. But often it is only in the comfort and familiarity of home surroundings that intimate feelings and personal problems are fully and freely disclosed.

The matter of delegation or sharing should not be overlooked. Clearly pastoral visiting is not the sole preserve of the professional and the clergy. Some visiting can be delegated to, and shared with, others provided that they are both competent and committed. Much useful pastoral care can be given by simple and sympathetic befriending (q.v.) where trust and friendship can be built up into something lasting and worthwhile. When such 'team' work is undertaken there should be regular discussion and exchange of information amongst those involved. Confidentiality (q.v.) must be observed, and adequate records (q.v.) maintained.

Baxter, Richard, *The Reformed Pastor* (J. Nisbet, 1860), pp. 138–42. Clinebell, Howard, J., *Basic Types of Pastoral Counselling* (Abingdon, 1966), pp. 80–5.

ANDREW F. ANDERSON

See also: LAY PASTORAL CARE; RECORD-KEEPING; STRUCTURE; SUSTAINING.

VOCATION

From the Latin *vocare* – to call; the process of being summoned by God either to a special relationship with him, or to a specific task within that relationship, e.g. a priest, prophet, monk, nun, healer, teacher or artist. In the first instance it is often closely related to conversion, particularly within the Puritan

and Evangelical traditions.

The word is also used in a technical sense as a shorthand expression for calls to the priesthood or to religious orders, so that Christians will speak of having 'many vocations' or a 'dearth of vocations'.

Both the Jewish and Christian traditions have innumerable stories of people 'summoned' by God – for example: that of Moses (in Exod. 3), when he saw the 'angel of the Lord' in the form of a burning bush; that of the child, and future prophet, Samuel, when he heard the voice of God calling him as he lay in bed (1 Sam. 3); or of Saul on the Damascus road (Acts 9). Sometimes the vocation is collective, as when the Hebrew people knew themselves to be 'chosen' by God to fulfil a special task.

Not infrequently 'calls' take the form of an actual voice, as in Saul's experience, or in the incident in St Augustine's *Confessions* when he heard 'from a neighbouring house, a voice, as of boy or girl. I know not, chanting, and oft repeating, "Take up and read; Take up and read." ' Augustine took up the Bible and opened it at the Pauline passage about giving up of careless dissipation and 'putting on the Lord Jesus' and this utterly changed his life. Sometimes the voice is accompanied by, or replaced by, a vision (q.v.), of God, Christ, the Virgin Mary or an angel. Sometimes, instead, a particular incident seems to indicate that an inner change has taken place and a new, deep commitment has begun, as when St Francis saw a leper in the road, got down from his horse and embraced him; only later, as the leper vanished, did St Francis know that he had embraced Christ himself, but he had already discovered his own total identification with the poor and outcast. The 19th-century reformer, Lord Shaftesbury, had a rather reminiscent experience when, as a schoolboy at Harrow, he happened to witness a pauper funeral in all its squalor and indignity. The shock remained with him and helped to initiate a remarkable series of Victorian legislative Acts of Parliament which relieved some of the worst abuses inflicted on the poor.

At least one great work of art, *The Pilgrim's Progress* by John Bunyan, is about Christian vocation. Thomas Merton's *The Seven Storey Mountain* is a modern account of how a young man in the 1930s was called first to Catholicism, and then to life as a Trappist monk and a priest.

The word 'vocation' is also a secular term, sometimes though less and less frequently, used as a synonym for a person's life's work. C.G. Jung, linking vocation to the process of inner growth, wrote at length about 'individuation' (q.v.), the call that took the recipient away from collective, mass or 'herd' norms and responses, to the loneliness and fulfilment of full personal differentiation and responsibility. 'Call', in his sense, is inextricably mixed up with personal choices and the movement towards integration of conflicting parts of the personality.

Various modern writers have tended to seek psychological explanations for vocation and to point out that there is often a certain inevitability about our choice to follow in a particular path (see: FREEDOM AND DETERMINISM). We are shaped, or pushed, by our genetic inheritance, our temperament, our upbringing, our problems, handicaps, conflicts and fears. It often seems as if, heroically or otherwise, we 'can do no other'

than follow the course that attracts us in pursuit of self-giving and 'meaning'. This does not in itself undermine the supernatural quality of vocation; rather it can mean that we discover the hand of God at work on a deeper and wider level which includes, yet transcends, our personal destiny. We are 'chosen' and yet we ourselves also choose by perceiving the role that is ours to play within an evolutionary and historical context. It is this which gives meaning to our lives.

Abbott, W. and **Gallagher, J.** (eds.), *Documents of Vatican II*: 'Pastoral Constitution of the Church in the Modern World' and 'Dogmatic Constitution on the Church' (G. Chapman, 1966). **Bonhoeffer, Dietrich,** *Life Together* (SCM, 1954); *Cost of Discipleship* (SCM, 1964). **Wingren, Gustaf,** *The Christian's Calling* (Oliver and Boyd, 1958).

MONICA FURLONG

See also: FAITH; REVELATION; VISIONS; WORK.

W

WOMEN: ORDINATION

Women played a significant role in ministering to Jesus, caring for him in their homes (Luke 20.38–42), remaining with him at the cross (Mark 15.40), following his body to the sepulchre (Mark 15.47), preparing to anoint it (Luke 23.55–6), and being the first to know about the resurrection and report the good news (Luke 24.1–10).

In the NT church there were women deacons. Women deacons ministered to women and men deacons to men. As far as we know they had identical status and duties: teaching catechumens, anointing them with oil at baptism, collecting and distributing offerings, administering Holy Communion to the sick. In time the women came to be called deaconess, later abbess, and gradually the title and job of deaconess was lost, and with it women's original share in the diaconate. So women's share in holy orders gradually fell into disuse until modern times.

The Roman Catholic Church is still adamant that it will not ordain women. In October 1976 the Congregation for the Doctrine of the Faith (the former Holy Office) published a Declaration known as *Inter insigniores*, which came to the conclusion that 'the Sacred Congregation for the Doctrine of the Faith judges it necessary to recall that the Church, in fidelity to the example of the Lord, does not consider herself authorized to admit women to priestly ordination'.

While a highly authoritative document, the Declaration is not 'infallible'. It is not impossible that the Church's position will change or develop, though at present it is probably true that only for the most radical Roman Catholics is the ordination of women a live issue.

Because of the significance within churches with a 'high' doctrine of the sacraments of the priest or minister as president at the Eucharist, the debate tends to be much more fierce within these churches. (In addition, a concern to maintain the possibility of a reunion with the Roman Catholic Church can be used as an argument to oppose the ordination of women.) Churches in the Reformed tradition, however, although sometimes inhibited by biblical injunctions against women speaking in church, have, in the majority, been persuaded by theological arguments regarding the oneness in Christ of men and women. For a number of years now women ministers have served in the United Reformed Church in England and Wales, in the Church of Scotland and the Congregational Church in Scotland and in the Presbyterian Church of Northern Ireland.

The Church of England, and indeed the Anglican Communion as a whole, have a more mixed history. Deaconesses were restored in 1862 by Bishop Tait, but in 1921 Dr Frank Weston claimed that these were not in holy orders, nor equivalent to male deacons. Recently, however, the General Synod has passed a measure which will admit women to the order of deacons.

For a number of years women have been asking the Church to test their vocation to the priesthood. In 1944, in the Diocese of Hong Kong, Bishop R.O. Hall ordained Florence Li Tim Oi to the priesthood because of the exigencies of war. After the war Li Tim Oi was forced to set aside her orders because of pressure on Bishop Hall (she resumed them in 1971) but a breach had been made.

In 1971 the Anglican Consultative Council passed the controversial Resolution 28, which encouraged debate on women's orders throughout Anglican churches, and permitted bishops to ordain women with the approval of their provinces. The new bishop of Hong Kong, Bishop Baker, at once ordained two women.

In 1974 eleven women of the Episcopal Church of the USA were irregularly ordained at Philadelphia by sympathetic bishops. Within the next few years women were legally ordained in the United States, New Zealand and Canada, and more recently these Episcopalian churches have been joined by those in Uganda and Kenya.

In 1975 the General Synod of the Church of England decided that there were 'no fundamental objections to the ordination of women to the priesthood', but in 1978 they voted against removing the legal barriers. This rejection caused a large group of bishops, clergy and lay people to found the Movement for the Ordination of Women (MOW) in 1979, a movement which, since then, has worked for canonical change.

Objections to the ordination of women are on grounds of tradition, of the genital difference which makes it (it is claimed) impossible for a woman to be 'representative' of Christ at the altar, or women's biological make-up which makes it impossible for a woman to 'initiate' (a male and godlike prerogative), and of the ecumenical difficulties which may arise from the Roman Catholic and Greek Orthodox refusal to ordain women. There is also (from Evangelicals) objection on biblical grounds, particularly for the reason that women's ordination will violate the 'headship' of men.

Those in favour of women's ordination claim that baptism makes women no less representative of Christ than men, and that lack of opportunity for their ordination earlier in Christian history is due more to misogyny, social convention, and oppression than any theological, intellectual, pastoral or biological lack in women. They feel that women will make as positive and useful a contribution as they have already made in medicine, teaching, social work, law and other professions and that their energy and insights may bring a new completeness to the priesthood. (There are now nearly 700 women ordained in the Anglican Communion.)

In other areas – reading, preaching, serving, administering, being sidesmen or church wardens, singing in the choir – from which women had been excluded until recent times, women are discovering a fuller ministry in the Church; in the past it was only in the mission field that women enjoyed something like a comparable responsibility with men, even though many women have worked faithfully in Britain as parish workers and Church Army sisters. Late in its history the Church has discovered that it has deprived itself (as well as generations of women) of the full ministry that women can offer.

Canham, Elizabeth, *Pilgrimage to Priesthood* (SPCK, 1983). **Dowell, S.** and **Hurcombe, L.,** *Dispossessed Daughters of Eve* (SCM, 1981). **Furlong, Monica** (ed.), *Feminine in the Church* (SPCK, 1984). **Maitland, Sara,** *A Map of the New Country* (Routledge, 1983). **Ruether, Rosemary,** *Sexism and God-talk* (Beacon Press, Boston, 1983).

MONICA FURLONG

See also: FEMININITY/MASCULINITY; MINISTRY, DOCTRINE OF; SEXISM.

WORK

Purposeful and indispensable activity to meet human needs and aspirations. For Christians, this has often meant sharing in God's creative and redemptive activity.

In modern society work is synonymous with paid employment as developed through industrialization and the emergence of wage labour and the division of labour. (Conversely, time spent in other than paid employment is seen as free time or leisure). As the provider of economic resources for individuals, families and societies, and a major source of attitudes and values, a proper understanding of work is essential for adequate Christian caring in all spheres of life. Such understanding includes ideas about work, the contribution of work to personal formation, and the changing realities of work.

Over the centuries ideas about work have changed radically. The Greeks regarded it as a means to leisure (work was non-leisure) and, with the Romans, developed a civilization dependent on slave labour. The medieval tradition of Aquinas also regarded contemplation as a higher human pursuit. The 16th and 17th centuries saw a radical change in the valuation of work. Luther's extension of vocation (q.v.) from the religious life to all work was completed by the Calvinists' use of success in work as a sign of election. Work was given a moral value, leisure was dethroned, and 'economic man' developed out of the convergence between capitalism and Western Christianity. The commitment to a work ethic is equally central to the Communist tradition.

Contemporary work meets many major human needs. It is the principal source of income, identity (q.v.) and status in society, an important opportunity for social interaction, and the major outlet for purposeful and creative activity. People obviously vary in their experiences of work. For example, middle-class jobs are often more purposeful and creative, and working-class jobs more concerned with income-provision and physical activity. If work is badly organized or paid, then it can be a cause of alienation (q.v.), stress-related diseases (see STRESS) like alcoholism, and tension within families.

In a period of economic and social dislocation, important changes occur around the

issue of work as paid employment, with
implications for views of work and life and
responses to them (including caring). These
changes include: (1) The decline of traditional manufacturing industry, the introduction of labour-saving technologies and the rise
of service employment resulting in the greater
majority being employed in service jobs and a
minority in manufacturing (with major implications for unemployed manual workers and
their communities, the association of work
with labour and manufacturing, and society's
ability to fund collective caring). (2) The
major entry of married women into work,
especially part-time, with implications for
family life. (3) The growing international
nature of economic life typified by the increasing dominance of multi-national corporations
and a declining local ability to influence
decision-making (reflected in the continuing
debate over religion and capitalism). (4) The
powerful interdependence of the modern
economy and the industrialization of the
caring services makes good industrial relations a necessity (with important implications
for hospital chaplains). (5) The recent
growth of low paid jobs with damaging
effects on family life (see POVERTY).

Contemporary changes are also eroding the
dominant place of work as paid employment
in society by: (1) Reducing working time and
increasing leisure time. (2) Enlarging the
informal economy, including the black
economy. (3) Increasing large-scale long-
term unemployment (q.v.). (4) Separating
income from paid employment, through the
emergence of the Welfare State. (5) Fostering the growing recognition that work is more
than paid employment and includes work in
the informal and household economy and in
the voluntary sector (as voluntary caring, the
latter may increase in importance as state
caring provision diminishes).

All these changes are reflected in theological ethics with growing interest in a
distribution ethic (to distribute limited paid
employment more fairly), a leisure ethic and a
life ethic (to replace the work ethic).

The Church's response to work-related
issues has been dominated by industrial
chaplaincies (q.v.), although there has been a
continuous struggle, largely unsuccessful, to
develop the role of the laity.

Anthony, P.D., *The Ideology of Work* (Tavistock,
1977). **Clarke, R.,** *Work in Crisis* (Saint Andrew

Press, 1982). **Preston, R.H.,** *Church and Society in
the Late Twentieth Century* (SCM, 1983).

JOHN R. ATHERTON

See also: RETIREMENT; UNEMPLOYMENT.

WORK-RELATED MINISTRIES
The exercise of a Christian ministry, in either
an ordained or a lay capacity, within a work
setting.

There are three main areas.

(1) On the basis of an incarnational theology,
work-based ministry will be concerned with
trying to establish rates of pay and conditions
of work compatible with human dignity. This
ministry has been largely undertaken by
trades unions, often in the face of bitter
opposition from the established church,
which in England in the 19th century was
generally aligned with employers. (It is worth
noting that denominational differences in
both town and country often reflect social and
political rather than theological differences.)
The unions however, now show a reluctance
to be concerned with broader implications of
trade, as for example, in and with developing
countries, and also with the implications of
apparently permanent and growing numbers
of unemployed. An important Christian
ministry, then, lies in the work of the unions.
(2) The other main area of ministry concerns
relations within industry, notably those
between management and workers. In so far
as Christians are present among both, they
have their own ministry of reconciliation to
work out in their particular work situations,
and their church membership should help to
equip them for this.
(3) There is also an important theological
ministry for the whole Church in analysing
wider issues of work and non-work and
trying to speak prophetically, in the tradition
of COPEC, the Conference on Politics, Economics and Citizenship which in 1924 launched
the ecumenical movement.

Who, then, are the ministers for such a
ministry?
(1) In a broad sense, all lay persons are
involved, and lay training ought to equip
them for these responsibilities. It is not easy
for clergy to administer this training, because
few of them have the necessary experience or
expertise. It is best done by groups of laity
involved in similar situations meeting to
discuss the issues they have to face, assisted

by clerics who can feed in insights from the whole Christian tradition.

(2) More particularly, ordained ministers are now more closely involved in the world of work. Chaplains are appointed for industry (see INDUSTRIAL CHAPLAINCY), as indeed they are also for agriculture, for leisure, and for tourism. Their appointment is approved jointly by management and unions, and here they have to maintain a scrupulous impartiality. They have a personal care for all members of the enterprise, which can be exercised more effectively in the light of their detailed knowledge of the strains and pressures of its operation. Their advice may be sought by either side concerning personal and corporate ethical issues. They are in a position to interpret the Church to the world and also the world to the Church. They are, nevertheless, outsiders, in the sense that they are not natives to the scene.

(3) The most significant experience since (and occasioned by) the Second World War of a more 'inside' operation by ordained men has been the worker-priest movement of the Roman Catholic Church in France. There, experienced parish priests entered industrial concerns as workers, often of the lowest grades, as life-long vocation since it involved total identification with working-class culture. They did not reveal their identities unless asked. They always worked in teams of three or more to overcome the inevitable loneliness, and they saw the Eucharist as the centre of their ministry – often in their own lodgings. They accepted office in trades unions (generally Communist-dominated ones) as a mark of confidence from their fellow-workers. They were reluctant to commend their work-mates to the local parish church because this meant the adoption of an alien culture. Not surprisingly such a policy has generated, and continues to generate, strains within that communion.

(4) Rather different is the exercise of non-stipendiary ministry (NSM), officially authorized by the bishops of the Church of England in 1970, and taken up by other churches since then. NSMs are selected in the same way as their stipendiary colleagues and trained on part-residential courses, that is, in their spare time while they continue in their secular occupations. Thus after ordination they are native to the scene, and most of them would say that their work continues much as before. Why then be ordained? Because the fact of

their official church authorization alters their standing at work. They are consulted on personal matters by fellow-workers in a way they were not before; and they are consulted by management on wider ethical issues, or are expected to offer particularly Christian insights in such issues. They also have a pastoral ministry to offer to the Church dispersed in the factory or office or wherever (and that is necessarily ecumenical), both for mutual personal care and for raising levels of Christian awareness. They find some lay associations of Christians unhelpful because they are turned in on themselves in a privatized pietism.

It is ironical that Christians are beginning to take work-based ministry seriously at a time when it seems likely that work (as traditionally understood) is never going to be available to several million of Britain's population (see UNEMPLOYMENT). The experience of redundancy for the traditional worker often produces depression (q.v.), illness, and even suicide (q.v.), and the prospect of prolonged unemployment for school and college leavers is not much less grievous. Unemployment is undoubtedly one factor in the present widespread social malaise, erupting in outbursts of violence (q.v.). This is such a radically new situation that the Church is ill-equipped to meet it. Many local churches are responding energetically with drop-in centres, counselling facilities, and not least the supportive fellowship of congregations who can demonstrate the fact that a person's status and worth is not to be measured by his or her employment. There is a challenge here to discover, or recover, a deep spirituality of the desert, a recourse to 'One who turneth the wilderness into a standing water, and dry ground into watersprings'.

Baum, G. (ed.), Work and Religion (T. & T. Clark, 1980). Hodge, M., Non-stipendiary Ministry in the Church of England (CIO, 1983). Industrial Mission Association, The End of Work (1980). Jenkins, C. and Sherman B., The Collapse of Work (Eyre Methuen, 1979). John Paul II, Laborem Exercens (Catholic Truth Soc., 1981). Markall, G., The Best Years of their Lives (William Temple Foundation, 1980). Phipps, S., God on Monday (Hodder, 1966). Siefer, G., The Church and Industrial Society (orig. Die Mission der Arbeiterpriester (Darton Longman and Todd, 1964).

M.A.H. MELINSKY

See also: INDUSTRIAL CHAPLAINCY; SOCIAL STRUCTURES; UNEMPLOYMENT; WORK.

WORSHIP AND PASTORAL CARE

Pastoral care needs to be grounded in a community's worship if it is to be safeguarded from perversion. In isolation it is too easily reduced to one-to-one relationships with all that that implies about the privatization of religion and about neglect of both the social dimension of human personality and the context of care. Indeed pastoral care, often exclusively and mistakenly identified with pastoral counselling (q.v.), can soon become no more than secular therapy if it is without a liturgical reference – it then falls short of its proper scope. The command to tend and feed Christ's sheep in John 21 implies more than helping troubled individuals – that is the negative aspect of pastoral care, i.e. assistance in facing problems and overcoming them, whereas the positive side requires the development of a Christian life style, progress in wholeness, and the edification or building up of a faithful Christian community, all of which are promoted by worship. This is not to say that worship is to be used as a technique to achieve pastoral goals; rather that worship by its very nature should function as pastoral care. It can do this in a number of ways, as regards both individuals and the entire fellowship of believers.

Individuals as they grow towards and develop in maturity pass through many critical stages. Liturgy ritualizes these (*see* LITURGY AND RITUAL), enabling partici-pants to cope with them and to share them with others. Indeed several forms of Christian worship fall into the category of rites of passage, which facilitate and give meaning to change of status. So baptism (q.v.) and thanksgiving for childbirth mark an important turning point in a family's life. Confirmation has many of the features of a puberty rite. The celebration of a wedding educates in the meaning of matrimony. A funeral (q.v.) is in part to be understood as a help towards working through grief; it can be an aid to those present in coming to terms with a situation of bereavement (q.v.). In these ways worship provides a pattern of behaviour, focusing attention on beliefs and standards and giving significance to the events exper-ienced. Indeed, worship as pastoral care can mediate encouragement and consolation (q.v.); it can be a teaching medium and a way of Bible study; it can give guidance and be a school of prayer (q.v.). Worship enables us to accept God's will and to enter into com-munion with him in whose presence we live. It thus fosters, as should pastoral care, an awareness of a dimension of existence that should be part of the whole of life whether inside or outside a church building.

As a corporate act, worship strengthens the fellowship, bringing it to a greater knowledge of its own identity as it serves the needs of individual and communal integration. The Lord's Supper (*see* COMMUNION) in partic-ular is a ritual of meeting, through which separateness is transcended and loneliness overcome, and the Church becomes its true self and *shalom* (q.v.) is shared. 'If,' said Augustine, addressing members of the Body of Christ about to partake of the sacramental body, 'if you have received well, you are that which you have received.'

To understand pastoral care in this light is not to restrict it unduly, as if worship relates only to a very small part of human activity. On the contrary worship is central to life, illuminating it from within and bringing awareness of its true character and purpose with which pastoral care is equally concerned. Of human existence in general it can be said that it is under a 'law', viz. the law that life is secured through death. Scientific advance, for example, is only possible through the giving up of old certainties and the confession of ignorance in order to discover new truths. Political and economic progress cannot be achieved unless people overcome their desire to retain what they have and to conserve the past rather than allowing it to die. Human happiness is realized largely through the death of self-love. Healthy natural life in all its varieties thus reveals a sacrificial rhythm, and the prototype of this is clearly to be found in the paschal event – in the suffering, death and resurrection of Jesus, which are at the basis of the Christian sacraments. In baptism we die and rise with Christ; in the Eucharist there is a renewed participation in his death and resurrection. In other words, worship reveals to us and draws us into the paschal pattern which in its turn is the fullness of all life as well as being the goal of all pastoral care. Indeed this sacrificial dying to live is to be related to each of the functions of pastoral care: healing, reconciling, guiding, sustaining.

While healing is and can be connected with special healing services (yet another liturgical connection), in its widest sense it refers to wholeness or, to use a different terminology which means the same, to salvation (q.v.).

But baptism so identifies us with Christ in his redemptive act that it can be said to 'save' us (1 Pet. 3.21), and the Eucharist renews us by allowing participation in the fruits of his sacrifice. 'Life through death' would be an apt title for the benefit of communion. Reconciliation (q.v.) is to be understood as a process, fostered by pastoral care but advanced and sealed in liturgical action whereby forgiveness of sins is conveyed and ever renewed through the cross of Christ. Guidance is concerned with making plain the proper direction of our lives and the liturgy unites us with Christ who is both the way and the good pastor, going before his flock and giving his life for the sheep. Sustenance takes the form of a present partaking of the new life in Christ who is himself the resurrection and the life. We are sustained by drawing upon this source, and it is precisely to this continuing nurture that pastoral care should be directed, with worship constantly holding up its proper goals before it.

Willimon, W.H., *Worship as Pastoral Care* (Abingdon, 1979).

J.G. DAVIES

See also: LITURGY AND RITUAL; PREACHING AND PASTORAL CARE; RITES AND RITUALS; SYMBOLS.

WRATH
See: ANGER AND HOSTILITY.